D1824642

Nottingham Trent University
BOOTS LIBRARY
www.ntu.ac.uk/llr

Enquiries: 0115 848 2175

International Human Rights

Series Editor
Stephen Hoadley
University of Auckland
Auckland, New Zealand

This series improves our understanding of why and how human rights norms are violated, and how violations can be minimized and human rights can be protected more effectively. The series covers the human rights and civil liberties outlined in intergovernmental treaties, protocols, resolutions, and declarations, and it analyzes how they are adjudicated by international tribunals and implemented by governments or intergovernmental institutions such as the United Nations.

The academic reader will discover authoritative, timely information, and current insights on international human rights, as well as emerging issues for further research. The human rights activist will find examples of mitigation of violations by institutional, political, and popular initiatives and learn how to use or improve on those initiatives. Potential or actual victims and their advocates will learn how violations arise and, hopefully, how to anticipate and counter or evade them.

More information about this series at http://www.springer.com/series/15218

Gerd Oberleitner
Editor

International Human Rights Institutions, Tribunals, and Courts

 Springer

Editor
Gerd Oberleitner
Faculty of Law
University of Graz
Graz, Austria

ISSN 2523-8841   ISSN 2523-885X (electronic)
ISBN 978-981-10-5205-7   ISBN 978-981-10-5206-4 (eBook)
ISBN 978-981-10-5207-1 (print and electronic bundle)
https://doi.org/10.1007/978-981-10-5206-4

Library of Congress Control Number: 2018950538

This Springer imprint is published by the registered company Springer Nature Singapore Pte Ltd.
The registered company address is: 152 Beach Road, #21-01/04 Gateway East, Singapore 189721,
Singapore

Series Preface

Welcome to the latest volume in this Springer Nature series of reference handbooks on International Human Rights. This series arose from the conviction by the series editor, shared by chapter contributors and the Springer editorial staff, that protection of human rights not only is, but increasingly ought to be, an essential element in the policies of all governments, international organizations, and civil society associations. Therefore, Springer Nature has sponsored this series of reference handbooks under the title International Human Rights and has successfully solicited the participation of handbook editors and contributors who share a central conviction: that human rights are important and their protection and enhancement should be given high priority.

Why "international"? While it is true that human rights protection is primarily the responsibility of governments, it is also true that governments take their cues from human rights standards that are set out in international treaties, declarations, and initiatives. Even governments that fail, deliberately or inadvertently, to achieve high standards of human rights protection for their citizens are aware, through participation in the Human Rights Council and other UN and regional bodies, and international conferences and courts, of those standards. Through education, emulation, and response to public opinion, it is to be hoped that governments' behavior will gradually converge with international standards.

It is fitting that the volume "International Human Rights of Children" to emerge in this series is devoted to the human rights of the most vulnerable of human beings, children. It is fitting also that the volume "International Human Rights of Women" is devoted to the largest category of human beings, women. The editors are well aware of the linkage that the denial of children's human rights can follow directly from the denial of rights to the women who care for children. Their contributors explore these linkages, although from the perspective of children's rights on the one hand and women's rights on the other. Two premier treaties the Convention on the Rights of the Child and the Convention on the Elimination of all Forms of Discrimination Against Women are the recognized beacons of the two volumes. But the contributors' analysis of children's and women's rights, and their enhancement in the face of persistent violations, goes beyond legal treaty obligations to encompass political, economic, social, and moral nuances. To both volumes the dedicated editors have attracted a worldwide set of chapter authors, many of whom bring to their contributions practical experience as well as skills of academic analysis and official policy formulation.

Agreement on high standards of human rights is a necessary first step but not sufficient without effective action. While governments are expected to apply high standards, it is often international institutions that give them voice and energy. The volume "International Human Rights Institutions, Tribunals, and Courts" in this series, on international institutions devoted to human rights, provides not only an anatomy of institutions but also information, analysis, and assessment of their initiatives, processes, and achievements. The volume editor, a senior academic and frequent advisor to governments and international institutions, has assembled contributions traversing the institutional landscape from UN treaty and Charter bodies through international and regional courts and tribunals.

The volume "International Human Rights and Terrorism" in the series is the troubled policy realm of counter-terrorism, troubled because the policies that governments so often are obliged to carry out under pressure of time and outrage can intrude into the legitimate activities of their citizens. Invasion of privacy is but one violation, albeit the most widespread one. More serious are curtailment of civil liberties, arbitrary arrest and prolonged detention, and targeted killings. Also, alleged terrorists have human rights. The contributors to this volume, drawn from experts around the globe, delineate the interface between counter-terrorism and human rights and suggest guidelines and limits.

As series editor, and on behalf of the volume editors and the Springer Nature editorial staff, let me commend these reference handbooks to you and to your colleagues, students, and libraries. Our aim is to provide the most current thinking and information on the issues surrounding the human rights of children and women, the international institutions that set and implement standards, and the dilemmas endemic on counter-terrorism and war.

Auckland, New Zealand   Stephen Hoadley
                                                                   Series Editor

Volume Preface

This volume introduces readers to the past, present, and future of major global and regional human rights institutions, courts, and tribunals. It assesses the legacy of these institutions and discusses the promise they hold for realizing human rights as well as the challenges they face in doing so. The chapters, written by leading academics, analysts, advocates, and practitioners, trace the rationale of setting up of international human rights institutions, present their historic development, and critically analyze their respective contributions to the promotion and protection of human rights. The broad geographical coverage combines historic analysis with a presentation of contemporary trends and future perspectives and weaves together the law and politics of human rights. In their contributions, the authors explore through different theoretical, practical, and geographical approaches and perspectives the potential of these institutions for safeguarding human rights in light of continuing human rights violations and recent global trends in human rights and international law and politics.

The introductory chapter discusses the legitimacy and authority of international human rights bodies. This is followed by a presentation of human rights institutions created within the framework of the United Nations since the adoption of the Universal Declaration of Human Rights in 1948. This section goes beyond the core human rights institutions (the UN Human Rights Council, the High Commissioner of Human Rights, and the human rights treaty bodies) and includes a gender perspective of the UN's human rights system as well as an analysis of the role of human rights in the International Labour Organization and in UNESCO, the UN's educational, scientific, and cultural organization. It also discusses the suggestion of setting up a world court of human rights.

The second part of the volume assesses how international criminal courts and tribunals have reframed human rights violations as individual criminal acts. The chapters range from the legacy of Nuremberg and Tokyo war crime tribunals and the international criminal tribunals for the former Yugoslavia and Rwanda to the International Criminal Court. This part includes also a reflection on the enforcement of international humanitarian law and a chapter on the past and future role of truth and reconciliation commissions. The third part of the volume is devoted to (established and emerging) regional human rights bodies and courts in Europe, the Americas,

Africa, Asia, and in the Arab world and ends with some notes on a possible agenda for strengthening global and regional human rights institutions.

Graz, Austria   Gerd Oberleitner
                                                                                    Editor

Contents

Introduction to Human Rights Institutions: Legitimacy and
Authority   1
Steven Wheatley

Part I   United Nations Human Rights Institutions **23**

The Universal Declaration of Human Rights: Politics and
Provisions (1945–1948)   25
Roland Burke and James Kirby

The UN Human Rights Council: Achievements and Challenges in
Its First Decade   49
Humberto Cantú Rivera

The UN High Commissioner for Human Rights and Field
Operations   69
William G. O'Neill

The UN Human Rights Treaty Bodies: Impact and Future   95
Lutz Oette

The UN Human Rights Committee 117
Anja Seibert Fohr

The UN Committee on Economic, Social, and Cultural Rights 143
Fons Coomans

Gender in the UN: CEDAW and the Commission on the Status of
Women 169
Jane Connors

The UN Security Council and Human Rights 199
Joanna Weschler and Lindiwe Knutson

International Labour Organization 227
Maria Victoria Cabrera-Ormaza

UNESCO and Human Rights   251
Yvonne Donders

A World Court of Human Rights   271
Manfred Nowak

National Human Rights Institutions   291
Kirsten Roberts Lyer

**Part II Human Rights Violations as Crimes: International
Courts and Tribunals** **317**

Human Rights: The Nuremberg Legacy   319
Miriam Cohen

Human Rights: Future of Ad Hoc Tribunals   333
Milena Sterio

**The International Criminal Court between Human Rights and
Realpolitik**   355
Luigi Daniele

Enforcement of International Humanitarian Law   377
Gentian Zyberi

**Transitional Justice for Human Rights: The Legacy and Future of
Truth and Reconciliation Commissions**   401
Elin Skaar

Part III Regional Human Rights Systems **421**

**The European Court of Human Rights: Achievements and
Prospects**   423
Philip Leach

The European Union Fundamental Rights Agency   443
Gabriel N. Toggenburg

The Inter-American Commission and Court of Human Rights   461
Veronica Gomez

**The African Commission and Court on Human and Peoples'
Rights**   479
Manisuli Ssenyonjo

**Human Rights Mechanisms in the Arab World: Politics and
Protection**   511
Zaid Eyadat and Hani Okasheh

ASEAN Human Rights Mechanisms 527
Sriprapha Petcharamesree

Agenda for Strengthening Human Rights Institutions 551
Gerd Oberleitner

Selected Human Rights Instruments 571

Index 615

About the Series Editor

Stephen Hoadley This International Human Rights series of five reference handbooks is coordinated by Series Editor Dr. Stephen Hoadley, Associate Professor of Politics and International Relations at the University of Auckland. He has 15 years of experience in directing the graduate degree of Master of Professional Studies in International Relations and Human Rights. Stephen Hoadley is a graduate of the University of California at Santa Barbara and has taught at universities in the United States, Japan, Hong Kong, and New Zealand. He is the author of nine books on international affairs, is a commentator on TV and radio as well as a speaker to civic groups, and has served on three government advisory committees.

About the Editor

Gerd Oberleitner is Professor of international law and UNESCO Chair in Human Rights and Human Security at the Faculty of Law, University of Graz, Austria; Head of the Institute of International Law and International Relations; and Director of the European Training and Research Centre for Human Rights and Democracy at the University of Graz.

Contributors

Roland Burke La Trobe University, Melbourne, VIC, Australia

Maria Victoria Cabrera-Ormaza Faculty of Law, Universidad Espíritu Santo-Ecuador, Samborondón, Ecuador

Humberto Cantú Rivera University of Monterrey, Monterrey, Mexico

Miriam Cohen Université de Montréal, Montreal, QC, Canada

Jane Connors International Advocacy, Amnesty International, Geneva, Switzerland

Fons Coomans Department of International and European Law, Maastricht University, Maastricht, The Netherlands

Luigi Daniele Nottingham Trent University, Nottingham, UK
University of the Studies of Naples Federico II, Naples, Italy

Yvonne Donders Faculty of Law, Department of International and European Law, University of Amsterdam, Amsterdam, Netherlands

Zaid Eyadat Human Rights Centre, University of Connecticut, Storrs, Connecticut, USA

Veronica Gomez Centro Internacional de Estudios Politicos, Universidad Nacional de San Martin, Buenos Aires, Argentina

James Kirby Durham University, Durham, UK

Lindiwe Knutson Security Council Report, New York, NY, USA

Philip Leach European Human Rights Advocacy Centre (EHRAC), Middlesex University, London, UK

Manfred Nowak University of Vienna, Vienna, Austria
European Inter-University Institute for Human Rights and Democracy, Venice, Italy

William G. O'Neill Human Rights and Humanitarian Law Brooklyn, New York, NY, USA

Gerd Oberleitner Faculty of Law, University of Graz, Graz, Austria

Lutz Oette SOAS, University of London, London, UK

Hani Okasheh University of Jordan, Amman, Jordan

Sriprapha Petcharamesree Institute of Human Rights and Peace Studies, Mahidol University, Salaya, Thailand

Kirsten Roberts Lyer School of Public Policy, Central European University, Budapest, Hungary

Anja Seibert-Fohr University of Heidelberg, Heidelberg, Germany

Elin Skaar Chr. Michelsen Institute (CMI), Bergen, Norway

Manisuli Ssenyonjo Brunel Law School, Brunel University London, London, UK

Milena Sterio Cleveland-Marshall College of Law, Cleveland, OH, USA

Gabriel N. Toggenburg Office of the Director of the European Union Agency for Fundamental Rights (FRA), Vienna, Austria

Joanna Weschler Security Council Report, New York, NY, USA

Steven Wheatley Law School, University of Lancaster, Lancaster, UK

Gentian Zyberi Norwegian Centre for Human Rights, University of Oslo, Oslo, Norway

Introduction to Human Rights Institutions: Legitimacy and Authority

Steven Wheatley

Contents

Introduction 2
On the Authority and Legitimacy of Global Human Rights Institutions 3
A Moral Code of Human Rights 5
Secondary Agents of Justice 6
Charter Bodies 7
Treaty Bodies 10
Having the Final Say 11
When the Treaty Body Pronouncements Are Conclusive 13
When the Treaty Body Pronouncements Are Persuasive 15
On the Persuasiveness of the Human Rights Treaty Bodies 17
Conclusion 19
References 20

Abstract

This chapter considers the legitimacy authority of global human rights institutions, their right to have the final say on a question of human rights. It shows how human rights was transformed from a moral code to a set of binding international law obligations in the aftermath of the 1960 Sharpeville Massacre, allowing a role for "Charter bodies" and "Treaty bodies" to monitor the human rights situations in states. The main Charter body is the United Nations Human Rights Council; the nine core human rights treaties each have their own bespoke Treaty body, although these operate in similar ways. This work focuses on the interpretive authority of the Treaty bodies, which depends on the acceptance of that role by the states parties, a form of sociological legitimacy. This in turn relies on a recognition of their normative legitimacy, understood variously in terms of the Treaty bodies

S. Wheatley (✉)
Law School, University of Lancaster, Lancaster, UK
e-mail: s.wheatley@lancaster.ac.uk

© Springer Nature Singapore Pte Ltd. 2018
G. Oberleitner (ed.), *International Human Rights Institutions, Tribunals, and Courts*,
International Human Rights, https://doi.org/10.1007/978-981-10-5206-4_1

working within the constraints of the rules for interpretation outlined in the Vienna Convention on the Law of Treaties (legitimacy as legality), the need to adopt a pro homine ("in favor of the individual") approach to interpretation (welfare enhancing, or output, legitimacy), the requirement to show the positions of the Treaty bodies are the result of their expert knowledge, following review of the states parties' reports (epistemic legitimacy), and that the Treaty bodies reach their conclusions in a considered manner (procedural legitimacy). The chapter concludes that the legitimacy authority of the Treaty bodies depends on their ability to persuade, not to command.

Keywords
United Nations · UN Charter · Legitimacy · Authority · Secondary agents of justice · UN Treaty bodies · Interpretive authority · Persuasive authority

Introduction

This chapter examines the legitimate authority of global human rights institutions, i.e., the claim of United Nations human rights Charter and Treaty bodies to have the final say on the subject of human rights. The idea of legitimate authority includes both the notion of authority, the ability of an actor to tell another what to do, and that of legitimacy, the justification for accepting that one actor has the right to determine the normative position of another. Looking to the human rights textbooks, it would seem the pronouncements of human rights institutions have been particularly important in explaining the meaning of human rights. Consider, for example, the position of the Committee on the Elimination of all Forms of Discrimination against Women (in its General recommendation No 35, para. 10) that the Women's Convention establishes an obligation for states parties to take positive measures to protect women from gender-based violence, whether occurring in public or in private life, notwithstanding the fact the Convention does not contain a provision on the issue. The Committee has also criticized Hungary in 2005 (in the case of Ms. A. T. v. Hungary, Communication No 2/2003, para. 9.6) for not protecting a woman from her violent common-law husband. But why should we accept the Committee's reading of the Convention? After all, the parties did not include a provision on gender-based violence, and they have not amended the treaty, or adopted an optional protocol, to remedy the deficiency of its exclusion. The status of the Committee's pronouncements depends on how we conceptualize its statements on the meaning of Convention terms, which in turn depends on its claim to legitimate interpretive authority.

This chapter begins by explaining the notions of legitimacy and authority and the ways they relate to the work of the global human rights institutions. Authority can be divided between legislative authority (the ability to make the rules) and interpretive authority (the ability to explain what the rules mean); it concerns the ability of an actor to determine the normative position of others. Legitimacy relates to the reasons for accepting that an actor has the right to tell others what to do. Legislative authority on human rights rests with the UN Member States, who agreed on the inclusion of the human rights clauses in the Charter and adopted the Universal Declaration of Human Rights and the core human rights treaties. In the early years of the United Nations, human rights was a moral code that explained the proper relationship between the government and the individual, and there was no role for "secondary agents of justice" to monitor the human rights performance of states. All that changed after the 1960 Sharpeville Massacre, when 69 unarmed civilians were killed by armed police in apartheid-era South Africa. The United Nations Organization then moved to establish "Charter bodies," which work under the auspices of the United Nations Charter, and "Treaty bodies," created by the core UN human rights treaties. The Charter bodies include the Special Procedures and the work of the United Nations Human Rights Council, especially the process of Universal Periodic Review, whereby the human rights performance of Member States is evaluated against the standards in the Universal Declaration. The nine core Treaty bodies are all different, having been created as bespoke mechanisms under their respective instruments, but they share many similarities in approach, evaluating the human rights performance of states against the standards in the conventions and adopting General Comments to explain the meaning of treaty terms.

There is no question of recognizing the interpretive authority of the Charter bodies, whose function is to hold states to account for their human rights performance. The ability of Treaty bodies to have the final say on the meaning of convention terms depends on an acceptance of their interpretive positions by the states parties (a form of sociological legitimacy), but that acceptance depends in turn on a recognition of their normative legitimacy in the sense of the Treaty bodies working within the relevant legal framework (legitimacy as legality), drawing on the lessons of the review of the reports of state practice (epistemic legitimacy); their methodologies for drawing up General Comments (procedural legitimacy); and the welfare-enhancing benefits of their work (output legitimacy). Where the position of the Treaty bodies is not accepted by the states parties, there remains the possibility it will influence the interpretive community of human rights lawyers and scholars working on and with the treaty, but again this will depend on the same conceptions of normative authority. The legitimate authority of the Treaty bodies, as we will see, depends on their ability to persuade, not their ability to command.

On the Authority and Legitimacy of Global Human Rights Institutions

Authority is concerned with the ability of an actor to rule, to determine the normative position of other actors. The commands of authorities are reasons for action, because they are the orders of an authority. They do not constitute "advice," suggestions about the right thing to do, taking into account other considerations; the pronouncements of authorities are a reason for action, *because* they are the orders of an authority (nothing more) (Raz 1979, pp. 14–15). Robert Paul Wolff puts the point this way: "Obedience is not a matter of doing what someone tells you to do. It is a matter of doing what he tells you to do *because he tells you to do it*"

(Wolff 1970, p. 9 (emphasis in original)). Authority concerns, then, the right of an actor to determine the normative position of another and the pronouncements of the authority are taken as sufficient reason for action by the other, without the need to examine the underlying reasons behind the pronouncements. When an authority says to a subject, "Do 'X,'" we expect the subject to "do 'X'" simply because the authority said so (nothing more is required).

Legitimacy is related to, but different from, authority. The sovereign authority of the State has, for example, traditionally been explained by the factual existence of a political community with the capacity for effective self-government through law (Austin 1885, pp. 88 and 220). The justification for the exercise of sovereign authority, the notion of *legitimate* political authority, is often explained by the existence of a social contract, whereby free individuals in the state of nature recognized their interests and natural rights would be better protected by the establishment of a coercive system of government (Hobbes [1651], pp. 185 and 228; Locke [1689], Bk II § 99).

Authority is the ability of an actor to determine the normative position of others; legitimacy explains the reasons why we should accept the rightness of this situation. Legitimate authority concerns both the ability to rule and an explanation as why we should accept that power to rule. One difference often drawn is that between sociological and normative conceptions of legitimacy. Sociological legitimacy describes a situation in which, as an observable fact, subjects accept the commands of an authority as a content-independent reason for action, that is, a reason for action simply because they are the commands of the authority. Normative legitimacy, on the other hand, is focused on the rationale for accepting the rightness of an actor to make decisions on behalf of another. The two issues are often related and conflated, as it would be unusual for an actor to accept the commands of another without there being a good reason to accept the exercise of authority.

There are five main grounds for accepting the normative legitimacy of political actors, of recognizing the rightness of them determining the position of others

First, consent-based arguments that focus on the agreement of subjects to the exercise of authority. This can include consent to the establishment of authority and agreement to the ongoing exercise of authority

Second, approaches that conceptualize legitimacy in terms of legality, that is, an actor enjoys legitimate authority where it operates in accordance with the relevant legal framework

Third, accounts that focus on the benefits of the exercise of authority for the subjects, normally expressed in terms of outcome or welfare-enhancing legitimacy

Fourth, there can be knowledge-based grounds for accepting the commands of others, whereby the authority can decide for others because it has a special expertise (the notion of epistemic authority)

Finally, there are the arguments that focus on the mechanisms through, and procedures by, which the authority reaches its decisions, with the outcome of a rule-making or rule-interpreting process seen as legitimate because of the mechanisms and procedures used, often tied to democratic or deliberative forms of decision-making.

As we have already noted, authority can be divided between rule-making authority, the ability to write the rules, and interpretive authority, the right to explain what the rules really mean. In the case of global human rights, rule-making authority is possessed by the United Nations "Charter system" and the nine core UN "Treaty systems." Thus, we expect states not to use torture, even in a "ticking time bomb" scenario, where its use might save countless lives, because the prohibition on torture is a rule of the United Nations human rights system and the core human rights treaty systems (nothing more – there is no need to interrogate the underlying rationale for the absolute prohibition).

The authority of global human rights institutions rests on their interpretive authority, the right to have the final say on the meaning of words and phrases in the UN Charter, the Universal Declaration of Human Rights, and the human rights treaties. Thus, in our "ticking time bomb" scenario, we might look to these institutions to explain whether the positive duty to protect the lives of innocent victims can override the negative duty not to use torture or whether some forms of enhanced interrogation techniques fall below the threshold required to be categorized as torture. The focus here is whether the pronouncements of the global human rights institutions count as "advice," one more opinion to be considered when trying to make sense of the content of global human rights, or a "command" about how to interpret the provisions in the UN Charter, Universal Declaration, and core human rights treaties, in the sense of having the final, definitive, say on the meaning of these words and phrases.

A Moral Code of Human Rights

The idea and language of "human rights" emerged following World War II as one part of a settlement that rejected the absolute claims of sovereignty that had allowed Nazi leader Herman Goering to proclaim on the subject of the Holocaust: "But that was our right! We were a sovereign State and that was strictly our business" (Quoted Lauren 2003, pp. 202–204). The dystopian fascist regime had demonstrated the problem of understanding sovereign authority exclusively in terms of the de facto exercise of political power, and the new world order recognized the importance of protecting the individual while still safeguarding the state from unjustified interference in its internal affairs. This is reflected in the Charter of the United Nations, which requires that the Organization "promote... universal respect for, and observance of, human rights" (Article 55(c)) while not intervening in matters essentially within the domestic jurisdiction of the Member States (Article 2(7)).

The meaning of the abstract term "human rights" was explained with the adoption of the Universal Declaration of Human Rights (UDHR) on 10 December 1948, which is primarily concerned with the relationship between the government and the individual. Whilst it can be read as a list of civil and political and economic, social, and cultural rights, we can see five moral principles underpinning the Declaration: the equal status of human persons; the need for the protection of the physical and psychological integrity of the person; the right to meaningful agency; the requirement for full participation in the political, economic, social, cultural, scientific, etc. life of the society; and the right to minimum welfare. These notions give expression to the importance of "being human" in a political community like the state.

The importance of equal status is clear from the first two provisions: Article 1 provides that "All human beings are born free and equal in dignity and rights," while Article 2 establishes that the rights in the Declaration are to be enjoyed "without distinction of any kind." Physical integrity concerns harm to "me," interferences in my bodily integrity or restrictions on my person; it is protected by the rights to life, liberty, and security of person (Article 3, UDHR); the prohibitions on slavery (Article 4), torture (Article 5), and arbitrary arrest (Article 9); and the right to freedom of movement (Article 13). Psychological integrity concerns harm to things that are an extension of "me," my personal space and property, for example, with the Declaration prohibiting arbitrary interference with my privacy, family, home, or correspondence (Article 12) and protecting my right to my property (Article 17). The right to personhood, or meaningful agency, is seen in the right to marry and to found a family (Article 16) and rights to freedom of thought, conscience and religion (Article 18), and opinion and expression (Article 19), along with the right to education, which "shall be directed to the full development of the human personality" (Article 26). The Declaration further recognizes that meaningful agency can only be enjoyed in community with others, with the establishment of the rights to political participation (Article 21); to work (Article 23); to rest and leisure, including periodic holidays with pay (Article 24); and to participate in the cultural life of the state (Article 27). Finally, the Universal Declaration affirms the need for minimum welfare, recognizing the right to an adequate standard of living, including food, clothing, housing, and medical care, and the right to social security in the event of circumstances beyond the individual's control (Article 25(1)).

Secondary Agents of Justice

When the Universal Declaration of Human Rights was adopted in 1948, it was a nonbinding moral code that did not require UN Members to change their domestic laws. Hersch Lauterpacht concluded: "Not being a legal instrument, the Declaration would appear to be outside international law" (Lauterpacht 1948, p. 369). Originally it was left to the state to decide what (if any) measures of protection were required to give effect to the moral rights in the Universal Declaration. There was no role for, what the philosopher Onora O'Neill calls, "secondary agents of justice" (O'Neill 2001, p. 181) to monitor the human rights performance of states and intervene where necessary.

All this changed in the aftermath of the Sharpeville Massacre. The 21 March 1960 had been chosen by the Pan Africanist Congress (PAC) to protest the pass laws that required every black South African to carry an internal document that controlled their movements. An estimated 20,000 people gathered outside the police station in Sharpeville township, some 30 miles south of Johannesburg. All the evidence points to it being a peaceful assembly. Nonetheless, the police ordered the crowd to go home. During an altercation between the police officer in charge and the PAC leaders, a shot was heard. A police officer shouted in Afrikaans "skiet" or "n'skiet," which translates as "shot" or "shoot." One officer interpreted this as an order and opened fire; others followed, discharging their guns into the crowd. By the end of the day, 69 people lay dead or dying, with hundreds more injured (Lodge 2011, p. 105).

After "Sharpeville," the United Nations Organization introduced a series of measures targeting the apartheid state, establishing two important precedents: the human rights provisions in the Charter created binding obligations for UN Member States, and the international community could establish oversight mechanisms in the form of "Charter bodies" and "Treaty bodies" to monitor the human rights performance of states.

Charter Bodies

The human rights obligations of UN Member States are established in the constituent instrument of the Organization, with the Charter requiring the United Nations to "promote" human rights (Articles 1(3) and 55). The meaning of the phrase "human rights" was explained with the adoption of the Universal Declaration of Human Rights, and in 1968, states confirmed that the rights in the Universal Declaration established legal obligations for UN Members with the adoption of the Proclamation of Tehran (United Nations 1968, para. 2). The existence of a set of international law rules does not require the establishment of institutional mechanisms to ensure the rules are enforced. In the case of human rights, there was no role for secondary agents of justice until the 1960s, when the United Nations Organization moved to deal with the problem of apartheid South Africa.

The shock of the Sharpeville Massacre resulted in the United Nations adopting a position that rejected South Africa's argument that its system of government was an internal affair. On 1 April 1960, 11 days after the killings, the UN Security Council adopted Resolution 134 (1960), which determined that the situation in South Africa "had led to international friction and if continued might endanger international peace and security" (para. 1). The General Assembly was not sitting, but it took the opportunity at its next session to adopt, on 12 December 1960, Resolution 1510 (XV) on "Manifestations of racial and national hatred," which condemned (in its para. 1) all manifestations and practices of racial hatred in the political life of a society as violations of the Charter and Universal Declaration of Human Rights, and (on 13 April 1961) Resolution 1598 (XV) on the "Question of race conflict in South Africa resulting from the policies of apartheid of the Government of the Union of South Africa," which deplored (in its para. 2) South Africa's disregard of the demands of the United Nations to end the policy of apartheid. The argument against apartheid was now framed as a specific manifestation of a wider battle against racial discrimination, and the General Assembly tasked the United Nations Commission on Human Rights to prepare a declaration on the elimination of all forms of racial discrimination and a convention on the same subject (Preparation of a draft declaration and a draft convention on the elimination of all forms of racial discrimination, UNGA Res 1780(XVII) (7 Dec 1962), para. 1).

The circumstances of apartheid were initially regarded as exceptional, but the United Nations' focus soon turned to situations of "gross and systematic" violations of human rights anywhere in the world. The key was the adoption by the Commission on Human Rights of the "1235" (1967) and "1503" (1970) procedures. ECOSOC Resolution 1235 (XLII) authorized the Commission to examine complaints about "gross violations of human rights" and make public recommendations on "situations which reveal a consistent pattern of violations of human rights." ECOSOC Resolution 1503 (1970) established a private procedure under which a working group could consider, on a confidential basis, communications that appeared to show "a consistent pattern of gross and reliably attested violations of human rights." The Commission could then decide whether to make a study under the "1235" procedure or establish an ad hoc independent committee with the consent of the target state to report in confidence. The "1235" and "1503" procedures made clear some human rights issues did not fall within the reserved domain of UN Member States, but they were limited in scope to situations where there was evidence of "gross and systematic violations" of human rights.

The UN's concern for human rights in a specific country (and with pervasive issues or problems) is now primarily dealt with under the Special Procedures mechanisms under the United Nations Human Rights Council. As of 1 August 2017, there were 12 country mandates and 44 thematic mandates. The special pro-cedures all have different mandates and go under different titles, including Special Rapporteur or independent expert. Their function is to investigate, examine, monitor, advise, and report and make recommendations to the United Nations Human Rights Council on the subject of the mandate (Kothari 2013, p. 607). While there is some evidence the Special Procedures, especially the special rapporteurs, have looked to explain the meaning of human rights through the adoption of "soft law" guidelines or "guiding principles" (Subedi et al. 2011, p. 159), there is no question of recognizing the binding nature of these statements. The United Nations has not allocated rule-making or rule-interpreting authority to the Special Procedures, and while the special rapporteurs and working groups are highly knowledgeable on the subject of their mandate, this expertise cannot justify an enhancement of their status beyond the confines of the individual mandates. The Special Procedures are what they are, mechanisms to report and advise on human rights.

By the new millennium, the United Nations Commission on Human Rights had fallen into disrepute because of the problem of politicization, with the concern being that some states appeared to be immune from criticism because of the problem of majority voting or the fact they had been elected to the Commission. In 2006, the Commission on Human Rights was replaced by the United Nations Human Rights Council with 47 UN Member States elected by the General Assembly. The function of the Human Rights Council is to promote "universal respect for the protection of all human rights and fundamental freedoms for all" (UN General Assembly resolution 60/251, 2006, para. 2). All human rights include all "civil, political, economic, social and cultural rights, including the right to development" (UN General Assembly resolution 60/251, 2006, para. 4).

The main innovation was the introduction of the Universal Periodic Review ("UPR"). General Assembly Resolution 60/251, which established the Human

Rights Council, tasked the body to "Undertake a universal periodic review, based on objective and reliable information, of the fulfilment by each State of its human rights obligations and commitments" (para. 5(e)). The Human Rights Council decided that the standards for the purposes of review would be those contained in (a) the United Nations Charter, (b) the Universal Declaration of Human Rights, and (c) the human rights treaties to which a Member State was party, along with (d) any other voluntary pledges and commitments (Human Rights Council resolution 5/1, 2007, para. 1). The important point is that, following the innovation of the Universal Periodic Review, all UN Member States, including those that have not signed the core United Nations human rights treaties, find their human rights performance subject to review against the range of standards in the Universal Declaration of Human Rights.

Under the Universal Periodic Review, UN Member States have agreed to have "presented and openly discussed their human rights record before the international community" (Chauville 2015, p. 87). The process has been described variously as a secular trial (Kälin 2015, p. 26), a truth-telling mechanism (Billaud 2015, p. 73), and a public audit ritual, in which the state under review gives an account of its human rights performance (Cowan 2015, p. 42). Christian Tomuschat explains the idea this way: the Universal Periodic Review "is a procedure that seeks to advance the cause of human rights by persuasion. It cannot be called an enforcement procedure. The states under review are not defendants. [...] However they are made accountable" (Tomuschat 2011, p. 626).

The objective of the Universal Periodic Review is to provide feedback to Member States on their human rights performance. Review is based on information provided by the state, material supplied by the Office of the High Commissioner for Human Rights on the state, and reports from national stakeholders, such as human rights institutions and nongovernmental organizations. The outcome of the Universal Periodic Review is a series of recommendations for action by other UN Member States to the state under review, which can either accept a recommendation, with a view to implementation, or note a recommendation. The large majority of recommendations are accepted by states. In terms of implementation, Karolina Milewicz and Robert Goodin make the point that countries often act on recommendations in the run-up to their next Universal Periodic Review (Milewicz and Goodin 2018, p. 527), suggesting the process might be an effective mechanism for the promotion of human rights.

In terms of developing our understanding of the rights in the Universal Declaration of Human Rights, Walter Kälin makes the point that every time a country makes a recommendation, it implicitly recognizes the validity of the proposed understanding and will, therefore, be prevented from rejecting the same conceptualization of the norm when it is subject to review. What develops is "a formal, albeit weak, consensus on the meaning and content of human rights" (Kälin 2015, p. 33). The process allows for the possibility of new understandings to emerge, with, for example, some countries promoting sexual orientation and gender identity rights, although, as Rosa Freedman notes, this has met with resistance by others, with Pakistan arguing that these do not concern "universally recognised human rights principles" (Freedman 2011, p. 310). For a new understanding of the rights in the Universal

Declaration of Human Rights to be established by way of Universal Periodic Review, there would need to be clear evidence of a consensus on the new meaning, evidence by agreement on the meaning of human rights or at least silence on the subject when a response might have been expected, and evidence those standards are being relied on in subsequent periodic reviews of the human rights performance of UN Member States.

Treaty Bodies

We have seen how the United Nations human rights system evolved in the aftermath of the 1960 Sharpeville Massacre with the establishment of oversight mechanism in the form of the "1235" (1967) and "1503" (1970) procedures focused on the most serious human rights violations. The United Nations also adopted an International Convention on the Elimination of All Forms of Racial Discrimination – the first global human rights treaty. Before the Sharpeville Massacre, attempts to transform the Universal Declaration of Human Rights into a binding international law instrument had been caught up in Cold War tensions. The adoption of the 1965 Race Convention showed that agreement on global human rights treaties was possible and it was followed 1 year later by the International Covenants on Economic, Social and Cultural Rights and on Civil and Political Rights, adopted to give effect to the rights in the Universal Declaration. No other United Nations human rights treaty was concluded until the Convention on the Elimination of all Forms of Discrimination against Women in 1981.

There are now nine core United Nations human rights treaties. Five deal with a range of issues: the International Covenant on Economic, Social and Cultural Rights, International Covenant on Civil and Political Rights, Convention on the Rights of the Child, International Convention on the Protection of the Rights of All Migrant Workers and Members of Their Families, and the Convention on the Rights of Persons with Disabilities. The other four focus on a specific human rights problem: the International Convention on the Elimination of All Forms of Racial Discrimination; Convention on the Elimination of all Forms of Discrimination against Women; Convention Against Torture and Other Cruel, Inhuman or Degrading Treatment or Punishment; and International Convention for the Protection of All Persons from Enforced Disappearance.

The adoption of the 1965 Convention on the Elimination of All Forms of Racial Discrimination set a precedent that was followed by the other human rights treaties, comprising a list of substantive rights and establishing a bespoke supervisory mechanism: the Committee on the Elimination of Racial Discrimination. The other Treaty bodies are the Human Rights Committee (established under the International Covenant on Civil and Political Rights); Committee on Economic, Social and Cultural Rights; Committee on the Elimination of All Forms of Discrimination against Women; Committee Against Torture; Committee on Migrant Workers; Committee on the Rights of the Child; and Committee on the Rights of Persons with Disabilities.

Having the Final Say

An actor, normally a court or tribunal, enjoys interpretive authority where its constituent instrument says this is the case. Thus, for example, Article 32 (1) of the European Convention on Human Rights establishes that "[t]he jurisdiction of the Court shall extend to all matters concerning the interpretation and application of the Convention." The European Court of Human Rights has the right to the final, definitive, say on the meaning of treaty terms because the European Convention provides this is the case. States parties have delegated interpretive authority, the right to explain the meaning of treaty terms, to the European Court of Human Rights, with the result that its judgments on the meaning of convention rights are, ipso jure, always correct, even if subject to substantial criticism.

This is not the case in relation to the core UN human rights bodies, given the lack of formal delegation of interpretive authority. Sir Nigel Rodley, former chair of the Human Rights Committee, explains the point this way: "It is self-evident that the UN treaty bodies are not courts and, accordingly, that their outputs are not of themselves binding on States" (Rodley 2015, p. 88) There is a need then to examine the practice of the Treaty bodies under the treaties to make sense of the status of their pronouncements, which come in one of three forms: Concluding Observations on the reports of the states parties, Opinions and Views on individual complaints, and General Comments on the provisions of the conventions.

First, states parties are required to submit a report to the relevant Treaty body on the measures taken to ensure compliance with the convention. There is then a public meeting between a delegation sent by the state party and the Treaty body to discuss the report. After the conclusion of the oral dialogue, the country rapporteur on the Committee drafts a report which is then adopted and approved by the whole committee in a private meeting, before the Concluding Observations are made public (Rodley 2013, pp. 627–629). The main objective of the Concluding Observations, as the former UN High Commissioner for Human Rights, Navanethem Pillay, points out, is to identify "the problems and challenges that exist in States parties to the protection of human rights and to [make] recommendations for action" (Pillay 2012, p. 60).

There has been some debate about the legal nature of these Concluding Observations, especially in relation to the Human Rights Committee, established under the International Covenant on Civil and Political Rights. Jack Goldsmith, for example, argues that the Human Rights Committee "does not have official judicial or enforcement authority in connection with state party reports" (Goldsmith 2000, p. 331), whereas Thomas Buergenthal takes the opposition position, holding that Concluding Observations "must be viewed as authoritative pronouncements on whether a particular state has or has not complied with its obligations under the Covenant" (Buergenthal 2001, p. 351). David Kretzmer steers a middle ground, with the view that while Concluding Observations "are not binding on States or international judicial institutions, they play an important role in the developing law of international human rights. They are frequently cited in judicial decisions and in academic writing on this law" (Kretzmer 2008, para. 28).

Second, the core UN human rights treaties allow for the possibility of hearing a complaint that a state party has not complied with its Convention obligations. Some allow for the possibility of interstate complaint (Ulfstein 2011, para. 5), but this is rarely (if ever) invoked (Rodley 2013, p. 633). More importantly, the treaties can allow individuals to bring a complaint to the Treaty body where they have been a victim of a human rights violation (Shelton 2006, para. 49). In arriving at a view on an individual application, the Treaty body is required to interpret the scope and content of a convention right and evaluate its application in the particular case. Rodley puts the point this way: "Dealing with individual complaints is the most court-like function of the treaty bodies, because it leads to a specific decision about claimed violations" (Rodley 2013, p. 634). The adoption of a number of Views and Opinions on a provision can allow for the development of a coherent jurisprudence as the Treaty body explains the legal reasoning for its decision.

Again the status of these pronouncements has been the subject of scholarly disagreement, with some writers observing that Views and Opinions cannot, by definition, be legally binding (Cole 2011, p. 987), while others observe the quasi-judicial nature of the mechanism (Crawford 1997, p. 257; Buergenthal 2001, p. 368). It is noteworthy that a factsheet produced by the United Nations describes the views adopted by the Human Rights Committee as reflecting the binary (judicial) divide between "either a finding of violation, or a finding of non-violation" (Office of the High Commissioner for Human Rights 2005, p. 26). In its General Comment No. 33 (25 June 2009), the Human Rights Committee pointed out that its Views represent an "authoritative determination" (para. 13) of the legal position of states parties, giving the impression, as Geir Ulfstein states that, "to the [Committee] at least, its Views are tantamount to legally binding decisions" (Ulfstein 2012, p. 441). This understanding is, to some extent, supported by the International Court of Justice, which concluded in the case of Ahmadou Sadio Diallo (Republic of Guinea v. Democratic Republic of Congo) that it "should ascribe great weight to the interpretation adopted by this independent body that was established specifically to supervise the application of that treaty" (International Court of Justice 2010, para. 66).

Third, the Treaty bodies have developed a practice of adopting "General Comments" (the Committee on the Elimination of Racial Discrimination and Committee on the Elimination of all Forms of Discrimination against Women refer to these as "General Recommendations") explaining the content of the primary convention rights and secondary rules concerning, for example, reservations, continuity of obligations, and the nature of the legal obligations imposed on states parties. A report by Navanethem Pillay makes the point that these General Comments "have evolved in length and complexity and now constitute detailed and comprehensive commentaries on specific provisions of the treaties and on the relationship between the articles of the treaty and specific themes/issues" (Pillay 2012, p. 82).

In relation to the General Comments adopted by the Human Rights Committee, there is an emerging consensus that these have some degree of legal authority, although the point is disputed by certain states parties. Academic opinions differ as to the legal status of General Comments more generally. Some commentators regard them as valuable indications of the content of treaty provisions, while a small number regard them as authoritative (Mechlem 2009, pp. 929–930). Sandy Ghandhi maintains that General Comments "are not in themselves strictly speaking binding. However, they constitute an authoritative guidance and interpretation of a legally binding treaty that requires the most serious consideration by States Parties" (Ghandhi 2011, pp. 534–535). Buergenthal disagrees, arguing that the General Comment has become a "distinct juridical instrument," enabling the Treaty body to announce "its interpretation of different provisions of the Covenant" (Buergenthal 2001, p. 386). It is though important to introduce a note of caution here, with Bruno Simma making the point that General Comments are "all too often marked by a dearth of proper legal analysis compensated by an overdose of wishful thinking" (Simma 2012, p. 27). The clearest example of this can be found in the Human Rights Committee's General Comment No. 14 (1984), which concluded (without analysis or explanation) that "[t]he production, testing, possession, deployment and use of nuclear weapons should be prohibited and recognized as crimes against humanity" (para. 6).

When the Treaty Body Pronouncements Are Conclusive

The pronouncements of the UN human rights Treaty bodies come in one of three forms, then: Concluding Observations on the reports of states parties on their compliance with the convention, Views or Opinions on individual complaints, and General Comments explaining the meaning of the treaty provisions. Looking to academic and practitioner texts on the treaties, there is consensus these pronouncements help us make sense of the human rights conventions (otherwise, human rights lawyers would not make reference to them), and the UN High Commissioner for Human Rights, Zeid Ra'ad Al Hussein, has stated before the International Law Commission (on 21 July 2015) that the work of the Treaty bodies has "an important role in establishing the normative content of human rights." The problem is that this claimed role is difficult to explain, given the lack of delegation of interpretive authority, that is, the right of the Treaty bodies to have the final say on the meaning of the provisions of the core human rights treaties.

To make sense of the role of the Treaty bodies, we have to look to the rules on interpretation in the Vienna Convention on the Law of Treaties. Article 31 lays out the "general rule." Subsection (1) provides the following: "A treaty shall be interpreted in good faith in accordance with the ordinary meaning to be given to the terms of the treaty in their context and in the light of its object and purpose." Context is limited by Subsection (2) to the instrument itself and any agreement or instrument adopted in connection with the conclusion of the treaty. Subsection (3) requires that any subsequent agreement or practice that establishes the meaning of the instrument shall be taken into account, along with relevant rules of international law. All of the elements in Article 31 are to be understood as "a single combined operation," and they must all be "thrown into the crucible [to] give the legally relevant interpretation" (United Nations 1967, pp. 219–220 [8]).

Article 32 of the Vienna Convention further allows recourse to supplementary means of interpretation to confirm a meaning resulting from an application of Article 31 where there is more than one possible reading and to determine meaning when Article 31 leaves it ambiguous or obscure or results in an interpretation that is manifestly absurd or unreasonable. Beyond reference to the *travaux préparatoires* (the drafts and records of discussions leading to the adoption of the treaty), the supplementary means are not defined, although they are generally understood to be limited to the approaches listed in Article 31.

Article 31(3)(b) of the Vienna Convention on the Law of Treaties directs us to have recourse to "Any subsequent practice in the application of the treaty which establishes the agreement of the parties regarding its interpretation." Subsequent practice can include the measures taken by the states parties in the application of the treaty, and where that practice changes so does the meaning of treaty terms. Thus, in the cases of Mr. Yeo-Bum Yoon and Mr. Myung-Jin Choi v. Republic of Korea, the Human Rights Committee concluded that the International Covenant on Civil and Political Rights included a right to conscientious objection (having previously concluded the opposite) on the ground that "an increasing number of those States parties to the Covenant which have retained compulsory military service have introduced alternatives to compulsory military service" (Human Rights Committee 2006, para. 8.4).

Subsequent practice can also include the work of the supervisory bodies established under the human rights treaties, given that their pronouncements in the form of Concluding Observations, Views and Opinions, and General Comments are the result of them carrying out the responsibilities allocated to them under the treaty. Ad hoc invocations of interpretive positions on the meaning of Convention terms by the Treaty body are not sufficient (even if there is no dissent). We must be able to see the Treaty body relying on its considered position in its own subsequent practice, when, for example, reviewing the reports of states parties or when adopting Views and Opinions.

Under Article 31(3)(b) of the Vienna Convention, those interpreting a treaty are required to take into account "subsequent practice," with a revised understanding emerging where the practice "establishes the agreement of the parties regarding its interpretation." It follows that the pronouncements of the human rights bodies only provide a definitive interpretation of the treaty where they are accepted by the states parties or where the states parties remain silent where a response might have been expected. It all depends, then, on how the states parties respond to the pronouncements of the Treaty bodies.

States parties will be aware when a General Comment has been adopted and can be expected to respond where they disagree with the understanding of the Treaty body. The same cannot be said about a Concluding Observation directed at another state, as it would be unrealistic to expect states to examine all Concluding Observations for evidence of an approach to interpretation they did not agree with. The adoption of Opinions and Views sits somewhere between the two, but there is not compelling evidence the Treaty bodies use their "judgments" in individual applications as a benchmark against which to evaluate the actions and inactions of the states parties.

Where one or more states parties challenge the position of the Treaty bodies, we are unable to conclude there is a "subsequent practice in the application of the treaty which establishes the agreement of the parties regarding its interpretation" (Article 31(3)(c) Vienna Convention on the Law of Treaties). So, for example, when the United States disagreed with the interpretation of the Human Rights Committee that Article 7 of the International Covenant on Civil and Political Rights (prohibition on torture) provided an implied right to non-refoulement (Bantekas and Oette 2016, p. 201), this prevented that interpretation being established by way of subsequent practice. Where there is not sufficient evidence to demonstrate a consensus between the Treaty body and the states parties, the pronouncements of the Treaty bodies contribute to our understanding of the treaty system by way of a supplementary means of interpretation (Article 32 Vienna Convention on the Law of Treaties), to confirm a meaning resulting from an application of Article 31 where there is more than one possible reading.

When the Treaty Body Pronouncements Are Persuasive

There are two circumstances, then, when the pronouncements of a UN human rights Treaty body establish the correct way to interpret the convention: where the treaty allocates interpretive authority to the body and where the states parties accept the interpretation proposed by the Treaty body. In either of these conditions, the pronouncements of the Treaty body establish *the* correct reading of the convention. Any other interpretation reading is wrong, as a matter of law.

In all other situations, no single actor has the right to establish the correct reading of the treaty. The proper interpretation emerges from the work of those international human rights lawyers working on, and with, the convention, including international law scholars and practitioners, who together form an interpretive community (Waibel 2015, p. 147). This interpretive community is defined by its shared approach to making sense of the words and phrases in the relevant instrument. That shared approach is outlined in the Vienna Convention on the Law of Treaties. Those interpreting the treaty must look to establish the ordinary meaning of the terms, taking into account the requirements of the *pro homine* ("in favor of the individual") approach, and any evolution in the ordinary meaning.

Once a human rights lawyer is convinced she has the correct interpretation, the next task is to demonstrate to other members of the interpretive community that she has established the proper understanding of convention terms. The position of each member of the interpretive community establishes *a* reading of the treaty, with *the* correct meaning emerging from the communications of practitioners and academics. The more a Treaty body pronouncement is accepted as the proper interpretation of the treaty within the interpretive community, the more likely it is to be the correct reading. Establishing the definitive interpretation, as John Tobin points out, depends on developing a reading that "attracts and achieves dominance over all other alternative understandings within the relevant interpretive community" (Tobin 2010, p. 7).

When interpreting a treaty, the primary focus is on the text, which is presumed, in the words of the International Law Commission, to be "the authentic expression of the intentions of the parties" (United Nations 1967, p. 220 [11]). Human rights treaties are understood to be different, with a focus on the object and purpose of the convention as a treaty for the protection of human rights, leading to a "*pro homine*" approach to interpretation, requiring that treaty norms are interpreted in favor of the individual. The *pro homine* methodology is particularly associated with the regional human rights bodies, but it has also been applied by the UN human rights bodies (Fitzmaurice 2013, p. 761).

As well as a pro homine approach to interpretation, the Treaty bodies have also relied on an evolutionary approach to make sense of treaty terms. The standard approach to interpretation is to establish what the parties intended at the moment of the conclusion of the instrument, with that intention reflected in the text. The purpose of interpretation is to establish "What did these words and phrases (then) mean to the states parties?" Evolutionary interpretation, on the other hand, directs us to ask, "What do these words and phrases (now) mean?" and the approach to interpretation has central to the development of human rights treaties, recognizing that the ordinary meaning of words can change over time.

Again, the methodology is associated mainly with the regional human rights courts, but the United Nations human rights bodies have also relied on evolutionary interpretation. The Committee Against Torture has, for example, observed in its General Comment No. 2 of 24 January 2008 that its understanding of the Convention Against Torture is "in a process of continual evolution" (para. 4). This has allowed the Committee to determine that the Convention includes implied rights of detainees to be informed of their rights, to receive independent legal and medical assistance, and to contact relatives (para. 13) and that states parties have an implied obligation to prevent acts of torture or ill-treatment by private actors, including instances of gender-based violence, such as rape, domestic violence, female genital mutilation, and human trafficking (para. 18). In justifying this expansive reading, the Committee stated that "[e]xperience since the Convention came into force has enhanced [its] understanding of the scope and nature of the prohibition against torture[,] as well as of evolving effective measures to prevent it in different contexts" (para. 14).

Under the regional human rights treaties, the states parties have allocated interpretive authority to a commission or court to answer the question: "What do these words and phrases in the treaty (now) mean?" The bodies look to technical and scientific developments, changes in societal understandings, and adaptions in regulatory approaches to see if there has been an evolution in the meaning of words and phrases in the convention. The positions of these human rights bodies may be subject to critical comment by academics and other commentators, but their judgments are nonetheless a correct statement of the law. This conclusion follows a simple process of deductive reasoning: if a human rights treaty gives a body interpretive authority, then any interpretation adopted by that body is correct as a matter of law (provided it acts in accordance with the treaty). The same cannot be said about the UN human rights Treaty bodies, which do have the final say on interpretation. It is not, then, sufficient for Treaty bodies to say that a new understanding has emerged because of developments in technical or scientific knowledge, changes in societal attitudes, or new international regulatory approaches. The supervisory bodies must show this is the case by providing the relevant evidence, including by drawing on their own work in reviewing states parties reports.

On the Persuasiveness of the Human Rights Treaty Bodies

Where the pronouncements of the Treaty body are accepted by the states parties, this establishes an authoritative interpretation by way of "subsequent practice" (normally through the adoption of a General Comment or General Recommendation). Consensus is important here; in the absence of agreement, a treaty cannot be modified by subsequent practice. The legitimacy of an interpretive approach that focuses on subsequent practices is explained by the consent of the states parties to the interpretation proposed by the Treaty body; this is a form of sociological legitimacy, evidenced by the fact of the acceptance of the pronouncements by the states parties.

Where there is not sufficient evidence that the states parties have accepted the position of the Treaty body by way of subsequent practice, establishing the (legally correct) meaning of treaty provisions, the pronouncements of the Treaty bodies are one factor to be taken into account in the interpretation of the treaty as a "supplementary means" under Article 32 of the Vienna Convention on the Law of Treaties. Given the lack of delegation of interpretive authority to a particular actor, the (legally correct) meaning of treaty provisions is an emergent property of the communications of international human rights lawyers trying to make sense of treaty terms. The influence of the pronouncements of Treaty bodies will depend, then, on how the Concluding Observations, Views or Opinions, and General Comments are received by the interpretive community of lawyers (academics and practitioners) working on and with the treaty.

The interpretive authority of the global human rights Treaty bodies depends, then, on their ability to convince others, to persuade the states parties to accept their position on the interpretation of the treaty and therefore to establish the (legally correct) reading by way of subsequent practice or to persuade the interpretive community of human rights lawyers working on and with the treaty to accept the pronouncements of the Treaty body, thus leading to a shared understanding about the correct way of understanding the convention.

But why would the states parties and international law practitioners and scholars defer to the position of the Treaty bodies in preference to their own reading of the human rights treaties? The Treaty bodies are not courts, and they have not been given the right to have the final say on the meaning of treaty terms. The persuasiveness of their interpretive positions will depend on how they carry out the responsibilities allocated to them under the relevant convention, and this will depend on the extent to which they are perceived as legitimate.

Four grounds of legitimacy are relevant when considering the persuasive authority of the Treaty bodies: legitimacy as legality, legitimacy as welfare enhancing, legitimacy as epistemic authority, and the legitimacy that flows from process.

The notion of legitimacy as legality refers to the idea that a body is legitimate to the extent it has lawful authority or acts within a legal framework. In the case of the human rights Treaty bodies, the fact they all take the Vienna Convention on the Law of Treaties as the basis for interpretation shows they are operating within the disciplinary constraints of international law and not seeking to impose their own subjective reading. Thomas Buergenthal, a former member of the Human Rights Committee, has explained the need for the Treaty body to be seen as an "independent, non-political body of experts that interprets and applies the Covenant in an objective and legally sound manner" (Buergenthal 2001, p. 395). That "legally sound manner" is explained in the Vienna Convention. By using the standard approach of international lawyers to interpretation, the Treaty bodies make clear they are operating within the international law system and in accordance with its rules for making sense of words and phrases.

By looking to "the ordinary meaning to be given to the terms of the treaty in their context" (Article 31 Vienna Convention on the Law of Treaties), the Treaty bodies can explain the meaning that the states parties intended the words and phrases to have at the point of the conclusions of the treaty. But, as we have seen, scholars and practitioners have identified a *pro homine* approach to the interpretation of human rights treaties that looks to adopt the approach most favorable to the individual, even if this was not what the states parties had in mind at the time of the conclusion of the convention. This is explained by the need to interpret words and phrases in a human rights treaty "in the light of its object and purpose" as a convention for the protection of human rights (again, Article 31 Vienna Convention on the Law of Treaties). The legitimacy of this approach is explained in terms of the outcome, the need to adopt a position that will enhance the welfare of those individuals who are the ultimate beneficiaries of the human rights regime.

There is also the need for the Treaty bodies to take into account the possibility the meaning of treaty terms can change over time with developments in the world outside the treaty system. Evolutionary interpretation allows for "the ordinary meaning to be given to the terms of the treaty" to evolve with developments in science and technology, alterations in societal attitudes, and new regulatory approaches. For the UN human rights Treaty bodies to persuade the states parties and the interpretive community working on and with the treaty that there has been an evolution in the ordinary meaning of treaty terms because of developments in the outside world, they must provide evidence this is the case. It is not enough for a Treaty body to say that a new meaning has emerged.

The epistemic authority of the Treaty bodies can be broken down into two component elements: the fact the Treaty bodies are comprised of individuals appointed for their expertise on human rights (often their expertise on human rights *law*) and the collective knowledge gained by the Treaty body on the practice of human rights through their review of the reports of states parties, allowing the Treaty body to gain an insight into any changes in the "real world" relating to developments in technical or scientific knowledge, changes in societal attitudes, or new regulatory approaches.

The procedural legitimacy of the Treaty bodies is provided by the process of drafting and adopting the General Comments that explain the meaning of the convention terms. As Rodley points out, the function of the General Comments is to provide a clear statement of "each committee's accrued experience, both from its reviews of states' periodic reports and the 'views' it has issued on its examination of individual complaints. It will effectively amount to something close to a codification of evolving practice" (Rodley 2013, p. 631). The drafting of General Comments normally proceeds by a three-state process: first, the Treaty body consults widely and publically with other UN bodies, states, international nongovernmental organizations, and academics to produce a draft that is placed on its website for notice and comment; second, one member of the committee will produce a second draft, which is intended for further discussion by the Treaty body and interested parties; and third, the revised draft of the General Comment is formally adopted by the Treaty body in plenary session (Office of the United Nations High Commissioner for Human Rights 2010, para. 122). As Cecilia Medina Quiroga observes, the adoption of a General Comment by the Treaty body depends on a collective process in which each member can contribute, with the Comments normally being adopted by way of consensus. The legitimacy of the process is further enhanced by the heterogeneous composition of the Treaty bodies, with representatives from many parts of the world and many different cultures (Quiroga 2013, p. 655).

The influence of the Treaty bodies depends on how their pronouncements are received by others. Where the positions of the Treaty bodies are accepted by the states parties, this establishes the correct way to interpret the convention by way of subsequent practice; where this is not the case, but the pronouncements are accepted by the interpretive community of scholars and practitioners, this provides the most likely correct reading of the treaty. The persuasiveness of the Treaty bodies depends on their normative legitimacy. As we have seen, this can be broken down into four component elements. First, the Treaty bodies must operate within the interpretive framework established by the Vienna Convention on the Law of Treaties. Second, they must adopt a pro homine ("in favor of the individual") approach to interpretation, focused on the object and purpose of the human rights treaties, to ensure output legitimacy for the ultimate beneficiaries of the convention rights. Third, the Treaty bodies must demonstrate their epistemic authority by providing evidence, through the reading of the states parties' reports of the human rights practices within states along with any changes in science and technology, societal attitudes, and regulatory approaches. Finally, through an open, transparent, and deliberative process of drafting General Comments, the Treaty bodies can demonstrate the procedural legitimacy of the interpretive positions that will inform the future practices of the Treaty bodies.

Conclusion

The human rights obligations of states are contained in the Charter of the United Nations, along with the Universal Declaration of Human Rights, and the core UN human rights treaties. These texts establish the international law obligations of states and correlative human rights for individuals. Of course, the meaning of these human rights depends on how we read the words and phrases in these instruments. In the absence of an authoritative interpretive body, a court or tribunal with the right to have the final, and therefore definitive, say on the meaning of provisions, our understanding of human rights is an emergent property of the communications of states, human rights bodies, academics, and practitioners who must follow the process outlined in the Vienna Convention on the Law of Treaties and look for the ordinary meaning of the words used, in the context of the instrument, in light of its object and purpose.

The review of the human rights performance of states is undertaken by global human rights institutions, which fall into one of two types: Charter bodies, established under the United Nations Charter, and Treaty bodies created under the core human rights treaties. The Charter bodies are concerned with the human rights obligations of UN Member States, with the Universal Periodic Review evaluating the human rights performance of states against the standard in the Universal Declaration. This is an accountability mechanism that does not allow for formal agreement on a revised understanding of human rights norms by way of subsequent practice. This is not the case under the human rights conventions, whereby the pronouncements of the Treaty bodies can establish the legally correct way of interpreting the covenants, where they are accepted by the states parties.

Given the lack of formal delegation of interpretive authority, the Treaty bodies must persuade the states parties to accept their position, and this will depend on their claim to legitimate authority, which in turn depends on four factors. The requirement for the Treaty body to operate within the constraints of the rules for interpretation in the Vienna Convention on the Law of Treaties (legitimacy as legality); the need to adopt a pro homine ("in favor of the individual") approach to interpretation (welfare enhancing, or output, legitimacy); the requirement to show the positions of the Treaty bodies are the result of their expert knowledge of the human rights situations within states, following review of the states parties' reports (epistemic legitimacy); and the mechanism by which General Comments are adopted (procedural legitimacy). Where the position of the Treaty body is accepted by the states parties, it establishes the legally correct way to interpret the convention. Where this is not the case, the pronouncements of the Treaty bodies reflect one way of interpreting the treaty, and where their position is accepted by scholars and practitioners as being the right way to read the treaty, we can regard the pronouncements as authoritative, but (again) the persuasiveness of a Treaty body's position will depend on its legitimacy. Having the final say on the meaning of human rights depends on the Treaty bodies persuading others that they should have the final say – and explaining why this should be the case.

References

Austin J (1885) Lectures on jurisprudence, 5th edn. John Murray, London
Bantekas I, Oette L (2016) International human rights law and practice, 2nd edn. Cambridge University Press, Cambridge
Billaud J (2015) Keepers of the truth: producing "transparent" documents for the Universal Periodic Review. In: Charlesworth H, Larking E (eds) Human rights and the Universal Periodic Review. Cambridge University Press, Cambridge, pp 63–83

Buergenthal T (2001) The UN Human Rights Committee. In: Frowein JA, Wolfrum R (eds) Max Planck yearbook of United Nations law and International Law, Heidelberg. vol 5. pp 341–398. http://www.mpil.de/en/pub/publications/periodic-publications/max-planck-yearbook/volume-5.cfm

Chauville R (2015) The Universal Periodic Review's first cycle: successes and failures. In: Charlesworth H, Larking E (eds) Human rights and the Universal Periodic Review. Cambridge University Press, Cambridge, pp 87–108

Cole W (2011) Individuals v states: the correlates of Human Rights Committee rulings, 1979–2007. Soc Sci Res 40:985–1000

Cowan J (2015) The Universal Periodic Review as a public audit ritual. In: Charlesworth H, Larkin E (eds) Human rights and the Universal Periodic Review. Cambridge University Press, Cambridge, pp 42–62

Crawford J (1997) An international criminal court? Conn J Int Law 12:255–264

Fitzmaurice M (2013) Interpretation of human rights treaties. In: Shelton D (ed) The Oxford handbook of international human rights law. Oxford University Press, Oxford, pp 739–771

Freedman R (2011) New mechanisms of the UN Human Rights Council. Neth Q Hum Rights 29:289–323

Ghandhi S (2011) Human rights and the International Court of Justice in the Ahmadou Sadio Diallo case. Hum Rights Law Rev 11:527–555

Goldsmith J (2000) Should international human rights law trump us domestic law? Chic J Int Law 1:327–339

Hobbes T [1651] (1968) Leviathan. Edited with an introduction by C.B. Macpherson. Penguin, London

Human Rights Committee (2006) Mr. Yeo-Bum Yoon and Mr. Myung-Jin Choi v. Republic of Korea, Communication Nos. 1321/2004 and 1322/2004, U.N. Doc. CCPR/C/88/D/1321-1322/2004

Human Rights Council resolution 5/1 (2007) Institution-building of the United Nations Human Rights Council, 18 June 2007

International Court of Justice (2010) Case concerning Ahmadou Sadio Diallo (Republic of Guinea v. Democratic Republic of Congo), judgment 30 November 2010

Kälin W (2015) Ritual and ritualism at the Universal Periodic Review: a preliminary appraisal. In: Charlesworth H, Larking E (eds) Human rights and the Universal Periodic Review. Cambridge University Press, Cambridge, pp 25–41

Kothari M (2013) From Commission to the Council: evolution of UN charter bodies. In: Shelton D (ed) The Oxford handbook of international human rights law. Oxford University Press, Oxford, pp 587–620

Kretzmer D (2008) Human rights, state reports. Max Planck encyclopedia of public international law. Available at http://opil.ouplaw.com/home/EPIL. Accessed 5 Apr 2018

Lauren P (2003) The evolution of international human rights, 2nd edn. University of Pennsylvania Press, Philadelphia

Lauterpacht H (1948) The Universal Declaration of Human Rights. Br Year Book Int Law 25:354–381

Locke J [1689] (1960) John Locke, two treatises of government. Edited with an introduction by Peter Laslett. Cambridge University Press, Cambridge

Lodge T (2011) Sharpeville: an apartheid massacre and its consequences. Oxford University Press, Oxford

Mechlem K (2009) Treaty bodies and the interpretation of human rights. Vanderbilt J Transnatl Law 42:905–947

Milewicz K, Goodin R (2018) Deliberative capacity building through international organizations: the case of the Universal Periodic Review of human rights. Br J Polit Sci 48(2):513–533

O'Neill O (2001) Agents of justice. Metaphilosophy 32:180–195

Office of the High Commissioner for Human Rights (2005) Factsheet No. 15 (Rev) Civil and political rights: the Human Rights Committee. United Nations, Geneva

Office of the High Commissioner for Human Rights (2010) Report on the working methods of the human rights treaty bodies relating to the State party reporting process, UN Doc. HRI/ICM/2010/2, 10 May 2010

Pillay N (2012) Strengthening the United Nations human rights treaty body system. Available at http://www2.ohchr.org/english/bodies/HRTD/docs/HCReportTBStrengthening.pdf. Accessed 28 Mar 2018

Quiroga CM (2013) The role of international tribunals: law-making or creative interpretation? In: Shelton D (ed) The Oxford handbook of international human rights law. Oxford University Press, Oxford, pp 649–669

Raz J (1979) The authority of law. Clarendon Press, Oxford

Rodley N (2013) The role and impact of treaty bodies. In: Shelton D (ed) The Oxford handbook of international human rights law. Oxford University Press, Oxford, pp 621–648

Rodley N (2015) The International Court of Justice and Human Rights Treaty Bodies. In: Andenas M, Bjorge E (eds) A farewell to fragmentation: reassertion and convergence in international law. Cambridge University Press, Cambridge, pp 87–108

Shelton D (2006) Human rights, individual communications/complaints. Max Planck encyclopedia of public international law. Available at http://opil.ouplaw.com/home/EPIL. Accessed 5 Apr 2018

Simma B (2012) Mainstreaming Human Rights: The Contribution of the International Court of Justice. Journal of International Dispute Settlement 3(1):7

Subedi S, Wheatley S et al (2011) The role of the special rapporteurs of the United Nations Human Rights Council in the development and promotion of international human rights norms. Int J Hum Rights 15:155–161

Tobin J (2010) Seeking to persuade: a constructive approach to human rights treaty interpretation. Harv Hum Rights J 23:1–50

Tomuschat C (2011) Universal Periodic Review: a new system of international law with specific ground rules? In: Fastenrath U et al (eds) From bilateralism to community interest: essays in honour of Judge Bruno Simma. Oxford University Press, Oxford, pp 609–628

Ulfstein G (2011) Human rights, state complaints. Max Planck encyclopedia of public international law. Available at http://opil.ouplaw.com/home/EPIL. Accessed 5 Apr 2018

Ulfstein G (2012) Treaty bodies and regimes. In: Hollis D (ed) The Oxford guide to treaties. Oxford University Press, Oxford, pp 428–447

UN General Assembly resolution 60/251 (2006) UN Doc. A/RES/60/251, 15 Mar 2006

United Nations (1967) Yearbook of the International Law Commission 1966, vol II. United Nations, New York

United Nations (1968) Proclamation of Teheran, Final Act of the International Conference on Human Rights, Teheran, 22 April to 13 May 1968, UN Doc. A/CONF.32/41

Waibel M (2015) Interpretive communities in international law. In: Bianchi A et al (eds) Interpretation in international law. Oxford University Press, Oxford, pp 147–165

Wolff RP (1970) In defence of anarchism. University of California Press, Berkeley

Part I

United Nations Human Rights Institutions

The Universal Declaration of Human Rights: Politics and Provisions (1945–1948)

Roland Burke and James Kirby

Contents

Introduction 26
Declaration Drafting: Setting Moral Standards for "A World Made New" 27
A Common Standard of Achievement: The Nature and Content of
the Universal Declaration 30
Declaration Debates: Arguing the Appropriate Shape for Utopia 31
Universalism and Universality 35
Legacies and Legalities 39
Conclusion 44
References 45

Abstract

The 1948 Universal Declaration of Human Rights established an international standard for measuring the enjoyment or violation of the rights entitled to all members of the human family. The final 30-article text emerged out of a protracted drafting process entangled by the philosophical idealism, sovereign self-interest, and bureaucratic politics of national delegates. Discussions began in the United Nations Commission on Human Rights in January 1947, ending in an overwhelming vote of endorsement in the General Assembly on 10 December 1948. The Declaration embodied an organic unity between civil, political, economic, and social rights that were equal, inherent, and inalienable for all persons. Delegates reached broad agreement on the synthesis between political liberalism and social democratic thought, while divisions lingered on the sequencing of

R. Burke (✉)
La Trobe University, Melbourne, VIC, Australia
e-mail: R.Burke@latrobe.edu.au

J. Kirby
Durham University, Durham, UK
e-mail: J.Kirby@latrobe.edu.au

© Springer Nature Singapore Pte Ltd. 2018   25
G. Oberleitner (ed.), *International Human Rights Institutions, Tribunals, and Courts*,
International Human Rights, https://doi.org/10.1007/978-981-10-5206-4_2

political and civil rights before socioeconomic rights, and the silence on collective rights. All articles were universal in scope, reaching out to all without discrimination. The final draft, short of being universal in geographic input and cultural perspectives, far from precluded a wide space for plurality. The debates were influenced by ideas of Western, Soviet, Islamic, Latin American, and Confucian origin. The decades after 1948 exhibited the Declaration's power in norms and customary law, as well as its limits as a nonbinding instrument vulnerable to outright abuse by states and hypocrisy by advocates. The vision of 10 December 1948 did not solve the problem of preventing human rights abuses but offered a pathway for such a world to be imagined.

Keywords
Universal Declaration of Human Rights · United Nations · United Nations Commission on Human Rights · Eleanor Roosevelt · John P. Humphrey · René Cassin · Colonialism · Cold War

Introduction

The 1948 Universal Declaration of Human Rights (UDHR) has been celebrated as a triumphant moment in the history of human rights. For those optimistic about its impact, the UDHR was, in the words of coarchitect Eleanor Roosevelt, the dawn of "a world made new" – a promise which activists sought to make real, and diplomats sought to make practical (Glendon 2002, p. 202). Drafted in the shadow of the most destructive war yet seen, and adopted without a formal dissenting vote, it proclaimed a soaring new set of international norms, with individuals recognized as the bearers of a globally shared, and expansive, set of rights. The content of those rights, their limits, and their enforcement had been the focus of 3 years of relentless debate – with deep philosophical differences often registered in contests over a single clause. In Paris, Geneva, and New York, delegates formulated a text which would make a fundamental claim about the nature of humanity, and seek a profound shift in the dynamic between the state, society, and the individual. Its transformative potential was self-evident, yet so too was its threat – one perceived acutely by various autocrats, be they Soviet, Saudi, or South African. No states voted against the UDHR. Nevertheless, those 48 states which affirmed it ceded no sovereignty. The document was not legally binding and no mechanisms for enforcement were established by the United Nations (UN). This nonjuridical quality, critiqued widely by contemporary observers, also proved an asset, allowing an elaboration of human rights that was less complex, and a message less leaden with legalism. In the decades which followed, its legal effect was ambiguous, but its moral weight, and popular embrace, grew in ways most unlike conventional instruments of international law.

Despite resting on moral exhortation, the content of the UDHR held sufficient power to initiate a decades-long revolution. In an era of ascendant totalitarian rule in Eastern Europe, a Western colonialism which seemed far from dead, and with legislative racism and sexism structural features even among the most liberal states, an unqualified statement of universally held equal rights belonging to all in every state was striking in its radicalism. While international mechanisms for translating this luminous vision into lived experience were sharply impeded by the Great Powers, both Western and Soviet, the text itself would prove, in countless instances, to be almost self-activating. Diplomats, jurists, and philosophers reshaped the relationship between the state and its citizens on the page. Subjects, citizens, and eventually, transnational activists, would reshape it on the ground. By adding a crystalline international standard for treating all members of the human family, the UDHR did not solve the problem of preventing human rights abuses, but offered a pathway for such a world to be imagined.

Declaration Drafting: Setting Moral Standards for "A World Made New"

Although the vision set out in the UDHR was characterized by its elegance, the path to its completion was protracted – involving a distinctive mixture of philosophical idealism, sovereign self-interest, and bureaucratic politics. The UN Charter, signed on 26 June 1945 in San Francisco, mentioned human rights seven times, but without definition of the term. It mandated the Economic and Social Council (ECOSOC) to create a permanent Commission on Human Rights (UNCHR), which commenced operation in January 1947. The UNCHR's 18 government representatives were tasked with drafting an international bill of human rights, an enterprise which began weeks later at Lake Success, with an executive group discussion of a preliminary draft. Many of the future icons of the UN program assembled, John P. Humphrey, Canadian international law scholar and director of the UN Secretary-General's Human Rights Division; Eleanor Roosevelt, the former First Lady of the United States (US) and Chair of the UNCHR; Peng Chun Chang, a Chinese philosopher and Vice-Chair; and Charles Malik, a Lebanese academic and Rapporteur. Preparation of the first draft fell to Humphrey, who kept a voluminous diary on the Declaration's drafting, and the myriad challenges of the early years (Humphrey et al. 1994). The director drew upon a vast array of texts and bills of rights, national and transnational, including those written by the American Law Institute, the Inter-American Juridical Committee, and Hersch Lauterpacht, a Polish-British international lawyer. Such diversity lent resilience to Humphrey's draft. The ecumenism of its various national origins formed a normative bedrock for the future evolution of the document.

Confronted with Humphrey's weighty "draft outline" in June 1947, an enlarged Drafting Committee called upon René Cassin, an outstanding French jurist who had fled Nazism, to rearrange the prosaic compilation of rights into an intuitive structure, a role which would become the basis for the myth, later ratified by the Nobel Committee, that Cassin was the "author" of the text (Glendon 2002, pp. 65–66). Cassin's stylish draft, which retained much of Humphrey's substance, formed the basis of the Drafting Committee's final recommendation to the UNCHR's Second

Session in December. The next gathering in Geneva became more inclusive. It invited nongovernmental organizations (NGOs) to be present at all sessions, and accepted submissions from NGOs, private individuals, and other UN members who not represented (Korey 1998). With a wider and more idealistic collection of voices, the ambition of the UN's project grew: The "Geneva Draft" resolved that the international bill should be made up of a declaration, a binding convention, and steps for implementing the rights that had been agreed. The more specified and substantial the term "human rights" came to mean in the discussions, the less the Charter's quick reference to human rights could be dismissed as decorative platitude. It was clear by this stage that states would be tested on their commitment to the international protection of human rights, while representatives would have to balance the demands of domestic and international politics, and very often, their own conscience. Questions on sovereignty and international legitimacy had become inescapable by the time of the UNCHR's Third Session held across May to June 1948. The delegates concluded, after vigorous discussions and genuine conflict, that they would produce merely a declaration, and delay immediate action on a covenant, or any implementation measures. Utopian visions of universal human rights remained intact, but the means for its realization was deferred.

With the basic contours of the draft text mapped out by the UNCHR, the UDHR arrived into the General Assembly (UNGA), a decidedly less juridical forum. Already notorious for its fractious and candidly political character, the UN General Assembly's Third Committee on social, humanitarian, and cultural issues met from September to December to debate the declaration's contents, exposing the careful phrase of the philosophically oriented UNCHR to a less genteel audience. Over 50 government representatives, in 85 meetings and 20 subcommittee meetings, deliberated on 186 resolutions with amendments to the drafts. The Third Committee, chaired by Malik, exhibited much of the most heated and meaningful debates of the drafting process. Agreement was reached on almost all articles, with disputes resolved by a mixture of contest and compromise, and at least periodically, simple exhaustion of the participants. The Third Committee approved the declaration before its submission to the Third General Assembly's Plenary Session on 9–10 December 1948 in Paris. The delegates, when canvassed in the UNGA, unanimously approved of 23 of the 30 articles (Glendon 2002, pp. 170–171).

The UDHR was adopted that evening. Endorsement was overwhelming: 48 states for, zero against, eight abstentions, and two absences. All of the Communist states abstained, the Union of Soviet Socialist Republics (USSR), the Ukrainian Soviet Socialist Republic (UKSSR), the Byelorussian Soviet Socialist Republic (BSSR), Poland, Czechoslovakia, and Yugoslavia. Soviet-aligned representatives protested the conception of human rights outside the state, itself a fundamental aspect of the concept; a purported Western bias toward individual rights; and the lack of reference to fascism and Nazism, categories which had a somewhat flexible meaning in Soviet rhetoric. Saudi Arabia's abstention set out a litany of complaints, within a framework that conformed to the patterns of cultural and religious relativism. Its voluble representative, Jamil Baroody, protested the inclusion of equal marriage rights, the right to change one's religion, and the supposed secularism of the Declaration. In an objection that would grow much louder in the years that followed, Baroody also lamented the absence of any article on collective colonial liberation. South Africa's abstention was perhaps the frankest of them all. It disagreed with the foundational precept of human equality, a rejection dictated by a defining principle of the emerging apartheid regime, which organized the entire society around officially categorized racial difference. The Honduran and Yemeni delegations simply did not attend, the latter due to a scheduling conflict with a concert. Despite dissent which expressed profound reservations about the text, none elected to cast a negative vote against the UDHR. Reservations, often fundamental, were expressed – but none found value in an official, recorded vote of rejection. As elliptical, fragile, and partial as it was, the fledgling international aspiration for human rights had already acquired a degree of normative power and prestige, balanced precariously above numerous lines of ideological, religious, cultural, and socioeconomic division (Morsink 1999b, pp. 4–28; Lauren 2003, pp. 210–236).

Along with the strength of its adoptive vote, the Declaration's capacity to make a plausible claim to universality was, at least in part, a consequence of the cohort which was engaged in its production. Unlike the pretensions to all humankind, fantastically pronounced by the deputies which drafted the 1789 Declaration of the Rights of Man, the range of personnel which shaped the draft drew upon numerous emancipatory traditions, spiritual systems, and political projects (Kley 1994). Along-side the iconic Roosevelt, and future Nobel Laureate Cassin, were figures which arrived with distinctive voices, and their own conception of human rights. Foremost among them were Malik, a Thomist philosopher from Lebanon, and Chang, a Confucianist. Despite obvious personal enmity, their voices – be it the often-Delphic quotations from Chang, or Catholic disquisitions on the nature of human personhood from Malik – coproduced the most fundamental underpinnings of the text. For Humphrey, who himself had a deep appreciation for the fragility of the human person, after the loss of his parents, and of his arm, as a child, these two figures were the deepest intellectual elements – neither of them from the political West. Nor was Indian feminist, Hansa Mehta, who had fought British rule, and traditional oppressions, and took leave from her work in the newly independent India. Mehta was ardently universalistic in orientation, and equally emphatic that human rights had to have meaning for the ordinary citizenry of the world. Carlos Romulo, a Pulitzer Prize winner, was vehemently opposed to colonialism and equally skeptical of any claims of Asian or African difference when human rights were at issue – a position he sadly walked away from in later decades. From the wider British Commonwealth, there was Roy Hodgson, who had been disabled in the Allied campaign at Gallipoli three decades earlier. Despite Australia's own domestic liabilities, he proposed a stunning system of enforcement (Devereux 2005). The very title of the final text, a "universal declaration," a development that occurred in the final weeks of the process was arrived at with the help of Emile Saint-Lot from Haiti. Perhaps, the most compelling testament to its global character was loud complaints from Catholic reactionaries and American conservatives – both of which protested that the text deferred far too little to the "Western tradition" of liberty (d'Aleth 1949; Bricker 1948; Holman 1949).

A Common Standard of Achievement: The Nature and Content of the Universal Declaration

The UDHR is made up of 30 articles that define the essential content of human rights and fundamental freedoms. Encompassing a panoply of civil, political, economic, and social rights, the document was sufficiently sweeping and universalistic that few qualitative novelties emerged in successor instruments. Such standards for ensuring human dignity, according to the Declaration, were equal, inherent, and inalienable for all persons (Donnelly 2013). Signatories were not merely recognizing these principles, but affirming their commitment to human rights. The Declaration was "a common standard of achievement," with state practice now measurable against the rights they professed to endorse. There was no longer a plausible claim to ignorance of human rights, or at this stage, a credible argument for national exceptionalism (Hunt 2007, pp. 203–204). Human rights were timeless. They existed before the state and preceded its prerogative (Mayers 2015, p. 447). State legitimacy rested upon its performance in securing rights for its citizenry, a feature which reflected the prevailing confidence that states would serve as the first-line mechanism for protecting human rights, and bitter recent experience of states which violated this trust grotesquely. The UDHR's language transcended the present and trumped the particular. Specific circumstances and traditions could not legitimize the restriction of its rights beyond a well-considered set of limits (Wildenthal 2011, p. 125).

Across the Declaration, rights were held as coequal with the most privileged objective of the early UN – the prevention of any return to war. World peace depended upon a respect for human rights, yet human rights only had value when fulfilled as ends in themselves. Not even the maintenance of peace, still an urgent and exalted goal for a world exhausted by two ruinous total wars, could be used by states to justify the abuse of human rights – much as the Soviet bloc sought to inscribe vaguely phrased prohibitions on "war propaganda." Freedom was a precondition for peace; and peace was an enabling condition for freedom. The Declaration was simple and concise, which made it accessible to people with little familiarity with constitutionalism, moral philosophy, or international relations. Even those without literacy were the subject of a global outreach campaign, via radio programs which spanned the distance from the marble of Geneva to the scrublands of Liberia. Language was no barrier. The UDHR became the most translated document in human history – and early exceptions, notably the absence of indigenous language versions in apartheid South Africa, tended to affirm the power of its message (Lauren 2003, p. 234).

Although the UDHR spanned subjects from clothing to conscience, its authors conceived of the Declaration as a unitary system. Its articles were interdependent and indivisible, a structure which would not permit disassembly into components. Each of its rights was relational, a facet of the whole text, and not an autonomous entity that could be cleaved out. Despite being enumerated, the sequence of the rights did not explicitly reflect prioritization. While those provisions with the most total application to their siblings, principally equality, were the first items stated, one set of rights often depended on others to be fulfilled. Article 25 on the right to an adequate standard of living, for instance, may be necessary to secure Article 3 on the right to life. A truly dignified existence required the provision of the full catalogue of rights. This made the UDHR more than the sum of its parts, indeed, its parts only held their meaning if they were integrated as a system: the securing of one right furthered or enabled the enjoyment of others. Such organic unity could only be found through a painstaking drafting process that dealt with competing agendas, hierarchies, and philosophies of rights. Such a process was itself only possible for a handful of years after the war, when hopeful visions could, albeit barely, outpace and withstand growing tension and conflict among the victorious Allied powers.

Declaration Debates: Arguing the Appropriate Shape for Utopia

Agreement on the final draft was only found through meticulous debates over its content and phraseology. Finely wrought language, negotiated over the course of months, transformed seemingly hard divisions into precarious agreements. Delegates carefully considered the ramifications of proposed texts and amendments article-by-article, line-by-line, and word-by-word. Among the principal debates were those on economic, social, and cultural rights. The UDHR was heavily grounded in political and civil rights, which had commonalities with Western antecedents such as the 1789 French Declaration of the Rights of Man and Citizen and the 1789 US Bill of Rights. These rights set out the boundaries of state power – while another set, generally regarded as more modern, laid down the material conditions that humans required to enjoy real freedom. Articles 1–21 of the UDHR dealt with the former, while Articles 22–27 covered the latter. Humphrey's draft incorporated both sets of rights on equal footing (Mayers 2015). His preference for an implied parity was influenced by the April 1948 American Declaration of the Rights and Duties of Man, adopted at the first meeting of the Organization of American States in Bogota. Consensus on this equilibrium among the UN representatives was elusive. Britain failed to include the "new rights" in its initial proposal, despite being amid the creation of a full-scale welfare state at home. Similarly, the USA opposed the mentioning of such rights, even though they had been a feature of New Deal progressivism for more than a decade. This narrow Anglo-American approach was defeated by delegates from the Soviet bloc, Latin America, Asia, and the Middle East, as well as the voices of NGOs. More than a mere revision of Atlantic Revolutions, it represented a synthesis between political liberalism and social democratic thought.

The coequal place of economic and social and civil and political sets of rights, although superficially an accommodation of stereotypical Soviet and Western interests, was much more intricate. Inclusion did not necessarily imply full parity, and the precise relationship between rights old and "new" was a perennial source of division – or evasion. The sequencing of political and civil rights before economic, social, and cultural rights signaled, for some delegates, that the more "traditional rights" were more fundamental than the others (Morsink 1984, pp. 325–332). Cassin, who supported economic and social rights, contended that political and civil rights must come first as they could be achieved more readily through virtuous but inexpensive state behavior; a position shared by the UK and many others who were similarly sympathetic to some recognition of the "new" rights. Economic and social rights, they argued, require more time, and presupposed well-developed national polities, and assumed an international order that would furnish the material resources needed to fulfil Articles 22–27.

Their reasoning mapped to prevailing notions of progress within Western liberal thought. "New rights," which were still "new" in material fact even in the wealthiest countries, arose out of the "old rights" as a logical next step. They represented several centuries of political struggle. Chief opponent of any such implicit priority for civil and political rights was the Soviet Union, which instead proposed precisely the reverse: Political and civil rights could not be enjoyed without a basic standard of living. For Stalinist functionaries like UN representative Alexei Pavlov, political and civil rights presumed a tension between state and people. Soviet philosophy posited the alignment of people and state – a condition where restraints on governmental power made little sense. Less provocative, and with origins in Catholic and conventional labor socialist milieu, various Latin American delegates tried – and failed – in their attempts to integrate notions of personal socioeconomic security in the UDHR. Their proposal to situate the "new rights" before the "traditional" ones fell well short of adoption. Nonetheless, Arab and Asian enthusiasm for economic and social rights, framed in terms distinct from the Soviet model, did have some impact. Malik, for instance, whose anticommunist orientation was unmistakable, did find ways of augmenting the material dimension to rights and initiated a successful move to attach what became Article 28. This articulated the need for a social and international order that would fulfil the UDHR's mission (Normand and Zaidi 2008, pp. 188–192).

Despite being agreed in principle, even those most basic elements of social and economic rights had a more precarious course to adoption than the "classical" political freedoms. Provision of the right to food, clothing, shelter, and health care (Article 25), an omnibus of the barest material requirements, were at first neglected, then carefully qualified. Humphrey's draft, inspired by Latin American proposals and constitutions, tabled the rights to food, shelter, and medical attention at the outset. Panama's representatives clarified that food and housing could be secured in minimalist terms, in safeguards against poor food standards and unaffordable prices. It reflected an acceptance of the limits of each state's resources, and the need for the individual to make the most of their opportunities for adequate food and housing. Humphrey's suggested "right to medical care" was diluted in Cassin's rewrite, which adopted the "best health conditions." It almost disappeared in the US draft, which strived merely for the "highest attainable standard" of medical care. The Soviet delegate objected to this attempted shift and Carlos Romulo, well aware of the misery in his own country, returned the discussion back to an absolute right to adequate food, housing, and medical care, as well as (for the first time) clothing. Britain and India made progress in the UNCHR's Third Session with an article that combined the right to medical care with the rights to social security, and the protection of motherhood and childhood. The International Labour Organization (ILO), which had previously undertaken work on economic and social rights, offered a paragraph that would have left out explicit reference to food, clothing, housing, and medical care (Maul 2012). Their inclusion required the intervention of Chang and Pavlov (Morsink 1999b, pp. 191–199). The debates reveal the crucial role of non-Western states in introducing and supporting these rights, and the nuanced view regarding the balance between state obligations and the restrictions of domestic circumstances.

Ideological conflicts between capitalism and socialism weighed heavily on the construction of workers' rights, a group which resided at the intersection of the two types of rights. Delegates agreed that all persons are at least somewhat independent and should choose their employment. Such individual labor autonomy was limited in Humphrey's draft, which expressed "a duty to work," and Cassin's rewrites, which added the right to self-development of one's personality. Drafters abandoned provisions for "the duty to work" due to concerns over the postwar job market. The place of trade unions, and freedoms of association, were challenging, especially for Labor governments protective of this key constituency. Still more divisive was a putative obligation of states to provide employment. The Soviet bloc, at the start of the Working Group of the Second Session, pressed for governments to take "all necessary measures" to achieve full employment. Their proposal was approved, but only with the clarification that states would not be held entirely responsible for employment, with the final text suggesting a milder level of state oversight

By the latter phases of the drafting process, the division on rights "old" and "new" was characterized by differences in the relative emphasis on economic and social rights, and precise nature of state responsibility. The UK and India cut the state duties paragraphs. They believed a concise article on the right to work and satisfactory conditions would intrinsically imply state duties, much like the rest of the Declaration. The trade unions represented at the talks disputed this logic, noting that prevention of unemployment was newer; a feature of the nascent Keynesian economic settlement then emerging, one which required a distinct right. The matter was brought to a head at a drafting committee. Malik added "protection against unemployment" to Article 23, which implied all measures be taken by states to ensure continued employment, and Article 22 articulated the obligations of states. Articles 22 and 29, which frame the socioeconomic rights section, incorporate a socialist ethos into the UDHR where one's rights and duties are given meaning within a wider economic community (Morsink 1999b, pp. 157–168).

Despite employment and welfare provisions eventually finding many supporters, and an uneasy entente with the communist legations, the Soviet viewpoint was less easily reconciled with respect to property rights. Somehow the article had to accommodate two different economic systems, capitalism, and socialism, and all the assorted species of thought on property that resided between these polar models. Confronted with a range of alternatives, ranging from a strong individually oriented claim, to a barely extant Soviet provision, which assumed near total state flexibility to define property in national law, consensus was not easily secured. Such latitude for domestic law meant no threat to Soviet practice – and, perversely, given Soviet posturing as anticolonial champion, full sanction for imperial confiscations, and restrictions it railed against. The Union of South Africa, where property was arbitrarily denied to Africans, and the Soviet Union, where property was defined by the dispensation of the state, were both consistent with their respective domestic legislation. Adept at linguistic innovations, the Third Committee arrived at a dual right. Property could be owned either alone or in association with others, permitting the individual to decide what form it should take, and included the home, private property, and profit-making enterprise. Almost all economic systems could find compliance with terms so broad. In an era when even the more liberal capitalist parties accepted a large role for the state, restrictions of some kind were assumed. Depression, full wartime mobilization, and postwar reconstruction had demonstrated the inadequacy of the market as a means for securing human rights. It was agreed in the Third Committee that Article 29 provided adequate limits against individuals who may exploit their capacity for mass ownership at the expense of the community – a provision in which Western governments could see their history of the struggle against monopolies; the newly independent states could see their hopes for radical land reform; and the Soviet bloc could see its own triumphs, real and imagined. Agreement on property rights, a locus for the global symbolic conflict, demonstrated the dynamic of the early Cold War – which shaped the text, but failed to paralyze or fully fracture the drafting process (Morsink 1999b, pp. 146–156).

Not all controversial elements survived, especially minority rights. The UDHR did not address any protections for human collectives or vulnerable racial, religious, ethnic, or linguistic minority groups. This exclusion was a conscious and well-studied choice, and indicative of the disposition of many in the immediate postwar period – who looked upon the patchwork of Minority Rights Treaties under the League as not merely a failed initiative, but a flawed philosophy (Burke 2017, pp. 287–314). The silence on collective rights was considered by some scholars as the gravest flaw of the UDHR (Morsink 1999a, p. 1057; Hoffmann 2011, p. 14; Simpson 2001, pp. 441–442, 450–444; Dolinger 2016, pp. 167, 196–197, 199). Raphael Lemkin, the principal force behind the 1948 Genocide Convention, and the first to fully define the concept of genocide, lamented the UDHR had eclipsed his own convention. For Lemkin, protection for universalized individuals was insufficient to ensure the survival of distinctive collective groups (Mayers 2015, p. 457). In its more free-form early months, there was the promise of both group and individual as the subject of rights. Humphrey's draft offered a detailed article on protections for racial, ethnic, linguistic, and religious minorities. The article was carried through into Cassin's draft and supported by the Sub-Commission on Minorities, a specialist group that worked adjacent to the UNCHR, with added limits to preserve public order and a stricter qualification for determining a minority group.

Ultimately, the provision stalled well before the final draft text. Eleanor Roosevelt claimed "minority questions did not exist in the American continent" and the French representative said that he spoke on behalf of a homogenous state that respected the human rights of all peoples within its territory. Even Latin American delegations feared the article would upset their policies of assimilation and threaten national unity. Only the Soviet bloc consistently supported minority rights in the drafting committee, but with what often seemed a transparently instrumental purpose, as a vector for sharpening divisions on nationalism and colonialism (UN General Assembly Third Committee 1948, pp. 717–718). They were joined episodically in the Third Committee by the delegates of Yugoslavia, Denmark, and Belgium, but made little impression. Minorities and collectives were inconsistent with the philosophical frames of the late 1940s human rights idea, though this would begin to shift by the time of the draft Covenant (Simpson 2001, pp. 441–442, 450; Morsink 1999a). This paucity of enthusiasm for collective human rights protection was, in retrospect, striking – given the UDHR was prepared so proximate to the Holocaust, and the first reckoning with the crimes of Nazism at Nuremberg. Much of the collective rights component was apportioned to the sibling Genocide Convention, passed one day earlier; and the presumptive adequacy of protections that orbited the individual (Robertson 2006, p. 36). Nevertheless, the focus on the horror and atrocity of totalitarianism and total war, as opposed to a recognition of the unique quality of the Holocaust and its victims, remains an unusual ellipsis in the text, which seems almost too universal and transcendent of its context when encountered over half a century later (Duranti 2012, p. 169).

Universalism and Universality

The UDHR's normative strength is found in the universality of its proclamations, and the near universal list of emancipatory struggles which would invoke it in the decades after 1948. The text applies to "all members of the human family" and "all peoples and all nations." This was not merely an international declaration or a diplomatic agreement among states, but a universal declaration with humanity as its subject. Article 2 articulates the UDHR's nondiscriminatory framework. Human rights are inherent to all, it proclaims, "without discrimination" such as race, sex, language, religion, or other statuses. This precept shaped the expression of all rights and freedoms in the Declaration. The drafters treated it as a basic principle to begin each Article, which featured the definitive words of "all," "everyone," and "no one." Its use of nongendered terms bolstered its universality – and also reflected the cross-cultural process of its formulation. It was women from outside the political West who protested that "all men" or "mankind" did not sufficiently include women. Only Articles 23 and 25 refer to the rights of "himself" as the breadwinner of the family (Morsink 1991, pp. 229–256). Crucially, the second sentence of Article 2 stipulated that non-discrimination also applied to those in colonial dependencies and trust territories.

Although less troubled by the exhortatory Declaration, the colonial powers worked during the debates to attach a colonial clause within the proposed human rights covenant, which would have impaired the direct applicability of human rights to colonial dependencies (Roberts 2015, pp. 128–136). The proposal failed decisively in 1950, but reflected the anxiety of colonial powers about the wider consequences of genuine universality. The compatibility between the UDHR's vision and colonialism was debatable, even if Article 2 did not deny that European imperial powers could protect the human rights of their subjects, a position only broadly conceded in the late 1950s. The Soviet bloc found rich terrain for political advantage on the issue of colonialism at the UN, and the USA did not want to alienate prospective partners in the colonial and postcolonial world. A growing list of newly independent states spoke with conviction on imperial abuses. The UNCHR, therefore, was one arena where colonial powers could not effectively defend any moral claims for empire. Universality, as a norm that now defined human equality and dignity, involved deep tension with the ideals of empire, and frank contradiction with colonial practice.

Assertions of a sweeping universality represented an epochal development. They did not, however, necessarily mean there was a complete universality of input and cultural perspectives. Fifty eight states were UN members during the vote on the UDHR, only some of whom were small non-Western states. Those ruled under European colonialism in Africa and South-East Asia, or defeated by the Allies in World War II, were unrepresented – though the latter exception was opined by few in the 1940s. The USA enjoyed a preponderance of power, which was exercised in the debates, though with less effect than elsewhere in the UN. For those academic critics of the project, even the array of influential figures from non-Western states were of debatable value. Malik's and Chang's Western education, for instance, was ample cause for doubt among some scholars about the multicultural credentials of the UDHR (Moyn 2010, p. 66; Mutua 2002, pp. 154–155; Normand and Zaidi 2008, pp. 195–196). Makau Mutua, a Kenyan-American legal scholar, exemplifies this critique of the UDHR's proclaimed universality. The Declaration, he argues, attempted to universalize the political and civil rights of Western liberal democracy. Individuals aside, the exercise was one carried out in the terms and structures of Western political thought (Mutua 2002, p. 46).

Such protests on the UDHR's lack of cultural relativism were made by contemporaries, though ironically, the most strident was not from Asia, Africa, or the Arab world, but from the American Anthropological Association (AAA) in its submission to the UNCHR. Their statement objected to the primacy of the individual as the focus of rights. Apparently unconvinced by the centrality of Malik, Chang, and numerous others in the proceedings, the AAA warned that a Declaration drawn up from a single culture would exclude and deny the rights of other groups. Their concern was with the interaction between human groups and the need to assert "the right of man to live in terms of their own traditions" (AAA 1947, pp. 539–543). Plausible in the terms of the interwar cultural relativist movement that dominated American anthropology, the AAA position presumed a highly questionable narrative of Western dominance over the emergence of human rights as a postwar project, and an oddly essentialist idea of tradition.

An abundance of Western voices far from precluded there being a wide space for plurality in the final draft. It was insufficient to control the process, with a final text that departed in meaningful ways from American, British, and French priorities. The Declaration incorporated a vast breadth of ideas in politics, religion, philosophy, and law, ranging from the US Bill of Rights, the Soviet Constitution, Anglo-Saxon common law, Islamic welfare systems, Confucianism, secular humanism, and

Catholic ideas of welfare and natural rights. Some of the most effective contributors to the UNCHR were non-Westerners like Chang, Malik, Romulo, Mehta, and Santa Cruz. The Third Committee's line-by-line discussion of the draft included six members from Latin America, six from the Communist-bloc, six from Asia, and 11 from states where the Islamic religion was strong or in the majority. It must be noted that only two representatives were from Sub-Saharan Africa, Ethiopia, and Liberia, thereby explaining the paucity of any distinctly African traditions or cultures in the UDHR debates. Nevertheless, liberal anticolonial movements across Africa embraced the text – which seemed more a weapon against empire than a tool for its extension (Burke 2010). By contrast, even by the 1950s, the UDHR was the subject of bitter rejection by influential voices within the US political and legal establishment – who condemned it as "alien" to American traditions, and drafted by a group which was not representative of US values (Holman 1954; Tananbaum 1988).

A Western education among many of the Asian and Arab delegates did not preclude their capacity for cross-cultural perspective and understanding. Chang, as Lydia Liu has demonstrated, traversed across both Confucian moral philosophy and European Enlightenment ideas during the debates. In so doing, he imparted a new plane of universalism to the UDHR's concept of human rights based on his translingual abilities and his use of a "new humanism" to transcend debates about references to God or nature. Neither of those two older wellsprings, nature and deity, foundational to preceding concepts of rights, ended up in the final draft; which rested instead on a web of human connection and mutual dependence (Liu 2014, pp. 404–414). Lebanon's Charles Malik, who argued vigorously with Chang, was a similarly decisive framer of the text. His own outlook, steeped in Western and Christian philosophy, and, more experientially, in encountering Nazism first hand during his studies in Germany, represented an unusual cosmopolitanism – not the unthinking recitation of a transplanted Western liberalism. Deep confidence and familiarity with Western thought allowed these figures a means of synthesis; one that was less readily accessed by Roosevelt, Cassin, or Humphrey. The fact that less than a decade after the UDHR was adopted, it was affirmed at the foundational conference of the Asian-African Movement, held in April 1955 in Bandung, amid uncompromising denunciations of imperialism, suggests its content appealed to those well outside the political West (Burke 2006, pp. 947–965). That over 500 translations of the UDHR are today offered by the UN represents a further testament to the extraordinary breadth of linguistic, philosophical, and cultural traditions that have engaged with the text.

While less apparent than the almost peerless Chang and Malik, many other individuals contributed to the building of the UDHR. Latin American delegates inspired many of the Articles included in the UDHR and served as a bridge between other geopolitical and cultural spheres. Humphrey's draft drew heavily upon the submissions of Panama and Chile. Panama presented the work of the US-based American Law Institute (ALI), which created a "Statement of Essential Human Rights." The document sought to identify a list of rights that could be agreed upon by lawyers, jurists, statesmen, and other educated professionals from around the world (ALI 1945). Chile submitted a 1945 version of what would become the

Bogota Declaration, which was similarly based on a diverse collection of sources. Humphrey directly borrowed from the rights and wording of Panama's and Chile's proposals. This Latin American contribution not only added an important geographical setting for the UDHR's origins, it also helped to make the final draft more appealing to other non-Western delegates. Neither Western individualism nor monolithic Soviet state-centric collectivism were sufficient to find broad compatibility. These submissions enhanced the Declaration's global appeal by elevating the role of the family unit, incorporating duties to a list of rights, and bringing together both political and civil rights and socioeconomic freedoms. The Latin American representatives would later insist upon amending the draft in the Third Committee to include more elements of the Bogota Declaration. The Dominican Republic succeeded in having both men and women referenced in the Preamble, Cuba attached the right to remuneration sufficient for families in Article 23, Ecuador inserted safeguards against arbitrary exile in Article 9, and Mexico pioneered Article 8's right to an effective remedy for rights violations (Glendon 2003, pp. 27–40). These contributions were both evidence of the UDHR's varied sources, and of the appreciable enhancements this diversity facilitated.

Representatives from the Muslim world stretched further the catalog of traditions and ideas featured in the UDHR. Delegations representing large Muslim populations were prominent in advancing amendments and ideas, though less unified than Latin America. India's Hansa Mehta, who represented 40 million Muslims in post-Partition India, joined the Dominican Republic in removing sexist language from the text. Mindful of the need for precision, Mehta also demanded that gender equality be spelled out in the workplace, political participation, judicial system, and marriage. This latter aspect, marriage, was fiercely contended, yet it was a division that ran within the Muslim delegates, and not a position which defined the group. Saudi Arabia, with support from Syria and Lebanon, wanted the eligibility for marriage and equality within the marriage to be determined by national laws. Pakistan's delegate, Shaista Ikramullah, a veteran of the independence struggle, joint founder of the women's wing of the Muslim League, and member of Pakistan's first parliament, was sympathetic to much of Saudi Arabia's position but insisted the relevant Article was needed to protect against child marriage and marriage without consent, and to provide freedom for women after divorce. Much of the text was broadly acceptable to the group, with articles on economic and social rights finding good support from the Muslim world, who invoked equivalents in their own systems of redistribution, which operated as a religious precept.

Most controversial for the Muslim states was the right to change one's religion, which was the prime objection raised in Saudi Arabia's abstention from the UDHR vote. Jamil Baroody of Saudi Arabia attempted to remove the provision from Article 18, which served as a proxy for a wider skepticism about Western influence, and reflected a supposed lack of consultation with Muslim NGOs. Some of the Muslim representatives, like India and Egypt, did not fully agree and either disputed Baroody's interpretation or registered their reservation. So too did Pakistan, a state founded on the promise of a home for the subcontinent's Muslim communities (Waltz 2004 pp. 799–844; Waltz 2002, pp. 437–448). Such examples show the vigor of non-Western engagement in the debates. Small-state actors like these could exert real agency on the final text; and equally, to dissent from features that were regarded as objectionable to their societies. That ultimately only one would do so, in the company of a Western-aligned racialized dictatorship, apartheid South Africa, and a bloc of Soviet totalitarian regimes, spoke more to the nature of Saudi Arabia's monarchy than it did to an exclusivist Western orientation to the Declaration. As diverse as it was, in comparative terms, the process invariably fell short of universal representation. Yet this did little to diminish the universal appeal of the text – which soon found enthusiastic endorsement, and a demand for its application, from those who had not participated. Exclusion from the process was a marginal concern for those, particularly under colonial rule, who demanded inclusion in the promised outcome, a universalized set of equal human rights.

Legacies and Legalities

The UDHR exerted exceptional influence upon the shape, and the very existence, of the postwar human rights movement. It did not resolve the tensions and ambiguities within the concept of human rights, but its eloquence and moral heft was readily drawn upon by those undertaking their own struggles, at the national, regional, and international level. It sits in a foundational position in almost every major text with a human rights aspect adopted after 1948, from the 1950 European Convention on Human Rights (ECHR), to the two human rights Covenants, adopted in 1966, to the Convention on the Rights of Persons with Disabilities (2006), born almost half a century later. The instruments with at least some deference to the UDHR are almost too voluminous to recite even in excerpt, but notable examples include the two international human rights covenants (1966), the Refugee Convention (1951), the Declaration on the Granting of Independence to Colonial Countries and Peoples (1960), the 1965 International Convention on the Elimination of All Forms of Racial Discrimination (1965), the Convention on the Elimination of All-Forms of Discrimination Against Women (1979), the African Charter on Human and Peoples' Rights (1981), the Convention Against Torture (1984), the Declaration on the Right to Development (1986), and the Convention on the Rights of the Child (1990) (Hannum 1995/1996, pp. 287–397). For at least some eminent historians of human rights, even the two Covenants, which had rather more ambitious purpose, as notionally binding treaties, proved not to be as influential as the text they sought to consolidate into law (Borgwardt 2005, p. 265; Glendon 2002, p. 216–217). From Soviet dissidents to LGBTQ activism worldwide, the UDHR has served as a common reference point for almost every human rights campaign and institution. Each article contributes to the legal, political, and everyday lexicon of human rights in the modern era. It is the almost fully naturalized base upon which rights claims rest, the calibration standard for national human rights institutions, and the over-arching frame for the UN's Universal Periodic Review of state performance. While almost every state in the world falls, at best, somewhat short, and countless regimes have attacked and obstructed human rights promotion, direct repudiation of the

UDHR has been comparatively limited. Human rights violations are innumerable – but only a handful of overt attacks on the UDHR itself have been undertaken. While a grim testament to its normative prestige, the fact that even the most authoritarian governments employ strategies that rest predominantly on faux deference to its standards, and subversion of its substance, speaks to the unique durability of the text.

In the simplicity of its purpose and sweep of its prose, the UDHR enunciated a transformative ambition with appeal for a vast section of humanity. In its silence on the practicalities of implementation, it devolved this ambition to humans, states, and the ever-nebulous global community. Born in a fleeting moment of weary optimism and redemptive sentiment, the text arrived into maturity amid a world with new crises and new tensions. The UDHR was adopted on the cusp of two decades-long conflicts, both of which would frequently curtail, and more episodically cultivate its vision. Barely escaping the slow freeze from postwar to Cold War, and only just preceding a cresting wave of anticolonial revolutions, the UDHR, and the rights it promised, was promptly drawn into contests between East and West, and North and South. Although, it had never been insulated from hard political calculation, across the 1950s, 1960s, and 1970s, the intensity and consistency with which human rights were drawn into geopolitical causes and interests became almost obscuring of their content. A predictable catalog of violations were instrumentalized: the Western states typically pointed to forced labor, the absence of freedoms of speech and association, freedom of movement, and generalized political repression within the Soviet bloc and its global satellites. Undeterred by their own abstention on the UDHR, Soviet-aligned legations endlessly directed invective against Western racism, unemployment, and colonialism. There was plenty of substance for both sides to work with, but the West often found itself at a tactical disadvantage owing to its comparatively open societies, domestic dissent and activism, and in its better moments, some degree of good faith and honesty in its responses. These rarely were an impediment faced by the Soviet bloc – which gleefully denounced imperialism as it crushed popular revolutions in Hungary in 1956, and, in 1968, the International Year for Human Rights, in Czechoslovakia.

Paradoxically, the Cold War instrumentalization of human rights also served to elevate their place in global debate. Precisely because the UDHR, and the rights it contained, were an exalted objective, observance, or perceived observance, held real utility in superpower competition. Respect for human rights were the notional underpinning of the legitimacy of each side, a reality that was readily grasped by civil rights activists in the USA, and later by a collection of Soviet writers, scientists, and artists who protested the routine violation of their most basic freedoms. The eventual loss of that legitimacy for the Soviet system, heralded by the emergence of a prominent dissident movement within the Soviet bloc, and accelerated by the mechanisms established in the 1975 Helsinki Final Act, was among the most dramatic developments of the twentieth-century (Foot 2010, pp. 445–465; Keys and Burke 2013, pp. 486–502). Under the terms of Helsinki, both superpowers promised to "act in conformity … with the Universal Declaration of Human Rights" (Conference on Security and Co-Operation in Europe 1975). The Soviet governments of Brezhnev, Andropov, and Chernenko were never disposed to much concern about such conformity – but a brave collection of their citizens acted otherwise (Thomas 2001; Snyder 2011).

With a few exceptions, notably emigration, interstate instrumentalization of human rights was fruitless, but transnational cooperation between citizens and activists often won, with immense suffering, meaningful success. The explosion of nongovernmental organizations devoted to human rights, and almost always resting on the UDHR itself, established a novel force in international affairs. Exemplified by Amnesty International (1961), these transnational human rights movements built their networks on interhuman solidarity, not interstate bargaining (Clark 2007; Sikkink, Keck 1998). Their conspicuous efforts at studied impartiality between repression from governments of the left and the right conferred upon them a credibility, and tool for moral suasion, that states mostly lacked. Their birth coincided with a renascent period for citizen-led activism, one which trafficked across borders, and both within and around conventional party politics in the West. From the civil rights and antiracism campaigns of the 1960s, to second-wave feminism and gay liberation in the 1970s, people mobilized using the various freedoms available in their respective societies to claim the rights promised to them, and where possible, to assist their counterparts overseas, many of which faced both different obstacles and less hospitable political conditions. Governments had proclaimed the UDHR was a guiding principle; their people sought to make it governmental practice.

Alongside the East-West axis, and interacting with the embryonic transnational human rights NGO movement, the anticolonial movement also seized upon the UDHR. Loud advertisement of faith in human rights were an exquisite hypocrisy for those who lived under European imperial rule. Almost every provision revealed European colonial deficiency in Asia and Africa, be it in political freedoms, individual legal protections, and national economic development.

While a widespread feature of anticolonial campaigns worldwide, UN Trust Territories were especially vulnerable to charges of human rights violation. The International Trusteeship System supervised territories placed under it according to agreements with the administering powers. Chapter 13, Article 76, of the UN Charter made a fundamental objective of the Trusteeship System "to encourage respect for human rights and for fundamental freedoms," as defined later by the UDHR. Using an avenue for redress foreclosed to other citizens until the late 1960s, and barely operational even in the 1970s, tens of thousands of petitions, for example, were sent to the UN Trusteeship Council from the French and British Cameroons in 1956 alone (Terretta 2012, pp. 329–360). The increasingly manifest incompatibility between imperial rule and human rights steadily eroded the mythology of humanitarian tutelage that underwrote imperial claims.

Colonial human rights violations, and by the mid-1950s, colonialism itself, was routinely declared inconsistent with respect for the rights of the UDHR (Burke 2010). By contrast, nationalist leaders paired their collective struggles with pursuit of human rights, and a number specified the UDHR as an animating objective. In Tanganyika, another UN Trust Territory, Julius Nyerere used the UDHR to help justify his independence movement. He spoke at the UNGA on 14 December 1961, a few days after Tanganyika's independence, on his aims regarding the UDHR. The document would be used "as a basis for both our external and our internal policies." He added some caution to his promise, however, by admitting that his government could not yet offer all the UDHR promised to its citizens and that the Declaration was more of a goal still to be attained (UN General Assembly Official Records 1961). Tragically, Nyerere also served as an example of what became a wider phenomenon among independence governments. Within only a few years, he curtailed individual protections, adopted a one-party state, and aligned with an African Socialist philosophy seemingly far removed from rights-talk (Kirby 2015, pp. 112–133).

This pattern was repeated elsewhere, as rights that were important enough to overthrow colonial powers were apparently no longer worthy of fulfilment once newly independent governments faced national security and economic challenges. The founding document of the Organisation of African Unity (OAU), adopted in May 1963, committed members to promote the UDHR (Heads of African States and Governments 1963). Many signatories would turn this into only a partial commitment, perceiving a hierarchy of rights. Development programs, to be fulfilled through the consolidation of state power, would mean political and civil rights would have to wait until the right to bread and protection from poverty could be secured (Howard 1983, pp. 467–490). Much of the Global South began to focus more on rights not explicitly included in the UDHR, such as the right to national self-determination and the right to development. Not all in the postcolonial world subscribed to such a rationale for human rights violations. President Seretse Khama of Botswana achieved his preindependence commitment to use the UDHR as a bedrock to build a nonracial society (Kirby 2017). Many anticolonial activists who did not win power, but saw national liberation as tied to individual freedoms, continued to fight for the cause from below (Terretta 2013, pp. 389–416). The UDHR offered genuine hope to the decolonization movement, even if newly independent states were only sporadically and sparsely loyal custodians of the Declaration.

UN members assented to no mandatory requirements when they voted on the Declaration. Statehood and domestic sovereignty remained, for practical purposes, nearly inviolable. The chief downfall of the UDHR was that it was, indeed, merely a declaration. It was not binding international law and it placed few measurable obligations upon states. The UDHR was very much unlike the ECHR, for instance, which was binding under international law, and backed by a stunningly intrusive enforcement body, and the first serious model for supranational human rights institutions (Duranti 2017, p. 160). Victims could only find comfort, or perhaps righteous frustration, in the UDHR's statements on what should be the human experience. The quest to fulfil these ideals depended on faith and goodwill, without any effective machinery for enforcement. What recourse there was rested largely in the hands of the people. The Preamble stated that UN members pledged to promote respect for and observance of the UDHR; yet accountability for these undertakings was dispersed so widely and imprecisely that the remedy was far from straightforward. Ad-hoc mobilizations, global campaigns, and opportunistic use of other forums and supplemental institutions were a less reliable and reassuring protection than a court in Strasbourg.

Much of this situation was the result of a compromise to ensure agreement among the international community. An expansive set of rights, proclaimed universally, had been purchased with a tactical elision when speaking of enforcement. For sibling human rights instruments, most obviously the ECHR, the possibilities afforded by a narrow and more harmonious community of states, and narrower catalog of freedoms, were very much distinct. The US-Soviet axis, at the very early stages of the Cold War, was united in their rejection of any coercive means for implementation. A nonbinding instrument was too weak for some observers to make a virtue out of necessity. Furthermore, arguments to suggest there were legal implications in the UDHR were not entirely persuasive. Cassin claimed the UDHR gave definition to the mission, outlined in the UN Charter, to promote and encourage respect for human rights and fundamental freedoms. This was a matter for international concern, Cassin argued, that superseded the UN Charter's safeguards for domestic jurisdiction. Hersch Lauterpacht, who was dramatically disappointed with the UDHR, was unconvinced. To attach the UDHR to the UN Charter in such a way, according to Lauterpacht, would only diminish the legal standing of the latter without adding any legality to the former. A nonbinding document could not be an authoritative interpretation of a legally binding Charter. Lauterpacht struggled to see how the UDHR could possibly be treated as an enforceable instrument without doing damage to the integrity of the entire UN system. If state sincerity on human rights guarantees was to be measured by their sacrifice for these ideals, they appeared depressingly deficient. The moral force of the UDHR's universality is undermined, for Lauterpacht, when one finds the basis for this in the universal agreement that obligations are forced upon no one (Lauterpacht 1968, pp. 394–428). States who were free in action could not be trusted to advance the cause of human freedom.

The UDHR has developed greater significance in international and domestic law than was expected by the critics at the time of its formation. It has had tangible ripple effects that have advanced human rights protections in the real world, in a diversity of ways and localities. National laws and constitutions adopted the language and principles of the Declaration, sometimes verbatim, across all continents. Well over 90 countries have had or maintained constitutions that refer to basic rights, many of which directly refer to the UDHR. In Africa, after a wave of postcolonial transitions in the late 1950s and early 1960s, there were at least 20 national constitutions that invoked human rights and fundamental freedoms. The Declaration has proven useful in domestic courts of law. Judges and legal practitioners may refer to it to clarify customary international law; interpret domestic human rights laws; define national policy in relation to international obligations; or, alternatively, to reject the applicability of the UDHR in domestic legal cases. Legal institutions scarcely oppose national laws based on a perceived incompatibility with the UDHR, but it is regularly referred to in judicial decisions related to fundamental rights within domestic legal codes. Judgments and national cases that cite the UDHR are found across the globe in countries as diverse as Argentina, Australia, Botswana, France, India, Israel, Mauritius, the UK, and the USA (Hannum 1995/1996, pp. 355–391). The Declaration remains a pertinent statement of human rights in both the international and domestic context.

The common view among many scholars has grown distant from Lauterpacht's dismissive take several decades ago. There is much more agreement that the UDHR is binding customary international law or an authoritative interpretation of the Articles on human rights in the UN Charter (Simpson 2001, p. 11; Sohn 1982, pp. 15–17; Simma, Alston 1988, p. 84–85). The UDHR aimed to protect citizens from state power, but human rights and domestic sovereignty are not necessarily antithetical. States, in the modern world, depend increasingly on international legitimacy for their jurisdiction to be fully recognized by other states. An egregious abuse of human rights, as defined by the Declaration, may in fact undermine the validity of a national government. The opposite is also true, as a strong human rights record can show a state is a fair and well-behaved member of the international community. Greater moral authority can mean greater cooperative links and economic partnerships and, therefore, more prosperous and stable governments. Sovereignty may therefore be reinforced by respect for international proclamations, even if they are without legally binding force. The UDHR's power in norms and customary law, however, lacking in their own realms, are mutually reinforcing. These attributes guarantee that the triumphant moment of 1948 still reverberates in the current day context.

Conclusion

At seventy, the UDHR has survived and witnessed the same historical milestones as any other septuagenarian. Unlike any human life, the UDHR is commonly judged on its strengths and weaknesses at birth. Furthermore, unlike many constitutions, it has not been reformed or amended. This adds to the timelessness of the UDHR's principles, but also risks irrelevancy as certain ideals can easily become outdated through the passage of time. The longer the UDHR endures as a utopia for human life, still seemingly far away and out of reach, the more observers may become cynical about the feasibility of human rights in an international system of sovereign states. The question is whether the UDHR is to blame for the failings of the present, just as much as it can be linked to successes like the Helsinki Final Act. The problem of evaluating the UDHR must be incorporated into an assessment, as this volume seeks to achieve, of the institutions, tribunals, and courts established in the decades after its creation. The UDHR's outcomes were forever destined to be dependent on how states, organizations, and individuals would live up to its vision. Its far-reaching rhetoric did not explain the consequences of transgressing these fundamental human freedoms, dignities, and protections. Perhaps, it did not have to. The Declaration, as much as it can be dissected and critiqued today, was itself a tool for evaluation and judgment. The mission to safeguard the UDHR was always one propelled predominantly by moral force. The UDHR, while merely claiming to adhere to timeless values at the moment of its drafting, now has genuine historical pedigree for the activists, lawyers, journalists, and policy-makers born after 1948.

The greatest challenge for the UDHR's claim to universality is whether it can transcend even further generations and the constant changes in global politics, economics, and culture. The human rights movement has had to adapt to the opportunities and difficulties of the modern world. Yet, the strength of the UDHR is its reminder that temporal, as well as national, context is no valid basis for violating inherent rights. Year 1948 remains the most significant year for human rights, short of any prospect for a universally binding and enforceable human rights bill. Its legacy is determined by the power of its advocates and descendants. The UDHR remains formative for those conceptualizing human rights for the first time in childhood or young adulthood. Ignorance, according to the UNCHR, is not possible. The Declaration's universal mandate is automatically passed down to the actors with agency to effect change. Its continued use as a source point for rights terminology and campaign offers hope for the world and, for those keeping score, provides evidence of durability. The UDHR's mission, far from fulfilled, is undoubtedly ongoing. The Declaration retains its relevance as long as it is unrealized and its reverence as it continues to offer guidance for relieving human suffering in all its forms.

References

American Anthropological Association (1947) Statement on human rights. Am Anthropol 49(4):539–543

American Law Institute (1945) Statement of essential human rights. Americans United for World Organisation, New York

Borgwardt E (2005) A new deal for the world: America's vision for human rights. Belknap Press of Harvard University Press, Cambridge

Bricker J (1948) An 'International Bill of Rights': proposals have dangerous implications for U.S. Am Bar Assoc J 34:984–986. 1078–1081

Burke R (2006) 'The compelling dialogue of freedom': human rights at the 1955 Bandung conference. Hum Rights Q 28:947–965. https://doi.org/10.1353/hrq.2006.0041

Burke R (2010) Decolonization and the evolution of international human rights. University of Pennsylvania Press, Philadelphia

Burke R (2017) Human rights internationalism. In: Clavin P, Amrith S, Sluga G (eds) Internationalisms: a twentieth-century history. Cambridge University Press, Cambridge, pp 287–314

Clark AM (2007) Diplomacy of conscience: Amnesty International and changing human rights. Princeton University Press, Princeton

Conference on Security and Co-Operation in Europe Final Act (1975) Helsinki final act. Available via Organization for Security and Co-operation in Europe, http://www.osce.org/helsinki-final-act. Accessed 26 Nov 2017

d'Aleth P (1949) A UNESCO exhibition. In: The tablet: The international catholic news weekly. Available via The Tablet archive. http://archive.thetablet.co.uk/issue/26th-november-1949/8/18530/a-unesco-exhibition. Accessed 10 Nov 2017

Devereux AM (2005) Australia and the birth of the international bill of human rights 1946–1966. Federation Press, Annandale

Dolinger J (2016) The failure of the Universal Declaration of Human Rights. Univ Miami Inter-Am Law Rev 47(2):164–199

Donnelly J (2013) Universal human rights in theory and practice. Cornell University Press, Ithaca

Duranti M (2012) The Holocaust, the legacy of 1789 and the birth of international human rights law: revisiting the foundation myth. J Genocide Res 14:159–186. https://doi.org/10.1080/14623528.2012.677760

Duranti M (2017) The conservative human rights revolution: European identity, transnational politics, and the origins of the European Convention. Oxford University Press, New York

Foot R (2010) The Cold War and human rights. In: Leffler MP, Westad OA (eds) The Cambridge history of the Cold War. Cambridge University Press, New York, pp 445–465

Glendon MA (2002) A world made new: Eleanor Roosevelt and the Universal Declaration of Human Rights. Random House, New York

Glendon MA (2003) The forgotten crucible: the Latin American influence on the universal human rights idea. Harvard Hum Rights J 16:27–40

Hannum H (1995/1996) The status of the Universal Declaration of Human Rights in national and international law'. Ga J Intl Comp L 25:287–397

Heads of African States and Governments (1963) Charter of the organization of African Unity. Available via University of Minnesota Human Rights Library. http://hrlibrary.umn.edu/africa/OAU_Charter_1993.html. Accessed 30 Nov 2017

Hoffmann SL (2011) Genealogies of human rights. In: Hoffmann SL (ed) Human rights in the twentieth century. Cambridge University Press, New York, pp 1–26

Holman FE (1949) International proposals affecting so-called human rights. Law Contemp Probl 14:479–489

Holman F (1954) Story of the 'Bricker' amendment. Committee for Constitutional Government, New York

Howard RE (1983) The full-belly thesis: should economic rights take priority over civil and political rights? Evidence from Sub-Saharan Africa. Hum Rights Q 5:467–490

Humphrey J, Hobbins AJ, Piatti L (1994) On the edge of greatness: the diaries of John Humphrey, first Director of the United Nations Division of Human Rights. McGill University Libraries, Montreal

Hunt L (2007) Inventing human rights: a history. Norton & Company, New York

Keys B, Burke R (2013) Human rights. In: Immerman RH, Goedde P (eds) The Oxford handbook of the Cold War. Oxford University Press, Oxford, pp 486–502

Kirby J (2015) 'Our ideals must guide us, not blind us': examining the abuse of human rights in Tanzania, 1960-75. Melbourne Historical Journal 43:112–133

Kirby J (2017) 'Our Bantustans are better than yours': Botswana, the United States, and human rights idealism in the 1970s. Int Hist Rev 29:860–884. https://doi.org/10.1080/07075332.2017.1283641

Kley DV (ed) (1994) The French idea of freedom: the old regime and the Declaration of Rights of 1789. Stanford University Press, Stanford

Korey W (1998) NGOs and the Universal Declaration of Human Rights: 'a curious grapevine'. St. Martin's Press, New York

Lauren PG (2003) The evolution of international human rights: visions seen. University of Pennsylvania Press, Philadelphia

Lauterpacht H (1968) International law and human rights. Archon Books, Hamden

Liu L (2014) Shadows of universalism: the untold story of human rights around 1948. Critical Inquiry 40:385–417. https://doi.org/10.1086/676413

Maul D (2012) Human Rights, Development and Decolonization: The International Labour Organization, 1940–70. Palgrave Macmillan, New York

Mayers D (2015) Humanity in 1948: the Genocide Convention and the Universal Declaration of Human Rights. Diplomacy & Statecraft 26:446–472. https://doi.org/10.1080/09592296.2015.1067522

Morsink J (1984) The philosophy of the Universal Declaration. Hum Rights Q 6:309–334

Morsink J (1991) Women's rights in the Universal Declaration. Hum Rights Q 13:229–256

Morsink J (1999a) Cultural genocide, the Universal Declaration, and minority rights. Hum Rights Q 21:1009–1060

Morsink J (1999b) The Universal Declaration of Human Rights: origins, drafting, and intent. University of Pennsylvania Press, Philadelphia

Moyn S (2010) The last utopia: human rights in history. The Belknap Press of Harvard University Press, Cambridge

Mutua M (2002) Human rights: a political & cultural critique. University of Pennsylvania Press, Philadelphia

Normand R, Zaidi S (2008) Human rights at the UN: the political history of universal justice. Indiana University Press, Bloomington

Roberts CNJ (2015) The contentious history of the International Bill of Human Rights. Cambridge University Press, New York

Robertson G (2006) Crimes against humanity: the struggle for global justice. Penguin Books, London

Sikkink K, Keck M (1998) Activists beyond borders: advocacy networks in international politics. Cornell University Press, Ithaca

Simma B, Alston P (1988) The sources of human rights law: custom, jus cogens, and general principles. Aust YbIL 12:84–85

Simpson AWB (2001) Human rights and the end of empire: Britain and the genesis of the European Convention. Oxford University Press, New York

Snyder S (2011) Human rights activism and the end of the Cold War. Cambridge University Press, New York

Sohn LB (1982) The new international law: protection of the rights of individuals rather than states. Am Univ Law Rev 32:1–64

Tananbaum D (1988) The Bricker amendment controversy. Cornell University Press, Ithaca

Terretta M (2012) 'We had been fooled into thinking that the UN watches over the entire world': human rights, UN trust territories, and Africa's decolonization. Hum Rights Q 34:329–360. https://doi.org/10.1353/hrq.2012.0022

Terretta M (2013) From below and to the left? Human rights and liberation politics in Africa's postcolonial age. J World History 24:389–416. https://doi.org/10.1353/jwh.2013.0041

Thomas DC (2001) The Helsinki effect: international norms, human rights, and the demise of communism. Princeton University Press, Princeton

UN General Assembly Official Records (1961) 1078th plenary meeting (16th session), UN Doc. A/PV.1078, 14 Dec 1961

UN General Assembly Third Committee (1948) UN Doc. GAOR, A/C.3/SR.161, 27 Nov 1948

Waltz S (2002) Reclaiming and rebuilding the history of the Universal Declaration of Human Rights. Third World Q 23:437–448

Waltz S (2004) Universal human rights: the contribution of Muslim States. Hum Rights Q 26(4):799–844. https://doi.org/10.1353/hrq.2004.0059

Wildenthal L (2011) Rudolf Laun and the human rights of Germans in Occupied and Early West Germany. In: Hoffmann SL (ed) Human tights in the twentieth century. Cambridge University Press, New York, pp 125–144

The UN Human Rights Council: Achievements and Challenges in Its First Decade

Humberto Cantú Rivera

Contents

Introduction 50
Achievements of the Human Rights Council 52
Human Rights Standard-Setting: Evolution and Political Legitimacy 52
The Universal Periodic Review in Balance: A (Short) Assessment of Its Experience 56
Challenges for the Human Rights Council 59
Limiting the Independence and Functions of Special Procedures Mandate-Holders 60
The (Limited?) Functions of the Advisory Committee to the Human Rights Council 62
Election to the Human Rights Council, or the Need for Higher Standards of Human Rights
Observance 64
Concluding Thoughts 65
References 66

Abstract

As the tenth anniversary of the Human Rights Council took place in 2016, it is useful to reflect on the different contributions made by this UN organ in the field of human rights. Its participation in the development and consolidation of human rights norms through its standard-setting function, in addition to its role as the institution to oversee the effective implementation of the Universal Periodic Review, the stalwart of this intergovernmental body, have ensured continuity from the working methods of the Commission while adding another layer of institutional monitoring capacity. And yet, 10 years after its creation, several shortcomings have been apparent, as a result of the inherent criticism deriving from the work of the Special Procedures system, from the limitation of its own subsidiary bodies, and of the politicization that undeniably and inevitably surrounds any intergovernmental body. This chapter aims to discuss some of the

H. Cantú Rivera (✉)
University of Monterrey, Monterrey, Mexico
e-mail: humberto.cantu.r@gmail.com

© Springer Nature Singapore Pte Ltd. 2018
G. Oberleitner (ed.), *International Human Rights Institutions, Tribunals, and Courts*,
International Human Rights, https://doi.org/10.1007/978-981-10-5206-4_3

most important achievements and challenges of the Human Rights Council during its first decade, as it sails into its second decade of existence with the purpose of effectively protecting and promoting human rights worldwide.

Keywords

Human rights · United Nations · Human Rights Council · Special procedures · Advisory Committee

Introduction

The establishment of the Human Rights Council in 2006 marked an important step in the consolidation of human rights as a pillar of the United Nations. However, the first step in this area was taken many decades before, as the international community tried to figure out how to move forward from the horrors of World War II (Tomuschat 2014, pp. 27–29). Indeed, the Charter of the United Nations explicitly foresaw in its preamble, as well as in its purposes and principles, the importance of the promotion and protection of human rights, dignity, and equality (United Nations Charter (UN Charter) 1945), as the basis for global progress. This basic tenet of the United Nations would eventually give rise to an important global architecture consisting of treaties, bodies, and organs in charge of securing a minimum of human dignity to peoples across the globe.

These principles would be made operational by the Charter in articles 62.2 and 68, relating to the attributions of the Economic and Social Council (ECOSOC) to make recommendations for the promotion and observance of human rights, and to establish commissions for that purpose. In the words of Hersch Lauterpacht, the relevance of this provision "is partly indicated by the fact that it is the only Commission specifically referred to in the Charter" (Lauterpacht 1947, p. 56). In that regard, a committee created for the organization of the ECOSOC adopted a report on 15 February 1946, conceiving the establishment of a Commission on Human Rights whose mandate would consist of providing the Council with advice, proposals, and reports in relation to four central questions: the development of an international bill of rights; international declarations or conventions on different matters of concern for human dignity (such as civil liberties, the status of women, freedom of information, etc.); the protection of minorities; and the prevention of discrimination (Report of the Committee on the organization of the Economic and Social Council 1946, par. 7(a)). This mandate would be eventually implemented, constituting the basis for the drafting of the Universal Declaration of Human Rights, of the 1966 covenants and of other human rights conventions and instruments (Cantú Rivera 2015, pp. 4–5).

The drafting of the Universal Declaration of Human Rights by the Commission on Human Rights, one of the most important nonbinding international instruments, would only be one of its first steps in a long list of achievements of this subsidiary body to ECOSOC (Smith 2010, p. 220). The Commission contributed directly to the development of international human rights law, overseeing during its existence the negotiation and adoption of conventions addressing minorities (on migrant workers or children's rights, for example), prevention of discrimination (on racial or gender basis), and atrocious human rights violations (notably torture) amounting to international crimes (Tomuschat 2014, p. 36). It also contributed to the refinement of international human rights standards through the work undertaken by Special Procedures mandate holders on numerous subjects. In addition, it received communications from victims denouncing alleged human rights violations, setting up an international follow-up mechanism – although perhaps not as effective as required, for that matter.

However, despite important contributions to the advancement of international human rights law, the Commission on Human Rights was an intergovernmental (political) body, a situation that crippled its functioning and led to double standards, bloc voting, and membership with the aim of shielding States from criticism from the inside (Alston 2006, pp. 191–192; Pinheiro 2006, pp. 108–111; Callejón 2006, pp. 88–89; Alston and Goodman 2013, p. 695; A More Secure World: Our Shared Responsibility, Report of the High-level Panel on Threats, Challenges and Change transmitted to the UN Secretary-General 2004, paras. 283–291). The loss of credibility on the Commission resulting from these practices led to a call for the redesign of the UN human rights machinery (In Larger Freedom: Towards Development, Security and Human Rights for All. Report of the Secretary-General 2005, pars. 182–183; De Alba and Genina 2016, pp. 34–36), in an effort to reposition the human rights pillar within the United Nations.

As such, the General Assembly adopted resolution 60/251 on 15 March 2006, substituting the Commission on Human Rights for the Human Rights Council (HRC), which would have a different – smaller – composition, and which would try to distance itself from the practices that led to the discredit of the Commission. Resolution 60/251 determined, among other things, that the Human Rights Council would become a subsidiary body of the General Assembly (instead of ECOSOC; Alston and Goodman 2013, p. 691), thus partially raising its political standing in the UN machinery (Bossuyt and Decaux 2005, p. 4); that it should submit recommendations to the General Assembly for the development of international human rights law; and that it would undertake a universal periodic review regarding the implementation of human rights obligations by States. It also established the need to review and rationalize the work of the Commission on Human Rights (especially of its mandates and mechanisms), and a reconfiguration of the membership of the Commission, reducing it to 47 members (despite a proposal to make its membership universal: A More Secure World: Our Shared Responsibility, Report of the High-level Panel on Threats, Challenges and Change transmitted to the UN Secretary-General, 2004 paras. 283–291) and redistributing the seats available per regional group. The *renaissance* of this human rights institution intended to mark a new era in which human rights would occupy a more prominent place in the structure of the United Nations, and contribute to its mainstreaming in other organs and processes. However, as the French adage goes, *plus ça change, plus ça reste la même chose*: criticism to some of the changes introduced by the Human Rights Council clearly reflected how, despite the good intentions to improve the functioning of the Commission, it would still be outmatched by the political considerations and limitations imposed by States on the effectiveness of the Council (Decaux 2006).

This contribution aims to reflect on the achievements and challenges in the first decade of existence of the Human Rights Council. Thus, it proceeds in two stages: first, it will analyze some of the progress made in fulfilling the objectives of resolution 60/251, notably in relation to the promotion of human rights, the continued evolution of human rights standards, and in implementing the flagship of the Council, the Universal Periodic Review. Secondly, it will analyze some of the most important challenges to the effectiveness of the Council to contribute to the development of international human rights law, particularly in relation to the inherent limitation of Special Procedures' mandate-holders independence, to the limited capacity of its think tank, the Advisory Committee, and finally, to the "membership issue" for States wishing to become a part of the Human Rights Council.

Achievements of the Human Rights Council

Taking into consideration the political turmoil that surrounded the context leading to the replacement of the Commission by the Human Rights Council – including the much-criticized election of Libya to the Presidency of the Commission (Tomuschat 2014, pp. 184–185) – the start of a new human rights body raised important concerns as to what could be improved in practice vis-à-vis its predecessor. As the first President of the HRC (Mexican Ambassador Luis Alfonso de Alba) points out, it was a particularly difficult challenge to navigate the complex diplomatic environment to organize the functioning of the Council and its definitive working methods (De Alba and Genina 2016), which would be adopted at the fifth session. However, two of the most important achievements of the Human Rights Council in its first decade of existence have been the continuous evolution of international human rights standards and their political legitimacy, and the establishment and early reform of the Universal Periodic Review, with the aim of making it more functional and less encumbering for States.

Human Rights Standard-Setting: Evolution and Political Legitimacy

One of the main concerns in relation to the activities undertaken by the Commission on Human Rights (and now by the Council) has been the work in relation to standard-setting, one of its most important functions in the early days of international human rights law. This work allowed the Commission to directly contribute to the evolution of human rights standards – as mandated by the Economic and Social Council in the resolution creating the Commission – notably through the adoption of the Universal Declaration on Human Rights and of the International Covenants of 1966. However, "at least since the entry into force of the two Covenants in 1976, the need for additional standards has often been questioned" (Alston and Goodman 2013, p. 702).

Indeed, the Covenants provided a large framework of human rights, with the aim of ensuring that the rights contained therein would be respected and protected by States without discrimination of any kind, a situation which begs the question whether it was necessary – or even desirable – to continue expanding the scope of human rights standards. However, despite those concerns, the Commission (and its member States, either implicitly or explicitly) continued to enlarge the international regulatory framework dealing with human dignity, by focusing on three categories or groups: grave human rights violations (which would focus notably on torture), discrimination (against women or in relation to race), and vulnerable groups (migrant workers, women, children). Several of these regulatory frameworks (which were adopted in the form of conventions, under the direction of the Commission) were accompanied by optional protocols, instituting complaints procedures or focusing on other aspects related to specific human rights issues. Such is the case on the Second Optional Protocol to the International Covenant on Civil and Political Rights on the abolition of the death penalty, or of the optional protocols established by the Committees on Racial Discrimination or Discrimination Against Women, creating individual complaints procedures. This continued evolution suggested that despite the general protection in relation to all human rights by the standards set forth in the Covenants, specific norms protecting individuals or groups from particular challenges or situations would be needed, in order to adapt the instruments of protection to the gaps created by or resulting from social evolution. This is an area where clear actions and initiatives are required to ensure that the standards initially conceived in the 1940s and 1950s continue to have practical effects for human rights protection against the challenges of the twenty-first century (and which is complemented by other processes, notably Special Procedures mandates, explained *infra*). As stated by the International Council on Human Rights Policy in 2006, ". . .there are limits to the extension of existing standards: new standards will continue to be needed in the future. Society is continually changing and human rights laws must also change when gaps in protection appear" (International Council on Human Rights Policy 2006, p. 3).

The replacement of the Commission by the Human Rights Council in 2006 did not stop that trend. One of the key issues in the transition was precisely securing the adoption of two particularly relevant international human rights instruments that had been negotiated under the Commission: the Declaration on the Rights of Indigenous Peoples, on the one hand, and the International Convention for the Protection of all Persons from Enforced Disappearance, on the other hand (De Alba and Genina 2016, pp. 77–87). Both instruments were adopted in the first session of the Council, and several others continued to be negotiated or adopted in the following sessions, including the International Convention on the Rights of Persons with Disabilities (also adopted in 2006, although in an ad hoc committee operating separate from the Commission or Council), and two optional protocols establishing communications procedures in relation to the International Covenant on Economic, Social and Cultural Rights (2008), and to the Convention on the Rights of the Child (2011).

In addition to these conventional instruments, several other instances devoted to analyzing the feasibility and convenience of enlarging the international human rights conventional framework have been created in relation to the questions of human rights and transnational corporations and other business enterprises, on the role of private military and security companies, on gaps in the International Convention on the Elimination of Racial Discrimination, and on declarations on the right to peace, and on the right of peasants and other people working in rural areas. As it can be observed, the work of the Council and its subsidiary bodies to continue developing international human rights law has allowed for the refinement of the rights of persons and groups in specific situations or scenarios, and of the obligations of States in relation to the promotion and protection of human rights. Nevertheless, not all of the standard-setting work has been made through conventional instruments.

The standard-setting activity has been especially complemented by the work undertaken by one of the most important mechanisms in the field of human rights: the Special Procedures mandate-holders (de Frouville 1996, p. 15). The UN Special Procedures "are a series of mandates entrusted to experts who work independently from any State or organization, and whose general purpose is the development of specific issues of international human rights law, to monitor the application and respect of human rights in States, and in many cases to receive communications regarding alleged human rights violations that may work as quasi-jurisdictional procedures at the international level" (Cantú Rivera 2015, p. 9). As independent experts working on specific thematic issues or country situations, their work has been lauded as the "crown jewel" of the United Nations system, given that they have contributed enormously to develop and advance human rights standards worldwide, through thematic reports, country visits, or individual communications. Indeed, they have a particularly relevant advantage vis-à-vis other human rights bodies (notably treaty-monitoring bodies): they do not depend on the ratification of an instrument by any given State to act in relation to the (general or specific) domestic or thematic human rights situation. This aspect has been explored by mandates whose areas of work address topics included in one of the international human rights conventions, such as in the case of enforced disappearances (de Frouville 2015, pp. 109–111), where a Working Group and a Committee coexist, or in the case of torture and other inhuman, cruel, or degrading treatments, where a Special Rapporteur, a Committee, and a Sub-Committee coincide (Evans 2017).

The Special Procedures of the Commission on Human Rights appeared in the context of the grave crisis of enforced disappearances in Latin America during the 1970s and 1980s (Decaux 2015, p. xi), through the creation of the Working Group on Enforced or Involuntary Disappearances (1980), and were soon complemented by other mandates, established either as working groups or as individual special rapporteurships. Three of the most relevant examples of the first "generation" of Special Procedures are the Special Rapporteur on summary or arbitrary executions, established in 1982; the Special Rapporteur on torture and other cruel, inhuman or degrading treatment, created in 1985; and the Working Group on Arbitrary Detention, established in 1991. These initial mandates (and others, such as those on religious intolerance or freedom of expression), would be followed by a second "wave" establishing procedures on issues relating to economic, social, and cultural rights, most notably on the rights to food (2000), to health (2002), to adequate housing (2000), or to education (1998), among others. The first two decades of the 2000s – including after the transition from Commission to Council – have seen a further expansion in the number and areas of work of special procedures mandates, a sort of third "wave" addressing issues such as business and human rights (2005 and 2011), the right to a healthy environment (2012), the right to development (2016), persons with leprosy (2017), transitional justice (2011), or discrimination based on sexual orientation and gender identity (2016). At the time of writing, thematic mandates of the Human Rights Council are 44 in total.

As it can be observed from the different "waves" in the creation of these mandates, the topics addressed by the Special Procedures mandate-holders can be considered to be of a double nature (Cantú Rivera 2015, p. 10): those addressing specific questions and rights, which are prone to more effective human rights protection through the individual communications procedure (including those on torture, arbitrary detention, enforced disappearances, housing, water, food, health and others); and those related to ascertainable rights, oriented to the definition of human rights perspectives of issues of a broader nature (such as those on transitional justice, international solidarity, extreme poverty and human rights, or the human rights implications of foreign debt, for example). Furthermore, this classification of procedures on "actionable rights" and "ascertainable rights" can be also equated to the "generational theory" of human rights (Domínguez-Redondo 2017, pp. 45–46): in that sense, those issues addressed in the mandates created in the 1980s and early 1990s revolve around civil and political rights ("first-generation" rights); those in the late 1990s and early 2000s mostly address issues related to economic, social, and cultural rights ("second-generation" rights); and those from the late 2000s and the present decade address questions of a broader nature that can have specific impacts on human rights ("third-generation" rights).

Most of the standard-setting work developed by Special Procedures mandate holders derives from their annual thematic reports to the Human Rights Council, and in many cases also to the General Assembly. Through them, they have been able to analyze the specific nuances of potential human rights violations, or the contours of the rights they've been entrusted to explore, thus systematically assessing the political, social, economic or technological developments in relation to the human rights standards included in international human rights treaties or in the Universal Declaration of Human Rights. Examples of this effect have started to become more and more visible in the first decade of existence of the Human Rights Council, where the work of several mandate-holders has progressively become more action-oriented: the Special Rapporteur on extreme poverty and human rights, for example, issued the Guiding Principles on Extreme Poverty and Human Rights (Final draft of the Guiding Principles on Extreme Poverty and Human Rights: Report of the Special Rapporteur on Extreme Poverty and Human Rights 2012; Carmona Sepúlveda 2015, pp. 121–125), in an effort to clearly determine the scope of human rights obligations of States to combat structural conditions that generate or perpetuate extreme poverty. The Special Rapporteur on the right to food also presented the Human Rights Council with a set of Guiding Principles on human rights impact assessments of trade and investment agreements (Guiding principles on human rights impact assessments of trade and investment agreements: Report of the Special Rapporteur on the right to food 2011), in order to guide the work of States to prevent violations to the right to food resulting from foreign investment or trade.

But perhaps the most notable example of standard-setting that has generated direct action by many States and non-State actors alike are the Guiding Principles on Business and Human Rights (Guiding Principles on Business and Human Rights: Operationalizing the "Protect, Respect and Remedy" Framework. Report of the Special Representative of the Secretary-General on the issue of human rights and transnational corporations and other business enterprises 2011), a set of recommendatory measures endorsed by the Human Rights Council that have generated regional and domestic State initiatives on this issue in different parts of the world, as well as sectoral or transversal projects involving businesses, NGOs, and other actors (Alston and Goodman 2013, pp. 703–704). Another element deriving from the Guiding Principles on Business and Human Rights that has generated State action is the 2014 report of the Working Group on the issue of human rights and transnational corporations and other business enterprises to the General Assembly, addressing the elements and focus that "National Action Plans" on business and human rights should have (Human rights and transnational corporations and other business enterprises. Note by the Secretary-General 2014). At the time of writing, 19 States from different regions of the world (although mostly those in Europe) have adopted National Action Plans on business and human rights, with at least 19 other countries being in the process of developing such initiatives. This clearly reflects how the standard-setting work developed by the Special Procedures of the Human Rights Council is slowly transitioning from a particularly declarative approach to a more action-oriented focus, which also represents – to some extent, at least – the political legitimacy that the work of mandate-holders can enjoy, from both States and other actors, enabling them to become direct harbingers of international human rights standards.

These are two of the major achievements of the Human Rights Council in its first decade of existence: the fact that it has permitted the continuous promotion of human rights, by renewing the mandates of most thematic procedures since 2006, and by expanding the scope of analysis and actions through the creation of new mandates. This, in turn, has permitted that international standards developed by mandate-holders enjoy political legitimacy, which has also generated the possibility of suggesting operational measures to improve human rights protection at the domestic and regional levels, while still focusing on refining the interpretation of normative standards contained in conventional or declarative instruments.

The Universal Periodic Review in Balance: A (Short) Assessment of Its Experience

The Universal Periodic Review (UPR) is considered the flagship of the UN Human Rights Council, and was conceived as the instrument that would help the Council to combat the politicization that plagued the Commission on Human Rights throughout its existence. Indeed, it was thought that it would be instrumental in fighting the double standards, bloc voting, and selectivity that crippled the effectiveness and moral standing of the Commission. As per its terms of reference in General Assembly resolution 60/251, the Council was entrusted to "[u]ndertake a universal periodic review, based on objective and reliable information, of the fulfillment by each State of its human rights obligations and commitments in a manner which ensures universality of coverage and equal treatment with respect to all States. . ." (Human Rights Council, 2006 para. 5(e)). For Alston and Goodman, "[t]he primary significance of the innovation was to ensure that every state, and not only those accused of serious violations, would need to account to the Council." (Alston and Goodman 2013, p. 737). The General Assembly tasked the Council with developing the modalities and working methods of the UPR within one year of its first session, a situation that was accomplished with the adoption of resolution 5/1 of the Human Rights Council (Institution-Building of the Human Rights Council 2007).

The "Institution-Building Package," as resolution 5/1 is known, determined that the UPR would be a Member-driven mechanism with the aim of ensuring full participation of the State under review (as opposed to their interaction with expert bodies or mandates, which routinely generate some degree of friction), and mostly, to improve the human rights situation on the ground. Through the review of three documents (a national report prepared by the State, and a compilation of recommendations to the State under review by UN human rights mechanisms and a separate document including other sources of information, mostly by NGOs, both prepared by the Office of the High Commissioner for Human Rights) and a three-hour interactive session facilitated by a *troika*, the State would receive comments and recommendations from peer member States, which it could freely accept or reject. Through (initially) four-year cycles, the goal of this mechanism is to incentivize State action vis-à-vis its international human rights obligations and commitments, and to measure the level of advancement in their fulfillment.

In accordance with paragraph 16 of resolution 60/251, the Human Rights Council undertook a review of its work and functioning in 2011, which served to further refine the working modalities of the Universal Periodic Review, and to address deficiencies noted throughout the first cycle. Some of the relevant changes to be implemented from the second session onward are the focus of the exercise, which should be centered on accepted recommendations from a prior cycle and in the positive development of the human rights situation on the ground (thus, avoiding what States consider as unnecessary criticism, which they already receive from other human rights bodies); the obligation for States to communicate in writing its position regarding recommendations made by other States in the course of its review; and finally, that the UPR cycle should be extended to 4.5 years, in order to allow sufficient time for the examination and interactive dialogue between the Working Group of the UPR (the Council in plenary) and the State under review (Review of the work and functioning of the Human Rights Council 2011).

As it could be guessed for any intergovernmental mechanism, its appraisal has been both positive and negative (Chauville 2014). For example, some argue that it has prompted State action and commitments at the domestic level, which are reflected through the cyclical and interim reports that States under review provide, as well as engagement with non-State actors on different human rights issues (de la Vega and Lewis 2011, p. 358). For Philip Alston, "the Human Rights Council has been operating in a way that is surprisingly balanced in the last few years," despite the fact that some of the permanent members of the Security Council "have both made it clear that they stand ready to introduce or to re-introduce major "reforms" of the Council, a prospect which is hardly grounds for cheer" (Alston 2017). Others have lauded the fact that it allows to follow-up on State obligations and commitments (Viegas e Silva 2013, pp. 105–107), as well as NGO participation, in addition to intersystemic cooperation between the regional and international human rights mechanisms (Tenorio Obando 2015 pp. 544–546). Yet another positive aspect is that "the UPR process has the potential to bring countries that might otherwise be marginalized or ignored in international rights debates into a common dialogue" (Charlesworth and Larking 2014, p. 13).

However, others are less optimistic, and even skeptical regarding the UPR: Andrew Clapham suggests that mixed reactions to the UPR process reflect doubts on whether it will bring relevant change, or if this process is being used to water down standards and scrutiny achieved under other UN human rights mechanisms (Clapham 2013 p. 160). Olivier de Frouville, for example, passionately argues that the UPR has become the mainstream, most visible process of the Human Rights Council, despite the many more satisfactory outcomes achieved by Special Procedures and Treaty Bodies; that it takes away many of the Office of the High Commissioner for Human Rights' limited (human and financial) resources; and that the "global efficiency of the mechanism is wholly dependent upon the good will of the state under review," which has prompted that States actually committed to the promotion and protection of human rights are more severely criticized than those whose intentions are less good-natured. Indeed, he points out, "the honest state is punished while the dishonest state is rewarded" (de Frouville 2011, p. 250).

Tenorio Obando points out that the main challenge (as is usually the case in the interaction between international and domestic law) is to go from rhetoric to practice, most notably for those States who use the UPR to evade their responsibilities or to justify the commission of human rights violations within their jurisdiction (Tenorio Obando 2015, pp. 565–567). Viegas e Silva identifies two more challenges in the UPR process: to strike a balance between diplomatic dialogue and constructive criticism, in order to make the assessment accurate and practicable for the State, and the need to follow-up effectively on State commitments in future cycles (Viegas e Silva 2013, pp. 105–107). But perhaps the most important criticism is that of Christian Tomuschat, who considers that the main participants in the Universal Periodic Review are diplomats, which will invariably taint the process with political considerations, a situation that paired with its brevity (an important issue given the many human rights aspects and situations that need to be reviewed for every State), "will not permit any in-depth inquiry into situations" where systemic human rights abuse exists (Tomuschat 2014, pp. 192–193).

An objective consideration of the Universal Periodic Review would definitely identify as its most positive trademark the fact that States under review are subjected to scrutiny in relation to all the rights contained in the Universal Declaration of Human Rights, thus setting the benchmark higher for all Member States than their current (selective) status as parties of the different international human rights treaties. Thus, for States that prioritize civil and political rights, this means that their actions and omissions on economic, social and cultural rights can also be scrutinized. The same applies to those that give preference to social rights over civil liberties and political rights. Yet another important aspect is that at least an abridged version of the recommendations issued by treaty bodies and special procedures mandates to States are analyzed, which may render a truthful image as to the level of implementation of human rights obligations and recommendations by States. However, the fact that human rights scrutiny is subjected to the political considerations of States, and that even acceptance of the recommendations depends entirely on the goodwill of States under review, undermines the legitimacy and impartiality that this process is supposed to represent.

The same can be said of follow-up measures, which is the Achilles heel of the vast majority of international human rights mechanisms. In order for the UPR to be effective, pressure must come not only from domestic civil society, but also from those States that are effectively committed to the promotion and protection of human rights. Conditioning bilateral or multilateral arrangements of different kinds to following-up on human rights obligations derived from international mechanisms, including the UPR, is an alternative worth exploring, particularly by those countries whose human rights records are slightly less tainted. While this would of course not be a panacea, and some States could even take advantage of this persuasion tool to blame other States on the lack of implementation of their human rights obligations, it could potentially help those States that are more inclined to – at least rhetorically – promote and protect human rights to act on their international commitments. At the end of the day, as Philip Alston puts it, "[d]efending human rights has never been a consensus project and has almost always been the product of struggle" (Alston 2017). In this regard, the outcome reviews of the UPR and the follow-up to accepted recommendations should be the basis to reduce that struggle and contribute to the advancement of human rights provisions on the ground.

Challenges for the Human Rights Council

Despite the several achievements of the Human Rights Council in its first decade of existence, including a successful transition from the Commission's working methods and functions, important challenges remain to ensure its effectiveness as a forum for international dialogue, promotion, and protection of human rights. As it was mentioned before, some of these obstacles derive from the intent of some member States to challenge the legitimacy and powers of Council procedures, as it was clear from the establishment of a code of conduct for Special Procedures mandate-holders, or on the effort to legally challenge the legality of the sexual orientation and gender identity mandate. Other important obstacles to the effectiveness of the Human Rights Council result from the limitations imposed on the successor to the Sub-Commission for the Promotion and Protection of Human Rights, the Advisory Committee, whose prior function as a *genuine* think tank for the Commission was eroded in the transition, or even from the election of UN Member States to the Council, which was intended to ensure a genuine commitment with the promotion and protection of human rights, but which has not necessarily been the case as a result of political tensions among delegations. In order for the Council to act more effectively in the promotion and protection of human rights, these – and other – challenges need to be addressed in a manner consistent with the mandate and spirit of human rights protection in accordance to its founding resolution and the UN Charter.

Limiting the Independence and Functions of Special Procedures Mandate-Holders

On 18 June 2007, the Human Rights Council adopted a Code of Conduct for Special Procedures Mandate-Holders, with the aim of "spell[ing]out, complete and increase the visibility of the rules and principles governing the behavior of mandate-holders." This decision, as the Council noted in its resolution, was not based on the desire to question or limit the independence of mandate-holders, which it described as being "absolute in nature," but rather to "enhance the cooperation between Governments and mandate-holders which is essential for the effective functioning of the system. . ." (Code of Conduct for Special Procedures Mandate-holders of the Human Rights Council 2007). Nevertheless, the idea of developing a Code of Conduct, suggested by Algeria and then pursued by several members of the African Group and OIC States, was supported by numerous non-Western countries, in what became a clear effort to balance the independence of mandate-holders in the fulfill-ment of their missions and to ensure accountability for their actions (Limon and Power 2014, p. 15).

The idea was initially met with distrust, notably as a result of the probability of hindering the work of mandate-holders in the fulfillment of their duties and man-dates. The idea of governing "the professional behavior of mandate holders even as they called upon States to cooperate" with them (Gaer 2017, p. 102), would appear to result not from a generalized or recurring situation, but rather from specific instances in which governments felt that the criticisms of mandate-holders were biased or unfounded, or in one specific case, where the mandate-holder exceeded her mandate (De Alba and Genina 2016, pp. 214–220; Rodley 2011, pp. 319–320). Thus, instead of ensuring the continuation of the prudent and self-restrained behavior that had been generally shown by mandate-holders – who widely support self-regulation (Abebe 2013, p. 750) –, the project intended to establish an external limit to the manner in which special rapporteurs or independent experts conducted their mandates (De Alba and Genina 2015, p. 215).

The perception of States on the need to establish explicit limits to the conduct of special procedures mandate holders could be considered as a relatively normal reaction or perception, given that the work of UN Special Procedures typically consists of criticizing (as constructively as possible, of course) the actions or omissions of States that result in human rights violations (Alston 2011, p. 581). In that regard, the resolution proposing the elaboration of a Code of Conduct was voted favorably by a large margin, being thus inserted within the framework of the institution-building process. And yet, as several commentators note, it did not affect disproportionately the work undertaken by mandate-holders, but merely served to aggregate standards of best practices that had already been developed within the working methods and manual of special procedures in one single document (Kothari 2013; Rodley 2011, p. 321). Nevertheless, it was – and still is – a matter of concern the fact that many different States made such a concerted effort to limit the independence and impartiality of mandate-holders, and in some occasions, even their functioning, a concern that has materialized in different moments since the Code's adoption (Alston 2011, pp. 592–601). A more recent example of this position was observed in 2016, precisely on the tenth anniversary of the Human Rights Council, when the creation of a new human rights mandate based on nondiscrimination caused a similar reaction from Council members.

In June 2016, during the 32nd session of the Human Rights Council, a resolution to create the mandate of the Independent Expert on Sexual Orientation and Gender Identity was adopted by the Council by vote (23 in favor, 18 against, with six abstentions). This marked the first time that a mandate specifically tasked with overseeing the promotion and protection of human rights of the LGBTI community was adopted in the wider framework of international human rights law, a decision that was considered a positive bold step for the Council (Abebe 2013, p. 750). However, in November 2016, a resolution proposed by Botswana on behalf of the African Group contested the legality of the new mandate, basing its arguments on the fact that sexual orientation and gender identity are not universally recognized as human rights and have not been included in any human rights convention or treaty, nor are linked to them. It then called for the postponement of the mandate until consensus could be reached on the legal basis on which to base it.

The African proposal was countered by the introduction of an amendment to the resolution, proposed by eight Latin American States (seven of which had proposed the creation of the mandate). The amendment argued that it would set a dangerous precedent to challenge a special procedures mandate of the Human Rights Council with a fully functioning mandate holder, particularly by revisiting the Annual Report of the Human Rights Council in the Third Committee of the General Assembly to selectively identify and try to block a resolution. In practical terms, it would directly undermine the authority and mandate given to the Council by the General Assembly, who could then be used as a forum to challenge the legitimacy of decisions and resolutions adopted by the 47 member States to the Council (Ali et al. 2016a). In addition, the basis to challenge the legal foundations of the mandate would be contrary to an obligation that has, in many instances, been recognized as a *jus cogens* norm, such as that of nondiscrimination, which is an overarching principle of international human rights law. While only by a narrow margin (84 in favor, 77 against, and 17 abstentions, with 15 votes that were not cast), the Latin American amendment was passed, which lay the ground for the adoption of the amended resolution by the Third Committee of the General Assembly (Ali et al. 2016b).

The fact that the Council has wrestled, in different moments during its first decade, with these types of issues reveals the difficulties inherent to maintaining the independence and structure of human rights mandates. Tensions over specific issues denote the potential future conflicts and challenges that any special procedures mandate may face, either in practical terms as a result of a general lack of cooperation from States, or in relation to their legitimacy, which may reflect more nuanced cultural differences across the globe. This also reveals the delicate balance on which the work of mandate-holders rests, and the importance to constructively criticize and support the work of States in upholding and protecting international human rights standards.

The (Limited?) Functions of the Advisory Committee to the Human Rights Council

For Emmanuel Decaux, the former Sub-Commission for the Promotion and Protection of Human Rights received the *coup de grâce* with the reform that created the Human Rights Council and its Advisory Committee (Decaux 2006, p. 2). The Sub-Commission, the result of the fusion of several of the original subsidiary bodies (on minorities, or on freedom of information and of the press, for example) created by ECOSOC and the "nuclear" Commission on Human Rights, was a body that achieved most of its success as a result of the studies undertaken *motu proprio* throughout its several decades of existence, including on topics such as the administration of justice by military tribunals, the human rights obligations of transnational corporations, human rights education, and even on extreme poverty and human rights. It was also an active part of the UN human rights machinery before its reform, as the body in charge of receiving confidential communications from alleged victims of human rights abuses under the 1503 procedure (Zoller 2006, p. 131).

Before its reform, the Sub-Commission for the Promotion and Protection of Human Rights was the main subsidiary body of the Commission on Human Rights, composed of 26 independent experts who usually organized their activities in working groups. As a result of this, they undertook numerous analyses on the topics described above and other issues, usually with the aim of contributing to the development of international human rights law, or to the working methods of UN human rights procedures. A clear example of this, and one of the most contentious experiences it faced in its final years, were the Norms on the Responsibilities of Transnational Corporations and Other Business Enterprises with Regard to Human Rights, a document that was adopted in 2003 after several years of work by a Working Group on the issue (Decaux 2010, pp. 12–13). Through the Norms, the Sub-Commission intended to make a restatement of international human rights law, and to establish direct international human rights obligations for business enterprises. While the Sub-Commission had the possibility of initiating studies and submitting them and its recommendations to the Commission on Human Rights for examination and eventual adoption, the particularly controversial nature of the topic addressed by the Norms highlighted the existing disagreement between a body integrated mostly by independent experts, on the one hand, and a political body such as the Commission, on the other hand.

The result of the interaction between them resulted in the Commission on Human Rights discrediting the work undertaken by the Sub-Commission, by stating that it had not requested the Norms, and that they did not have any legal standing, thereby forbidding the Sub-Commission from taking any supervisory action in that regard. While it was not necessarily the cause for the transformation of the functions of the Sub-Commission, the possibility of undertaking studies *motu propio* by the Advisory Committee was one of the main changes introduced in the transition to the Human Rights Council, as a result of resolution 5/1 of 2007.

In accordance with the Institution-Building Package, the Advisory Committee "will function as a think-tank for the Council and work at its direction," and has explicit limitations as to the manner and form of the expertise it shall provide to the Council, and especially to the possibility of adopting resolutions or decisions, which is explicitly forbidden. In addition, resolution 5/1 also forbids the Advisory Committee to establish subsidiary bodies unless authorized by the Council, a situation that limits the collegial efforts previously undertaken by the Sub-Commission through its working groups, which at the very least provided room for consensus-building and for differences in opinion.

While on paper these changes would seem to directly limit the efficiency in the work of the Advisory Committee when compared to the Sub-Commission, in practice it has clearly established a hierarchy between the Committee and the Council, thus limiting the potential for disagreements that occurred between the Sub-Commission and the Commission on Human Rights, without necessarily hindering the work undertaken by the Committee members or its quality. For example, the Advisory Committee undertook studies (either from the start or inherited from the Sub-Commission) on issues such as contemporary forms of slavery, corruption, albinism, or terrorism, which eventually became mandates of the Human Rights Council entrusted to Special Procedures mandate-holders. In addition, the list of topics within the purview of the Advisory Committee has not diminished, but quite the opposite: since its establishment, the Committee has considered different issues such as local governments and their role in human rights protection, international cooperation, international solidarity, the right to peace, human rights education and training, or sports and the Olympic ideal, among many others, thus providing new avenues and issues on which to reflect on, particularly considering the added value or the relationship to the promotion and protection of human rights.

In a sense, the lack of "independence" of the Advisory Committee would seem to constitute an obstacle when compared to the work undertaken by different UN human rights bodies, which is clearly stipulated to be on a purely individual decision-making basis. This, of course, is quite notable in the current status of this subsidiary body, which has therefore become a forum to discuss issues that may be relevant for States sitting in the Human Rights Council, but not necessarily others which may be controversial or which may engender disapproval by States. However, the absence of any decision-making capacity by individual experts appointed to the Advisory Committee in relation to the topics they consider necessary to address may indeed represent the biggest setback in its functioning as a genuine think-tank.

Election to the Human Rights Council, or the Need for Higher Standards of Human Rights Observance

As it has been explained before, politicization, bloc voting, and other pernicious State practices led to calls for reform of the Commission on Human Rights, which had lost credibility. The creation of the Human Rights Council raised expectations in relation to the possibility of moving beyond those issues that had crippled the effective functioning of the Commission. However, as Freedman and Houghton aptly note, "[t]he Council has been politicised from its outset. Politicisation has been apparent through states advancing unrelated political objectives, groups shielding their allies from Council scrutiny and politically motivated attacks on some states that have obstructed similar action being taken on other, needed, situations." (Freedman and Houghton 2017, pp. 1–2). Of course, the existence and composition of an intergovernmental body, and the different political, economic, ideological, religious or military goals of its member States, have a tendency to result in some degree of disagreement and even confrontation among them, either to advance specific initiatives or to prevent others from achieving their objectives. This was apparent from the first years of existence of the Council, which saw an explicit focus on some situations of grave human rights violations as a result of this collision of interests and forces, while completely ignoring other situations requiring the same amount of attention. Such is the case of Israel and the Occupied Territories, which were even included in the agenda of the Council as a lone-standing item, a situation that would be contrary to the principles of impartiality and non-selectivity (De Alba and Genina 2016).

This situation, which cannot, however, be fully avoided in the context of an intergovernmental body, has been replicated to a great extent in an issue that was of concern during the transition from Commission to Council: the question of membership. In theory, reducing membership from 53 to 47 States should contribute to enhancing the human rights profile of those States wishing to become part of the Council. Such was the goal stated in resolution 60/251 establishing the Council, where in operative paragraphs eight and nine, the General Assembly determined that decision on membership should "take into account the contribution of candidates to the promotion and protection of human rights and their voluntary pledges and commitments made thereto," as well as that "members elected to the Council shall uphold the highest standards in the promotion and protection of human rights, shall fully cooperate with the Council and be reviewed under the universal periodic review mechanism during their term of membership." And yet, as Freedman and Houghton explain, the founding principles of the Human Rights Council have not curbed the behavior of States, nor the reformed membership addressed the issue of political alliances (Freedman and Houghton 2017, p. 5), an aspect that can difficultly be tackled in such an environment or through such mechanisms.

Beyond the issue of political connections across regional or ideological groups, the issue of membership has become an important source of disagreement: resulting from the election in the General Assembly, Member States to the Human Rights Council should in theory promote and protect human rights and pledge to genuinely contribute to the advancement of the international human rights agenda. However, as reality has shown, two different trends have appeared in that regard: first, States have resorted to bloc voting and to propose the exact number of candidates for the number of available seats for any regional group, in order to ensure their election to the Council. This has resulted in States such as Congo, Pakistan, the Philippines or Saudi Arabia becoming members of the Council, thus highlighting the political impasse to ensure that only those States with the highest respect for human rights can be successful in their candidatures. In the opinion of Ambassador de Alba, it is necessary for States to regain their sense of individual responsibility in the Council, instead of resorting to group positions and defensive attitudes (Outcome of the high-level panel discussion on the occasion of the tenth anniversary of the Human Rights Council 2016, par. 12).

Secondly, several States that have been selected to the Council have nevertheless been reluctant to comply with their pledges to uphold international human rights standards. A recent case was that of Australia, elected to the Council in 2017 despite its asylum policies (Doherty 2017), and even its refusal to develop a National Action Plan on business and human rights notwithstanding its announcement of an intention to do so in a multistakeholder platform prior to its election to the Human Rights Council. This also highlights the unachieved balance between political realities and legal requirements, particularly in international organizations, where member States enjoy important prerogatives without effective mechanisms to ensure their account-ability and compliance (Abebe 2013, p. 758).

Within the spectrum of States with diverse backgrounds, it is the role of those that are more moderate to participate in the mediation efforts to successfully advance the human rights agenda, while also contributing to avoid the functional crippling of the Human Rights Council (Freedman and Houghton 2017, p. 3; Abebe 2013, p. 759). Yet, it is necessary to contemplate that those frictions and disagreements among conflicting political views or objectives cannot be easily resolved in an intergovern-mental forum. To a large extent, the main cause that led to the demise of the Commission on Human Rights will unavoidably continue to be a consistent pattern in the functioning of the Human Rights Council.

Concluding Thoughts

As it has been argued throughout this chapter, the first decade of the Human Rights Council has resulted in several important achievements, starting with an effective transition from a body that became under intense scrutiny for failing to live up to its mandate, and continuing with maintaining the *acquis* of the Special Procedures system. In addition to these already important *réussites*, the Universal Periodic Review should be considered another milestone, particularly taking into consider-ation the fact that a universal participation was ensured, and that the peer-learning and dialogue processes have become more refined, thus allowing to have a (rela-tively accurate) picture of the state of human rights globally.

Nevertheless, the Council has also faced important obstacles, notably in terms of the independence of Special Procedures mandates, which have been challenged in several occasions throughout the first decade of this Charter-based body; of the limitations to the functioning and autonomy of the Advisory Committee to act as a genuine think tank; and finally, of the continued politicization that has resulted from conflicting objectives between States, and that has replicated even in the election processes to the Council. These, of course, are only a few traces of success and failure that the Human Rights Council has faced.

In general terms, the outcome of the first decade of the Human Rights Council has been positive, particularly in ensuring a more explicit focus on issues such as the realization of economic, social, and cultural rights, or even in the articulation of a strategy to promote and include within the scope of its work the achievement of the Sustainable Development Goals. These two interrelated aspects – one being a legal requirement established under human rights treaties, the other being a global public policy tool to contribute to the fulfillment of those legal obligations –, in addition to linking the fight against climate change with the protection of human rights, and focusing more clearly on effectively promoting and protecting human rights in emergency situations (such as in special sessions; Tabbal 2010) and on the ground, seem to be some of the main challenges facing the Council as it embarks in its second decade of existence.

Despite those important issues, there is hope that the perennial renewal of the Council may bring about the precise formula of States that are genuinely committed to the defense and promotion of human rights to truly address some of the most complex problems affecting vulnerable populations across the globe, leaving behind political confrontations and protective or defensive postures. It is only in that spirit that the efforts started in 1946 by the nuclear Commission on Human Rights, which reached a historic milestone on 10 December 1948 with the adoption of the Universal Declaration of Human Rights, will make this document a living instrument and a reality for peoples across the globe.

References

Abebe AM (2013) The role and future of the human rights council. In: Sheeran S, Rodley N (eds) Routledge handbook of international human rights law. Routledge, London

Ali M, McGregor L, Murray D, Palacios Zuloaga P, Rodley N, Sandoval C, Shaheed A (2016a) What is the future of the SOGI mandate and what does it mean for the UN human rights council? In: EJIL: talk! https://www.ejiltalk.org/what-is-the-future-of-the-sogi-mandate-and-what-does-it-mean-for-the-un-human-rights-council/. Accessed 20 Sep 2017

Ali M, McGregor L, Murray D, Palacios Zuloaga P, Rodley N, Sandoval C, Shaheed A (2016b) SOGI mandate passes third committee hurdle. In: EJIL: talk! https://www.ejiltalk.org/sogi-mandate-passes-third-committee-hurdle/. Accessed 20 Sep 2017

Alston P (2006) Reconceiving the UN human rights regime: challenges confronting the new UN human rights council. Melb J Int Law 7:185

Alston P (2011) Hobbling the monitors: should U.N. human rights monitors be accountable? Harv Int Law J 52:561

Alston P (2017) Human rights under siege. In: SUR 25. http://sur.conectas.org/en/human-rights-siege/. Accessed 10 Sep 2017

Alston P, Goodman R (2013) International human rights. Oxford University Press, New York

Bossuyt M, Decaux E (2005) Editorial: De la "Commission" au "Conseil" des droits de l'homme, un nom pour un autre? Droits fondamentaux 5

Callejón C (2006) Rapport général. In: Decaux E (ed) Les Nations Unies et les droits de l'homme. Pedone, Paris

Cantú Rivera H (2015) The United Nations human rights council: remarks on its history, procedures, challenges and perspectives. In: Cantú Rivera H (ed) The special procedures of the human rights council. Intersentia, Cambridge

Carmona Sepúlveda M (2015) Extreme poverty and human rights: a social struggle against a global issue. In: Cantú Rivera H (ed) The special procedures of the human rights council. Intersentia, Cambridge

Charlesworth H, Larking E (eds) (2014) Human rights and the universal periodic review: rituals and ritualism. Cambridge University Press, Cambridge

Chauville R (2014) The universal periodic review's first cycle: successes and failures. In: Charlesworth H, Larking E (eds) Human rights and the universal periodic review: rituals and ritualism. Cambridge University Press, Cambridge

Clapham A (2013) The use of international human rights law by civil society organizations. In: Sheeran S, Rodley N (eds) Routledge handbook of international human rights law. Routledge, London

De Alba LA, Genina V (2016) La creación del Consejo de Derechos Humanos de la ONU: crónica de una negociación multilateral. Instituto Matías Romero, Mexico

De Frouville O (1996) Les procédures thématiques: une contribution efficace des Nations Unies à la protection des droits de l'homme. Pedone, Paris

De Frouville O (2011) Building a universal system for the protection of human rights: the way forward. In: Bassiouni MC, Schabas WA (eds) New challenges for the UN human rights machinery. Intersentia, Cambridge

De Frouville O (2015) On the twentieth anniversary of the United Nations declaration for the protection of all persons against enforced disappearances. In: Cantú Rivera H (ed) The special procedures of the human rights council. Intersentia, Cambridge

De la Vega C, Lewis TN (2011) Peer review in the mix: how the UPR transforms human rights discourse. In: Bassiouni MC, Schabas WA (eds) New challenges for the UN human rights machinery. Intersentia, Cambridge

Decaux E (2006) Editorial: Le progrès des droits de l'homme. Droits fondamentaux 6

Decaux E (2010) Introduction. In: Decaux E (ed) La responsabilité des entreprises multinationales en matière de droits de l'homme. Bruylant, Brussels

Decaux E (2015) Foreword. In: Cantú Rivera H (ed) The special procedures of the human rights council. Intersentia, Cambridge

Doherty B (2017) Australia to be elected to powerful UN human rights council. In: The Guardian. https://www.theguardian.com/world/2017/oct/14/australia-to-be-elected-to-powerful-un-human-rights council?CMP−Share_iOSApp_Other. Accessed 20 Oct 2017

Domínguez-Redondo E (2017) The history of special procedures: a 'learning-by-doing' approach to human rights implementation. In: Nolan A, Freedman R, Murphy T (eds) The United Nations special procedures system. Brill, Leiden

Evans M (2017) The UN special rapporteur on torture in the developing architecture of UN torture protection. In: Nolan A, Freedman R, Murphy T (eds) The United Nations special procedures system. Brill, Leiden

Freedman R, Houghton R (2017) Two steps forward, one step back: politicisation of the human rights council. Hum Rights Law Rev 17:753

Gaer F (2017) Picking and choosing? Country visits by thematic special procedures. In: Nolan A, Freedman R, Murphy T (eds) The United Nations special procedures system. Brill, Leiden

International Council on Human Rights Policy (2006) Human rights standards: learning from experience. ICHRP, Geneva

Kothari M (2013) From commission to the council: evolution of UN charter bodies. In: Shelton D (ed) The Oxford handbook of international human rights law. Oxford University Press, Oxford

Lauterpacht H (1947) The international protection of human rights. Recueil des Cours 70

Limon M, Power H (2014) History of the United Nations special procedures mechanism: origins, evolution and reform. Universal Rights Group, Versoix

Pinheiro PS (2006) Les États au sein de la Commission des droits de l'homme, la politisation des groups. In: Decaux E (ed) Les Nations Unies et les droits de l'homme. Pedone, Paris

Rodley NS (2011) On the responsibility of special rapporteurs. Int J Hum Rights 15:319

Smith RKM (2010) The United Nations human rights system. In: Baderin MA, Ssenyonjo M (eds) International human rights law: six decades after the UDHR and beyond. Ashgate, Surrey

Tabbal M (2010) La douzième session extraordinaire du Conseil des droits de l'homme. Droits Fondamentaux 8

Tenorio Obando F (2015) Un examen al Examen: una aproximación a los resultados del Examen Periódico Universal. Anuario Mexicano de Derecho Internacional 51:539

Tomuschat C (2014) Human rights: between idealism and realism, 3rd edn. Oxford University Press, Oxford

Viegas e Silva M (2013) The United Nations human rights council: six years on. SUR Int J Hum Rights 10(18):97

Zoller A (2006) La procédure 1503. In: Decaux E (ed) Les Nations Unies et les droits de l'homme. Pedone, Paris

The UN High Commissioner for Human Rights and Field Operations

William G. O'Neill

Contents

Introduction 70
The UN Takes Stock After 25 Years 73
Capacity-Building and Human Rights 75
Exploding the Myths 76
"Good Practices" in Human Rights Field Operations 78
Use "Emblematic Cases" 78
Use Public Opinion Surveys to Identify Priorities and Generate Baseline Data ... 79
Twin Results-Based Monitoring with Results-Based Capacity-Building 79
Provide Program Budgets for Activities 79
Consult Beneficiaries Before Embarking on Assistance Efforts 80
Identify Allies as Senior as Possible in the Government Hierarchy 81
Work with Parliament and National Legislatures 82
Use Treaty Bodies and Special Procedures Strategically 82
Strengthen Local Ownership and Management and Leadership Skills 84
Colocate and Mentor/Coach 85
Develop Capacity to Handle Data 86
Link with UNCTs and "Mainstreaming" Human Rights 86
Register, Certify, and Vet Judicial and Security Personnel 87
See the Human Rights Section as a "Convener" 88
Include National Human Rights Officers 89
Focus on Youth 90
Assess Training's Impact on Performance 90
The Guiding Principles for Human Rights Field Officers Working in Conflict and
Post-conflict Environments 91
Conclusion 91
References 92

W. G. O'Neill (✉)
Human Rights and Humanitarian Law Brooklyn, New York, NY, USA
e-mail: William.oneill485@gmail.com

© Springer Nature Singapore Pte Ltd. 2018
G. Oberleitner (ed.), *International Human Rights Institutions, Tribunals, and Courts*,
International Human Rights, https://doi.org/10.1007/978-981-10-5206-4_4

Abstract

Human rights work by the UN for the organization's first 45 years consisted mostly of creating laws and standards and convening meetings in Geneva. It was only with the end of the Cold War that the UN started to move human rights work to the places where violations were occurring. This new focus on the field required the UN to learn to promote and protect human rights in a completely new and challenging way. Many mistakes were made, but over time the UN has identified several key principles and approaches that can lead to success: improved respect for human rights, prevention of further violations, and ending impunity. Much remains to be done, however, especially in this era where terrorism, national security, and mass forced displacement have generated new challenges for human rights field officers.

Keywords

United Nations · UN High Commissioner for Human Rights · Field operations · Peacekeeping · Peace missions · Rule of law · Monitoring · Capacity-building

Introduction

More than 25 years have passed since the first United Nations (UN) human rights field operation deployed to El Salvador. Over 100 international civilians, with nothing more than an agreement between the two warring parties brokered by negotiators from the UN Department of Political Affairs (DPA), arrived in a country still at war, with landmines, checkpoints, no-go areas, mass graves, and death squads roaming the landscape. UN human rights work involved the important task of drafting treaties and standards, organizing the annual meetings of the Human Rights Commission and its Sub-Commission, and supporting the work of a number of Special Rapporteurs and Working Groups, but the UN had never mounted such an operation in its then 45-year history.

While this standard-setting, annual meetings, and the work of "special procedures" of the UN Human Rights Council (and its predecessor, the Human Rights Commission) was crucial, it was fairly circumscribed and reactive and largely dependent on member state compliance. Moreover, the Human Rights Center, as it was then called, had always been located in Geneva in the days before faxes, email, and videoconferencing. In addition to the isolation, the Center received only a pittance from the UN regular budget and was led by a fairly low-ranking official. In an organization that prizes titles and hierarchy, this combination marginalized the UN's capacity for real engagement on human rights issues.

Things began to change with the demise of the Soviet Union and the end of the Cold War. The UN had more political space in which to raise human rights concerns, even at the Security Council. The creation of a High Commissioner for Human Rights in 1994 was also important in raising the profile of human rights. The first High Commissioner, Jose Ayala Lasso, immediately faced a major crisis on taking

office when the genocide in Rwanda erupted in April 1994. Previous field operations such as El Salvador mentioned above, Cambodia (1992), Haiti (1993), and Guatemala (1994) had all been managed by the UN in New York which at least had some experience mounting and overseeing field operations.

Identifying, recruiting, and then deploying civilians to a war zone were a radical departure from UN standard practice. These human rights officers would monitor, verify, and report on violations of human rights and the laws of war by both parties to the conflict. They would need vehicles, communications equipment, offices, housing, security officers, and other logistical support. Moreover, they would need guidance on how to do their work: how to interview victims, witnesses, and government officials. They would need to know how to conduct a proper prison visit, monitor a demonstration, observe a trial and then write a report that captured the key details, and propose recommendations to address the violations that they had documented. All this would have to take place in an environment where those committing the violations would not be receptive to cooperating with the human rights officers.

These officers, moreover, would not be there for just a week or so but would stay for months, even years, following up with visits, meetings, and other interventions. They were to enjoy functional diplomatic immunity, and their correspondence, offices, living quarters, and vehicles were immune from search or seizure, at least on paper. They established offices all over El Salvador and traveled freely, entered any place of detention without prior notice, examined case files, observed trials, and talked to local Salvadorans who were supposed to be protected from any threats or reprisals for having cooperated with the UN human rights officers. Although in reality this was not often respected and how to obtain information from victims and witnesses without further endangering them became and remains one of the toughest challenges for field work in human rights.

Where would the UN find people with the experience, skills, and language (Spanish in this case) ability to do such stressful, sensitive, and demanding work? Who would train them at the outset and what would the training include? No one had answers to these questions in 1991, yet time was of the essence. The war had been going on for 20 years, over 70,000 people had been killed, and a chance for peace was there but was fleeting. The UN Human Rights Center in Geneva had no role in the conception, organization, or realization of the first human rights field operation in UN history, ONUSAL (Spanish acronym for the UN Observer Mission in El Salvador). UN officials in New York, relying on their own personal network of leading human rights experts at organizations like Amnesty International, the Lawyers Committee for Human Rights, and Human Rights Watch, convened emergency meetings where human rights priorities, reporting, and recruiting personnel were discussed. The Mission soon began its work.

Barely 2 years later, in 1993, Haiti faced a crisis following a violent military coup in late 1991 that had chased from office the hugely popular and recently elected President, Jean-Bertrand Aristide. Gross human rights violations were rampant, with murder, disappearances, torture, and rape leading the way; the perpetrators were the Haitian army, police, and their paramilitary death squads. Again, due to political

negotiations lead by the UN's DPA, the Haitian military, in an effort to defuse the crippling sanctions imposed by the USA and the Organization of American States, agreed to the deployment of human rights officers to monitor and report on violations. This time, working off the Salvador template, UN officials in New York, with the same representatives of major human rights NGOs, hammered out "terms of reference" for the human rights officers who would be sent to Haiti. Challenges regarding recruitment, deployment, logistics, security, and securing agreement from the illegitimate de facto military regime to allow the officers to do their work proved daunting (Martin 1995). Yet with the experiences gained from El Salvador and a growing body of work and experience, the mission was on the ground in Haiti by February 1993.

The tidal wave of UN human rights field operations picked up speed throughout the 1990s. After El Salvador and Haiti came Guatemala, Bosnia-Herzegovina, Angola, Sierra Leone, the Democratic Republic of the Congo, Timor-Leste, Kosovo, Liberia, Chad, and the Central African Republic. As mentioned above, Rwanda in 1994, following the April genocide, marked the first time that the UN Human Rights Center in Geneva had responsibility for a human rights field operation, the Human Rights Field Operation in Rwanda. The Human Rights Center in Geneva had never deployed a major human rights field operations before, its only experience being the establishment of a one-person office in Bosnia in 1993 (O'Flaherty and Ulrich 2010). Deploying over 100 people to post-genocide Rwanda was an entirely different matter (Howland 1999).

The impetus to deploy human rights officers on the ground for extended periods of time did not end with the dawn of the new century. Human rights officers worked in Nepal, Iraq, Afghanistan, Côte d'Ivoire, Burundi, Haiti (again in 2004), Colombia, Darfur, South Sudan, Eritrea/Ethiopia, Southern Lebanon, Mali, Central African Republic, the Ukraine, and Libya, to name a few. While the UN Office of the High Commissioner (OHCHR) assumed a greater role in establishing and managing these operations over time, most human rights officers worked as part of UN peacekeeping operations, usually in a human rights department. The Department of Peacekeeping Operations in New York (DPKO) had primary operational responsibility, while OHCHR participated in recruiting and receiving regular reports from the unit. The real power and authority, however, remained with the Special Representative of the Secretary-General (SRSG), who in turn reported to the Secretary-General and the Security Council in New York (UN Secretary-General Report 2000).

When Louise Arbour took over as High Commissioner for Human Rights in 2004, she made increasing the number of field presences a priority (UN High Commissioner for Human Rights 2005). In addition to the human rights components in peace operations, Arbour wanted to establish stand-alone human rights teams and pushed for UN Country Teams (UNCTs) to include a human rights officer to assist in implementing then-UN Secretary-General Kofi Annan's directive to "mainstream" human rights in all the UN's work. As of the end of 2016, OHCHR had 14 stand-alone offices in Bolivia, Cambodia, Colombia, Guatemala, Guinea, Honduras, Mauritania, Mexico, the Occupied Palestinian Territories, Kosovo, Togo, Tunisia, Uganda, and Yemen (temporarily evacuated due to security concerns) (OHCHR 2017).

Also by the end of 2016, OHCHR had 28 Advisers and National Offices as part of UNCTs in Bangladesh, Barbados (UN Regional Team for Barbados and Eastern Caribbean Countries), Chad, Dominican Republic, Jamaica, Kenya, Madagascar, Malawi, Maldives, Moldova, Nigeria, Panama (UNDG-LAC), Papua New Guinea, Paraguay, the Philippines, Russia, Rwanda, Sierra Leone, Southern Caucasus (Tbilisi), Sri Lanka, Tajikistan, Tanzania, Timor-Leste, Thailand, the Ukraine, and Zambia, as well as two national Advisers in Serbia and FYR of Macedonia.

This rapid increase in on-the-ground long-term field presences in various guises working on human rights around the world represents a tectonic shift for the UN. It has brought human rights down from a high, conceptual – some would argue abstract level – to a much more concrete and pragmatic effort to improve people's lives in real and measurable ways. As with any venture that is so ambitious and sensitive, remember the UN Charter's proviso about not interfering in the domestic affairs of member states, and with ongoing resistance from some states to the very notion of human rights – despite Article 1 of the Charter, which states one of the purposes of the UN is "promoting and encouraging respect for human rights and for fundamental freedoms..." – there have been setbacks. The efforts continue, however, and the trend is now irreversible.

The UN Takes Stock After 25 Years

In 2015, as Secretary-General Ban Ki-Moon's 10-year tenure was winding down, he ordered two sweeping reviews of UN policy and practice relating to peace operations and post-conflict peacebuilding. The High-Level Independent Panel on Peace Operations issued its report "Uniting for Peace – Politics, Partnerships and People" on 16 June 2015. One month later, in July 2015, the Advisory Group of Experts submitted their report to the Secretary-General, entitled "The Challenge of Sustaining Peace" (Advisory Group of Experts 2015). Finally, a few years earlier, in July 2013, the Secretary-General's office issues a detailed Plan of Action to implement its new "Human Rights Up Front" policy. This initiative grew out of an Internal Review Panel assessed the UN's actions in the final stages of armed conflict in Sri Lanka as a "systemic failure," a judgment that the Secretary-General accepted (UN Secretary-General 2013).

These three reviews identified many common themes that relate to the UN's work on the ground to promote and protect human rights. Among them are human rights that are central to the UN's work – there will be no peace or development without respect for human rights, accountability for those who violate rights, and transparent governance. There is a need to understand the root causes of conflicts, and this requires a deep analysis of the human rights situation: whose rights are violated, by whom, and in what ways. The Rights Up Front initiative calls for regular, quarterly reviews by the entire UN system of cases of concern. This initiative hopes to address a continuing concern noted in all the reviews: the UN's fragmented, silo approach where human rights issues in particular are often marginalized and downplayed. All three initiatives call for the UN to consult and listen to local civil society actors and leaders and not just government officials. UN Country Teams must be integrated more into UN policy planning and analysis. And finally, the UN must find its voice on human rights and not be afraid to advocate for the victims and seek to hold perpetrators accountable. The UN should never cede the moral high ground (Advisory Group of Experts 2015).

The Sustainable Development Goals (SDGs) launched in 2015 also contain an important new element that was lacking in the 2000 Millennium Development goals. SDG 16 adds the dimension of human rights, accountability, good governance, and transparency to the more traditional development components. SDG 16 requires all states to *"Promote peaceful and inclusive societies for sustainable development, provide access to justice for all and build effective, accountable and inclusive institutions at all levels."* SDG 16 is well-tailored to human rights field work since it demands that states take measurable steps to reduce violence; end the abuse, exploitation, and trafficking of children; promote the rule of law and access to justice for all; reduce corruption and bribery; develop effective, accountable, and transparent institutions at all levels; insure responsive, inclusive, participatory, and representative decision-making at all levels; insure public access to information and protect fundamental freedoms, in accordance with national legislation and international agreements; strengthen relevant national institutions, including through international cooperation, for building capacity at all levels, in particular in developing countries; and promote and enforce nondiscriminatory laws and policies for sustainable development. Human rights officers, as part of their mandates and normal operating procedures, should be working on all of these issues: monitoring and gathering data, meeting with nongovernmental organizations, and working on reform of key institutions, including the vital task of building capacity so that state and non-state institutions can better protect human rights.

Human rights officers have important tools to help them assess SDG 16 and evaluate whether UN member state is actually delivering justice and promoting the rule of law. As one wise management consultant said: you can't improve what you can't measure. Up until very recently, however, the UN and most other outside actors had either few or inadequate measures to assess the impact of their work (Seymour 2010). For example, toting up the number of police receiving human rights training or the quantity of beds provided to the prisons tells you something but not what you really need to know about any change or progress in creating a rule of law culture.

The good news is that the UN, after an extensive study and drafting exercise largely directed by the highly regarded Vera Institute on Criminal Justice, unveiled the "Rule of Law Indicators" in 2012. Taking into account various legal systems (common law, civil law, Islamic law, customary practices, etc.), the expert drafters identified a series of indicators for each main sector (police, prisons, and courts). The indicators within each sector are then broken down into "baskets" assessing the performance of the institution, its integrity, treatment of vulnerable groups, and capacity. Used wisely and adapted to local conditions and priorities, these indicators will show the impact of specific projects that include the paramount elements of integrity, accountability, values, and incentive structures. The following are examples of indicators: To what extent do you agree that alleged incidents of police corruption or misconduct are seriously investigated and, when required by law, prosecuted? How often does it happen that people can avoid a conviction or receive a less severe punishment by paying a bribe to a judge, a prosecutor, or other court personnel? To what extent do you think that corrections officers use excessive force (e.g., use of excessive physical force, use of restraints as punishment) against prisoners (United Nations OROLSI Rule of Law Indicators 2011)?

For the first time, the UN will be able to measure any improvements or deterioration and identify the reasons for change. Real data (quantitative and qualitative), previously missing from the rule of law world, will be generated and used to assess and plan. Developing national capacity to manage data on police, courts, and crime is potentially a crucial by-product of this exercise that changes the prevailing culture which often favors impunity, nepotism, and brute power while penalizing accountability, competence, and fairness. Merely asking a wide number of people questions like the ones above could help change attitudes, values, and behavior and will involve a greater segment of the population in the reform effort.

Capacity-Building and Human Rights

A key development over the years in UN human rights field work is a focus on institutional reform through "capacity-building." In the words of Machiavelli, "there is nothing more difficult to take in hand, more perilous to conduct, or more uncertain of success, than to take the lead in the introduction of a new order of things" (Machiavelli 1513, Chap. VI). While monitoring and reporting on human rights violations remains essential, reporting is a means to an end and not an end in itself. By examining closely what is wrong, UN field officers can prescribe responses that should lead to improved human rights protection. The monitoring indicates what needs to be fixed in core institutions charged with protecting human rights like the police, the courts, and the prisons (International Council on Human Rights 2000). Initially, most attention was directed to the monitoring and reporting, and only with time and experience did UN human rights officers complete the cycle by using the information they had gathered to design programs to prevent further violations.

UN human rights field officers deployed in integrated peacekeeping operations literally face a smoldering, ravaged terrain and a terrified, often largely displaced population. Education and literacy levels among police, corrections, and even judicial officials are often very low. Rape has been used as a weapon of terror or ethnic cleansing, leaving a legacy of horror and trauma across huge swathes of the population. Corruption is often endemic, and the post-conflict governance vacuum has created a culture of criminality, often highly organized, well-funded, and lethal. Finally, the general population may have lost all faith in systems of government and justice, with good reason. The state has rarely respected human rights, and the relationship with the population has been one of mutual distrust and fear, often tinged with contempt.

This reality requires pragmatism, patience, and a fair dose of humility. Building capacity, giving technical advice, and reforming or creating institutions in

Afghanistan, Sierra Leone, and Burundi are a world apart from tinkering with some shortcomings in the judiciary, prisons, or police in countries like Chile, Slovakia, Jordan, or Mongolia.

UN human rights field officers enjoy several advantages over the "typical" UN advisory services or capacity-building initiatives undertaken by OHCHR or other UN agencies. The most important benefit is that they have firsthand information on the actual problems because of their monitoring. And second, they are there for the long-haul to design, implement, and evaluate programs and can then determine if they are having any impact on the human rights situation. This ongoing presence also puts pressure on local officials to do their jobs or else ongoing monitoring will show that the problems persist despite the UN's best efforts.

Human rights officers deploy to the mission country for comparatively long periods. This contrasts with other capacity-building or technical assistance missions that might last weeks at best and consist of episodic visits. A lengthy presence offers the possibility for the human rights officer to develop an in-depth knowledge of the country, including an understanding of what went wrong and the urgent priorities for fixing the problem. When officers leave for a new assignment, their successors pick up the work.

In most mission countries, human rights officers are present throughout the territory. Even in vast countries like Sudan and DRC, human rights officers can be found in even the most remote provinces. In the Democratic Republic of the Congo, for example, outside of its headquarters in Kinshasa, the UN Mission has 15 field offices throughout the country. Their presence for sustained periods allows them to create working relationships with local partners, to gain their trust by demonstrating competence, perseverance, and good faith. And the importance of consistent follow-up should never be underestimated. When the prosecutor knows, for example, that the human rights officer will be back next week and the week after that to check on the status of cases, the odds of seeing real action and accountability for inaction increase. Officers respond to questions and requests while enlisting support from other UN actors. Forging relationships with civil society, especially local human rights defenders, develops since UN human rights officers live in their town, understand the reality, and will be there for advice, constructive criticism, and support.

Another advantage resides in the existence of the other sections of the UN integrated peace missions. Learning how to leverage the greater numbers and resources of UN military, UN police, and the various humanitarian and development agencies, and tapping into their expertise, is an important skill.

Exploding the Myths

Several myths persist about the work of human rights field officers, even after more than 25 years of experience. The first myth is that monitoring is a separate activity from technical assistance or capacity-building. This myth is widespread and dangerous. Monitoring the human rights situation is a prerequisite for effective programming to strengthen institutions. Without an understanding of the weaknesses in the judiciary, police, or other state institutions, capacity-building efforts are likely to fail. Monitoring provides the diagnosis of the problem which must then help define the cure (International Council on Human Rights 2000). Monitoring also reveals whether the cure is working; without ongoing investigations into the situation, the human rights officers will not know whether their training programs, logistical support, oversight capacity-building, or awareness-raising campaigns are having a positive impact on the ground so that people enjoy greater respect for their human rights. A related myth is that capacity-building initiatives should come later in a mission cycle and that only monitoring occurs at the start. From the earliest days in a mission, officers should exploit opportunities for capacity-building, often with limited or no resources. Building links and trust with locals via project activities must start immediately.

The second myth is that capacity-building efforts must focus on government entities only. Human rights officers should work with members of civil society, strengthening their ability to monitor, advocate, and promote human rights. Addressing the "demand" side, in addition to the "supply" side, is critical. Helping civil society to develop ways to push the authorities to do their jobs (*responsabiliser l'état* in the French formulation) must be part of capacity-building.

Third, many working in peace operations believe they cannot work on economic, social, and cultural rights and emphasize civil and political rights. While these latter rights may be priorities, especially in the early phases of a peace operation, some human rights officers have used creative approaches to engage both state and non-state actors in programs on food, shelter, education, and medical care, enlisting UN agencies, development and humanitarian organizations, and bilateral donors to support projects. Finally, detecting discrimination in access to education, food, shelter, and medical care is a crucial component of the field officer's work and can help prevent further conflict while assuring equitable enjoyment of these human rights.

Fourth, human rights are often seen as a specialist task, best left to the human rights section, and in particular, lawyers. Human rights officers need to overcome this myth by forging alliances with other parts of the UN. These partnerships can be especially fruitful in the areas of economic, social, and cultural rights. Learning how to leverage the larger resources and greater numbers of people in other parts of the UN Mission increases the impact of the human rights section.

Fifth, many in the host society and even in the UN family see human rights as essentially "confrontational." For them, human rights mean naming, shaming, and public criticism. While these may be important tools, they are not the only ones and it is by designing effective programs to assist government institutions and their civil society counterparts to promote and protect human rights that the field officers can best defuse this myth. "We have to show them that we are here to try to help them and not only to criticize them," says one experienced human rights officer in Haiti. Another noted, "We must convince them that we are not here only to bother them" (Interview with UN Official, November 2007).

Sixth, another myth holds that "capacity-building" essentially means training local counterparts to do their jobs. While training is necessary, it is not sufficient to insure that both capacity-building and institutional reforms occur. Human rights officers should adopt the approach used by their counterparts in the development world: the project cycle of assessment, analysis, design, implementation, monitoring, and evaluation. All are crucial to successful human rights programming. And one should always ask: Which capacity are we trying to build and what is our overall strategy? How does what we are doing mesh with efforts by the UNCT, bilateral donors, and the international financial institutions (World Bank, regional banks, IMF) (Seymour 2010)? And lastly, the goal should be for human rights officers to work themselves out of their jobs, to make themselves obsolete or superfluous because local counterparts will take over, the sooner the better.

"Good Practices" in Human Rights Field Operations

Over the years, a range of good practices have been developed in human rights field operations. They will be discussed below to show first, how human rights field work constantly evolves and adapts to changing conditions and second, that while each situation is unique and one should avoid mindlessly copying experiences from one human rights field operation to another, certain core principles and tested approaches are worth keeping in mind.

Use "Emblematic Cases"

Human rights officers have identified an "emblematic case," whether for the courts, police, prison administration, or the military, as a way to identify institutional weaknesses and strengths, test the state's commitment to reform, judge whether it is "safe" to perform your job properly, and engage civil society. For example, UN human rights officers in the OHCHR office in Nepal investigated a case of a young girl who was raped while in detention at an army base. The office provided its findings to the Military Prosecutor and the courts. It offered to supply evidence and testimony it had gathered and to find additional expertise to help in the prosecution. The office also used the case to advocate for changes in the way the military operated, especially concerning arrest, detention, and conditions of detention. The government and the army for a long time failed to respond to these initiatives, thus showing that the political will for change was not there (Sharma 2011). This is a crucial factor since why bother with training, providing equipment, or offering study programs abroad if the institution itself is not really interested in reform. This high visibility case also showed the donors that the army was not interested in protecting rights so their programs needed to reflect this reality. Unless the girl's case was treated seriously, all technical assistance and capacity-building risked being a waste of time and money.

Use Public Opinion Surveys to Identify Priorities and Generate Baseline Data

Several human rights departments have conducted public opinion surveys to gauge the population's concerns, goals, and perceptions of the state's performance. As with monitoring, these surveys are tools for human rights officers to pinpoint problems or weaknesses in all areas of rights. For example, in Afghanistan, the human rights section and UNHCR, in partnership with local groups, created and distributed a questionnaire for IDPs that generated solid information to base programming on, especially for economic, social, and cultural rights (World Bank 2011).

The human rights officers in Abkhazia used a questionnaire to get information about the nature and extent of violence against children and then used this information along with UNICEF to design training and education campaigns for officials and NGOs (Lynch et al. 2008). Without this data and the relationships that developed from the very process of gathering information, the programs and the capacity of local counterparts would have been weaker. This program had the additional positive impact of enhancing the government's capacity to gather, maintain, analyze, and then use data. Without the first survey, there would be no way to measure the impact of the training or other initiatives.

Twin Results-Based Monitoring with Results-Based Capacity-Building

Monitoring is a means to an end and not an end in itself. The main purpose of monitoring is to lead to improved protection and promotion of rights. Similarly, capacity-building and institutional reform is more than just a series of training activities or logistical and financial support. The activities must lead to identifiable change in performance. This culture of "results" has often been lacking in UN human rights field work, but there are signs that a new rigor and sense of accountability are emerging. Consider an example: a UN human rights officer met with the Chief Prosecutor of Guinea-Bissau and requested that they conduct joint visits to detention centers with magistrates. A number of issues previously pointed out to the prosecutor in meetings and in training programs for magistrates still needed follow-up and had not been addressed. The Chief Prosecutor agreed that the magistrates would from now on have to submit written reports to him regularly on their activities, including prison visits.

Provide Program Budgets for Activities

All UN field presences, whether as part of a peace operation, a stand-alone office, or even a solitary human rights officer in a country team, need money for programs and not only for staff salaries. If the human rights presences bring nothing to the table, only monitoring and reporting, they will lose credibility, access, and ability to effect change. UN human rights work must be more than just denouncing violations.

"We must be able to say: we are here to help solve these problems and prevent future violations; it's paradoxical that human rights offices don't have program budgets since it must be central to what we are doing" according to a UN humanitarian officer in Burundi who supported human rights and saw its importance to the overall success of the UN in Burundi (Interview with UN official, Bujumbura, November 2007).

Having something to offer also buys goodwill from the national authorities and makes it easier to raise the inevitable criticisms and "negative" news. A UNICEF official in Burundi noted, "There is a lot of human rights talk, but you need money to do this work, human rights do not come cheap, yet the human rights section is always the poor cousin" (Interview with UN official, Bujumbura, November 2007).

Human rights officers with even a minimal budget for programming (Burundi, Haiti, and Nepal) have seen greater impact, results, and thus success. With just $300/month per province in Burundi (about $30,000/year), the section was able to conduct important promotion and protection activities (OHCHR 2013). Financing must be flexible and quickly available. For the UN field operation in Rwanda in 1997, $10,000/month for programming made a crucial difference to its work and made criticisms of government performance more palatable for all sides.

The Ethiopian Women's Lawyers Association (EWLA) used funding from the UN to promote public awareness of domestic violence and to prevent child abuse. EWLA resolved 90% of the complaints it received through the courts or mediation. EWLA also ran an awareness-raising campaign on women's rights, especially early marriage, property and inheritance rights, and female genital mutilation; due to effective advocacy by EWLA, 26 underage marriages were canceled in Eastern Tigray. This shows how small amounts of money strategically deployed can have a major impact.

As a last resort, literally, human rights sections should plan to hand over as much as possible to local counterparts when a peace operation is winding down. In addition to the intellectual component, for example, the human rights section in the peacekeeping mission in Liberia is planning to transfer equipment, office furniture, computers, and books to local Liberian human rights organizations before it leaves at the end of 2017 (UNMIL 2017). OHCHR should be more assertive at the mission planning stage and in staffing and budgetary discussions for peace operations and in programming among the agencies comprising the UNCTs. The need for an assured budget line for human rights programming cannot be overstated.

Consult Beneficiaries Before Embarking on Assistance Efforts

Sometimes human rights officers, in an excess of enthusiasm, design programs that they think are priorities without first consulting the intended beneficiaries. "Participation" is too often honored in the breach. Meaningful, early participation with key stakeholders is always a good practice. Human rights officers should take the time to identify who are the most important local counterparts, governmental and civil society actors, and insure that they participate in every stage of the project. This is time-consuming but essential.

Addressing female genital mutilation in Eritrea, the human rights section of the United Nations Mission in Ethiopia and Eritrea (UNMEE) worked closely with the National Union of Eritrean Women who engaged with women's organizations to conduct a needs assessment and gathered reliable data. These efforts contributed to the Eritrean government banning female genital mutilation (FGM) in 2007 (Eritrea Gov. Proclamation, 2007). Along with UNICEF, the human rights section supported meetings with local government and civil society (including religious leaders) to design a campaign to combat FGM. For HIV/AIDs, local youth groups led awareness-raising campaigns as part of a "human rights week." These groups learned how to gather information, analyze it, and honed their advocacy skills.

The UN human rights section in UNMEE participated in designing and delivering courses on international human rights law at the law schools. But before starting, the section met with law students to ask them what were the most important human rights issues and how could they best be taught. After teaching the course for the first time, the UN met again with students and faculty to assess the quality and relevance of the course and made necessary adjustments based on the feedback. The course was made more practical and less theoretical, and the students recommended that police, military, and local government officials be invited to participate to make the discussions more "real"; this was done in later iterations with great success.

Identify Allies as Senior as Possible in the Government Hierarchy

Identifying allies as senior as possible in the government hierarchy is especially important in organizations like the police, intelligence services, and the military where command structures are paramount. Without their leaders' support for institutional change, it doesn't matter how many human rights workshops, how many people you train, or the thousands of copies of the Universal Declaration of Human Rights that you distribute.

One police reform expert emphasizes the importance of "integrity management" which requires managers and administrators in a police force to enforce constantly the rules that govern police behavior. It is not enough to have policies in place, written up, nicely included in procedural manuals. Unless managers make integrity a top priority and take action when necessary to address corruption or abuse of power, then slowly integrity will erode due to peer pressure and demands from outsiders who offer opportunities for material gain and symbolic rewards. This holds equally true for the judiciary, penal administration, and other state bodies.

"You have to get the senior leaders on board, then they will pass the orders down the hierarchy," noted a UN human rights officer in Burundi. Otherwise, "the training will go in one ear and out the other once they are back in their workplace" (Interview with UN official, Bujumbura, November 2007). An officer in the Haitian National Police's Inspector General's office echoed this advice: "You have to have the right person in the Station Command post. He or she sets the tone for everything and is responsible for discipline and good order" (Interview with UN official). Selecting the right people for key posts is crucial, as will be explained in the section on registration, certification, and vetting below.

Work with Parliament and National Legislatures

National parliaments should protect and promote human rights. In addition to helping parliamentarians draft and review laws to insure they are consistent with international human rights standards and the state's treaty obligations, human rights officers should help legislatures meet their responsibilities to oversee behavior by government ministries. Human rights sections in Haiti, Burundi, Timor-Leste, Liberia, and Kosovo have worked to enhance the skills of parliamentarians to investigate human rights issues, hold hearings, draft laws, and write reports.

In Sudan, the Human Rights Division of UNMISS has worked with parliament on analyzing national budgets. The members of parliament (MPs) have learned to assess financial information so that they can question the executive branch. This is important for economic, social, and cultural rights. "A human rights-based approach to budget monitoring" insists on progressive realization of rights and examines whether "maximum available resources" are being devoted to education, housing, health care, and access to clean water as required by the International Covenant on Economic, Social and Cultural Rights. Greater public debate on how government funds are spent, priorities identified, and increased transparency and accountability for spending decisions leads to greater knowledge and capacity of MPs. The impact of this capacity-building means better governance as MPs engage in the budget process and probe for information and demand explanations from the ministries.

The Burundi Bar Association, judges, prosecutors, Ministry of Justice officials, law professors, and members of parliament and of civil society participated in "Validation Workshops" organized by the human rights and justice sections of the United Nations Integrated Office in Burundi (BINUB) to review changes to the Penal Code and Code of Criminal Procedure. These workshops also covered questions of judicial ethics. This initiative not only strengthened the capacities of several institutions but also encouraged them to collaborate, which had rarely occurred before.

Use Treaty Bodies and Special Procedures Strategically

Human rights officers should use treaty bodies' conclusions and recommendations and the reporting process and visits and findings by Special Rapporteurs and Working Groups. In the early days of human rights field work, there was a divorce between the work on the ground and the whole treaty body and special procedures world. Designing a process to channel treaty body and special procedures' findings into programming should become routine practice for human rights officers.

The concluding observations and recommendations provide an entry point for human rights officers to raise delicate issues with the authorities.

The recommendations and conclusions should become the basis for programming to address the deficiencies identified by the experts. In Sudan, the human rights section has used the reporting process under the Convention on the Elimination of All Forms of Discrimination against Women (CEDAW) to launch a national discussion on the relationship between Shari'a and women's rights. The human rights section's role has also made it "safer" to have such discussions on sensitive issues.

The report of the Independent Expert on Haiti helped establish the human rights section's priorities when the UN Stabilization Mission in Haiti (MINUSTAH) deployed in 2004. Later reports by the Expert led to funding from one UN member state to address priorities like establishing a legal aid program and intensifying human rights promotion. The human rights section funded a 10-segment radio program produced by a well-known Haitian author and filmmaker on human rights and law enforcement; the programs used characters based on Haitian reality speaking Créole to convey important lessons about the police, judiciary, and the citizen's role. In recent years, the Independent Expert and the human rights team in MINUSTAH exchange information and analysis with the Expert relying on the priorities identified by officers on the ground (UN Human Rights Council 2012).

The Special Rapporteurs on torture and internally displaced persons (IDPs) came to Abkhazia, and their visits started a dialogue with the authorities, which were supported by the human rights team. Both Rapporteurs offered to return to run workshops for the authorities on how to implement their respective recommendations. Also, the other members of the UNCT are now involved in this dialogue, so the special procedures have helped integrate further human rights within the UN family.

A good practice developed by the Timor-Leste human rights section in their 2008–2009 strategy was to include special procedures-related indicators: number of communications and missions/visits by mandate holders, percentage of government responses to communications from mandate holders, number of invitations by government to Special Rapporteurs and Working Groups, percentage of special procedures recommendations implemented by government, NGOs' follow-up on special procedures recommendations, NGOs submitting information to mandate holders, and the level of UN agencies' participation in supporting the work of mandate holders (OHCHR, Timor-Leste, 2008 and 2009). The section also had a goal of supporting the submission of at least two "shadow reports" to treaty bodies.

National parliaments are often unaware of the treaty body conclusions or recommendations by the Special Rapporteurs. Human rights officers should provide parliament with relevant recommendations from the treaty bodies and special procedures and advise on implementing these relevant findings. The teams in the Sudan and DRC have done this, and others should be encouraged to do likewise. The Universal Periodic Review (UPR) of the Human Rights Council, although relatively new, establishes another promising tool for human rights field officers to feed information and analyses to the review process. Officers are also well-placed to assess the implementation of recommendations that the UPR generates.

Strengthen Local Ownership and Management and Leadership Skills

"Stay one step behind the locals, let them take the credit and gain the visibility, even if the UN has done all the work" said one experienced field officer (Interview with UN official). And the sooner the locals can do the bulk of the work the better. The team in Haiti adopted this approach, providing all of the documents, materials, and logistical support for Haiti's national human rights institution's events celebrating International Human Rights Day, while staying in the background and allowing the *Office de Protection du Citoyen* (OPC) to get visibility and credit. The team also provided support for OPC investigations (logistics, material, and personnel) with the goal of raising the OPC's stature so that more people will use it, have confidence in it, and funders will see that it is worth supporting.

United Nations Police (UNPOL) in Haiti provides logistical and material support to the Haitian National Police (HNP) to increase their presence: on patrol, directing traffic, visiting schools, and interacting more with the public (UN Office of Internal Oversight 2012). The population gained confidence in the HNP, while the HNP likewise gained competence and confidence in itself. Some units demanded even more training so they would not be "left behind," and the UNPOL deputy police commissioner noted a "cultural change" in the HNP. The incentives have changed, and officers see that competence and good behavior are rewarded, while incompetence and malfeasance are punished. This builds capacity leading to long-term institutional change and illustrates "integrity management" described above.

The UN human rights officers in Abkhazia developed good practices even in that difficult environment before they were expelled in late 2008. All human rights projects were implemented directly by local partners. The UN human rights team provided advice and sometimes support (documents, access to experts, and limited financial help). Training on project management, fund-raising, and reporting to donors and budgeting made these local NGOs more self-sufficient, independent, and effective. They were also well-placed to raise certain "taboo" topics like domestic violence that international observers would have found hard to do. One local NGO established a "hotline" and received over 130 calls for domestic violence incidents in the first few weeks. Police later received specialized training on how to handle domestic violence.

In the Central African Republic, the *Chef de Quartier* has enormous prestige and influence on the people residing in his jurisdiction. The UN human rights office in the early 2000s worked closely with the Chefs, building their knowledge of human rights, and tying this to local priorities as identified by the Chef and the people. The office then helped the Chef prepare workshops, speeches, and radio programs where human rights issues are raised and discussed. Similarly, the office has helped organize local women's organizations into a *Collectif des Femmes* who have identified women to run in local elections and for parliament. Finally, these women's organizations helped lobby parliament to pass a law allowing the prosecutor to bring cases of sexual violence without a complaint from the victim who was often afraid to lodge a complaint for fear of reprisals.

In Sierra Leone, the human rights section of the UN Integrated Office for Sierra Leone (UNIOSIL) supported the creation of an umbrella organization of human rights NGOs in 14 districts (UN Integrated Office in Sierra Leone 2008). UNDP's financial support allowed the office to hold workshops on monitoring and reporting, advocacy, and how to intervene with the authorities.

The UNIOSIL human rights section documented greater activity by local organizations and intensified reporting which led to the removal of several local officials for corruption and abuse of power. Civil society grew more assertive about demanding rights and accountability from the authorities. "We support and they lead" said a UN official in Freetown (Interview with UN official).

In Burundi, UNIFEM and the human rights section/office work jointly with the local traditional leaders ("Bashingantahe") on sensitive issues like women's rights, inheritance, early marriage, and HIV/AIDS (UNIFEM 2009). Without the leadership from these local chiefs, raising awareness and the capacity of local organizations to discuss these issues and seek change would be unthinkable.

Colocate and Mentor/Coach

As a follow-up to more formal classroom training, placing experts as mentors inside institutions, government, and non-state has produced positive results. The opportunity to observe and react quickly to local counterparts' actions has an immediate and lasting impact on performance. In Timor-Leste, human rights officers worked alongside colleagues in the *Provedoria's* (Ombudsman's) office for several years. Applying the mantra "reinforce, not replace," the mentors advise national officers on complaint handling, hearing procedures, report writing, and human rights education. Study after study shows that adults learn best by doing, so what better way to build capacity than to provide advice and constructive criticism while someone is "on the job."

Experience in Burundi also underscores the importance of building strong leadership, oversight capacity, and putting a premium on integrity. Without these, mere training and mentoring will not be enough. For example, one senior UN official in Burundi summed up the challenge: "How do we insure a transfer of what is learned in the class room to the work place and the skills and knowledge from the training does not get drowned out in the daily routine?" (interview with UN official). The police in Burundi continue to commit abuses despite many training sessions and workshops. One officer who had just received his certificate following a UN-sponsored human rights training session beat and nearly tortured a politician to death. When asked how he could do this after all he had learned, he responded, "I went back into the system, and the system was the same."

This only underscores the importance of reinforcing what is learned in training at the workplace through rigorous mentoring and oversight. For example, in Kosovo

UNPOL created a "Field Officer's Training Manual" which shows the mentor how to advise and assess the local officer's performance and contains checklists for each police function and questions to pose to the officers to insure they understand their tasks (Rausch 2007).

Develop Capacity to Handle Data

As was mentioned, you can't improve what you can't measure. The capacity to gather, analyze, maintain, retrieve, and use sound data is a fundamental part of all human rights work. An important lesson is that the amount of time and effort spent on helping the state and NGOs to handle all aspects of data is a worthwhile investment. The human rights teams in Haiti and Timor-Leste have helped the national human rights institutions in both countries, the *Provedoria* and the *Office de Protection du Citoyen*, to establish databases and have trained officers on how to use the software and the UN HURIDOCS system. The team in Liberia helped the Justice Ministry to develop a database on trends, patterns, and concerns within the judiciary on harmful traditional practices that will help define a strategy to address this problem along with extensive analyses of rape and sexual violence (UN DPKO 2017). And as the UN Rule of Law Indicators are rolled out in more and more countries, the data gathering, management, and analysis required will further reinforce a "data culture" in rule of law and human rights field work.

Link with UNCTs and "Mainstreaming" Human Rights

Human rights officers must try to forge closer links with the UNCT. This includes possibilities for increased programming on economic, social, and cultural rights. In Sudan, human rights officers worked with the UNCT to promote awareness of economic, social, and cultural rights among the population in the south and the government of South Sudan. Burundi's human rights officers have trained other UNCT members on the rights-based approach and participated in CCA-UNDAF formulations to insure that there is human rights content in these core planning documents.

In the Democratic Republic of the Congo (DRC), the human rights officers of MONUC (the UN Mission in the Democratic Republic of the Congo) informed UNCT members of the work of the Special Experts and their recommendations and arranged for meetings with UNCT during experts' visits. The officers have also set as a target that at least 30% of UN agencies' country programs incorporate a human rights perspective. "Pick a right – water, food, housing, health, education – then team up with a UN agency, budget programs in your cost plan, and then tackle economic, social and cultural rights you have targeted" a human rights field officer recommends, offering a sound formula that should be regular good practice in all missions (Interview with UN official).

Register, Certify, and Vet Judicial and Security Personnel

Many government institutions in post-conflict countries do not even know how many staff they have, where they are deployed, and their backgrounds, qualifications, or past performance records. Registration and certification programs can strengthen institutions by identifying all personnel, revealing their qualifications and providing information on gender, ethnic, religious, and racial composition. This capacity to know and manage your staff is crucial, especially for insuring competence, integrity, and diversity.

In Haiti, the human rights section supported a registration and certification program for the police. The head of the Haitian National Police had no idea how many officers he had, where they were stationed, and whether they had been appointed legally. And this was true before the devastating January 2010 earthquake. Many people claimed to be police officers who really were not. A significant number were implicated in serious human rights abuses and criminal activity. So a registration program was crucial for all further reform work. Building a solid database on all personnel was a capacity that the HNP never had before. Just knowing who is a police officer and who is not, how many are there, and where are they stationed was a major advance.

Vetting serving officers is a bridge between addressing impunity and reforming institutions. Any government official who by his/her past behavior is unworthy of continuing in office should be removed following a fair and open procedure. The population and the organization itself sees that the old ways will not be accepted and those vetted out pay a price for their crimes by losing a good job.

Vetting, however, is time-consuming and resource-intensive and can be controversial (UN Special Rapporteur on the Promotion of Truth 2015). Powerful people, or their friends and relatives, may lose their jobs some of which are lucrative and also provide the opportunity to extract bribes and graft. Donors sometimes shy away from funding vetting programs for precisely these reasons. One in particular is that most donors demand fast, concrete, and demonstrable results, and these are more likely to be obtained if the focus is on light, easy, and noncontroversial activities like training judges, providing cars for the police, and drafting new penal laws. The risk, however, in that approach is that by failing to address the root causes of why the institution does not work correctly – the values/incentive/organization culture – the reform effort fails to tackle foundational problems.

The UN is not alone in this approach. The United States Agency for International Development (USAID), the European Union, the UK's Department for International Development (DFID), and the Organisation for Security and Cooperation in Europe (OSCE), among others, also go for the relatively quick and easy quantifiable results. What can be done about this? How can the UN, especially given the short-term nature of most peace operations and special political missions, incorporate in their projects some elements that begin to address the long-term task of changing values and attitudes within and toward core institutions like the police, courts, and prisons?

Principles of Institutional Reform

Not just operational
effectiveness and service
delivery but also …

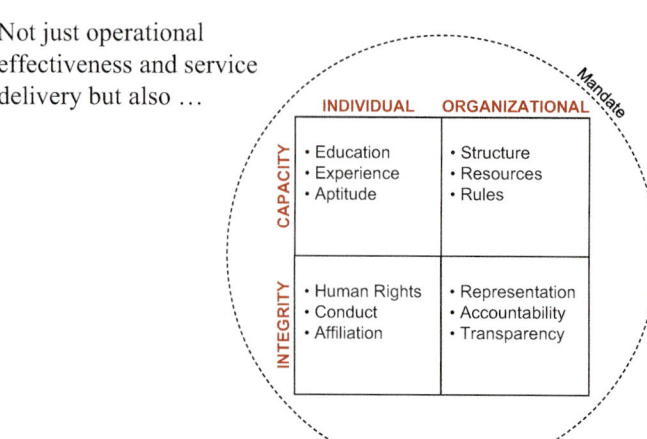

Source: OECD DAC Handbook 2007

An experienced human rights and security sector reform practitioner, Alexander Mayer-Rieckh, has designed an approach that helps to mitigate the now almost automatic tendency to focus on logistics, management, and technical training. He identifies an important principle that is rarely practiced by the UN or others: integrity. Mayer-Rieckh stresses the importance of identifying, supporting, and rewarding integrity for both the individuals in the police, judiciary, and prison service but also building the overall integrity of the institution itself. Moreover, he identifies the crucial principle of accountability as part of an institution's integrity. Reforms will only succeed when there is a price to pay for misconduct or abuse of power and whether good job performance is recognized and rewarded and bad performance is punished (Rea et al. 2010).

See the Human Rights Section as a "Convener"

UN human rights officers can exploit their role as "outsiders" to bring together institutions that often have not worked together or even communicated much before. This facilitating role can help strengthen the state's ability to identify problems, forge concerted action to respond, and create programs to prevent future violations. The mere fact of getting people in the same room to discuss issues can enhance government performance and reinforce links to civil society, whose representatives should be included whenever possible. The human rights and justice sections in Burundi regularly convened meetings between the Ministry of Justice and the Ministry of Human Rights to discuss common problems. This had rarely happened before, and it quickly yielded results, such as collaboration between the two in reforming the penal and criminal procedure codes. The Office also held periodic workshops for human rights groups, trade unions, political parties, and the press (Bašagic 2008). Much less expensive and time-consuming than formal training sessions, these workshops provided an opportunity to build the knowledge and skills of local counterparts and habituate them to consulting and communicating across sectors. They offered a regular forum to meet for follow-up and included more people than a formal training would have allowed. Formulating arguments and learning how to make demands on the government are skills that were honed in these meetings.

Another good practice employed by the OHCHR Office in Burundi was the weekly "protection meeting" chaired by the Office and attended by senior representatives of the police, army, intelligence service, and security service, the International Committee of the Red Cross, and a few international NGOs. These meetings became mini-training sessions in themselves where human rights officers conveyed to their government counterparts certain key principles and garnered their "buy-in" to prevent violations and punish those responsible for violations. One participant noted that "The weekly protection meetings help build government capacity by pressing the army, police and intelligence services to do their jobs the right way and to take corrective action when needed. And we are there to remind them each week of their responsibilities" (Interview with UN official).

The public prosecutor and the police had a horrible relationship in Haiti. Each accused the other of corruption and incompetence. The human rights section brought them together for a workshop, and soon they were exchanging information. The prosecutor started coming to the police academy to give a presentation to the new cadets and invited them to visit his office. The Police Inspector General started referring cases to the prosecutor for follow-up. A UN human rights officer noted: "We're a facilitator, we bring people together who should be talking but are not" (Interview with UN official).

Include National Human Rights Officers

One of the most effective, efficient, and sustainable ways of building capacity is to include nationals in the UN's human rights mission teams. In some places and times, certain issues cannot be assigned to nationals for reasons of their security or for broader concerns about confidential information. But these are often the exceptional situations. Most times national human rights officers can and should do just about anything that internationals do. The advantages of national officers are obvious: language ability, knowledge of local history, culture, the patterns and sources of human rights violations, and good contacts with key local players. Most national officers will stay in the country when the mission departs, so one of the most important legacies a human rights office can leave is a well-trained corps of national human rights professionals who will take their knowledge, skills, and work ethic into a variety of jobs, including national human rights institutions, government posts, or with nongovernmental organizations. The UN could learn a lot from the OSCE, an organization that has pioneered the use of national human rights officers (OSCE/ODIHR 2012). The ultimate goal of all UN human rights officers should be to make themselves obsolete, to work themselves out of their jobs and who better to hand the work over to than national counterparts.

Focus on Youth

The human rights section of the UN Mission in Liberia (UNMIL) has supported "Human Rights Clubs" in high schools throughout the country. Using teachers and NGOs, the section has provided guidance, materials, and financial support to these clubs. The goal is to make the clubs completely self-sufficient and self-governing.

In Abkhazia, the human rights officers worked with local NGOs specializing in children's rights (OHCHR Quarterly Report 2005). One in Sokhumi had children write and produce a puppet play that conveyed human rights problems and principles using traditional Abkhaz stories and characters. Enormously popular with children and adults, the puppets will be used for future human rights activities.

The team in Timor-Leste integrated human rights into the primary school curriculum and trained trainers at the Ministry of Education on human rights issues (UNICEF 2010). The office has joined UNICEF to lead a national campaign for children's rights.

Assess Training's Impact on Performance

Human rights officers must identify ways to evaluate how training achieves the goal of improving capacity, knowledge, and commitment leading to improved performance by those trained. It is not enough to pass around a questionnaire at the end of a workshop asking people what they think of the training. Periodic evaluations to gauge the impact of training are necessary. Effective human rights officers link their overall monitoring to issues covered in various trainings. Their monitoring strategy includes obtaining information showing whether or not training improves the performance of those trained. For example, has a workshop for judges on international human rights law has led to an increased use of these laws in the judges' work?

In Sierra Leone, after the workshops held for the police on juvenile justice and the Convention on the Rights of the Child, follow-up monitoring by the section has shown that prisons and police lockup facilities now refuse to admit juveniles and insist that they be taken back to court and assigned to appropriate juvenile facilities or released. In Burundi, the National Intelligence Service (SNR) was implicated in serious cases of rights violations, including routine beatings of detainees and holding people incommunicado for long periods. SNR leaders attend weekly meetings convened by the UN Human Rights Office in Burundi where serious cases were raised with government officials, including representatives of the army, police, and SNR (Human Rights Watch 2009). The SNR leadership requested training for its agents on the rights of detainees and the proper use of force. Human rights officers helped organize these training sessions based on real cases. Afterward, they noted a decrease in cases alleging violations by the SNP. Inspections showed that cells were not overcrowded and detainees were treated humanely. SIN improved its capacity and its will to investigate and bring perpetrators to justice. One officer noted, "I can see the impact, I review the orders given by commanding officers and they have improved and include references to human rights and humanitarian law principles where they never did before" (Interview with UN official). Another effective tool is to create after each training session a "Comité de Suivi" or "follow-up committee" which should include some participants, the UN human rights officers, and relevant government or NGO officers.

The Guiding Principles for Human Rights Field Officers Working in Conflict and Post-conflict Environments

Much of the preceding analysis has been distilled into ten *Guiding Principles for Human Rights Field Officers Working in Conflict and Post-Conflict Environments* (GPs) (O'Neill 2009). A group of leading experts on human rights field work reviewed and commented on early drafts of the GPs, culminating in a day-long meeting at the Scuola Sant'Anna in Pisa in March 2008. Senior officials from OHCHR participated in every phase of the development of the GPs, and they were officially introduced in Geneva in 2009. They "do not purport to be a comprehensive field manual or to exhaustively address every aspect of the issues explored. They are intended to provide a professional framework for the individual HRFO – in the main reflecting consensus as to international law and practice, but also pointing critically to how field practice may be enhanced."

Initial reactions from practitioners to the GPs have been positive with most noting the GPs are practical, attuned to field realities, being both accessible and comprehensive. One mystery, however, is OHCHR's ambivalent attitude toward the GPs. Despite significant and sustained participation by OHCHR officials, the office has not fully embraced the GPs nor, more importantly, used them or made them available to UN human rights field officers. The High Commissioner should formally endorse the GPs and the office and incorporate them into training, doctrine, and evaluations of field work. Greater awareness and application of the GPs would only help to improve the quality of UN human rights field work while also helping instill a more coherent, consistent, and effective approach while allowing for the variation in context that is the essence of field work. The challenge of doing principled work in diverse environments is precisely what makes human rights field work so difficult and rewarding. The GPs, though they came first, would also help realize the goals identified in the HIPPO and AGE reports and be fully consistent with the Rights Up Front approach.

Conclusion

Human rights fieldwork by the United Nations and indeed by the African Union, the European Union, the Organization for Security and Cooperation in Europe, and indeed for all major institutions must continue to adapt and evolve. The growth in number, size, and lethality of non-state actors poses enormous challenges. Climate change, in particular the declining access to water and arable land, and the conflict that this can help generate is another new factor. Terrorism itself is a horrible human rights violation, along with efforts to counter terrorism, which also all too often leads to human rights violations and complicates the work of human rights professionals. The sclerotic nature of the UN Security Council presents a deep political problem, particularly with permanent members like Russia and China who consistently block or undermine UN efforts to deploy human rights officers or even consider their reports. Nevertheless, the growth of civil society around the world and the demand for dignity and respect for human rights make the work of on-the-ground monitors all the more crucial. That they do their work competently and professionally is essential.

References

Advisory Group of Experts (2015) The challenge of sustaining peace. Available at http://www.providingforpeacekeeping.org/project/the-challenge-of-sustaining-peace-report-of-the-advisory-group-of-experts-on-the-review-of-the-un-peacebuilding-architecture-2015. Accessed 12 Feb 2018

Bašagic Z (2008) UN integration in Burundi in the context of the peacebuilding office BINUB: taking stock and lessons learned from June 2006 to November 2007. Available at https://reliefweb.int/sites/reliefweb.int/files/resources/901F358C1EEE02CC852575E700679405-Full_Report.pdf. Accessed 12 Feb 2018

Bell C (2002) Peace agreements and human rights. Oxford University Press, Oxford

DCAF/The International Security Sector Advisory Team (ISSAT) (2012) SSR in a nutshell: manual for introductory training on security sector reform. Available at https://issat.dcaf.ch/mkd/download/2970/25352/ISSAT%20LEVEL%201%20TRAINING%20MANUAL%20-%20SSR%20IN%20A%20NUTSHELL%20-%205.3.pdf. Accessed 26 Mar 2018

Eritrea Government Proclamation 158/2007 (2007) A proclamation to abolish female circumcision [Eritrea], No. 158/2007, 20 March 2007

Farkas E (2011) Bridging the gap: finding alternatives to the oil revenue. United Nations Mission in Sudan (June 2011): 6, https://unmis.unmissions.org/sites/default/files/insudan-june-2011-eng-web.pdf. Accessed 26 Mar 2018

High Level Independent Panel on United Nations Peace Operations (HIPPO) (2015) United Nations. Available at https://reliefweb.int/sites/reliefweb.int/files/resources/HIPPO_Report_1_June_2015.pdf. Accessed 26 Mar 2018

Howland T (1999) Mirage magic, or mixed bag? The United Nations High Commissioner for Human Rights' Field Operation in Rwanda. Human Rights Quarterly 21(1):1–55. http://www.refworld.org/docid/48578c812.html. Accessed 12 Feb 2018

Human Rights Watch (2009) Pursuit of power: political violence and repression in Burundi. Human Rights Watch, New York. Available at https://www.hrw.org/report/2009/06/03/pursuit-power/political-violence-and-repression-burundi. Accessed 12 Feb 2018

Inter-Agency Standing Committee (2000) Note of guidance of the secretary-general on relations between representatives of the secretary-general, Resident Coordinators and Humanitarian Coordinators, news release, 1 October 2000 UN Security Council, Report of the Secretary-General on the situation in Abkhazia, Georgia, UN Doc S/2008/219, 2 April 2008

International Council on Human Rights Policy (2000) Local perspectives: foreign aid to the justice sector. International Council of Human Rights Policy, Versoix. Available at http://www.ichrp.org/files/reports/9/104_report_en.pdf. Accessed 12 Feb 2018

Lynch M, Saralidze L, Goguadze N, Zolotor A (2008) National study on violence against children in Georgia. UNICEF Georgia, Tbilisi. Available at http://www.mes.gov.ge/upload/multi/geo/1230185414_School_Violence_ENG.pdf. Accessed 26 Mar 2018

Machiavelli N (1513) [2011] The prince. Penguin Books, New York

Marshall D (ed) (2014) The international rule of law movement. Harvard University Press, Harvard

Martin I (1995) Paper versus steel: the first phase of the international civilian mission in Haiti. In: Henkin A (ed) Honoring human rights and keeping the peace. Kluwer, The Hague, pp 73–118

O'Flaherty M, Ulrich G (2010) The professionalization of human rights field work. Journal of Human Rights Practice 2(1):1–27

O'Neill W (2009) Guiding principles for human rights field officers working in conflict and post-conflict environments. University of Nottingham, Human Rights Law Centre. Available at https://reliefweb.int/sites/reliefweb.int/files/resources/7827EC3BF46AB9FAC125749600687EE5-Guiding%20Principles.pdf. Accessed 26 Mar 2018

Office of the High Commissioner for Human Rights (2005) Quarterly reports of field offices: Europe Central Asia, and North America region, report (June 2005): 26–27

Office of the High Commissioner for Human Rights (2017) OHCHR in the World. Available at http://www.ohchr.org/EN/Countries/Pages/WorkInField.aspx. Accessed 12 Feb 2018

Office of the High Commissioner for Human Rights in Timor-Leste (2008-2009) OHCHR in Timor-Leste. Available at http://www.ohchr.org/EN/Countries/AsiaRegion/Pages/TLSummary0809.aspx. Accessed 12 Feb 2018

Office of the High Commissioner for Human Rights and United Nations Integrated Mission in Timor-Leste (UNMIT) (2009) Report on Human Rights Developments in Timor-Leste: 1 July 2008 to 30 June 2009. Available at http://www.ohchr.org/Documents/Countries/UNMIT01072008_300609.pdf. Accessed 12 Feb 2018

Organisation for Economic Co-operation and Development (2007). The OECD DAC handbook on security system reform: supporting security and justice. Available at https://www.eda.admin.ch/dam/deza/en/documents/themen/fragile-kontexte/224402-oecd-handbook-security-system-reform_EN.pdf. Accessed 26 Mar 2018

Organization for Security and Co-operation in Europe/Office of Democratic Institutions and Human Rights (OSCE/ODIHR) (2012) Annual Report. Available at https://www.osce.org/odihr/93799?download=true. Accessed 12 Feb 2018

Ratcliffe R (2017) UN calls on Nepal to investigate civil war case of gang-rape and torture by soldier. Available at https://www.theguardian.com/global-development/2017/aug/09/un-calls-on-nepal-to-investigate-civil-war-case-of-gang-rape-and-torture-by-soldiers. Accessed 12 Feb 2018

Rausch C (2007) From elation to disappointment: justice and security reform in Kosovo. In: Call C (ed) Constructing justice and security after war. United States Institute of Peace, Washington, pp 271–312

Rea D, Bradley D, Gilligan B (2010) Public accountability: the Policing Board and the District Policing Partnerships in policing the narrow ground. In: Doyle J (ed) Policing the Narrow Ground. Royal Irish Academy, Dublin, pp 128–144

Seymour (2010) New models for human rights capacity-building in the field: human rights field officers and relief and development professionals. In: O'Flaherty M, Ulrich G (eds) The professional identity of the human rights field officer. Ashgate, Aldershot, pp 115–131

Sharma M (2011) Transitional justice and vetting from the perspective of the TCC in strengthening the rule of law through the United Nations security council. Australia National University. Available at http://regnet.anu.edu.au/sites/default/files/publications/attachments/2015-05/Sharma_1.4_0.pdf. Accessed 12 Feb 2018

UN Commission on Human Rights (2002) Situation of human rights in Haiti, UN Doc E/CN4/2003/116, 23 December 2002

UN Department of Peacekeeping Operations (2017) Justice Update. Available at http://www.un.org/en/peacekeeping/publications/cljas/justice042010.pdf. Accessed 12 Feb 2018

UN Development Programme (2014) Strengthening the rule of law in crisis affected countries. Global Report 2014:83–87

UN High Commissioner for Human Rights (2005) The OHCHR plan of action: protection and empowerment. Available at http://www2.ohchr.org/english/planaction.pdf. Accessed 12 Feb 2018

UN High Commissioner for Human Rights (2013) UNHCR Global Appeal 2013 update – Burundi. Available at http://www.unhcr.org/50a9f81db02.html. Accessed 12 Feb 2018

UN Human Rights Council (2012) Report of the independent expert on the situation of human rights in Haiti, Michel Forst, UN Doc A/HRC/20/35, 23 April 2012

UN Integrated Office in Sierra Leone (UNIOSIL) (2008) Review of Sierra Leone media reports. Available at https://appablog.wordpress.com/2008/04/14/review-of-sierra-leone-media-reports-14-april-2008/. Accessed 26 Mar 2018

UN Office of Internal Oversight Services, Internal Audit Division (2012) The Haitian National Police development programme in MINUSTAH, internal audit report, assignment no. AP2011/683/10

UN Office on Drugs and Crime (2011) Law enforcement officers receive computer-based training in Timor-Leste, News release. Available at https://www.unodc.org/southeastasiaandpacific/en/2011/01/cbt-timor-leste/story.html. Accessed 26 Mar 2018

UN Secretary-General (2013) Rights up front. Detailed Plan of Action. On file with the author

UN Special Rapporteur on Truth, Justice and Reparations and Guarantees of Non-recurrence (2015) UN Doc. A/70/438

UNICEF (2010) Evaluation of UNICEF's education programme in Timor Leste. United Nations Children's Fund, New York

UNIFEM (2009) Annual Report 2008–2009. United Nations Development Fund for Women, New York. Available at http://www.peacewomen.org/assets/file/Resources/UNReports/unifem_annualreport_2008-2009.pdf. Accessed 26 Mar 2018

United Nations Integrated Peacebuilding Office in Sierra Leone (2017) Second DHRC National Consultative Conference and training takes place in Bo. News release. Available at https://unipsil.unmissions.org/second-dhrc-national-consultative-conference-and-training-takes-place-bo. Accessed 26 Mar 2018

United Nations OROLSI Rule of Law Indicators (2011) Available at http://www.un.org/en/peacekeeping/publications/un_rule_of_law_indicators.pdf. Accessed 12 Feb 2018

UNMIL (2017) UNMIL donates equipment and publications to support promotion of human rights in Liberia. News release. Available at https://unmil.unmissions.org/unmil-donates-equipment-and-publications-support-promotion-human-rights-liberia. Accessed 26 Mar 2018

World Bank and the African Development Bank Group (2017) How the project cycle works. Available at http://www.worldbank.org/en/projects-operations/products-and-services/brief/projectcycle. Accessed 26 Mar 2018

World Bank and UNHCR Afghanistan (2011) Research study on IDPs in urban settings – Afghanistan. Available at http://siteresources.worldbank.org/EXTSOCIALDEVELOPMENT/Resources/244362-1265299949041/6766328-1265299960363/WB-UNHCR-IDP_Full-Report.pdf. Accessed 12 Feb 2018

The UN Human Rights Treaty Bodies: Impact and Future

Lutz Oette

Contents

Introduction 96
Development and Mandate 98
Reporting 100
General Comments and General Recommendations 103
Complaints Procedures 104
Inquiry Procedure 106
The OPCAT as an Alternative Model 108
Achievements 108
Challenges and Future Potential 110
Conclusion 112
References 113

Abstract

The United Nations human rights treaty bodies have, from modest beginnings, developed monitoring practices, particularly consideration of States Parties' reports, individual complaints procedures, and inquiries, which cover a broad range of rights and issues. This development, in particular increasingly participatory procedures, has been lauded as an example of "human rights experimentalism." The treaty bodies have thereby contributed to the interpretation of international human rights law, though not without some weaknesses, and to the protection of human rights, at least to some extent. While treaty bodies have undoubtedly become an integral part of the UN's human rights system, they face considerable challenges in terms of their efficiency, effectiveness, and legitimacy. Their proliferation, and the consequent increase in the number of States Parties' reports and cases, has prompted an ongoing review process. It calls into question

L. Oette (✉)
SOAS, University of London, London, UK
e-mail: lo8@soas.ac.uk

© Springer Nature Singapore Pte Ltd. 2018
G. Oberleitner (ed.), *International Human Rights Institutions, Tribunals, and Courts*,
International Human Rights, https://doi.org/10.1007/978-981-10-5206-4_5

the future of the system in its present form and entails that treaty bodies and their record will remain under close scrutiny. Treaty bodies will have to continue navigating conflicting demands and expectations from States Parties, within the United Nations, and civil society organizations. In a world where inequality, conflict, and instability are rife and the very notion of human rights is frequently sidelined if not criticized, treaty bodies face a considerable challenge to ensure effective monitoring and ultimately the protection of human rights. Combining a clear conceptual focus and attention to context with closer institutional alignment and holistic and effective forms of engagement will be critical in meeting this challenge.

Keywords
United Nations · Treaty bodies · Human rights · Monitoring · Institutional reforms

Introduction

The genesis of the United Nations (UN) human rights treaty bodies system could be portrayed as a success story of steady progress. The beginnings were modest, with many States opposed to strong monitoring mechanisms that were viewed as undue encroachment on their sovereignty. Subsequently, treaty bodies have succeeded in carving out an important role within the broader UN human rights architecture. They have contributed to the development of UN human rights practice by using their respective mandates to develop monitoring tools and interpret their respective treaties. The proliferation of treaty bodies, whose mandates now covers a range of rights, demonstrates that treaty body monitoring is a viable model that has the support of States Parties and the UN as an organization (Oberleitner 2007). While the implementation of treaty bodies' recommendations and decisions has been inconsistent, there is considerable evidence that they have resulted in positive change at the domestic level (Creamer and Simmons 2015). The treaty bodies could just as easily be perceived as a failure. Instead of being at the heart of the UN human rights system, exercising robust and effective monitoring, bodies have proliferated with limited coordination, visibility, and impact, due to weaknesses in institutional design, working methods, and inadequate financial support. They are at risk of being marginalized within the broader human rights field, particularly if contrasted with the regional human rights systems and UN charter bodies, with a proactive Human Rights Council (HRC) in place. The never-ending debates surrounding treaty body reform is testimony that the model is in permanent crisis (Bayefsky 2001; Morijn 2011). Both perspectives can claim some validity. What the competing views demonstrate, though, is the difficulty of assessing the impact of treaty bodies.

The literature on treaty bodies has for a considerable period been dominated by insiders, that is, those who have participated in the system (e.g., Alston, Buergenthal, Kälin, Keller, Nowak, O'Flaherty, Rodley, Scheinin, Schöpp-Schilling). Its focus has been on particular functions exercised by treaty bodies, such as reporting

(Kälin 2012), general comments (Keller and Grover 2012), complaints procedures (Ulfstein 2012; Van Alebeek and Nollkaemper 2012), and questions of interpretation (Mechlem 2009; Schlütter 2012). At the same time, there has been a growing body of literature, particularly commentaries, on individual treaties and their monitoring bodies (e.g., Thornberry 2016; Della Fina et al. 2017). With the proliferation of treaty bodies and complaints procedures, attention has focused on the efficiency and effectiveness of treaty bodies in discharging their monitoring functions. The debate about the reform, or strengthening of treaty bodies, has centered on questions of institutional design and working methods, particularly numbers and types of treaty bodies, their composition, functional efficiency, and impact (Office of the High Commissioner for Human Rights 2006; O'Flaherty and O'Brien 2007; Morijn 2011; Pillay 2012). The ongoing scrutiny also includes how the work of treaty bodies relates to other bodies and procedures, especially the HRC's universal periodic review (UPR) and special procedures (Rodley 2009, 2012; O'Flaherty 2011). Several observers have raised broader questions about the treaty body system, particularly in respect of its responsiveness to human rights challenges in a fast-changing world, and its impact in promoting and protecting human rights (Kelly 2009; Mutua 2016). Research by legal and international relations scholars has provided important theoretical and empirical insights on compliance with treaty commitments and the role and impact of treaty bodies (Heyns and Viljoen 2002; de Gaer 2011; de Búrca 2017). The various strands of research and commentary form part of a wider inquiry into treaty bodies' legitimacy in terms of their position vis-à-vis States Parties (Keller and Ulfstein 2012), composition and attitudes (Kelly 2009), relationship with civil society organizations and the victims of human rights violations (Kelly 2009; Craemer and Simmons 2015; Levin 2016), and gender dimension (Johnstone 2006).

This brief overview shows the multiple challenges that an assessment of the impact and future of UN human rights treaty bodies poses. A useful starting point in any analysis is to focus on how well the bodies perform their functions, particularly the consideration of reports and complaints, under their respective treaty mandate. The common features of the monitoring system allow for a largely generic analysis, with the exception of the recently established Subcommittee on Prevention of Torture and Other Cruel, Inhuman or Degrading Treatment or Punishment (SPT). Its governing treaty sets out a unique, tailored mandate, which provides a model as to how the mandates and functions of treaty bodies could be framed or how various treaty bodies could complement each other. A focus on fulfilment of functions, that is, the effectiveness of monitoring within the confines of the system, would be incomplete without a wider inquiry into treaty bodies' contribution to the promotion and protection of human rights (law). Ultimately, "enhanced protection of human rights at the domestic level" must be "the purpose of all forms of reform of the treaty body system" (Aidoo et al. 2009, para. 7).

This chapter sets out a contextual understanding of treaty bodies that identifies underlying factors and the role of various actors in shaping developments. It situates treaty bodies within the wider human rights framework and infrastructure and explores a series of in-built tensions. This includes the hybrid nature of treaty bodies as both creatures of States *and* independent monitoring bodies, specificity versus coherence, and monitoring as ritual versus responsiveness to the individuals and target groups that treaty bodies are meant to protect. The chapter examines both the internal institutional and operational dimension of treaty bodies, such as their composition, functions, and working practice, and their external dimension, particularly their relationships with States Parties, other UN bodies, civil society organizations, and victims of human rights violations. These dimensions are at the heart of ongoing debates about the reform or strengthening of treaty bodies that are analyzed further. The chapter also locates treaty bodies in broader developments within the field of human rights, including how they have responded to the critical interrogation of the international human rights system by multiple actors.

Development and Mandate

The development of international human rights law in the period following the end of World War II was marked by an emphasis on setting out general human rights standards, and debates surrounding the binding nature, and effectiveness of rights (Lauterpacht 1945). Bodies mandated to exercise monitoring functions were not unknown, such as the International Labour Organization's petition system (Oberleitner 2007; Kälin 2012). However, States jealous of their sovereignty proved initially reluctant to establish treaty bodies with strong monitoring functions. It was after sustained institutional debates within the UN, particularly the then Commission on Human Rights, that the current human rights treaty system began to take shape, with its monitoring functions only becoming more effective following the end of the Cold War (O'Flaherty and Tsai 2011; Kälin 2012). The Committee on the Elimination of Racial Discrimination (CERD) was the first treaty body to be established in 1969, followed by the Human Rights Committee (HRCttee) in 1976, the Committee on the Elimination of Discrimination against Women (CEDAW) in 1982, and the Committee on Economic, Social, and Cultural Rights (CESCR) in 1985, which was, anomalously, set up as an UN Economic and Social Council (ECOSOC) body. Since then, the total number has risen to ten treaty bodies to date. This includes the Committee against Torture (CAT), 1987; the Committee on the Rights of the Child (CRC), 1991; the Committee on Migrant Workers (CMW), 2003; the Committee on the Rights of Persons with Disabilities (CRPD), 2008; and the Committee on Enforced Disappearances (CED), 2011. The SPT, established under the Optional Protocol to the Convention against Torture and Other Cruel, Inhuman or Degrading Treatment or Punishment (OPCAT) in 2006, is a separate treaty body, its potentially misleading name notwithstanding. This development may be construed as evidence of an inexorable rise in the number of treaty bodies. However, by their nature, the existence of such bodies is premised on a treaty. The momentum for the adoption of new treaties, and treaty bodies, has visibly slowed in the last decade. A number of factors account for this development, but concerns over the sustainability of the treaty body system in its current form suggest that there is limited appetite for substantial further expansion.

Most treaty bodies share a number of features; they are, with the exception of the CESCR, established by States Parties and derive their respective mandate and functions from the founding treaty. Other than the SPT, treaty bodies have a set of common core functions, namely, consideration of States Parties reports and of individual complaints, and the adoption of general comments/recommendations. Treaty bodies are composed of between 10 and 25 independent experts who serve in an individual capacity and are elected at the meetings of States Parties or ECOSOC (in the case of CESCR). Treaty bodies report to the UN General Assembly (or, in the case of CESCR, to ECOSOC), are financed out of the UN budget and voluntary contributions, and are being serviced by the Office of the High Commissioner for Human Rights (OHCHR). These features make them an integral part of the broader UN human rights system (Office of the High Commissioner for Human Rights 2015). Yet, UN human rights treaty bodies are by no means uniform. There are substantial differences in respect of their historical development, particularly the CESCR and CEDAW, and the significance of their governing treaty. The latter depends on the subject matter and number of States Parties and the nature of the body concerned, including size, composition (individual expertise, gender, origin, independence, and workload), its functions, and record. Several bodies have only recently begun to consider individual complaints (CRPD, CRC, CESCR, CED), while others have no such competence, such as CMW, where the complaints mechanism is not yet in force, or SPT, where no such mechanism is envisaged. Equally, only some bodies have the power to conduct inquiries (CAT, CEDAW, CED, CRPD, CESCR, CRC) or to use urgent action procedures (CED) or early warning procedures (CERD). The SPT, for its part, follows a fundamentally different model based on monitoring visits, advice and assistance to States Parties and National Preventive Mechanisms, and cooperation with a cross section of actors. These differences matter as any assessment and reform proposals doing justice to the nature and work of the committees will have to consider both common features and discrete elements of the treaty body or bodies in question.

The powers of treaty bodies are circumscribed by their mandate, i.e., the authority to carry out certain functions. Delineating the scope of a body's mandate poses a well-known challenge of interpretation, which will invariably have a bearing on the relationship between the body and States Parties. Is the body merely, or primarily, the implementing organ of its "masters," that is, States Parties, or does it have considerable latitude to foster the objects and purposes of the treaty? Treaty bodies are generally mandated to carry out specific functions as set out in their respective treaties. Some of the bodies are also vested with a wider mandate of reviewing the "progress made in the implementation" of the treaty (Art. 17(1) Convention on the Elimination of All Forms of Discrimination against Women), the "realisation of the obligations undertaken" (Art. 43(1) Convention on the Rights of the Child), or "the application of the present Convention" (Art. 72(1)(a) International Convention on the Protection of the Rights of All Migrant Workers and Members of their Family). This laconic, functional approach means that treaties largely do not spell out the purposes that the functions are meant to serve (Rodley 2009). The treaty bodies have also not been given any explicit powers to interpret authoritatively the respective treaty or to reach binding decisions (Keller and Ulfstein 2012). This apparent structural shortcoming might be perceived as ensuring the inherent and perpetual weakness of treaty bodies. However, such reading would ignore the potential, and reality that treaty bodies play an important role in the interpretation of their respective treaties, and international human rights law more broadly. Treaty bodies have exercised their functions in a manner that ostensibly went considerably beyond what many States had envisaged during the drafting stage of the governing treaties and have, some misgivings notwithstanding, developed their legitimacy in so doing.

Human rights treaties are instruments agreed upon multilaterally by States to advance common, shared goals, which are ultimately aimed at protecting the right holders covered by the treaty. Treaty bodies may in this context be understood as international guardians who are mandated to advance the cause of the promotion and protection of the human rights falling within their remit. While the human rights committees and their members have been vested with a degree of autonomy (Oberleitner 2007), the factors mentioned above have, to date, not led to a wholesale reversal in the relationship between treaty bodies and States Parties. The UN human rights system depends on States, and treaty bodies may resemble diplomatic actors (O'Flaherty 2011) more than courts, having to "oscillate between the desire to supervise and the need to cooperate" (Rajagopal 2003, 66–67).

Reporting

The consideration of regular reports by States Parties is a core function of most treaty bodies, with the exception of CED, as Article 29 of the International Convention for the Protection of All Persons from Enforced Disappearance (CPED) provides for initial reports only and later reports upon request by the Committee, and SPT. The reporting procedure enables treaty bodies to monitor States Parties' compliance with their treaty obligations in regular intervals. It has been aptly referred to as a "complex cyclical process" (Morijn 2011, 309), the purpose of which is to examine the measures taken by States Parties to implement their treaty obligations. The OHCHR identified four purposes of reporting, including giving a "holistic perspective of human rights," reaffirmation of commitment to treaties, review of national implementation, and "constructive dialogue at the international level" (Kälin 2012, 38–39). The reporting procedure is more than a purely binary process between the respective Committee members and State Party representatives. It provides an opportunity for States Parties to evaluate any progress made, to identify gaps and challenges in respect of relevant human rights obligations, and to develop and adopt the policies and measures needed to enhance compliance. It also provides a forum for various national and international actors to share information and analysis. This allows subjecting the performance of the State Party concerned to close scrutiny with a view to prompting improvements where needed. Ideally, the reporting procedure therefore creates an enabling environment for States Parties whereby the treaty bodies act as both assessors and facilitators.

The reporting procedure is central to treaty body monitoring. Yet, the general wording of relevant provisions provides limited guidance on the format of reports and the process of review. Article 19(1) of the Convention against Torture and Other Cruel, Inhuman or Degrading Treatment or Punishment (UNCAT), for example, stipulates that "States Parties shall submit to the Committee... reports on the measures they have taken to give effect to their undertakings under this Convention," which the Committee shall consider, pursuant to Article 19(3), and "make such general comments on the report as it may consider appropriate and shall forward these to the State Party concerned..." The question of the format of consideration of reports was initially not solely a technical matter, though, as some committee members also objected to any process overly critical of States Parties' record (Kälin 2012). The first task of treaty bodies was therefore to clarify the reporting obligations of States Parties, primarily by means of adopting general comments (HRC, General Comment 1 (1981), subsequently replaced by General Comment 30 (2002), and General Comment 2 (1981, superseded by CCPR/C/66/GUI, Consolidated guidelines for State reports under the International Covenant on Civil and Political Rights (ICCPR) (29 September 1999)). To date, treaty bodies follow a similar though by no means uniform format in their reporting procedure. In their practice, treaty bodies examine States Parties' reports in light of information received, such as by UN agencies, national human rights institutions, and civil society organizations, and commonly draw up a list of issues to facilitate the dialogue with the States Parties' representatives. The review cycle ends with the adoption of concluding observations, which cover, with some variation, positive developments, areas of concern, and recommendations.

Concluding observations are at the heart of the review process, providing a baseline for subsequent reports and acting as critical reference points for States Parties' record over time. It is generally agreed that they do not create any legal obligation by means of a binding interpretation (O'Flaherty 2006). Nonetheless, they do have a special status as an authoritative pronouncement by the body mandated to monitor States Parties' compliance (O'Flaherty 2006). Concluding observations have been repeatedly objected to, including on legal grounds where States Parties disagreed with the interpretation of treaty provisions put forward by the Committee concerned. They have also been criticized for the lack of setting clear priorities, specificity, and coherence (O'Flaherty 2006; Mechlem 2009). These are critical factors as they impact the authority of the Committee concerned and influence the likelihood of implementation of the recommendations in question. Such implementation has been inconsistent in practice, also due to the weakness of follow-up procedures (de Gaer 2011). The extent to which recommendations are implemented is difficult to establish in the absence of systematic, qualitative assessment and review (Morijn 2011; Kälin 2012).

The lack of timely and adequate reporting by states on how they have complied with their treaty obligations is a long-standing, systemic challenge (Pillay 2012; UN Secretary-General 2016). It has been the subject of ongoing debates over the last three decades that has intensified with the growing number of States becoming parties to treaties (Alston and Crawford 2000; Bayefsky 2001; Morijn 2011).

The failure to adequately report in time can be attributed to a number of factors, including limited capacity of States Parties, multiple reporting obligations, and the lack of incentive in the absence of political costs for non-compliance (Le Blanc et al. 2010; Kälin 2012; Creamer and Simmons 2015). Human rights treaty bodies and the OHCHR have responded to this situation by seeking to build the reporting capacity of States Parties; simplifying the reporting procedure, particularly by focusing on lists of issues; and considering country situations in the absence of reports that have been long overdue (Pillay 2012). While the measures largely focusing on States Parties have led to some improvements, the treaty bodies themselves also face systemic problems. They have limited time and resources to review reports and to follow up in systematic fashion while facing an increasing backlog (Pillay 2012). These challenges of input (States Party reports), analysis (review and concluding observations), and output (by treaty bodies) combine to adversely affect the impact of treaty bodies (O'Flaherty and Tsai 2011). They thereby form part of broader concerns about the accessibility, quality, coherence, and effectiveness of the system (Morijn 2011). This situation has resulted in an ongoing review of the treaty body system and changes to make the reporting procedure more efficient.

The reporting procedure of treaty bodies cannot be seen in isolation of other UN human rights charter mechanisms, not least those that further add to States' reporting obligations. This applies particularly to the UPR, which has a number of markedly different features. It is a regular, wide-ranging review process of States' human rights obligations and commitments with clear timelines, is based on the notion of peer review, is viewed as less antagonistic, and allows States to accept, and reject, recommendations (UN General Assembly resolution 60/251 (2006)). The initial concerns that the UPR might result in undermining the treaty bodies' reporting procedures have largely not been borne out (O'Flaherty and Tsai 2011). It has been viewed as providing a positive, complementary dimension by allowing "the concerns of the treaty bodies to be taken up at the inter-governmental level" (Rodley 2012, 330). Nonetheless, it is undeniable that the UPR has contributed to the proliferation of reporting review processes. It has added further complexity to the ongoing reform debates, particularly on the relationship between treaty bodies and UN charter bodies (Rodley 2009).

Being equipped with limited legal guidance or institutional experience, and facing internal divisions in their early years, treaty bodies have taken a series of steps to strengthen the reporting procedure in terms of quality of reports, timely submission and consideration, and follow-up. The reporting procedure has also become more participatory and accessible through means such as materials and search functions on the OHCHR's website (www.ohchr.org) as well as webcasting (UN Secretary-General 2016). It provides an important forum and symbolic and practical focal point for the identification, deliberation, and potential resolution of human rights challenges. It is also a critical tool for local and other actors advocating changes to improve human rights standards. Yet, the impact of the reporting proce-dure is difficult to assess (Heyns and Viljoen 2002; Kälin 2012). It is limited by systemic challenges and the in-built constraints of monitoring as routine and bureau-cratic exercise. Any further reforms will need to move beyond concerns over the efficiency of the current system and focus on how to bridge the gap between diplomatic "ritual" (Kelly 2015) and the situation on the ground. This entails making follow-up and practical engagement with key actors in the country concerned more effective (O'Flaherty 2011; Evans 2017), including by means of targeted, and field-based follow-up recommendations (de Gaer 2011).

General Comments and General Recommendations

General comments, referred to as general recommendations by CEDAW and CERD, are "detailed and comprehensive commentaries on specific treaty provisions or on the relationship between treaty provisions and specific themes" (UN Doc. HRI/MC/2015/4 (2015), para. 2). They are adopted by treaty bodies "to facilitate the interpretation of the treaties and thereby advance implementation by States Parties of the treaty provisions for the benefit of rights holders" (UN Doc. HRI/MC/2015/4 (2015), para. 4). The adoption of general comments grew out of treaty bodies' power to make "general recommendations based on the consideration of the reports and information received from the States Parties" (Art. 9(2) ICERD). Treaty bodies initially used general comments to specify States Parties' reporting obligations and have thereafter employed them as a means to interpret treaty provisions and elaborate on States Parties obligations. However, the practice of treaty bodies varies considerably; CERD and HRCtee have each adopted 35 general recommendations/general comments, respectively, while CAT and CMW have adopted a mere three general comments each to date. General comments have become increasingly detailed and have addressed general obligations of States Parties, including implementation of treaties; specific provisions, including those containing fundamental principles such as non-discrimination (HRC, General Comment 18 (1989)); "new" rights, such as the right to water (CESCR, General Comment 15 (2003)); as well as crosscutting issues (such as the gender-related dimensions of refugee status, asylum, nationality and statelessness of women (CEDAW, General Recommendation 32 (2014)). Treaty bodies have also begun to issue joint general recommendations/general comments, such as on harmful practices (CEDAW, General Recommendation 31/CRC, General Comment 18 (2014)). The process of drafting general comments has become more participatory. This development has enabled civil society organizations and others to make submissions and contribute to debates (UN Doc. HRI/MC/2015/4 (2015)), which has made the resulting general comments more attentive to conceptual and practical challenges. The process of drafting the HRCtee's General Comment on Article 6 of the ICCPR – Right to life, which commenced in 2015, is an example of this practice.

   The fact that general comments do not have a formal, binding, legal status does not mean that they lack legal significance. General comments set out an interpretation of the rights and obligations of States Parties under the respective treaty, in which the respective committee draws on its jurisprudence and other relevant sources to elaborate on its understanding of treaty provisions and relevant issues. The authoritative status of treaty bodies as interpreter of their respective treaty has at times been questioned by States Parties (Mechlem 2009; Keller and Grover 2012). There is also an apparent risk that treaty bodies use such instruments in a questionable fashion to enhance their authority and legitimize certain interpretations of the treaty concerned. Yet, it is equally clear that general comments can serve as important reference documents and authoritative Committee statements and have proved influential in the development of the jurisprudence of national and international bodies (Van Alebeek and Nollkaemper 2012; Keller and Grover 2012).

The impact of general comments varies considerably, and their legitimacy depends on a series of factors. In the context of the HRCtee, these factors have been described as determinacy, symbolic validation, coherence, adherence, and democratic decision-making (Keller and Grover 2012). A detailed study of the role of the HRCtee's general comments found that they provide legal analysis and valuable policy and practice direction (Keller and Grover 2012). General comments assume a particular importance where an individual complaints procedure is not available, which allows a treaty body to interpret treaty obligations in its jurisprudence. The CRC and CESCR in particular have made ample use of general comments to set out their interpretation of the nature and scope of rights and obligations of States Parties under the Convention on the Rights of the Child and International Covenant on Economic, Social, and Cultural Rights (ICESCR), respectively (20 and 22 general comments, respectively). The CESCR's general comments have sought to clarify the nature of rights and obligations in respect of a contested and complex field; set the ground for developing an individual complaints procedure, namely, the Optional Protocol to ICESCR (OPICESCR); and influenced national jurisprudence (Abashidze 2011). The Committee has thereby contributed significantly to the development and acceptance of economic, social, and cultural rights (critical Mechlem 2009). Judging by experiences to date, general comments can be expected to become an even more important instrument for treaty bodies to develop the interpretation of international human rights law and to address important and crosscutting themes, including by means of closer cooperation between treaty bodies.

Complaints Procedures

Eight of the ten treaty bodies except ICRM, where the procedure is not yet in force, and SPT have the competence to consider individual complaints. This competence is provided for either under the treaties establishing the treaty body or under an Optional Protocol to that treaty (ICCPR, ICESCR, Optional Protocol to the Convention on the Rights of the Child on a Communications Procedure (OPCRCIC)). In contrast to the mandatory reporting procedure, individual complaints can only be brought against a State Party that has accepted the competence of the Committee in question. This reflects the traditional reluctance of States to subject themselves to the jurisdiction of any supranational body. Seven treaty bodies (except CEDAW, CPRD and SPT) may consider interstate complaints or disputes. This procedure has remained dormant, even though a number of States Parties have accepted the competence of treaty bodies to consider interstate complaints. This lack of recourse can be attributed to States' preference to resort to political and diplomatic means to address human rights concerns. However, the number of interstate cases concerning alleged breaches of human rights obligations brought before the European Court of Human Rights and the International Court of Justice (ICJ) suggests that States may be willing to resort to litigation where the outcome is binding and is viewed as carrying significant weight.

The individual complaints procedure serves multiple purposes. In contrast to related fields such as international humanitarian law and international refugee law, the procedure provides a remedy at the international level for persons alleging a violation of their rights. It enables treaty bodies to monitor compliance in respect of individual cases and to interpret the rights and obligations under the treaty concerned. The jurisprudence of treaty bodies is also increasingly reflected in general comments and thereby informs guidance given to States Parties on the implementation of treaties in respect of specific rights or issues.

Individuals can bring complaints against States Parties that have accepted the competence of the Committee concerned. In practice, many States Parties have done so, often in addition to recognizing the competence of regional human rights treaty bodies to consider individual complaints. However, acceptance is far from universal, as several major States, such as the United States of America, India, and China, and States in certain regions, such as the Middle East, have not accepted any individual complaints procedures (Bantekas and Oette 2016).

The individual complaints procedure is quasi-judicial (HRCtee, General Comment 33(2009), para. 11). In contrast to judicial bodies, treaty bodies are typically not entirely composed of lawyers, do not conduct fact-finding or hearings (Kletzel et al. 2011), and rely primarily on written materials (Ulfstein 2012). Their views or opinions are not formally binding. Opinions are divided as to whether these decisions are purely recommendatory, or effectively binding, as suggested in the HRCtee's general comment on the subject (Human Rights Committee, General Comment 33 (2009), para. 13). Most courts, including the ICJ and several national courts, agree that the interpretation adopted by treaty bodies such as the HRCtee should be accorded "great weight" (International Court of Justice 2010, para. 66) and that their decisions be considered relevant (Van Alebeek and Nollkaemper 2012). The decisions therefore have legal significance and should be given serious consideration by States Parties and judicial bodies (Ulfstein 2012; Van Alebeek and Nollkaemper 2012).

Several treaty bodies, particularly the HRCtee, have a well-developed jurisprudence, which has addressed important issues and influenced the practice of other bodies at the international, regional, and national level (Van Alebeek and Nollkaemper 2012). Yet, there are a number of apparent challenges and shortcomings. Several individual complaints procedures only came into force recently. This has rendered the system uneven, particularly reflecting for a long time the effectively weak status of economic, social, and cultural rights, thereby calling into question the supposed indivisibility of rights. Conversely, the growth in complaints procedures and increase in complaints, while indicating an enhanced use of the system, has resulted in a backlog of cases (Report of the Secretary-General 2016). Proceedings are time-consuming and are not particularly accessible and victim friendly, and treaty bodies do not undertake fact-finding (Kletzel et al. 2011). Treaty bodies decisions have been criticized for their "methodological weaknesses and lack of coherence and analytical rigor" (Mechlem 2009, 905). They often provide limited legal reasoning that would set out underlying principles and contribute to the development of a systematic approach. Remedies set out in decisions are frequently generic. Compliance with the decisions of treaty bodies is inconsistent and generally weak (Ulfstein 2012; Morijn 2011). This can be attributed to the non-binding nature of decisions, their non-specificity, the lack of national legal frameworks that would facilitate implementation, and ineffective follow-up procedures (Ulfstein 2012; Van Alebeek and Nollkaemper 2012). Follow-up procedures often consist of sending, at times seemingly endless, reminders to States Parties in the, frequently futile, hope that the latter will take action. Nonetheless, in some countries, national actors have been able to use the jurisprudence of treaty bodies to vindicate individuals' claims, highlight systemic shortcomings, and strengthen advocacy campaigns, such as Nepal before the HRCtee (Bantekas and Oette 2016).

Unsurprisingly, the challenges experienced in respect of individual complaints procedures have brought them firmly within the scope of reform discussions. In the short- and mid-term, a major focus will be on how the treaty bodies concerned, particularly CRPD, CED, CESCR, and CRC, will be developing their recently established individual complaints procedure. Caseload and limited effectiveness are serious, systemic challenges facing all committees. Yet, treaty bodies have considerable scope to advance international human rights law, particularly in areas that have so far been largely neglected in national, regional, and international jurisprudence, and to strengthen follow-up procedures to enhance the prospect of implementation (de Gaer 2011; Kletzel et al. 2011).

Inquiry Procedure

Several treaty bodies are vested with a mandate to conduct confidential inquiries in respect of systematic, grave, or serious violations. The inquiry procedure under Article 20 of the UNCAT provides the "model for later human rights treaties" (Nowak and McArthur 2008, 660). Subsequently, inquiry procedures were included in Article 8 of the Optional Protocol to the Convention on the Elimination of Discrimination against Women (OPCEDAW); Article 6 of the Optional Protocol to the Convention on the Rights of Persons with Disabilities (OPCRPD); Article 33 of the CPED; Article 11 of the OPICESCR; and Article 13 of the OPCRCIC. States Parties are subject to the inquiry procedure unless they opt out at the time of signature, ratification, or accession.

An inquiry can be initiated by the Committee concerned either ex officio or upon complaint following receipt of "reliable information" meeting the required threshold of violations. As information is typically provided by NGOs, the procedure has been likened to an actio popularis (Nowak and McArthur 2008, 661). The threshold for inquiries varies slightly. UNCAT requires that torture is systematically practiced;

under OPCEDAW, OPCRPD, OPCRCIC, and OPICESCR, violations must be grave or systematic and under CPED seriously violating the provision of this Convention. Inquiry procedures have been usefully described as consisting of four phases (Nowak and McArthur 2008). The evaluation of source information forms the basis for the decision whether to undertake an inquiry. If the threshold is considered to be met, the treaty body in question conducts a confidential inquiry, which may include a visit to the State Party concerned. Thereafter, the body adopts and transmits the finding of the inquiry, including whether it has found violations, and a set of recommendations. The findings may be published by way of a summary account or, with the consent of the State Party, as a full report. To date, CAT has carried out ten inquiries (Turkey, Egypt (twice), Peru, Sri Lanka, Mexico, the Federal Republic of Yugoslavia, Brazil, Nepal, and Lebanon), CEDAW four inquiries (Mexico, Canada, the Philippines and the United Kingdom), and CRPD one inquiry (the United Kingdom).

The inquiry procedure is an important mechanism that enables the relevant committees to respond to allegations of systematic, grave, or serious violations. It is complementary to both the reporting and individual complaints procedure because its fact-finding dimension provides treaty bodies with greater scope to engage with the State Party concerned in detail on the alleged violations (Rodley 2009). Inquiries carried out to date have cast the spotlight on a number of countries and issues, thereby reinforcing concerns that had been either raised already by the committee concerned or in other fora. Examples are CEDAW's inquiry concerning high levels of violence experienced by aboriginal women and girls in Canada (UN Doc. CEDAW/C/OP.8/CAN/1 (2015)); its inquiry concerning "the provision of sexual and reproductive health rights, services and commodities in Manila," Philippines (UN Doc. CEDAW/C/OP.8/PHL/1 (2015)); and the CRPD inquiry concerning the "cumulative impact of legislation, policies and measures adopted by the State Party [United Kingdom] on social security schemes and on work and employment . . . directed to or affecting the enjoyment by persons with disabilities of [several] of their rights. . ." (UN Doc. CRPD/C/15/R.2/Rev.1 (2016), para.1). Inquiries therefore constitute a valuable, authoritative source on their subject matter, and their findings and recommendations can serve as advocacy tools for civil society although they have been problematic where they resulted in controversial findings, such as that there was no evidence of a systematic practice of torture in Sri Lanka (UN Doc. A/57/44 (SUPP) (2002), para. 181). However, inquiries have been few in numbers and are subject to limitations due to their confidentiality and the possibility that they may only result in the publication of summary accounts. Inquiries follow a traditional format that is limited in its effectiveness, particularly if compared with the numerous commissions of inquiry set up by the HRC in recent years, which have produced detailed reports and findings that are typically brought to the attention of a broader public. The treaty procedures, including inquiries, are based on consent, and hence unlikely to undergo radical changes. In practice, therefore, their utility and impact will largely depend on their use by NGOs and others, their thoroughness and quality, and a concerted follow-up on their findings and recommendations. This is both within the treaty setting and beyond, such as through the UPR or other measures at the HRC or other UN bodies.

The OPCAT as an Alternative Model

The SPT, operational since 2007, represents an innovative treaty body approach. It has two major operational functions, namely, undertaking visits to places of detention within the jurisdiction of States Parties and providing assistance and guidance on the establishment and the work of National Preventive Mechanisms under Article 11 OPCAT. According to its website, it "is a new kind of treaty body" that "has a preventive mandate focused on an innovative, sustained and proactive approach to the prevention of torture and ill treatment" (www.ohchr.org/EN/HRBodies/OPCAT/Pages/Brief.aspx). Its approach differs from the rather formalistic reporting procedure. It is based on an ongoing dialogue that is "flexible and responsive" (as stated by the Chairperson of the SPT at the 70th session of the General Assembly on 20 October 2015) and allows the SPT to be proactive in identifying and seeking to address structural and specific challenges, instead of relying on a drawn-out, second-level monitoring process. In his statement at the 72nd session of the General Assembly on 18 October 2016, the SPT's Chairperson Sir Malcolm Evans referred to the need for fluid, discursive, and engaged discussion with those directly working in the relevant field, which differs markedly from the constructive dialogue of other treaty bodies with delegates representing the State Party in diplomatic fora. The OPCAT model has also benefited from the complementarity and close cooperation of CAT, SPT, and the Special Rapporteur on Torture. This suggests scope for enhanced effectiveness through a division of labor between treaty bodies relying on more traditional monitoring procedures and more operational, parallel bodies, particularly with a preventive mandate, which have greater scope for flexibility and a cooperative, contextual approach. Such a model appears easier to establish in relation to a specific prohibition, such as torture or enforced disappearance, but there are no intrinsic reasons why it could not be utilized for all treaty bodies. However, the SPT has experienced challenges in seeking to discharge its mandate effectively. States Parties have refused access, and its Chairperson has repeatedly raised concerns about the lack of availability of sufficient resources, which are particularly important for a body of this nature that relies on close engagement, including through visits to States Parties.

Achievements

The UN treaty bodies have gradually developed a monitoring system that covers a broad range of treaty rights. Treaty bodies developed haphazardly, being essentially dependent on States' willingness to adopt treaties with an integral monitoring body. Yet, the UN has been able to build a functioning system, albeit one seemingly in constant need of adjustment. Within this framework, treaty bodies have provided an important forum for dialogue, critical scrutiny, and awareness raising. The increasingly participatory nature of processes, particularly the reporting procedure, and the authority of treaty bodies have made their findings, decisions, and recommendations important advocacy tools for civil society and national institutions worldwide. The monitoring tools have enabled treaty bodies to become a repository of a wealth of documentation and information concerning the human rights record of States Parties. Treaty bodies have clarified and elaborated on the meaning and scope of rights and obligations under their respective treaties, drawing on a range of sources. Their practice has led to several positive changes in respect of human rights protection in States Parties. It has also resulted in reparation, both by means of upholding individual complaints in relevant complaints procedures and by setting out forms of reparation that States Parties – where compliant – have provided to victims of human rights violations. The treaty bodies are therefore an integral part of the international human rights system, having contributed and continuing to contribute to its development through interpreting human rights law and monitoring the implementation of States Parties' human rights obligations.

Scholars have celebrated "the growing participatory dimension" of treaty bodies as an example of largely successful "human rights experimentalism" (de Búrca 2017, 288). This applies particularly to the engagement between national and international actors, as "[l]ocal actors are in a position to articulate their specific claims and concerns and to provide contextualized knowledge and feedback to the international actors and institutions which rely on such feedback, and on the other hand they are in a position to adapt or vernacularize international standards within domestic and local contexts" (de Búrca 2017, 280).

Giving latitude to local actors in the process of treaty implementation may in this context be seen as a potential strength, rather than an inherent weakness that leads to inconsistencies and lack of compliance. Civil society organizations in particular play a crucial role in providing information, pursuing individual complaints, following up on concluding observations and decisions, and engaging in raising awareness and cultural translation (Lynch and Schokman 2011); they also help providing like-minded officials with valuable tools, such as recommendations in concluding observations, which might be used to promote domestic reforms (Bantekas and Oette 2016; Levin 2016). Recent studies suggest that treaty ratification, and subsequent practice, particularly in the context of reporting, has resulted in improved human rights standards at the national level (de Gaer 2011; de Búrca 2017). Strong local civil society and institutions and a "certain minimum level of commitment to human rights in the domestic system" are critical factors that enhance the impact of the treaty and treaty monitoring body (Heyns and Viljoen 2002, 35). Conversely, intimidation and reprisals against individuals and groups who seek to cooperate or are cooperating with treaty bodies have become an increasing concern, both in terms of protection and effectiveness of engagement. This development provides a note of caution against painting an overly harmonious picture of participation in practice, as the Guidelines against intimidation or reprisals ("San Jose Guidelines"), adopted by the Chairs of the Treaty Bodies in 2015, demonstrate.

Close observers of treaty bodies have provided fresh perspectives on the nature of committees' work. They argue that what has been viewed as weakness of treaty bodies is part of their essence and potential strength, namely, that they are diplomatic actors (O'Flaherty 2011) and engage in rituals (Kelly 2015). A diplomatic approach with a pragmatic focus can enhance persuasion (O'Flaherty 2011) and might be more effective than "naming and shaming" strategies, particularly where the focus is on achievable outcomes in the context at hand (Levin 2016). While rituals come at the expense of a greater "voice" for victims, they can help in creating an enabling environment to promote human rights compliance (Kelly 2015).

Challenges and Future Potential

These achievements, important as they are, cannot obscure the considerable challenges facing treaty bodies. The reform or strengthening (Pillay 2012) of the system is the most apparent systemic challenge. It has been on the UN's agenda since the late 1980s (www.ohchr.org/EN/HRBodies/HRTD/Pages/TBStrengthening.aspx). Calls for changes have centered on several interrelated, recurring themes. The lack of efficiency, particularly delays, backlogs, and bureaucracy; transparency and accessibility; impact, particularly in terms of enhancing the protection of human rights; coherence of the system; and legitimacy have been particularly prominent (Morjin 2011; Keller and Ulfstein 2012). The challenge of a system increasingly seen as not fit for purpose and unsustainable prompted the UN and other actors to engage in a concerted process of how to strengthen the system of treaty bodies. In 2006, the OHCHR proposed that a unified standing treaty body be established (UN Doc. HRI/MC/2006/2 2006). Such a body would, it argued, provide "a framework for a comprehensive, cross-cutting and holistic approach to implementation," which would make the process more visible and "would be more likely to attract heightened attention from political bodies such as . . . [the] Human Rights Council or the Security Council" (UN Doc. HRI/MC/2006/2 2006, para. 36). This proposal triggered intense debates, and considerable opposition, based on concerns that such a body would weaken the focus and expertise on the protection of specific rights (Morjin 2011). These reactions prompted a change in approach that was markedly less ambitious. In 2009, the High Commissioner for Human Rights invited key stakeholders to work toward strengthening treaty bodies, particularly in terms of measures to harmonize their working methods. In her subsequent report, the High Commissioner made a number of recommendations, which focused on the availability of resources, increasing accessibility and visibility, streamlining of reporting and working methods, and improving coordination between the treaty bodies (Pillay 2012). This report was followed by UN General Assembly resolution 68/268 in 2014, which provides the framework for a periodic review of measures to be put in place, and their effectiveness (with an overall review to take place no later than 2020). The measures contemplated in the Pillay report and the 2014 General Assembly resolution have already resulted in improvements (Report of the Secretary-General 2016). Closer alignment of working methods, taking the form of an institutional bottom-up approach, holds some promise of making the system more effective (Evans 2017). The piecemeal nature of measures raises the question, though, whether the challenges of fragmented mandates, insufficient powers and resources, and cumbersome modus operandi led by independent experts working effectively pro bono on a part-time basis condemn the treaty bodies to perpetuate what is by many viewed as a flawed system. Establishing a unified standing treaty body, or a World Court of Human Rights, the idea of which has been repeatedly mooted would dramatically enhance visibility and probably impact. Such a step would, however, carry the risk that the more contextual, rights-specific engagement before the specialized treaty bodies is lost. In any case, there is seemingly limited political appetite for more far-reaching changes, with the very idea of human rights and the international human rights system being challenged, including by States that have been erstwhile supporters.

An overly narrow focus in the debate surrounding the strengthening of treaty bodies risks obscuring some broader questions concerning the nature of human rights engagement. This applies in particular to the often antagonistic nature of the monitoring processes, notwithstanding the supposedly constructive dialogue, and to strategies of naming and shaming whose effectiveness is or may be limited. The SPT may provide a model of a more practical, outcome-oriented engagement that avoids some of the apparent pitfalls of a ritualistic engagement. These considerations are important, as the treaty bodies, in common with other supranational human rights treaty bodies and courts, face the persistent challenge of a lack of implementation. The nature of States Parties' responses to the controversial interpretation of treaties and pronouncements by national courts suggest that the lack of clarity concerning the legal nature of outputs and decisions, and their non-binding nature, has given treaty bodies a lesser status compared to judicial bodies, such as regional human rights courts and the ICJ (Van Alebeek and Nollkaemper 2012). While this legal ambiguity remains a challenge, it is less certain that changes to make treaty bodies' decisions binding would significantly enhance implementation by States Parties, with the value of treaty monitoring lying between "the strictly legal and purely political" (Morijn 2011, 312; O'Flaherty 2011). What is clear, though, is that legal recognition and/or strong institutional mechanisms at the national level are pivotal in enhancing the prospect of implementation (International Law Association 2004). In the absence of a strong legal mandate and national mechanisms of this kind, treaty bodies will have to rely on their legitimacy, persuasion, and often the intervention of other actors, be it States, regional or international organizations, or civil society, including transnational networks, to add weight to their interpretations, findings, and recommendations.

The question of appropriate models of monitoring and engagement is largely of an institutional nature. A broader assessment of the future of treaty bodies also needs to inquire into their capacity to respond to demands from wider constituencies, particularly those who have suffered, or are at risk of suffering, human rights violations, as well as those critically engaging with the work of the committees. This includes addressing inherent structural shortcomings in a process that is largely based not on direct inspection but monitoring by means of examination of second-hand information (Kelly 2009). Questions of awareness and visibility of procedures, accessibility (Lynch and Schokman 2011), and greater proximity of treaty bodies to developments on the ground (de Gaer 2011) are critical in this regard. Treaty bodies must also be mindful of any biases in their work. CAT, for example, has been criticized for its liberal bias, showing deference to "developed" countries (Kelly 2009), which echoes broader concerns over a human rights system in which saviors

(Western liberals) condemn savages (non-Western governments and actors) to save victims (in non-Western countries that lack agency) (Mutua 2001). Treaty bodies' legitimacy also demands, both in terms of the procedure and substance of their work, that they are attentive to issues at the forefront of human rights concerns, such as race, inequality, gender (Johnstone 2006; Edwards 2011), cross-cultural dimensions (Addo 2010), and marginalization, including of noncitizens. This includes a close focus on the interrelated nature of rights, their collective dimension, and a contextual approach that addresses structural factors causing, or contributing to, adverse impacts on the human rights of those affected. While it is a trite observation that treaty bodies operate within the confines of their governing treaties and their relationship with States Parties and other actors in the system, there is considerable scope to develop a more theoretically grounded, analytical, and contextual practice of interpretation and engagement. This would hold considerable potential to make the work of the treaty bodies more authoritative and to address the criticism that human rights actors largely perpetuate a state-centric, (neo)liberal status quo that fails both to address key issues, such as economic factors, and to improve the situation of individuals at the receiving end of myriad injustices (Mutua 2001, 2016; Kennedy 2002). It is important that a participatory model takes shape. Equally, closer cooperation among various UN bodies, a stronger focus on national actors, and the factors and modalities of implementation will be crucial for the treaty bodies to achieve their potential, provided, of course, they are vested with the necessary resources and support within the system. In this regard, it would be wise to heed the call that when considering the future of human rights protection, we "ought not to be thinking so much of the jurisprudence of international mechanisms, or of their working practices and procedures, but of how the multilayered systems of dialogue and delivery of human rights compliance work across national, regional, and international divides, embracing as it does a multitude of potential players" (Evans 2017, 541–542).

Conclusion

As the guardians of the core human rights instruments, treaty bodies occupy an important space in the UN human rights architecture. They have grown in numbers and have steadily developed their practice and thereby contributed to the development of international human rights law and the protection of human rights. Yet, treaty bodies do not have the undisputed authority, or legitimacy, that this trajectory suggests. They constantly have to navigate multiple and often conflicting expectations and demands from various key actors. A number of States Parties have either challenged treaty bodies' authority or undermined the committees' work through non-reporting or other non-compliance. The UN administration, also influenced by demands of States, is under-resourced but has also at times frustrated members of treaty bodies with what is viewed as excessive bureaucracy. Civil society organizations may welcome the more participatory work of treaty bodies and their outputs but despair at the often slow pace and apparent limits of implementation and hence lack of effectiveness. The victims, or persons at risk of human rights violations, are for their parts often at risk of intimidation and reprisals and/or remote if not altogether invisible in the diplomatic rituals taking place far away from the ground. These conflicting demands, and realities, provide the context that explains the tensions and dynamics experienced by treaty bodies. Even though political developments world-wide are at present not particularly favorable to the very idea of international cooperation to promote and protect human rights, the treaty bodies' place appears too firmly established to be at risk of drastic changes. It can be assumed that treaty bodies will remain the subject of ongoing debates on how best to strengthen the system. A self-reflective and proactive practice on the part of treaty bodies and other institutions within the UN system is pivotal for their future and future impact. Enhancing the effectiveness of treaty bodies' work and attention to structural challenges and contextual factors, including the role of various actors in the protection of human rights, will be critical to fulfill the promise contained in Article 55 (c) of the Charter of the United Nations, namely, to promote "universal respect for, and observance of, human rights and fundamental freedoms for all without distinction as to race, sex, language, or religion." Treaty bodies are at the heart of this endeavor, which is as critical as ever in a twenty-first-century context characterized by inequality, conflict, instability, and attendant human rights violations.

References

Abashidze A (2011) The complementary role of general comments in enhancing the implementation of treaty bodies' recommendations and views (the example of CESCR). In: Bassiouni CM, Schabas W (eds) New challenges for the human rights treaty machinery. Intersentia, Cambridge, pp 137–148

Addo MK (2010) Practice of United Nations human rights treaty bodies in the reconciliation of cultural diversity with universal respect for human rights. Hum Rights Q 32:601–664

Aidoo AA et al (2009) The Dublin statement on the process of strengthening of the United Nations human rights treaty body system, at. www2.ohchr.org/English/bodies/HRTD/docs/DublinStatement.pdf. Accessed 30 Aug 2017

Alston P, Crawford J (eds) (2000) The future of UN human rights treaty monitoring. Cambridge University Press, Cambridge

Bantekas I, Oette L (2016) International human rights law and practice, 2nd edn. Cambridge University Press, Cambridge

Bayefsky AF (2001) The UN human rights system: universality at the crossroads. Kluwer Law International, The Hague

Creamer C, Simmons B (2015) Ratification, reporting, and rights: quality of participation in the convention against torture. Hum Rights Q 37:579–608

de Búrca, G (2017) Human rights experimentalism, AJIL 111:277-316

de Gaer F (2011) Implementing treaty body recommendations: establishing better follow-up procedures. In: Bassiouni CM, Schabas W (eds) New challenges for the human rights treaty machinery. Intersentia, Cambridge, pp 107–121

Della Fina V, Cera R, Palmisano G (eds) (2017) The United Nations convention on the rights of persons with disabilities: a commentary. Springer, Cham

Edwards A (2011) Universal suffrage and the international human rights treaty bodies: where are the women? In: Bassiouni CM, Schabas W (eds) New challenges for the human rights treaty machinery. Intersentia, Cambridge, pp 151–170

Evans MD (2017) Co-existence and confidentiality: the experience of the optional protocol to the convention against torture, harmony and human rights: the music of the spheres. In: Buckley CM, Donald A, Leach P (eds) Towards convergence in international human rights law: approaches of regional and international systems. Brill Nijhoff, Leiden, pp 516–542

Heyns C, Viljoen F (2002) The impact of the United Nations human rights treaties on the domestic level. Kluwer Law International, The Hague

International Court of Justice (2010) Case concerning Ahmadou Sadio Diallo, Republic of Guinea v. Democratic Republic of the Congo, Merits, Judgment, ICJ Reports 2010, p 639

International Law Association (2004) Final report on the impact of findings of the United Nations human rights treaty bodies. In International Law Association, Report of the Seventy-First Conference, pp 621–702

Johnstone RL (2006) Feminist influences on the United Nations human rights treaty bodies. Hum Rights Q 28:148–185

Kälin W (2012) Examination of state reports. In: Keller H, Ulfstein G (eds) UN human rights treaty bodies: law and legitimacy. Cambridge University Press, Cambridge, pp 16–72

Keller H, Grover L (2012) General comments of the human rights committee and their legitimacy. In: Keller H, Ulfstein G (eds) UN human rights treaty bodies: law and legitimacy. Cambridge University Press, Cambridge, pp 116–198

Keller H, Ulfstein G (2012) UN human rights treaty bodies: law and legitimacy. Cambridge University Press, Cambridge

Kelly T (2009) The UN Committee against torture: human rights monitoring and the legal recognition of cruelty. Hum Rights Q 31:777–800

Kelly T (2015) Two cheers for ritual: the UN committee against torture. Paper delivered at 'The Rituals of Human Rights' Workshop, Centre for International Governance and Justice, RegNet, Australian University, Canberra, Australia, 25–27 June 2014, available online at www.regnet. anu.edu.au/research/publications/6121/rituals-human-rights-workshop-working-paper-no-7-two-cheers-ritual. Accessed 29 Nov 2017

Kennedy D (2002) The international human rights movement: part of the problem. Harv Hum Rights J 15:101–126

Kletzel G, Barretto Maia C, Zwaig M (2011) Strengthening of the UN treaty bodies' complaints procedures: elements for a reform agenda from an NGO perspective. In: Bassiouni CM, Schabas W (eds) New challenges for the human rights treaty machinery. Intersentia, Cambridge, pp 193–236

Lauterpacht H (1945) An international bill of the rights of man. Oxford University Press, Oxford

LeBlanc LJ et al (2010) Compliance with the reporting requirements of human rights conventions. Int J Hum Rights 14:789–807

Levin A (2016) The reporting cycle to the United Nations human rights treaty bodies: creating a dialogue between the state and civil society- the Israeli case study. George Washington Int Law Rev 48:315–376

Lynch P, Schokman B (2011) Taking human rights from the grassroots to Geneva . . . and back: strengthening the relationship between UN treaty bodies and NGOs. In: Bassiouni CM, Schabas W (eds) New challenges for the human rights treaty machinery. Intersentia, Cambridge, pp 173–192

Mechlem K (2009) Treaty bodies and the interpretation of human rights. Vanderbilt J Transl Law 42:905–947

Morijn J (2011) Reforming United Nations human rights treaty monitoring system. Neth Int Law Rev LVIII:295–333

Mutua M (2001) Savages, victims, and saviors: the metaphor of human rights. Harv Int Law J 42:201–245

Mutua M (2016) Human rights standards: hegemony, law and politics. State University of New York Press, New York

Nowak M, McArthur E (2008) The United Nations convention against torture: a commentary. Oxford University Press, Oxford

O'Flaherty M (2006) The concluding observations of United Nations human rights treaty bodies. Hum Rights Law Rev 6:27–52

O'Flaherty M (2011) The United Nations human rights treaty bodies as diplomatic actors. In: O'Flaherty M et al (eds) Human rights diplomacy: contemporary perspectives. Martinus Nijhoff Publishers, Leiden, pp 155–171

O'Flaherty M, O'Brien C (2007) Reform of UN human rights treaty monitoring bodies: a critique of the concept paper on the high Commissioner's proposal for a unified standing treaty body. Hum Rights Law Rev 7:147–172

O'Flaherty M, Tsai P-L (2011) Periodic reporting: the backbone of the UN treaty body review procedures. In: Bassiouni CM, Schabas W (eds) New challenges for the human rights treaty machinery. Intersentia, Cambridge, pp 37–56

Oberleitner G (2007) Global human rights institutions: between remedy and ritual. Polity, Cambridge

Office of the High Commissioner for Human Rights (2006) Concept Paper on the High Commissioner's Proposal for a Unified Standing Treaty Body. UN Doc. HRI/MC/2006/2

Pillay N (2012) Strengthening the United Nations Human Rights Treaty Bodies: A report by the United Nations High Commissioner for Human Rights, at: www2.ohchr.org/English/bodies/HRTD/docs/HCreportTBStrengthening.pdf. Accessed 29 Aug 2017

Rajagopal B (2003) International law from below: development, social movements, and third world resistance. Cambridge University Press, Cambridge

Rodley N (2009) The United Nations human rights council, its special procedure, and its relationship with the treaty bodies: complementarity or competition? In: Boyle K (ed) New institutions for human rights protection. Oxford University Press, Oxford, pp 49–73

Rodley N (2012) UN treaty bodies and the human rights council. In: Keller H, Ulfstein G (eds) UN human rights treaty bodies: law and legitimacy. Cambridge University Press, Cambridge, pp 320–355

Schlütter B (2012) Aspects of human rights interpretation by the UN treaty bodies. In: Keller H, Ulfstein G (eds) UN human rights treaty bodies: law and legitimacy. Cambridge University Press, Cambridge, pp 261–319

Thornberry P (2016) The international convention on the elimination of all forms of racial discrimination: a commentary. Oxford University Press, Oxford

Ulfstein G (2012) Individual complaints. In: Keller H, Ulfstein G (eds) UN human rights treaty bodies: law and legitimacy. Cambridge University Press, Cambridge, pp 73–115

United Nations Human Rights Office of the High Commissioner (2015) Handbook for human rights treaty body members. United Nations, New York

United Nations Secretary-General (2016) Status of the human rights treaty body system. UN Doc. A/71/118

Van Alebeek R, Nollkaemper A (2012) The legal status of decisions by human rights treaty bodies in national law. In: Keller H, Ulfstein G (eds) UN human rights treaty bodies: law and legitimacy. Cambridge University Press, Cambridge, pp 356–413

The UN Human Rights Committee

Anja Seibert-Fohr

Contents

Introduction 118
Historical Background 119
Membership and Composition 120
Functions 123
    State Reporting 123
    General Comments 127
    Individual Communications and State Communications 130
Challenges and Promises 133
The Committee's Legacy: A Critical Assessment 135
References 137

Abstract

The UN Human Rights Committee, which is recognized for its legal expertise in human rights law, belongs to the most prominent institutions for the oversight of international human rights. The Committee was the first universal body with a mandate to examine individual communications. Among the international treaty bodies it continues to receive the highest number of individual petitions. Through the course of its four decades of existence, the Committee has developed a considerable body of jurisprudence affecting the interpretation of human rights by domestic and international institutions, including the International Court of Justice. The present chapter introduces readers to the work of this quasi-judicial expert body from the perspective of a former Committee member. It locates the Committee's institutional place in the overall structure of the human rights system

The author was a member of the Human Rights Committee from 2013 to 2018. The views expressed in this chapter are solely those of the author and do not claim to represent the position of the Committee.

A. Seibert-Fohr (✉)
University of Heidelberg, Heidelberg, Germany

© Springer Nature Singapore Pte Ltd. 2018
G. Oberleitner (ed.), *International Human Rights Institutions, Tribunals, and Courts*,
International Human Rights, https://doi.org/10.1007/978-981-10-5206-4_6

and describes current challenges and developments. The author offers an in-depth assessment of the Committee's legacy and makes proposals on how the Committee can refine its procedures and methodology.

Keywords

Human rights · Treaty bodies · Compliance · Individual complaints · Monitoring · General comments

Introduction

The Human Rights Committee is the body currently tasked by 170 States parties to monitor their compliance and domestic implementation of the International Covenant on Civil and Political Rights (Articles 40 et seq. ICCPR; International Covenant on Civil and Political Rights 1966; McGoldrick 1994; Nowak 2005). This treaty provides a wide array of rights, ranging from the right to life over the prohibition of discrimination to the protection of persons belonging to minorities. With its mandate to monitor these treaty rights, the Committee is among the most prominent institutions for the oversight of universal human rights. The International Court of Justice (ICJ) recognized the Committee in the *Diallo* case as an "independent body that was established *specifically* to supervise the application of that treaty [the ICCPR]" and that accordingly the Court "should ascribe great weight to the interpretation adopted by this independent body" (International Court of Justice 2010, *Case Concerning Ahmadou Sadio Diallo* para 66).

The Committee is treaty-based and thus not a formal organ of the United Nations (UN). It is, however, procedurally and financially closely linked to the UN system since the Secretary-General provides the necessary staff and facilities for the functioning of the Committee, acts as the depository of the Covenant, and convenes the meetings of the States parties. As a body composed of renowned, typically legally experienced, and independent experts, it differs institutionally and functionally from UN bodies with a political composition, such as the Human Rights Council.

The Committee's primary task is to interpret the Covenant and to monitor its implementation. For States parties, which also have ratified or acceded to the Second Optional Protocol, the Committee's monitoring function includes the oversight over the abolition of the death penalty. On the basis of the Covenant and its First Optional Protocol (Optional Protocol to the ICCPR 1966), the Committee has developed three main pillars of its work: the review of state reports under Article 40 ICCPR, the review of individual communications under the Optional Protocol, and the compilation of its interpretation of the Covenant in General Comments. The state communication procedure, which is also foreseen in Article 41 of the Covenant, has not been resorted to since the ICCPR entered into force in 1976.

Whereas the Committee's pronouncements are not considered legally binding, its legal basis (ICCPR), the adversarial decision-making process, and its procedural safeguards arguably render the individual communication procedure quasi-judicial.

The Committee's attempt in draft General Comment 33 to attribute Views a legally binding effect met with strong opposition from States parties and eventually is excluded from the text finally adopted. The Committee instead described its role as follows: "While the function of the Human Rights Committee in considering individual communications is not, as such, that of a judicial body, the views issued by the Committee under the Optional Protocol exhibit some important characteristics of a judicial decision. They are arrived at in a judicial spirit, including the impartiality and independence of Committee members, the considered interpretation of the language of the Covenant, and the determinative character of the decisions" (General Comment No. 33, para 11). Thus the Committee's Views, even though not per se legally binding, at least require States parties to substantively engage with its legal findings. Mere denial without argumentative rebuttal would be irreconcilable with the object and purpose of the Covenant's monitoring system.

Whereas the Views, which the Committee adopts upon the review of an individual complaint, result in findings of law, the Concluding Observations under the reporting procedure reflect the Committee's examination of the Covenant's domestic implementation in the respective States parties more generally. The conclusions are recommendatory in nature (Klein 2011, p. 547) and suggest measures of implementation without rendering them legally binding (Neuman 2018, p. 4). This is in accordance with Article 2, paragraph 3 of the Covenant, which provides that each State party undertakes "to take the necessary steps, in accordance with its constitutional processes and with the provisions of the present Covenant, to adopt such laws or other measures as may be necessary to give effect to the rights recognized in the present Covenant. "This provision leaves States parties room to identify context-specific means of implementation without dictating specific measures.

General Comments, the third pillar of the Committee's activities, consider thematic issues more broadly without focusing on particular States parties. In the past, they have served as sources for the interpretation of the Covenant in international and domestic settings (ILA Report 2004, p. 624 et seq.). The UN General Assembly, for example, has referred to General Comments in several resolutions (see, e.g., UN Doc A/RES/60/149) so has the International Tribunal for the Former Yugoslavia (IT-95-17/1-T, paras 153 et seq.) and the ILC (UN Doc A/52/10, para 130 et seq.).

Historical Background

The establishment of the Human Rights Committee was a significant achievement when the General Assembly adopted the International Covenant on Civil and Political Rights on 16 December 1966. During the drafting of the Covenant, the proposal of a monitoring body met with strong opposition by communist countries in the Human Rights Commission and in the Third Committee of the General Assembly. They considered the implementation of human rights to fall under the exclusive competence of the States parties (UN Doc E/CN.4/353, p. 2; UN Doc. A/1576, Annexes). The Soviet Union and its allies insisted on state sovereignty and opposed any kind of enforcement regime including the review of reports, which they feared would interfere with the prohibition of intervening in matters essentially within the domestic jurisdiction of any State pursuant to Article 2 (7) UNC (UN Doc A/5655, p. 30; UN Doc E/CN.4/SR.429). This opposition to any form of review, however, was rejected by the General Assembly (UN Doc A/1559, para 60).

The drafters reached a compromise in order to allow some form of international monitoring while ensuring the Covenant's broad ratification (UN Doc A/6546, para 53). The Covenant therefore provides for a reporting procedure as the only compulsory review mechanism, complemented by an optional state communication procedure. Furthermore, the (First) Optional Protocol establishes an individual communication procedure for States parties ratifying or acceding thereto.

Institutionally the Human Rights Commission opted for the establishment of the Human Rights Committee as the sole body entrusted with these tasks. Earlier proposals had ranged from the establishment of a judicial body over a permanent independent organ to ad hoc commissions of inquiry. After its adoption it took another decade for the Covenant to enter into force on 23 March 1976. The Optional Protocol (OP I) entered into force on the same date, whereas the state communication procedure under Article 41 (2) of the Covenant became operative as of 28 March 1979.

The discussion about the role of the Committee continued even after the relevant procedures became operative. When the Human Rights Committee had met for its first session in March 1977, its work was hampered by the Cold War. Since members from communist countries opposed the adoption of state-specific recommendations in the reporting procedure (Ando 2007, p. 18, 21 et seq., 26), the Committee in 1981 started only adopting General Comments on procedural and thematic issues, including on the interpretation of substantive rights without, however, addressing the particular human rights situations of individual countries. Members could only share their individual evaluation and recommendations with the delegations at the end of each dialogue. It was only after the fall of the Berlin Wall that the Committee started formally adopting Concluding Observations following the consideration of state reports in 1992 (UN Doc A/48/49, Volume I). Since then the Committee has continuously refined its procedure in its Rules of Procedure in order to improve its effectiveness.

Membership and Composition

The 18 members of the Committee, who shall be of "high moral character and recognized competence in the field of human rights" (Article 28(2) ICCPR), are elected for a renewable 4-year term by the States parties to the Covenant and serve in their personal capacity. Legal experience is pertinent in particular for the individual complaint procedure. The Committee's performance and legitimacy depend on the election of renowned experts who represent different legal traditions and merit trust and professional authority. It is in the States parties' interest to exercise due diligence in the nomination and election process in order to sustain the highest level of independent legal expertise.

The Committee's membership has traditionally been composed of law professors, judges, diplomats, civil servants, and other legal professionals including such from nongovernmental organizations. Though concerns have been raised that the renewable term could have a detrimental effect on members' independence, this does not appear to play a role in practice. In any case, this issue could only be addressed by introducing a longer single term, which would allow for the necessary continuity in the Committee's composition.

According to a recent study on the question of political or regional biases, in practice members of the Committee for the most part act in their personal capacity (Shikhelman 2015). This study further found that despite certain geopolitical voting patterns during individual communications, these usually do not affect the Committee's final decision, and its decisions on individual communications can generally be regarded as unbiased. Even though members are independent from their countries of origin, nothing prevents them from pursuing their own political agenda. However, taking into account that the Committee members are elected for their recognized expertise in human rights law, it falls upon each expert member to take decisions on the basis of the Covenant as the relevant point of reference. This is in the interest of sustaining the Committee's expert authority and to distinguish the Committee from political bodies within the United Nations system.

Candidates are nominated by the States parties whose nationals they are. They are elected by the meeting of the States parties in New York. This procedure has been criticized as nontransparent and influenced by diplomatic considerations (Crawford 2000, p. 9; UN Doc A/66/860, p. 74). Therefore, in an effort to improve transparency before the 2016 elections, a number of candidates responded to a detailed questionnaire by the Centre for Civil and Political Rights, an NGO, which provides valuable information on the Committee's work and links it to civil society. The questionnaire addressed issues, such as the qualification of the candidate, current position, and relevant experience in the field of human rights, motivation, and potential conflicts of interest.

The States parties determine the overall composition of the Committee. Gender balance has improved over the past decade so that the Committee is currently composed of seven women. But there are no persons with disabilities on the Committee yet (UN Doc A/Res/68/268, para 13). Though Article 31 of the Covenant requires States parties to consider equitable geographical distribution, there is no regional quota, and some regions have been underrepresented in the membership of the Committee compared to the respective number of Covenant ratifications (Buergenthal 2001, p. 345). A balanced representation of all regions can enhance the Committee's comprehension of the relevant context in which human rights are implemented and thus further the Committee's persuasive legitimacy and claim of universality. For this purpose, the Committee's chair has traditionally rotated among the different regions. The regional rotation helps the Committee to gain the necessary respect from all regions represented by the States parties. The function of the chairperson is primarily to represent the Committee and to coordinate and facilitate the Committee's work as primus/prima inter pares. It is not a political function requiring a policy agenda. This is in line with the Committee's mandate as a universal expert body.

Half of the members are elected biannually. Whereas in the past some members have served over several decades, in more recent elections, about one third of the Committee's members has been replaced every 2 years. In order to provide for more continuity and enhance the efficiency of the Committee's work while allowing for the necessary innovation, a staggered model of newly elected posts over the course of a longer period of time would be feasible. For example, if five new members were elected after 2 and 4 years, respectively, and four new members after 6 and 8 years, members could serve for two terms. This would result in a 25% average rate of new membership on the Committee every 2 years. In the interest of more continuity, the election of only three new members every 2 years would be preferable. However, with the current workload and extensive meeting time of the Committee, it is unlikely that members will be in a position to serve for the corresponding 12 years on the Committee resulting from this rotation model.

In order to ensure the Committee's proper functioning, its members are entitled to the privileges and immunities of experts on mission for the UN as set forth in the 1946 Convention on the Privileges and Immunities of the United Nations (International Court of Justice 1989, Applicability of Article VI, Section 22, of the Convention on the Privileges and Immunities of the United Nations (Advisory Opinion), p. 177). The members' independence is reinforced by the 2011 Addis Ababa Guidelines, a code of ethics, which the Committee has pledged to observe in order to avoid real or perceived conflicts of interest (UN Doc A/67/222). The observance of the guidelines, which is essential for the Committee's legitimacy, falls primarily within the member's individual responsibility and can be safeguarded also by measures adopted by the Committee as a whole. In the interest of independence and impartiality, members shall partake neither in the consideration of reports or individual communications relating to their country of nationality nor in the consideration of communications which relate to a decision in which a member has previously participated.

According to the guidelines, the independence and impartiality of a member is compromised by the political nature of his or her affiliation with the executive branch of the State. Members shall not undertake activities in nongovernmental or State-related organizations, which may appear not to be readily reconcilable with the perception of independence and impartiality. In practice, acting diplomats and members of the executive continue to serve on the Committee. This is a matter that already deserves more attention in the nomination and election process because members of the Committee are not remunerated for their work on the Committee (UN Doc A/Res/56/272) and thus continue to depend on the income from their regular positions when elected. Therefore, resignation from political office is unlikely to happen after the election. For this reason, the human rights treaty bodies' chairs have called on States parties to refrain from nominating or electing persons to the treaty bodies whose independence and impartiality is compromised by the political nature of their affiliation with the executive branch of the State (UN Doc. A/72/17, para 39).

While distance from the States parties' political branch is necessary to preserve impartiality, less attention has been given so far to relations to other stakeholders (for the actual practice, see Keller and Grover 2012, p. 187). In order to preserve the

Committee's legitimacy as an independent expert body, proposals have been made to also regulate in more detail the interaction of individual Committee members with the nongovernmental sector (Davala 2012, p. 131). It is in the Committee's interest to avoid any appearance of bias. Transparency and avoiding ex parte communications by individual members can play an important role in this respect. The Committee's secretariat at the Office of the High Commissioner of Human Rights can serve a valuable purpose by serving as the sole focal point of contact for all information provided to the Committee while taking all necessary measures (including guarantees of confidentiality) to protect human rights defenders against repercussions and reprisals for their communication with the Committee. For this matter the Committee adopted the Guidelines Against Intimidation or Reprisals (the San José Guidelines, UN Doc HRI/MC/2015/6) at its 117th session (UN Doc A/72/40, para 51).

Functions

From the beginning of its existence in 1977, the Committee has been meeting in three sessions per year. Over the past years, due to its increased workload, meeting time has been extended by the General Assembly to 4 instead of 3 weeks per session. While originally holding one session per year at the UN Headquarters in New York, in recent years the Committee, because of financial constraints, has convened exclusively at the seat of the High Commissioner in Geneva where the Committee's secretariat is domiciled. Public sessions are webcasted nowadays in order to enhance access to the Committee's work worldwide.

Decision-making is normally by consensus, otherwise by majority vote (UN Doc CCPR/C/3/Rev.10, Rule 51; Article 39 ICCPR). Consensus does not necessarily require unanimity or active endorsement by all members but absence of formal objection (Klein and Kretzmer 2015, p. 223). This modus operandi has protected the Committee in the past against politization and allowed for gradual interpretative progress (Buergenthal 2001, p. 342-3). The traditional attempt to reach decisions by consensus requires members to take on a spirit of collegiality and compromise. As a collective body, rather than the aggregate of individualists, the Committee tried to accommodate serious reservations by Committee members in the past. With respect to General Comments and Concluding Observations, which both do not foresee individual opinions, aspiring for consensus can render their adoption less controversial (Young 2002, p. 48 et seq.). At the same time, it enhances the persuasive force of the Committee as a universal expert body which is sought to represent different cultures and legal systems (Rodley 2013, p. 626).

State Reporting

Each State party has undertaken to submit a report on the implementation of the Covenant within 1 year of the entry into force of the Covenant and subsequently in accordance with the periodicity decided by the Committee, depending on the deficiencies found to exist between 3 and 6 years (UN Doc HRI/MC/2006/3). While originally the Committee reviewed four reports per session, it has increased the number of reports to seven in recent years in order to reduce the backlog of reports waiting for review. As a result of these efforts, there is currently (as of November 2017) no longer a backlog of reports waiting for review.

Nevertheless, periodicity remains a major challenge because of the insufficient procedural compliance of States parties with their reporting obligations, in particular due to the late submission of state reports. There is still a 36% rate of overdue reports, despite efforts to facilitate the reporting procedure and the word limit for reports imposed by the UN General Assembly in Resolution 68/268 (UN Doc HRI/MC/2017/2, Table 6). As of 7 November 2017, there were 16 initial reports which had not been received. Eighteen States had failed to submit a periodic review with a delay of 10 years or more (UN Doc A/72/40, Annex II).

If a State party fails to submit a report despite reminders, the Committee may examine the human rights situation in the absence of a report from material available to it in a public session upon prior notification of the State party in the so-called review procedure (UN Doc CCPR/C/3/Rev.10, Rule 70). The notification of this procedure has prompted some States parties with overdue reports to submit a report, which then served as the basis of the subsequent dialogue (UN Doc A/72/40, para 67) or at least to send a delegation that sought to respond to questions by Committee members. The Committee started to schedule at least one review per session in order to consider the situation in non-reporting states.

In some cases the Committee in the 1990s requested reports with respect to situations requiring immediate attention to prevent or limit serious violations of the Covenant, such as in the case of the former Yugoslavia, Angola, Burundi, Rwanda, Haiti, and Nigeria (UN Doc CCPR/C/3/Rev.10, Rule 66 (2); e.g., UN Doc A/48/49, Annex VII (Bosnia and Herzegovina, Croatia, Yugoslavia)). This practice, however, has not been pursued over the past two decades since other institutions including the UN High Commissioner and the Human Rights Council are in a better position to deal ad hoc with such situations (Buergenthal 2001, p. 359). Given the time constraints under which the Committee operates and the deteriorating human rights situations in many States worldwide, a deviation from the periodic examination would risk that the Committee could be considered selective in its approach. However, this has not prevented the Committee from requesting States parties with a deteriorating human rights record to submit overdue reports for periodic examination.

Absent fact-finding capacities or on-site inspections, the Committee receives information provided by the States parties and other stakeholders. In preparation of the examination in public meeting, the Committee forwards a list of issues to obtain more detailed information on specific human rights concerns usually one session in advance, which the State party is invited to respond to in writing before the meeting. This allows the delegation to prepare for the dialogue and to be cognizant of pertinent issues the Committee will address during the meeting. Specialized UN agencies, who are invited to address the Committee in a public meeting before the reporting procedure, present additional information. Reports of the UN Human Rights Council's special procedures and its Universal Periodic Review provide additional information. The sources of information have gradually been extended in order to enable the Committee to also confront the States parties with concerns raised by civil society and other stakeholders and to ask pertinent questions (Lintel and Ryngaert 2013, p. 366 et seq.).

Nongovernmental organizations and National Human Rights Institutions (NHRIs) contribute to the reporting procedure through the submission of additional information relating to the implementation of the treaties and the follow-up on Concluding Observations in the country reviewed (UN Doc. CCPR/C/104/3). According to its Working Methods, the Committee invites nongovernmental organizations and NHRIs to provide reports containing country-specific information in order to ensure that it is well informed. Such information should be submitted in writing, preferably well in advance of the relevant session. The Committee sets aside the first morning meeting of each plenary session to enable representatives of nongovernmental organizations and of NHRIs to provide oral information and answer members' questions in a formal closed meeting preceding the examination of the State party's report. In addition, nongovernmental organizations organize informal lunchtime briefings to provide Committee members with further information before the examination of the state report (HRC, Working Methods, VIII).

Additional information allows the Committee to cross-check reports and to become aware of issues which may be included in the list of issues or the list of issues prior to reporting and to be discussed with the relevant State party. While NGO's role is to sensitize the Committee, it is in the interest of its legitimacy that the Committee processes information with the necessary caution, independence, impartiality, and transparency while taking all necessary precautions against reprisals targeting human rights defenders. For this purpose, a more formalized procedure has been proposed to introduce more transparency in NGO reporting and to avoid the impression that the Committee's agenda was political in nature (Tyagi 2011, p. 225, 822). In any event, the Committee needs to confront and verify information received by other sources in the dialogue with the delegations by giving State representatives the opportunity to respond thereto. If a State party fails to respond, the Committee will draw adequate conclusions.

During the public examination of the report, which usually lasts for two meetings of 3 h each, the Committee seeks all sorts of additional information about the implementation of the Covenant. More time is allocated for the examination of initial reports. A task force of usually five to six members is primarily responsible for the preparation of the dialogue including the list of issues drafted by a rapporteur and for asking pertinent questions. This division of labor allows the Committee to be more efficient and knowledgeable. Other members may complement the questions. The participating members seek to engage in a constructive dialogue with the State party's delegates. This requires a certain degree of sensitivity and an understanding of the legal as well as sociocultural context. However, constructive does not mean uncritical. Usually members ask probing questions about concrete measures taken to protect the rights under the Covenant, about the legal and institutional framework, and confront delegations with reports of human rights violations, inviting them to respond. Members are required to allow the state representatives to answer all questions asked. Whether the dialogue is indeed constructive depends on both sides. Members may ask follow-up questions in a second round to seek further clarification. The State party is allowed to complement answers in writing within 48 h after the dialogue has been completed.

The Concluding Observations, which are adopted in a private session, identify positive aspects and matters of concern including recommendations proposing measures to be adopted for dealing with the concern. Whereas the individual communication procedure considers the question whether an individual right is violated, the reporting procedure examines the situation in the State party more broadly and evaluates to what extent prevailing circumstances may be conducive or detrimental to human rights protection in general (Klein 2011, p. 554). Kretzmer and Klein, two former Committee members, have advised the Committee to concentrate on monitoring State compliance with the Covenant and to adopt a modicum of modesty in relation to its capacity to make recommendations in light of the complex situations in the States parties (Kretzmer and Klein 2015, p. 165).

In order to ease the burden in reporting, the Committee decided to make a new procedure available, the list of issues prior to reporting (LOIPR) in October 2009. It allows States parties, subsequent to their initial report, to respond to a list of specific issues by the Committee instead of furnishing a comprehensive report (UN Doc CCPR/C/99/4). The first review under this procedure was conducted in 2013. Since then about one fourth of the States parties have agreed to the LOIPR procedure.

The LOIPR is based on the last state report, the common core document, the Committee's latest Concluding Observations, follow-up information, and the Committee's Views under the Optional Protocol if applicable. In addition, other treaty bodies' Concluding Observations or recommendations, reports of special procedures, universal periodic review documents, documents from regional organizations, information by the United Nations including the Office of the UN High Commissioner, and reports from NHRIs and from nongovernmental organizations may also provide relevant information for the preparation of the list of issues prior to reporting. The list identifies areas of particular concern and includes questions focusing on areas seen as priority issues. The answers to these questions provide the basis for the Committee's subsequent dialogue with the State party. At its 114th session in 2015, the Human Rights Committee decided, when determining the periodicity for future reports, that States submitting reports under the simplified reporting procedure would be given an extra year to do so compared to those submitting reports under the standard reporting procedure. The additional time seeks to ensure fairness between States parties using the different procedures because the regular procedure takes longer and thus leads to a longer reporting cycle. Without the additional year, States parties preferring a longer cycle would be reluctant to accept the list of issue prior to reporting procedure (UN Doc HRI/MC/ 2017/2).

The most recent innovation regarding periodic reports is the consideration in dual chambers. It allows the 18 Committee members to divide labor and to consider more reports within a session. During the 118th session, the Committee examined four State party reports in double chambers. The plenary then adopted the Concluding Observations.

In order to promote implementation of the recommendations and to maintain the dialogue with the State party, the Committee already introduced a follow-up procedure in 2001 (Schmidt 2011). The Committee in its Concluding Observations asks States parties to provide follow-up information within 2 years on the implementation of selected observations, which are of particular concern. For this purpose, the Committee identifies two to four recommendations which are serious and urgent and can be achieved within a short period of time. The State party's follow-up information enables the Committee to evaluate the degree of implementation in its subsequent follow-up report (Mutzenberg 2014). States parties are at least expected to engage with the Committee, by taking the Concluding Observations into account, and to send information as requested. The complete failure by a considerable number of States to respond to the requested follow-up arguably violates their good faith obligation under the Covenant.

In order to assess implementation, the Committee introduced a grading scheme. Absent enforcement powers, the system operates on the basis of "naming and shaming." States parties' procedural and substantive compliance is measured on the basis of grades which range from "A, reply/action largely satisfactory; B, reply/action partially satisfactory; C, reply/action not satisfactory; D, no cooperation with the Committee to E, the information or measures taken that are contrary to or reflect rejection of the recommendation."

General Comments

Pursuant to Article 40 (4) of the Covenant, the Committee shall transmit General Comments as it may consider appropriate to the States parties. General Comments summarize the Committee's interpretation of the Covenant in abstract terms (Keller and Grover 2012). They are normally directed at all States parties but are equally relevant to other stakeholders, including NGOs, attorneys, and international human rights institutions, as well as States planning to become parties to the Covenant. Contrary to Concluding Observations, these comments elaborate on issues of a general nature, not only individual States. While they were originally conceived to guide States in their reporting by identifying relevant questions to be answered in periodic reports and to stimulate State activities in the promotion of human rights, more recent comments concentrate primarily on the substantive meaning of the Covenant by elaborating on the content of the obligations assumed by the States parties and recommending means of implementation. The latter aspect with respect to implementation provides guidance for States parties on how to foster the enjoyment of Covenant rights. The former aspect involves a legal analytical function. By providing objective standards for monitoring compliance with the Covenant, General Comments serve as a point of reference for the Committee during individual communications and state reporting, and thus their scope extends beyond the reporting procedure. Accordingly, General Comments have developed into a separate instrument, which is probably the best-known part of the Committee's work.

Until 2014, the Committee adopted 35 General Comments. At the time of writing (November 2017), the Committee was in the process of adopting a new General Comment on Article 6. With their growing depth and the aim to reach more and more substantive questions comprehensively, the length of General Comments has significantly increased over time. While most Comments consider the interpretation of individual rights, General Comment No. 15 deals with the position of aliens under the Covenant considering all relevant articles. Some General Comments deal with more abstract issues, such as General Comment No. 26 on issues relating to the continuity of obligations to the ICCPR, General Comment No. 29 on states of emergency, General Comment No. 33 on obligations of States parties under the Optional Protocol, and General Comment No. 31 on the nature of the general legal obligation imposed on States parties to the Covenant. The latter reaffirmed that States incur both negative and positive obligations to ensure the effective enjoyment of the rights protected under the Covenant (General Comment No. 31, para 6). The positive dimension of human rights protection also affects the Committee's role in its oversight of State party implementation.

With the passage of time, some early General Comments have been replaced by more elaborate comments, including subsequent experience gained by the Committee. Examples are the General Comment No. 20 on the Nature of the General Legal Obligation Imposed on States Parties to the Covenant, which replaced former General Comment No. 7, and General Comment No. 28 on the Equality of Rights between Men and Women, which replaced General Comment No. 4. Some articles of the Covenant, such as the right of peaceful assembly and the freedom of association, have so far not been subjects of a General Comments. The General Comment on Reservations attracted particular attention and has prompted France, the United Kingdom, and the United States to object to the Committee's authority to determine the permissibility of specific reservations and their legal effects (UN Doc HRI/GEN/1/ Rev.2, p. 42).

The principal object of General Comments is to consolidate, harmonize, and systematize the Committee's interpretation of the Covenant based on earlier pronouncements. General Comments on rights protected under the Covenant have traditionally been limited to prior statements instead of seeking a comprehensive commentary on all problems related to the relevant article (Klein and Kretzmer 2015, p. 219). Accordingly, Views adopted in the individual complaint procedure are a primary source for General Comments since they are adopted after full legal argument, result from a thorough legal analysis, and are found after consideration of genuine cases. Concluding Observations are less suitable in this regard, because they are recommendatory in nature and do not necessarily claim to result from legal analysis but to a certain degree give policy directions. Even if the Committee expresses its concern in Concluding Observations, it does not definitely commit to finding a violation. They do not offer a legal reasoning. Furthermore, Concluding Observations seek to propose ways of implementation which appear suitable in the context of a particular State party without claiming to be generalizable or the exclusive mandatory means of implementation. Keller and Grover thus recommend that the Committee add interpretative reasoning when it refers to Concluding Observations in its General Comments (Keller and Grover 2012, p. 166).

The legal significance of General Comments has been controversially discussed for some time, including the issue of whether they constitute soft law documents (Keller and Grover 2012, p.129) or whether they – or acquiescence by States parties to General Comments – can be considered subsequent practice pursuant to Article 31 (3) (b) Vienna Convention of the Law of Treaties (Mechlem 2009). Some commentators have considered General Comments as an authoritative interpretation of the Covenant (Klein and Kretzmer 2015, p. 209). Others have been more critical. According to Tomuschat, former member of the Committee, "some general comments stand out on account either of their political or of their legal importance"(Tomuschat 2010, para 18). Simma characterized them as "all too often marked by a dearth of proper legal analysis compensated for by an overdose of wishful thinking" (Simma 2013, p. 601).

Ultimately, the legal value of General Comments depends on their methodology. It depends on the Committee to either strengthen the legal impact of its General Comments by refining its methodology for the adoption of General Comments with respect to its sources and legal analysis (like restatements) and resist external lawmaking expectations or to pursue a more active path promoting new avenues of human rights policy. To the extent that General Comments are the result of a legal analysis by an expert body established to interpret the Covenant, they require States parties to duly consider the obligations specified therein. To the extent that they function as policy recommendations, they are advisory in nature. Admittedly, the difference is not always easy to discern. A relevant indicator is the use of permissive language ("may," "recommend) or mandatory language ("must," "shall").

Since the Covenant regime lacks enforcement powers its implementation relies considerably on its legitimacy and persuasive force. There are thus good reasons for the Committee to solidly ground General Comments on its prior experience based on legal analysis. Progressiveness does not necessarily translate into effectiveness, which depends to a large degree on acceptance. Experience shows that those Comments, which have gone beyond the Committee's previous practice seeking to make general statements and promoting new aspects of human rights protection, such as the General Comment on Article 6 with respect to nuclear weapons and the General Comment on Reservations, which went beyond the interpretation of the Covenant, have attracted most controversy and were arguably less influential internationally and domestically.

The adoption of a General Comment involves a multistage procedure. When the Committee chooses a topic for a General Comment, it takes into account issues particularly relevant to its practice and the timespan since the adoption of an earlier General Comment on the same subject. A rapporteur prepares a draft, which is shared with States parties and the general public. Specialized agencies, non-governmental organizations, NHRIs, academics, and other human rights treaty bodies, including UN Special Rapporteurs, are also invited to provide input into the process of elaboration of the General Comment. In some instances, a public meeting is held to give stakeholders the opportunity to give input for or to comment on the initial draft before the first reading. Since 2002 the Committee has gradually extended the process of consultations and enhanced transparency of this procedure.

The discussion in the first round of reading follows the draft's paragraphs and includes controversial debates. These meetings are open to the general public and form part of the Committee's summary records which as *travaux préparatoires* give important insights regarding the finally adopted text. Once a text is finalized after the first reading, there is another round of consultations before the General Comment is adopted upon its second reading. The second round is intended to consolidate and to take into account the comments submitted by States and other stakeholders during the consultation process. General Comments are adopted by consensus (Neuman 2018, p. 9). This enhances the Comment's persuasiveness and may at times require that highly controversial statements are modified or even that particular issues are dropped if consensus cannot be reached.

While the general parameters of the adoption procedure are more or less settled, its concrete design varies and has been criticized as ad hoc. Keller and Grover have therefore suggested to standardize the object of General Comments, the selection of topics, and their adoption process in order to enhance their persuasive force and legitimacy (Keller and Grover 2012, p. 192).

Individual Communications and State Communications

The Human Rights Committee was the first universal body with a mandate to examine individual communications (Article 1 OP I). It continues to receive the highest number of individual petitions among the treaty bodies. The individual communication procedure has become operative for two thirds of the States parties after having ratified or acceded to the (First) Optional Protocol. About 3000 cases have been registered since 1977. Many more have not passed the threshold for registration when they failed to meet the most basic requirements under the Protocol, because they failed to make an arguable case under the Covenant (Article 2 OP I), were anonymous or abusive (Article 3 OP I).

Considering the relatively small number of complaints brought to the Human Rights Committee compared to cases before the European Court of Human Rights (UNCHR 2016, Statistical survey), its contribution to individual justice is practically limited. Obstacles for the submission of petitions are the insufficient visibility of the individual complaint mechanism in the States parties and fear of retribution or harassment that victims face in several countries for the submission of complaints (Shikhelman 2017, p. 33, 42).

Unfortunately, the current system is not capable of handling more communications. The backlog of individual communications is one of the most pressing challenges the Committee is faced with (UN Doc A/72/40, para 27; Navanethem 2012; UN Doc A/66/860). Since 2014, the number of newly registered cases has been twice as high compared to prior years. As of December 2016, 645 cases were pending. Most of these cases come from countries of the Western European and Others Group (WEOG) (Shikhelman 2017, p. 22).

Whereas the system, due to its institutional and logistical shortcomings, can hardly claim to generally ensure individual access to justice worldwide, its major impact is on the interpretation of the Covenant, which is relevant not only for individual cases but also more broadly for the implementation of the Covenant in the States parties. The Committee's legal interpretation in its Views helps to clarify the meaning of the rights protected under the Covenant. Furthermore, individual communications draw the Committee's attention to issues, which can also be relevant for the reporting procedure.

The submission of a case does not require legal representation. The procedure is simplified, and according to a recent study, the lack of legal representation does not influence the outcome of a case (Shikhelman 2017, p. 26). In order to avoid irreparable harm, for example, in death penalty or non-refoulement cases, the Committee takes interim measures of protection requesting States to adopt measures to prevent the violation of the Covenant (e.g., by refraining from executing or deporting the author of a communication). Interim measures are issued by the rapporteur on new communications who is also the first to review incoming communications and who may decide to split the consideration of admissibility from the review of the merits. The Committee considers interim measures binding because States are obliged under the Optional Protocol to act in good faith with the individual complaints procedure. Disregard of interim measures leading to irreparable harm would deprive the complaint procedure of any real meaning (HRC 2000, Piandiong et al. v The Philippines, Communication No. 869/1999). Most of the States therefore abide by these measures (Rieter 2010, p. 952 et seq.).

As long as a communication is under review, the Optional Protocol provides for confidentiality. This, however, does not prevent the Committee from publishing its Views after adoption and transmission to the parties and to make other decisions, including the order of interim measures, public. The procedure has traditionally been in writing and does not provide for the taking of evidence. At its 118th session, the Committee decided to develop a pilot process for inviting the parties in selected communications to offer oral comments on the other party's submissions in closed session (UN Doc A/72/40, para 36). The idea of an oral hearing is not new, but it had failed so far because, according to the Optional Protocol, the Committee "shall hold closed meetings when examining communications" (Article 5 (3) OP). It is doubtful that this provision is meant to only apply to the Committee's deliberations. After all, confidential deliberation is a necessary feature of every judicial and quasi-judicial body irrespective of such a provision. Furthermore, Article 5 (1) of the Optional Protocol provides that "the Committee shall consider communications received under the present Protocol in the light of all *written* information made available to it by the individual and by the State Party concerned" (Tomuschat 2010, para 32). Whether single States parties can waive this procedural rule by agreeing to an oral hearing is open to debate. The new procedure introduces novel inquisitorial elements, affects the institutional role of the Committee more generally, and is thus arguably not at the disposition of single parties. At any rate, the Committee, while being aware of its time constraints as a nonpermanent body, should ensure that all petitioners have access to the same procedural entitlements and that such hearings are not only to the benefit of a few individuals represented by nongovernmental organizations which can afford to travel to Geneva.

Most of the cases submitted to the Committee not only raise issues of law but also issues of facts. Due to a lack of fact-finding capacities, the Committee has to rely on party submissions. Many decisions are therefore based on findings of burden of proof. Once the author of a communication has substantiated allegations of a violation, States parties are expected to respond specifically to the petitioner's allegations and to provide details on factual contentions (HRC 1980, Grille Motta v Uruguay, Communication No. 11/1977, para 14) and on grounds of justification. Absent any investigation by the State party, the facts as presented by the author are given due weight. In many cases this leads the Committee to conclude that the author's allegations are true provided they appear from all the circumstances to be substantiated (General Comment No. 33, para 10). Though the Committee has eased the burden of proof when the alleged facts lie outside the control of the petitioner, e.g., in case of enforced disappearance or ill-treatment in custody (HRC 1982, Bleier v Uruguay, Communication No. 39/1978, para 13.3), the inability of the Committee to establish the true facts limits its capacity to make factual findings and thus arguably constrains its ability to render full justice.

The procedure for the adoption of Views is multistaged. Cases are decided on the basis of the Covenant after a thorough legal analysis (de Zayas 2001). Each case is assigned a rapporteur who prepares a draft decision to be discussed in a presession working group. The working group presents a revised draft to the plenary, which then reviews the case and renders a decision. The Committee usually considers admissibility and the merits of the case together, unless serious admissibility questions arise which warrant a split of the phases. Admissibility is determined on the basis of the requirements set out in the Optional Protocol. Among these, the requirement to exhaust local remedies ensures that the communication procedure before the Committee is only subsidiary (Article 5 (2) (b) Optional Protocol). Exception is made if domestic remedies are ineffective or unreasonably prolonged. Furthermore, in accordance with the lis pendens rule, the Committee may not deal with cases pending before another procedure of international investigation or settlement (Article 5 (2) (a) OP I). Several European States parties have declared a reservation to this provision extending inadmissibility to cases, which *have been* examined by another international procedure. The author of a communication is required to make factual submissions and adduce relevant material supporting the alleged violation. Communications, which are insufficiently substantiated, are declared inadmissible pursuant to Article 2 of the Optional Protocol.

The legal analysis concludes with the adoption of the Committee's Views, which are forwarded to the State party concerned and the individual petitioner (Article 5 (4) OP I). The Committee's decisions have been criticized for a lack of detailed legal reasoning (Hakki 2002, p. 97). However, the 10,700 word limit imposed by the General Assembly (UN Doc A/Res/68/268) does not allow for much leeway in this respect. Whether the exceeding length of some individual opinions is able to compensate this constraint is debatable and depends on members' self-perception. While the Committee generally aims to adopt decisions by consensus, if no agreement is reached, it adopts its Views by majority vote. Members may append individual opinions, indicating their dissent or concurrence with the majority. However, influencing the analysis and the legal reasoning of a decision is the highest impact that a member of the Committee can have, albeit less visible on the outside. Furthermore, the absence of an individual opinion does not necessarily indicate unanimity.

If the Committee finds a violation, it usually indicates appropriate measures of individual redress (David 2014). In some cases the Committee also asks for general measures, arguably blurring the lines between individual communications and the state reporting procedures. States parties are expected to consider the Views in good faith. Since the Optional Protocol lacks an enforcement mechanism comparable to the procedure before the Council of Europe's Committee of Ministers, where the Department for the Execution of Judgements of the European Court of Human Rights oversees the implementation, the Committee itself established a follow-up procedure for its Views in 1990. The Committee was the first universal treaty body introducing such a procedure. Since then the Committee requests States parties in its Views to provide within 180 days information concerning the measures taken to give effect to the Views. The responses are evaluated on the basis of the same grading scheme as the one adopted for the follow-up on Concluding Observations. Though the Views are not legally binding under the Optional Protocol, the Committee refers to the right to an effective remedy under Article 2 (3) of the Covenant in order to strengthen the normative character of its remedial holding.

Whereas the Human Rights Committee has had the opportunity to develop a substantial body of jurisprudence under the individual communication procedure over the years, the state complaint procedure has played no role at all over the past four decades. Not a single State so far has taken the opportunity to bring a formal communication to the attention of another State party claiming that it is not fulfilling its obligations under the Covenant and to refer the matter to the Committee pursuant to Article 41 ICCPR. Though more than a fourth of all States parties have accepted the competence of the Human Rights Committee to receive and consider such communications, the procedure remains mute.

Challenges and Promises

Despite considerable procedural developments, the Committee faces several institutional challenges – a phenomenon, which will require more attention by the States parties in the future. For over two decades, commentators have criticized a mismatch between the Committee's tasks and working capacity (Buergenthal 2001; Tomuschat 2010, para 21; Shany 2013, p. 1322). The increasing number of States parties creates challenges for the Committee as a nonpermanent body. Though recently the backlog of reports has been diminished as a result of increased meeting time allocated by the General Assembly (UN Doc A/Res/68/268), the high ration of overdue reporting by one third of the States parties remains a matter of concern (UN Doc A/66/860, p. 20 et seq.; UN Doc HRI/MC/2017/2, para 9, Table 6). If all reports were submitted on time, the Committee, under the currently allotted meeting time, would only be able to consider them on an 8-year cycle.

Furthermore, the growing number of ratifications of the Optional Protocol, an increase in new communications, and the still insufficient number of support staff have led to a mounting backlog of individual communications over many years (UN Doc A/71/118, para 36). An additional increase of meeting time from currently 14.7 weeks per year (2017) to 19,8 weeks per year (as of 2018) for a part-time Committee composed of renowned experts who depend on their regular positions as a source of income is not a viable solution. According to a commentator, "it can hardly be expected that highly qualified experts will spend several months of their time in Geneva while being paid just one symbolic US dollar per year" (Tomuschat 2010, para 37). In any event a mandate that involves more than three months of absence is hard to reconcile with full-time professional obligations.

Finally, the coordination with the Universal Periodic Review mechanism to the Human Rights Council and the considerable overlap with the mandate of the other human rights treaty bodies will need to be addressed (Tistounet 2000, p. 383 et seq.), presumably through a major institutional overhaul of the entire treaty body framework (Kozma et al. 2010; Riedel 2013; Nowak 2013).

In light of these challenges, the Committee needs to use its mandate and resources as efficiently as possible. Pursuant to Article 39 (2) ICCPR, the Committee is entitled to develop its rules of procedure. This competence provides it with some leeway within the outer boundaries of the Covenant (Klein 2011, p. 542). At the same time, it requires a constant review of the methods of work and necessary refinements. In the past, the Committee used this competence to introduce the follow-up procedures for individual communications and Concluding Observations as well as the list of issues prior to reporting procedures. The institutionalization of dual chambers is an avenue worth considering in the future to enable the Committee to fulfill its mandate within the confines of its institutional setup. A body of 18 experts is well-equipped to diversify its procedure, distribute different tasks among its membership, draft decisions in chambers, and reserve the approval of such decisions and the adoption of controversial decisions to the plenary (Buergenthal 2001, p. 394).

It is not only up to the Human Rights Committee to defend the validity of the Covenant. This is a task that the Committee shares with the community of States parties. A human rights system can only be as effective as its main stakeholders allow it to be. This primarily concerns the institutional capacity to issue legally binding decisions, the availability of enforcement mechanisms, and its structural capacity. Recognizing that human rights are universal not only requires international norm-setting but active measures to preserve the integrity of the Covenant enforcement regime and a collective approach in terms of implementation and enforcement (Seibert-Fohr 2012. p. 547). States parties not only carry the responsibility for the composition of the Committee as an independent body of experts and for its structural capacities and legal competences, but they also have a role to play as trustees of universal human rights engagement. In accordance with their *erga omnes partes* obligations under the Covenant, a more active complementarity approach by the States parties would render the system more effective (Seibert-Fohr 2012, p. 547 et seq.). An appropriate step into this direction would be for

States parties to resort to the so far dormant state communication procedure, to induce States to finally comply with their reporting obligations and to take a more active stance with respect to reservations incompatible with the object and purpose of the Covenant (Klein 2011, p. 549; Seibert-Fohr 2004, p. 194, 207, 210 et seq.).

The Committee's Legacy: A Critical Assessment

For more than four decades, the Committee has performed its task of monitoring State compliance and implementation with the International Covenant on Civil and Political Rights despite various challenges. It has gradually shaped and developed the substantive meaning of the Covenant. Furthermore it has refined its procedures in order to render monitoring more stringent and enhance transparency. While its early performance was influenced by the Cold War, more recently the Committee's main challenges in performing its international monitoring task are structural in nature. The rising number of States parties to the Covenant since its entry into force and the increase in individual communications under the (First) Optional Protocol provide ample evidence for the growing demand for universal oversight. Accordingly, victims and civil society have placed high hopes in the Committee.

As a universal monitoring body, the Committee's role can only be assessed on the basis of a connected view, which considers its interaction with all relevant stakeholders. The Committee identifies generic problems and asks States to remedy them. Other bodies, such as the Human Rights Council and the High Commissioner, can play a valuable role in prompting States to implement the Committee's pronouncements. Through the course of its existence, the Committee in its effort to enhance the universal protection of human rights has affected the interpretation of the Covenant by various UN organs including Special Rapporteurs and Special Procedures.

The Committee's role needs to be considered also in relation to regional human rights mechanisms. Regional and universal bodies engage in mutual cross-fertilization. Regional human rights courts have drawn from the Committee's jurisprudence, likewise national courts (Seibert-Fohr 2014; Killander 2014). The Committee's role is primarily complementary and of particular practical relevance in those States parties, which are not or no longer covered by a regional system. Recent denunciations from the American Convention of Human Rights, e.g., by Venezuela and the Dominican Republic, render the oversight under the International Covenant on Civil and Political Rights even more pertinent. Since the Covenant does not allow for such denunciation, it holds a residual function (General Comment No. 26).

Whereas the Committee is a facilitator for the implementation of international human rights, the effectiveness of the Committee's work in everyday life depends essentially on factual implementation. The onus to exercise a stronger commitment to treaty implementation and enforcement lies on each State party. States parties need to strengthen their legal remedies and implementation mechanisms, including procedures, which feed the Committee's interpretation and decisions into the domestic process (Klein 2011, p. 548). This is a matter of linking the international and the domestic level, both substantively and procedurally. In order to render universal monitoring more effective, it is necessary to develop national mechanisms connecting the outcome of the communication and reporting procedure to the relevant national institutions so that they can translate it into the domestic system. The effectiveness of the Committee's task depends on domestic multipliers. National Human Rights Institutions can play a valuable role in this respect. Furthermore, pursuant to Article 2 (3) of the Covenant, the primary task to provide for access to justice is with the States parties, whereas the role of the Committee can be subsidiary at best (Kretzmer 2000). It is therefore important that the Committee require States parties to establish an independent effective judiciary in accordance with Article 14 of the Covenant. When domestic courts take the International Covenant on Civil and Political Rights and its interpretation into account, they can multiply its impact. Finally, nongovernmental organizations can serve a valuable role in raising awareness of the Committee's work and engaging in the domestic oversight of treaty implementation (Lintel and Rygaert 2013).

In this context, the Committee's work can help mobilize domestic processes (Simmons 2011). Nevertheless, the Committee should be aware of its limits, namely, that it cannot assume the role of a constitutional court. International human rights protection provides for universally applicable standards. The density of these obligations does not equal constitutional standards, and States parties are free to surpass these standards domestically. The Committee thus needs to grant States necessary constitutional leeway while exercising a residual function where the domestic order fails to protect universally accepted human rights norms.

Irrespective of the Committee's efforts, State party compliance with the Covenant obligations remains a major concern (Hathaway 2002; UN Doc A/72/40, para 39). This is a problem faced by all human rights treaty bodies. A recent study only found a 24% rate of positive responses for all universal treaty bodies (Fox Principi 2018: 4). At times even bona fide considerations of the Committee's pronouncements are lacking (Tomuschat 1995, p. 623 et seq.). On the other hand, there are also positive examples. Some findings of the Committee in the individual complaint procedure have led to legislative amendments affecting the population at large. Kate Fox, a former secretary of the Human Rights Committee, in her study identified a total of 27 cases, in which treaty body decisions, mostly from the Human Rights Committee, led to new legislation in labor law, criminal procedure, minority rights, migration, language, education, violence against women, and discrimination (Fox Principi 2018: 7). In addition, there are adjustments which are less direct and visible because the Committee's pronouncements feed into a long-term international or domestic political process or affect judicial decision-making. As a result, the Committee's real impact is difficult to measure (Kretzmer and Klein 2015, p. 138 et seq.).

Taking into account the Committee's limited resources and legal competencies, one cannot evaluate the Committee's performance simply on the basis of State compliance with their human rights obligations. Absent the necessary enforcement tools, the Committee can only restate the law, give advice, and rely on persuasion. In light of the institutional weakness of the universal human rights system, namely, the absence of a universal human rights court, weak enforcement, and the fact that the Optional Protocol fails to accord legally binding effect to the decisions of the Committee, the utmost that the Committee can do to promote the effectiveness of its activities is to reemphasize its efforts to strengthen the legitimacy of its decisions. The Committee needs to recognize that the nature and effect of the Committee's pronouncements depend significantly on the methodology applied. The higher the emphasis on the legal foundation and respective sound legal reasoning, the more likely the Committee will be recognized as a quasi-judicial organ and its interpretation considered authoritative. As the Committee depends on the persuasive force of its pronouncements, a cautious but steadily evolving approach may be more effective than an activist line of reasoning. Ultimately, the legitimacy of its interpretation depends on the Committee's independence, legal reasoning, and ability to render the Covenant's meaning truly universal. Therefore, it is up to the Committee to find a balance between progress and consolidation taking into account that as an independent expert body, it lacks legitimation and accountability for political decision-making.

In order to preserve its legacy as a central player in universal human rights protection, the Human Rights Committee is also called upon to refine its place in the overall structure of the human rights system by emphasizing its unique features and special competences. In the absence of a universal human rights court, the Committee as a body of independent experts, which is recognized for its legal expertise in human rights law, should make full use of its interpretative powers and feed its interpretation of the Covenant into other human rights mechanism. Other bodies, such as the Human Rights Council, could play a more active role in the oversight of implementation and enforcement comparable to the Committee of Ministers of the Council of Europe and thus relieve the Committee from the burden of follow-up procedures. The Human Rights Council, Special Rapporteurs, and Special Procedures are also better equipped to react ad hoc to human rights emergencies.

While the Committee can provide advice on how to implement the Covenant, the Committee's essential role lies in interpreting the Covenant as a common point of reference for all States parties and to update the meaning of the Covenant as a living instrument in line with present-day conditions. Accordingly its main achievement as an independent treaty body established by the States parties for the purpose of monitoring is its consolidated interpretation which has been referred to as a universal standard by international and domestic institutions. Throughout the years, the Committee has developed a considerable body of jurisprudence, which clarifies the obligations that States parties have undertaken under the Covenant. In times of increasing challenges of international human rights, its principal objective is to defend the integrity of the Covenant as a legally binding instrument, to continuously remind States parties of their legal obligations, and to maintain a norm-based dialogue with them.

References

Ando N (2007) The development of the Human Rights Committee's procedure to consider the States Parties' reports under Article 40 of the International Covenant on Civil and Political Rights. In: Kohen MG (ed) Promoting justice, human rights and conflict resolution through international law/La promotion de la justice, des droits de l'homme et du règlement des conflits par le droit international: Liber Amicorum Lucius Caflisch. Brill, Leiden, pp 17–32

Buergenthal T (2001) The U.N. Human Rights Committee. Max Planck Yearb U N Law 5:341–398

Crawford J (2000) The UN human rights treaty system: a system in crisis? In: Alston P, Crawford J (eds) The future of UN-human rights treaty monitoring. Cambridge University Press, Cambridge, pp 1–12

Davala M (2012) Conflict of interest in universal human rights bodies. In: Peters A, Handschin L (eds) Conflict of interest in global, public and corporate overnance. Cambridge University Press, Cambridge, pp 125–141

David V (2014) Reparations at the Human Rights Committee. Neth Q Hum Rights 32:8–43

De Zayas A (2001) The examination of individual complaints by the United Nations Human Rights Committee under the optional protocol to the international covenant on civil and political rights. In: Alfredsson G et al (eds) International human rights monitoring mechanisms. Martinus Nijhoff Publishers, The Hague, pp 67–121

Fox Principi K (2018) United Nations individual complaint procedures – how do states comply? A categorized study based on 268 cases of "satisfactory" implementation under the follow-up procedure, mainly of the UN Human Rights Committee. Hum Rights Law J, 37:1–31

Hakki MM (2002) The silver anniversary of the Human Rights Committee: anything to celebrate? Int J Hum Rights 6(3):85–102. https://doi.org/10.1080/714003771

Hathaway OA (2002) Do human rights treaties make a difference? Yale Law J 11(8):1935–2042

HRC. Grille Motta v Uruguay. Communication No. 11/1977 (29 July 1980)

HRC. Bleier v Uruguay. Communication No. 30/1978 (29 March 1982)

HRC. General Comment No. 26: general comment on issues relating to the continuity of obligations to the International Covenant on Civil and Political Rights (8 December 1997) UN Doc CCPR/C/21/Rev.1/Add.8/Rev.1

HRC. Piandiong et al v. The Philippines. Communication No. 869/1999 (15 June 1999)

HRC. General Comment No. 31: the nature of the general legal obligation imposed on States Parties to the Covenant (29 March 2004) UN Doc CCPR/C/21/Rev.1/Add.13

HRC. General Comment No. 33: the obligations of States Parties under the Optional Protocol to the International Covenant on Civil and Political Rights (5 November 2008) UN Doc CCPR/C/GC/33

HRC. The relationship of the Human Rights Committee with non-governmental organizations (4 June 2012) 104th Session, UN Doc CCPR/C/104/3

HRC. Working methods of the Human Rights Committee. Available at http://www.ohchr.org/EN/HRBodies/CCPR/Pages/WorkingMethods.aspx. Accessed 28 Nov 2017

HRC (1994) Procedural Decisions of the Human Rights Committee, UN Doc A/48/49, Annex VII (1994). (Bosnia and Herzegovina, Croatia, Yugoslavia)

ILA (2004) International human rights law and practice: final report on the impact of findings of the United Nations human rights treaty bodies. In: Report of the seventy-first conference held in Berlin (16–21 August 2004). International Law Association, London, pp 621–702

ILC. Yearbook of the International Law Commission 1997, Volume II, Part Two, UN Doc A/52/10

International Court of Justice. Applicability of Article VI, Section 22, of the Convention on the Privileges and Immunities of the United Nations (Advisory Opinion) (1989) ICJ Rep 177

International Criminal Tribunal for the former Yugoslavia. Prosecutor v Anto Furundzija (Judgment in the Trial Chamber) Case No. IT-95-17/1-T (10 December 1998)

International Court of Justice. Case Concerning Ahmadou Sadio Diallo (Republic of Guinea v Democratic Republic of the Congo) (Judgment) (2010) ICJ Rep 639

International Covenant on Civil and Political Rights (adopted 16 December 1966, entered into force 23 March 1976) 999 UNTS 171 (ICCPR)

Keller H, Grover L (2012) General comments of the Human Rights Committee and their legitimacy. In: Keller H, Ulfstein G (eds) Human rights treaty bodies. Cambridge University Press, Cambridge, pp 116–198

Killander M (2014) Jurisprudential dialogue in supranational human rights litigation in Africa. In: Reinisch A et al (eds) International law and… select proceedings of the European Society of International Law, Volume 5. Bloomsbury Publishing, London, pp 25–42

Klein E (2011) Stimmen Zweck und Mittel des internationalen Menschenrechtsschutzes überein? In: Wittinger M et al (eds) Verfassung – Völkerrecht – Kulturgüterschutz. Duncker & Humblot, Berlin, pp 541–555

Klein E, Kretzmer D (2015) The UN Human Rights Committee: the general comments – the evolution of an autonomous monitoring instrument. Ger Yearb Int Law 58:189–229

Kozma J, Nowak M, Scheinin M (2010) A world court of human rights: consolidated statute and commentary. Neuer Wissenschaftlicher Verlag, Wien/Graz

Kretzmer D (2000) Commentary on complaint processes by Human Rights Committee and Torture Committee Members: the Human Rights Committee. In: Bayefsky A (ed) The UN human rights treaty system in the 21st century. Kluwer Law International, The Hague/London/Boston, pp 163–166

Kretzmer D, Klein E (2015) The UN Human Rights Committee: monitoring states parties reports. Isr Yearb Hum Rights 45:133–167

Lintel I, Rygaert C (2013) The interface between non-governmental organisations and the Human Rights Committee. Int Community Law Rev 15:359–379. https://doi.org/10.1163/18719732-12341257

McGoldrick D (1994) The Human Rights Committee: its role in the development of the international covenant on civil and political rights. Clarendon Press, Oxford

Mechlem K (2009) Treaty bodies and the interpretation of human rights. Vanderbilt J Transl Law 42:905–947

Mutzenberg P (2014) Agir pour la mise en oeuvre des droits civils et politiques: L'apport du Comité des droits de l'homme. Editions L'Harmattan, Paris

Navanethem P (2012) Strengthening the United Nations human rights system: a report by the United Nations High Commissioner for Human Rights. Available at http://www2.ohchr.org/english/bodies/HRTD/docs/HCReportTBStrengthening.pdf. Accessed 28 Nov 2017

Neuman GL (2018) Giving meaning and effect to human rights: the contributions of Human Rights Committee Members. In: Moeckli D, Keller H (eds) The UN Human Rights Covenants at 50. Oxford University Press, Oxford

Nowak M (2005) U.N. Covenant on civil and political rights: CCPR commentary. N.P. Engel Verlag, Kehl

Nowak M (2013) Comments on the High Commissioner's proposals aimed at strengthening the UN human rights treaty body system. Neth Q Hum Rights 31:133–167

Optional Protocol to the International Covenant on Civil and Political Rights (adopted 16 December 1966, entered into force 23 March 1976) 999 UNTS 171 (Optional Protocol to the ICCPR)

Riedel E (2013) Global human rights at the crossroads: strengthening or reforming the system. In: Breuer M et al (eds) Der Staat im Recht. Duncker & Humblot, Berlin, pp 1289–1306

Rieter E (2010) Preventing irreparable harm: provisional measures in international human rights adjudication. Intersentia, Cambridge

Rodley N (2013) The role and impact of treaty bodies. In: Shelton D (ed) The Oxford handbook of international human rights law. Oxford University Press, Oxford, pp 621–648

Schmidt MG (2011) Follow-up procedures to individual complaints and periodic state reporting mechanisms. In: Alfredsson G et al (eds) International human rights monitoring mechanisms. Martinus Nijhoff Publishers, The Hague, pp 201–215

Seibert-Fohr A (2004) The potentials of the Vienna convention on the law of treaties with respect to reservations to human rights treaties. In: Ziemele I (ed) Reservations to human rights treaties and the Vienna convention regime: conflict, harmony or reconciliation. Martinus Nijhoff Publishers, The Hague, pp 183–211

Seibert-Fohr A (2012) The International Covenant on Civil and Political Rights: moving from coexistence to cooperation and solidarity. In: Hestermeyer H et al (eds) Coexistence, cooperation and solidarity: Liber Amicorum Rüdiger Wolfrum. Martinus Nijhoff Publishers, Leiden/Boston, pp 521–553

Seibert-Fohr A (2014) Judicial engagment in international human rights comparativism. In: Reinisch A et al (eds) International law and…select proceedings of the European Society of International Law, Volume 5. Bloomsbury Publishing, London, pp 7–24

Shany Y (2013) The effectiveness of the Human Rights Committee and the treaty body reform.
    In: Breuer M et al (eds) Der Staat im Recht. Duncker & Humblot, Berlin, pp 1307–1323
Shikhelman V (2015) Impartiality, geopolitics and culture in the United Nations Human Rights
    Committee. Available via SSRN. Available at https://ssrn.com/abstract=2616026. Accessed 28
    Nov 2017
Shikhelman V (2017) Access to justice in the United Nations Human Rights Committee. Mich J Int
    Law 3. Available at https://ssrn.com/abstract=2999668. Accessed 28 Nov 2017
Simma B (2013) Human rights before the international court of justice: community interest coming
    to life? In: Tams CJ, Sloan J (eds) The development of international law by the international
    court of justice. Oxford University Publisher, Oxford, pp 577–603
Simmons BA (2011) Mobilizing for human rights: international law in domestic politics.
    Cambridge University Press, Cambridge
Tistounet E (2000) The problem of overlapping among different treaty bodies. In: Alston P,
    Crawford J (eds) The future of UN-human rights treaty monitoring. Cambridge University
    Press, Cambridge, pp 383–401
Tomuschat C (1995) Making individual communications an effective tool for the protection of
    human rights. In: Beyerlin U et al (eds) Recht zwischen Umbruch und Bewahrung: Festschrift
    für Rudolf Bernhardt. Springer, Heidelberg, pp 615–634
Tomuschat C (2010) Human Rights Committee. Max Planck Encyclopedia of Public International
    Law. Available via at http://opil.ouplaw.com/view/10.1093/law:epil/9780199231690/law-
    9780199231690-e813?prd=EPIL. Accessed 28 Nov 2017
Tyagi Y (2011) The UN Human Rights Committee. Cambridge University Press, Cambridge
UN Economic and Social Council. Comments of Governments on the Draft International Covenant
    on human rights and measures of implementation, (29 December 1949) UN Doc E/CN.4/353
UN International Human Rights Instruments. Compilation of general comments and general
    recommendations adopted by human rights treaty bodies (29 March 1996) General Comment
    No. 24: General comment on issues relating to reservations made upon ratification or accession
    to the Covenant or the Optional Protocols thereto, or in relation to declarations under article 41
    of the Covenant, UN Doc HRI/GEN/1/Rev.2
UN International Human Rights Instruments. Harmonized guidelines on reporting under the
    international human rights treaties, including guidelines on a common core document and treaty
    specific documents (10 May 2006) UN Doc HRI/MC/2006/3
UN International Human Rights Instruments. Twenty-seventh meeting of chairpersons of the
    human rights treaty bodies: guidelines against Intimidation or Reprisals ("San José Guidelines")
    (30 July 2015) UN Doc HRI/MC/2015/6
UN International Human Rights Instruments. Compliance by States parties with their reporting
    obligations to international human rights treaty bodies: Note by the Secretariat, (2 May 2017)
    29th Meeting of Chairs, Item 8 of the provisional agenda, UN Doc HRI/MC/2017/2
UN International Human Rights Instruments. Twenty-ninth meeting of Chairs of the human rights
    treaty bodies: compliance by State parties with their reporting obligations to international human
    rights treaty bodies (2 May 2017) UN Doc HRI/MC/2017/2
UNCHR. Focused reports based on replied to lists of issues prior to reporting (LOIPR): implemen-
    tation of the new optional reporting procedure (LOIPR procedure), (29 September 2010) 99th
    Session, UN Doc CCPR/C/99/4
UNCHR. Rules of procedure of the Human Rights Committee (11 January 2012) UN Doc CCPR/C/
    3/Rev.10
UNCHR. Statistical survey of individual complaints dealt with by the Human Rights Committee
    under the Optional Protocol to the International Covenant on Civil and Political Rights
    (March 2016). Available at http://www.ohchr.org/_layouts/15/WopiFrame.aspx?sourcedoc=/
    Documents/HRBodies/CCPR/StatisticalSurvey.xls&action=default&DefaultItemOpen=1.
    Accessed 28 Nov 2017
UNGA. Draft First International Covenant on Human Rights and measures of implementation
    (1 December 1950), GAOR (V), Agenda item 63, UN Doc A/1576

UNGA. Draft First International Covenant on Human Rights: report of the third committee (20 November 1950) GAOR (V), Agenda item 63, UN Doc A/1559

UNGA. Draft International Covenants on Human Rights: report of the third committee (10 December 1963) GAOR (XVIII), Agenda item 48, UN Doc A/5655

UNGA. Draft International Covenants on Human Rights: report of the third committee (13 December 1966) GAOR (XXI), Agenda item 62, UN Doc A/6546

UNGA. Resolutions and Decisions adopted by the General Assembly during its forty-eighth session Volume I (21 September–23 December 1993) GAOR (XLVIII), UN Doc A/48/49

UNGA. Resolution 56/272: comprehensive study of the question of honorariums payable to members of organs and subsidiary organs of the United Nations (23 April 2002) GAOR (LVI), Agenda item 122, UN Doc A/Res/56/272

UNGA. Resolution 60/149: International Covenants on Human Rights (16 December 2005) Agenda item 71 (a), UN Doc A/Res/60/149

UNGA. Implementation of human rights instruments. Note by the Secretary General (2 August 2012) GAOR (LXVII), Agenda item 70 (a) of the provisional agenda, UN Doc A/67/222

UNGA. United Nations reform: measures and proposals. Note by the Secretary General (26 June 2012) GAOR (LXVI), Agenda item 124, UN Doc A/66/860

UNGA. Resolution 68/268: strengthening and enhancing the effective functioning of the human rights treaty body system (9 April 2014) GAOR (LXVIII), Agenda item 125, UN Doc A/Res/68/268

UNGA. Status of the human rights treaty body system: Report of the Secretary-General (18 July 2016) GAOR (LXXI), Items 69 (a) and 124 of the provisional agenda, UN Doc A/71/118

UNGA. Report of the Human Rights Committee: 117th – 119th session (2017) GAOR (LXXII), UN Doc A/72/40

UNGA. Report of the United Nations Commission on International Trade Law (3–21 July 2017) GAOR (L), UN Doc A/72/17

Young KA (2002) The law and process of the U.N. Human Rights Committee. Transnational Publishers, Ardsley

The UN Committee on Economic, Social, and Cultural Rights

Fons Coomans

Contents

Introduction 144
Background, Mandate, and Composition of the Committee on Economic, Social, and
Cultural Rights 145
The Committee's Working Methods 146
Clarifying States' Obligations with Regard to Economic, Social, and Cultural Rights 149
A "Violations Approach" to Economic, Social, and Cultural Rights 151
A Right to Individual Complaints 152
The Extraterritorial Scope of Application of the Covenant 155
The Committee and the Extraterritorial Application of the Covenant 157
Extraterritorial Obligations and Business Activities Abroad 160
Future Potential 161
Challenges Ahead 162
Concluding Remarks 165
References 165

Abstract

This chapter will deal with the activities and achievements of one of the UN human rights monitoring bodies, namely, the United Nations Committee on Economic, Social and Cultural Rights which was established to monitor implementation of the International Covenant on Economic, Social and Cultural Rights. It will discuss the mandate and functioning of the Committee, assess its achievements over the years, and in light of challenges ahead, discuss its future potential and limitations. As an approach, this chapter will apply an analysis and discussion of the output of the Committee in terms of documents adopted. The Committee has been active in making the Covenant from a stepchild to full member of the UN human rights family and strengthening the status of economic,

F. Coomans (✉)
Department of International and European Law, Maastricht University, The Netherlands
e-mail: fons.coomans@maastrichtuniversity.nl

© Springer Nature Singapore Pte Ltd. 2018
G. Oberleitner (ed.), *International Human Rights Institutions, Tribunals, and Courts*,
International Human Rights, https://doi.org/10.1007/978-981-10-5206-4_7

social, and cultural rights as human rights. It has clarified the normative content of economic, social and cultural rights and relating obligations by using and applying ideas and suggestions from academic discourse. A dynamic interpretation of the Covenant has been developed which emphasizes the key importance and relevance of economic, social, and cultural rights as touchstone for legislation, policy, and practice in societies in the North and the South. Especially through its General Comments, and to a lesser extent its Concluding Observations, has the Committee been able to explain and highlight that the protection of economic, social, and cultural rights is a key element of human dignity. However, the Committee still has to deal with skeptic views of governments who question the legal nature of economic, social, and cultural rights as human rights.

Keywords

Economic, social, and cultural rights · International Covenant on Economic, Social and Cultural Rights · UN Committee on Economic, Social and Cultural Rights · State reports · General Comments · Optional Protocol · Justiciability · Violations · Extraterritorial human rights obligations

Introduction

This chapter will deal with the activities and achievements of a UN human rights monitoring body which is, to some extent, different from other human rights treaty bodies. The United Nations Committee on Economic, Social and Cultural Rights (UNCESCR or Committee) was not established when the International Covenant on Economic, Social and Cultural Rights (ICESCR or Covenant) was adopted in 1966. The Committee only came into existence in 1987 following a decision by the Economic and Social Council of the UN. Since then the Committee has been very active in making the Covenant from a stepchild to full member of the UN human rights family and strengthening the status of economic, social, and cultural rights as human rights. This was needed, because for a long time economic, social, and cultural rights were considered to be less legal and of having an inferior status compared to civil and political rights. Through its activities, the Committee has operated as a vehicle to make the Covenant more familiar with States parties and hold the latter accountable for their actions and failures to implement economic, social, and cultural rights at the domestic level. In its work, the Committee got support from other actors, such as nongovernmental organizations (NGOs) and civil society organizations and members from the academic community. This chapter will discuss the mandate and functioning of the Committee, assess its achievements over the years, and in light of challenges ahead, discuss its future potential and limitations. As an approach, this chapter will apply an analysis and discussion of the output of the Committee in terms of documents adopted. It will employ a combination of a descriptive and evaluative research method. In doing so, the chapter will use academic sources in substantiating and supporting its findings.

Background, Mandate, and Composition of the Committee on Economic, Social, and Cultural Rights

As a result of the 1952 decision of the UN General Assembly to draft two separate Covenants because of the inherent differences between civil and political rights and economic, social, and cultural rights, the ICESCR only had a state reporting system as a way of monitoring states' compliance with their obligations. According to Article 16 ICESCR, States parties undertake to submit reports on the measures taken and the progress made in achieving the observance of the Covenant rights. Such reports may indicate factors and difficulties affecting the degree of fulfillment of obligations (Art. 17(2) ICESCR). Reports should be submitted to the UN and one of its principal organs, the Economic and Social Council (ECOSOC), was entrusted with the task of considering these reports. ECOSOC established a Working Group of Governmental Experts to deal with the state reports, but its actual role was left unclear (ECOSOC 1978). The Covenant itself did not provide for the creation of a supervisory committee as is the case with the International Covenant on Civil and Political Rights (ICCPR) which provides for the legal basis of the Human Rights Committee (Art. 28 ICCPR). The record of this Working Group in examining state reports was poor. The main criticism related to the politicized nature of the discussions, as the Group was composed of governmental experts, not of independents representatives, and the Group failed to establish standards for the evaluation of state reports (Craven 1995). In 1985, as a response to this unsatisfactory situation, ECOSOC established a new supervisory body to be composed of experts, acting in their personal capacity (ECOSOC 1985). The new body was to be named the Committee on Economic, Social and Cultural Rights and is a subsidiary body of ECOSOC, so not a treaty body similar to the Human Rights Committee. This means that members are elected by ECOSOC, not by the State parties to the ICESCR. This may raise questions about the legitimacy of the Committee (Khaliq and Churchill 2012). In 2007, the Human Rights Council adopted a resolution "to initiate a process to rectify, in accordance with international law, in particular the law of international treaties, the legal status of the Committee on Economic, Social and Cultural Rights, with the aim of placing the Committee on a par with all other treaty monitoring bodies" (Human Rights Council 2007). However, so far no decision has been taken on rectifying the legal status of the Committee (Human Rights Council 2007).

The new Committee began its work in 1987. It now meets twice or three times a year for sessions of 3 weeks. Over the years, its mandate, composition, and working methods have developed according to those of the other UN human rights treaty bodies with respect to the consideration of state reports. In addition, the Committee gave a fresh impetus to the examination of state reports. Some of these new developments will be discussed below. In 2013, an optional complaints procedure for individual complaints entered into force which grants individuals the right to submit complaints about alleged violations of economic, social, and cultural rights to the Committee. This was the final stage of a long-awaited process of bringing the Covenant to a par with the ICCPR in terms of providing for a remedy at the international level for cases of alleged violations of rights. The latter development will be discussed below.

The composition of the Committee is based on a geographical distribution of its members. These should be persons of high moral character and have recognized competence in the field of human rights. Members are elected by ECOSOC for 4 years with the possibility of re-election. The composition of the Committee in 2017 was such that the big majority of members had a legal background, i.e., professors of law or judges, while social scientists and economists were quite underrepresented. Although the Committee is performing legal functions and legal expertise is certainly required, it has quite rightly been argued by some commentators that more expertise on economic, health, social, and educational matters is very much desirable (Craven 1995; Dowell-Jones 2004). Such expertise would enrich the Committee's work and deepen its understanding of the nonlegal obstacles countries face in realizing the rights.

The Committee's Working Methods

The Committee engages in a so-called "constructive" dialogue with representatives of a State party whose periodic report is subject to examination (Coomans 2009a). State reports should be drafted in accordance with guidelines established by the Committee. These contain requests to provide detailed information about the extent to which a particular right has been realized in a country. For example, on the right to adequate food, a government should provide information on whether hunger and/or malnutrition exists in a country, with specific attention for the situation of vulnerable groups, such as the urban poor, children, and elderly people (UNCESCR Revised guidelines for reporting 2008). The dialogue is an oral exchange of views between members of the Committee and representatives of a government, usually in the form of questions and answers. This exchange of views is not meant to be confrontational but rather to assist a State party to better implement the Covenant rights. In order to prepare this dialogue, the Committee will establish a presessional working group, composed of five members, which is in charge of drafting a list of issues and questions that will constitute the principal focus of the dialogue with the reporting state (UNCESCR 2017d). The state is requested to answer these questions in writing before the public consideration of the state report takes place. This list of issues certainly has an added value, because it gives the Committee the opportunity to go beyond the often rather generally worded, descriptive and legalistic sections in the state report. It may ask for clarification and an exposition of the real difficulties affecting implementation of the Covenant. With a view to strengthening the effectiveness and efficiency of working methods, the Committee has decided to pilot a simplified reporting procedure by preparing lists of issues prior to reporting for states whose periodic reports were due in 2017. This means that states are asked to report on those specific issues in the state report, instead of presenting a general and comprehensive overview of law, policy, and practice of all economic, social, and cultural rights. The Human Rights Committee under the ICCPR has already quite some experience with this simplified reporting procedure.

The examination of the state report concludes with the adoption of Concluding Observations by the Committee. These contain an assessment of the progress made and obstacles encountered by the State party in realizing the rights. This document mentions positive developments, principal issues of concern, and suggestions and recommendations aimed at a better implementation of the Covenant provisions. Recommendations may deal with policy issues and legislative issues. Concluding Observations are not legally binding, but they do have authority, because they were adopted by the treaty body in charge of reviewing states' implementation of treaty obligations. States have the possibility to comment on Concluding Observations. According to O'Flaherty, the authority of Concluding Observations is stronger when a treaty body is of the view that a particular situation is a violation of the state's obligations, while the authority is weaker when a Concluding Observation only contains general advice aimed at a better implementation of the Covenant (O'Flaherty 2006). Through the constructive dialogue and the Concluding Observations, the Committee has potentially contributed to strengthening State parties accountability for their acts and omissions in the area of economic, social, and cultural rights implementation. However, the reporting procedure is a relatively weak mechanism as it is based on persuasion and its recommendations are non-enforceable. A detailed empirical study of 2014 on the domestic impact and effectiveness of Concluding Observations of six UN human treaties in the Netherlands, New Zealand, and Finland concluded that those of the UNCESCR have been negligible and ineffective (Krommendijk 2014). The reasons for this were, among others, that economic, social, and cultural rights were seen as aspirational and programmatic by the respective governments. The authority and quality of the Concluding Observations and the Committee were also questioned by the said governments. Finally, very few domestic actors in the three states mobilized and lobbied for the implementation of the Concluding Observations (Krommendijk 2014, 163).

Furthermore, States parties are often (very) late in submitting their periodic reports, but after reminders have been sent, governments may still be persuaded to submit a report. However, there are a number of countries whose reports are very significantly overdue. For these types of cases, the Committee has adopted a special procedure which entails that it will consider these countries in the absence of a state report but in the light of alternative information. This information may come from other UN human rights monitoring procedures, NGOs, specialized agencies, newspapers, magazines, research institutes, etc. The Committee has announced that it will consider the situation of nonreporting States parties and considerably overdue reports in 2017.

There are ample possibilities for NGOs to contribute to the consideration of state reports by the Committee. As the Committee is a subsidiary body of ECOSOC, the rules for NGO participation that apply to ECOSOC also apply to the Committee. This means that NGOs in general or in special consultative status with ECOSOC or on the UN Roster may submit a written statement to the Committee at the reporting session. An NGO without consultative status with ECOSOC may also submit a written statement, provided that it is sponsored by an NGO in consultative status with ECOSOC. NGOs may also participate in the work of the presessional working group by submitting written parallel or shadow reports, or by making an oral statement to the working group, or to the country rapporteur prior to its meeting. Finally, during each session of the Committee, one or more hearings are organized during which NGOs can voice their concerns in an oral statement about one of the countries whose report will be subject to examination at that session. NGOs, however, cannot participate in the dialogue between the Committee and representatives of governments.

Another important tool of the Committee is the adoption of General Comments. These are authoritative explanations and interpretations of the nature, content, and scope of treaty provisions, in particular substantive rights. These are based on the examination of state reports and are meant to assist state parties in the implementation of the Covenant at the domestic level and provide guidance to governments. They explain what is to be expected from states in terms of obligations and policy objectives seen through the lens of the Covenant. Over the years, the Committee has adopted General Comments on most of the rights included in the ICESCR, or on specific issues, such as the right to sexual and reproductive health (UNCESCR 2016c). Input for General Comments also comes from so-called Days of General Discussion that are organized during each session. Specialized agencies, NGOs, academics, UN Special Rapporteurs, and individual experts may submit written and oral information that might help the Committee in getting a proper understanding of substantive issues. For example, in February 2017, during its 60th session, the Committee held a Day of General Discussion on the draft General Comment on State obligations under the Covenant in the context of business activities. Over the years, General Comments have been adopted on most of the rights included in the Covenant. A recent and important one is General Comment 24 on obligations of States under the Covenant in the context of business activities (UNCESCR, General Comment 24 2017b). Some sections of this Comment will be discussed later on.

Still another tool that the Committee has used is the adoption of Statements to clarify and confirm its position on developments and topical issues that relate to Covenant obligations. They provide an opportunity for the Committee to stress that States parties act in a way that is in conformity with the ICESCR obligations. Similar to General Comments, Statements are meant to give direction to the legislation and policy of governments. Recent Statements relate to human rights defenders and economic, social, and cultural rights (2016b); the duties of States towards refugees and migrants under the ICESCR (2017e); public debt, austerity measures, and the ICESCR (2016b); and social protection floors (2015c). The Statement on the duties of States towards refugees and migrants under the Covenant (2017e) is important, because it confirms the Committee's view that economic, social, and cultural rights apply to everyone, irrespective one's legal status. The Committee said that "[a]ll people under the jurisdiction of the State concerned should enjoy Covenant rights. That includes asylum seekers and refugees, as well as other migrants, even when their situation in the country concerned is irregular" (UNCESCR, Statement on the duties of States towards refugees and migrants under the Covenant 2017e).

Clarifying States' Obligations with Regard to Economic, Social, and Cultural Rights

From the outset, it was clear that the Committee, which began its work in 1987, should focus on clarifying the normative content of the rights in the Covenant (Coomans 2009a). The first Chairperson of the Committee, Philip Alston, made some important proposals in this respect which served as a source of inspiration for the Committee in its future work (Alston 1987). One of the main challenges for the Committee was to clarify the nature of States parties' obligations resulting from Article 2(1) of the Covenant. This major issue was discussed at an academic expert meeting which took place in Maastricht, The Netherlands, in 1986. The outcome of this meeting was the so-called Limburg Principles on the Implementation of the International Covenant on Economic, Social and Cultural Rights (Coomans 2009b). They provide an interpretation of the nature and scope of States parties' obligations under Articles 2–5 in particular. These Principles were used by the Committee as inspiration and input when it started drafting a General Comment on Article 2(1). This key General Comment 3 was adopted in 1990 at the fifth session. It laid the foundation for the future normative and monitoring activities of the Committee. The importance of this General Comment is great and needs to be discussed here in some detail. The text of Article 2(1) ICESCR is as follows: "Each State Party to the present Covenant undertakes to take steps, individually and through international assistance and co-operation, especially economic and technical, to the maximum of its available resources, with a view to achieving progressively the full realization of the rights recognized in the present Covenant by all appropriate means, including particularly the adoption of legislative measures."

The Committee begins its General Comment 3 by clarifying the meaning of the obligation "to take steps." It is of the view that, although the full realization of the Covenant rights may be realized progressively, a State Party must begin to take measures aimed at implementing the rights shortly after the Covenant gets into force for that particular state. Such measures should be "deliberate, concrete, and targeted as clearly as possible" towards meeting its obligations (UNCESCR 1991, para. 10). This means that a government may not lean back and take a passive attitude once it has ratified the Covenant. After all, the ICESCR is aimed at realizing higher levels of realization of the substantive rights. However, the Article 2(1) clause "achieving progressively the full realization of the rights" means that the drafters were aware of the fact that in many countries full realization will not be achieved in a short period of time. Therefore, in the view of the Committee, on the one hand progressive realization is "a necessary flexibility device" which reflects the realities and difficulties of the real world (UNCESCR 1991, para. 10). On the other hand, the object and main feature of the Covenant is that it lays down obligations for States aimed at the full realization of rights. Consequently, the phrase "progressive realization" imposes an obligation to move as expeditiously and effectively as possible towards full realization. Deliberately retrogressive measures which imply a step backwards in the level of enjoyment of rights would require careful consideration and full justification in light of object and purpose of the Covenant.

In General Comment 3, the Committee introduces a new concept that is meant to lay down some minimum level of enjoyment of a right that should be guaranteed under all circumstances. This is the notion of "minimum core obligations to ensure the satisfaction of, at the very least, minimum essential levels of each of the rights" (UNCESCR 1991). Thus, each right has a minimum or core content which must be observed under all circumstances. If such a minimum level cannot be realized, a human right would lose its raison d'être. In other words, the core content of a right refers to the essential elements of a right in terms of protecting human dignity. The Committee argued that "a State party in which any significant number of individuals is deprived of essential foodstuffs, of essential primary health care, of basic shelter and housing, or of the most basic forms of education, is prima facie, failing to discharge its obligations under the Covenant" (UNCESCR 1991, para. 10). The Committee also thinks that, in light of the obligation to take steps to the maximum of its available resources, states must give priority to the satisfaction of minimum core obligations. In this respect, it is important to note that "available resources" both refer to domestic resources and those from the international community through international cooperation and assistance. It may also imply that a state must reorient national priorities, for example, from spending on military equipment to health issues. In addition, a government may be obliged to reallocate resources within one sector, for example, from higher education to primary education. In times of severe resource constraints, a government may also be required to adopt low-cost targeted programs or safety nets to protect the most vulnerable members of society. The 2016 Committee Statement on Public Debt, Austerity Measures and the ICESCR should be read and understood in light of General Comment 3. The final clause to be mentioned here is the obligation to take steps "by all appropriate means." Legislative measures are singled out in Article 2(1), but other measures may also be appropriate, depending on the domestic situation. One may think of judicial remedies, financial measures such as a progressive income policy, a housing policy facilitated by allowances for low-income households, or the distribution of food to those in need who are unable to take care of themselves.

General Comment 3 has been influential, because some of its key notions have been applied in other General Comments on substantive rights. An example is the notion of core obligations which is included in all General Comments since 1999. Most General Comments on substantive rights have been structured along similar lines. They include, in addition to an introductory part, sections on the normative content of a right, obligations of States parties, violations, implementation at the national level, and obligations of actors other than States. Each part is divided into subsections on specific issues, such as nondiscrimination and equality, monitoring domestic implementation and remedies, and accountability. As already mentioned, General Comments are meant to assist States parties in fulfilling their obligations under the Covenant. They primarily have an interpretative function; however, in the view of some authors, "some General Comments seem to go beyond interpretation and appear to be quasi-legislative in nature" (Khaliq and Churchill 2012, 206). The Committee broke new ground by drafting a General Comment on a right which is not included in the Covenant. This is about the right to water whose legal basis, according to the Committee, can be found in

Article 11(1), the right of everyone to an adequate standard of living and Article 12, the right to health (General Comment 15 2002). This General Comment has been criticized for creating a new right which states have not recognized and which did not exist in international law. In addition, the template used for drafting General Comments was said to focus too much on a State-centric model, largely excluding the role and responsibilities of the private sector (Tully 2005). This General Comment has been characterized as having an even stronger legislative nature (Khaliq and Churchill 2012). All General Comments can be seen as soft law documents.

There are other concepts and notions that have been developed in the academic debate on economic, social, and cultural rights and subsequently applied in General Comments. These include the so-called typology of obligations – to respect, to protect, and to fulfill – meant to clarify and specify obligations of States parties (Sepúlveda 2003). Each General Comment on a substantive right uses this typology to define negative and positive state obligations. For example, the obligation to respect the right to social security requires States parties to refrain from interfering directly or indirectly with the enjoyment of the right to social security. The obligation to protect requires that States parties prevent third parties, such as employers, from interfering with the enjoyment of the right to social security. Finally, the obligation to fulfill requires States parties to adopt the necessary measures, such as the establishment and implementation of a social security scheme, directed towards the full realization of this right.

A "Violations Approach" to Economic, Social, and Cultural Rights

Another approach developed by academics and subsequently applied by the Committee in General Comments is the so-called violations approach to economic, social, and cultural rights (Coomans 2009a). The idea to identify violations of economic, social, and cultural rights came up as response to the problems encountered in measuring progressive realization of human rights. After all, Article 2(1) ICESCR grants considerable discretion to governments in taking measures to realize the rights. In addition, there was a lack of an agreed methodology and reliable indicators and statistical information to assess whether a state was complying with its obligation to realize progressively the rights (Robertson 1994; Chapman 2007) Consequently, there was a lack of effective monitoring of states' performance. An alternative approach was suggested by Audrey Chapman (Chapman 1996). Building on the Limburg Principles, which already contained a few criteria for identifying violations of economic, social, and cultural rights (Limburg Principles 1987, paras. 70–72), she proposed to distinguish between three types of violations: violations resulting from actions and policies on the part of governments, violations related to patterns of discrimination, and violations related to a state's failure to fulfill minimum core obligations emanating from rights (Chapman 1996). This violations approach was not meant to replace measuring progressive realization but rather to complement it. Early in 1997, an expert meeting was held in Maastricht whose objective was to draft guidelines for identifying violations of economic, social, and cultural rights. Such guidelines could be of assistance to monitoring expert and judicial bodies at the national, regional, and international levels. The outcome of this meeting was the adoption of the Maastricht Guidelines on Violations of Economic, Social and Cultural Rights of 1998. These Guidelines distinguish between violations as a consequence of active interference (acts of commission) by the State and a failure to act (acts of omission) by the State. Examples of the former include forced evictions of people from their home or land or forced closure of schools. Examples of the latter are a failure to adopt a law on nondiscrimination and equal treatment in labor matters or the failure to take steps to address the negative consequences of the privatization of health systems (reduced accessibility due to higher fees). Furthermore, violations related to patterns of discrimination are also referred to in the Maastricht Guidelines. An example is the exclusion and discrimination of people from Roma descent in schools and housing policy in a number of European countries. Finally, violations of minimum core obligations are identified as a type of violations in the Maastricht Guidelines. An example is the failure to make primary education compulsory and free to all as required by Article 13(2)(a) and 14 ICESCR.

However, not all of these acts or failures amount to violations of economic, social, and cultural rights. The Maastricht Guidelines distinguish between the inability of a state to comply and its unwillingness to comply with treaty obligations. The former may be due to an objective lack of resources as a result of a natural disaster. There is thus an objective justification for not complying with treaty provisions. Such a situation may call for international assistance and cooperation. The unwillingness of a State to comply may be caused by a lack of political will, deliberately made policy choices, retrogressive measures, and corruption. Such a situation would certainly qualify as a human rights violation. A good example were the deliberate actions of the Nigerian authorities violating the right to health, housing, food, and a healthy environment of the Ogoni people in the Niger delta in the 1990s. These acts were qualified as violations by the African Commission on Human and Peoples' Rights (Coomans 2003).

This so-called violations approach was adopted by the Committee in its General Comments, starting with the General Comment on the right to health by explaining what a violation of this right means (UNCESCR, General Comment 14 2000). However, in its Concluding Observations on the examination of periodic state reports, the Committee is quite hesitant to use the language of violation because such language would not fit within the so-called constructive dialogue approach between the Committee and the government of the reporting state. Instead, it uses language which expresses (deep) concern about a particular situation. However, the careful listener will understand that the Committee is often referring to situations which amount to a violation of economic, social, and cultural rights.

A Right to Individual Complaints

The fact that the ICESCR lacked an individual complaints procedure for a long time has its roots in discussions about the nature of civil and political versus economic, social, and cultural rights in the 1950s, when the Covenant was drafted, as mentioned above. The Committee took up the issue of developing an Optional Protocol to the Covenant providing for a complaints procedure in the early 1990s. These efforts were meant to restore the imbalance in the supervisory mechanisms between the two Covenants. This was deemed to be necessary in light of the principle expressed in the 1993 Vienna Declaration of the Second World Conference on Human Rights that all human rights must be treated in a fair and equal manner, on the same footing and with the same emphasis. Also Article 8 of the Universal Declaration of Human Rights requires establishing effective remedies in case of alleged violations of human rights, thus including economic, social, and cultural rights. The ratio for having a complaints protocol to the Covenant was well expressed by the Committee. It said: "As long as the majority of the provisions of the Covenant (and most notably those relating to education, health care, food and nutrition, and housing) are not the subject of any detailed jurisprudential scrutiny at the international level, it is most unlikely that they will be subject to such examination at the national level either" (UNCESCR, Towards an Optional Protocol 1992, para. 24).

Over the years, the question of adding a complaints procedure to the ICESCR led to an intense debate in academic circles, among governments and in UN bodies. Some have emphasized the need to close the "protection gap" in the area of economic, social, and cultural rights (Alston 1991), while others have argued that, taking into account the nature of economic, social and cultural rights, a quasi-judicial procedure is not a suitable mechanism for vindicating these rights (Tomuschat 2005; Dennis & Stewart 2004). In addition, some governments remain opposed to accepting a complaints procedure at the international level for rights which they consider as primarily directed at governments and therefore not justiciable. Many NGOs, on the other hand, strongly advocated the adoption of a complaints procedure to the ICESCR. Over the years, several proposals have been made containing draft texts for a Protocol, both by academics (Arambulo 1999) and the Committee itself (UNCESCR 1997).

The debate got a fresh impetus when the UN Commission on Human Rights in 2003 decided to establish an "Open-Ended Working Group," with the mandate to discuss options for the elaboration of an Optional Protocol to the ICESCR. In April 2008, after 4 years of intensive discussions, the Working Group was able to submit a text for a Protocol to the Human Rights Council. This text was adopted by the Council on 18 June 2008 and by the General Assembly on 10 December 2008 with resolution 63/117 (UNGA 2008). The Protocol entered into force on 5 May 2013. At the time of writing, the Protocol has 23 States parties.

In addition to the general concerns about the justiciability of economic, social, and cultural rights, a number of specific issues were raised during the discussions in the Working Group. The first one was whether, in addition to individual complaints, collective complaints would also be possible under the Protocol. This would give NGOs, either national or international, the right to submit a communication, more or less similar to the Collective Complaints Procedure under the European Social Charter. Another issue was the scope, ratione materiae, of the right to complain. This relates to several questions, namely, whether the Protocol should apply to all of the substantive rights listed in Part III of the Covenant, whether complaints about the general clause of progressive realization in Article 2(1) should be included, whether States should be free to choose the rights or provisions to which the right to complain should apply (the so-called à la carte approach), or alternatively whether a State could declare that it does not recognize the competence of the Committee to consider communications under certain provisions (the so-called opt-out clause). Another key issue was how the Committee should deal with complaints alleging that a State has failed to progressively realize the rights as provided for in Article 2(1). What type of standard should be used to assess an alleged violation of the notion of progressive realization?

In the text that was finally adopted by the Open-Ended Working Group and the Human Rights Council, the right to complain is limited to communications by individuals. The possibility of lodging collective complaints was not accepted (Article 2). Communications may deal with alleged violations of any of the right set forth in Part II and Part III of the Covenant, thus excluding the right of self-determination in Part I. This means that both an à la carte approach and an opt-out possibility were rejected. In Article 3, the Protocol provides for admissibility criteria, including the exhaustion of domestic remedies. The solution found for reviewing complaints alleging a violation of the obligation to progressively realize one or more of the rights is included in Article 8(4) on the examination of the merits of a communication. The article reads as follows: "When examining communications under the present Protocol, the Committee shall consider the reasonableness of the steps taken by the State Party in accordance with Part II of the Covenant. In doing so, the Committee shall bear in mind that the State Party may adopt a range of possible policy measures for the implementation of the rights set in the Covenant."

The concept of reasonableness as a standard of review was probably copied from the jurisprudence of the Constitutional Court of South Africa which applies this standard for assessing the extent to which the government has complied with its obligation to progressively realize a number of economic, social, and cultural rights listed in the South African Constitution (Liebenberg 2010). The Committee is also in favor of applying some form of reasonableness review and it has elaborated on this in a 2007 Statement. In that Statement, the Committee mentioned several criteria to be applied in evaluating whether States have complied with the obligation to take steps to the maximum of available resources when examining cases under an optional Protocol (UNCESCR, Statement 2007). In that Statement, the Committee also said that it would respect the margin of appreciation of a State Party to determine the optimum use of its resources and to adopt national policies and prioritize certain resource demands over others (UNCESCR, Statement 2007). This Statement is important, because it is clearly meant to reassure especially Western states that the Committee would not interfere with policy decisions in the field of economic, social, and cultural rights, provided these measures are reasonable. Finally, the Protocol provides for an interstate communications procedure (Article 10) an inquiry procedure (Article 11) and the possibility of so-called interim measures aimed at avoiding irreparable damage to victims (Article 5).

The Protocol is a logical step aimed a remedying a long-term gap in human rights protection on the international level. This is the more so now that international complaints under other treaties may already deal with alleged violations of economic, social, and cultural rights. These include special communications procedures in the International Labour Organisation, the collective complaints procedure adopted under the Protocol to the European Social Charter and the Optional Protocol to the UN Convention on the Elimination of All Forms of Discrimination Against Women. States have thus already voluntarily accepted the possibility to bring alleged violations of economic, social, and cultural rights before an international quasi-judicial body of experts. The optional complaints procedure therefore acknowledges and reaffirms the indivisibility of all human rights.

In addition, the Protocol is important for a number of other reasons. First of all, a complaints procedure at the international level strengthens the accountability of governments before an international body for complying with their treaty obligations. These governments come under a strong pressure to justify their policies, their acts, or their failure to act. In addition, a Protocol to the Covenant allows NGOs and lawyers to support victims of violations of economic, social, and cultural rights and bring their claims before an international quasi-judicial body. Finally, and perhaps most importantly, in some cases, a complaint lodged with the Committee and the views or findings adopted by it may lead to a remedy for the victim. This can be the halt of the violation; compensation for the harm incurred; a commitment by the government to observe its treaty obligations, for example, by amending domestic legislation; and the actual enjoyment of a right, for example, getting access to a school, health service, or housing program. These possible outcomes depend, of course, on the willingness of the government to implement in good faith the views of the Committee which are authoritative but strictly speaking nonbinding under international law.

At the time of writing, 20 communications have been submitted against two States: 16 against Spain and 4 against Ecuador. The total number of complaints lodged was 23 (January 2018). The majority of the cases have been declared inadmissible by the Committee and only very few cases ended with views on the merits. Some cases against Spain dealt with an alleged violation of the right to adequate housing as a result of an eviction of individuals from their home. A good example is a case in which the Committee concluded that Spain had violated the right to housing of a family with young children, who were evicted from a rented room in a flat without being provided with alternative housing. In 2012, the family stopped receiving unemployment benefits and was unable to continue paying the rent. In its findings in case 5/2015, the Committee noted that although the eviction by court order was legal, the authorities had not taken all the necessary steps to provide the family with alternative housing. The Committee reviewed the complaint in light of the economic and financial crisis in the country and asked the government of Spain to put into operation a comprehensive plan to guarantee the right to adequate housing for people with low incomes (UNCESCR 2015a). These are promising views in an important case which have the potential of setting a trend for future cases.

The Extraterritorial Scope of Application of the Covenant

Realization of economic, social, and cultural rights essentially has primarily a territorial scope as it normally takes place on the territory of States. As laid down in Article 2(1) of the Covenant, each of the 167 States parties (as of January 2018) is under an obligation to take all appropriate measures to progressively realize the economic, social, and cultural rights listed in the treaty. However, states do not exist in isolation. As members of the community of States, they are dependent on international relations and cooperation to deal with problems that go beyond national borders. The need for international cooperation is a key principle of present-day life in the era of globalization in which we live. The process of globalization is crucial for a proper understanding of the international dimensions of the realization of economic, social, and cultural rights. Globalization as an economic and social phenomenon is characterized by an increase in international transactions between a growing number of actors, such as companies, individuals (through worldwide migration), international governmental organizations, nongovernmental organizations, and States. The nature of involvement of actors in this process is also changing; we witness an increase in the role and responsibilities of private actors in economic life, a diminishing role of the State with trends towards privatization, and a stronger involvement of international governmental organizations and international market forces in the economic and financial policy of states in situations of financial and economic austerity and through adjustment programs propagated by the European Union, the International Monetary Fund, and the World Bank. The process of economic globalization has also led to an unequal distribution of the positive effects of globalization between people living in the North and those in the South. In other words, the realization of economic, social, and cultural rights increasingly has international dimensions (Kinley 2009).

Furthermore, since the end of the Second World War, the nature of international law has changed dramatically. Not only did the law of cooperation between states develop alongside the law of co-existence. The more recent process of globalization has also led to a trend towards a wider interpretation of concepts traditionally related to territory, such as jurisdiction and national sovereignty in matters of human rights (Langford et al. 2013). What then is the relationship between developments towards globalization and the universal protection of economic, social, and cultural rights? The UNCESCR has noted that in itself globalization as a social phenomenon is not incompatible with the idea of social, economic, and cultural rights. However, "taken together ... and if not complemented by appropriate additional policies, globalisation risks downgrading the central place accorded to human rights by the Charter of the United Nations and the International Bill of Human Rights in particular" (UNCESCR, Statement on Globalisation 1999, para. 92). In other words, the changed (and changing) nature and pattern of economic and financial transactions worldwide may jeopardise the enjoyment of economic, social, and cultural rights in many countries. The challenge then is to make the ICESCR fit for the era of globalization and to reach beyond traditional concepts of state sovereignty in order to provide for international solidarity and achieve global justice. At the time when the treaty was drafted, only States were the principal actors on the international plane. The role of the State as the principal actor responsible and accountable for the realization of these rights is still paramount but other actors, such as international organizations or companies may also have an impact on the actual enjoyment or lack of enjoyment of these rights. The question then is how the State, as a State Party to the ICESCR, can be held responsible for the conduct of these nonstate actors who often act extraterritorially or whose conduct has extraterritorial effects. For example, if the World Bank intends to financially support the construction of a dam in a developing country and if, as a consequence of this project, indigenous people face eviction from their land and homes: has a Western donor State an obligation under human rights law to oppose approval of this project by the competent body of the World Bank? Also, the actions of States outside their own territory through, for example, concluding investment and tax treaties or facilitating international trade deals may have human rights effects in other countries. Does the State have human rights obligations due to an extraterritorial application of the ICESCR? What does international human rights law have to say about this?

Over the years, the Committee has dealt with the extraterritorial scope of the ICESCR. It has indicated that the Covenant may have an effect beyond the borders of States parties, meaning that States may be bound by their obligations under the treaty when acting extraterritorially. This idea has been developed cautiously but progressively in the General Comments, the Statements, and Concluding Observations adopted by the Committee. The following section will study how the Committee has used this notion in its work. It will focus in particular on the recent General Comment 24 on state obligations under the ICESCR in the context of business activities.

The Committee and the Extraterritorial Application of the Covenant

Article 2(1) ICESCR refers to the obligation of every State Party "to take steps, individually and through international assistance and cooperation, especially economic and technical, to the maximum of its available resources, with a view to achieving progressively the full realisation of the rights recognised in the present Covenant by all appropriate means." The ICESCR does not mention territory or jurisdiction as delimiting criteria for the scope of application of the treaty. Instead, it refers to the international or transnational dimensions of the realization of economic, social, and cultural rights. Therefore it is suggested that a certain extraterritorial (in the sense of international) scope was intended by the drafters and is part of the treaty (Craven, 144). This is also clear from the Preamble of the Covenant which contains a reference to the obligation of States under the Charter of the United Nations to promote universal respect for, and observance of, human rights and freedoms. There was consequently no need to limit explicitly the protection of economic, social, and cultural rights to those people resident in the territory of a State party only.

The UNCESCR began to develop its views on the extraterritorial reach of the ICESCR in a number of General Comments that were adopted in the early 1990s. These Comments dealt mainly with the nature of States parties' obligations resulting from the key provision of the Covenant, Article 2(1). A number of Statements on topical issues also contain references to the notion of the international reach of the Covenant, such as the one on poverty and economic, social, and cultural rights

(UNCESCR, Statement on Poverty 2001). A number of General Comments on substantive rights deal with the obligation of a State party to regulate and monitor the activities of transnational corporations based in that country who, through their activities in other countries, may affect the rights of the local residents. In General Comments and Concluding Observations, the Committee also calls upon States to take into account their obligations resulting from the ICESCR as members of intergovernmental organizations, such as the International Monetary Fund and the World Bank. In addition, the Committee deals with the international scope of the Covenant in its Concluding Observations when it calls upon States to allocate 0.7% of its Gross National Product (GNP) to development cooperation. Finally, the Committee occasionally discusses the extraterritorial application of the Covenant in the framework of a situation of occupation of foreign territory by a State party. A case in point is the occupation of the Palestinian Territories by Israel (Coomans 2011).

In General Comment 3 on the nature of States' Parties obligations, adopted in December 1990, the Committee dealt for the first time with the international scope of the Covenant. It referred to the obligation of States included in Article 2(1) to take steps, individually and through international assistance and cooperation, especially economic and technical aimed at the full realization of economic, social, and cultural rights. It is helpful to quote here the relevant parts of this General Comment:

> 13. The Committee notes that the phrase 'to the maximum of its available resources' was intended by the drafters of the Covenant to refer to both the resources existing within a State and those available from the international community through international cooperation and assistance. Moreover, the essential role of such cooperation in facilitating the full realization of the relevant rights is further underlined by the specific provisions contained in articles 11, 15, 22 and 23. With respect to article 22 the Committee has already drawn attention, in General Comment 2 (1990), to some of the opportunities and responsibilities that exist in relation to international cooperation. Article 23 also specifically identifies 'the furnishing of technical assistance' as well as other activities, as being among the means of 'international action for the achievement of the rights recognized...'
>
> 14. The Committee wishes to emphasize that in accordance with Articles 55 and 56 of the Charter of the United Nations, with well-established principles of international law, and with the provisions of the Covenant itself, international cooperation for development and thus for the realization of economic, social and cultural rights is an obligation of all States. It is particularly incumbent upon those States which are in a position to assist others in this regard. The Committee notes in particular the importance of the Declaration on the Right to Development adopted by the General Assembly in its resolution 41/128 of 4 December 1986 and the need for States parties to take full account of all of the principles recognized therein. It emphasizes that, in the absence of an active programme of international assistance and cooperation on the part of all those States that are in a position to undertake one, the full realization of economic, social and cultural rights will remain an unfulfilled aspiration in many countries. In this respect, the Committee also recalls the terms of its General Comment 2 (1990).

The focus of the Committee in these two paragraphs is on the obligation of international cooperation, which is a duty for States under general international law. Cooperation and assistance should be aimed at contributing to the realization of economic, social, and cultural rights in other countries. One may assume that cooperation and assistance entail positive measures requiring the allocation of resources. The Committee does not distinguish between cooperation and assistance.

One would argue that cooperation is the wider term meaning a relationship providing for mutual advantages for the participating States while providing assistance is a unilateral act requiring efforts from one State to the benefit of another State (Craven, 147). The latter is often in a dependent and weak position.

The Committee has developed the concept of international assistance and cooperation further in the context of the eradication of poverty. It has used the notion of core obligations to clarify what is required from developed States and others that are in a position to assist. The Committee explained that "the core obligations of economic, social and cultural rights have a crucial role to play in national and international developmental policies, including anti-poverty strategies. When grouped together, the core obligations establish an international minimum threshold that all developmental policies should be designed to respect. In accordance with General Comment No. 14 [on the right to health], it is particularly incumbent on all those who can assist, to help developing countries respect this international minimum threshold. If a national or international anti-poverty strategy does not reflect this minimum threshold, it is inconsistent with the legally binding obligations of the State party" (UNCESCR, Statement on Poverty 2001, para. 17).

It is not clear whether the Committee is of the view that developed countries have a legal obligation to assist other countries in implementing poverty elimination policies with a view to fulfilling core obligations resulting from economic, social, and cultural rights. Core obligations have been qualified as nonderogable by the Committee. Core obligations give rise to international responsibilities for developed States (Statement on Poverty 2001, para. 16). It added that "because poverty is a global phenomenon, core obligations have great relevance to some individuals and communities living in the richest States" (UNCESCR, Statement on Poverty 2001, para. 18). It should be noted that, in the view of the Committee, the fulfillment of core obligations in a country that has to cope with severe poverty does not give rise to obligations for developed States but merely to responsibilities. The Committee may have been aware of this inconsistency but was perhaps reluctant to impose hard obligations on rich States that cannot be based directly and unambiguously on Covenant provisions. However, the meaning of responsibilities is vague: is it possible to impose and enforce the fulfillment of responsibilities?

In addition, the question may be raised how the Committee will assess whether a (rich) State and others are "in a position to assist." Will it look at the GDP of such States, their voting power in the International Monetary Fund and the World Bank and/or its Official Development Assistance? Furthermore, the qualification of core obligations as nonderogable would greatly strengthen their legal character. It would mean that their legal nature goes much further than mere responsibilities and would apply under all circumstances. This is something to which developed States would object. It should be recalled that the principal obligations to guarantee human rights lie with the national States. International obligations by other States are of a complementary nature. Finally, it is not clear what is meant by the clause that core obligations have great relevance to some individuals and communities living in the richest States. Does the Committee have The Bill and Melissa Gates Foundation, George Soros and the business community in mind?

Extraterritorial Obligations and Business Activities Abroad

In its General Comments and Concluding Observations, the Committee has paid attention to different dimensions of the extraterritorial scope of the ICESCR as a consequence of measures and actions by States parties and other actors which have an effect on economic, social, and cultural rights of persons residing in other countries. It has dealt with, inter alia, UN sanctions, military occupation, international assistance, and (development) cooperation as well as with the activities of companies abroad (Coomans 2011).

Recently, the focus has been put on specifying State obligations in the context of business activities. General Comment 24 deals with this issue. Its goal is to clarify the duties of States parties to ensure compliance with human rights in situations in which corporate activities over which States exercise control negatively affect economic, social, and cultural rights domestically and abroad (UNCESCR, General Comment 24 2017b). Section III.C. of this General Comment deals with extraterritorial obligations. In the Committee's view, extraterritorial obligations follow from the fact that the obligations of States according to Article 2(1) are not restricted to individuals within the territory or subject to the jurisdiction of State parties. In addition, that same provision refers to "international assistance and cooperation" as ways of realizing the Covenant rights. The rationale for extraterritorial obligations flowing from the "international assistance and cooperation" clause in Article 2(1) to regulate companies is that "it would be contradictory ... to allow a State to remain passive where an actor domiciled in its territory and/or jurisdiction, and thus under its control and authority, harms the rights of others in other States, or where conduct by such an actor may lead to foreseeable harm being caused" (UNCESCR, General Comment 24 2017b, para. 27). The Committee identifies an extraterritorial obligation to protect which requires States to take measures to "prevent and redress infringements of the Covenant rights that occur outside their territories due to the activities of business entities over which they can exercise control" (UNCESCR, General Comment 24, para. 30). Such an obligation to protect also requires home States to ensure that corporations act with due diligence in regulating and overseeing the activities of their subsidiaries and business partners (such as subcontractors) in the host State. Although the language used in this General Comment is not mandatory and leaves discretion to States to take measures, it goes further than the UN Guiding Principles on Business and Human Rights (Ruggie Principles) according to which States should set out clearly the expectation that all business enterprises domiciled in their territory and/or jurisdiction respect human rights throughout their operations. According to Ruggie, States are at present not generally required under international human rights law to regulate the extraterritorial activities of business domiciled in their territory and/or jurisdiction (Ruggie Principles I.A.2 and Commentary 2011). The UNCESCR, for its part, clearly identifies such an obligation. It is likely that the drafters of this General Comment found inspiration in the Maastricht Principles on the Extraterritorial Obligations of States in the Area of Economic, Social and Cultural Rights to which the General Comment also refers. In particular, the obligation to protect of the home state of corporations has been explained in the Principles. These are drawn from international law and aim to clarify the content of extraterritorial State obligations (Maastricht Principles 2011). One could conclude that in the Committee's view the extraterritorial obligation to protect is essentially a home State obligation with an extraterritorial effect. It does not entail the exercise of extraterritorial jurisdiction. In its Concluding Observations, the Committee seems to have adopted a similar view, emphasizing the need for a due diligence approach by the home State of multinational companies. The Committee did so in its Concluding Observations on Belgium (2013a), Norway (2013b), China (2014), Canada (2016a), and The Netherlands (2017g). General Comment 24 constitutes an important contribution to setting a normative framework for regulating the activities of business activities through the obligations of States. It has a strong focus on extraterritorial obligations which makes sense in an era characterized by economic globalization and the need to regulate the activities of companies abroad. The Committee's approach in this Comment is progressive in the sense of going beyond the Ruggie Principles framework.

Future Potential

The future potential of the Committee lies in particular in its ability to contribute to making the implementation of economic, social, and cultural rights stronger at the domestic level. This can be done through the reporting procedure by focusing on the follow-up given by States parties to Concluding Observations. The Committee recently adopted a procedure aimed at assessing whether a State party has given follow-up to a selected number of recommendations that require urgent action (UNCESCR, Follow-up procedure 2017c; UNCESCR, Concluding Observations on the Netherlands 2017g). A State party is required to respond to the request for urgent action within 18 months. Follow-up reports submitted by the State will be assessed in terms of sufficient/insufficient progress made in response to the recommendations. This procedure will raise the pressure on States and help in furthering that Concluding Observations will be picked up by civil society organizations as tools to hold the government accountable.

Another potential that the Committee is able to pursue is to give a fresh impetus to the justiciability of economic, social, and cultural rights at the domestic level through the examination of cases under the Optional Protocol. The decision to become a State party is a voluntary sovereign act; however, once ratified, it should have consequences at the domestic level: "[T]he mere possibility that complaints might be brought before an international forum may or even should stimulate governments to ensure that effective remedies are available at the national level. A complaints procedure at the international level would also strengthen the recognition of economic, social and cultural rights. It would also stimulate a government to adopt and implement legislative and policy measures to comply with obligations under the Covenant, because in case it does not, there will be a risk of facing one or more complaints" (Coomans 2002, 197).

So far, the number of State parties to the Optional Protocol is rather small. This may gradually increase over the years. The number of cases submitted and the number of State parties involved is also quite small. However, the expectation may be voiced that the development of a good body of case law based on a reasonableness review of the merits of the cases and authoritative interpretations of the Covenant could help to confirm that cases of alleged violations of economic, social, and cultural rights can be fully justiciable. Views of the Committee can become powerful legal opinions which cannot easily be ignored by a State. Recently, the Committee has adopted a procedure on the Committee's follow-up to views under the Optional Protocol. The aim is to keep the pressure on the State Party to foster that recommendations relating to the position of the victim as well as recommendations of a more general nature are being implemented (UNCESCR, Working methods concerning follow-up to Views 2017f).

Now that the Committee has recently adopted General Comment 24 on State obligations in the context of business activities, it is in a better position to assess the measures taken by States to regulate, monitor, and sanction the activities of business at home and abroad which negatively impact on economic, social, and cultural rights. The next step should be that Concluding Observations on States about business activities of companies over which States exercise control are specific and provide clear and concrete guidance for measures by States. The Committee has cautiously embarked on such an approach in its Concluding Observations on China (2014), The Netherlands (2017g), and Australia (2017a). However, this should be expanded and strengthened by being more explicit on the nature of the obligation and measures to be taken by the State. The Committee may also recommend the type of remedy that is most appropriate in such a case. Such an approach would help in making the rather vague due diligence obligation tangible and concrete and consequently easier to translate to the domestic level. It would also contribute to making the ICESCR fit for the challenges of economic globalization.

Challenges Ahead

One issue which has received little attention from the Committee is the relationship with UN specialized agencies and other intergovernmental organizations competent in the field of economic, social, and cultural issues, such as the World Health Organisation (WHO), the International Labour Organisation (ILO), UNESCO (the UN Organisation for Education, Science and Culture), the Food and Agricultural Organization (FAO), and the International Monetary Fund and the World Bank (Alston 1979). This may also include the World Trade Organisation and the European Union. Article 18 ICESCR deals with the relationship with specialized agencies but has largely remained a dead letter. The Committee should begin an ongoing dialogue with such international organizations whose standard-setting activities, policies, and operational activities may impact on economic, social, and cultural rights, either positively or negatively. Many of those organizations are engaged in international assistance and cooperation but usually do not do so from an economic, social, and cultural rights point of view. For example, the World Bank has been criticized strongly for its inability to engage in a meaningful manner with the international human rights framework and to assist its member States in complying with their human rights obligations (Alston 2015). The obligations of States when they act as members of international organizations have also received little attention from the Committee (Coomans 2007). This applies in particular when States vote in favor of so-called "destructive acts" (in the sense of violating economic, social, and cultural rights) as members of a decision-making body of an international organization, especially when it would have been foreseeable that such a decision negatively impacts economic, social, and cultural rights. The Committee has occasionally addressed this issue in its Concluding Observations and in a Statement (UNCESCR, Statement on Public Debt 2016b) but had done so only in general terms. So far the Committee has not paid in-depth and detailed attention to the plurality of actors involved and the diversity and division of obligations and responsibilities between the different actors in specific situations or cases. In light of the increasing role of international financial institutions in financing for development and reorganizing the finances and the economy of debtor states, more attention should be given by the Committee to the relevance and practical meaning of the ICESCR in such situations.

Another thematic issue that deserves attention from the Committee is the question how the UN Sustainable Development Goals (SDGs), which strongly relate to economic, social, and cultural rights, can be implemented at the domestic level by adopting a human rights-based approach. In other words, how can the SDGs be translated into human rights language? At the same time, a critical assessment of the SDGs would be necessary because they fail to indicate a clear division of labor between duty-holders for eradicating poverty (Pogge and Sengupta 2016). The Committee should take up that question and devote a Statement to it. In addition, the Committee could address the implementation of the SDGs when examining State reports.

So far the Committee has not dealt in a structural way with the issue of climate change and human rights, in particular the protection of economic, social, and cultural rights. Many economic, social, and cultural rights will be affected as a result of climate change, such as the right to food, work, health, and housing. The Committee could engage with this challenge by discussing and designing a human rights-based approach aimed at guiding global policies and measures to address climate change and promote respect for economic, social, and cultural rights. This could be done through a discussion of reports of States which are vulnerable to the effects of climate change, such as island-states, but also through a General Comment devoted to this issue.

The question has been raised whether the ICESCR with its strong reliance on the State as provider of welfare services is perhaps outdated in a situation where market forces play a key role and individuals have a responsibility for their own destiny (Tomuschat 2008). It is true that the Covenant was drafted and adopted more than 50 years ago when there was world-wide optimism about rising levels of welfare all over the world. Does this mean that in an unstable global market economy the State can no longer be seen as the protector of economic, social, and cultural rights, now that its role has been reduced? It is submitted that this is not the case. Especially during a domestic and international economic and financial crisis, the State, in accordance with its treaty obligations under the ICESCR, has to ensure that minimum essential levels of economic, social, and cultural rights are protected, especially for vulnerable and marginalized groups. Austerity measures with retrogressive effects on the enjoyment of economic, social, and cultural rights, cuts in the budgets and decreasing levels of welfare need to be justified and scrutinized in light of human rights obligations of States. Prior human rights impact assessments of such measures need to be undertaken. The Committee can play a key role in holding States accountable for the effects of such measures and has actually done so when examining the State reports of Spain and Greece (UNCESCR, Concluding Observations on Spain 2012 and on Greece 2015b). In the case of Greece, the Committee recommended the State party to "further ensure that its obligations under the Covenant are duly taken into account when negotiating financial assistance projects and programmes, including with international financial institutions" (UNCESCR, Concluding Observations on Greece 2015b, para. 9). The Committee can also point to the danger of turning economic, social, and cultural rights into goods and services which can be bought and sold on the market. As monitoring body under the ICESCR, the Committee has the responsibility to stress the value of economic, social, and cultural rights for protecting human dignity. It means that with a view to strengthening the legal status of economic, social, and cultural rights at the domestic level it must push States to fully recognize and institutionalize these as justiciable and enforceable human rights. This can be done through strong General Comments, detailed and specific Concluding Observations, and progressive and at the same time reasonable views in complaints under the Optional Protocol.

Perhaps the biggest challenge ahead is how the Committee will deal with difficult cases under the Optional Protocol involving alleged violations of economic, social, and cultural rights as a result of breaches by the State party of obligations to fulfill. These could include cases about retrogressive measures taken by the State, such as the reduction of funding for social assistance and grants as a result of a political decision to reorganize public finances. How will the Committee apply the criterion of reasonableness as provided for in Article 8(4) of the Optional Protocol when reviewing such measures (Porter 2009)? To what extent will the 2007 Committee Statement on evaluating the obligation to take steps to the "maximum of available resources" be useful as guidance for the Committee? Cases where austerity measures with a retrogressive effect have been taken by States which negatively impact upon the enjoyment of economic, social, and cultural rights would lend themselves for applying a reasonableness review. Questions like these will only be answered when more States accede to the Optional Protocol and more complaints are lodged.

A final issue relates to the question whether alleged violations of economic, social, and cultural rights as a result of a breach of an extraterritorial obligation of a State party to the Protocol can be reviewed by the Committee (Sepúlveda and Courtis 2009). Pursuant to Article 2 of the Protocol, victims have to be under the jurisdiction of a State party. It is most likely that victims in such types of cases will be residing in another State and not be subject to the territorial jurisdiction of the said State party. Will the Committee apply a limited interpretation of the term jurisdiction (i.e., exercise of authority or effective control) or will it be willing to expand the meaning of jurisdiction to include situations where acts and/or omissions of a State party had foreseeable effects on economic, social, and cultural rights of persons outside its territory? The Maastricht Principles on the Extraterritorial Obligations of States provide for such a broader meaning and scope of the concept of jurisdiction (Maastricht Principle 9). If the Committee would be willing to follow such a dynamic approach, it would make the ICESCR fit to deal with the consequences of economic globalization on economic, social, and cultural rights. However, it is more likely that the Committee will adopt a more cautious approach with a view to not to deter States from acceding to the Protocol or questioning the legitimacy of the Committee to deal with complaints.

Concluding Remarks

One can conclude that the ICESCR has evolved from stepchild to full member of the UN human rights family, thanks to the work of the Committee. It has clarified the normative content of economic, social, and cultural rights and relating obligations by using and applying ideas and suggestions from academic discourse. A dynamic interpretation of the Covenant as a living instrument has been developed which emphasizes the key importance and relevance of economic, social, and cultural rights as touchstone for legislation, policy, and practice in societies in the North and the South. Especially through its General Comments – and to a lesser extent its Concluding Observations – has the Committee been able to explain and highlight that the protection of economic, social, and cultural rights is a key element of human dignity. In particular, the economic, social, and cultural rights of members of vulnerable and marginalized groups in society deserve attention from governments, members of parliament, and policy-makers. The justiciability and enforceability of economic, social, and cultural rights is still underdeveloped in many countries. This phenomenon is also reflective of the still rather negative attitude of governments towards economic, social, and cultural rights, in particular their alleged weak legal nature compared to civil and political rights. This reluctant attitude still dominates the status of economic, social, and cultural rights in many countries. The UNCESCR has the potential to adjust this traditional approach through a straightforward but reasonable review of cases under the complaints procedure of the Optional Protocol. It is to be hoped that States show political will to allow the Committee to review and assess its domestic legislation, policies, and practices through individual complaints.

References

Alston P (1979–1980) The United Nations' specialized agencies and implementation of the International Covenant on Economic, Social and Cultural Rights. Columbia J Transnation Law 18:79–118

Alston P (1987) Out of the Abyss: the challenges confronting the new U.N. Committee on economic, social and cultural rights. Hum Rights Q 9:332–381

Alston P (1991) No right to complain about being poor: the need for an optional protocol to the economic rights covenant. In: Eide A, Hegelsen J (eds) The future of human rights protection in a changing world – essays in honour of Torkel Opsahl. Norwegian University Press, Oslo, pp 79–100

Arambulo K (1999) Strengthening the supervision of the International Covenant on Economic, Social and Cultural Rights. Intersentia/Hart, Antwerpen/Oxford

Chapman A (1996) A 'violations approach' for monitoring the International Covenant on Economic, Social and Cultural Rights. Hum Rights Q 18:23–66

Chapman A (2007) The status of efforts to monitor economic, social and cultural rights. In: Hertel S, Minkler L (eds) Economic rights – conceptual, measurement, and policy issues. Cambridge University Press, Cambridge, pp 143–164

Coomans F (2002) The role of the UN Committee on economic, social and cultural rights in strengthening implementation and supervision of the International Covenant on Economic, Social and Cultural Rights. Verfassung und Recht in Übersee 35:182–200

Coomans F (2003) The Ogoni case before the African commission on human and peoples' rights. Int Comp Law Q 52:749–760

Coomans F (2007) Application of the International Covenant on Economic, Social and Cultural Rights in the framework of international organisations. Max Planck Yearb U N Law 11:359–390

Coomans F (2009a) The International Covenant on Economic, Social and Cultural Rights - from stepchild to full member of the human rights family. In: Gómez Isa F and De Feyter K (eds) International human rights law in a global context, University of Deusto, Bilbao, pp 293–317

Coomans F (2009b) The Limburg principles on socio-economic rights. In: Forsythe D (ed) Encyclopedia of human rights, vol 3. Oxford University Press, Oxford, pp 448–452

Coomans F (2011) The extraterritorial scope of the International Covenant on Economic, Social and Cultural Rights in the work of the United Nations Committee on economic, social and cultural rights. Hum Rights Law Rev 11:1–35

Craven MCR (1995) The International Covenant on Economic, Social and Cultural Rights – a perspective on its development. Clarendon Press, Oxford

Dennis MJ, Stewart DP (2004) Justiciability of economic, social and cultural rights. Am J Int Law 98:462–515

Dowell-Jones D (2004) Contextualising the International Covenant on Economic, Social and Cultural Rights: assessing the economic deficit. Nijhoff, Leiden/Boston

ECOSOC (1978) Res. 1978/10 of 3 May 1978

ECOSOC (1985) Res. 1985/17 of 28 May 1985

Guiding Principles on Business and Human Rights (Ruggie Principles) (2011) UN Doc. A/HRC/17/31

Human Rights Council (2007) Report of the Office of the UN High Commissioner for Human Rights on the rectification of the legal status of the Committee on economic, social and cultural rights. UN Doc. A/HRC/6/21, 7 Nov 2007

Khaliq U and Churchill R (2012) The protection of economic and social rights: a particular challenge? In: Keller H and Ulfstein G (eds) UN Human rights treaty bodies - law and legitimacy, Cambridge University Press, Cambridge, pp 199–260

Kinley D (2009) Civilising globalisation – human rights and the global economy. Cambridge University Press, Cambridge

Krommendijk J (2014) The domestic impact and effectiveness of the process of state reporting under UN human rights treaties in the Netherlands, New Zealand and Finland. Intersentia, Antwerp

Langford M, Vandenhole W, Scheinin M, van Genugten W (2013) Global justice, state duties – the extraterritorial scope of economic, social and cultural rights in international law. Cambridge University Press, Cambridge

Liebenberg S (2010) Socio-economic rights: adjudication under a transformative constitution. Juta & Co., Cape Town

Limburg Principles on the Implementation of the International Covenant on Economic, Social and Cultural Rights. UN Doc. E/CN.4/1987/17, annex. Also published (1987) Hum Rights Q 9:122–135, together with a commentary and preparatory papers, p 136–273

Maastricht Guidelines on Violations of Economic, Social and Cultural Rights (1998) Hum Rights Q 20:691–705

Maastricht Principles on the Extraterritorial Obligations of States in the Area of Economic, Social and Cultural Rights (2011) www.etoconsortium.org. Accessed 29 Nov 2017

O'Flaherty M (2006) The Concluding Observations of United Nations human rights bodies. Hum Rights Law Rev 6:27–52

Pogge T, Sengupta M (2016) Assessing the sustainable development goals from a human rights perspective. J Int Comp Soc Policy 32:83–97

Porter B (2009) The reasonableness of article 8(4) – adjudicating claims from the margins. Nord J Hum Rights 27:40–54

Report by the UN special rapporteur on extreme poverty and human rights, Philip Alston, UN Doc. A/70/274 (4 Aug 2015)

Robertson M (1994) Measuring state compliance with the obligation to devote the 'maximum available resources' to realizing economic, social and cultural rights. Hum Rights Q 16:693–714

Sepúlveda M (2003) The nature of the obligations under the International Covenant on Economic, Social and Cultural Rights. Intersentia, Antwerp/Oxford

Sepúlveda M, Courtis C (2009) Are extra-territorial obligations reviewable under the optional protocol to the ICESCR? Nord J Hum Rights 27:55–64

Tomuschat C (2005) An optional protocol for the International Covenant on Economic, Social and Cultural Rights? In: Dicke K et al (eds) Weltinnenrecht – Liber Amicorum Jost Delbrück. Duncker & Humblot, Berlin, pp 815–834

Tomuschat C (2008) Human rights between idealism and realism, 2nd edn. Oxford University Press, Oxford

Tully S (2005) A human right to access water? A critique of General Comment no. 15. Neth Q Hum Rights 23:35–63

UNCESCR (1991) General comment 3, the nature of states parties' obligations (Art. 2, par. 1). UN Doc. E/1991/23, annex III

UNCESCR (1992) Towards an optional protocol to the International Covenant on Economic, Social and Cultural Rights, analytical paper adopted by the Committee at its seventh session, 11 Dec 1992, UN Doc. A/CONF.157/PC/62/Add.5, annex II

UNCESCR (1997) Draft optional protocol to the International Covenant on Economic, Social and Cultural Rights, UN Doc. E/C.12/1994/12 and E/CN.4/1997/105

UNCESCR (1999) Statement on globalisation and its impact on the enjoyment of economic, social and cultural rights, May 1998, UN Doc. E/1999/22

UNCESCR (2000) General comment 14 on the right to the highest attainable standard of health, UN Doc. E/C.12/2000/4

UNCESCR (2001) Statement on poverty and the ICESCR, UN Doc. E/C.12/2001/10

UNCESCR (2002) General comment 15 on the right to water, UN Doc. E/C.12/2002/11

UNCESCR (2007) Statement on an evaluation of the obligation to take steps to the 'maximum of available resources' under an optional protocol to the Covenant, UN Doc. E/C.12/2007/1

UNCESCR (2008) Revised general guidelines regarding the form and contents of reports to be submitted by states parties under articles 16 and 17 of the ICESCR, UN Doc. E/C.12/2008/2, adopted 18 Nov 2008

UNCESCR (2012) Concluding observations on periodic state report by Spain, UN Doc. E/C.12/ESP/CO/5

UNCESCR (2013a) Concluding observations on periodic state report by Belgium, UN Doc. E/C.12/BEL/CO/4

UNCESCR (2013b) Concluding observations on periodic state report by Norway, UN Doc. E/C.12/NOR/CO/5

UNCESCR (2014) Concluding observations on periodic state report by China, UN Doc. E/C.12/CHN/CO/2

UNCESCR (2015a) Case of Mohamed Ben Djazia and Naouel Bellili v. Spain, 05/2015, views of 21 July 2015, UN Doc. E/C.12/61/D/5/2015

UNCESCR (2015b) Concluding observations on periodic state report by Greece, UN Doc. E/C.12/GRC/CO/2

UNCESCR (2015c) Statement on social protection floors, UN Doc. E/C.12/2015/1

UNCESCR (2016a) Concluding observations on periodic state report by Canada, UN Doc. E/C.12/CAN/CO/6

UNCESCR (2016b) Statement on public debt, austerity measures and the International Covenant on Economic, Social and Cultural Rights, UN Doc. E/C.12/2016/1

UNCESCR (2016c) General comment 22, on the right to sexual and reproductive health, UN Doc. E/C.12/GC/22

UNCESCR (2017a) Concluding observations on periodic state report by Australia, UN Doc. E/C.12/AUS/CO/5

UNCESCR (2017b) General comment 24, state obligations under the ICESCR in the context of business activities, UN Doc. E/C.12/GC/24

UNCESCR (2017c) Note on the procedure for follow-up to concluding observations, adopted by the Committee at its 61st session (29 May – 23 June 2017)

UNCESCR (2017d) Report on the fifty-seventh, fifty-eighth and fifty-ninth sessions (2016), UN Doc. E/2017/22

UNCESCR (2017e) Statement on the duties of states towards refugees and migrants under the ICESCR, UN Doc. E/C.12/2017/1

UNCESCR (2017f) Working methods concerning the Committee's follow-up to views under the optional protocol to the International Covenant on Economic, Social and Cultural Rights, adopted by the Committee at its 61st session (29 May – 23 June 2017)

UNCESCR (2017g) Concluding observations on periodic state report by The Netherlands, UN Doc. E/C.12/NLD/CO/6

UNGA (2008) Resolution on the optional protocol to the International Covenant on Economic, Social and Cultural Rights, 63/117, 10 Dec 2008

Gender in the UN: CEDAW and the Commission on the Status of Women

Jane Connors

Contents

Introduction 170
Recurrent Themes 171
Establishment of the Commission on the Status of Women 173
Membership, Mandate, and Working Methods 174
The Working Group on Communications on the Status of Women 177
Relationship with UN Entities and Civil Society 179
Assessment of the Commission on the Status of Women 181
Committee on the Elimination of Discrimination Against Women 182
  Establishment and Composition 182
  Competence 183
  The Reporting Procedure 184
  General Recommendations 186
The Optional Protocol to the Convention on the Elimination of All Forms of
Discrimination Against Women 188
Conclusion 192
References 193

Abstract

This chapter introduces the development and competence of the Commission on the Status of Women, the main UN intergovernmental body, responsible for the advancement of women. Among its major achievements is the elaboration of the draft Convention on the Elimination of All Forms of Discrimination Against Women and its Optional Protocol. The Convention is overseen by the Committee on the Elimination of Discrimination Against Women, whose competence and work are also described.

J. Connors (✉)
International Advocacy, Amnesty International, Geneva, Switzerland
e-mail: jconnors@bluewin.ch

© Springer Nature Singapore Pte Ltd. 2018
G. Oberleitner (ed.), *International Human Rights Institutions, Tribunals, and Courts,*
International Human Rights, https://doi.org/10.1007/978-981-10-5206-4_8

169

Keywords

UN mechanisms · Women's human rights · Gender equality · Commission on the Status of Women · Convention on the Elimination of All Forms of Discrimination Against Women · CSW · CEDAW

Introduction

Early multilateral diplomatic conferences, the International Labour Organization (ILO) and the League of Nations engaged in international standard setting on the rights of women and girls in the period prior to, and during, the early twentieth century. Examples are the International Agreement for the suppression of the "White Slave Trade" (1904) and the international convention of the same name (League of Nations Treaty Series I, p. 84–94), the International Convention for the Suppression of Traffic in Women and Children (League of Nations Treaty Series ix, p. 416–33), the International Convention for the Suppression of Traffic in Women of Full Age (League of Nations Treaty Series cl, p. 431–43), the Convention Concerning the Employment of Women Before and After Childbirth (Convention 3) of 1919, the ILO Convention Concerning Employment of Women During the Night (Convention no 4) of 1919, the ILO Convention Concerning the Employment of Women in Underground Work in Mines of All Kinds (Convention 45) of 1935, the Hague Convention on the Conflict of Nationality Laws of 1930, and the Montevideo Convention on the Nationality of Women of 1933.

But it was the 1945 Charter of the United Nations (UN) which provided the impetus for the creation of dedicated international standards and mechanisms directed to the equal rights of women and men and the elimination of discrimination against women on the basis of sex. Spurred on by the efforts of civil society and the support of sympathetic States, often inspired by developments in their regions, and individuals in the secretariat itself, proposals to achieve these objectives were introduced at the United Nations Conference on International Organization (the San Francisco Conference) which met in San Francisco, USA, from 25 April to 26 June 1945 to draw up the Charter of the new world body (Skard 2008). As a result, the Charter's preamble reaffirms the equal rights of men and women, Article 1 provides that the achievement of international cooperation in promoting and encouraging respect for human rights and fundamental freedoms for all without distinction as to sex and other grounds is one of the UNs purposes, Article 8 sets out that the UN shall not restrict the eligibility of men and women to participate in any capacity and under conditions of equality in its organs, while three other provisions – Article 13(1)(b), 55(c), and 76(c) – establish nondistinction on the basis of sex in efforts to realize human rights and fundamental freedoms as a principle underpinning other aspects of the Organization's work.

The years since the entry into force of the Charter on 24 October 1945 have seen UN engagement in many areas, but perhaps the quest to eliminate discrimination on the basis of sex and achieve women's equality with men has attracted more commitment, support and excitement than other endeavors. As a result, there is now an intricate web of international legal standards and principles, intergovernmental bodies and expert mechanisms, and UN entities dedicated to these objectives. The quest now encompasses the achievement of gender equality in development, peace, security, and human rights, defined by the Charter as the UNs three pillars.

This chapter introduces two fundamental building blocks in the UN gender equality architecture: the Commission on the Status of Women (CSW), the peak UN intergovernmental body dedicated to promoting women's advancement and the enjoyment of their human rights, and the Committee on the Elimination of Discrimination Against Women (CEDAW), the expert body established by the 1979 Convention on the Elimination of All Forms of Discrimination Against Women (the Convention), initiated and largely drafted by the CSW, now ratified by, or acceded to, 189 States.

Recurrent Themes

There is a number of common themes which recur in relation to UN efforts to achieve gender equality which have affected the development and influence of both these bodies and related initiatives. First, even before the negotiations to create the UN, those engaged in the women's human rights/status of women struggle quickly recognized and understood the potential of a world body to constitute a forum in which the powerless could pressure States to make legislative, policy and programmatic change and a site in which States could be held to account for their actions at the national level. Accordingly, the UN became a place where women's non-governmental organizations (NGOs) brought issues ignored at the national level into the international arena and have them recognized and often acted upon, because they spoke about women's lives and realities.

As a result, the UN became an important factor in the foundation and expansion of the global women's movement, giving it a legitimacy that it might have otherwise lacked. This movement was, and remains, multifaceted and multicultural, with its members drawn from international, regional, national, local and grass-roots civil society, UN Member States' delegations, and the UN Secretariat itself. From the San Francisco Conference and the first session of the UN General Assembly in January 1946, those – and they have in the main been women – who have championed women's human right, their empowerment and involvement in all areas of international activity on an equal basis with men have, more than in any other area of UN work, worked together across the different functions of delegate, expert and UN entity staff member, and frequently moved across these functions. The engagement and influence of civil society, especially from the grass roots, are also significant. Both the CSW and the CEDAW owe their existence in large part to civil society efforts and have been generous and open to its participation in their work. In turn, civil society has been crucial in the evolution of these bodies and has profoundly contributed to their visibility and influence.

Importantly also, although UN commitment to the promotion and protection of the rights of women was part of the foundation of the world body and grew and developed as it matured, the institutions, policies, and programs directed towards these objectives were created and evolved separately and parallel to those directed to the promotion and protection of human rights. This separation was compounded in 1973 and 1979, respectively, when the CSW secretariat was moved from the Division of Human Rights within the Department of Political and General Assembly Affairs to the Centre for Social and Development and Humanitarian Affairs within the Department of Economic and Social Affairs, and the secretariat of CSW, which later included that of CEDAW, was moved from New York to Vienna. These secretariat entities, and the bodies they supported, have generally been endowed with fewer financial and human resources than those provided to the human rights program. Indeed, as will be seen below, the time available for the CSW to meet is significantly less than the Human Rights Council (HRC) and its predecessor, the CSWs sister body, the Commission on Human Rights (CHR). Notably, the CSW was authorized to meet only biennially between 1972 and 1986, and in 1980, an unsuccessful resolution was introduced at the thirty-fifth session of the General Assembly to abolish it and transfer its functions to the ECOSOC (Reanda 1992, p. 295).

At that session, the UN General Assembly adopted resolution 35/136 was adopted which, inter alia, requested the Secretary-General to consider appropriate measures to enable the CSW to discharge the functions assigned to it for the implementation of the 1975 World Plan of Action for the Implementation of the Objectives of the International Women's Year (E/CONF.66/34(76.IV.1) and the 1980 Programme of Action for the Second Half of the UN Decade for Women (A/CONF.94/35 (80.IV.3) and take immediate action to strengthen the CSWs secretariat (UN General Assembly resolution 35/136 1980). Similarly, unlike other human rights treaties, the Convention on the Elimination of All Forms of Discrimination Against Women limits the CEDAWs meeting time to 2 weeks annually (Article 20 CEDAW). As a result, some perceived these bodies as weak and removed from what they saw as "the mainstream." Ironically, also, the existence of what are considered to be the "women's institutions" allowed UN human rights bodies and traditional human rights nongovernmental organizations to neglect issues of concern to women, as they were able to point to the CSW and the CEDAW as the bodies responsible for these issues.

A turning point occurred in 1993, when, much as the result of organized pressure from women's human rights groups, the World Conference on Human Rights proclaimed the human rights of women and girls to be an inalienable, integral, and indivisible part of universal human rights and called for their integration into the mainstream of UN system-wide activity (Vienna Declaration and Programme of Action 1993, para. 18 and paras. 36–44; Connors 1996, p. 169–173). The UN policy of "gender mainstreaming," identified by the 1995 Beijing Declaration and Platform for Action, adopted by the Fourth World Conference on Women, as a critical and strategic approach to achieve gender equality, elaborated in the UN Economic and Social Council's (ECOSOC) agreed conclusions 1997/2, endorsed by numerous UN resolutions, including in para. 20 of the 2030 Agenda for Sustainable Development also seeks to ensure that women's rights and gender equality is at the center of all UN activity.

Much progress has been made, including since the operationalization, on 1 January 2011, of the UN Entity for Gender Equality and Empowerment of

Women (UN Women), now responsible for the substantive and technical servicing and other support of the Commission on the Status of Women and the UN advancement of women agenda (Charlesworth and Chinkin 2013, p. 1–36). The transfer in 2008 of responsibility for supporting the CEDAW from the Division for the Advancement of Women to the Office of the High Commissioner for Human Rights so that it could interact closely with and inform the UN human rights program and particularly the nine other human rights treaty bodies has also been helpful (OHCHR 2008). Nonetheless, a disconnect between these essential and important streams of work still remains, including because the UN institutional responsibility for them is located in different UN entities and geographical centers, and the intergovernmental and expert mechanisms dedicated to these issues are distinct. Continued concerted and sustained efforts are necessary to ensure these essential streams of work are, and perceived to be, inextricably linked.

Establishment of the Commission on the Status of Women

Although the Inter-American Commission on Women to examine the status of women in Latin America had been created by the Pan American Union in 1928 (Statute of the Inter-American Commission of Women 2016), the CSW is the first global intergovernmental body dedicated to promoting women's rights in the political, social, and educational fields (ECOSOC resolution E/RES/2/11 1946). It finds its roots in a proposal presented at the San Francisco Conference by Bertha Lutz, a Brazilian delegate and one of the four women who signed the Charter (the others were Minerva Bernadino, Dominican Republic, Virginia Gildersleeve, USA, and Wu Yi Fang, China) recommending the creation of a commission to study conditions and prepare reports on the political, civil and economic status, and opportunity of women with special reference to discrimination and limitations placed on them on account of their sex. Although the proposal garnered much support, it was opposed by several powerful delegations which suggested that a separate women's commission would be discriminatory and unnecessary as their concerns could be dealt with by a commission on human rights and proved unsuccessful (Skard 2008, p. 47–55; Jain 2005, p. 17–18).

However, in February 1946, the inaugural meeting of the General Assembly, perhaps influenced by the "Letter to the Women of the World," read by UN delegate Eleanor Roosevelt, expressed enthusiastic support for the establishment of a subsidiary body to the Commission on Human Rights to address the status of women. A few days later, on 16 February, ECOSOC established the CHR and its subsidiary, the Sub-commission on the Status of Women. The Sub-Commission was short-lived, as its members and supporters were determined to see its status elevated to a full commission so its suggestions could go directly to the ECOSOC rather than to it through the CHR. The Sub-Commission's Chair, Bodil Begtrup of Denmark, President of the Danish Council of Women, made a formal proposal to this effect to the second session of the ECOSOC, pointing out that the Sub-Commission's mandate addressed the condition of half the population of the world and should thus not be dependent on another commission. She countered suggestions that women's problems should not be separated from those of men, arguing that this view was "idealistic," but "purely unrealistic and academic," and that it would, in the opinion of the Sub-Commission's members, "be a tragedy to spoil this unique opportunity by confusing the wish with the fact" (Begtrup 1946).

Ms. Begtrup's advocacy proved compelling, as on 21 June 1946, the ECOSOC decided to confer on the Sub-commission the status of a full commission to be known as the Commission on the Status of Women reporting directly to the ECOSOC (ECOSOC resolution E/RES/2/11). As such, it is one of the eight functional commissions created by the ECOSOC pursuant to Article 68 of the Charter. The others are the Commission for Social Development, the Commission on Narcotic Drugs, the Commission on Crime Prevention and Criminal Justice, the Statistical Commission, the Commission on Population and Development the Forum on Forests, and the Commission on Science and Technology for Development.

Membership, Mandate, and Working Methods

Originally comprised of 15 members, the Commission has expanded over time as the number of UN Member States has grown. It is now made up of 45 UN Member States elected by the ECOSOC in biennial elections for 4-year terms in line with a formula to ensure balanced equitable geographic representation of the UN recognized regional groups: 13 members from Africa, 11 from Asia, 9 from Latin America and the Caribbean, 8 from Western European and other States, and 4 from Eastern European States. The most recent enlargement was through ECOSOC resolution 1989/45. Apart from geography, unlike under paras. 8 and 9 of UN General Assembly resolution 60/251 of 2006 which set up the Human Rights Council, there are no criteria for membership nor is there a provision for suspension of members. The election in 2017 of Saudi Arabia by the ECOSOC on an uncompetitive geographic slate attracted comment from civil society and others in light of its record on women's human rights. The UN practice of conducting elections to UN intergovernmental and other bodies through secret ballot, ruling out scrutiny of States' decision-making, was also criticized (UN Watch 2017; Butler-Dines 2017; Finlay 2014). Similar concerns were raised following the election of the Islamic Republic of Iran in 2014 (Finlay 2014).

Each Member State of the Commission, in consultation with the UN Secretary-General, designates a representative to serve on the CSW, who is then subject to formal confirmation by the ECOSOC (ECOSOC decision 2002/234). Thus, CSW representatives, who can be replaced at any time, are not independent experts but reflect their State's political positions. However, from its early sessions, commentators have pointed out that the CSW has evoked more personal commitment from its delegates than any other UN body, with John Humphrey, the first Director of the UN Human Rights Division in which the Section on the Status of Women which supported the work of the CSW was located, and a key force in the elaboration of the Universal Declaration of Human Rights describing the Commission as a "kind of lobby for the women of the world" (Humphrey 1983, p. 387–405). This may be because those chosen to represent their countries at the Commission have usually been women, with only a handful being men. Additionally, most appointees have been invested in the CSWs mission and have relied on the political, intellectual, and moral support of women's national and international nongovernmental organizations, from which many have been drawn.

A five-member bureau, made up of a chairperson and four vice-chairpersons, drawn from each regional group, is elected at the first meeting of each session which is convened immediately after the closure of the previous session for the sole purpose of this election (ECOSOC resolution 2015/6, paras. 11, 12, 22 and 23). Bureau members serve for 2 years and are expected to be actively involved in the preparation of and follow-up to sessions during their tenure, including through regular briefings and consultations with Member States. The Bureau is also tasked with identifying, in collaboration with all stakeholders, an emerging issue, trend, focus area or new approach to be discussed by each Commission session which will be summarized by the Chair and is encouraged to propose interactive dialogues and other formats which engage all stakeholders and encourage dialogue and enhance the impact of the CSWs work (ECOSOC resolution 2015/6, paras. 11, 12, 22, and 23).

The Commission's original mandate was twofold: to prepare recommendations and reports for the ECOSOC on matters concerning the promotion of women's rights in the political, economic, civil, social, and educational fields and make recommendations on problems requiring immediate attention in the field of women's rights. This mandate expanded incrementally, and ultimately was extended formally by ECOSOC resolutions 1987/22 and 1996/6 in response to the outcomes of the Third and Fourth World Conferences on Women held in 1985 and 1995, respectively to include advocacy of equality, development, and peace; monitoring the implementation of internationally agreed measures for the advancement of women; and reviewing and appraising progress at the national, subregional, sectoral, and global levels. In 1995 and 2000, also, the General Assembly devolved on the Commission the central responsibility of monitoring the implementation of the Beijing Platform for Action adopted by the Fourth World Conference on Women and the 5-year review of that Conference by the twenty-third Special Session of the General Assembly and mainstreaming a gender perspective in all UN activities (UN General Assembly resolution 50/203 of 1995 and UN General Assembly resolution 55/71 of 2000). Follow-up to the 2030 Agenda for Sustainable Development is also an important part of the CSWs work, and it contributes to the thematic reviews of progress on the Sustainable Development Goals which take place annually at the high-level forum on sustainable development (ECOSOC resolution 2016/3).

Since 1987, the CSW has formulated a multiyear program of work delineating priority themes to be taken up at its sessions (ECOSOC resolution 1987/24). Its current, and seventh, program of work remains in force until the end of its sixty-third session in 2019. As in the case of programs adopted since 2006, it requires the CSW at each session to take up one priority and review theme, with the latter allowing it to evaluate its conclusions on a priority discussed at an earlier session. In 2018, its priority theme will be the challenges and opportunities in achieving gender equality and the empowerment of rural women and girls, and it will review the participation and access of women to the media and information and communications technologies as an instrument of advancement of women discussed at it forty-seventh session. In 2019, the priority theme will be social protection systems, access to public services and sustainable infrastructure for gender equality and the empowerment of women and girls, and women's empowerment and sustainable development of women and girls as its review theme (Begtrup 1946).

With the exception of the years between 1972 and 1986, when it was authorized to meet once only every 2 years, the CSW meets annually, bringing together thousands of representatives of Member States, UN entities, and civil society organizations from all over the world. Sessions have convened at UN headquarters in New York since 1994 and usually take place from late February to mid-March. They typically last for 10 working days (ECOSOC resolution 1987/21 and ECOSOC resolution 1999/257) although they have sometimes lasted longer or resumed to complete outstanding work when authorized to do so by the ECOSOC. On rare occasions, the CSW has convened informal intersessional working groups, such as in September 1992 to finalize the draft of UN Declaration on Violence Against Women and during the preparations for the Fourth World Conference on Women. The time the CSW is authorized to meet should be contrasted with that allotted to the Commission on Human Rights, which met for 6 weeks annually and also convened special sessions, and its successor, the Human Rights Council which is required to meet for no fewer than three sessions per year for a minimum of 10 weeks annually, and may, where warranted, convene special sessions (UN General Assembly resolution 60/251, para. 10).

The CSWs working methods have evolved, and particularly since it has been supported by UN Women and now highlight its central role in the international institutional framework to advance the status of women and girls. They are set out in ECOSOC resolution 2015/6 which reaffirms that the CSWs primary responsibility is to follow-up the outcomes of the Fourth World Conference on Women and its 5-year review in 2000, and include policy-making and coordinating the implementation and monitoring of the Beijing Declaration and Platform for Action and, since 2016, follow-up Agenda 2030 to accelerate the realization of gender equality and empowerment of women. These tasks are conducted through a variety of formats: a ministerial segment, including a ministerial discussion; ministerial roundtables; and high-level interactive dialogues designed to ensure that the Commission's deliberations attract high-level engagement and visibility. General discussions and interactive expert panels take place on the priority and review themes, emerging issues, trends, focus areas, and new approaches affecting women and gender mainstreaming in respect of which it has a catalytic role. At its sixty-first session in 2017, the empowerment of indigenous women was discussed as an emerging/focus theme (United Nations, Report of the Commission on the Status of Women 2017). As from 2016, Member States have made voluntary presentations on lessons-learned, challenges, and best practices in realizing implementation of the review theme.

The CSW formulates its principal output, short, succinct negotiated agreed conclusions on the session's priority theme which focus on action-oriented recommendations directed at Member States and other stakeholders in plenary and informal meetings. It also adopts resolutions and decisions on women's rights issues and considers in closed meetings the report of the Working Group on Communications which is described below. Until 1986, all decisions and resolutions adopted by the CSW were submitted to the ECOSOC for approval and were occasionally rejected or sent back for further consideration (Reanda 1992, p. 271). Currently, although it brings its agreed conclusions and most resolutions to the attention of the Council, some resolutions and decisions, in particular those with budgetary implications, including its long-term program of work are submitted to the ECOSOC for its approval and action (Begtrup 1946).

Unlike the HRC, and the CHR before it, the CSW has shied away from creating subsidiary mechanisms, such as working groups, special rapporteurs, or representatives. Exceptionally, it created a special rapporteur on the status of women and family planning in 1968 (Commission on the Status of Women resolution 7(XXI) E/4472. Chapter XVIII; ECOSOC resolution 1326). It also recommended that ECOSOC requests the Secretary-General to prepare a report on the implementation of the Convention for the Suppression of the Traffic in persons and of the Exploitation of the Prostitution of Others (Commission on the Status of Women resolution XXVII 1978; Commission on the Status of Women draft resolution 1982; United Nations, Report of the Special Rapporteur on the exploitation and prostitution of others to the ECOSOC 1983). This was carried out by a special rapporteur appointed by the UN Secretary-General who reported to the ECOSOC in 1983. Proposals that the CSW create a special rapporteur to study laws which discriminate against women were made in the late twentieth and early twenty-first centuries, but gained no traction, but succeeded in the HRC which established the Working Group on Discrimination Against Women in Law and in Practice in 2010 (Banda 2013a, p. 65–81; Human Rights Council resolution 15/23 2010). Currently, the Working Group on Communications on the Status of Women, discussed below, is the CSWs only subsidiary body.

The Working Group on Communications on the Status of Women

It will be recalled that the CSWs original mandate included a capacity to make urgent recommendations to the ECOSOC on problems requiring immediate attention in the field of women's rights, and at its first session, the CSW appointed a subcommittee, consisting of the representatives of China, Guatemala, and the United States, to consider how to deal with communications concerning the status of women. On the recommendation of the subcommittee and the CSW itself (United Nations, Report of the Commission on the Status of Women to the ECOSOC on its first session 1947, Chap. III), the ECOSOC decided to request the Secretary-General to compile a confidential list of communications concerning the status of women, with a brief indication of the substance of each and not revealing the identity of their authors, which would be forwarded to the CSWs members at least 14 days before the opening of each session (ECOSOC resolution 76 (V) 1947, amended by ECOSOC resolution 304 I (XI) 1950). Members of the CSW were entitled to consult the original communications, and their authors would be informed that their petitions had been received and duly noted for consideration in accordance with UN procedures. In the same resolution, however, ECOSOC made clear that, like the CHR, the CSW had no power to take any action on complaints concerning the status of women.

In 1983, the ECOSOC adopted resolution 1983/27 directed to strengthening the CSWs capacity to deal with communications. It requested the Secretary-General to submit to the CSW a report on confidential and nonconfidential communications on the status of women, including communications received in line with resolution 76(V), with any comments of the States concerned and communications received by UN entities, with information on action that that might have been taken following their receipt. The CSW was authorized to appoint a working group of not more than five members, based on geographical distribution, to meet in closed meetings during each session, whose function was to consider the communications and any Government replies with a view to bringing the Commission's attention to those which appeared to reveal a consistent pattern of reliably attested injustice and discriminatory practices against women. The Working Group was also mandated to prepare a report, based on its analysis of the communications indicating the categories in which communications are most frequently submitted to the CSW. The Commission's sole power, following its examination of the Working Group's report, was to make recommendations to the ECOSOC, which would decide on the appropriate action on the emerging trends and patterns of the communications.

Successive ECOSOC resolutions have slightly adjusted the procedure set out in ECOSOC resolution 1983/27 (ECOSOC resolutions 1992/19, 1993/11, 2009/16 and ECOSOC decision 2002/235), but it remains broadly the same, although the Working Group, whose members serve for 2 years, now convene in closed meetings prior to each Commission session to consider the communications and any Government replies. Notably, the outcome of the procedure has not changed, being confined to identification of trends and patterns relating injustice and discrimination against women (United Nations, Report of the Commission on the Status of Women 2016) often without recommendations for action, and providing neither individual relief nor remedies to victims. Although it may be argued that information on trends and patterns may assist the CSW in its thematic work, it is clear the procedure offers little to victims. Further, only a minority of States provides comments or responses on communications which concern them, suggesting that the procedure is regarded as unimportant to them, and accordingly has little potential for domestic impact. These factors, as well as the fact that the Committee on the Elimination of Discrimination Against Women is now able to receive and consider individual petitions as outlined below, may explain why in recent years less than 100 communications have been dealt with by the Working Group annually.

The ECOSOCs approach to communications on the status of women contrasts starkly with its approach to those on human rights. In 1967, it authorized the CHR to act in situations which revealed a consistent pattern of violations of human rights

(ECOSOC resolution 1235 1967), while in 1970, it authorized the CHRs Sub-Commission on Prevention of Discrimination and Protection of Minorities to appoint a Working Group to consider all communications and bring those, and any replies from Governments, which appear to reveal a consistent pattern of gross and reliably attested violations of human rights and fundamental freedoms to the Sub-Commission's attention. The Sub-Commission was also empowered to refer situations to the CHR, which could mandate a study by the Commission, a report and recommendation to the ECOSOC and an investigation by an *ad hoc* committee appointed by the CHR (ECOSOC resolution 1503 1970).

The Sub-Commission's procedure, now replaced by the HRCs' Complaint Procedure (Human Rights Council resolution 5/1 2007, Chap. IV), the first universal complaint procedure covering all human rights and fundamental freedoms in all States and its outcomes, inspired attempts by some members of the CSW to make its procedure more robust. Reports with recommendations to achieve this goal have been placed before sessions of the CSW (United Nations, Reports of the Secretary-General 1991; 2001; 2003; 2004; 2008) but had almost no impact. Some delegations managed to postpone discussion of their substance and successfully blocked change by suggesting this might lead to duplication across the UN system. Ironically, similar arguments were raised by delegations not known for supporting human rights mechanisms during the CSWs twenty-fifth session aimed at excluding communications on women's rights from the CSWs procedure on the basis that the CHR 1503 procedure should deal with all communications on human rights, including those relating to women (Commission on the Status of Women, Report of the Twenty-fifth Session 1974, p. 52). The proposal was adopted by the CSW and ECOSOC requested reconsideration of this decision (ECOSOC decision 86/5683).

Relationship with UN Entities and Civil Society

From its first session, the CSW forged relationships with UN entities, including civil society and UN entities, such as specialized agencies and other UN system bodies (Commission on the Status of Women 1947, Chaps. IV, V, and IX). As highlighted above, women's NGOs were active during the elaboration of the Charter and lobbied for the creation of the Commission. Once the system for consultative status envisaged in Article 71 of the UN Charter was operational, women's organizations, including the International Alliance of Women, the International Council of Women, the International Federation of Business and Professional Women, and the World Association of Girls Guides and Girl Scouts, were among the first NGOs recognized (ECOSOC List of nongovernmental organizations 2016).

Civil society representatives attended the CSW from its first session, where statements were made by 12 NGOs. Since then, NGOs have monitored the CSWs work and lobbied it to accelerate women's advancement and their enjoyment of human rights, leading one commentator to observe early on that "in no organ of the United Nations do international non-governmental organisations play a more active and influential role that in the Commission" (Boulding 1975, p. 340–346). NGOs contributed to the CSWs standard-setting work, particularly the Convention on the Elimination of All Forms of Discrimination Against Women and its Optional Protocol, through submission of written comments and advocacy during and between sessions both at international level and on the ground (Connors 1996, p. 155–162). They initiated the idea, taken up by the twenty-fourth session of the CSW in 1972 (Commission on the Status of Women resolution 10 (XXIV) 1972) and agreed by the General Assembly later that year (UN General Assembly resolution 3010 (XXVII) 1972), that 1975 be designated "International Women's Year" (Peitilä 2007, p. 38–39). They pressured the Commission and the General Assembly to convene the four UN conferences on women and engaged with the CSW as it acted as the preparatory committee for the conferences held in Nairobi and Beijing in 1985 and 1995, respectively. NGOs closely monitor follow-up by the CSW of the Beijing Platform for Action and Beijing+5, and participated in the political reviews of implementation of both these documents which took place in 2010 and 2015.

Currently, NGOs accredited as being in consultative status by the ECOSOC, in line with its resolution 1996/31, may participate in annual sessions and submit written statements in advance on the themes to be considered. A limited number is also able to make oral interventions during the session's panels. Those with or without consultative status may organize and attend parallel events held outside UN premises. They also participate, either as observers or experts in light of their expertise, in expert group meetings mandated by the Commission, and organized by UN Women, to prepare the CSWs work. Civil society interest in the CSW has grown and is testified to by the fact that its sixty-first meeting in March 2017 attracted more than 3900 civil society participants from more than 580 organizations and 138 countries which submitted 131 written statements and participated in over 600 side events hosted by States, UN entities, and NGOs (Puri 2017). Notably, also, almost 1000 women's NGOs from around the world reacted to the CSW draft declaration on twentieth anniversary of the Fourth World Conference on Women (https://iwhc.org/resources/womens-statement-20th-anniversary-fourth-world-conference-women). Many who attend the CSW also participate in the annual consultations convened immediately prior to the Commission session organized by the NGO Committee on the Status of Women, made up of a group of New York-based women's NGOs in consultative status with ECOSOC, which also coordinates activities during the session. Younger representatives also participate in the CSW Youth Forum which has also met before the session since 2016.

Since its first session, also, the CSW has worked in close partnership with UN system entities, including the secretariat, specialized agencies, funds, and programs. The UN "Blue Book" on the United Nations and Advancement of Women (United Nations 1996) points to its collaboration with bodies such as the International Labour Organization; the UN Educational, Scientific and Cultural Organization; the World Health Organization; and the Food and Agriculture Organization. At each CSW session, representatives of these and other UN bodies participate in high-level panels and roundtables and make statements reflecting their close cooperation, they frequently collaborate in the organization of expert group meetings and were closely involved in the CSWs standard-setting work. For example, the Food and Agriculture Organization was instrumental in the inclusion of Article 14 on rural women in the Convention on the Elimination of All Forms of Discrimination Against Women (Banda 2013b, p. 361).

In its early years, the CSW participated in the development of the UN human rights architecture. Representatives of the CSW participated in the drafting of the Universal Declaration of Human Rights and made explicit drafting suggestions. ECOSOC transmitted the suggestions of the CSW for amendments to the draft Declaration which were ultimately reflected in the text. Similarly, the CSW suggested amendments to the CHR on the draft Covenants on Economic, Social and Cultural Rights and Civil and Political Rights directed to ensuring that the rights they enshrined stated explicitly that they applied equally to women and men (United Nations 1996). In the late-1990s, the chairpersons of the CSW and the CHR adopted the practice of addressing their respective sessions as a strategy to accelerate the integration of women's human rights into the human rights framework, but, unfortunately, with the creation of the Human Rights Council, this practice has not continued. However, a number of the Special Procedures of the Human Rights Council has developed close linkages with the CSW. Indeed, the constituent resolutions of the Special Rapporteurs on Violence Against Women, its causes and consequences and the right to education (Commission on Human Rights 1998) and the Working Group on Discrimination Against Women in Law and in Practice require their reports to be made available to the CSW. The Special Rapporteur on Violence Against Women and a member of the Working Group also address the Commission at its annual sessions and participate in its other formats, as well as side-events.

Assessment of the Commission on the Status of Women

Laura Reanda's detailed analysis of the CSW identifies three phases in its work: the "equal rights" orientation, the "development" orientation, and the "mainstreaming" strategy (Reanda 1992, p. 275–300). She recognizes that there is overlap among these phases, but points out that during the first phase, the Commission focused on standard-setting, legal studies and promotional activities, with its most significant achievement being the elaboration of the Convention on the Elimination of Discrimination Against Women, whose Committee is discussed below; the second, on ensuring that women equally participated in, and benefited from, social and economic development in their countries and internationally, while the third was directed to women's empowerment and ensuring they were a full part of what is referred to as the "mainstream" (Reanda 1992, p. 275).

The CSW is now in its fourth stage, bringing together the themes of equality, development and mainstreaming. This stage focusses on follow-up to the critical areas of concern identified in the Beijing Platform for Actions and serving as a global catalyst for the empowerment of women and integration of a gender perspective in all contexts. Now supported by UN Women, a strengthened and very visible UN entity, the CSW annual sessions providing the main international venue where good practices and challenges to women's empowerment and enjoyment of their human rights are discussed by a multitude of different actors and strategies crafted to move these objectives forward. Despite the current security of its position, however, its limited meeting time and authority to deal with women's rights violations serve to undermine its role in the realization of women's human rights.

Committee on the Elimination of Discrimination Against Women

Establishment and Composition

The Committee on the Elimination of Discrimination Against Women (CEDAW) is established by Article 17 of the Convention on the Elimination of All Forms of Discrimination Against Women, the first comprehensive international treaty on discrimination against women on the basis of sex, was discussed and elaborated by the CSW and the Third Committee of the General Assembly from 1972 to 1979 (Chinkin and Freeman 2012, p. 6–8). A number of comprehensive accounts, including those of Ineke Boerefijn (Boerefijn 2013a and 2013b) and Andrew Byrnes (Byrnes 2013, p. 27–61), describes the drafting history of provisions of the Convention which relate to the Committee, its competence, work, and achievements, and the brief survey below is merely introductory.

The questions of whether the Convention should have an oversight body and what shape any such body should take sparked much debate during its negotiation (Boerefijn 2013a and 2013b). Some States considered there should be no oversight body, others favored giving oversight to the CSW, or a working group composed of CSW members which were States parties to the Convention to emphasize the CSWs central role. Others proposed a body of experts established by the Convention, along the lines of the Committee on the Elimination of Racial Discrimination (CERD) established by the International Convention on the Elimination of All Forms of Racial Discrimination adopted in 1969 and on which the Convention on the Elimination of All Forms of Discrimination Against Women itself was largely modeled. Ultimately, the CSW proposed an oversight mechanism which would operate under its authority, but the General Assembly decided on a committee of independent experts elected by States parties on the lines of the CERD and the Human Rights Committee established by the International Covenant on Civil and Political Rights. Apart from Article 21(2), which provides that CEDAWs reports are to be transmitted to the CSW for information, the Convention envisages no role for the CSW. A conference room paper on the results of CEDAW sessions is transmitted to each CSW session, and in its early days, the ECOSOC requested that the timing of CEDAW sessions be arranged so the CSW would gain optimal benefit from its output.

The Committee's purpose is to consider the progress made in the implementation of the Convention. It is made up of 23 "experts of high moral standing and competence in the field covered by the Convention" (Article 17, para. 1), nominated and elected by States parties to the Convention, but who serve in their personal capacity. However, as in the case of other human rights treaty bodies, some experts have served simultaneously as ambassadors or held high-level Government posts while holding Committee membership. For some, this engenders a perception of lack of independence and has led to criticism inspiring the meeting of human rights chairpersons to adopt the Addis Ababa Guidelines on independence and impartiality of members of human rights treaty bodies (United Nations, Report of the Chairs of human rights treaty bodies on their twenty-fourth meeting 2012). There is no formal geographic quota governing membership, but in elections, which occur biennially at UN headquarters in New York, and are conducted by secret ballot, consideration is to be given to equitable geographic distribution and the representation of the different forms of civilization, as well as the principal legal systems. Experts are elected for 4-year terms, and there is no limit on the number of times they may be reelected. Many have served for long, uninterrupted periods, while some have returned to the Committee after a break. Casual vacancies are filled by the State party whose expert has ceased to function from among its nationals, rather than by election.

One hundred and thirty-five experts have served on the Committee since it began its work in 1982. Unlike other human rights treaty bodies, with five exceptions, all members have been women, drawn from diverse backgrounds, rather than predominantly from the legal field. The majority has been profoundly committed to the objectives of the Convention and has significant expertise in the issues it addresses. As in the case of members of the CSW, they have frequently had a background in civil society activism on women's rights. The quality and commitment of the Committee's membership allowed it to develop its apparently narrow mandate imaginatively and expansively and advocate for the elimination of discrimination against women and recognition of their human rights not only with States parties but in UN policy-making and beyond.

The responsibility of providing the necessary staff and facilities for the effective performance of the functions of the Committee is devolved by the Convention on the UN Secretary-General. As noted earlier, this was fulfilled through the Branch and the Division for the Advancement of Women until 2008, when this responsibility was transferred to the Office of the High Commissioner for Human Rights. In large part, this transfer responded to the Secretary-General's desire for the ten human rights treaty bodies to streamline their work and harmonize their approaches to create an integrated human rights treaty body system. Pressure from civil society directed at strengthening CEDAW and securing it as central and crucial part of the UN human rights treaty discourse and machinery also played a significant role in the decision.

Competence

The Convention limits the competence of the Committee to consider progress made in its implementation to a reporting procedure set out in Article 18. This competence is supplemented by Article 21, which gives the Committee power to make suggestions and general recommendations based on the examination of reports and information received from States parties. In 1999, the General Assembly adopted an Optional Protocol to the Convention on the Elimination of All Forms of

Discrimination Against Women which added two further capacities: the competence to receive and consider individual communications claiming violations by a States party of any of the rights in the Convention and conduct confidential inquiries into reliable information indicating gave or systematic violations of the rights in the Convention by a State party. These are described below.

The Reporting Procedure

Article 18 provides that States parties undertake to submit reports on the legislative, judicial, administrative, or other measures they have adopted to give effect to the Convention and progress made within 1 year of entry into force for the State concerned and then every 4 years thereafter. The Committee may also request a report at any time, a power it has used rarely in exceptional situations such as conflict or economic crisis. Examples for the former are the situation in the (former) Federal Republic of Yugoslavia (Serbia and Montenegro) in its thirteenth session in 1994, in Bosnia and Herzegovina in its thirteenth session in 1994, in Croatia in its fourteenth session 1995, in Rwanda in its sixteenth session in 1996, and in the Democratic Republic of the Congo in its sixteenth and seventeenth sessions, respectively in 1997. An example of the latter is the report on the economic crisis in Argentina (CEDAW Committee, Follow-up report on Argentina 2004).

The Committee has adopted guidelines for reports which ask States parties to submit a "common core document," compiling general information on the human rights framework of the State relevant for all human rights treaty bodies, and a CEDAW-specific report (United Nations, Report of the Secretary General 2009, p. 3–26 and p. 65–71). The report is examined by a presessional working group two sessions before the report will be considered by the Committee, which draws up a list of issues and questions to which the State is asked to respond in writing well before the consideration. Since 2015, the Committee has offered States whose initial reports have been considered the option of using a "simplified" reporting procedure, as long as they have an up-to-date common core document. Under this procedure, the State is not required to submit a new CEDAW-specific report, as its answers to the list of issues and questions fulfill its subsequent reporting obligation (OHCHR/CEDAW 2015).

In line with the practice of all human rights treaty bodies, the Committee considers reports, along with the answers to the lists of issues and questions, in public meetings, in what is termed a "constructive dialogue" with representatives of the reporting State, sometimes some participating through video-technology, during which the member designated as the country rapporteur and other Committee members, most part of a country "task-force," pose questions to which the State responds. This process lasts for approximately six hours, after which the Committee adopts "concluding observations" specific to the State concerned. These are prepared by the country rapporteur with the support of the Secretariat.

The concluding observations follow a standard pattern, with some standard paragraphs and themes, which now include a section on the implementation of the Sustainable Development Goals. They are designed to provide the State with concrete guidance on strengthening implementation of the Convention. Accordingly, although reference is made to positive developments, their primary focus is on areas of concern and recommendations for action. They also indicate when the next report should be submitted, and, importantly, identify up to two "follow-up items" for short-term action, and ask States to provide information on these within 1 or 2 years, depending on their urgency. After the session, the concluding observations are transmitted to the State, which is asked to translate them into its official languages and disseminate them widely, including to relevant State institutions, such as the parliament and the judiciary. On occasion, States comment on the concluding observations in writing. Such comments are provided to the Committee members and the fact of their receipt mentioned in its annual report, with the full comments being uploaded on the OHCHR website if the State party so requests (Byrnes 2013, p. 38).

The Committee has invested considerable energy into honing its approach to concluding observations and the follow-up procedure. It appoints a rapporteur and an alternate rapporteur on follow-up to concluding observations, adopted a detailed methodology and regularly assesses the procedure. Guidelines for follow-up reports for States parties and stakeholders, which are all available publicly, have been developed, as has a system to grade the State's implementation of the follow-up items. In addition, the issue is accorded a separate agenda item at each Committee session, and a report on its follow-up activities is included in its annual report to the General Assembly. Methodology of the follow-up procedure to concluding observations has been described in detail by the Committee (United Nations, Report of the Committee on the Elimination of Discrimination Against Women on its 54th session 2013).

The guidelines for the common core document describe the objective of the reporting procedure, including preparation of the report, the dialogue with the Committee and follow-up, as an opportunity for the State to take stock of the state of human rights protection within their jurisdiction for the purpose of policy planning and implementation. They also indicate that the process should encourage national level public scrutiny of government policies and constructive engagement with relevant actors of civil society which should be conducted in a spirit of cooperation and mutual respect to advance the enjoyment by all of the rights protected in the treaty. CEDAW encourages States to include civil society in the preparation of the report and follow-up to concluding observations. It also includes it in all its processes in order to ensure that it has information to provide it with a full overview of national implementation (CEDAW Committee, Statement by the Committee on the Elimination of Discrimination Against Women on its relationship with nongovernmental organizations 2018a).

Thus, preparation of the lists and issues in the presessional working group and in the context of the simplified reporting procedure is informed by input from nongovernmental organizations and national human rights institutions, provided in writing and closed briefings. This information is also welcomed by the Committee during sessions, and NGOs are given a slot during formal meetings to brief it on the States under consideration. In addition, informal briefings of the Committee as a whole or particular member are convened. NGOs are also able to submit reports in the context of the follow-up procedure. CEDAW also recognizes that it and those

National Human Rights Institutions (NHRIs) which adhere to the Paris Principles (UN General Assembly resolution 48/134 1993) share the common goal of protecting, promoting, and fulfilling the human rights of women and girls and accordingly encourages NHRIs to provide country-specific information in writing and through oral briefings in formal meetings on States under consideration to the presessional working group and plenary sessions (CEDAW Committee, Statement of the Committee on the Elimination of Discrimination Against Women on its relationship with national human rights institutions 2008) as well as engage in its follow-up procedure, including through written reports.

United Nations specialized agencies, funds and programs, and other bodies, such as the Inter-Parliamentary Union, also participate in the reporting procedure. Article 22 of the Convention provides that specialized agencies may be represented at the consideration of implementation of provisions which fall within the scope of their activities and submit reports. Initially, such reports tended to be thematic but in line with the Committee's decisions are now country-specific (CEDAW Committee, Report of the Committee on the Elimination of Discrimination Against Women on its 34th, 35th, and 36th sessions 2006, part I, annex II, 79–80). Information is also provided in closed briefings, and the entities which transmit reports or otherwise engage go well beyond specialized agencies, and may include the relevant UN country team, sometimes through video-link, and the Human Rights Council's country rapporteurs.

Since its first session, CEDAW has worked hard to make its reporting mandate a dynamic force for change, in particular at the national level. As in the case of other human rights treaty bodies, however, it has faced the twin challenges of delayed submission of reports by States parties and a backlog of reports awaiting review, which became particularly acute as the number of States parties grew rapidly and its meeting time was strictly limited. The backlog has been addressed to a large extent by the General Assembly's approval of incremental increases in the Committee's meeting time beyond the 2 weeks envisaged in the Convention to the current three 3-week annual sessions and additional time for its various working groups. There has also been a significant improvement in reporting compliance, assisted by the Committee allowing reports to combine reporting rounds, the introduction of the simplified reporting procedure and the use of strategies such as consideration of the Convention's implementation in a State party in the absence of a report (Report of the Committee on the Elimination of Discrimination Against Women on its 34th, 35th, and 36th sessions, A/61/38, part I, annex II, 79–80, 2006). The OHCHRs human rights treaty capacity-building program, in which CEDAW members participate, has also enhanced State compliance.

General Recommendations

In addition to requiring the Committee to report annually to the General Assembly, via the ECOSOC, Article 21, paragraph 1 of the Convention indicates that it may make suggestions and general recommendations based in on the examination of reports and information received from States parties. There was much debate during CEDAWs early sessions as to the scope of this provision, and at its fifth session on 1986, it adopted its first general recommendation directed at all States parties on the reporting obligation set out in Article 18 (Boerefijn 2013b, p. 522–523). Most of its initial recommendations were brief and tentative, but they have now evolved in substance and complexity and provide authoritative guidance on measures required to implement the Convention and contribute to the development of international law. By the end of its sixty-seventh session in July 2017, the Committee had adopted 35 general recommendations on individual articles of the Convention and cross-cutting themes, and several are in an advanced stage of preparation (OHCHR/CEDAW 2014). One general recommendation, 35 on gender-based violence against women updates general recommendation 19 adopted 25 years ago in 1992 (CEDAW Committee General recommendation No. 35 2017a). Importantly also, general recommendation 31 on harmful practices, adopted with the Committee on the Rights of the Child, is the first joint general recommendation to be adopted by the human rights treaty body system (CEDAW Committee and CRC Committee Joint general recommendation No. 31 2014).

Usually, the topics chosen for general recommendations emerge through the information and experience gained by the Committee through the reporting process, including through the input of the UN system and civil society. Potential themes are often suggested by UN entities and civil society, including academia, which may support the process by providing background papers and the organization of meetings and other events. The Centre for Women, Peace and Security at the London School of Economics and Political Science convened two expert group meetings to assist in the development of this general recommendation. Individual Committee members also advocate for particular areas of focus. The Committee's procedure for elaborating general recommendations is highly consultative and inclusive of States and all stakeholders relevant to the subject of the recommendation. It also incorporates the elements proposed in 2015 by the treaty body chairs directed at aligning the practices of all the human rights treaty bodies in this context (United Nations, Report of the Chairs of the human rights treaty bodies on their 27th meeting 2015b, paras. 90–91). Thus, after deciding to embark on the general recommendation, the Committee generally prepares a concept note and convenes a half-day discussion, usually featuring expert commentators, with States, UN entities, civil society, and other interested parties. A working group of the Committee formulates a draft which may be made available to other human rights treaty bodies and relevant special rapporteurs for input to encourage coherence in human rights interpretation. Thereafter, the draft recommendation is uploaded on the OHCHR website and comments solicited. These, also posted on the website, are considered by the working group, which may revise the draft. The final draft is then considered for adoption in the Committee plenary.

Several general recommendations have had influence on the development of human rights law at the international and regional levels, laws, policies, and programs in States parties and civil society advocacy and interventions. General recommendation 19 on violence against women has been especially important as its categorization of gender-based violence as a form of discrimination against women on the basis of sex fills the glaring omission of this issue from the Convention and locates the issue squarely within in the framework of international human rights law (Chinkin 2012, p. 443–474). The language and analysis in this general recommendation underpin UN work on gender-based violence against women, including that of the Special Rapporteur on Violence Against Women, while regional and domestic courts have also cited its terms (European Court of Human Rights 2009, para. 25; Inter-American Court 2009, paras. 394–5; Supreme Court of India 1977, para. 13). The broad participation the Committee advocates in the preparation of these documents and their implementation is likely to deepen their influence (Swaine and O'Rourke 2015, p. 1–28).

In addition to general recommendations, the Committee adopts "suggestions," which usually relate to procedural matters, "statements" and what it describes as "open letters" (OHCHR/CEDAW 2017). Statements, which are sometimes joint, are difficult to categorize as they can relate to themes; the situation of women and girls in particular countries or territories; UN processes, for example, the elaboration of the Sustainable Development Goals or treaty body strengthening; and relationships with UN entities, such as UN Women. "Open letters" are similarly difficult to categorize, as are the Committee's decisions and occasional resolutions which are published in its reports. An example is the resolution on the guidelines on independence and impartiality of members of the human rights bodies (CEDAW Committee, Report of the Committee on the Elimination of Discrimination Against Women on its 52nd session 2013, Part I, Annex).

The Optional Protocol to the Convention on the Elimination of All Forms of Discrimination Against Women

The background to the Optional Protocol and the work of the Committee in respect of its procedures to the end of 2010 has been described by the current author and others and will not be repeated here. Suffice it to say, although during the Convention's drafting three delegations suggested inclusion of an individual petition procedure along the lines of those available to the Human Rights Committee and the Committee on the Elimination of Racial Discrimination, these suggestions were not followed. Indeed, several delegations considered that such a procedure would be inappropriate as there was a distinction between treaties on serious international crimes, such as apartheid and racial discrimination and those dealing with discrimination against women where States had begun to cooperate (Connors 2012, p. 608–609).

The campaign to strengthen the Committee's oversight capacity began almost as soon as its first session, as commentators began to describe it as the poor relation of the treaty body family, and CEDAW itself began to demand more tools. Advocacy began in earnest in the lead-up to the World Conference on Human Rights and the Fourth World Conference on Women, with the outcome of both calling for strengthening of CEDAW generally, and for early adoption of a petitions procedure, in particular. Coordinated and determined pressure from sympathetic and skilled members of the CSW, CEDAW, and well-prepared civil society resulted in the launch of a negotiation process on a draft which provided for both an individual petitions procedure and an inquiry procedure. This successfully concluded after 4 years and was followed by rapid entry of the instrument into force. At the time of writing, there are 109 States parties to the Optional Protocol drawn from all regions of the world. Of these, four, Bangladesh, Belize, Colombia, and Tajikistan, have chosen, as allowed by the treaty, to opt out of the inquiry procedure.

The Optional Protocol's petitions and inquiry procedures are modeled on similar procedures in earlier treaties, but good practices developed by their respective treaty bodies, such as CEDAWs power to request interim measures to avoid irreparable harm to victims and means to follow-up the outcome of both procedures, are explicitly set out in the Protocol. There are also novel provisions, including that no reservations are permitted to the Protocol, and that the State party shall take all appropriate steps to ensure that individuals under its jurisdiction are not subjected to ill-treatment or intimidation as a consequence of using its procedures. The latter provision is now particularly pertinent as the incidence of intimidation of and reprisals against those who use or seek to access human rights procedures and remedies has become commonplace. Indeed, in 2015, the treaty body chairs adopted the San José Guidelines on Reprisals (United Nations, Guidelines on Intimidation or Reprisals 2015a), while CEDAW itself addressed China on the issue in the concluding observations when it reported in 2014 (CEDAW Committee, Concluding Observations 2014c, paras. 32–33).

By the end of its sixty-seventh session in July 2017, CEDAW had adopted 65 decisions on petitions under the Optional Protocol. Of these, 35 were held to be inadmissible in line with the admissibility criteria set out in its Articles 2 and 4. The threshold requirement for admissibility is that the petitioner or petitioners (or any petition transmitted on their behalf) must claim to be a victim of a violation of any of the rights in the Convention by a State party to both the Convention and the Protocol. In addition, all available domestic remedies must be exhausted, unless the application of such remedies is unreasonably prolonged or unlikely to bring effective relief. The Committee is also required to declare a communication inadmissible where it has already examined the same matter or the matter has been or is being examined under another procedure of international investigation or settlement; it is incompatible with the provisions in the Convention, manifestly ill-founded or not sufficiently substantiated or an abuse of the right to petition or the facts relied on occurred prior to the entry into force of the Protocol for the State party unless they are considered to have continued. Predominantly, CEDAW has found claims inadmissible because of lack of substantiation and failure to exhaust domestic remedies. In two cases relating to family names (CEDAW Committee, Communication No. 12/2007 Group d'Intérêt pour le Matronyme v France 2009a; and Communication No. 13/2007 SOS Sexisme v France 2009b), it concluded the complainants were not victims of a violation but sought to address systemic discrimination against women related to the issue. A similar decision was made in claim for relief for systemic discrimination against foreign women in child custody cases where the petitioner had gained custody of her child (CEDAW Committee, Communication No. 44/2012 M.KD-AA v Denmark 2013). In another, held inadmissible by the majority of the Committee on the ground that the facts occurred prior to the entry into force of the Protocol, the minority found a claim by a woman of discrimination on the basis of sex resulting from her younger brother's succession to a title of nobility to be incompatible with the Convention. This decision was based on the view that a title of nobility was purely symbolic and honorific, and any claim of succession was incompatible with the objective of the Convention to protect women from discrimination which has the effect or purpose of impairing or nullifying the recognition, enjoyment or exercise by women on a basis of equality of men and women of human rights and fundamental freedoms in all fields (CEDAW Committee, Communication No. 7/2005 Munoz-Varas y Sainz de Vicuna v Spain 2007c). Unsurprisingly, this view has been criticized.

CEDAWs decisions, which Article 7 of the Optional Protocol terms "views," in admissible cases, although technically not legally binding, have profoundly contributed to the growing body of women's rights jurisprudence. Some relief has also been given to victims, or where they are deceased, their families, through reparations, including compensation.

To date, most petitions have concerned gender-based violence, including sexual harassment in the workplace, and reproductive health rights. The Committee's views on these, which include detailed recommendations, outline the obligations of States parties in respect of their actions and those of their agents, such as law enforcement personnel, prison officials, the judiciary, and public health providers. Building on Article 2(e) of Convention which requires States parties to take all appropriate measures to eliminate discrimination against women by any person, organization or enterprise and relevant general recommendations, views explain the obligation of States parties to act with due diligence to prevent violations of rights result from the acts of non-State actors, as well as to investigate and punish such violations and provide compensation so as to avoid impunity. Strong guidance has been provided to States parties on their accountability for violence against women and girls, including domestic and sexual violence (CEDAW Committee, Communications No. 2/2008 AT v Hungary 2005; No. 5/2005 Şahide Goekce v Austria 2005; No. 6/2005 Yildirim v Austria 2007b; No. 29/2008 VK v Bulgaria 2012e; No. 31/2011 SPP v Bulgaria 2012c; No. 32/2011 Isatou Jallow v Bulgaria 2012d; No. 47/2012 González Carreňo v Spain 2014b; and No. 29/2009 X and Y v Georgia 2015a). Where reproductive health is concerned, the Committee has drawn on its general recommendation 24 on women and health and held States parties accountable for their failures to meet the distinctive health needs of women. It has also made clear that States parties have an obligation of due diligence to ensure that private actors implement health policies and practices appropriately, an obligation they cannot evade by outsourcing medical services to the private sector (CEDAW Committee, Communications No. 17/2008 Alyne da Silva Pimentel Teixera v Brazil 2011a; and No. 22/209 LC v Peru 2009). Several decisions provide pioneering analysis of stereotypes and ideologies which are at the root of discrimination against women may be at the root of violations, especially if relied on by the judiciary when deciding sexual violence cases (CEDAW Committee, Communications No. 18/2008 Vertido v the Philippines 2010; No. 34/2011 RPB v the Philippines 2014a; and No. 28/2010 RKB v Turkey 2012b). Most explore the obligations States have implement measures in place to address compounded, intersectional, or multiple discrimination arising, for example, from the interplay of discrimination based on disability and race with discrimination on the basis of sex (CEDAW Committee, Communication No. 19/2008 Kell v Canada 2012a).

The Optional Protocol provides that the State party which has been the subject of a successful communication should transmit a written response including information on action it has taken in this context 6 months after receiving the Committee's views. CEDAW may request further information, including in Article 18 reports. Just as with its concluding observations, CEDAW has been active in following up the implementation of its recommendations where it finds a violation. Its approach is tailored to each case and may include requesting further information on the steps that the State has taken and meeting with its representatives to discuss its action. Follow-up may continue until a satisfactory resolution has been reached, at which point it will be declared closed. The results of follow-up, which suggest that most States respond positively to the Committee's recommendations, are reported on in CEDAWs annual report. CEDAW is also active in implementing its interim measures competence, with decisions in this context being taken in the light of the gender-based and other constraints, such as those resulting from intersectional discrimination, petitioners might face.

Article 8 to 10 of the Optional Protocol set out the parameters of CEDAWs inquiry competence. An inquiry is generated where the Committee receives reliable information indicating grave or systematic violations of the rights in the Convention in a State which is party to the Convention and the Optional Protocol but has not taken advantage of the possibility set out in Article 10 that it does not recognize the Committee's inquiry competence. Information in this context may be submitted by any source, including individuals, women's rights groups and other civil society organizations and the initial task of the Committee, which it devolves at the outset on its working group on inquiries, is to determine whether the information is reliable. It must then determine whether the information suggests the high threshold of "grave" or "systematic" violations of the Convention, in other words very serious forms of discrimination, which may be isolated, or broad patterns of structural discrimination. Notably, the threshold is not cumulative, so the violations need not be both grave and systematic. If the Committee considers the threshold met, which is not always the case, the information is transmitted to the State party for its comments. Thereafter, the initial information, the State's response, and any other reliable information available to the Committee, which might include UN material, is examined and the Committee's decides whether to conduct an inquiry. If it decides to do so, it devolves this responsibility on one or more of its members, who may, where warranted and with the consent of the State party, visit its territory. The findings of the inquiry are then examined by the Committee and these are transmitted to the State, along with any recommendations. Thereafter, the State has 3 months in which to provide its observations to the Committee.

At the end of July 2017, the Committee had conducted four inquiries, of which the results of three (Canada: disappearance of indigenous women; Mexico: disappearance of women; and the Philippines: reproductive health rights) had been published (OHCHR/CEDAW 2013). A further 13 were at various stages of the procedure (CEDAW Committee, Report of the Committee on the Elimination of Discrimination Against Women on its 67th session 2017b, Appendix I, Annex 2, para. 5). The objective of the inquiry procedure is to bring about structural change at national level to address very serious patterns of discrimination against women, and its hallmarks are confidentiality and the cooperation of the State throughout all stages of the process. Follow-up includes the possibility that the Committee will invite the State to provide information on steps it has taken to respond to the inquiry and/or include such information in its next report under Article 18 of the Convention (Article 9). It is the Committee's practice to publish the full report of any inquiry along with the comments of the State party, where the latter agrees. Where it does not do so, the Committee publishes a summary report (CEDAW Committee, Summary of the Philippines inquiry 2015b).

Conclusion

Since its establishment, like the CSW, CEDAWs visibility and influence has expanded and deepened. Once described as marginal and weak, its Convention is almost universally ratified, and it is a full member of the human rights treaty body family, enjoying all the competencies of such a body and fully engaged in the work of the system. It has built strong relationships with its sister treaty bodies and participates fully in the human rights treaty body strengthening process. It has a broad constituency among UN bodies and collaborates closely with the HRC special procedures system, in particular the Special Rapporteur on Violence Against Women and the Working Group on Discrimination Against Women in Law and in Practice and other human rights mechanisms such as the HRC Universal Periodic Review. It maintains a close relationship with the CSW and by engaging with the 2030 Agenda, including through its CEDAW-UN Women/SDGs Working Group and its contributions to the High-level Political Forum on Sustainable Development. CEDAW bridges the human rights and development agendas. It has crafted relationships with bodies outside the UN system, such as the IPU, and, perhaps more than any other human rights treaty body, has a broad and varied civil society following, including from the grass roots.

Nonetheless, there are challenges. Much as a result of its visibility, and the promise it offers women all over the world, it has an almost insurmountable workload. This has increased as it expanded its reach to take on new tasks and crafts new outputs, including general recommendations on multifaceted topics. Where once CEDAW was disappointed at the limited use of the Optional Protocol, it now faces a large backlog of communications and inquiry requests. Another challenge facing the Committee, particularly as more women turn to the Optional Protocol, is consistency of interpretation and rigorous analysis of gender-based discrimination in all contexts. The Committee's approach to communications where gender-based discrimination is clear, such as violence against women and reproductive health rights is strong. Where this is less clear, as in relation to titles of nobility or complex pension entitlements, it appears less so.

This chapter has briefly traced the development of the peak intergovernmental and expert bodies dedicated to the realization of women's human rights. It has sought to underline the communalities between them, while at the same time showing that they have different, but linked objectives, with the CSW focused on women's empowerment and gender mainstreaming, and CEDAW the promotion and protection of the rights set out in the Convention. It has not addressed a fundamental challenge that faces both: the maintenance of a universal approach in a world of diversity of culture, religion, and opinion. This challenge is debated annually as the CSW conducts its detailed review of implementation of the Beijing Declaration and Platform for Action. It is a factor in CEDAWs dialogue and relationship with States parties, especially those which maintain objectionable reservations, and in the delivery of all its mandates.

References

Agenda for Sustainable Development (2015), UN Doc. A/RES/70/1

Banda F (2013a) The UN Working Group on discrimination against women. In: Hellum A, Sindig Aasen H (eds) Women's human rights: CEDAW in international, regional and national law. Cambridge University Press, Cambridge, pp 62–94

Banda F (2013b) Article 14: rural women. In: Freeman M, Chinkin C, Rudolf B (eds) The UN Convention on the Elimination of All Forms of Discrimination Against Women: a commentary. Oxford University Press, Oxford, pp 358–385

Begtrup B (1946) Statement of the chair of the Subcommission on the Status of Women. Bodil Begtrup to ECOSOC, UN Doc E/PV4 (28 May 1946)

Boerefijn I (2013a) Article 17. In: Freeman M, Chinkin C, Rudolf B (eds) The UN Convention on the Elimination of All Forms of Discrimination Against Women: a commentary. Oxford University Press, Oxford, pp 475–478

Boerefijn I (2013b) Article 21. In: Freeman M, Chinkin C, Rudolf B (eds) The UN Convention on the Elimination of All Forms of Discrimination Against Women: a commentary. Oxford University Press, Oxford, pp 522–523

Boulding E (1975) Female alternatives to hierarchical systems, past and present: a critique of women's NGO's in the light of history. International Associations 6-7:340–346

Butler-Dines K (2017) Saudi Arabia's election to the UN Commission on the Status of Women: UN blunder or new opportunity? Georgetown Institute for Women, Peace and Security (GIWPS) Available at: http://giwps.georgetown.edu/saudi-arabias-election-to-the-un-commission-on-the-status-of-women-un-blunder-or-new-opportunity-2. Accessed 13 February 2018

Byrnes A (2013) The Committee on the Elimination of Discrimination against Women. In: Hellum A, Sinding Aasen H (eds) Women's human rights: CEDAW in international, regional and national law. Cambridge University Press, Cambridge, pp 27–61

CEDAW Committee (2004) Follow-up report on Argentina, UN Doc. CEDAW/C/ARG/5/Add.1, 29 January 2004

CEDAW Committee (2005) Communication 2/2003 AT v Hungary, UN Doc. CEDAW/C/36/D/2/2003

CEDAW Committee (2006) Report of the Committee on the Elimination of Discrimination Against Women on its 34th, 35th and 36th sessions, UN Doc. A/61/38

CEDAW Committee (2007a) Communication No. 5/2005 Şahide Goekce v Austria, UN Doc. CEDAW/C/39/D/5/2005

CEDAW Committee (2007b) Communication No. 6/2005 Yildirim v Austria, UN Doc. CEDAW/C/39/D/6/2005

CEDAW Committee (2007c) Communication No. 7/2005 Munoz-Varas y Sainz de Vicuna v Spain, UN Doc. CEDAW/C/39/7/2005

CEDAW Committee (2009a) Communication No. 12/2007 Group d'Intérêt pour le Matronyme v France, UN Doc. CEDAW/C/44/D/12/2007

CEDAW Committee (2009b) Communication No. 13/2007 SOS Sexisme v France, UN Doc. CEDAW/C/44/D/13/2007

CEDAW Committee (2010) Communication No. 18/2008 Vertido v the Philippines, UN Doc. CEDAW/C/46/D/18/2008

CEDAW Committee (2011a) Communication No. 17/2008 Alyne da Silva Pimentel Teixera v Brazil, UN Doc. CEDAW/C/49/D/17/2008

CEDAW Committee (2011b), Communication No. 22/2009 LC v Peru, UN Doc. CEDAW/C/50/D/22/2009

CEDAW Committee (2012a) Communication No. 19/2008 Kell v Canada, UN Doc. CEDAW/C/51/D/19/2008

CEDAW Committee (2012b) Communication No. 23/2010 RKB v Turkey, UN Doc. CEDAW/C/51/D/28/2010

CEDAW Committee (2012c) Communication No. 31/2011 SPP v Bulgaria, UN Doc. CEDAW/C/53/D/31/2011

CEDAW Committee (2012d) Communication No. 32/2011 Isatou Jallow v Bulgaria, UN Doc. CEDAW/C/52/D/32/2011

CEDAW Committee (2012e) Communication No. No. 20/2008 VK v Bulgaria, UN Doc. CEDAW/C/49/D/20/2008

CEDAW Committee (2013) Communication No. 44/2012 M.KD-AA v Denmark, UN Doc. CEDAW/C/56/D/44/2012

CEDAW Committee (2014a) Communication No. 34/2011 RPB v the Philippines, UN Doc. CEDAW/C/57/D/34/2011

CEDAW Committee (2014b) Communication No. 7/2012 González Carreño v Spain, UN Doc. CEDAW/C/48/D/47/2012

CEDAW Committee (2014c) Concluding observations on the combined 7th and 8th periodic reports of China, UN Doc. CEDAW/C/CHIN/CO/7–8

CEDAW Committee (2015a) Communication No. 29/2009 X and Y v Georgia, UN Doc. CEDAW/C/61/D/29/2009

CEDAW Committee (2015b) Summary of the Philippines inquiry, UN Doc. CEDAW/C/OP.8/PHL/1/2015

CEDAW Committee (2017a) General recommendation No. 35 on gender-based violence against women, updating general recommendation No. 19, UN Doc. CEDAW/C/GC/35, 26 July 2017

CEDAW Committee (2017b) Report of the Committee on the Elimination of Discrimination Against Women on its 67th session, Informal Document, UN Doc. CEDAW/C/2017/II/CRP

CEDAW Committee (2018a) Statement by the Committee on the Elimination of Discrimination Against Women on its relationship with non-governmental organizations, http://www.ohchr.org/Documents/HRBodies/CEDAW/Statements/NGO.pdf. Accessed 13 January 2018

CEDAW Committee (2018b) Statement of the Committee on the Elimination of Discrimination Against Women on its relationship with national human rights institutions 2008, http://www.ohvhr.org/Documents/HRBodies/CEDAW/StatementOnNHRIs.pdf. Accessed 13 January 2018

CEDAW Committee and CRC Committee (2014) Joint general recommendation No. 31 of the Committee on the Elimination of Discrimination Against Women/General comment No. 18 of the Committee on the Rights of the Child on harmful practices, UN Doc. CEDAW/C/GR/31-CRC/C/GC/18, 4 November 2014

Charlesworth H, Chinkin C (2013) The new United Nations "gender architecture": the creation of UN women, RegNet research paper series, 2013/7, regulatory institutions network (RegNet). Australian National University, Centre for International Governance and Justice, pp 1–36

Chinkin C Freeman M (2012) introduction. In: Freeman M, Chinkin C. Rudolf B (eds) the UN Convention on the Elimination of All Forms of Discrimination Against Women: a commentary. Oxford University Press, Oxford, pp 1–33

Chinkin C, Freeman M (2012) Violence against women. In: Freeman M, Chinkin C, Rudolf B (eds) The UN Convention on the Elimination of All Forms of Discrimination Against Women: a commentary. Oxford University Press, Oxford, pp 443–474

Commission on Human Rights (1988) resolution 188/33 (April 1988) UN Doc E/CN4/Res/1998/33:17

Commission on the Status of Women (1947) Report of the Commission on the Status of Women on its first session (1947) UN Doc (February 1947) E/281/Rev 1:25

Commission on the Status of Women (1972) resolution 10 (XXIV) (February 1972) UN Doc E/CN 6(/568):29

Commission on the Status of Women (1974) Report of the twenty-fifth session, UN doc. In: E/5451

Commission on the Status of Women (1978) Resolution XXVII adopted at its twenty-seventh session, UN doc. E/1978/322/rev.1-E/CN.6/620/rev.1, ECOSOC official records 1978. Supplement No:2

Commission on the Status of Women (1982) draft resolution UN Doc. IV E/1982/14-E/CN.6/1982/14

Commission on the Status of Women (2016) Report of the Commission on the Status of Women on its sixtieth session for the types of trends identified, UN doc. In: E/CN.6/2016/22

Commission on the Status of Women (2017) Report of the Commission on the Status of Women on its sixty-first session, UN doc. In: E/2017/27-E/CN.6/2017/21

Commission on the Status of Women. resolution 7(XXI), UN Doc. E/4472

Connors J (1996) NGOs and the human rights of women at the UN. In: Willets P (ed) The conscience of the world: the influence of non-governmental organisations in the UN system. Hurst, London, pp 147–180

Connors J (2012) Optional Protocol. In: Freeman M, Chinkin C, Rudolf B (eds) The UN Convention on the Elimination of All Forms of Discrimination Against Women: a commentary. Oxford University Press, Oxford, pp 607–679

ECOSOC (2016) List of non-governmental organizations in consultative status with the Economic and Social Council as of 1 September 2016, UN Doc. E/2016/INF/5, 29 December 2016

ECOSOC. decision 2002/234, 24 July 2002

ECOSOC. decision 2002/235, 24 July 2002

ECOSOC. decision 86/5683, UN Doc. E/5683 (1975)

ECOSOC. draft resolution IV presented to the ECOSOC by the twenty-ninth session of the CSW, UN Doc. E/1982/14-E/CN.6/1982/14

ECOSOC resolution. 1235, UN Doc. E/4935 (1967)

ECOSOC resolution. 1326 (XLIV), 31 May 1968, UN Doc. A/7203

ECOSOC resolution. 1503, UN Doc. E/4832, Add.1 (1970)

ECOSOC resolution. 1987/21, UN Doc. E/RES/1987/21, 26 May 1987

ECOSOC resolution. 1987/24, UN Doc. E/RES/1987/24, 26 May 1987

ECOSOC resolution. 1992/19, UN Doc. E/RES/1992/19, 30 July 1992

ECOSOC resolution. 1993/11, UN Doc. E/RES/1993/11, 27 July 1993

ECOSOC resolution. 1999/257, UN Doc. E/RES/1999/257, 28 July 1999

ECOSOC resolution. 2009/16, UN Doc. E/RES/2009/16, 28 July 2009

ECOSOC resolution. 2015/6, UN Doc. E/RES/2015/6, 31 July 2015

ECOSOC resolution. 2016/3, Multi-year programme of work of the Commission on the Status of Women, UN Doc. E/RES/2016/3, 22 July 2016

ECOSOC resolution. 304 I (XI), UN Doc. E/1849, 14 and 17 July 1950

ECOSOC resolution. 76 (V) 1947, UN Doc. E/573, 5 August 1947

ECOSOC resolution E/RES/196 (VIII) (1949) calling for cooperation between the International Labour Organization and the Commission on the Status of Women, UN Doc. E/RES/196 (VIII), 18 February 1949

ECOSOC resolution E/RES/2/11 (1946) establishing the Commission on the Status of Women, UN Doc. E/RES/2/11, 21 June 1946

European Court of Human Rights., Opuz v Turkey, 33401/02, 9 June 2009

Finlay, L (2014) Having Iran as its standard-bearer for women's rights discredits UN. The Conversation. Available at: https://theconversation.com/having-iran-as-its-standard-bearer-for-womens-rights-discredits-un-26437. Accessed 13 February 2018

Human Rights Council resolution 15/23 (2010) UN doc. HRC/RES/15/23, 23 October 2010

Human Rights Council resolution 5/1 (2007) on the institution building of the Human Rights Council, UN Doc. A/RES/HRC/5/1, 18 June 2007

Humphrey JP (1983) The memoires of John P. Humphrey: the first director of the United Nations division for human rights. Human Rights Quarterly 5:387–405

Inter-American Court of Human Rights (2009) Gonzàlez et al ('Cotton Field') v Mexico, Series c, No 205, 16 November 2009

International Women's Health Coalition (n.d.) Statement on the political declaration on the occasion of the 20th anniversary of the Fourth World Conference on Women, https://iwhc.org/resources/womens-statement-20th-anniversary-fourth-world-conference-women. Accessed 15 February 2018

Jain D (2005) Women, development and the United Nations: a sixty-year quest for equality and justice. Indiana University Press, Bloomington, pp 17–18

OHCHR (2008) CEDAW now in Geneva. Available at http://www.ohchr.org/EN/NewsEvents/Pages/Cedaw.aspx. Accessed 15 February 2018

OHCHR/CEDAW (2014) General recommendations, Available at http://www.ohchr.org/EN/HRBodies/CEDAW/Pages/Recommendations.aspx. Accessed 15 February 2018

OHCHR/CEDAW (2015) Simplified reporting procedure, Available at http://www.ohchr.org/EN/HRBodies/CEDAW/Pages/ReportingProcedures.aspx. Accessed 15 February 2018

OHCHR/CEDAW (2017) Chairperson's and other statements. Available at http://www.ohchr.org/EN/HRBodies/CEDAW/Pages/Statements.aspx. Accessed 15 February 2018

OHCHR/CESCR (2013) Inquiry procedure, Available at: http://www.ohchr.org/EN/HRBodies/CESCR/Pages/InquiryProcedure.aspx. Accessed 15 February 2018

Peitilä, H (2007) The unfinished story of women and the United Nations, NGLS Development Dossier, Geneva, UNCTAD/NGLS/2007/1, p 38–39

Puri, L (2017) Report on CSW61 and analysis of the agreed conclusions, UN Women. Available at http://www.unwomen.org/en/digital-library/publications/2017/5/report-of-csw61-and-analysis-of-the-agreed-conclusions. Accessed 15 February 2018

Reanda L (1992) The Commission on the Status of Women. In: Alston P (ed) The United Nations and human rights: a critical appraisal. Oxford University Press, Oxford, pp 265–303

Skard T (2008) Getting our history right: how were the equal rights of women and men included in the charter of the United Nations? Forum for Development (1):37–60

Statute of the Inter-American Commission of Women (2016). Available at http://www.oas.org/en/cim/docs/CIMStatute-2016-EN.pdf. Accessed 28 Feb 2018

Supreme Court of India., Vishaka v The State of Rajasthan (AIR 1977 Supreme Court 3011)

Swaine Λ, O'Rourkc C (2015) Guidebook on CEDAW general recommendation no 30 and the UN security Council's resolutions on women, peace and security. Women, UN

UN General Assembly resolution 3010 (XXVII) (1972) UN Doc A/RES/3010 (XXVII), 18 December:1972

UN General Assembly resolution 35/136 (1980) UN Doc. A/RES/35/136, 11 December 1980

UN General Assembly resolution 48/134 (1993) Principles relating to the status of national institutions for the promotion and protection of human rights (Paris Principles), UN Doc. A/RES/48/134, annex, 20 December 1993

UN General Assembly resolution 50/203 (1995) UN Doc. A/RES/50/203, 22 December 1995

UN General Assembly resolution 55/71 (2001) UN Doc. A/RES/55/71, 8 February 2001

UN General Assembly resolution 60/251 (2006) UN Doc. A/RES/60/251, 3 April 2006

UN Watch (2017) No Joke: UN elects Saudi Arabia to Women's Rights Commission for 2018–2022 Term. Available at https://www.unwatch.org/no-joke-u-n-elects-saudi-arabia-womens-rights-commission. Accessed 13 January 2018

UN Women (2017) Communications Procedure, Available at: http://www.unwomen.org/en/csw/communications-procedure. Accessed 13 February 2018

United Nations (1948), UN Doc. E/RES/120 (VI), 3 March 1948

United Nations (1950) Report of the Secretary-General to the CSW on the UNESCO study of educational opportunities for women, UN Doc. E/CN.6/146, 9 May 1950

United Nations (1980) Programme of Action for the Second Half of the UN Decade for Women, UN Doc. A/CONF.94/35 (80.IV.3)

United Nations (1983) Report of the special rapporteur on the exploitation and prostitution of others to the ECOSOC, UN Doc. E/1983/7, 17 March 1983

United Nations (1991) Report of the Secretary-General: Monitoring the Implementation of the Nairobi Forward-looking Strategies for the Advancement of Women: examining existing communications mechanisms of the advancement of women, UN Doc. E/CN.6/1991/10

United Nations (1996) United Nations and advancement of women, UN publications series, vol VI. United Nations Publications, New York

United Nations (1997) Report of the Economic and Social Council, UN Doc. A/52/3, 18 September 1997

United Nations (2001) Report of the Secretary-General assessing the implications of the reforms of the mechanisms in the human rights area (1503 procedure) for communications concerning the status of women, UN Doc. E/CN.6/2001/12, 16 January 2001

United Nations (2002) Report of the Secretary-General assessing the implications of the reforms of mechanisms in the human rights area (1503 procedure) for communications concerning the status of women, UN Doc. E/CN.6/2002/12, 18 January 2002

United Nations (2004) Report of the Secretary-General on future work of the Working Group on Communications on the Status of Women, UN Doc. E/CN.6/2004/11, 22 December 2003, Add I, 16 January 2004, and Add II, 11 February 2004

United Nations (2009a) Report of the Secretary General, UN Doc. HRI/GEN/2/Rev.6, 3 June 2009

United Nations (2009b) Report of the Secretary-General on future work of the Working Group on Communications on the Status of Women, UN Doc. E/CN.6/2009/8, 1 December 2008

United Nations (2012) Report of the Chairs of human rights treaty bodies on their 24th meeting, Annex I, UN Doc. A/67/222

United Nations (2013) Report of the Committee on the Elimination of Discrimination Against Women on its 52nd session, UN Doc. A/68/38

United Nations (2015a) Guidelines on Intimidation or Reprisals (San José Guidelines), UN Doc. HRI/MC/2015/6, 30 July 2015

United Nations (2015b) Report of the Chairs of the human rights treaty bodies on their 27th meeting, UN Doc. A/70/302

Vienna Declaration and Programme of Action (1993), UN Doc. A/CONF.157/23

World Plan of Action for the Implementation of the Objectives of the International Women's Year (1975), UN Doc. E/CONF.66/34 (76.IV.1)

The UN Security Council and Human Rights

Joanna Weschler and Lindiwe Knutson

Contents

Introduction 200
The Early Years of the Security Council's Involvement with Human Rights 201
The Security Council and Human Rights Information 202
The Security Council's Interaction with UN Human Rights Investigators 205
The Security Council's Interaction with the UN High Commissioner for Human Rights 206
The Security Council's Discussions of Human Rights 208
The Security Council's Evolving Approach to Human Rights as a Theme 209
Human Rights Components in Peace Operations 210
Commissions of Inquiry 212
Judicial Mechanisms 213
Council Visiting Missions 214
Sanctions 216
Human Rights in Security Council Conflict Prevention Action 219
Council Dynamics 220
Conclusions and a Look Ahead 221
References 222

Abstract

The UN Security Council and Human Rights examines the relationship between peace and security and human rights and the role human rights have played in the thinking and action of the Security Council when addressing conflicts worldwide. Human rights feature prominently in the Charter of the United Nations. For decades, however, human rights were seen as being largely outside the scope of the Security Council. Over the past quarter of a century or so, the Security Council has indeed significantly changed its attitude to human rights. This chapter examines the evolution of the Security Council's approach to human

J. Weschler (✉) · L. Knutson
Security Council Report, New York, NY, USA
e-mail: j.weschler@securitycouncilreport.org; l.knutson@securitycouncilreport.org

© Springer Nature Singapore Pte Ltd. 2018   199
G. Oberleitner (ed.), *International Human Rights Institutions, Tribunals, and Courts*,
International Human Rights, https://doi.org/10.1007/978-981-10-5206-4_9

rights, including in relation to peace operations, visiting missions, and sanctions regimes. It also examines the relationship between the Security Council and the parts of the UN system specifically focused on human rights, in particular the Human Rights Council and the High Commissioner for Human Rights. This close examination suggests that the Security Council's resort to the different tools available and its follow-up has been uneven in relation to human rights. A conclusion reached is that meaningful human rights results on the ground in conflict situations are achieved when there is burden sharing both within the Security Council and among the different parts of the UN, maximizing all resources. Related to this conclusion is that human rights improvements are never just the success of one actor and that the different actors can reinforce each other's contribution.

Keywords

United Nations · Security Council · Human rights · High Commissioner for Human Rights · Human Rights Council

Introduction

Human rights feature prominently in the Charter of the United Nations. Its preamble says that the "Peoples of the United Nations" are determined to save succeeding generations from the scourge of war and reaffirm faith in fundamental human rights. Promoting the respect for human rights is included among the purposes and principles of the organization. Article 55 sees "universal respect for, and observance of, human rights" as integral to the "creation of conditions of stability and well-being which are necessary for peaceful and friendly relations among nations."

For decades, however, human rights were seen as being largely outside the scope of the Security Council and were seldom mentioned within its confines. Governments felt ambivalent about including a set of issues widely perceived as a matter of state sovereignty in their deliberations about international peace and security. But, after several decades when most items on the Council agenda had been conflicts between states, the nature of the situations the Council needed to address changed toward the end of the 1980s increasingly to internal conflicts. In these situations, human rights violations are often among the first warning signs of a looming conflict, they may be part of a conflict's root causes, and they are almost invariably a feature of the conflict as such. A failure to accept human rights as an aspect of the reality which the Council needed to deal with would, for purely pragmatic reasons, considerably hamper the Council's effectiveness.

Over the past quarter of a century or so, the Security Council has indeed significantly changed its attitude to human rights. From largely keeping human rights outside its scope, the Security Council today sees human rights as an important factor in the situations it is striving to address. Most missions created or authorized by the Council now have various human rights tasks in their mandates, and most missions have substantive human rights capacities or components. In addition, the

Council has used or developed an impressive range of tools – such as commissions of inquiry, judicial mechanisms, visiting missions, or sanctions – to achieve goals with an impact on human rights in different parts of the world.

This chapter will examine the evolution of the Security Council's approach to human rights. It will also examine the relationship between the Security Council and the parts of the UN system specifically focused on human rights, in particular the Human Rights Council and its predecessor, the Commission on Human Rights, as well as the High Commissioner for Human Rights.

The Early Years of the Security Council's Involvement with Human Rights

During the Cold War period, human rights were seen as a particularly sensitive topic that members were reluctant to pursue in the Council. However, while the end of the Cold War certainly created a new dynamic, human rights were not entirely absent from the Council even in the early decades. Human rights references were included in several Council resolutions, including those on the situation in Hungary in 1956, in the Congo in 1961, and in the Dominican Republic in 1965.

Starting in the early 1960s, several Council resolutions that were adopted in the context of decolonization had strong human rights language, and some invoked the Universal Declaration of Human Rights. The strongest human rights language in Council resolutions of the Cold War era concerned South Africa. Between 1963 and the late 1980s, the Council passed numerous resolutions that called on the government to take specific measures strictly dealing with the protection of human rights, such as the release of political prisoners (e.g., resolutions 181 and 182); stopping executions and granting amnesties for political prisoners (e.g., resolution 190); abolishing detention without charge, without access to counsel, and without the right to a prompt trial (e.g., resolution 191); or commutations of death sentences or stays of execution concerning a specific prisoner (e.g., resolution 547).

In January 1992, the Security Council held its first summit-level meeting on the topic of the responsibility of the Security Council in the maintenance of international peace and security (S/PV.3046 1992). Every head of state or government participating in the debate raised the issue of the appropriateness of the Council's addressing human rights; most were in full support. President Boris Yeltsin of Russia said that the "Security Council is called upon to underscore the civilized world's collective responsibility for the protection of human rights and freedoms," while President George H. W. Bush of the USA listed human rights among "the building blocks of peace and freedom." Most members as well as the Secretary-General were strongly supportive of the Council's concern with human rights. A few, however, expressed reluctance, foreshadowing the tension that would mark the Council's approach to human rights for several years to come. President Li Peng of China said that his country was "opposed to interference in the internal affairs of other countries using the human rights issue as an excuse." India wanted the Council "to delineate the parameters that harmonise the defence of national integrity with respect for human rights," while Zimbabwe cautioned that "great care has to be taken to see that these domestic conflicts are not used as a pretext for the intervention of big Powers in the legitimate domestic affairs of small States."

A presidential statement adopted at the meeting merely acknowledged that human rights verification had become one of the "integral parts of the Security Council's effort to maintain international peace and security" and welcomed this development (S/23500 1992).

The Security Council and Human Rights Information

Of the six principal organs of the UN, the UN Charter sees the Economic and Social Council (ECOSOC) as the body with key responsibility for human rights. Article 68 of the Charter says that ECOSOC "shall set up commissions in economic and social fields and for the promotion of human rights." In 1946, ECOSOC established its Commission on Human Rights (CHR), which first met in 1947 and then continued to meet in annual 6-week sessions until 2005. The first several decades of the work of the only UN political body devoted solely to human rights were focused largely on creating a normative system (starting with the Universal Declaration of Human Rights in 1948), rather than on investigating, condemning, or preventing human rights violations. Only in the late 1960s, largely due to the pressure coming from the young, newly independent African states and the pandemic human rights violations committed by apartheid South Africa and also by several Latin American dictatorships, did the CHR start discussing human rights violations in specific countries. From the point when the CHR started addressing violations in country-specific situations, there has always been an overlap in the situations which it and the Security Council were focused on. Even though until around the end of the Cold War there seemed to be very little interaction between the Security Council and the CHR, it was not entirely absent.

Fact-finding by the CHR grew considerably from the late 1980s on and became a tool readily available to the Security Council. An unusual aspect of the CHR fact-finding system, and later also the Human Rights Council (HRC), has been that holders of the investigative mandates, jointly referred to as special procedures, have not been UN employees (only their expenses and their support staff have been paid by the UN) and have had editorial control over their reporting and statements. This has resulted on numerous occasions in frank and hard-hitting reporting, otherwise difficult to achieve in UN documents. Furthermore, special procedures could act with considerable speed. The Council, however, has made direct use of this tool only infrequently. It was not until the height of the Balkan War – following the 13–14 August 1992 CHR first emergency session, which adopted a resolution appointing a special rapporteur on human rights in the former Yugoslavia and, in an unusual move, asked the Secretary-General to make the rapporteur's reports available to the Security Council – that the Council began receiving human rights information regularly. Subsequent CHR resolutions contained this request to the

Secretary-General, and as a result, between August 1992 and November 1996, the Council received 23 periodic reports on human rights violations in the former Yugoslavia, all of which were issued as Security Council documents.

The receipt of specialized and timely human rights information about countries on the Council agenda, however, has been more of an exception than the rule. The genocide in Rwanda provides one very powerful example for why it is critically important for the Security Council to take advantage of the available human rights information about situations on its agenda. It also illustrates the preventive potential of human rights information. In April 1993, a year before the full eruption of genocide, the CHR Special Rapporteur on extrajudicial, summary, or arbitrary executions, Bacre Wally Ndiaye, visited Rwanda to investigate the violence between the mainly Hutu government forces and the Tutsi-led Rwandese Patriotic Front, ongoing despite an accord signed by the two sides in Arusha in July 1992. His report was published on 11 August 1993 (E/CN.4/1994/7/Add.1 1993). In it, he depicted in great detail an alarming situation with genocide looming and stressed that "human rights must be the prime concern of any system for monitoring or implementing of the agreements."

A few months later, in October 1993, the Security Council established the UN Assistance Mission for Rwanda (UNAMIR) to help the parties implement the agreement, monitor its implementation, and support the transitional authorities. Human rights were not mentioned in resolution 872, which established UNAMIR, and the operation had no human rights component. The first Council reference to the activities of the UN human rights system came 2 months after the April 1994 onset of genocide, in resolution 925 of 8 June 1994, in which the Council welcomed the visit to Rwanda by the High Commissioner for Human Rights and took note of the 25 May 1994 appointment of a Special Rapporteur on human rights in Rwanda by a CHR emergency session. The resolution adopted at this session asked the Secretary-General to make the reports of the Special Rapporteur available to the Security Council. Accordingly, in 1994 and 1995, the reports of the Special Rapporteur on Human Rights in Rwanda were regularly transmitted to the Council by the Secretary-General and were issued as Security Council documents.

Information from the UN human rights investigative mechanisms, including special procedures, has since been included or referenced in some (though for different reasons not all) of the Secretary-General's periodic reports on the countries in question. But the full human rights reports have been forwarded to the Security Council only infrequently.

Since its establishment in 2006, the HRC, has referenced or welcomed Security Council resolutions in several of its resolutions but has stopped short of mandating that its investigators report regularly to the Security Council. However, in one particular area – the intersection of human rights with countering terrorism – the HRC mandated its Special Rapporteur and the relevant officials within the Office of the High Commissioner for Human Rights (OHCHR) to interact with the relevant subsidiary bodies of the Security Council. The mandate of the Special Rapporteur on the protection of human rights and fundamental freedoms while countering terrorism, created in April 2005 by the Commission on Human Rights in resolution 2005/80 and most recently extended by the HRC in 2016 for 3 years in resolution 31/3, requires the Rapporteur "to develop a regular dialogue and discuss possible areas of cooperation with... relevant United Nations bodies ... inter alia with the Counter-Terrorism Committee of the Security Council."

So far, however, the flow of human rights information from the HRC to the Security Council has been modest, except via the Secretary-General's periodic reports on different situations on the Council agenda that have regularly referenced the reports of the human rights special procedures. The 25 September 2014 resolution on Syria decided "to transmit all reports and oral updates of the commission of inquiry to all relevant bodies of the United Nations, including the General Assembly, and the Secretary-General for appropriate action"; thus, in October, the Secretary-General sent the report to the president of the Security Council and asked that the document be circulated to Council members (A/HRC/RES/27/16 2014). The first HRC request for forwarding the human rights findings regularly to the Security Council also concerned Syria and came in March 2015, when the Human Rights Council decided in resolution 28/20 "to transmit all reports and oral updates of the Commission of Inquiry to all relevant bodies of the United Nations" and recommended "that the Assembly submit the reports to the Security Council for appropriate action." The HRC also expressed its appreciation to the Commission of Inquiry for its briefings to members of the Security Council and recommended continuation of future briefings. Similar language was not consistently included in subsequent HRC resolutions on Syria.

The pattern that has emerged from examining the means for transmitting reports of the HRC to the Security Council suggests that the most effective way is a direct mandate from the HRC to the Secretary-General to transmit the reports to the Security Council. There is, however, also a possibility of this initiative coming from members of the Security Council, as illustrated by the approach to the human rights situation in the Democratic People's Republic of Korea (DPRK). On 28 March 2014, the HRC adopted a resolution in which it welcomed the report of its commission of inquiry on human rights in DPRK and recommended "that the General Assembly submit the report of the commission of inquiry to the Security Council for its consideration and appropriate action in order that those responsible for human rights violations, including those that may amount to crimes against humanity, are held to account" (A/HRC/RES/25/25 2014).

Without waiting for the General Assembly to act, permanent representatives of three members of the Security Council – Australia, France, and the USA – sent a letter on 14 April 2014 to the Council's president with a request to circulate an attached human rights report and issue it as a document of the Security Council (S/2014/276 2014). On 17 April 2014, the same Council members organized an informal briefing by the members of the Commission of Inquiry, held under the Arria-formula (S/2014/501 2014). Arria-formula briefings are informal gatherings of Security Council members to receive informative briefings and allowing an opportunity to engage in dialogue on a given topic. However, they are not always attended by all Council members, and there is usually no record and no outcome.

An 11 July 2014 letter from the same three permanent representatives transmitted a non-paper summarizing the briefing and the discussion that ensued (S/2005/490). And on 22 December 2014, a procedural vote (with China and Russia voting against and Chad and Nigeria abstaining) placed the situation in DPRK on the agenda of the Security Council. Once a year since, the Security Council has received a briefing on human rights in DPRK.

The Security Council's Interaction with UN Human Rights Investigators

Over the years, there has been a varying degree of reluctance in the Council to receive written human rights information. The reluctance to interact directly with human rights investigators has been considerably stronger. The Council has interacted directly with CHR- or HRC-mandated human rights investigators on several occasions, some of them repeatedly, but such interactions have been generally ad hoc and infrequent.

Organizing the first formal briefing by a human rights rapporteur was exceptionally politically challenging, as several members of the Council were adamantly opposed to holding such a meeting. On 7 August 1992, Belgium, France, the UK, and the USA each sent a letter to the president of the Security Council asking that the CHR Special Rapporteur on Iraq, Max van der Stoel, be allowed to address the Council. A meeting was indeed held on 11 August 1992, but at the outset of that session, four Council members signaled their deep displeasure (S/PV.3105 1992). At the meeting, the permanent representative of India argued: "Deviation from the Charter, in which the nations of the world have reposed their faith and support, could erode that confidence and have grave consequences for the future of the Organization as a whole. … The Council … cannot discuss human rights situations per se or make recommendations on matters outside its competence." The other three members opposed were China, Ecuador, and Zimbabwe.

Two more such meetings occurred before the end of 1992: on 13 November 1992, the Special Rapporteur of the CHR on the former Yugoslavia, Tadeusz Mazowiecki, was invited to brief the Council during a meeting on the situation in Bosnia and Herzegovina (S/PV.3134 1992), and on 23 November of the same year, van der Stoel briefed the Council again during a meeting on the situation between Iraq and Kuwait (S/PV.3139 1992). In both cases, China and Zimbabwe re-stated their reservations about the Security Council's focus on human rights. The fourth instance of a human rights special rapporteur's formal briefing to the Council occurred on 28 October 2014, when Chaloka Beyani, Special Rapporteur on the human rights of internally displaced persons (IDPs), briefed the Council during an open debate on women, peace, and security, with a special focus on displaced women and girls (S/PV.7289 2014). The fifth and at press time most recent interaction between the Security Council and a special rapporteur of the HRC took place during the 15 March 2017, during an open debate on trafficking in persons in conflict situations when Urmila Bhoola, Special Rapporteur on contemporary forms of slavery, including its causes and consequences, was invited to take part in the discussion (S/PV.7898 2017). All other interactions with human rights investigators appointed by the CHR or the HRC have been held under the Arria-formula format.

The first Arria-formula briefing by a human rights mandate holder most likely occurred in November 1999, when Roberto Garretón, CHR Special Rapporteur on human rights in the DRC, briefed the Council, with three more similar briefings during 2000 and 2001. Special rapporteurs on Afghanistan and Burundi briefed Council members under the Arria-formula format in 2001 and 2002. Starting with a 22 March 2012 Arria-formula briefing by members of the HRC International Commission of Inquiry on Syria, Council members have been receiving regular human rights updates from the Commission (on 12 October 2012, 21 June 2013, 25 July 2014, 20 February, 12 November 2015, and 21 April 2017). And, as mentioned earlier, on 17 April 2014, the Council was briefed on the human rights situation in the DPRK by members of the HRC Commission of Inquiry on human rights in the DPRK. Thematic human rights investigators have briefed under the Arria-formula format as well. The CHR Special Rapporteur on Violence against Women briefed on 8 March 2002; the CHR Special Rapporteur on extrajudicial, summary, or arbitrary executions briefed on Afghanistan (together with the country-specific mandate holder) on 6 November 2002; the HRC Special Rapporteur on the right to freedom of opinion and expression briefed on 13 December 2013; and the Special Rapporteur on the Human Rights of IDPs briefed on 30 May 2014.

The Security Council's Interaction with the UN High Commissioner for Human Rights

The 1993 General Assembly resolution creating the post of the High Commissioner for Human Rights was silent on the issue of the new official's interaction with the Security Council. But by then the Council had already ventured into human rights issues on several occasions, had been briefed by human rights investigators, and had acknowledged in its decisions links between repression and international peace and security. Proponents for the establishment of this post – member states, UN insiders, as well as NGOs – had assumed that the newly appointed Under-Secretary-General with a human rights mandate would become an immediate substantive interlocutor for the Security Council and that a mutually reinforcing working relationship would be established. Yet it took several years before the first direct contact occurred.

The reasons were complex; most but not all had to do with the reluctance on the part of the Security Council. The first High Commissioner, José Ayala Lasso, former permanent representative of Ecuador in New York, was not eager to pursue establishing a working relationship between his office and the Council. In fact, as an elected Security Council member in 1992, he had been one of the most vocal opponents of allowing a human rights rapporteur to brief the Council. Mary Robinson, former president of Ireland, succeeded Ayala Lasso and held the post from September 1997 to September 2002. Robinson launched an effort from the beginning of her term to establish direct contacts with the Security Council. After initial resistance on the part of some Council members, Robinson addressed the Council on 16 September 1999 at the invitation of Secretary-General Kofi Annan during the semiannual debate on protection of civilians in armed conflict (S/PV.4046 1999). She talked about human rights violations related to several situations on the Council's agenda, including Angola, Colombia, East Timor, and Sierra Leone. "Conflicts almost always lead to massive human rights violations, but also erupt because human rights are violated due to oppression, inequality, discrimination and poverty," she said. "The Security Council has a vital role to play, both at the prevention stage and, should that fail, in the deployment of peacekeepers to mini-mize the impact of conflict on civilians." That first meeting opened the way to eventual further contacts, though for several more years, the acceptance of the participation of the High Commissioner in Council meetings and the recognition of the High Commissioner's positive contribution to the Council's work were not universal and occasionally suffered setbacks.

From 1999 through 2005, the High Commissioner (or the Deputy or Acting High Commissioner) was invited to meet with the Council either in a formal meeting or in consultations a total of eight times. No meetings occurred in 2006 and 2008, and there was one in 2007. During that period, various Council members suggested hearing from the High Commissioner but encountered considerable resistance from their counterparts.

Things began to change in 2009, due to a sustained effort of an elected member, Austria. Serving on the Council in 2009–2010, Austria had the presidency of the Council in November 2009, when a periodic debate on protection of civilians in armed conflict was scheduled. The permanent representative decided to invite the High Commissioner as one of the briefers and secured the consent of all the members. Before the next protection of civilians debate was to be held in July 2010, the Austrian ambassador consulted informally with other members of the Council – in particular Russia and China, which had been most reluctant – and secured their consent to another briefing by the High Commissioner. From that point on, the High Commissioner started being invited regularly to the open debates on the protection of civilians in armed conflict.

What is more significant, the regular participation of the High Commissioner in the periodic open debates seems to have made Council members appreciate the usefulness of the High Commissioner as a resource in Council work, and the number of interactions increased dramatically. From 1999 through 2009, the High Commis-sioner addressed the Council 12 times, either in formal meetings or in consultations. In the period from the beginning of 2010 through 2017, the High Commissioner for Human Rights, the Deputy High Commissioner for Human Rights, or the Assistant Secretary-General for Human Rights (a post created to head the New York Office of the High Commissioner in 2010) addressed the Council at least 60 times, briefing repeatedly on situations such as Ukraine, Syria, Côte d'Ivoire, South Sudan, or Burundi. In addition, the High Commissioner or his or her representatives met with the Council several times in informal formats, such as retreats, workshops, and Arria-formula briefings.

The Security Council's Discussions of Human Rights

Prior to 2017, the Council had not held any formal meetings with a stated focus on human rights. Its members have, however, on several occasions discussed human rights informally in retreats, workshops, and Arria-formula briefings. In March 2001, the Council held a 2-day retreat outside New York at the initiative of the UK Permanent Representative at the time, Jeremy Greenstock, to specifically discuss human rights and the work of the Security Council. The High Commissioner for Human Rights, Mary Robinson, participated in the event, whose agenda was organized around three main topics: human rights and early warning, human rights in peacekeeping operations, and human rights in post-conflict situations. Ten of the fifteen Council members attended, at the level of permanent representative or deputy permanent representative: China, Colombia, France, Ireland, Jamaica, Norway, Russia, Singapore, the UK, and the USA. Bangladesh, Mali, Mauritius, Tunisia, and Ukraine were absent.

Human rights were also discussed during nearly all of the Finnish "Hitting the Ground Running" workshops held annually since 2003 to welcome into the Council its newly elected members. In 2008, the High Commissioner for Human Rights, Navi Pillay, was asked to be the keynote speaker at the dinner on the eve of the workshop, prompting a particularly rich discussion of human rights the following day (with the High Commissioner invited to stay on as a guest). One of the topics discussed during the 2012 Secretary-General's annual retreat with the Security Council was the tools that the Security Council can use and different approaches it can take when confronting situations where there have been gross human rights violations and mass atrocities.

Occasionally, some of these discussions would focus again on the appropriateness of the Council's concerning itself with human rights and echo the controversies that had arisen in 1992 when human rights rapporteurs had been invited to brief the Council formally. For a few years, approximately 2005–2008, human rights would be brought up in the context of discussions over the so-called "encroachment" problem, wherein some members both on and outside the Council argued that the Security Council should not encroach on areas that traditionally had been seen as the domain of other UN bodies. This controversy seems to have abated with the gradual acceptance of the changing nature of conflicts the Council needed to address and thus of the need to change and modify its scope and tools.

The Council held its first, and to date only, formal meeting with a stated focus on human rights on 18 April 2017 (S/PV.7926 2017). The public meeting, in briefing format, was titled "Maintenance of international peace and security: human rights and prevention of armed conflict." Secretary-General António Guterres briefed. A concept paper circulated to Council members by the USA on 3 April 2017 stated "the Security Council has never before held a meeting dedicated to and focused exclusively on human rights." The concept paper also asked whether the Council should receive regular briefings on emerging and current situations involving serious human rights violations and abuses.

Initially, the USA had wanted to hold the briefing under a new agenda item "Human rights and international peace and security." A procedural vote was expected in order to get agreement on holding the meeting as several members raised objections when the program of work was being adopted at the beginning of the month. As stated in rule 9 of the Council's rules of procedure, the first item of the provisional agenda for each meeting of the Council shall be the adoption of the agenda. It has been the practice of the Council to adopt the agenda without a vote unless an objection is raised. If differences over the agenda cannot be worked out among Council members ahead of time, they are resolved by a procedural vote. Procedural decisions, in order to be adopted, require nine votes in favor, and there is no veto.

As the date of the planned meeting approached, it appeared that a procedural vote to add a new agenda item might not be successful. China and Russia had all along been expected to oppose adding human rights as a new item to the agenda of the Security Council. Non-Aligned Movement (NAM) members Bolivia, Egypt, Ethiopia, and Senegal and NAM observer Kazakhstan signaled their opposition to adding human rights as a new thematic item to the Council agenda. It seems a compromise was reached to hold the meeting under the existing agenda item "Maintenance of international peace and security."

Four out of the last five procedural votes by the Council also concerned human rights. In December 2014, at the initiative of Australia, ten Council members requested that the situation in the Democratic People's Republic of Korea (DPRK) "be formally placed on the Council's agenda without prejudice to the item on non-proliferation" in the DPRK. China objected, and a vote was called for, with 11 members being in favor, 2 abstaining, and 2 permanent members, China and Russia, voting against. A similar scenario played itself out in December in 2015, 2016, and 2017, with respect to holding a human rights-focused meeting on the DPRK.

The Security Council's Evolving Approach to Human Rights as a Theme

Examining the Council's approach to human rights over the decades, including the April 2017 attempt to add human rights to the Council agenda, one phenomenon that becomes noteworthy in the early phase of this engagement is something that could be described as a certain "linguistic phobia." For several years starting in 1991, the Council was prepared to take action with considerable impact on human rights, while at the same time, some of its members had difficulties with using the term "human rights." One telling example is the Balkan conflict that loomed large on the Council agenda from late 1991 through 1995 (and remains on it, though with much less intensity, to this day). Even though the Council had already established a comprehensive human rights monitoring mission (in El Salvador) and created a peacekeeping operation with a human rights component (in Cambodia), it very persistently avoided using the term "human rights" in several of its Balkan War-related decisions. This was the case with resolutions establishing and developing further the mandate of the first UN-mandated peacekeeping operation with a protection of civilians' mandate, the UN Protection Force, UNPROFOR. In its subsequent resolutions on the Balkan conflict, the Council often condemned violations of international humanitarian law (IHL), but references to human rights were rare and mostly appeared in the context of some of the 23 reports of the Special Rapporteur of the CHR that were regularly transmitted to the Council from 1992 to 1996.

Similarly, following the outbreak of the genocide in Rwanda in April 1992, the Council was mute on the massive violations of human rights and began using the term initially only in the context of the activities of the High Commissioner for Human Rights or the Special Rapporteur appointed by an emergency session of the CHR in May 1994.

Starting in the late 1990s, the Council began focusing on certain forms of human rights violations, such as the impact of armed conflict on children (including their recruitment as soldiers), protection of civilians in armed conflict, or sexual violence in conflict, in a thematic way and without explicitly resorting to human rights vocabulary. The Council started examining these serious conflict-related phenomena across the board, rather than placing each specific conflict on the agenda. The theme as such became the agenda item, and this afforded the Council a possibility of discussing both the serious human rights violations and relevant situations not on the Council agenda. The Council started holding periodic open debates on these thematic issues and created a complex normative system on these matters over the years through the adoption of a series of resolutions and presidential statements.

Given that each of the themes is essentially an aspect of the overall human rights situation, the potential impact of this approach on human rights protection in places where Council-authorized missions are deployed is considerable, though the Council has not always been consistent when applying principles agreed upon in the abstract to concrete situations. However, these principles have been codified in Council decisions, and they can and occasionally have been resorted to in addressing specific crises when there is enough of a sense of urgency and political will has been mobilized.

Human Rights Components in Peace Operations

The Council's constant adaptability and considerable creativity during much of its history have led to its using some of its existing tools or establishing new ones for functions with a significant impact on human rights. Human rights components in peace operations, Commissions of Inquiry, judicial mechanisms, Council visiting missions, and sanctions are the most important among them. Field missions in conflict and post-conflict areas constitute a key tool with a potential for significant and often quick impact on human rights. The very presence of outsiders perceived as representative of the international community has often had a considerable preventive impact. In some cases, however, the presence alone was not enough to stop some of the most extreme violations of human rights, and some were committed literally under UN watch, such as the 1994 genocide in Rwanda and the mass executions of civilian men in 1995 in the former Yugoslavia. The evolution over the past two decades toward specific human rights mandates and more specialized staffing within Council-established missions has considerably enhanced the protective impact of peace operations.

The first human rights component of a peace operation was established through resolution 693 of 20 May 1991, in which the Council mandated the UN Observer Mission in El Salvador. The next peace operation with a human rights component was the UN Transitional Authority in Cambodia, established in resolution 745 of 28 February 1992. In April 1993, the General Assembly authorized the International Civilian Mission in Haiti (MICIVIH) deployed jointly by the UN and the Organization of the American States (OAS) with a mandate to verify the respect for human rights and to investigate allegations of violations. When the UN Mission in Haiti (UNMIH) was deployed in 1994, MICIVIH (as a joint mission with the OAS) was not integrated into UNMIH, but its head reported to the UN Special Representative of the Secretary-General, as well as to the Secretary-General of the OAS. (Human rights monitoring in Haiti continued through MICIVIH until April 2000.)

However, human rights components were to be a rarity in newly established missions for another several years. Thus, neither UNPROFOR in the former Yugoslavia established in late 1991 nor the UN Assistance Mission for Rwanda (UNAMIR) established in October 1993 had such components in their mandates, despite the fact that severe human rights violations were prevalent in both conflicts. Only around 1997, starting with the UN Observer Mission in Angola, did including a human rights component in a peace operation become more of a norm rather than an exception.

Today, nearly all peace operations have human rights-related tasks in their mandates, and currently there are more than 800 human rights staff members working in nine peacekeeping operations and five special political missions. Those without a human rights component tend to be older missions with predominantly or exclusively military mandates, such as the first UN peacekeeping operation, the UN Truce Supervision Organization, established in 1948 to monitor cease-fires and supervise armistice agreements in the Middle East, or the UN Disengagement Observer Force, established in 1974 following the agreed disengagement of the Israeli and Syrian forces in the Golan, or regional political missions, such as the UN Regional Center for Preventive Diplomacy for Central Asia or the UN Regional Office for Central Africa. A notable exception in this context has been the UN Mission for the Referendum in Western Sahara (MINURSO), established in 1991, which does not include human rights despite repeated attempts by different Council members to add it to MINURSO's mandate, due to staunch opposition from Morocco and support by at least one of the permanent members.

Since 2012, Security Council members have used closed Arria-formula format to meet with the heads of human rights components of different operations. Most recently, on 24 February 2017, Security Council members held a closed Arria-formula meeting with the heads of human rights components of three UN peace operations: the UN Organization Stabilization Mission in the Democratic Republic of the Congo (MONUSCO), the UN Mission in South Sudan (UNMISS), and the UN Assistance Mission in Somalia (UNSOM). Similar meetings occurred in January 2015 and March 2016.

Commissions of Inquiry

Under Article 34 of the UN Charter, the Council has the power to investigate "any situation which might lead to international friction." Such investigations can be done through different mechanisms described in the Council's Provisional Rules of Procedure and include rapporteurs, committees, or commissions appointed for a specific question. The Council has resorted to these tools on several occasions and at various times recommended the establishment of commissions of inquiry with a significant human rights mandate. Examples include the following:

A commission of experts was established under resolution 780 of 6 October 1992 to examine information regarding violations of laws of war, "ethnic cleansing," and other practices by the warring parties against civilians in the former Yugoslavia. The commission laid the ground for the establishment of the International Criminal Tribunal for the Former Yugoslavia (ICTY) in May 1993 through resolution 827.

On 1 July 1994 in resolution 935, the Council decided to establish a commission of experts to provide "conclusions on the evidence of grave violations of international humanitarian law committed in the territory of Rwanda, including the evidence of possible acts of genocide." Subsequently, in November 1994, the Council established the International Criminal Tribunal for Rwanda (ICTR). Through resolution 1012 of 28 August 1995, the Council established an international commission of inquiry into the 1993 coup attempt in Burundi and into the massacres that followed, stressing the need "to eradicate impunity and promote national reconciliation in Burundi." The commission's report was forwarded to the Council by the Secretary-General on 25 July 1996 and eventually issued as a public document on 22 August 1996 (S/1996/682 1996).

In a presidential statement of 25 May 2004, the Council condemned "the violations of human rights and international humanitarian law committed in Côte d'Ivoire" and expressed "its determination to ensure that those responsible for all these violations are identified and that the Ivorian Government brings them to justice" (S/PRST/2004/17 2004). It mandated the Secretary-General to establish a commission of inquiry to "investigate all human rights violations committed in Côte d'Ivoire since September 19, 2002, and determine responsibility." The nearly 45,000-word commission report was submitted to the Council in December 2004. It was never made public, nor was it acted upon.

Resolution 1564 adopted on 18 September 2004 mandated the establishment of an international commission of inquiry "in order immediately to investigate reports of violations of international humanitarian law and human rights law in Darfur by all parties, to determine also whether or not acts of genocide have occurred, and to identify the perpetrators of such violations with a view to ensuring that those responsible are held accountable." The commission submitted its report to the Secretary-General in January 2005, and he forwarded it to the Council on 31 January (S/2005/60 2005). On 31 March 2005 in resolution 1593, the Council referred the situation in Darfur to the International Criminal Court.

Following an 8 June 2006 letter from the Foreign Minister of Timor-Leste, José Ramos-Horta, to the Council asking it to establish an independent commission of inquiry into violent events that resulted in mass displacement of civilians earlier in the year, the Council, in resolution 1690 of 20 June, welcomed "the initiative of the Secretary-General to ask the High Commissioner for Human Rights to take the lead in establishing an independent special inquiry commission in response to the request" (S/2006/391 2006). The Secretary-General transmitted the report to the Council on 18 October (S/2006/822 2006). The Council referenced the report in several resolutions when renewing the mandate of the UN Integrated Mission in Timor-Leste.

Following a year of violent events in the Central African Republic (CAR), the Council decided on 5 December 2013 in resolution 2127 to "rapidly establish an international commission of inquiry for an initial period of one year, including experts in both international humanitarian law and human rights law, in order immediately to investigate reports of violations of international humanitarian law, international human rights law and abuses of human rights in CAR by all parties since 1 January 2013, to compile information, to help identify the perpetrators of such violations and abuses, to point to their possible criminal responsibility and to help ensure that those responsible are held accountable." The commission's report was submitted to the Council on 19 December 2014 (S/2014/928 2014), and its members briefed the Council in an informal interactive dialogue on 20 January 2015. In resolution 2217, renewing the mandate of the Integrated Multi-dimensional Mission in the CAR, the Council noted with concern the findings of the report and mandated the mission to support the implementation of the relevant recommendations of the Commission of Inquiry as part of its human rights mandate.

Judicial Mechanisms

From the early 1990s on, the Council has seen promoting accountability for the gravest crimes, including individual responsibility for violations of human rights laws, as important in the efforts aimed at the maintenance of international peace and security. A new tool it created specifically for the purpose of promoting individual criminal accountability was the international tribunal. The Council has to date authorized the establishment of three such judicial bodies with a particular impact on human rights.

Through resolution 827 of 25 May 1993, the Council established the ICTY. The Council expressed its grave alarm about the violations committed in the former Yugoslavia, including mass killings, massive and organized detention, rape of women, and the practice of "ethnic cleansing." The sole purpose of the court, according to the resolution, was to be "prosecuting persons responsible for serious violations of international humanitarian law committed in the territory of the former Yugoslavia between 1 January 1991 and a date to be determined by the Security Council upon the restoration of peace."

On 8 November 1994, the Council in resolution 955 established the ICTR. It decided "to establish an international tribunal for the sole purpose of prosecuting persons responsible for genocide and other serious violations of international humanitarian law committed in the territory of Rwanda and Rwandan citizens responsible for genocide and other such violations committed in the territory of neighbouring States, between 1 January 1994 and 31 December 1994." Among the resolution's other elements, the Council also took note of the reports of the Special Rapporteur for Rwanda of the CHR.

Responding to a June 2000 request from the president of Sierra Leone, the Council asked the Secretary-General in resolution 1315 of 14 August to negotiate with the country's government an agreement for the creation of an independent special court with personal jurisdiction over persons who bear the greatest responsibility for crimes against humanity, war crimes, and other serious violations of international humanitarian law committed during the civil war that tore the country during almost all of the 1990s.

Those responsible for gross violations of human rights in East Timor in connection with the 1999 referendum were brought to justice within the court system created by the UN Transitional Administration in East Timor (UNTAET), established by Council resolution 1272 of 25 October 1999. Both during and after the period of transitional administration, this was an exercise of domestic jurisdiction, but international judges sat on the Special Panels for Serious Crimes, and the Serious Crimes Unit responsible for conducting investigations and preparing indictments was headed by an international prosecutor. The Serious Crimes Unit was made part of the follow-on mission to UNTAET, the UN Mission of Support in East Timor, established in 2002 through Council resolution 1410. In 2005, the Serious Crimes Unit was shut down with most of its functions being passed on to the domestic prosecutions system. By that time, the unit had produced 95 indictments and charged 440 individuals.

Council Visiting Missions

The Council has undertaken visiting missions for a number of purposes, including preventive diplomacy, gathering of first-hand information, and supporting peace processes and mediation. In the period until the end of the Cold War, it resorted to this tool about a dozen times. From 1992 to 2017, the Council (either all of its members or a subset) has undertaken a visiting mission 60 times to at least 46 countries, 3 territories, and several headquarters of international bodies, some of which it has visited repeatedly.

Prior to June 2001, all the missions undertaken consisted of some but not all Council members. Virtually all were to places that either were in the midst of an active armed conflict or were emerging from one. They all showed a sense of urgency – the trip would occur within a few weeks or sometimes days (and in one case, hours) of the decision to undertake it. Reports from the missions would often be written on the flight back and presented to the Council within days. In some cases, an oral report would be given immediately after the mission's return and its recommendations promptly acted upon in Council decisions.

With their destinations being areas either ravaged by a bloody conflict or just emerging from it, nearly every mission brought back a wealth of human rights information, whether as part of the explicit mandate included in the mission's terms of reference or by virtue of witnessing conditions on the ground and collecting testimonies, and certainly played a role in sensitizing Council members to the human rights aspects of conflict. Several, especially in earlier years when conflict-related human rights violations were not regularly addressed by the Council, resulted in concrete human rights recommendations. Examples include the following:

The April 1993 mission to Bosnia and Herzegovina recommended several changes to the mandate of UNPROFOR with direct impact on civilians, in particular those in the UN-declared "safe areas" (S/25700 1993). Resolution 824 adopted in early May revised UNPROFOR's mandate and asked for regular monitoring of conditions in the safe-area towns. The August 1994 mission to Burundi recommended the deployment of human rights observers throughout the country (S/1994/1039 1994). In a presidential statement in October, the Council recognized "the work of the High Commissioner for Human Rights and the office he has established in Burundi" and noted "the important role human rights monitors might play" (S/PRST/1994/60 1994). The February 1995 mission to Rwanda recommended that the government allow unimpeded access for UN human rights monitors throughout the territory. The September 1999 mission to Jakarta and East Timor resulted in a number of recommendations, incorporated into subsequent Council decisions, with a significant impact on the human rights situation on the ground. The July 2003 visit to West Africa raised human rights concerns with interlocutors in all the countries visited. The visit took place less than a month after the indictment of then Liberian President Charles Taylor by the Special Court for Sierra Leone. In their contacts with top leaders of the countries in the region, members stressed the message that impunity for human rights abuses could not be tolerated. (Taylor stepped down as Liberia's president in August 2003 and fled to Nigeria. He was arrested there and subsequently transferred to The Hague for trial in 2006. In 2012 he was found guilty of planning, aiding, and abetting of crimes committed by rebel forces in Sierra Leone and received a 50-year prison sentence.)

The May 2009 visit to the DRC occurred at the time when sexual violence had become one of the most endemic human rights violations, in particular in the eastern part of the country, with several former rebel leaders responsible for such crimes being incorporated into the country's armed forces. The Council delegation raised specific cases of sexual violence committed by five high-ranking officers of the DRC armed forces in meetings with the country's president and prime minister. On certain occasions, a briefing from a mission would create an opportunity to discuss the situation in an open debate. One example is the 17 May 2000 open debate on the DRC following the Council's visit to the country from 3 to 8 May. Non-Council members from Africa, Asia, and Europe participated in the discussion, and rampant human rights violations were one of the key topics addressed (S/PV.4143 and Resumption 1 2000). Similarly, the presentation of the report from the Council's 20–29 June 2004 mission to West Africa created an opportunity for an open debate with the participation of members from Africa, Asia, and Europe, with several speakers addressing human rights (S/PV.5005 2004). The presentation of the report from the 11–16 November 2006 mission to Afghanistan, which had a considerable human rights focus, also resulted in a debate in which these concerns were raised (S/PV.5581 2006). A June 2010 mission to Afghanistan also provided the occasion for a debate in which representatives of non-Council member states from several regional groups participated and human rights concerns were raised by several speakers (S/PV.6351 2010).

In some cases, the Council's visiting missions provided an opportunity for action with direct human rights impact. The most far-reaching such situation was the 1999 trip to Jakarta and East Timor. Other examples include strategically planned Council visits to areas in the immediate aftermath of an acute conflict, thus signaling to the parties that the international community was watching their behaviors closely.

Council missions have also spurred some spontaneous action on human rights matters. One such relatively recent situation occurred during the 18–19 May 2009 visit to eastern DRC and Kinshasa, referred to above. Initially, even though individual responsibility for serious human rights violations and ensuring that their perpetrators were brought to justice were mentioned in the mission's terms of reference (S/2009/243 2009), these issues were not meant to feature prominently in the interaction with the authorities on the ground. However, after a visit to a hospital for rape victims in Goma and shaken by the lack of accountability for such crimes, members of the visiting mission decided on the spur of the moment to raise the names of five alleged perpetrators of sexual violence, all high-ranking officers within the DRC armed forces, in meetings with President Joseph Kabila and Prime Minister Adolphe Muzito the next day. Within weeks, all five officers were ordered to be relieved of their posts, and judicial proceedings were initiated against three. (One was acquitted by a military court for lack of evidence, another presumably fled the country, and the third, for whom there had already been an arrest warrant due to a rape conviction in Bukavu, continued commanding a battalion in Equateur province, where the commanding officer refused to transfer him to the military prosecutor.) On 5 July 2009, President Kabila announced a "zero-tolerance policy" within the Congolese Armed Forces with respect to the lack of discipline and human rights violations, including sexual and gender-based violence.

In more recent practice, Council missions, which now almost always include all 15 members, have tended to take longer to organize (e.g., a mission in response to the December 2013 coup in South Sudan took place in August 2014), their reports are often written several months after the trip (and in two cases – the 2011 mission to Sudan, Addis Ababa, and Nairobi and the 2012 mission to West Africa – nearly 2 years later), and oral reports by the missions' leaders tend to be limited to just a briefing with no public discussion to follow. Several of the missions have had some human rights focus, but their impact as a tool contributing to the prevention of major human rights violations appears to have diminished.

Sanctions

Sanctions have been an important tool, resorted to by the Council in numerous conflict situations and with a variety of purposes. These have included curtailing the ability of parties to arm themselves by applying arms embargoes, cutting off sources of income for insurgencies through commodity sanctions, or changing the behavior of decision-makers through comprehensive economic sanctions and later through individually targeted measures, such as travel bans or asset freezes.

Human rights violations have almost always been part of the overall landscape of the situation the Council was striving to ameliorate with the use of sanctions. Over the years, the Council has developed a sophisticated methodology for sanctions design and implementation, in particular when it moved from comprehensive sanctions (which often had the effect of harming the general population) to imposing measures targeting individuals with decision-making power or displaying specific types of behaviors.

References to human rights violations can be found in the earliest instances of the Security Council's use of sanctions. Resolution 253 of 29 May 1968, which imposed comprehensive economic sanctions on Southern Rhodesia, condemned "all measures of political repression, including arrests, detentions, trials and executions which violate fundamental freedoms and rights of the people of Southern Rhodesia," and explicitly stated among its goals to "enable the people to secure the enjoyment of their rights as set forth in the Charter of the United Nations." Resolution 418 of 4 November 1977, which established comprehensive sanctions against the apartheid regime of South Africa, condemned "the South African Government for its resort to massive violence against and killings of the African people, including schoolchildren and students and others opposing racial discrimination" and "for its acts of repression."

Some of the 11 sanctions regimes imposed during the 1990s had human rights language. For example, resolution 841 of 16 June 1993, which imposed a mandatory trade embargo on Haiti in the aftermath of a coup that overthrew a democratically elected government, expressed concern about "a climate of fear of persecution," and resolution 1267 of 15 October 1999, which imposed sanctions in Afghanistan, reiterated "deep concern over the continuing violations of international humanitarian law and of human rights."

By the late 1990s, the Council was moving toward more precise sanctions measures that would affect individuals rather than whole territories. Imposing such sanctions involved in most cases two steps: agreeing that particular actions would prompt the imposition of certain measures, with both the types of behaviors and the measures articulated in the resolution, and then agreeing on the list of individuals who would be placed under such sanctions. The latter step has usually been taken subsequently within the respective subsidiary body, the sanctions committee established to manage the particular set of sanctions.

Gradually, the Council has moved from referring to human rights in the preambular paragraphs of its sanctions resolutions to including human rights violations among the criteria that might land an individual on a sanctions list. Of the 14 sanctions regimes currently in existence, 8 have human rights violations among their listing criteria. Resolution 1591 of 29 March 2005 on the conflict in Darfur imposed travel bans and asset freezes on individuals who "commit violations of international humanitarian or human rights law or other atrocities," as designated by the sanctions committee based on information provided by sources that included the High Commissioner for Human Rights. In resolution 1698 of 31 July 2006 on the

DRC, the Council decided that sanctions imposed originally in 2005 through resolution 1596 would also apply to "political and military leaders recruiting or using children in armed conflict in violation of applicable international law" and "individuals committing serious violations of international law involving the targeting of children in situations of armed conflict, including killing and maiming, sexual violence, abduction and forced displacement." In its resolution 1807 of 31 March 2008, the Council extended the DRC sanctions criteria to also include individuals "committing serious violations of international law involving the targeting of children or women . . . including . . . sexual violence."

When imposing sanctions on Libya in resolution 1970 of 26 February 2011, the Council decided that travel bans and assets freezes would apply to individuals "involved in or complicit in ordering, controlling, or otherwise directing, the commission of serious human rights abuses against persons in the Libyan Arab Jamahiriya." An annex to resolution 1970 contained the names of 16 individuals to whom the sanctions would apply and included human rights violations among the criteria for listing Libyan leader Muammar Qaddafi, Director of Military Intelligence Abdullah Al-Senussi, and others. In July 2011, the Council added human rights violations to the criteria in the sanctions regime on Somalia and Eritrea. In resolution 2002, the Council decided that travel bans and assets freezes imposed in 2008 would also apply to individuals responsible for "violations of applicable international law in Somalia involving the targeting of civilians including children and women in situations of armed conflict, including killing and maiming, sexual and gender-based violence, attacks on schools and hospitals and abduction." In resolution 2134 of 28 January 2014, on the Central African Republic, the Council decided that travel bans and asset freezes could apply to "individuals involved in planning, directing, or committing acts that violate international human rights law or international humanitarian law, as applicable, or that constitute human rights abuses or violations, in the CAR, including acts involving sexual violence, targeting of civilians, ethnic- or religious-based attacks, attacks on schools and hospitals and abduction and forced displacement."

On 26 February 2014 in resolution 2140, the Council imposed sanctions on Yemen that include travel bans and asset freezes applicable to individuals engaged in "planning, directing or committing acts that violate applicable international human rights law or international humanitarian law or acts that constitute human rights abuses, in Yemen." On 3 March 2015 in resolution 2206, the Council decided to impose sanctions on South Sudan, with travel bans and asset freezes to apply to individuals engaged in "planning, directing, or committing acts that violate applicable international human rights law . . . or acts that constitute human rights abuses, in South Sudan," as well as those responsible for "targeting of civilians, including women and children, through the commission of acts of violence (including killing, maiming, torture or rape or other sexual violence)" or "conduct that would constitute a serious abuse or violation of human rights or a violation of international humanitarian law." On 5 September 2017, the Council adopted resolution 2374 imposing sanctions on Mali stating that activities such as "planning, directing or committing acvts in Mali that violate international human rights law . . . or that constitute human rights abuses or violations" may be subject to sanctions.

However, when analyzing Security Council sanctions, it is important to distinguish between the theoretical possibility of sanctioning persons for human rights violations as articulated in a resolution and applying sanctions in practice citing human rights violations among the reasons in specific listing cases, which is usually decided by consensus by the relevant sanctions committee. No individual has been listed solely on human rights grounds. Furthermore, the actual targeting has more often than not only taken place long after the adoption of the relevant sanctions resolution, and the human rights criteria have rarely been invoked in the narratives justifying the imposition of the measures.

Human Rights in Security Council Conflict Prevention Action

An increase in human rights violations has in numerous situations preceded the eruption of an acute conflict and as such could be considered an early warning that might allow for preventive action. The Council has vowed on many occasions to strive to work on preventing conflicts from occurring or expanding. In some cases, indeed, it could be argued that a Council action (such as a visit to the scene, a prompt deployment of an operation, sustained attention to a mediation process, or direct intervention with key decision-making actors) prevented a conflict from spreading or helped to end it. However, the Council has continued to be resistant to approaching prevention in a sustained and consistent manner. And, in particular, even with plenty of warning, the Council and the UN system more broadly were unable to prevent massive human rights violations even when there was a full-fledged peacekeeping operation on the scene, as in the cases of the 1994 genocide in Rwanda and the 1995 mass executions of male civilians in Srebrenica and other Bosnian towns designated by the UN as "safe areas."

Shortly before the tenth anniversary of the Rwanda genocide, Secretary-General Annan floated the idea of "establishing a Special Rapporteur on the prevention of genocide, who would be supported by the High Commissioner for Human Rights, but would report directly to the Security Council – making clear the link, which is often ignored until too late, between massive and systematic violations of human rights and threats to international peace and security." Since the first holder of the mandate, Juan Méndez, was duly appointed in 2004, followed by Francis Deng in 2007, and Adama Dieng in 2012, the Council's interaction with the Special Adviser on the Prevention of Genocide has been sporadic and limited, with briefings on average not more than once a year often in informal meetings. In this regard, the intended flow of information from the Special Rapporteur to the Security Council seems to have been stunted from the start.

Another notable initiative, in seeking to provide the Council with early warning-related information, came from the UK during its presidency, in November 2010. The UK organized the first so-called "horizon-scanning" briefing, inviting the head of the Department of Political Affairs (DPA) to brief Council members in consultations on emerging security issues in a number of countries, regardless of whether they were on the Council's agenda or not. For the next few years, such monthly briefings were held by nearly all presidencies (including four permanent members, the USA being the exception due to its unhappiness with the format). These briefings afforded an opportunity for the Council to discuss a number of situations that involved serious human rights violations either for the first time – such as the pre-2012 coup tensions in Guinea-Bissau, the situation in northern Mali, or the worrying developments in Yemen – or to discuss on an urgent basis unfolding events in places such as Syria, Iraq, or Libya. But the attempt at creating an early warning mechanism has proven politically sensitive both among some Council members and among governments that found themselves the object of such early scrutiny, and starting in 2013, "horizon-scanning" briefings have subsided.

In August 2014, the Council proclaimed once again its commitment to conflict prevention. In resolution 2171, it expressed "its willingness to give prompt consideration to early-warning cases brought to its attention by the Secretary-General, including to the dispatch, in appropriate circumstances, of preventive political missions." It went on to acknowledge that serious abuses and violations of human rights "can be an early indication of a descent into conflict or escalation of conflict" and recognized the important role the Office of the UN High Commissioner for Human Rights and human rights briefings to the Council can "play in contributing to early awareness of potential conflict." In recent years, while there are no longer "horizon-scanning" briefings, there has been, it appears, an increased use of the "any other business" agenda item during consultations (that come at the initiative of a member state) to discuss urgent and fast-evolving developments, which can in some instances be considered an early warning that might allow for preventive action.

Council Dynamics

Among the permanent members, China and Russia have historically been more reluctant than their Western counterparts to include human rights concerns in the Council's outlook. In any given context, they would be supported by some of the elected members of the Council. A number of resolutions with strong human rights language were jointly vetoed by China and Russia in the past several years. These included the January 2007 draft resolution on Myanmar (S/2007/14 2007), with Congo, Indonesia, and Qatar abstaining, and the July 2008 draft resolution on Zimbabwe (S/2008/447 2008), with Libya, South Africa, and Vietnam also voting against and Indonesia abstaining. Four draft resolutions on Syria had substantive human rights language and received the double veto: in October 2011 (S/2011/612 2011), with Brazil, India, Lebanon, and South Africa abstaining; in February 2012 (S/2012/77); in July 2012 (S/2012/538/Rev.2 n.d.), with Pakistan and South Africa abstaining; and in May 2014 (S/2014/348 2014). Russia alone vetoed a March 2014 draft resolution on Ukraine (S/2014/189 2014), with China abstaining, and a July 2015 draft resolution commemorating the 1995 genocide in Bosnia and Herzegovina (S/2015/508 2015), with Angola, China, Nigeria, and Venezuela abstaining. In 2016, draft resolutions on Syria containing human rights language were vetoed by Russia in October, with Venezuela voting against and China and Angola abstaining (S/2016/846), and by both Russia and China in December, with Venezuela voting against and

Angola abstaining (S/2016/1026). In 2017, five draft resolutions on Syria were vetoed by Russia alone in four cases and by both China and Russia in one instance; however, these drafts did not contain specific references to human rights.

But even with their historic disinclination to incorporate human rights into the Council's discourse, Russia and China have accepted their relevance in numerous Council decisions, and each has actively sought a briefing by the High Commissioner for Human Rights on at least one occasion: China, in May 2012, issued an official invitation for the High Commissioner to brief during an open debate on protection of civilians in armed conflict during its presidency; and Russia successfully argued for the need to receive a briefing in consultations on Libya in July 2012.

Securing the Council consensus to address human rights – in particular in the early post-Cold War period – usually required a degree of activism. At different points, Council members committed to advancing the Council's attention to human rights made a specific situation their cause and worked proactively and strategically to pave the way to achieving the assent of their more reluctant colleagues. Elected members played a particularly important role in that process, by taking the lead to ensure that the overall Council approach to conflicts where human rights violations were widespread would address this aspect of the conflict. This dynamic could perhaps be explained by the fact that elected members, because of the short duration of their Council terms, have had a greater sense of urgency and a strong motivation to see immediate impact. Human rights issues, in turn, are most effectively addressed early on, and if an intervention is successful, the impact is felt and seen immediately.

In the last few years, overall, the Council seems to be more prepared than was the case in the past to receive human rights information but less prepared to take action such as making an emergency visit to the site of conflict, promptly dispatching human rights monitors to the field or having consistent and ongoing attention to accountability for human rights abuses. There are probably several factors contributing to this change in the dynamics. One of them may be that with the emergence of the system, members other than the penholders are disinclined to make human rights in a particular conflict their cause, deferring to the lead country and its overall approach. Another factor contributing to the somewhat diminished pro-activity and a lesser sense of urgency may, ironically, be the general acceptance of the relevance of human rights to peace and security issues and the resulting perception of human rights becoming part of the Council routine and not an area in need of a champion among Council members.

Conclusions and a Look Ahead

The Council has undoubtedly come a long way in its evolution of the manner in which it treats human rights. After seeing human rights almost as a taboo for a number of decades, the Council now considers human rights as a part of the reality with which it needs to deal in its effort to maintain international peace and security. The story of the evolution of the Council's approach to human rights also illustrates several of the most interesting features of the Security Council: its adaptability, pragmatism, and creativity. Not all these features are seen at every point, and not every member displays them at any given moment, but it is safe to say that, collectively, the Security Council is probably the most pragmatic and adaptable international body. The Council's treatment of human rights provides one of the examples of its ability to accept the changing nature of the very phenomenon with which it works, i.e., conflict; and thus to modify one of its seemingly most inviolable tenets, i.e., that human rights fall strictly within states' sovereignty; and to invent or adapt its tools to better fit the changing nature of international peace and security.

Yet, looking at the various conflict situations, the Council's approach to them, and the impact of this approach specifically on the human rights of the people living in the different countries, some more critical thoughts also come to mind. A close examination of Council decisions and action with regard to human rights suggests that its resort to the different tools and its follow-up have been uneven and that a large proportion of human rights-related language in Council's resolutions is declaratory or hortative, rather than operative.

It seems that meaningful human rights results on the ground in conflict situations are achieved when there is burden sharing both within the Council and among the different parts of the UN, maximizing all resources. Follow-up and a close focus, sometimes for years at a time, are needed to produce lasting human rights improvements. Such long-term commitment is sometimes hard to maintain, especially when multiple crises compete for the Council's attention, and a sense of fatigue sets in when the conflict continues despite all the measures deployed.

It is also useful to appreciate that human rights improvements are never just one actor's success and that the different actors can reinforce each other's value added. In this context, what may often be useful is advocacy, not only from civil society alone but also from concerned member states and across the different UN bodies. Internal advocacy within the different parts of the UN, aimed at achieving synergies, maximizing the available resources and impact also appears to be a potentially useful tool. Flexibility and creativity are key to finding ways to address human rights challenges, and the Security Council with its almost limitless adaptability can in this context probably be seen as a model by other bodies. One final conclusion is that there is probably quite a high degree of unrealized potential within the Security Council for having a significant impact on human rights conditions in specific situations around the world.

References

Security Council Resolutions

S/RES/1012 (1995) Established an international commission of inquiry into the 1993 coup attempt in Burundi and into the massacres that followed
S/RES/120 (1956) Referred the situation in Hungary to the General Assembly
S/RES/1267 (1999) Established the Al-Qaida and Taliban committee and its sanctions mandate

S/RES/1272 (1999) Established UNTAET in East Timor

S/RES/1315 (2000) Requested the Secretary-General to negotiate an agreement to create the Special Court for Sierra Leone

S/RES/1410 (2002) Established the UN Mission of Support in East Timor and stressed the importance of ensuring that those who committed serious crimes should be brought to justice

S/RES/1564 (2004) Established the International Commission of Inquiry to investigate reports of violations of international humanitarian law and human rights law in Darfur

S/RES/1591 (2005) Created a committee and panel of experts and additional individually targeting measures

S/RES/1593 (2005) Referred the situation in Darfur to the International Criminal Court

S/RES/161 (1961) Was on the situation in the Congo following the killings of Congolese leaders Patrice Lumumba, Maurice Mpolo and Joseph Okito

S/RES/1690 (2006) Extended the UN Office in Timor-Leste (UNOTIL) until 20 August and requested a report with recommendations for a future UN presence by 7 August

S/RES/1698 (2006) Extended sanctions to individuals recruiting or targeting children in situations of armed conflict, expressed the intention to consider measures over natural resources, and renewed the sanctions regime and the mandate of the Group of Experts until 31 July 2007

S/RES/1807 (2008) Extended the sanctions regime on the DRC until 31 December 2008

S/RES/181 (1963) Called on South Africa to abandon the policies of apartheid and discrimination

S/RES/182 (1963) Called on South Africa to comply with resolution 181

S/RES/190 (1964) Urged South Africa to cease prosecution of the opponents of apartheid policy

S/RES/191 (1964) Related to the policies of apartheid by the Government of South Africa

S/RES/1970 (2011) Referred the situation in Libya to the International Criminal Court, imposed an arms embargo and targeted sanctions (assets freeze and travel ban) and established a sanctions committee

S/RES/2002 (2011) Extended the mandate of the monitoring group on Somalia and Eritrea for 12 months and expanded the criteria for targeted sanctions to include recruitment and use of children in armed conflict and targeting of civilians

S/RES/203 (1965) Was a resolution on the situation in the Dominican Republic

S/RES/2127 (2013) Asked the Secretary-General to establish an international commission of inquiry in order to investigate reports of violations of international humanitarian law, international human rights law and abuses of human rights in CAR

S/RES/2140 (2014) Expressed the Council's strong support for the next steps of the political transition and established sanctions against those threatening the peace, security or stability of Yemen

S/RES/2171 (2014) Requested the Secretary-General to submit a report to the Council on actions taken to "promote and strengthen conflict prevention tools within the United Nations system" by 31 August 2015

S/RES/2206 (2015) Established a sanctions regime for South Sudan

S/RES/253 (1968) Established the first Council sanctions committee to monitor the implementation of the sanctions measures in Southern Rhodesia

S/RES/418 (1977) Imposed a mandatory ban on all states from engaging in "any cooperation with South Africa in the manufacture and development of nuclear weapons"

S/RES/693 (1991) Mandated the UN Observer Mission in El Salvador to monitor the human rights situation in El Salvador

S/RES/745 (1992) Established UNTA

S/RES/780 (1992) Asked the Secretary-General to appoint an international commission to provide recommendations on how to address the situation in the former Yugoslavia

S/RES/824 (1993) Established safe areas in Bosnia and related UNPROFOR responsibilities

S/RES/827 (1993) Established the International Criminal Tribunal for the former Yugoslavia

S/RES/841 (1993) Imposed sanctions in connection with Haiti

S/RES/872 (1993) Established UNAMIR in Rwanda

S/RES/925 (1994) Extended the mandate of UNAMIR (Rwanda) for additional six months

S/RES/935 (1994) Requested the Secretary-General to establish a commission of experts to obtain
  information regarding grave violations of international law in Rwanda
S/RES/955 (1994) Established the International Criminal Tribunal for Rwanda

Security Council Presidential Statements

S/23500 (1992) Was adopted following the first Security Council meeting on the level of heads of
  state on 31 January 1992
S/PRST/1994/60 (1994) Was on the situation in Burundi
S/PRST/2004/17 (2004) Asked the Secretary-General to establish an international commission of
  inquiry to investigate all human rights violations committed in Côte d'Ivoire since 19 September
  2002 and determine responsibility

Security Council Reports

S/1996/682 (1996) Was a report of international commission of inquiry into the 1993 coup attempt
  in Burundi and into the massacres that followed established through Security Council resolution
  1012 of 28 August 1995
S/2005/60 (2005) Was the report of the International Commission of Inquiry on Darfur to the
  Secretary-General
S/2006/822 (2006) Was a report of the Independent Special Commission of Inquiry for Timor-Leste
S/2014/276 (2014) Was a letter to the Council from Australia, France and the US transmitting the
  report of the commission of inquiry on human rights in the DPRK
S/2014/928 (2014) Was the final report of the CAR Commission of Inquiry

Security Council Letters

S/2014/501 (2014) Was from Australia, France and the US summarising the Council's Arria-
  formula meeting on the CoI report on human rights in DPRK
S/24393 (1992) Was from Belgium requesting that the Security Council invite the CHR Special
  Rapporteur on Iraq, Max van der Stoel, to address the Council
S/24394 (1992) Was from France requesting that the Security Council invite the CHR Special
  Rapporteur on Iraq, Max van der Stoel, to address the Council
S/24395 (1992) Was from the UK requesting that the Council invite the CHR Special Rapporteur on
  Iraq, Max van der Stoel, to address the Council
S/24396 (1992) Was from the US requesting that the Security Council invite the CHR Special
  Rapporteur on Iraq, Max van der Stoel to address the Council

Security Council Meeting Records

S/PV.3046 (1992) Was the first Security Council meeting held at the level of heads of state
S/PV.3105 (1992) The Council decided for the first time to invite a Special Rapporteur of the UN
  Commission on Human Rights (Special Rapporteur on the human rights situation in Iraq Max
  Van der Stoel) to address the body during a meeting on the situation between Iraq and Kuwait

S/PV.3134 (1992) Special Rapporteur of the Commission on Human Rights on the former Yugo-slavia, Tadeusz Mazowiecki, was invited to address the Council during its consideration of the situation in Bosnia and Herzegovina

S/PV.3139 (1992) The Special Rapporteur on the human rights situation in Iraq, Max Van der Stoel, was invited to address the Council on the situation in between Kuwait and Iraq

S/PV.4046 (1999) Was semi-annual debate on the protection of civilians during which the High Commissioner for Human Right (Mary Robinson at the time) addressed the Security Council for the first time

S/PV.4143 and Resumption 1 (2000) Was an open debate on the DRC following the Council's visit to the country from 3 to 8 May

S/PV.5005 (2004) Was an open debate on the Security Council visiting mission to West Africa from 20 to 29 June 2004

S/PV.5581 (2006) Was on the report of the Council visiting mission to Afghanistan

S/PV.6351 (2010) Was on Afghanistan

S/PV.7289 (2014) Was the annual open debate on women, peace and security during which Chaloka Beyani, HRC Special Rapporteur on the human rights of internally displaced persons, was among the briefers

S/PV.7898 (2017) Was an open debate on trafficking in persons in conflict situations during which Urmila Bhoola, Special Rapporteur on contemporary forms of slavery, including its causes and consequences, was among the briefers

S/PV.7926 (2017) Was the first formal Security Council meeting with a stated focus on human rights

Other

S/1994/1039 (1994) Was the report of the Security Council's fact-finding mission to Burundi, on 13 and 14 August 1994

S/2006/391 (2006) Was an 8 June 2006 request by Timor Leste to the Council asking it to establish an independent commission of inquiry into violent events that resulted in mass displacement of civilians earlier in the year

S/2007/14 (2007) Was a draft resolution on the situation in Myanmar which was vetoed by China and Russia

S/2008/447 (2008) Was a draft resolution on the situation in Zimbabwe

S/2009/243 (2009) Was a letter containing the terms of reference for the Security Council mission to Africa in May 2009

S/2011/612 (2011) Was a vetoed draft Security Council resolution condemning the Syrian crack-down on protestors. Russia and China vetoed the draft resolution and Brazil, India, Lebanon and South Africa abstained

S/2012/538/Rev.2 (n.d.) Was a draft resolution on Syria that did not pass

S/2014/189 (2014) Was a draft resolution on Ukraine that was not adopted due to a veto by Russia

S/2014/348 (2014) Was a draft resolution referring situation in Syria to the ICC

S/2015/508 (2015) Was a draft resolution to commemorate the anniversary of the Srebrenica genocide that was vetoed by Russia and Angola. China, Nigeria and Venezuela abstained

S/25700 (1993) Was the report of the Security Council visiting mission to former Yugoslavia, including Sarajevo and Srebrenica

UN Human Rights Council/Commission on Human Rights

1992/S-1/1 (1992) Was a resolution adopted at the first special session of the CHS which requested the appointment of the Special Rapporteur to investigate the human rights situation on the territory of former Yugoslavia

A/HRC/RES/15/15 (2010) Was a Human Rights Council resolution extending the mandate of the Special Rapporteur on the protection of human rights and fundamental freedoms while countering terrorism

A/HRC/RES/25/25 (2014) Was a Human Rights Council resolution which welcomed the report of HRC commission of inquiry on human rights in DPRK and recommended that the General Assembly submit the report of the commission of inquiry to the Security Council

A/HRC/RES/27/16 (2014) Was Human Rights Council resolution on the human rights situation in Syria

A/HRC/RES/28/20 (2015) Was a Human Rights Council resolution on human rights and the humanitarian situation in Syria

A/HRC/RES/30/10 (2015) Was a Human Rights Council resolution on human rights and the humanitarian situation in Syria

E/CN.4/1994/7/Add/1 (1993) Was a report by the CHR Special Rapporteur on extrajudicial, summary or arbitrary executions regarding the situation in Rwanda

General Assembly

A/RES/3/217 A (1948) Was Universal Declaration of Human Rights

A/RES/48/141 (1993) Was a resolution that created the post of High Commissioner for Human Rights

A/RES/60/251 (2006) Was a resolution that established the Human Rights Council

International Labour Organization

Maria Victoria Cabrera-Ormaza

Contents

Introduction 228
The ILO Mandate and Institutional Framework 229
Tripartism 230
Organs 230
Standard-Setting Function 231
ILO Regular Supervisory System 233
Representations 234
Complaints 235
Special Procedures Concerning Freedom of Association 236
Freedom of Association and Trade Union Rights 237
Right to Collective Bargaining 239
Trade Union Rights and Other Civil Liberties 240
Trade Union Rights and Democracy 241
Impact of ILO Standards in International Human Rights Law 241
Indigenous Peoples' Rights 242
Indigenous Populations and the Idea of Integration 242
The Contribution of ILO Convention No. 169 244
Standard Review Initiatives 246
Conclusion 246
References 246

Abstract

Based on its commitment to social justice, the International Labour Organization (ILO) has been one of the most progressive institutions of the international community. A consolidated system of international labor standards and a vigorous supervisory system have helped the ILO to cement its role as a key player in the development of international human rights, mainly in the field of collective

M. V. Cabrera-Ormaza (✉)
Faculty of Law, Universidad Espíritu Santo-Ecuador, Samborondón, Ecuador
e-mail: marvic.co@gmail.com; mvcabrer@uees.edu.ec

© Springer Nature Singapore Pte Ltd. 2018   227
G. Oberleitner (ed.), *International Human Rights Institutions, Tribunals, and Courts*,
International Human Rights, https://doi.org/10.1007/978-981-10-5206-4_26

rights, namely trade unions' rights and indigenous peoples' rights. This chapter revisits the normative action of the ILO in these fields and shows how, in the performance of its normative function, the ILO has been confronting challenges that have hindered its ability to continue promoting advancements.

Keywords
International Labour Organization · ILO · Trade union · Freedom of association · Collective bargaining · Indigenous peoples

Introduction

The International Labour Organization (ILO) is one of the oldest international organizations with universal membership. It was established in 1919 with the promise of achieving universal peace through social justice (Treaty of Peace of Versailles, Part XIII, Preamble). Since its outset, the ILO has distinguished itself from other international organizations for its tripartite governance structure. This allows national and transnational employers' and workers' organizations to join governments in setting the agenda and conducting the activities of the organization. Tripartism is ingrained in the ILO as the most appropriate method of achieving the ILO's objectives (ILO Declaration 2008, Section I (iii)) and is reflected in the process of creating and supervising international labor standards, which deviates from the traditional inter-States law-making model (Lauterpacht 1955, p. 731). After the demise of the League of Nations in 1946, the ILO became part of the United Nations System as one of its specialized agencies in the field of social and economic rights.

In almost a century of its existence, the ILO has assumed the task of adopting conventions and recommendations containing international labor standards, while creating a "corpus juris of social justice" (Jenks 1963, p. 101). Two areas where the ILO has left an important legacy in human rights are trade union rights (freedom of association and the right to collective bargaining) and indigenous peoples' rights. International labor standards and the pronouncement of ILO supervisory bodies have heavily influenced the development of international and regional human rights instruments and jurisprudence in the field of labor rights (Ebert and Oelz 2012) as well as of indigenous peoples' rights (Cabrera 2017). Regarding trade union rights, the ILO has been actively protecting trade unions' autonomy from unlawful interference by the State or employers (Swepston 1998), and promoting respect for workers' right to collective bargaining as the "corollary of freedom of association" both in the public and private sector (ILO International Labour Office 2013a, para. 226). In this regard, it has also support recognition of a right to strike (Bellace 2014). With regards to indigenous peoples' rights, the ILO's initial task was that of guarantying fair labor conditions to indigenous workers and, over time, it has given new collective rights to indigenous groups based on their condition as historically socially disadvantaged group of the society.

Regardless of the fact that the work of the ILO in the fields of collective labor rights and indigenous rights can be traced back to the period of the League of

Nations, these two sets of rights have taken different roads of development over time and confronted different types of challenges. The action of the ILO with respect to freedom of association and collective bargaining has been constantly reinforced through the adoption of instruments with both binding and nonbinding legal effect as well as through the establishment of special procedures of supervision. One of these latter instruments is the 1998 ILO Declaration on Fundamental Principles and Rights at Work, which clearly reaffirms the obligation of every Member State of the ILO to respect, to promote and to realize, in good faith, the universal rights and principles of freedom of association and collective bargaining (ILO Declaration on Fundamental Principles and Rights at Work, 1998). On the other hand, the action of the ILO regarding indigenous peoples' rights has been characterized by debates over the limits of the organizations' capacity to deal with indigenous issues and the orientation of its standards. Even though the only two treaties dealing specifically with indigenous peoples have been adopted under the auspices of the ILO, they lack support of the majority of member States in terms of ratification. Furthermore, until now indigenous organizations can access the ILO system of regular supervision and complaints only when aided by a workers' or employers' organization.

This chapter briefly explains the functioning of the ILO and explores the contribution of this organization in relation to trade union rights and indigenous peoples' rights. In doing so, it starts exploring the role of the ILO in terms of its mandate, as well as of its norm production and supervision functions. Subsequently, the chapter outlines relevant aspects of ILO standards and jurisprudence relating to trade union rights and indigenous peoples' rights which have been crucial to furthering the development of these rights under international human rights law. This chapter concludes with some reflections on the current landscape of the organization.

The ILO Mandate and Institutional Framework

The preamble to Part XIII of the Treaty of Versailles, which contains the ILO foundational charter, proclaimed that "peace can be established only if it is based on social justice." Albert Thomas, who was the first Director General of the International Labour Office, was convinced that governments "must not regard labour problems as entirely internal matters without close connection with the great problems of international peace" (International Labour Office 1978). The ILO general commitment to social justice was further reaffirmed in the 1944 Declaration concerning the Aims and Purposes of the International Labour Organization, the so-called "Philadelphia Declaration," which today forms part of the ILO Constitution. Based on this commitment, the ILO's three constituents (governments', workers', and employers' organizations) set as one of the core objectives of the ILO promoting the right that all human beings have to pursue their material and spiritual development in conditions of freedom and dignity, economic security, and equal opportunity (Declaration of Philadelphia Section II). The Permanent

Court of International Justice recognized the comprehensive character of the ILO mandate and its broad field of work in two advisory decisions adopted in the 1920s (PCIJ 1922, 1926). As a result, it has been possible for the ILO to deal, in the course of its existence, with a very wide range of subjects; including labor conditions, social security, and indigenous peoples; as long as they were related to social justice, a term which ILO constituents have left undefined.

Tripartism

Since the inception of the ILO, workers', employers', and governments' representatives have taken part in its governance. Tripartism "is embedded in every aspect of the organization's institutional structure" (La Hovary 2015b, p. 210) as well as in its normative function. Workers' and employers' representatives are involved since the early stage of drafting international labor standards proposals, through their formal adoption by the plenary of the International Labour Conference until the process of their ratification (Standing Orders of the International Labour Conference, Section E). With regards to the monitoring of international labor standards, Article 22 of the ILO Constitution requires governments to communicate their reports on the implementation of ratified conventions to the representative organizations of workers and employers in order to allow them to provide their comments on such reports. Tripartism has been linked to the conviction that "voluntary interaction and dialogue among representatives of the various parties is vital for social and economic stability and progress" (Simpson 1994, p. 40). Nevertheless, tripartism has been criticized for limiting dynamism within the organization, putting the effectiveness of its work in jeopardy (La Hovary 2015a, p. 207). Indeed, in practice, tripartism has become a lock that has indirectly prevented other non-State actors from participating in the governance of the ILO, as is in the case with indigenous peoples' organizations which have always needed to find support from any of the tripartite constituents to submit their claims to the ILO, or the case of unorganized workers who cannot access to the ILO individually.

Organs

The ILO is composed of a political and an executive organ, as well as a secretariat. The International Labour Conference is the political body composed of accredited workers', employers' representatives – the so-called social partners – and government delegates. The Conference serves as a "forum for tripartite dialogue" (CAS Report 2017, 15 Part I/50) debating on issues of interest to the organization and the negotiation and adoption of international labor standards. The Conference also cooperates in the regular supervision of compliance with ILO conventions. In its annual meeting, it sets a conference committee known as the Committee on the Application of Standards (CAS) (Standing Orders of the International Labour Conference Article 7), which discusses general aspects relating to the application of international labor conventions. Since 1957, the CAS has put into practice the examination of individual cases of serious noncompliance with ILO standards (Landy 2004, p. 15). Within this procedure, governments have the opportunity to provide the CAS with information and to reply to the observations made by Conference members.

The Governing Body is the executive body of the ILO as it has "the responsibility of coordinating all the activities of the organization" (Valticos 1979, p. 36). It sets up the agenda of the International Labour Conference and selects possible topics for conventions and recommendations (Standing Orders of the International Labour Conference, Articles 34 and 43). Tripartism is also reflected in the composition of the Governing Body: 28 of its members represent governments, 14 members represent the employers, and 14 members represent the workers (ILO Constitution, Article 7).

The Governing Body may also impose some pressure on member States to implement international labor standards utilizing Article 19 of the ILO Constitution. According to this provision, the Governing Body can request all member States to provide information on the current state of its law and practice in regard to the matters pertaining to ILO Conventions, indicating the actions taken to give effect to them as well as the difficulties which prevent or delay their ratification. The use of this tool can lead to changes in the law and practice of States in conformity with international labor standards which have not yet been ratified by them. In addition, the Governing Body appoints the members of the Committee on Freedom of Association and of tripartite committees in charge of examining representations relating to concrete violations of ILO conventions. The functions of these bodies are explained below.

Finally, the International Labour Office acts as the secretariat of the International Labour Organization. Governed by a Director General, who is appointed by the Governing Body (ILO Constitution, Article 8), the Office is tasked with providing technical support to the Conference and the Governing Body. Upon decision of the Conference, it can also assist governments in framing laws and regulations, improving administrative practices and systems of inspection in conformity with ILO standards (ILO Constitution, Article 10). Over the years, the CAS has consistently recommended governments that have seriously failed to comply ratified ILO conventions to receive technical assistance of the International Labour Office. This has been regarded as a valuable tool in the search for the causes and solutions to implementation problems (Landy 2004, p. 16). On several occasions, the Office has provided opinions to member States on issues relating to international labor standards, but with a disclaimer that its views are not authoritative (Valticos 1988, p. 190).

Standard-Setting Function

Under Article 19 of the ILO Constitution, the International Labour Conference can adopt international labour standards in the form of conventions, which are treaties in a strict sense, or recommendations, which are instruments of nonbinding character. Up to now, the ILO has adopted a total of 189 conventions, 6 protocols, and 205 recommendations. The latter lacks binding effect, but in most of the cases contains guidelines to give effect to conventions. Notably the production of conventions appears to have decreased over time. Within the last 10 years, only one Convention and one Protocol were adopted by the ILO, whereas until the end of the 1990s, the ILO adopted an average one convention per year.

The standard-setting process is coordinated by the International Labour Office, which upon request of the Governing Body collects and analyses the information provided by governments and the comments of the social partners in relation to proposed subjects of conventions or recommendations (Standing Orders of the International Labour Conference, Article 39). Normally, the adoption of international standards is preceded by a double-discussion on the matter within the International Labour Conference. According to Article 19 (5) (b) of the ILO Constitution, once the Conference has adopted an instrument (whether a convention, a protocol, or a recommendation), member States have the obligation to put this instrument into consideration of the competent authorities, within a period of a year, "for the enactment of legislation or other action." The Committee of Experts on the Application of Conventions and Recommendations (CEACR), one of the ILO supervisory organs, has indicated that the rationale of this obligation "is to promote measures at the domestic level for the implementation of the instruments adopted by the Conference, but it does not imply an obligation to propose ratification of Conventions/ Protocols or acceptance of Recommendations" (International Labour Office 2015a, 31 para. 96).

For the ILO, international labor standards have to be flexible, both in their wording and means of implementation (Politakis 2004) in view of the diversity of national conditions of ILO member states (Valticos 1988, p. 182). However, workers' organizations have contended that such flexibility could render the standards meaningless (Politakis 2004, p. 469). In this regard, an effective supervision by ILO monitoring bodies could arguably mitigate the obscurity inherent in flexible standards (Valticos 1988, p. 192).

Following the adoption of the 1998 Declaration on Fundamental Principles and Rights at Work, the ILO introduced a classification or "normative hierarchy" (Alston 2004, p. 458). There is a group of fundamental conventions, which include those regulating the "core labour standards": Freedom of association and the right to collective bargaining, elimination of forced labor, abolition of child labor, and the elimination of discrimination with respect to employment. A second category of conventions is the so-called "governance conventions" as they are regarded as relevant from a point of view of governance, in line with the 2008 Declaration on Social Justice for a Fair Globalization (ILO Declaration 2008, Section II (B) (iii)). Conventions which are not included within these two categories are identified as technical conventions. The focus of this hierarchization of standards is to concentrate institutional efforts on achieving compliance with what the ILO regards as its fundamental norms through alternative means of supervision (so-called follow-up mechanism) introduced as an Annex the 1998 Declaration.

ILO Regular Supervisory System

The ILO's supervisory machinery has been of central importance to achieving ILO's objectives. The ILO monitors compliance with its international labor standards through a regular reporting mechanism and a set of adversarial proceedings. Regular supervision is carried out by the CEACR. Established by the Governing Body in 1926, the CEACR is a permanent expert and quasi-judicial body (Leary 1982, p. 19) composed of 20 jurists with recognized knowledge and expertise in the field of labor and social rights. Guided by the principles of independence, objectivity, and impartiality (International Labour Office 2013a), this body is tasked with supervising implementation of ratified conventions based on governments' reports that are due under Article 22 of the ILO Constitution. These reports contain information on the steps taken by governments to put into effect every provision of a Convention according to a report form approved by the Governing Body. These measures can include legislative and administrative regulations as well as judicial decisions. In the case of ILO fundamental labor conventions, reports are due every 3 years, whereas in the rest of the conventions, reports are due every 5 years, unless the CEACR considers it necessary to request reports at shorter intervals (International Labour Office 2012a, p. 22).

Tripartism is also reflected in the supervisory function of the ILO. Article 23 of the ILO Constitution imposes on member States the duty to communicate to the most representative organizations of workers and employers copies of the reports submitted under Article 22. In practice, this provision permits the workers' and employers' organizations to submit to the International Labour Office their comments on governments' reports. They may, for instance, draw attention to a discrepancy in law or practice regarding the application of a ratified Convention (International Labour Office 2017, p. 1). The CEACR assesses the information contained in governments' reports, taking into account the comments sent by the social partners. Depending on the results of its assessment, the CEACR can issue comments in the form of either "observations" or "direct requests." Observations "point to important discrepancies between the obligations under a Convention and the related law and/practice of member States," whereas direct requests are used by the CEACR to "engage in a continuing dialogue with governments on questions of rather technical nature" (International Labour Office 2017a, 14 para. 39). These comments constitute a form of soft-law jurisprudence (La Hovary 2015a).

The CEACR understands its mandate as entailing the main task of indicating "the extent to which each member State's legislation and practices are in conformity with ratified Conventions and the extent to which member States have fulfilled their obligations under the ILO Constitution in relation to standards" (International Labour Office 2017, p. 1). Notably, in 2012, employers' members of the International Labour Conference called into question the capacity of the CEACR to provide expansive interpretations of ILO Conventions when performing its supervisory function (International Labour Office 2012a, 19(Rev.) Part I/22). As shown later on, this criticism was connected to the CEACR's support for the recognition of the right to strike, as implicit in the ILO Convention concerning Freedom of Association and Protection of the Right to Organise (No. 87). For its part, the CEACR emphasized in 2013 that "in order to carry out its mandate of evaluating and assessing the application and interpretation of Conventions, it had to consider and express its views on the legal scope and meaning of the provisions of these Conventions" (International Labour Office 2013a, 10 para. 26). Furthermore, it maintained that "the Committee's non-binding opinions or conclusions are intended to guide the actions of ILO member States by virtue of their rationality and persuasiveness, their source of legitimacy (by which is meant the independence, experience, and expertise of the members), and their responsiveness to a set of national realities including the informational input of the social partners" (International Labour Office 2013a, 35 para. 14). Arguably, in some cases, the CEACR has even extended the scope of ILO Conventions beyond what was foreseen at the time of their adoption just as UN human rights treaty bodies do with respect to the conventions whose compliance they supervise (La Hovary 2015a, p. 318). However, the CEACR has denied having the capacity to give authoritative interpretations of ILO conventions, a competence which lies exclusively with the International Court of Justice, as provided for in Article 37 of the ILO Constitution.

The CEACR cooperates with the CAS in the supervision of ILO Conventions as its comments are taken as basis for the selection of individual cases to be discussed at the International Labour Conference. In this respect, the CAS has normally focused on the CEACR's notes contained in its observations, the so-called "footnotes," which are used to indicate serious, persistent, or urgent problems in relation to the application of a convention (International Labour Office 2017, Appendix I 15 Part I/ 53). Even though employers' members of the International Labour Conference have argued that the CEACR is subordinated to the work of the CAS, they have been allocated different though interrelated functions without any form of hierarchy of one over the other.

Representations

Article 24 of the ILO Constitution establishes that any industrial association of employers or workers can submit before the International Labour Office a representation against any member which has failed to comply with ratified conventions. Each case of a representation is examined first by a tripartite committee established by the Governing Body which is composed of one representative of each of the three ILO constituents. The conclusions of the tripartite committees have to be approved by the Governing Body before they are communicated to the State concerned (Standing orders concerning the procedure for the examination of representations under articles 24 and 25 of the Constitution of the ILO, paras. 17–19). These two aspects may arguably affect the impartiality of the procedure and its outcome, which finally rest on the constituents' positions rather than on the meaning of the conventions in light of the international rules of interpretation.

Representations can be submitted with respect to any convention and by any organization of workers or employers, regardless of its size. Yet, representations that concern any convention relating to freedom of association and collective bargaining may be referred to the Committee on Freedom of Association (Standing orders concerning the procedure for the examination of representations under articles 24 and 25 of the Constitution of the ILO, para. 12). In no case, exhaustion of domestic remedies is required.

Only workers' and employers' organizations are entitled to submit representations, whether they are local, national, or international associations. They do not need to be directly affected by a violation of a Convention to make use of this procedure. Because of this, all representations that have concerned violations of the provisions of the 1989 ILO Convention No. 169 on Indigenous and Tribal Peoples have been submitted by workers' organizations on behalf of affected indigenous groups. In practice, however, the procedure of representation has been marginalized (Maupain 2013, p. 134) arguably due to a transparency deficit, lack of legal expertise of tripartite committee's members, and a week follow-up mechanism.

Complaints

Complaints are regulated by Articles 26 to 29 of the ILO Constitution and are considered as the "most formal type of supervisory procedure in the ILO" (Valticos 1979, p. 245). They constitute the ultimate recourse that the ILO can use to exercise pressure on a government which has committed grave violations of ILO standards. A complaint can be filed by any state "if it is not satisfied that any other Member is securing the effective observance of any Convention which both have ratified" (ILO Constitution, Article 26). The complaint is examined by a Commission of Inquiry set up by the Governing Body, which is required to report on the findings on all questions relevant to the issues which are subject matter of the complaint and to make recommendations. Failure to comply with the recommendations of the Commission of Enquiry may be subject to sanctions established by the Governing Body, as it happened in the case of Myanmar in 1999. In that year, the International Labour Conference adopted a resolution in which it called on relevant bodies of the organization to reconsider in the light of the conclusions of the Commission of Inquiry any cooperation they were engaged in with Myanmar and to cease any activity that had the effect of directly or indirectly abetting the practice of forced or compulsory labor (International Labour Conference 1999).

A total of 13 complaints have been decided since the establishment of the ILO. Most of them have related to the violation of fundamental conventions, including Convention No. 87 (freedom of association) and Convention No. 98 (collective bargaining). Although it is possible for the Governing Body of the ILO to start a complaint procedure of its own motion or upon receipt of a complaint from a delegate to the Conference, this option has not been put in practice so far.

Special Procedures Concerning Freedom of Association

Freedom of association and collective bargaining has always received special treatment within the ILO, particularly in terms of mechanisms of supervision. In 1950, a Fact Finding and Conciliation Commission on Freedom of Association was established upon agreement between the ILO Governing Body and the Economic and Social Council of the United Nations. The role of this Commission was to undertake investigations of allegations concerning violations of freedom of association and the right to collective bargaining submitted by governments, workers', or employers' organizations (Gravel et al. 2001, p. 8). The Commission's main function is "to examine such cases of alleged infringements of trade union rights as may be referred to it, to ascertain the facts and to discuss the situation with the government concerned with a view to securing the adjustment of difficulties by agreement" (International Labour Office 1966, para. 2). Complaints examined by the Fact Finding and Conciliation Commission involve States members of the United Nations, irrespective of whether they are also members of the ILO (International Labour Office 2006, p. 2).

The Committee on Freedom of Association (CFA) was created in 1951 to support the work of the Fact-Finding and Conciliation Commission to carry out a preliminary examination of complaints with respect to violations of freedom of association and the right to collective bargaining (Governing Body 1951, 45–50). It is composed of nine members appointed by each of the three ILO constituents (three for each group) represented in the Governing Body, and an independent chairperson. Although it was conceived as an auxiliary body, over time the CFA assumed a more decisive role in the ILO, becoming the main body responsible for examining complaints concerning freedom of association (Gravel et al. 2001, p. 11). According to the Special Procedures for the Examination in the International Labour Organization of Complaints alleging Violation of Freedom of Association, issued by the Governing Body in 2009, the mandate of the CFA "consists in determining whether any given legislation or practice complies with the principles of freedom of association and collective bargaining laid down in the relevant Conventions." Within this mandate, the CFA shall examine allegations concerning possible violations of these principles and report to the Governing Body its findings and recommendations on such complaints. In this regard, it the main objective of the CFA procedure "is not to criticize certain governments, but rather to engage in constructive tripartite dialogue to promote respect for trade unions' and employers' associations' rights in law and practice" (International Labour Office 2016, para. 30). The CFA can support its assessment through direct missions, a practice which has been used to better understand the problems faced by the competent national authorities to implement trade unions' rights (Valticos 1981). Since its creation, the CFA has dealt with a total of more than 3000 complaints and has published for five occasions digests of its main decisions.

Tripartism in the CFA has been manifested in a practice of adopting decisions by consensus, trying to ensure a "judicious balance between the interests defended by the Government, Employer and Worker members" (Gravel et al. 2001, p. 12).

Contrary to the case of representations, the high number of cases that have been examined by the CFA since its creation reveals the importance attached to this mechanism within the ILO system. At the same time, the CFA has been criticized for limiting itself to pronounce the principles transgressed and to require providing information on any progress, without giving a deeper understanding of the issues under discussion (Simpson 2004, p. 69).

Freedom of Association and Trade Union Rights

The Treaty of Versailles proclaims the right of association for all lawful purposes by the employed as well as by the employers' as one of the principles to which the High Contracting Parties gave a "special and urgent" importance (Treaty of Versailles, Art. 427). The 1944 Philadelphia Declaration reaffirms that freedom of association is "essential to sustained progress" and recognizes as a solemn obligation of the ILO to achieve "the effective recognition of the right of collective bargaining" (Declaration of Philadelphia, Sections I and III).

In 1948, the International Labour Conference adopted the Convention concerning Freedom of Association and Protection of the Right to Organise (No. 87). This convention originated in a request made by the Economic and Social Council to the Governing Body to include the topic of freedom of association and industrial relations on the agenda of the Conference (International Labour Office 1948, p. 2). Before that, the only ILO instrument that recognized the principle of freedom of association was the Convention concerning the Rights of Association and Combination of Agricultural Workers, which, under its Article 1, requires States to secure to all those engaged in agriculture the same rights of association as to industrial workers. Article 2 of ILO Convention No. 87 defines freedom of association as the right of "workers and employers, without distinction whatsoever, to establish and, subject only to the rules of the organisation concerned, to join organisations of their own choosing without previous authorisation." The conception of this instrument was supported by the United Nations General Assembly, which, as early as in 1947, adopted a resolution that reaffirmed the existence of an inalienable right of trade union freedom of association as essential to the improvement of the standard of living of workers and to their economic well-being and called upon the ILO to take the necessary steps to safeguard trade union rights (United Nations General Assembly A/RES/128(II)). The obligations of States in relation to freedom of association imply the one of respecting, promoting, and realizing in good faith. These obligations are not only derived from Convention No. 87 but are obligations that are imposed on every member State of the ILO as is considered to be inherent in the ILO Constitution, as spelled out in the 1998 Declaration on Fundamental Principles and Rights at Work. The right to freedom of association has both an individual and a collective dimension. This is the right of every worker or employer to join an organization, and the right of the organization to join other organizations and to engage into trade union activities. The CFA has dealt with cases when governments impose, through labor legislation, a minimum number of workers in an enterprise to establish a trade union. In this regard, the CFA considered that "while a minimum membership requirement is not in itself incompatible with Convention No. 87, the number should be fixed in a reasonable manner so that the establishment of organizations is not hindered" (International Labour Office 2006, paras. 286–287).

In addition, the CFA has maintained that freedom of association also means the possibility for workers or employers to create more than one organization. The CFA has asserted: "A situation in which an individual is denied any possibility of choice between different organizations, by reason of the fact that the legislation permits the existence of only one organization in the area in which that individual carries on his or her occupation, is incompatible with the principles embodied in Convention No. 87" (International Labour Office 2006, para. 324). Even though Convention No. 87 does not impose a positive obligation of States to promote diversity of trade unions, it does require them to refrain from directly or indirectly imposing a trade union monopoly (Swepston 1998, p. 203).

A key element of freedom of association is the principle of nondiscrimination, as set forth in in Article 2 of Convention No. 87. This means mainly two things. Firstly, workers or employers cannot be discriminated in the exercise of this right for reasons of nationality, sex, political ideology, etc. Secondly, by virtue of the principle of nondiscrimination, every worker, regardless of the labor sector he belongs to, can enjoy these rights, though they can be subject to certain restrictions which have to be necessary and legitimate. The ILO has addressed situations of countries which have adopted measures aimed at systematically excluding workers of the public sector from the scope of freedom of association and collective bargaining. By way of example, in recent years, the CEACR has noted that constitutional reforms had been introduced in Ecuador intended to limit the exercise of freedom of association of public workers. One of these reforms stated that public workers could only be represented by a single trade union. In this respect, the CEACR reminded the government that public sector workers have the right, without discrimination, to create as many organizations as they deem necessary (CEACR Observation to Ecuador, Convention No. 87, 2015) and it required the government to revise this provision in conformity with Convention No. 87.

Another key condition for the effective and full realization of freedom of association is the autonomy of trade unions, which means the minimum possible level of interference of public authorities in trade union's activities. In other words, states have a negative obligation to abstain from interfering in the activities relating to the creation, administration, representation, and termination of trade unions and employer's organizations. This requirement derives from Articles 2 and 3 of Convention No. 87. The CEACR has observed that

> to guarantee fully the right of workers' and employers' organizations to draw up their constitutions and rules: (i) national legislation should only lay down formal requirements respecting trade union constitutions, except with regard to the need to follow a democratic process and to ensure a right of appeal for the members; and (ii) the constitutions and rules should only be subject to the verification of formal requirements by the authorities. (International Labour Office 2012c, para. 100)

The principle of autonomy also addresses employers, who should abstain from intervening in the exercise of freedom of association or collective bargaining of workers, for example, through the imposition of sanctions against those engaging in trade union activities (International Labour Office 2006, p. 338).

A permanent matter of controversy and tension among ILO constituents in relation to the principle of freedom of association is the right to strike. No ILO Convention expressly recognizes the existence of this right. Nevertheless, both the CFA and the CEACR have supported the existence of this right as an element that is inextricably linked to the right to freedom of association (Bellace 2014). In its 2012 General Survey on ILO Fundamental Conventions, the CEACR reaffirmed that "strikes are essential means available to workers and their organizations to protect their interests" and that strike action "is not an end in itself, but the last resort for workers' organizations" (International Labour Office 2012c, para. 117). To support this conclusion, the CEACR relied on the practice of member States, which have recognized their right to strike in their national legislations. Nevertheless, employers opposed the position of the CEACR in the context of the discussion around the general survey within the 2012 session of the CAS. On this occasion, the employers' group recalled that over time they had fundamentally objected to the Committee of Experts' opinions concerning the right to strike as soft law jurisprudence (International Labour Office 2012b, para. 82) and further observed that "the mandate of the Committee of Experts did not include giving definitive interpretations of Conventions" (International Labour Office 2012b, para. 85).

Following the above-mentioned debate, there have been much discussions about the limits of the mandate of the CEACR in the discharge of its supervisory function as well as on the implicit recognition of the right to strike under ILO Convention No. 87. This has led ILO constituents to consider the possibility of requesting an advisory opinion from the International Court of Justice (International Labour Office 2015b, para. 49). However, the Governing Body decided not to make use of this possibility (International Labour Office 2015b, para.25 (b)), leaving the controversy unsolved. For its part, the CEACR has continued addressing issues relating to the right to strike on the basis of previous comments, or national legislation that recognizes this right (CEACR Observation to Albania, ILO Convention No. 87 2016a; Observation to Bahamas, ILO Convention No. 87 2016b).

Right to Collective Bargaining

ILO Convention No. 87 is supplemented and reinforced by the Convention concerning the **Application of the Principles of the Right to Organise and to Bargain Collectively (No. 98),** which consecrates the right of trade unions to collective bargaining. This right constitutes a "fundamental aspect of the principle of freedom of association" (Gernigon et al. 2000, p. 40) and consists of the right of workers and employers organizations to negotiate the terms and conditions of employment by means of collective agreements (ILO Convention No. 98, Article 4). As in the case with freedom of association, collective bargaining is based on the notion of autonomy. In other words, public authorities should not intervene in the negotiation and drafting of collective agreements "unless it consists exclusively of technical aid" (International Labour Office 1996, para. 866). The CEACR has emphasized that if national legislation stipulates that any approval to collective agreements

> must be based on criteria such as compatibility with the general or economic policy of the government, or official directives on wages and conditions of employment, it in fact makes the entry into force of the agreement subject to prior approval, which is in violation of the principle of the autonomy of the parties. (International Labour Office 2012c, para. 201)

In addition to Convention No. 98, the ILO adopted in 1981 the Collective Bargaining Convention (No. 154) to regulate the exercise of the right to collective bargaining. Convention No. 154 indicates the issues that should be subject to collective negotiation and mentions the different means for the promotion and application of this right. Notably, it promotes, under Article 7, the development of collective bargaining between public authorities and public employees, reinforcing the protection of public workers' collective right offered by the 1978 Labour Relations (Public Service) Convention (No. 151). In this connection, the CEACR has noted that "recognition of the right to collective bargaining in the public service is a long-standing demand of the trade union movement, which has rightly criticized the unequal treatment of public employees in this regard" (International Labour Office 2013b, para. 226).

Trade Union Rights and Other Civil Liberties

The ILO has acknowledged that the realization of the right to freedom of association and collective bargaining depends on the respect for civil liberties. This was set forth in a resolution adopted by the International Labour Conference in 1970 concerning trade union rights and their relation to civil liberties. This resolution reaffirms

> the rights conferred upon workers' and employers' organizations must be based on respect for those civil liberties which have been enunciated in particular in the Universal Declaration of Human Rights and in the International Covenant on Civil and Political Rights and that the absence of these civil liberties removes all meaning from the concept of trade union rights. (International Labour Conference, 1970)

The resolution also mentions certain rights considered as essential for the exercise of freedom of association, which include: The right to freedom from arbitrary arrest and detention; freedom of opinion and expression and right to seek, receive, and impart information; freedom of assembly; the right to a fair trial; and the right to protection of the property of trade union organizations. The following year, in 1951, the Conference adopted the Workers' Representative Convention (No. 135) which, under its Article 1, provides trade unions' representatives "effective protection against any act prejudicial to them, including dismissal, based on their status or activities as a workers' representative or on union membership or participation in union activities."

Trade Union Rights and Democracy

Freedom of association serves democracy (Curtis 2004, p. 90). Particularly in Latin America, ratification of Convention No. 87 has "served as an impetus for improvements in collective rights following the demise of authoritarian rule and transitions towards democratic polity" (Brudney 2017, p. 21). However, there has been cases in which governments, in the name of democracy, have tried to limit trade union rights. This has been the case of Venezuela. Through a referendum, the Venezuelan government intended to impose a trade union unity rule in the public sector to dissolve unions that opposed the government. The CFA gave its pronouncement on this case concluding that this referendum constituted a grave breach of ILO standards on freedom of association and required the government to refrain "from carrying out referendums on matters directly affecting the trade union movement, disregarding the will of the trade unions and their confederations." (CFA Case 2067 Interim Report No. 325 2001, para. 589)

Impact of ILO Standards in International Human Rights Law

In the human rights context, ILO Convention No. 87 has a great normative value beyond the contours of the ILO. The last paragraph of Article 8 of the Covenant on Economic, Social, and Cultural Rights prevents "States Parties to the International Labour Organisation Convention of 1948 concerning Freedom of Association and Protection of the Right to Organize to take legislative measures which would prejudice, or apply the law in such a manner as would prejudice, the guarantees provided for in that Convention." Likewise, the Committee on Economic, Social, and Cultural Rights adopted its General Comment No. 18 on the right to work, drawing heavily on the work of the ILO (Riedel 2007, p. 5).

The ILO normative contribution in the field of freedom of association and collective bargaining has also been acknowledged in the jurisprudence of regional human rights courts. The European Court of Human Rights has made use of ILO instruments and the jurisprudence of ILO supervisory bodies in several occasions and in different ways (Ebert and Oelz 2012). For instance, in its 2014 judgment on the case "National Union of Rail, Maritime and Transport Workers v. The United Kingdom," the Court referred to the statements voiced by the CEACR and the CFA in relation to freedom of association and the right to strike (Application no. 31045/10, Judgement: 27). In particular, the Court considers the work of the CEACR to be "a point of reference and guidance for the interpretation of ILO conventions" (European Court of Human Rights 2014, para. 97). Also, the Inter-American Court of Human Rights in its 2001 judgment on the case Baena Ricardo v. Panama took into account the jurisprudence of the CFA to examine whether measures adopted by the government of Panama for the dismissal of trade union representatives of public workers associations were in violation of Article 16 of the American Convention of Human Rights (Inter-American Court of Human Rights 2001, paras. 163–165). In a recent advisory opinion, the Court further recognized that trade unions were legal entities covered by the American Convention on Human Rights referring, among others, to both Convention No. 87 and the 1998 ILO Declaration on Principles and Rights at Work (Inter-American Court of Human Rights 2016, paras. 87, 101, 102).

Indigenous Peoples' Rights

Another important contribution of the ILO to human rights law relates to the development of indigenous peoples' rights. To understand properly the ILO central role in the formation of indigenous rights, it is important to understand the origins of this commitment, which started with the adoption of the Treaty of Versailles in 1919. At that time, the colonial powers, which were members of the League of Nations, decided to assume an international obligation "to undertake to secure just treatment of native inhabitants living in non-independent territories" (Treaty of Versailles, Article 23 (b)). In addition, states committed themselves to report to the International Labour Office the actions taken by them to implement international labor conventions in their colonies, protectorates, and possessions (Treaty of Versailles, Art. 421). In 1930, the ILO adopted the Forced Labour Convention (No. 29), which was a response to the appalling conditions under which native workers were working in nonindependent territories, as witnessed by Albert Thomas, first Director General of the International Labour Office (Maul 2012, p. 17). ILO Convention No. 29 was not supposed to prohibit forced labor, but to regulate it in order to prevent it from rendering into slavery (Goudal 1929, p. 622). It conferred protection not only to the native workers, but also to their families and communities.

But it was not until 1936 when the ILO introduced the term "indigenous" into the lexicon of its international labor standards, albeit without defining it. Drawing upon the Forced Labour Convention, the ILO adopted the Recruitment of Indigenous Workers Convention (No. 50), which was designed to ensure fair conditions for recruited workers as well as to prevent disruption of the connections between the worker and his family and community. ILO Convention No. 50 was followed by the adoption in 1939 of further conventions relating to contracts of employment with indigenous workers (ILO Convention No. 64) and the penal sanctions that were usually included in such contracts (ILO Convention No. 65). Notably, Belgium and the United Kingdom, which, during the first half of the twentieth century, still exercised control over certain territories in Africa and Asia, were among the ratifying countries of ILO instruments on indigenous workers.

Indigenous Populations and the Idea of Integration

The ILO focus on indigenous workers began to be expanded when American member States of the ILO, which convened at an ILO regional conference in Santiago in 1936, adopted a resolution calling upon the International Labour Office to undertake studies on the economic and social problems affecting indigenous populations in the

American continent (Record of Proceedings of the Conference of American States members of the ILO in Santiago de Chile 1936, p. 383). The issue of indigenous populations continued to be present in the agenda of several regional meetings that followed the Santiago conference (Cabrera 2017, p. 28–30). During the 1940s, the indigenous question was central in the development agenda of several Latin American countries, and, in this context, the ILO was supposed to assume a crucial role.

As early as 1946, the ILO set forth a Committee of Experts on Indigenous Labour, which was tasked with examining the factors that prevented the integration of members of indigenous populations into the social and economic systems of the countries where they lived (Minutes of the 99th session of the Governing Body of the International 1946, p. 96). The Committee met in two occasions and adopted a set of recommendations. In one of these recommendations addressing indigenous forest dwellers, the Committee requested the Governing Body of the ILO to call the attention of the governments concerned to assist indigenous forest dwellers within the framework of a policy for their protection and gradual integration (International Labour Review 1954, p. 428).

The work of the Committee on Indigenous Labour set the grounds for the Indigenous and Tribal Populations Convention (No. 107) adopted by the ILO in 1957. This instrument broadened the scope and possibilities of action of the ILO with respect to indigenous populations. Its underlying idea was that only through the integration of indigenous population in their national communities, such groups could improve their living standards (Rodriguez-Piñero 2005, p. 175–215). Notably, Convention No. 107 was the first international instrument to define the term "indigenous" as one referring to descendants from populations

> which inhabited the country, or a geographical region to which the country belongs, at the time of conquest or colonisation and which, irrespective of their legal status, live more in conformity with the social, economic or cultural institutions of that time than with the institutions of the nation to which they belong. (ILO Convention No. 107, Article 1)

In addition, it expressly acknowledges the "right of ownership, collective or individual, of the members of the populations concerned over the lands which these populations traditionally occupy" (ILO Convention No. 107, Article 11). Notably, Convention No. 107 was adopted with the opposition of countries like Australia and the United Kingdom, which considered that this instrument fell outside the ILO mandate (International Labour Conference 1957, p. 406).

After its adoption, Convention No. 107 was strongly criticized for reinforcing States' assimilationist policies that threatened the maintenance of indigenous culture (Engle 2010, p. 67). José Martínez Cobo, who was appointed as Special Rapporteur for the preparation of a Study of the Problem of Discrimination against Indigenous Populations, observed in his report: "Convention No. 107 has not proven very effective in protecting and developing the human rights and fundamental freedoms of indigenous populations in countries which are parties to it" (Martinez-Cobo 1986, p. 335). He further recommended that ILO norms should place more emphasis on "ethno-development and independence or self-determination, instead of 'integration and protection'" (Martinez-Cobo 1986, p. 335).

In response to this criticism, the ILO undertook a thorough revision of Convention No. 107 and allowed the participation of indigenous organization within this process (International Labour Office 1987). There was a consensus among ILO constituents that integration was not acceptable as a core concept in an international legal instrument that was to meet the aspirations of indigenous peoples. The experts that were appointed by the ILO to revision of Convention No. 107 concluded that "indigenous and tribal peoples should enjoy as much control as possible over their economic, social and cultural development" and that states should recognize the right of these groups to "interact with the national society on an equal footing through their own institutions" (International Labour Office Appendix I 1987, para. 159 (3)). The result of the revision of ILO Convention No. 107 was the Indigenous and Tribal Peoples Convention (No. 169), which was adopted by the International Labour Conference in 1989.

The Contribution of ILO Convention No. 169

In general terms, ILO Convention No. 169 promotes and ensures respect for the indigenous culture, way of life, and institutions, especially in three ways. Firstly, it uses the term "indigenous peoples" instead of "indigenous populations" to emphasize their historically rooted distinct cultural, social, and political identity as a group (Anaya 2004, p. 100), albeit excluding any implications as regards the rights which may be attached to the term "peoples" under international law (ILO Convention No. 168, Article 1). Secondly, it sets forth the obligation of States to hold good faith consultations with indigenous peoples "through appropriate procedures and in particular through their representative institutions, whenever consideration is being given to legislative or administrative measures which may affect them directly" and "with the objective of achieving agreement or consent to the proposed measures" (Article 6 ILO Convention No. 169). This obligation has been regarded as a necessary requirement to eliminate the integrationist approach of ILO Convention No. 107 of the Convention (CEACR 2010). Furthermore, this procedural requirement helps realizing other rights recognized in Convention No. 169 such as land rights and educational rights. Thirdly, it recognizes indigenous peoples' right to use their own means of adjudication for sanctioning offences committed by their members and subject to the respect of human rights (ILO Convention No. 169, Article 9).

As it was the case with ILO standards on freedom of association, ILO Convention 169 has been crucial for the development of international human rights law, providing the basis for the UN Declaration on the Rights of Indigenous Peoples adopted by the General Assembly in 2007 (Gómez Isa 2016, p. 201) and international jurisprudence concerning indigenous rights. In its 2012 judgment on the case Sarayaku v. Ecuador, the Inter-American Court of Human Rights referred to Convention No. 169 as "particularly relevant to the recognition of the right to cultural identity of indigenous peoples" (Inter-American Court of Human Rights

2012, para. 215). In addition, in this decision, the Court referred in several to the pronouncements of the ILO tripartite committees concerning representations relating to ILO Convention No. 169 to understand the meaning of the requirement of consultation with indigenous peoples. (Inter-American Court of Human Rights 2012, paras. 181, 186).

Still, with 22 ratifications, ILO Convention No. 169 has failed to achieve more support from ILO member States than its predecessor. Fourteen Latin American countries have ratified this convention and some of them have granted them "constitutional rank" (Cabrera 2017, p. 75–88) within their national legal orders while in other regions of the world in Asia and Africa, the mere existence of indigenous peoples is still a contested matter.

ILO supervisory bodies have confronted themselves with contested substantial questions in relation to Convention No. 169. One such question relates to the meaning of the obligation to consult. Though the 2007 United Nations Declaration on the Rights of Indigenous Peoples may suggest that in certain circumstances states are required to obtain the free, prior, and informed consent of indigenous peoples (United Nations Declaration on the Rights of Indigenous Peoples, Article 32.2), in a General Observation issued in 2010, the CEACR reaffirmed that

> while Article 6 did not require consensus to have been reached in the process of prior consultation, it does stipulate that the peoples involved should have the opportunity to participate freely at all levels in the formulation, implementation and evaluation of measures and programmes that affect them directly. (CEACR, General Observation 2010)

The position of the CEACR may reflect the reluctance of the ILO to advance indigenous peoples' rights beyond the limits of Convention No. 169. This approach is consistent with the position of the employers group at the ILO which during the session of the CAS in 2010, referring to the records of the discussions held prior to the adoption of ILO Convention No. 169, observed that "it was clear that consultation did not equate to, or require the consent of the parties being consulted" (International Labour Office 2009, 16 Part II/103).

Furthermore, the substantive legal developments brought by Convention No. 169 have not been accompanied with norms allowing indigenous peoples access to the supervisory mechanisms. Until to date, indigenous organizations can only submit their observations to States' reports through workers organizations or when the State agrees on that, as it is the case with the Sami people of Norway. Likewise, indigenous peoples' organizations cannot lodge representations by themselves but need to be represented by an organization of workers or employers for this purpose.

Since the adoption of C169, the issue of indigenous peoples was absent in the agenda of the ILC. Yet, in 2018, members of the ILC are to decide on the abrogation of the set of indigenous workers conventions as proposed by the Governing Body. Notably, in 1996, the Governing Body had decided to shelve the Convention noting that the practices regulated by the ILO Conventions on indigenous workers had "largely disappeared" (International Labour Office 2018, p. 3–7).

Standard Review Initiatives

Cognizant of the difficulties faced by the ILO to keep its standard system relevant and responsive to the new social realities of the international community, the Governing Body of the ILO decided to adopt a Standard Review Policy on the eve of it century anniversary. A Standard Review Mechanism of a tripartite composition was created in 2011 within the framework of this policy. The objectives of the mechanism includes, among others, the determination of the status of current labor standards and the identification of those in need of revision or abrogation, and the determination of new subjects and approaches for standard-setting (International Labour Office 2011). A second component of the mechanism consists of a strategy to strengthen the ILO supervisory system encouraging tripartite support and improving its coherence, efficiency, and effectiveness. Two of the areas of action in this regard are the communication and cooperation among supervisory bodies and the improvement of transparency. With regard to the latter point, the chairpersons of the CEACR and CFA have defended the use of a more inclusive approach providing venues for the participation of other actors affected by international labor standards, as the case with informal workers (International Labour Office 2016, para. 129). This could also eventually lead to the creation of means for the participation of indigenous organizations in the standard-setting and supervisory activities of the ILO.

Conclusion

In sum, the International Labour Organization is an institution with a deeply rooted standard-setting function and a robust monitoring machinery that have sustained it for almost a century. It has played a significant role in the development of collective human rights in the field of freedom of association and collective bargaining, as well as indigenous peoples' rights. As has been shown in this chapter, these developments have not been free from controversies. For example, both in the case of trade unions' and indigenous peoples' rights, employers' groups have opposed that the ILO advance the content of these rights beyond the contours and wording of international labor conventions. Recognition of both sets of rights in other human rights forums, to a great extent influenced by the ILO, may also put aside the ILO as a reference institution, if its constituents prevent the organization from adapting it to future legal realities and other institutions may take over the leading role in the advancement of the described collective rights.

References

Alston P (2004) 'Core labour standards' and the transformation of the international labour rights regime. European Journal of International Law *15(3):457–521*. https://doi.org/10.1093/ejil/15.3.457
Anaya J (2004) Indigenous peoples in international law. Oxford University Press, Oxford

Bellace J (2014) The ILO and the right to strike. Int Labour Rev 153(1):29. https://doi.org/10.1111/j.1564-913X.2014.00196.x

Brudney J (2017) The internationalization of sources of labour law. University of Pennsylvania Journal of International Law 39(1) 64 pages

Cabrera M (2017) The requirement of consultation with indigenous peoples in the ILO. Brill Nijhoff, Leiden/Boston

Committee of Experts on the Application of Conventions and Recommendations (2015) Observation to Ecuador, Convention No 87. Available at http://www.ilo.org/dyn/normlex/en/f?p=1000:20010:::NO:::. Accessed 26 Feb 2018

Committee of Experts on the Application of Conventions and Recommendations (2016a) Observation to Albania, Convention No. Available at http://www.ilo.org/dyn/normlex/en/f?p=1000:20010:::NO:::. Accessed 26 Feb 2018

Committee of Experts on the Application of Conventions and Recommendations (2016b) Observation to Bahamas, Convention No. Available at http://www.ilo.org/dyn/normlex/en/f?p=1000:20010:::NO:::. Accessed 26 Feb 2018

Committee of Experts on the Application of Conventions and Recommendations (2010) General observation on ILO convention no. 169. Available at http://www.ilo.org/dyn/normlex/en/f?p=1000:20010:::NO:::. Accessed 26 Feb 2018

Committee on Freedom of Association (2001) Case 2067 Interim Report No. 325. Available at http://www.ilo.org/dyn/normlex/en/f?p=1000:20060::FIND:NO:::. Accessed 26 Feb 2018

Curtis K, Democracy, freedom of association and the ILO. In: Politakis G (ed) Les normes internationales du travail: un patrimoine pour l' avenir Mélanges en l' honneur de Nicolas Valticos. International Labour Office, Geneva

Declaration concerning the Aims and Purposes. of the International Labour Organisation (Declaration of Philadelphia)

Ebert F, Oelz M (2012) Bridging the gap between labour rights and human rights: the role of the ILO law in regional human right courts (Discussion paper). International Institute for Labour Studies

Engle K (2010) The elusive promise of indigenous development: rights, culture, strategy. Duke University Press, Durham

European Court of Human Rights (2014) Case of National Union of Rail, Maritime and Transport Workers v. The United Kingdom (Application no. 31045/10). Judgment, 8 April 2014

Gómez Isa F (2016) The role of soft law in the progressive development of indigenous peoples' rights. In: Lagoutte S, Gammeltoft-Hansen T, Cerone J (eds) Tracing the roles of soft law in human rights. Oxford University Press, Oxford. https://doi.org/10.1093/acprof:oso/9780198791409.003.0010

Goudal J (1929) The Question of Forced Labour before the International Labour Conference. International Labour Review Vol. xix Issue 5

Gravel E, Duplessis I, Gernigon V (2001) The committee on freedom of association: its impact over 50 years. International Labour Office, Geneva

Governing Body (1951) Minutes of the 117th session

Governing Body (1946) Minutes of the 99th session

Gernigon B, Odero A, Guido H (2000) ILO principles concerning collective bargaining. Int Labour Rev 139(1):33–55. https://doi.org/10.1111/j.1564-913X.2000.tb00401

Inter-American Court of Human Rights (2001) Case of Baena Ricardo et al v. Panama. Merits, Reparations and Costs. Judgments of February 2, 2001. Series C No. 72

Inter-American Court of Human Rights (2012) Case of the Kichwa Indigenous People of Sarayaku v. Ecuador (Merits and Reparations), Judgment of June 27, 2012. Series C No 245

Inter-American Court of Human Rights (2016) Entitlement of legal entities to hold rights under the inter-American human rights system (Interpretation and scope of Article 1(2), in relation to Articles 1(2), 8, 11(2), 13, 16, 21, 24, 25, 29, 30, 44, 46 and 62(3) of the American Convention on Human Rights, as well as of Article 8(1)(A) and (B) of the Protocol of San Salvador). Advisory Opinion OC-22/16 of February 26, 2016. Series A No 22

International Labour Conference (1957) Record of Proceedings of its 40th Session

International Labour Conference (1970) Resolution concerning Trade Union Rights and their relation to Civil Liberties

International Labour Conference (1999) Resolution concerning the measures recommended by the Governing Body under article 33 of the ILO Constitution on the subject of Myanmar

International Labour Office (1948) International labour conference 31st session. Freedom of Association and Protection of the Right to Organise

International Labour Office (1966) Official Bulletin Special Supplement Vol. XLIX, No. 1. Report of the fact-finding and conciliation Commission on Freedom of Association concerning persons employed in the public sector in Japan

International Labour Office (1978) Albert Thomas, 1878–1978

International Labour Office (1987) Partial revision of the indigenous and tribal populations convention, 1957 (No. 107), Report VI (I)

International Labour Office (1996) Freedom of Association, Digest of Decisions and Principles of the Freedom of Association Committee of the Governing Body of the ILO (Forth Revised edition)

International Labour Office (2006) Freedom of association. Digest of decisions and principles of the freedom of Association Committee of the Governing Body of the ILO (5th edition)

International Labour Office (2009) Report of the Committee on the Application of Standards of the International Labour Conference (99th Session)

International Labour Office (2011) Governing Body. Fifth item on the agenda. Improvements in the standards-related activities of the ILO. ILO standards policy: the establishment and the implementation of a standards review mechanism (GB.312/LILS/5)

International Labour Office (2012a) Handbook of procedures relating to international labour conventions and recommendations (2nd revised edition)

International Labour Office (2012b) Report of the Committee on the Application of Standards of the International Labour Conference (101th session)

International Labour Office (2012c) Giving globalization a human face. International labour conference (101th session)

International Labour Office (2013a) Report of the Committee of Experts on the Applications of Conventions and Recommendations. Report III (Part 1A)

International Labour Office (2013b) Collective bargaining in the public service: a way forward. International labour conference 102nd session

International Labour Office (2015a) Report of the Committee of Experts on the applications of conventions and recommendations. Report III (Part 1A)

International Labour Office (2015b), Fifth item on the agenda of the Governing Body. The Standards Initiative

International Labour Office (2016) The standards initiative: Joint report of the chairpersons of the Committee of Experts on the Application of Conventions and Recommendations and the Committee on Freedom of Association (GB.326/LILS/3/1)

International Labour Office (2017a) Report of the Committee of Experts on the Application of Conventions and Recommendations. Report III (Part 1A)

International Labour Office (2017b) Report of the Committee on the Application of Standards of the International Labour Conference (106th Session), Appendix I

International Labour Office (2018) International labour conference 107 session. Report VII(2) abrogation of six international labour conventions and withdrawal of three international labour recommendations

International Labour Review (1954) Reports and inquiries. The Second Session of the I.L.O. Committee of Experts on Indigenous Labour

ILO Declaration on Fundamental Principles and Rights at Work, 1998

ILO Declaration on Social Justice for a Fair Globalization, 2008

ILO. Constitution

Jenks W (1963) Law, freedom and welfare. Steven and Sons, London

La Hovary C (2015a) The ILO's supervisory bodies' 'soft-law jurisprudence. In: Blanckett A, Treblicock A (eds) Research handbook on transnational labour law. Edward Elgar Publishing, Cheltenham

La Hovary C (2015b) A challenging ménage à trois? Tripartism in the International Labour Organization. International Organizations Law Review 12:204–236. https://doi.org/10.1163/15723747-01201008

Landy E (2004) Shaping a dynamic ILO system of regular supervision: the Valticos years. In: Politakis G (ed) Les normes internationales du travail: un patrimoine pour l' avenir Mélanges en l' honneur de Nicolas Valticos. International Labour Office, Geneva

Lauterpacht H (ed) (1955) Oppenheim's international law – a treatise (8th edition) Volume I: Peace. Longmans Green and Co., London

Leary V (1982) International labour conventions and national law: the effectiveness of automatic incorporation of treaties in national legal systems. Nijhoff, Leiden

Maul D (2012) Human rights, development and decolonization: the International Labour Organization 1940–1970. Palgrave Macmillan, Houndmill

Maupain F (2013) The ILO regular supervisory system: a model in crisis? International Organizations Law Review 10:117–165. https://doi.org/10.1163/15723747-01001004

Permanent Court of International Justice (1922) Competence of the International Labour Organization in regard to international regulation of the conditions of the labour of persons employed in agriculture (advisory opinion) PCIJ Series B No. 2

Permanent Court of International Justice (1926) Competence of the International Labour Organization to Regulate, Incidentally, the Personal Work of the Employer (Advisory Opinion) PCIJ Series B No 13

Politakis G (2004) Deconstructing flexibility in international labour conventions. In: the Valticos years. In: Politakis G (ed) Les normes internationales du travail: un patrimoine pour l' avenir Mélanges en l' honneur de Nicolas Valticos. International Labour Office, Geneva

Riedel E (2007) Monitoring the 1966 international covenant on economic, social and cultural rights. In: Politakis G (ed) Protecting labour rights as human rights: present and future of international supervision. International Labour Office, Geneva

Rodríguez-Piñero L (2005) Indigenous Peoples, postcolonialism, and international Law: The ILO Regime (1919–1989). Oxford University Press, Oxford

Simpson W (1994) The ILO and tripartism: some reflections. Monthly Labour Review 17(9):40–45

Simpson W (2004) Standard-setting and supervision: a system in difficulty. In: Politakis G (ed) Les normes internationales du travail: un patrimoine pour l' avenir Mélanges en l' honneur de Nicolas Valticos. International Labour Office, Geneva

Special Procedures for the Examination in the International Labour Organization of Complaints alleging Violation of Freedom of Association (2009)

Standing Orders. of the International Labour Conference

Standing Orders. concerning the procedure for the examination of representations under articles 24 and 25 of the Constitution of the ILO

Martínez-Cobo J (1986) Study of the Problem of Discrimination against Indigenous Populations, Final Report: Conclusions, Proposals and recommendations (E/CN.4 Sub.2/1986/7/Add.4)

Swepston L (1998) Human rights law and freedom of association: development through ILO supervision. Int Labour Rev 137(2):169–194

Treaty of Versailles (1919)

United Nations Declaration on the Rights of Indigenous Peoples (2007)

United Nations General Assembly (1947) Trade Union Rights (Freedom of Association), UN Doc. A/RES/128(II)

Valticos N (1979) International Labour Law. Kluwer, Deventer

Valticos N (1981) Une nouvelle forme d'action internationale: les "contacts directs" de l'O.I.T. en matière d'application de conventions et de liberté syndicale. Annuaire français de droit international 2:477–489

Valticos N (1988) The sources of international labour law: recent trends. In: Heere W (ed) International law and its sources: liber amicorum Maarten Bos. Kluwer, Deventer/Antwerp/London/Frankfurt/Boston /New York

UNESCO and Human Rights

Yvonne Donders

Contents

Introduction 252
Structure and Functions of UNESCO 252
Human Rights Within UNESCO's Competence 254
Human Rights Standard Setting and Monitoring 257
UNESCO Procedure on Human Rights Violations: History and Purpose 258
Comparison with Other International Procedures 265
Concluding Remarks 267
References 268

Abstract

The United Nations Educational, Scientific, and Cultural Organization (UNESCO) was set up in November 1945 as an autonomous United Nations organization or specialized agency under Article 57 of the UN Charter. Human rights are at the heart of UNESCO's mandate. Article I(1) of UNESCO's Constitution states that the purpose of the organization is to contribute to peace and security by promoting collaboration among the nations through education, science, and culture in order to further universal respect for justice, for the rule of law, and for the human rights and fundamental freedoms which are affirmed for the peoples of the world, without distinction of race, sex, language, or religion, by the Charter of the United Nations. Following this mandate, Member States of UNESCO have adopted numerous legal instruments in the field of human rights, related to education, culture, and science of communication. UNESCO has further developed many programs and activities to advance and promote human

Y. Donders (✉)
Faculty of Law, Department of International and European Law, University of Amsterdam, Amsterdam, Netherlands
e-mail: y.m.donders@uva.nl

© Springer Nature Singapore Pte Ltd. 2018   251
G. Oberleitner (ed.), *International Human Rights Institutions, Tribunals, and Courts*,
International Human Rights, https://doi.org/10.1007/978-981-10-5206-4_25

rights in these fields. UNESCO also has a procedure to assess complaints about alleged human rights violations in its fields of competence. This chapter outlines the general structure and functioning of UNESCO; gives an overview of various instruments, strategy, and activities of UNESCO in relation to human rights; and discusses the communication procedure.

Keywords
UNESCO · Human rights · Education · Culture · Science · Freedom of expression

Introduction

The United Nations Educational, Scientific, and Cultural Organization (UNESCO) was set up in November 1945 as an autonomous United Nations (UN) organization or specialized agency under Article 57 of the UN Charter. Human rights are at the heart of UNESCO's mandate. Article I(1) of the UNESCO Constitution states that the purpose of the Organization is "...to contribute to peace and security by promoting collaboration among the nations through education, science and culture in order to further universal respect for justice, for the rule of law and for the human rights and fundamental freedoms which are affirmed for the peoples of the world, without distinction of race, sex, language or religion, by the Charter of the United Nations."

Following this mandate, Member States of UNESCO have adopted numerous legal instruments in the field of human rights, related to education, culture, science, and communication. UNESCO has further developed many programs and activities to advance and promote human rights in these fields. UNESCO also has a procedure to assess complaints about alleged human rights violations in its fields of competence.

Below first a short introduction into the general structure and functioning of UNESCO is given. This is followed by an overview of various instruments, strategies, and activities of UNESCO in relation to human rights. Subsequently the communications procedure is discussed in more detail and put within the framework of other UN mechanisms.

Structure and Functions of UNESCO

UNESCO is an autonomous UN organization, which means that its membership is separate from the membership of the UN. In fact, several States, such as the United States and the United Kingdom, have withdrawn from the Organization in the past (and rejoined afterward), whereas other States, such as Palestine, are Member States of UNESCO but not full members of the UN. UNESCO is further not funded out of the regular UN budget, but, instead, the Member States pay separate contributions to UNESCO.

UNESCO has three main organs: the General Conference, the Executive Board, and the Secretariat. The General Conference consists of representatives of all

Member States and determines the general policy line of UNESCO. Every Member State has one vote. In principle, it meets every 2 years, but, if the agenda so demands, it can assemble every year (UNESCO Constitution Article IV).

The Executive Board is elected by the General Conference and consists of 58 Member States, with regional distribution. In the past, the Executive Board consisted of independent experts. In 1954, the General Conference decided, at the proposal of the United Kingdom and the United States, to abolish the independence of the members of the Executive Board. They still had to be experts in the field of UNESCO's mandate, but they would no longer speak on personal title but on behalf of their state. In 1995, at the proposal of Japan, the General Conference decided that the Executive Board would consist of 58 government representatives, although these still have to be experts in (one of) the fields of competence of UNESCO (28 C/Resolutions). The Executive Board meets twice a year and prepares the agenda of the General Conference. It is further responsible for the execution of the work program and the budget adopted by the General Conference, and it can make recommendations to the General Conference (UNESCO Constitution Article V).

The Secretariat is headed by the Director-General, who participates in the General Conference without a vote. The Director-General prepares annual reports on the activities of the organization and makes proposals for activities to the General Conference and the Executive Board (UNESCO Constitution Article VI). The current Director-General is Ms. Audrey Azoulay (France) who took office in November 2017 for a term of 4 years.

The most recent Medium-Term Strategy 2014–2021 describes UNESCO's main functions as (a) serving as a laboratory of ideas and generating innovative proposals and policy advice in its fields of competence; (b) developing and reinforcing the global agenda in its fields of competence through policy analysis, monitoring, and benchmarking; (c) setting norms and standards in its fields of competence and supporting and monitoring their implementation; (d) strengthening international and regional cooperation in its fields of competence and fostering alliances, intellectual cooperation, knowledge sharing, and operational partnerships; and (e) providing advice for policy development and implementation and developing institutional and human capacities (General Conference resolution 37 C/Res.1 and Executive Board 194 EX/Decision 18, UNESCO 37 C/4, p. 14).

UNESCO has a unique aspect in its relationship with Member States. According to Article VII of the UNESCO Constitution, Member States should establish so-called National Commissions for UNESCO to associate national organizations in the fields of education, science, culture, and communication with the work of UNESCO. Such National Commissions are expected to advise national governments as well as their delegations to the General Conference and the Executive Board on aspects related to the work of UNESCO. The Charter of National Commissions for UNESCO, adopted by the General Conference in 1978, outlines that functions of the National Commissions include to "disseminate information on the objectives, programme and activities of UNESCO," "participate in the planning and execution of activities of UNESCO," and "undertake on their own initiative other activities related to the general objectives of UNESCO" (UNESCO Doc. 20 C/Resolutions, pp. 116–19).

Presently, there are 199 National Commissions for UNESCO across the world. There is no single model of a National Commission. Each Member State defines its National Commission's structure in accordance with its own priorities and needs, and therefore the nature, composition, and capacities of National Commissions are very diverse. They do however play a significant role in the liaison with partners and the promotion of UNESCO's visibility at the country level (Review of the Cooperation of UNESCO's Secretariat with the National Commissions for UNESCO, IOS/EVS/PI/112, December 2011).

UNESCO further hosts two networks closely related to human rights: the UNESCO Chairs and the UNESCO Associated Schools. The UNITWIN/UNESCO Chairs Programme was launched in 1992 and nowadays involves over 700 institutions in 116 countries. The program promotes international interuniversity cooperation and networking to enhance institutional capacities through knowledge sharing and collaboration. UNESCO Chair and UNITWIN Networks are established in key priority areas related to UNESCO's fields of competence – i.e., in education, natural and social sciences, culture, and communication. There are many UNESCO Chairs on human rights or on human rights-related topics such as gender, education, migration, cultural diversity, and sustainable development. The UNESCO Associated Schools Network links more than 10,000 educational institutions in over 180 countries. The Network develops and disseminates innovative educational materials and promotes new teaching and learning approaches based on UNESCO's core values and priorities, such as international understanding, peace, intercultural dialogue, sustainable development, and quality education, and it promotes exchange of experiences, knowledge, and good practices among schools, individuals, communities, policy-makers, and society as a whole.

Human Rights Within UNESCO's Competence

As stated above, the advancement of human rights is explicitly mentioned as part of the mandate of UNESCO. Since its establishment, the Organization has been active in the field of human rights, in particular, in relation to education, science, culture, and communication. UNESCO was instrumental in the elaboration of the Universal Declaration of Human Rights, and it took an active part in the drafting of human rights treaties (Marks 1999, p. 42; Coomans 1999, p. 221). In its efforts to advance human rights, UNESCO focuses on those human rights that are directly within its sphere of competence. These rights include the right to education, the right to participate freely in cultural life and share in scientific advancement, and the right to freedom of opinion and expression, including the right to information.

In the broad fields of education, culture, science, and communication, UNESCO and its Member States have adopted legal instruments and have developed a variety of activities and projects related to human rights. In 2003 UNESCO adopted a Human Rights Strategy to guide the activities of the Organization in the years to come. The Strategy followed the broader developments in the UN concerning the mainstreaming and integration of human rights throughout the system. It provided a road map for the Organization, defining its objectives and main lines of activities in the field of human rights, thereby also ensuring a better division of labor within the UN system.

The Strategy confirmed the dedication of UNESCO to integrate a human rights-based approach into all its programs, which implies that basic human rights principles, such as equality, participation, and accountability, together with human rights standards, should guide the elaboration, implementation, and evaluation of all programs. In terms of activities to advance human rights, the Strategy reaffirms UNESCO's traditional functions: encouraging theoretical and empirical research and disseminating knowledge on human rights, further promoting human rights education as an integral part of the right to education, and developing and implementing UNESCO's human rights standards. UNESCO thereby gives priority to the promotion of human rights of women and the equal participation of women in all spheres of life.

The Medium-Term Strategy 2014–2021 reaffirmed UNESCO's mission ". . .to contribute to the building of peace, the eradication of poverty, and sustainable development and intercultural dialogue through education, the sciences, culture, communication and information" (UNESCO Doc. 37 C/4, p. 13). The Organization has identified two global priorities, namely, Africa and gender equality, and nine strategic objectives, all of which have a link with human rights. The ones with the most direct link are objective 3 on advancing education for all, objective 6 on supporting inclusive social development and promoting ethical principles, and objective 9 on the promotion of freedom of expression and access to information.

UNESCO has a long track record in the promotion of human rights education as an integral part of the right to education. Within UNESCO the first international legally binding instrument was adopted on the right to education, namely, the Convention Against Discrimination in Education (1960). This instrument formed a crucial reference in the further elaboration of this right in many other international instruments. The Convention encompasses the idea that education is a fundamental right, and it underscores the state's obligation to proscribe any form of discrimination in education while promoting equality of educational opportunities.

UNESCO also played a lead role in the development and implementation of the UN Decade for Human Rights Education (1995–2004). It further promotes the principle of Education for All (EFA) and has, in 2007, together with UNICEF, developed the Guidelines for a Human Rights-Based Approach to EFA (UNESCO and UNICEF, A Human Rights Based Approach to Education for All 2007), which provides a framework for the realization of children's right to education and rights within education. UNESCO also links education to its other fields of interest, in particular, culture. It has developed Guidelines on Intercultural Education (UNESCO Guidelines on Intercultural Education) and a Conceptual and Operational Framework on Intercultural Competences (UNESCO, Intercultural Competencies – Conceptual and Operational Framework).

Following the UN Decade, the UN Member States proclaimed the World Programme on Human Rights Education (2005–ongoing) to advance the implementation of human rights education programs in all sectors (General Assembly resolution

59/113, 10 December 2004). The first two phases of the World Programme focused, respectively, on human rights education in the primary and secondary school systems (2005–2009) and on human rights education for higher education and on human rights training programs for teachers and educators, civil servants, law enforcement officials, and military personnel (2010–2014). The third phase (2015–2019) focuses on strengthening the implementation of the first two phases and promoting human rights training for media professionals and journalists. UNESCO plays an important role in the implementation of this program together with the Office of the High Commissioner for Human Rights (OHCHR).

Another human rights field where UNESCO is very active is press freedom and the protection of journalists. The Organization provides legal and policy advice to states on media laws, and it develops training programs for journalists, security forces, and the judiciary in media freedom. UNESCO further organizes every year World Press Freedom Day on 3 May, and it hands out the World Press Freedom Prize to promote and publicize the importance of free, independent, and pluralistic media in print, broadcast, and online.

UNESCO's work in the field of the protection of cultural heritage and cultural diversity also has important links with human rights. From its establishment the Organization has worked on cultural heritage, mainly from the idea that States should protect cultural heritage because of its significance for humanity and as a means of international cooperation. In the UNESCO heritage instruments, increasing emphasis is placed on the importance of cultural heritage for the construction and expression of cultural identity and on the link between cultural heritage and cultural diversity. Accordingly, elements of a human rights approach, including the value of human dignity and the principles of participation, contribution, and access can be increasingly found in these instruments.

Whereas the Convention concerning the Protection of the World Cultural and Natural Heritage (1972) and the Convention on the Protection of the Underwater Cultural Heritage (2001) mainly focused on the protection of cultural heritage for the public at large and emphasis on the sovereignty and rights of States, the Convention on the Safeguarding of the Intangible Cultural Heritage (2003) takes the perspective of the protection of cultural heritage of and for specific cultural communities as part of their cultural identity, involving them in the process of identification and protection. Important instruments promoting cultural diversity are the Universal Declaration on Cultural Diversity (2001) and the Convention on the Protection and Promotion of the Diversity of Cultural Expressions (2005).

In the field of sciences, UNESCO also has a long-standing involvement in bioethics and ethics of science. UNESCO has contributed to the formulation of basic principles in bioethics through, in particular, the Universal Declaration on the Human Genome and Human Rights, adopted by UNESCO's General Conference in 1997 and endorsed by the UN General Assembly in 1998, and the International Declaration on Human Genetic Data (2003). Another important instrument adopted by UNESCO is the Universal Declaration on Bioethics and Human Rights, reaffirming the interrelation between ethics and human rights in the specific field of bioethics.

Human Rights Standard Setting and Monitoring

The Member States of UNESCO can, according to Article IV(4) of its Constitution, adopt conventions, which are binding upon the Member States, and recommendations, which are not legally binding but do have a legal effect in that they should be implemented by States. The possibility of adopting declarations and other, nonbinding, instruments was added later by an amendment of the General Conference at its seventh session in 1952 (UNESCO Constitution Articles IV(2), (3), and (5)). Apart from these instruments adopted by the General Conference, international conferences under the auspices of UNESCO can adopt conventions, treaties, agreements, recommendations, or declarations.

In general, the standard setting procedure within UNESCO is as follows: first, the Director-General, or any other person invited to do so, prepares a preliminary study of the technical and legal aspects of the question involved. This study is submitted to the Executive Board for prior consideration. The Executive Board can put the proposal for an international regulation on the agenda of the General Conference. The General Conference decides on the desirability of the regulation and on the form that it should take, e.g., a convention, a recommendation, or a declaration. The Director-General is then instructed to prepare a preliminary report including an outline of the problem and the possible action of regulation. The Member States are invited to present their comments and observations, on the basis of which the Director-General prepares a final report. This final report is submitted to the General Conference or, if the Conference so decides, to a committee of experts. The General Conference finally considers the draft texts submitted and adopts the instrument. Recommendations are adopted by a simple majority, while a two-thirds majority is required for the adoption of conventions. (UNESCO Constitution Article IV(4) and Rules of Procedure concerning Recommendations to Member States and International Conventions covered by the terms of Article IV(4) of the Constitution, para. 12).

The implementation and monitoring mechanism of UNESCO consists of a reporting procedure, described in Article VIII of the Constitution, and a communications procedure adopted by Decision 3.3 of the Executive Board in 1978.

The reporting procedure implies that Member States must periodically submit a report on the action taken in the field of the recommendations and conventions adopted by UNESCO (General Conference Rules of Procedure Part VI). One of the first instruments that required State reports was the Convention on Discrimination in Education, which includes in Article 7 that "[t]he States Parties to this Convention shall in their periodic reports submitted to the General Conference of [UNESCO] on dates and in a manner to be determined by it, give information on the legislative and administrative provisions which they have adopted and other action which they have taken for the application of this Convention."

UNESCO's General Conference invited the Executive Board in 1968 to establish a subsidiary organ of the Board to examine the State reports (15 C/Resolution 12.2). Rule 16.1 of its Rules of Procedure allows the Executive Board to establish permanent commissions and committees from among its Members that can assist it in the execution of its tasks. The Board accordingly established in 1966 the Special

Committee on Discrimination in Education to examine State reports on the implementation of the Convention and Recommendation against Discrimination in Education (71 EX/Decision 3.2). The name of the Committee was changed in 1969 into Committee on Conventions and Recommendations in Education when it was entrusted to also examine reports on the Recommendation concerning the Status of Teachers (82 EX/Decision 4.2.4).

The Committee was again renamed in 1978 Committee on Conventions and Recommendations (CR) when the Executive Board decided to add to its mandate the consideration of communications received by UNESCO concerning cases and questions of alleged violations of human rights within UNESCO's fields of competence (104 EX/Decision 3.3). In 1985, the CR became a permanent Committee of the Executive Board (104 EX/Decisions 3.3 1978, paras. 13, 14; UNESCO, The Right to Education: Monitoring standard-setting instruments of UNESCO 2008).

The CR considers the reports without a dialogue with the Member States. It drafts a report on its findings to the Executive Board, which sends it with its comments to the General Conference. States have not always consistently respected their reporting obligations. Reports have come in with irregular intervals, and they are of different quality. The 2017 consultation on the implementation of the Convention and Recommendation against Discrimination in Education, covering the period 2012–2016, was prepared on the basis of 67 national reports (UNESCO Doc. 39 C/24, 23 October 2017). This makes the monitoring task of the CR difficult at times. The Executive Board recognized already in 2002 "the need to improve the effectiveness of the mandate of the CR, and of the reporting system on UNESCO conventions and recommendations in general" and consistently reminds Member States "to respect their legal obligations under the UNESCO Constitution concerning periodic reports on the follow-up to conventions and recommendations" (165 EX/Decision 6.2).

The current CR is composed of 30 members from all electoral groups representing one of the Member States of the Executive Board. The CR meets in principle twice a year on the occasion of the sessions of the Executive Board. Extraordinary sessions may also be convened when the Executive Board considers it necessary. Apart from considering the State reports on the implementation of UNESCO's standard-setting instruments, the CR is mandated to examining communications relating to cases and questions concerning the exercise of human rights in UNESCO's fields of competence. The communications procedure was adopted by Decision 3.3 of the Executive Board in 1978. This procedure is not well-known, and its effectiveness has been questioned. It is dealt with in more detail below.

UNESCO Procedure on Human Rights Violations: History and Purpose

From its establishment, UNESCO received communications drawing its attention to situations relating to human rights (181 EX/CR/2 Rev 2016). Individuals and groups turned to UNESCO in an attempt to have their human rights situation addressed. Already in 1952 the Executive Board noted that "the Chairman of the Board and the

Director-General receive communications from private persons or associations alleging violation by States, members or non-members of UNESCO, of certain human rights, and, in particular, of educational and cultural rights" but that "having regard to the present provisions of the Constitution and regulations of the Organization, no cognizance can be taken of these communications" (29 EX/Decision 11.3 1952, Item I). At the next session in 1953, the Executive Board expressed its wish to "define the procedure whereby it can take cognizance of these complaints and take suitable action in regard to them so far as it is within its power to do so" (30 EX/Decision 11 1953).

The discussion in the Executive Board was however postponed until the adoption in 1966 of the two UN human rights covenants, the International Covenant on Civil and Political Rights (ICCPR) and the International Covenant on Economic, Social, and Cultural Rights (ICESCR). In 1967 the Executive Board adopted 77 EX/Decision 8.3, which put in place a more elaborate procedure for the action to be taken on communications relating to individual cases invoking human rights in the fields of education, science, and culture. This procedure broadly followed the earlier adopted procedure by the UN Commission on Human Rights (ECOSOC Resolution 728F, 27 May 1970). The most important feature of the UNESCO procedure was its confidentiality, established in 1967 and maintained ever since (UNESCO's Procedure for the Protection of Human Rights 2009, p. 5–6; Marks 1999 p. 103–104).

The procedure turned out not to be entirely satisfactory. The decision by the Executive Board mainly set out the terms under which certain communications would be brought to its attention, without indicating a procedure to be followed in considering them. Adjustments were however not made until 1976. In that year the General Conference invited the Executive Board and the Director-General to map the existing procedures within the UN system concerning the examination of individual complaints, which could be used as a model for a more effective system in UNESCO (UNESCO's Procedure for the Protection of Human Rights 2009, p. 5–6, 84; UNESCO Doc. 19C/Res 12.1). In 1977 the Director-General presented to the Executive Board the requested study (UNESCO Doc. 102 EX/19 1977). The Executive Board established an ad hoc working party composed of 13 of its Member States, which, in consultation with the other members of the Board, drafted the famous Decision 104 EX/Decision 3.3 which was adopted by the Executive Board on 26 April 1978. This decision was brought to the attention of the General Conference but not formally adopted and therefore retains the status of a decision and not of an international convention (Partsch and Hufner 2003, p. 116).

One of the main discussion points in the General Conference was to what extent UNESCO should follow the model of the (then) Human Rights Commission and its complaints procedures 1235 and 1503, which dealt with alleged gross and systematic violations of human rights in general and through communications or whether the Organization could also deal with individual cases. Eastern States favored the first option, preferring that UNESCO would merely deal with situations in which human rights are violated on a massive and systematic scale. Western States favored the second option, focusing on individual cases. The compromise was to include both (Weissbrodt and Farley 1994, p. 396; Marks 1999, p.115; Partsch and Hufner 2003, p. 115; 104 EX/Decisions 3.3 1978, para. 14).

The subsidiary body of the Executive Board that at that time was most directly involved in human rights issues was the above-described Committee examining the periodic reports of the State parties to the Convention and Recommendation against Discrimination in Education. Individual communications were sent to this Committee, but as indicated above, the Executive Board was of the opinion that UNESCO was not authorized to assess such communications let alone to take measures upon them. The Committee accordingly merely drafted a list of these communications, informed Member States involved, and asked them for their comments (Partsch and Hufner 2003, p. 114).

In 1978 the confidential procedure to examine communications concerning alleged violations of human rights in its fields of competence, namely, education, science, culture, and communication, was established, and the renamed Committee on Conventions and Recommendations (CR) became the body dealing with the communications (104 EX/Decisions 3.3 1978, para.13).

According to the Decision establishing it, the procedure fits in the general mandate of UNESCO in the field of human rights. The Decision refers to UNESCO's Constitution as well as to "the Universal Declaration of Human Rights, the international covenants on human rights and the various conventions and recommendations adopted by UNESCO" (104 EX/Decision 3.3 1978, para. 2).

The UNESCO procedure is not based on or limited to a specific treaty. Communications can concern (alleged) violations of human rights in one or more of these instruments. The text speaks of "the international covenants on human rights" most likely referring to the ICESCR and the ICCPR. This reference could also be seen as a more general reference to UN human rights treaties, which would make it possible to include in the procedure other treaties, such as the Convention on the Elimination of Racial Discrimination, the Convention on the Elimination of All Forms of Discrimination against Women, or the Convention on the Rights of Persons with Disabilities.

The Decision firstly reaffirms that UNESCO is prohibited from intervening in matters which are essentially within the domestic jurisdiction of the Member States (para. 6). The Decision is further very clear on the nature of the communications procedure and the role of the CR. It is stated that "in matters concerning human rights within its fields of competence, UNESCO, basing its efforts on moral considerations and its specific competence, should act in a spirit of international cooperation, conciliation and mutual understanding, and ... not play the role of an international judicial body" (para. 7).

The main purpose of the procedure is for the CR to help to bring about a friendly solution to all communications brought before it (para 14(k)). There is no procedure to appeal or reopen a case. The author may however present new facts or amend a communication, after which the CR may decide to consider this a new communication (Marks 1999, pp. 111–112).

The communications procedure includes two possible sorts of complaints: (1) "cases concerning violations of human rights which are individual and specific" and (2) "questions of massive, systematic or flagrant violations of human rights which result either from a policy contrary to human rights applied de jure or de facto by a State or from an accumulation of individual cases forming a consistent pattern" (para.10).

The latter type may include "for example, those perpetrated as a result of policies of aggression, interference in the internal affairs of States, occupation of foreign territory and implementation of a policy of colonialism, genocide, apartheid, racialism, or national and social oppression" (para. 18). This is a very wide description of massive and flagrant violations of human rights. Moreover, some of them, for instance, interference in the internal affairs of States, can be interpreted in different ways.

Following the other procedures in the UN system, the Executive Board decided that not only individuals but also NGOs could submit communications. These NGOs should however prove to have a legitimate interest in doing so, for instance, when the alleged victim is a member of that organization or when the organization is broadly working to advance human rights (102 EX/19 1977, para. 136). There was also discussion whether States should be able to submit communications, but this option was rejected, since States were found to have sufficient access to the main organs of UNESCO, the General Conference, and the Executive Board, and that it would therefore be inappropriate to have such a procedure before a subsidiary organ of one of them (102 EX/19 1977, para. 135).

Accordingly, communications may be submitted by "a person or a group of persons who, it can be reasonably presumed, are victims of an alleged violation of any of the human rights. . .It may also originate from any person, group of persons or organization having reliable knowledge of those violations" (104 EX/Decisions 3.3 1978, para. 14(ii)). Alleged violations should concern the rights "falling within UNESCO's competence in the fields of education, science, culture and information and must not be motivated exclusively by other considerations" (104 EX/Decisions 3.3 1978, para. 14(iii)). The fact that the last part was added implies that there is some room for other human rights to be referred to but that the core of the communication should concern one or more of the rights within UNESCO's competence. Although these rights are not specified in the Decision, it is clear from UNESCO's documents and website that these rights include the right to education; the right to freedom of expression, including the right to seek, receive, and impart information; the right to take part in cultural life; and the right to enjoy the benefits of scientific progress. Other, related rights could be added such as the right to freedom of religion, assembly, association, and movement as well as author's rights.

Communications can be submitted against all States. This includes of course the Member States of UNESCO, but it is not excluded that communications against non-Member States can be submitted. The CR then needs to see whether the State in question is willing to cooperate and accept the conditions of the procedure. If so the CR can follow its regular procedure. If not, it may be difficult to establish a dialogue with that State in order to reach a friendly solution (Partsch and Hufner 2003, p. 118; Marks 1999, p. 112). Most likely such cases will be declared inadmissible.

After a communication is submitted, the Director-General of UNESCO must ascertain that the author of the communication does not object to this communication being brought to the attention of the government concerned as well as the CR. If there is no such objection, the communication will be forwarded to the government concerned informing it that it will also be sent to the CR, "together with any reply the government may wish to take" (104 EX/Decisions 3.3 1978, paras. 14(b)(ii) and (iii)).

The CR examines the communications in private sessions. The government concerned "may attend" the meetings of the CR to provide additional information or answer questions from CR members (104 EX/Decisions 3.3 1978, para. 14(e)). Although this formulation focuses on the option governments have, in practice governments and warmly invited by the CR to attend and most of them indeed accept the invitation and attend the session. Authors of the communications or human rights organizations are not invited nor allowed to attend the sessions, except in extraordinary circumstances for which the CR needs special authorization from the Executive Board (104 EX/Decisions 3.3 1978, para. 14(g); Marks 1999, p. 113; Partsch and Hufner 2003, p. 125).

The CR bases its deliberations on the information provided by the author and the government, but it may also "avail itself of the relevant information at the disposal of the Director-General" (104 EX/Decisions 3.3 1978, para. 14(f)). Such information may include reports by UN Special Rapporteurs or UN treaty bodies and in some cases information by NGOs.

Confidentiality is at the heart of the procedure. According to UNESCO, "what is perhaps the overriding characteristic of the UNESCO procedure is the emphasis, or indeed the insistence, on its strictly confidential nature, even after cases have been settled. No publicity has ever been given to the successes achieved through the UNESCO procedure, in order to sustain the confidence of the State concerned and secure its cooperation. The desire for confidentiality has even been taken to the point of declaring inadmissible those communications whose confidentiality had clearly been breached by their authors" (181 EX/CR/2 Rev., Information Report 2016, para. 53).

The confidential character of the procedure means that only general information is shared. The website of UNESCO contains an outline of the procedure as well as the forms to be used to submit communications. All National Commissions for UNESCO are regularly informed of the procedure and encouraged to bring the procedure to the attention of NGOs and other human rights organizations. The Executive Board decided at its one hundred seventy-first session in 1987 that the documents of the Committee would be published or made accessible to the public "after a period of 20 years . . . so as to ensure that the Committee's achievements were more widely known" (181 EX/CR/2 Rev., Information Report 2016, para. 55). This information is however not easily accessible and, for instance, cannot be found on the UNESCO website. It may be available upon request at the secretariat, but this is not an easy or accessible route for individuals and organizations.

The communications procedure is composed of two stages: the admissibility phase and the merits phase. In the admissibility phase, the CR assesses whether the communication fulfils certain procedural conditions (104 EX/Decisions 3.3 1978, para. 14(a)). For instance, the communication may not be anonymous and must be submitted within a reasonable time after the facts have taken place or continue to take place (104 EX/Decisions 3.3 1978, para. 14(a)(i) and 14(a)(viii)). The communication may furthermore not be against the principles of UNESCO or offensive or based exclusively on information stemming from the mass media (104 EX/Decisions 3.3 1978, para. 14(a)(iv), 14(vi) and 14(a)(vii)). Communications can further be dismissed as non-admissible if they are manifestly ill-founded or when the matter at hand is already settled by the States concerned (104 EX/Decisions 3.3 1978, para. 14(a)(v) and 14(a)(x)).

It is noteworthy that one of the admissibility criteria familiar to all international and regional monitoring procedures, namely, the exhaustion of local remedies, is not strong in the UNESCO procedure. Instead of obliging authors to exhaust local remedies before a communication can be submitted to this procedure, it is stated in the Decision that "the communication must *indicate whether an attempt has been made to exhaust available domestic remedies* with regard to the facts which constitute the subject-matter of the communication and the result of such an attempt, if any" (104 EX/Decisions 3.3 1978, para. 14(a)(ix), emphasis added by the author). Most likely this was found to be sufficient for a procedure which its main purpose is to seek a friendly settlement with the State concerned and does not have the judicial character that other communications procedures have. It gives the CR more flexibility and avoids that the CR has to examine the local remedies in Member States. It does however seem unlikely that communications are declared admissible if no procedure whatsoever to seek redress at national level has been followed (Partsch and Hufner 2003, p. 123; Marks 1999, p. 107).

There is no provision in the Decision that prohibits the submission of communications to UNESCO if the same communication has been submitted and/or dealt with under another international procedure. Most other international communications procedures prohibit that the same matter has been or is being examined by another international body. Because of the special character of the UNESCO procedure, it was not found to be necessary to include this in the procedure. Practice is that the Secretariat checks whether a case has already been or is being dealt with by another body. If so, but moreover if the case was settled by the State, the CR will not consider the case (146 EX/7 1995 para. 48).

The Director-General shall notify the author of the communication and the government of the decision taken by the CR on the admissibility of the case (104 EX/Decisions 3.3 1978, para. 14(i)). The admissibility phase and the merits phase are not always clearly separated, partially because of the substantive character of some of the admissibility criteria (for instance, 104 EX/Decisions 3.3 1978, para. 14(a)(i), (ii), (iii), (iv), and (v)). This mingling of the two phases results in the fact that the seeking of a friendly solution, formally part of the merits phase, sometimes already enters the admissibility phase, which can lead to lengthy delays in the consideration of cases. The CR tends to leave cases pending for a long time in the admissibility phase in order to try and reach a friendly settlement, instead of taking a decision on that and moving to the merits phase, where reaching a friendly settlement is actually meant to be (Weissbrodt and Farley 1994, p. 398; Marks 1999, p. 108).

The CR submits confidential reports to the Executive Board before each session, containing information on its examination of communications. These reports may also contain general recommendations or recommendations regarding a particular communication under consideration. The Executive Board considers these reports also in private sessions (104 EX/Decisions 3.3 1978, paras. 15–16). The possibility of issuing recommendations to the Executive Board was meant to provide a tool that would be equivalent of the Concluding Observations or General Comments adopted by the UN treaty bodies. The CR does however not seem to have made use of this tool (Marks 1999, p. 114).

If a communication concerns a question of massive, systematic, or flagrant violations of human rights, both the Executive Board and the General Conference should consider the reports of the CR in public meetings (104 EX/Decisions 3.3 1978, para. 18). There is no particular procedure prescribed for the General Conference to consider these communications. Although many "questions" have been submitted to the CR, there are no examples of the Executive Board or the General Conference taking up these questions (Saba 1982, p. 421; Partsch and Hufner 2003, p. 127; Marks 1999, p. 115).

The communications submitted to UNESCO on (alleged) violations of human rights usually have a double link within UNESCO's field of competence. Most of the authors are professionals working in UNESCO's areas of education, science, culture, or information. They are, for instance, teachers, professors, researchers, academics, writers, or journalists. Furthermore, the alleged violations of their human rights are connected to their activities in the fields of education, science, culture, or information, for instance, the refusal of travel permits or study grants; imprisonment or expulsion of students or professors, academics, or journalists arbitrarily deprived of their employment; publication bans; lack of access to education; etc. (Beiter 2006, p. 240; Dumont 1990, p. 44). In recent years, cases mostly concern imprisonment of academics or journalists.

The website of UNESCO shows some figures of the communications procedure. From 1978 to 2015, the CR considered 597 communications, of which 381 communications were settled. Included in these are a few famous cases: The Argentinian pianist Miguel Angel Estrella, who was freed from prison in 1980; Professor Andrei Sakharov, Nobel Peace Prize winner (1975); and Vaclav Havel, former President of the Republic of Czechoslovakia (Dumont 1990, p. 44). The 216 remaining cases concern communications that are inadmissible or whose examination has been suspended or is under way.

Most cases were settled by the release of the person involved (224 cases). Others were settled because of the completion of the sentence (21). In other cases, persons were authorized to leave the country (21) or to return to the country (35). Cases also were settled because persons were able to resume their employment or activity (15), to resume a banned publication or broadcast program (14), to resume studies (9), or to resume a normal life after cessation of threats (5). Finally, cases were settled because persons were able to benefit from changes in education laws discriminatory toward ethnic minorities (10) or because persons belonging to religious minorities were able to obtain passports and/or grants or receive diplomas (12).

Comparison with Other International Procedures

How and where does the UNESCO procedure fit in the group of UN communications procedures? Which elements are similar to these other procedures, and which are unique for the UNESCO procedure? And what are comparable advantages and disadvantages of the UNESCO procedure compared to others?

In an information document on the UNESCO procedure adopted by the Executive Board, the special character of the UNESCO procedure in comparison with other human rights procedures within the UN was outlined as follows:

> It will also be noted that the various aspects of UNESCO's procedure are not, taken separately, either very original or very new. It is the combination of these aspects and the spirit in which they are applied that give the procedure its originality. While the other procedures seem most often to take a conflictual and accusatory form, the UNESCO procedure – although it is largely similar – has from the very beginning been deliberately applied exclusively with a view to seeking a solution with the State concerned. For this reason, everything has always been done to avoid reaching the conclusion that a State has violated human rights. Such a conclusion would in fact mean a deadlock, preventing the continued search for a solution. This is the background against which the many and varied stages of the procedure before the CR must be understood, since each stage represents a further level of dialogue with the State concerned and, consequently, another opportunity to find a satisfactory solution. The desire shown by the Committee to take its decisions solely by consensus is no doubt a reflection of the same concern. (181 EX/CR/2 Rev, Information Report 2016, para. 52)

In other words, the Executive Board stresses and also values the non-accusatory character of the procedure, avoiding a concrete conclusion on a violation of human rights. The confidentiality of the procedure, as well as the important aspect of dialogue with the State as well as the consensus in the CR in decision-making, are all reflective of this character. The CR therefore also does not possess the power to investigate, since this would be seen as illegal interference in the domestic affairs of States.

The UNESCO procedure has several similarities with the complaints procedure of the Human Rights Council. Firstly, the composition of the bodies leading the procedures is the same. Both the CR and the HR Council are composed of States representatives. This implies that the monitoring has an important political element. Secondly, both communications procedures are confidential. The sessions in which the communications are discussed are fully private, and documents relating to the communications are provided to the Member States of the CR and HR Council only and may not be shared. In the case of the HR Council procedure, the alleged victim is after submission of the complaint not even informed anymore about the status of the procedure or any possible outcome. Within the UNESCO procedure, the author of the communication is kept informed about the stage of the procedure, for instance, if the communication is declared admissible. No information is provided on the discussion of the content of the case in the CR or on the dialogue with the State.

The HR Council procedure only deals with situations of gross and systematic violations. The procedure is not meant for individual situations or individual redress. The UNESCO procedure is open for two types of communications: cases on individual communications and questions of (alleged) systematic violations.

The core of the procedures in both the HR Council and the CR is dialogue with the State, and both bodies try to reach a friendly settlement with the State. The procedures are not meant to file judgments or come to binding conclusions. An important tool of the HR Council is its Special Procedures, which it can establish and use in case no progress is made in a certain State.

The UNESCO procedure was the first and for some time only international/ universal procedure that dealt with (alleged) violations of economic, social, and cultural rights. Until the adoption of the Optional Protocol to the IVESCR in 2013, there was no individual complaints procedure under this Covenant. Some of the rights protected by this Covenant that are within UNESCO's competence, such as the right to education, the right to take part in cultural life, and the right to science and thereby, are potentially part of the UNESCO procedure.

In terms of process, the CR procedure is very different from the individual communications procedures of the UN treaty bodies. The treaty bodies are composed of independent experts, not representatives of States. The procedures in the treaty bodies are not entirely confidential. While the communications are examined by the treaty bodies in closed session and all working documents related to the communications remain confidential (Rules of Procedure Rule 102(1) and (2), UN Doc. CCPR/C/3/Rev.10), the final views on communications shall be made public (Rule 102(5)). The treaty bodies communications procedure has further a different character. Although treaty bodies also always try to reach a friendly settlement with the State concerned, if such settlement is not reached, the treaty body will conclude whether the State has complied with its obligations under the treaty or whether it has violated the treaty. Although this outcome is not legally binding but presented as a View, it does provide the victim as well as the State an answer whether the treaty was violated. Such statement by an independent monitoring body cannot be easily ignored and is broadly accepted by States as being of a very authoritative nature.

The independence of the monitoring body as well as the concrete outcome of the cases is however the reason why the communications procedures for the treaty bodies have to be separately accepted by States, by their ratification of an optional protocol or by declaring their acceptance. Such specific acceptance is not needed for the UNESCO procedure, which is part of its general rules and procedures.

Another important procedural difference is the exhaustion of local remedies. Such exhaustion, although with some possibilities for exception, for instance, when it is clear that such remedies do not exist or are ineffective, is compulsory for all international procedures, except for the UNESCO procedure. Within the UNESCO procedure, it suffices to indicate in the communication whether an attempt has been made to exhaust available domestic remedies. This was considered to be sufficient, bearing in mind the nonjudicial character of the procedure whereby a friendly solution with the state is sought.

The nonparticipation of the author of the communication is another important difference and seen by many as a problematic part of the UNESCO procedure. The whole procedure is intergovernmental whereby the author is kept informed to a certain extent, but she is not allowed to actively participate in the dialogue or present her views.

Concluding Remarks

UNESCO is a specialized and autonomous agency within the UN, with separate (although largely overlapping) State membership and an independent budget and institutional framework. Based on its Constitution, the Organization has a clear mandate in the field of human rights, in particular, the rights related to education, science, culture, and communication. Within the UN system, UNESCO has traditionally been seen as the "intellectual arm" of the UN, because of its focus on education, science, culture, and communication and its traditional link to professionals working in these fields. Accordingly, central functions of UNESCO include being a laboratory of ideas, a clearing house, and a capacity builder for Member States. A great number of programs and activities related to human rights and education, science, culture, and communication bear witness of these functions.

UNESCO also has a standard-setting function, and Member States have adopted numerous conventions, recommendations, and declarations related to human rights. These instruments typically do not contain substantive human rights to be invoked by individuals or communities, but they reflect strong human rights dimensions. Examples include the instruments on education, cultural heritage, cultural diversity, and bioethics. The monitoring of these treaties is done by reporting procedures.

UNESCO further has a procedure to assess communications submitted by individuals and NGOs on alleged human rights violations in its areas of competence. This procedure is not often used; figures show that the amount of communications is very low compared to the procedures for the treaty bodies. This may have to do with the fact that the procedure is not well-known. Its confidential nature as well as the general limited knowledge of UNESCO and its role in the field of human rights also contributes to this. It may also have to do with a lack of confidence in this procedure. Victims or NGOs may not have trust in an intergovernmental procedure that is confidential and does not lead to a concrete end unless a friendly settlement is reached. Authors of communications are not involved in the procedure, so although such a friendly settlement may be a good outcome, it may also be that the author is not as satisfied with the settlement as the CR and the State involved are.

Despite these critical remarks, the UNESCO procedure should certainly be made more widely known in order for alleged victims and NGOs to be able to file their communications if they wish to do so. The procedure, despite its imperfections, has a place in the group of international procedures for the protection of human rights. It is however only a small part of the many programs and activities that UNESCO undertakes in the field of human rights. Its core themes of education, science, culture, and communication have manifold links to human rights, which gives UNESCO a justified role in the advancement of human rights in the world.

References

Beiter KD (2006) The protection of the right to education by international law: including a systematic analysis of article 13 of the International Covenant on Economic, Social and Cultural Rights. Martinus Nijhoff Publishers, The Hague

Coomans F (1999) UNESCO and human rights. In: Hanski R, Suksi M (eds) An introduction to the international protection of human rights, 2nd edn. Institute for Human Rights at Abo Akademi University, Turku, pp 219–230

Donders Y (forthcoming 2018) UNESCO's communications procedure on human rights. In: Rodley N, Van Ho T (eds) Research handbook on human rights institutions and enforcement. Edward Elgar Publishing, London

Dumont GH (1990) A behind-the-scenes struggle for human rights. The UNESCO Courier, Paris, pp 43–45

Executive Board, Committee on Conventions and Recommendations, Information Report, UNESCO Doc. 181 EX/CR/2 Rev, Paris, 18 Mar 2016. Available at http://unesdoc.unesco.org/images/0024/002439/243902e.pdf. Accessed 8 Mar 2018

Marks SP (1999) The complaints procedure of the United Nations educational, scientific and cultural organization. In: Hannum H (ed) Guide to international human rights law practice, 3rd edn. Transnational Publishers, Ardsley, pp 103–118

Partsch KJ, Hufner K (2003) UNESCO procedures for the protection of human rights. In: Symonides J (ed) Human rights: international protection, monitoring, enforcement. UNESCO/ Ashgate Publishing, Paris, pp 111–132

Saba H (1982) UNESCO and human rights. In: Alston P, Vasak K (eds) The international dimensions of human rights: volume 1. UNESCO Publishing & Greenwood Press, Paris/Westport, pp 401–427

UNESCO and UNICEF, A Human Rights Based Approach to Education for All. Available at http://unesdoc.unesco.org/images/0015/001548/154861E.pdf. Accessed 8 Mar 2018

UNESCO Guidelines on Intercultural Education. Available at http://unesdoc.unesco.org/images/0014/001478/147878e.pdf. Accessed 8 Mar 2018

UNESCO, Intercultural Competencies – Conceptual and Operational Framework. Available at http://unesdoc.unesco.org/images/0021/002197/219768e.pdf. Accessed 8 Mar 2018

Weissbrodt D, Farley R (1994) The UNESCO human rights procedure: an evaluation. Hum Rts Q 16:391–414

UN and UNESCO Documents

14 EX/Decision 11.3 (1952) Action to be taken on communications addressed to UNESCO alleging violations of human rights, in particular educational and cultural rights, Item I

15 EX/Decision 11 (1953) Action to be taken on communications addressed to UNESCO alleging violations of human rights, in particular educational and cultural rights

18 EX/19 (7 Apr 1977) Study of the procedures which should be followed in the examination of cases and questions which might be submitted to UNESCO concerning the exercise of human

Note: Parts of this chapter are published in Donders Y (forthcoming 2018) UNESCO's Communications Procedure on Human Rights. In Rodley N and Van Ho T (eds) Research Handbook on Human Rights Institutions and Enforcement. Edward Elgar Publishing, London.

rights in the spheres of its competence, in order to make its action more effective: report of the working party of the executive board

19 EX/Decisions 3.3 (1978) Study of the procedures which should be followed in the examination of cases and questions which might be submitted to UNESCO concerning the exercise of human rights in the spheres of its competence, in order to make its action more effective: report of the working party of the executive board

19C/Res 12.1 (1976) UNESCO's contribution to peace and its tasks with respect to the promotion of human rights and the elimination of colonialism and racialism; long-term programme of measures whereby UNESCO can contribute to the strengthening of peace

20 EX/7 (25 Feb 1995) Questions relating to the methods of work of the committee on conventions and recommendations

22 EX/CR/2 Rev (18 Mar 2016) Executive board, committee on conventions and recommendations information report

ECOSOC Resolution 728 (27 May 1970) Procedure for dealing with communications relating to violations of human rights and fundamental freedoms 1503

UNESCO's (Mar 2009) Procedure for the protection of human rights, the legislative history of the 104 EX/3.3 procedure. UNESCO, Paris. http://unesdoc.unesco.org/images/0018/001818/181839e.pdf. Accessed 8 Mar 2018

A World Court of Human Rights

Manfred Nowak

Contents

Introduction 272
Why Is the World Court of Human Rights a Good Idea? 273
Main Features of the Draft Statute of a World Court of Human Rights 275
Philip Alston's Fundamental Critique of the Proposed World Court of Human Rights 276
Concern of Scale: Justiciability of all Human Rights 277
Concern of Scale: Universality 278
Concern of Scale: Budget 279
Concern of Power: Fact-Finding Powers 279
Concern of Power: Exhaustion of Domestic Remedies 280
Interim Measures 281
Concern of Power: "Bindingness" 282
Concern of Power: Advisory Opinions 284
Concerns of Vision 284
Legalism 284
Hierarchy 285
Entities 286
Universality 286
Philip Alston's Conclusions 287
Final Remarks 288
References 289

Abstract

Already in 1947, Australia proposed in the UN Commission on Human Rights the establishment of an International Court of Human Rights. While regional human rights courts were created in the following decades in Europe, the Americas, and

M. Nowak (✉)
University of Vienna, Vienna, Austria

European Inter-University Institute for Human Rights and Democracy, Venice, Italy
e-mail: manfred.nowak@univie.ac.at; manfred.nowak@eiuc.org

© Springer Nature Singapore Pte Ltd. 2018
G. Oberleitner (ed.), *International Human Rights Institutions, Tribunals, and Courts*,
International Human Rights, https://doi.org/10.1007/978-981-10-5206-4_10

271

Africa, the United Nations so far has entrusted only quasi-judicial treaty monitoring bodies with the examination of individual complaints, whose decisions are,
however, nonbinding under international law. This is the reason why the author of
this chapter, together with Julia Kozma and Martin Scheinin, drafted a Statute for
a World Court of Human Rights in the framework of a Swiss initiative aimed at
preparing a new Agenda for Human Rights on the occasion of the 60th anniversary of the Universal Declaration of Human Rights. This proposal goes beyond
the model of regional human rights courts and also provides for an optional
competence to hold international organizations, transnational corporations, and
other non-State actors accountable for human rights violations. Despite the fact
that the current political climate is not very favorable to innovative and future-
oriented ideas to strengthen international human rights protection, this initiative
was well-received by civil society and the academic community. There is,
however, one significant exception: Philip Alston, one of the most prominent
human rights scholars of our time, launched a fundamental attack on the very idea
of a World Court of Human Rights, calling it a "truly bad idea." After a short
overview of the main reasons for a World Court and the main features of the draft
statute, this chapter examines the various reasons put forward by Philip Alston
against the World Court and subjects them to a critical review.

Keywords
World Court of Human Rights · Philip Alston · Non-state actors · Remedies ·
Individual complaints

Introduction

In contrast to the other human rights institutions, courts, and tribunals described in
the present volume, the World Court of Human Rights (WCHR) does not yet exist.
The idea of a WCHR is not new. Already in 1947, when the newly established UN
Commission on Human Rights was developing ideas how the United Nations could
best implement the commitment of its member States in the UN Charter to promote
human rights, the Australian Government proposed an International Court of Human
Rights (UN Doc. E/CN.4/15 1947; Devereux 2002, p. 47). During the Cold War,
there was no chance of realizing this proposal despite various efforts to revive it (Li
2017, p. 11). With the end of the Cold War, a new window of opportunity emerged
for more ambitious ideas. During the 1990s, two other future-oriented proposals
dating back to the 1940s, the UN High Commissioner for Human Rights and the
International Criminal Court (ICC), were finally put into practice.

That is the background why Martin Scheinin and the author of this chapter
decided in 2000 that the time was ripe for a new initiative to push for the establishment of a WCHR. Their efforts were supported by the Panel of Eminent Persons
under the chair of Mary Robinson and Paulo Sergio Pinheiro, which was requested
by the Swiss Government on the occasion of the 60th anniversary of the Universal
Declaration of Human Rights to prepare a new Agenda for Human Rights in the

twenty-first century (Panel of Eminent Persons). The Panel requested to prepare a detailed draft Statute with a Commentary, which was finalized with the assistance of Julia Kozma from the Ludwig Boltzmann Institute of Human Rights in Vienna (Kozma et al. 2010). This proposal provoked much scholarly debate but little support from governments so far. Most comments from scholars are supportive, despite the fact that the international climate is currently not very favorable to ambitious and future-oriented ideas to strengthen the international protection of human rights (International Commission of Jurists 2011; Ssenyonjo 2016; Cassese 2012; Kirkpatrick 2014). There is, however, one significant exception: on several occasions, one of the most prominent human rights scholars of our time, Philip Alston, launched a fundamental attack on the very idea of a WCHR (Alston 2013, 2014a, 197; 2014b; Alston and Tessitore 2014). In the following, some of the main reasons for the proposal of a WCHR will be recalled, and the main features of the WCHR as outlined in the draft statute will be discussed. The main part of this chapter will, however, respond to some of the arguments which Philip Alston has advanced against the WCHR.

Why Is the World Court of Human Rights a Good Idea?

The arguments for a WCHR can be summarized as follows (Nowak 2007, p. 251, 2009, p. 697, 2012a, p. 17, 2012b, p. 257, 2013a, p. 531, 2013b, p. 3, 2014, p. 3): First, the very idea of any subjective right means that the rights holder must have a remedy against the duty bearer before an independent court in case the duty bearer violates the right. This applies in all fields of law, including human rights law. Otherwise, the right would be meaningless. Second, the monitoring system of the UN human rights treaties constitutes the lowest common denominator between States during the time of the Cold War when the Soviet Union and other Communist States were strictly against the very idea of individual complaints. Nevertheless, Article 14 of the International Convention on the Elimination of All Forms of Racial Discrimination of 1965 and the first Optional Protocol to the International Covenant on Civil and Political Rights of 1966 contain at least an individual communication procedure before quasi-judicial independent treaty bodies (Racial Discrimination Committee and Human Rights Committee). The Communist States insisted, however, that these treaty bodies were not courts and that their decisions ("suggestions," "recommendations," or "final views") were not legally binding under international law. Despite the fact that the Soviet Union and its satellite States in Europe collapsed almost 30 years ago, the United Nations has continued to adopt treaties with the same weak individual communication procedures as if we were still living in the times of the Cold War. The most recent examples are Article 31 of the International Convention for the Protection from Enforced Disappearance 2006 as well as the respective Optional Protocols to the Convention on the Rights of Persons with Disabilities 2006, to the International Covenant on Economic, Social and Cultural Rights 2008, and to the Convention on the Rights of the Child 2011. The Human Rights Committee and the other UN treaty monitoring bodies have developed best practices in following the procedure and jurisprudence of regional human rights courts, but their decisions simply do not carry the same weight as legally binding judgments and are, therefore, easier to be ignored by States.

Furthermore, the three regional intergovernmental organizations, which have developed a meaningful system for the protection of human rights, i.e., the Council of Europe, the Organization of American States, and the Organization of African Unity/African Union, created regional human rights courts (the European Court of Human Rights, the Inter-American Court of Human Rights, and the African Court of Human and Peoples' Rights). They are entrusted with the power to decide in a legally binding manner on individual and other complaints. Since the entry into force of the 11th Additional Protocol to the European Convention on Human Rights in 1998, the European Court in Strasbourg even has been working as a full-time professional court, which hands down thousands of judgments per year in relation to the 47 member States of the Council of Europe.

While the UN Charter-based system for the protection of human rights has undergone a major structural reform with the creation of the UN Human Rights Council in 2005/2006 and with the introduction of the Universal Periodic Review of the human rights performance of all UN member States, the treaty body system, despite all its well-known weaknesses, is still waiting for a meaningful reform. The next attempt for such a reform is envisaged for the year 2020. Why not establish a judicial WCHR as a counterpart to the political UN Human Rights Council consisting of States?

Most of the more far-reaching proposals for the reform of the UN treaty body system would require amendments of the existing treaties, which are very difficult to achieve. The creation of a WCHR would not require any treaty amendment. It can be achieved by adopting a new treaty (Statute of the WCHR), similar to the Rome Statute of the ICC of 1998. This also means that the existing ten UN human rights treaty monitoring bodies shall not be replaced by the new WCHR. As the ratification process of the WCHR Statute would proceed, they would gradually lose their competence to decide about individual complaints and could therefore fully concentrate their limited time on the examination of State reports and other functions under the respective treaties. For the State reporting procedure, the multidisciplinary composition of the current treaty bodies and the special expertise of their members on the rights of women, children, migrant workers, or persons with disabilities on torture, racial discrimination, enforced disappearances, or various economic, social, and cultural rights is certainly an asset. However, the decision on individual complaints about alleged violations of human rights by States parties requires special legal expertise and should, therefore, better be entrusted to judges with a solid legal background.

One of the major weaknesses of the current international human rights system is the lack of legal accountability of intergovernmental organizations and non-State actors. Intergovernmental organizations (United Nations, European Union, NATO, or the World Bank and the International Monetary Fund), transnational corporations, and other non-State actors have gained significant power in times of globalization. Similar to States, they often violate human rights but are, at the same time, willing to assume increasing responsibility for the promotion and protection of human rights as part of their corporate social responsibility. Legally speaking, there are strong arguments that intergovernmental organizations and certain non-State actors are even bound by current international human rights treaties. Nevertheless, they cannot be held accountable before any international treaty monitoring body. This significant gap in international law can and will be filled by the creation of a WCHR, and the joint draft Statute does contain provisions to this effect.

In 2005, the UN General Assembly adopted the UN Basic Principles and Guidelines on the Right to a Remedy and Reparation for Victims of Gross Violations of International Human Rights Law and Serious Violations of International Humanitarian Law (UN General Assembly Resolution 60/147 of 16 December 2005). They foresee a variety of different forms of reparation adequate to the respective human rights violations, such as restitution, rehabilitation, compensation, satisfaction, and guarantees of non-repetition. In reality, UN treaty bodies, however, have no power to grant victims adequate reparation for the harm suffered, which is a fundamental aspect of the right of victims to an effective remedy. This constitutes another serious weakness of the international human rights protection system, which could easily be remedied by the creation of a WCHR, as suggested in the draft Statute.

Main Features of the Draft Statute of a World Court of Human Rights

The consolidated draft Statute for a WCHR is based on two earlier drafts, one by Martin Scheinin, the other by Julia Kozma and the author of this chapter, which were later merged (Kozma et al. 2010, p. 9, 69 and 87). It consists of 54 Articles. The Statute proposes a permanent court with international legal personality, based in Geneva with the power to decide in a legally binding manner on all complaints about alleged human rights violations brought before it in accordance with this Statute. The court should have 21 judges to be elected by the States parties to the Statute, sitting as a plenary court, in chambers of seven and committees of three judges, similar to the European Court of Human Rights (European Court of Human Rights). The Court shall render binding judgments on individual complaints, declare complaints inadmissible, facilitate friendly settlements, order interim measures, or strike out complaints, similar to other human rights courts. It shall also be entrusted with the power to provide advisory opinions upon request of States, the UN Secretary General, and the UN High Commissioner for Human Rights, similar to the Inter-American Court of Human Rights. Final judgments of the court are binding under international law. Their implementation by States shall be supervised by the UN High Commissioner for Human Rights, who may seize the Human Rights Council or, in exceptional cases through the UN Secretary General, the Security Council, with a request to take the necessary measures that will bring about the enforcement of the judgment (Article 18).

The Statute does not create any new substantive human rights obligations for States parties. As applicable law, Article 5 defines a total of 21 existing human rights treaties of the United Nations. Of course, the provisions of these treaties are only applicable if the State concerned is also a party to the respective treaty in addition to having ratified the Statute of the WCHR. In addition, Article 50 contains an opting-out clause which provides any State party to the WCHR with the right to declare that it does not recognize the jurisdiction of the Court in relation to certain human rights treaties or certain provisions thereof. This Article was inserted in order to make it easier for States to ratify the Statute. If a State is, e.g., party to both Covenants but wishes to allow complaints to the WCHR only in relation to one of the Covenants, it may issue, at the time of ratification, a reservation under Article 50(1) excluding the other one (Kozma et al. 2010, p. 65). This reservation can be withdrawn at any time thereafter in order to broaden the jurisdiction of the Court.

For "Entities," which are defined in Article 4 as "any inter-governmental organization or non-State actor, including any business corporation, which has recognized the jurisdiction of the Court in accordance with Article 51," the Statute envisages a special "opting in" clause. Such "Entities" cannot usually become parties to any international human rights treaty. The possibility for regional integration organizations, such as the European Union, to become a party to the Convention on the Rights of Persons with Disabilities in accordance with Article 44 of this UN treaty, is an exception. In fact, the EU has made use of this possibility. Under the draft Statute of the WCHR, such Entities are invited to voluntarily declare under Article 51 that they recognize the competence of the WCHR to "receive and examine complaints from any person, non-governmental organization or group of individuals claiming to be the victim of a violation by the respective Entity of any human right provided for in any human rights treaty listed in Article 5(1)." When making such a declaration, the "Entity" may specify under Article 51(2) which human rights treaties and which provisions thereof shall be subject to the jurisdiction of the Court. The Commentary suggests that members of the UN Global Compact should be specifically encouraged to make such a declaration and accept, e.g., the jurisdiction of the Court over certain economic rights, such as trade union freedoms and conditions of work (Kozma et al. 2010, p. 65).

Finally, there is no hierarchy between the proposed WCHR and regional human rights courts. As other similar treaties, the draft Statute requires as admissibility criteria the exhaustion of domestic remedies (Article 9) and various other criteria, including in Article 19(1)(b) the pre-condition that the same matter has not "already been examined in substance by the Court or by any other procedure of international investigation and settlement, including before a regional human rights court." In other words, applicants must make up their minds whether they prefer to lodge a complaint, after having exhausted all domestic remedies, with the WCHR or with a regional human rights court, if applicable. Consequently, there will be no review of a judgment of a regional court by the WCHR if it concerns the same matter.

Philip Alston's Fundamental Critique of the Proposed World Court of Human Rights

A number of commentators have criticized the establishment of a WCHR. Antonio Cassese said that "[t]o consider an international court as the final guarantor may today seem hopelessly naive, not to say unrealistic, but this destination is simply the logical development of the project to protect human rights through international law" (Cassese 2012, p. 323). Stefan Trechsel argued that "[r]ealistically speaking, the creation of a world court for human rights is, at the present time, neither desirable, nor necessary, nor probable" (Trechsel 2004, p. 18). Like these authors, Philip Alston stresses that the current time with all its crises and problems is not particularly conducive for the realization of highly ambitious projects like the WCHR. However, his critique is of a much more fundamental nature and goes far beyond pragmatic reasons when he says:

> But a World Court of this type is not just an idea whose time has not yet come. The very idea fundamentally misconceives the nature of the challenges confronting an international community dedicated to eliminating major human rights violations. And, if it were ever realized, it would concentrate frighteningly broad powers in the hands of a tiny number of judges without the slightest consideration of the implications for the legitimate role of the state. (Alston 2014, p. 197)

In fact, Alston distinguishes concerns of scale, concerns of power, and concerns of vision. They need to be addressed one by one.

Concern of Scale: Justiciability of all Human Rights

Philip Alston starts by saying that:

> the sheer scale of the project raises a number of concerns, but it will suffice to identify three . . . the court is given jurisdiction over alleged violations of any of the rights contained in a whopping twenty-one separate existing human rights treaties . . . the prospect that every right in every one of the treaties that a given state has ratified would be subject to binding international adjudication would in fact provoke hugely contentious debates in any society that takes the rule of law seriously. In addition, such a far-ranging jurisdiction would give rise to very difficult challenges for judges in terms of reconciling complex, diverse, overlapping, and perhaps inconsistent treaty provisions. (Alston 2015, p. 201–202)

He thus criticizes that the proponents of the draft Statute included too many treaties when they defined the applicable law in Article 5 of the draft Statute. Which treaties should have been deleted? In fact, all nine core UN human rights treaties plus additional protocols are included, which today are all subject to individual communication procedures before quasi-judicial treaty monitoring bodies. In addition, a few earlier UN human rights treaties were included, such as the Slavery Conventions, the Genocide Convention, and the Geneva Refugee Convention. If a State has ratified all these treaties and does not opt out of any of them in accordance with Article 50 of the Statute at the time of ratification or accession, then it is indeed true that any person subject to this State's jurisdiction may lodge a complaint before the WCHR in relation to alleged violations of any of the rights enlisted in these 21 treaties. It is also true that the judges might be faced with difficult challenges and perhaps inconsistent treaty provisions. However, solving these challenges is precisely the task of professional judges, whether as judges of national supreme or constitutional courts, of the European or International Court of Justice or of any other court with broad jurisdiction. Under Article 64 of the American Convention on Human Rights, the Inter-American Court of Human Rights may be requested to render an advisory opinion regarding the interpretation of the American Convention or of any other (international or inter-American) treaty concerning the protection of human rights in the American states. Many UN human rights treaties contain a specific clause enabling States parties to refer any dispute concerning the interpretation or application of the respective treaty to the International Court of Justice (ICJ).

However, Philip Alston seems to argue that not every right contained in these 21 UN treaties would be justiciable before an international court. This is a much more fundamental challenge. Unfortunately, he does not provide any example of a human right which, in his opinion, would not be justiciable. Usually, when the question of justiciability of human rights is brought up in scholarly debates, it is questioned in relation to economic, social, and cultural rights, such as the right to work or the right to an adequate standard of living. Since Philip Alston was a long-term member and chair of the UN Committee on Economic, Social and Cultural Rights and in fact did campaign for the adoption of an Optional Protocol to this Covenant enabling individuals to lodge individual complaints or "communications" before the Committee, one should not assume that he would have these rights in mind when challenging the justiciability of certain human rights. Perhaps he is not even fully challenging the justiciability but is simply of the opinion that there would be contentious debates within societies when confronted with a judgment of the WCHR telling domestic judges and legislators that human rights must be taken seriously. But is this not the very purpose of international human rights law? When the European Court of Human Rights handed down its first judgments in the 1960s and 1970s, there were fierce debates about sovereignty and interference in domestic matters. Even more recently, the British Prime Minister David Cameron said in response to the judgment of the European Court in the case of Hirst versus the United Kingdom (European Court of Human Rights, Hirst v UK 2005) that it makes him feel sick if he would have to give the right to vote to prisoners in order to execute this judgment (BBC News 2012). Similar debates take place in Brazil and other Latin American States with respect to the jurisprudence of the Inter-American Court and also with respect to the case law of the Human Rights Committee and other UN treaty bodies.

Concern of Scale: Universality

Philip Alston continues by saying that:

> [t]he second concern is whether the court would be competent to deal with the domestic legal systems of every state in the world, which are tremendously varied. It is one thing for a treaty body, such as the Human Rights Committee, to formulate essentially nonbinding 'views' or general recommendations that take adequate account of the particularities of legal systems from Afghanistan to Zimbabwe, or Austria to Uruguay. But it is quite another for a court to hand down binding judgments on domestically controversial and contested issues to a large group of states with hugely diverse legal systems. (Alston 2014, p. 202)

This argument presents a severe critique of the Human Rights Committee and other UN treaty bodies, which do their utmost to interpret their limited competences in the best quasi-judicial manner. Alston conveys the troublesome message that decisions of UN treaty bodies in individual communication procedures do not need to be taken seriously and, therefore, can simply be ignored. However, with binding judgments of the WCHR, this would be a different matter. After all, States accept legally binding obligations when becoming parties to human rights treaties, and the monitoring bodies have been entrusted with the task of interpreting these binding obligations and to tell States whether they comply with international human rights law or not. Whether these "final views" or "general comments" are themselves legally binding or not is not the decisive question, as these are authoritative interpretations of States' legal obligations. That the WCHR will have to deal with a tremendous variety of domestic legal systems is uncontested. However, this is not different from the current practice of UN treaty bodies or international courts, such as the ICC (when assessing the complementarity principle) or the ICJ.

Concern of Scale: Budget

"The third magnitude-related concern is cost" (Alston 2014, p. 202). Compared to the budget of the ICC (US $ 132 million in 2011), the International Criminal Tribunal for the former Yugoslavia (US $ 143 million), and the European Court of Human Rights (US $ 90 million in 2013), Philip Alston arrives at "a nearly billion dollar price tag for a global human rights court" and concludes that "governmental commitments of that magnitude seem highly improbable" (Alston 2014, p. 202).

One may well question if this estimate is realistic. It is true that a permanent court of highly professional full-time judges requires a substantial amount of resources. If the European Court of Human Rights with 47 judges, which deals with hundreds of thousands of cases, can perform its tasks with roughly US $ 100 million, i.e., less than the ICC, which is investigating and prosecuting a very limited number of cases, then it will take a fairly long time until the budget of the WCHR with only 21 judges will exceed that of the European Court of Human Rights. It would have been more appropriate to take the budget of the International Court of Justice as a basis of comparison, which for the biennium of 2016–2017 is around US $ 46 million (International Court of Justice 2016). This would still be a lot of money, but States have accepted higher financial burdens with respect to other international courts, above all criminal courts.

Concern of Power: Fact-Finding Powers

Philip Alston criticizes that the WCHR Statute "in fact adopts a maximalist approach in relation to many of the most controversial procedural dimensions of international human rights adjudication, and in so doing would produce a radically more powerful tribunal than any that currently exists" (Alston 2014, p. 203). He illustrates this argument with five different examples on fact-finding powers, the exhaust of domestic remedies, interim measure, the "bindingness" of judgments, and advisory opinions.

First, he argues that the fact-finding powers envisaged for the WCHR would constitute "a huge leap in terms of powers that states would see as infringing on their sovereignty. The vesting of comprehensive investigative powers plus very extensive judicial authority in a single body would be without precedent at the international level" (Alston 2014, p. 203). It is true that the draft Statute provides far-reaching powers to the WCHR when the court considers it necessary to carry out a fact-finding mission for the sake of clarifying the facts in a particularly disputed case. According to Article 14(3) of the draft Statute, the State party concerned "shall provide all necessary cooperation and facilitate the investigation, including by granting access to all places of detention and other facilities." This provision is supplemented by the general obligation of States parties under Article 40(1) to "cooperate fully with the Court in its examination of complaints." This obligation is specified in Article 40(2) as follows: "In particular, the Court shall enjoy full freedom of movement and inquiry throughout the territory of the State Party, unrestricted access to State authorities, documents and case files as well as the right of access to all places of detention and the right to hold confidential interviews with detainees, victims, experts and witnesses."

On the other hand, these fact-finding powers are not as unprecedented under existing international law as Philip Alston claims. Article 38 ECHR authorizes the European Court of Human Rights to "undertake an investigation, for the effective conduct of which the High Contracting Parties concerned shall furnish all necessary facilities." Experience shows that, for reasons of time, personal, and financial resources, such in-depth investigations and fact-finding missions only take place in exceptional cases. This will certainly also be the practice of any future WCHR (Kozma et al. 2010, p. 43; Leach et al. 2009). The Rome Statute of the ICC devotes an entire Part (Part 9) to international cooperation and judicial assistance, and Article 93 of the ICC Statute contains a fairly comprehensive list of duties of States parties aimed at assisting the ICC in investigating the facts of suspected crimes.

Concern of Power: Exhaustion of Domestic Remedies

All international and regional human rights treaties which allow for individual complaints or communications establish as one of the conditions for admissibility that the applicants must exhaust all available domestic remedies before lodging a complaint before an international court or other monitoring body. This can, for example, be found in Art. 5(2)(b) of the 1st Optional Protocol to the International Covenant on Civil and Political Rights, Art. 3(1) Optional Protocol to the International Covenant on Economic, Social and Cultural Rights, Art. 35(1) of the European Convention on Human Rights, and Art. 46(1)(a) of the American Convention of Human Rights. This requirement follows from the well-established principle of subsidiarity under international law. The primary responsibility for protecting human rights rests with States and any violation of human rights by State authorities shall, therefore, be remedied first by domestic courts, which should properly investigate such allegations, decide whether they amount to a violation, and, if so, provide the victims with an appropriate reparation for the harm suffered. This obligation of States to ensure a right to an effective remedy before domestic courts and other domestic authorities can be found, e.g., in Art. 2(3) of the International Covenant on Civil and Political Rights, Art. 13 of the European Convention on Human Right and Art. 25 American Convention of Human Rights.

With respect to the WCHR, Philip Alston criticizes that "the statute actually expands dramatically the range of situations in which such recourse can be had" (Alston 2014, p. 203). He is right, but as the Commentary to the draft Statute of the WCHR explains, there are good reasons why Article 9 puts a special emphasis on the requirement of the applicants to exhaust domestic remedies and on the obligation of States to provide for effective judicial remedies in their domestic legal systems. An analogy can be drawn to the principle of complementarity in the Statute of the ICC. The drafters of the draft Statute of the WCHR have explained that:

> [t]he ICC is only competent to try a person for a particular crime if the respective State authorities are either unwilling or unable to prosecute the person concerned. This principle serves a double function. It respects State sovereignty and prevents the ICC to become overloaded with cases. At the same time, it shall serve as an incentive for the domestic criminal justice authorities to prosecute persons suspected of having committed war crimes, genocide and crimes against humanity. (Kozma et al. 2010, p. 38–39)

The obligation of States parties in Article 9(1) of the draft Statute "to ensure that all applicants have access to effective judicial remedies in relation to all human rights enshrined in the applicable human rights treaties" shall serve as an incentive for States to improve their domestic judicial systems for the protection of human rights. It shall thus provide victims of human rights violations with an effective, prompt, and not too expensive remedy before domestic courts and at the same time ensure that the WCHR will not be overloaded with too many cases. To facilitate this objective, we also envisage in Article 39 the establishment of a trust fund with the task of, inter alia, assisting States parties "to improve their domestic judicial remedies in accordance with Article 9." The insertion of the trust fund into the Statute goes back to a proposal by Mary Robinson in the Panel of Eminent Persons established by the Swiss Government mentioned above. The criticism of Philip Alston is in fact less concerned with the requirement of the exhaustion of domestic remedies but is rather based on his highly questionable assumption outlined above that not all of the rights covered by the 21 human rights treaties are in fact justiciable before domestic courts (Alston 2014, p. 203–204).

Interim Measures

Article 19(1) of the draft Statute provides that the WCHR "may transmit to the State Party or Entity concerned an order that the State or Entity take such interim measures as may be necessary in exceptional circumstances to avoid possible irreparable damages to the victim or victims of the alleged human rights violations." According to Article 19(4) of the draft Statute, such orders for interim measures "are binding with immediate effect upon the respondent party and shall be enforced in the same manner as judgments in accordance with Article 18." Again, there is nothing revolutionary in this provision, which can also be found in the law and practice of the ICJ and regional human rights courts (Frowein 2002, p. 55). Rule 39 of the Rules of the European Court of Human Rights, Art. 63(2) of the American Convention of Human Rights, Art 27(2) of the Protocol to the African Charter on Human and Peoples' Rights on the Establishment of an African Court on Human and Peoples' Rights, and Art 41(1) of the ICJ Statute are examples thereof (International Court of Justice, Genocide Case 1993, p. 325; International Court of Justice 2001; Frowein 2002, p. 55). Orders for interim measures are usually issued to prevent irreparable damages, such as in death penalty cases to avoid execution or in expulsion cases to prevent torture.

Nevertheless, Philip Alston feels the need to criticize this provision with the argument that "few issues have proven more controversial, as was illustrated most dramatically in 2012 by Brazil's furious reaction to interim measures proposed by the Inter-American Commission of Human Rights in relation to the construction of the Belo Horizonte hydroelectric power plant" (Alston 2014, p. 204). It is true that certain orders for interim measures have in practice been ignored by States. It must be doubted, however, whether this is a convincing argument against the need for provisional measures for the purpose of preventing irreparable harm. It is also true that States have repeatedly challenged the legally binding effect of such measures if the respective provisions were not clear. This prompted the proponents of the draft Statute to make clear beyond any reasonable doubt that such interim measures are legally binding with immediate effect.

Concern of Power: "Bindingness"

The arguments of Philip Alston against the "bindingness" (a term used by him) of judgments of a future WCHR are the most striking ones in his critique of the WCHR. He starts his argument as follows:

> After almost fifty years in existence, the ECHR system moved in 1998 to characterize its judgments as being binding on the state concerned, although the 'enforcement' measures it applies continue to be filtered through the Committee of Ministers, which is a political body and acts accordingly. Judgments often take many years to be enforced and are frequently sidestepped. (Alston 2014, p. 204)

First of all, Philip Alston is wrong in so far as the judgments of the European Court of Human Rights were already legally binding since the establishment of the "old" Court in the late 1950s and not only since the creation of the "new" Court by the Additional Protocol No. 11 to the European Convention on Human Rights in 1998. Secondly, the enforcement measures are not filtered through the Committee of Ministers, but Article 46 ECHR entrusts the Committee of Ministers as the highest political body of the Council of Europe with the task of supervising the execution of the Court's judgments. Who else should perform this task? Of course, sometimes it may take States years to execute the judgments of the Court, as comprehensive legislative measures may be needed and/or final judgments of domestic courts may need to be set aside. Austria was, e.g., required in more than one case to amend its constitution in order to comply with the judgments of the European Court of Human Rights. This took several years, but Austria finally did comply. Sometimes, States such as Turkey or the Russian Federation may "sidestep" judgments of the Court, but in general, Council of Europe member States do comply with the Court's judgments, thanks to the supervisory role and practice of the Committee of Ministers.

What is most surprising in Philip Alston's criticism is, however, that he seems to argue against the very idea that judgments of the WCHR are foreseen to be final and binding (Alston 2014, 204). After having described a range of concerns relating to the political feasibility, magnitude, and expansiveness of the proposed WCHR, he suggests that "many if not all of these concerns could be dealt with by adjusting the model in various ways" (Alston 2014, p. 205). One of these adjustments he proposes is that "judgments could be made nonbinding" (Alston 2014, p. 205). It is unclear what the purpose of courts that hand down "nonbinding" judgments would be. On the contrary, courts have been established on the domestic and international level for the very purpose to decide in a legally binding manner about legal disputes of a civil, criminal, constitutional, or international character. What is the sense of a domestic or international criminal court convicting a person found guilty of a criminal offense in a judgment which is not legally binding? Or would Philip Alston apply his proposal of "nonbinding" judgments only to human rights courts? If so, are human rights complaints in his opinion less important than any other legal dispute of a civil or constitutional nature so that they do not deserve a legally binding judgment?

Article 18 of the draft Statute, which provides that the judgments of the WCHR shall be "final and binding," entrusts the supervision of the execution of the Court's judgments to the UN High Commissioner for Human Rights. Since the High Commissioner has no powers to enforce the judgments, Article 18(5) envisages that the High Commissioner, after concluding that any State party fails to abide by or enforce any judgment, "shall seize the Human Rights Council or, if he or she deems it necessary, through the Secretary General the Security Council with a request to take the necessary measures that will bring about the enforcement of the judgment." This provision is modeled on the system of the European Convention on Human Rights under which an independent court decides on the admissibility and merits of human rights complaints and the highest political body is entrusted to supervise the execution of the judgments. Since Philip Aston disapproves of the system of the European Convention of Human Rights, he consequently also disapproves of the system proposed in the draft statute of a WCHR. One of his arguments is that "the veto-wielding members of the Security Council would be effectively immune from any such initiative, unless they choose to submit themselves to it" (Alston 2014, p. 204). This is of course true as long as the current composition and powers of the Security Council stay as they are. It is, however, not a convincing argument against entrusting the highest political bodies of the United Nations with the enforcement of the legally binding judgments of a future WCHR. Philip Alston fails to provide a convincing alternative in accordance with the current UN Charter.

Concern of Power: Advisory Opinions

Philip Alston alleges that the "statute provides that the International Court of Justice may be requested to give an advisory opinion in relation to the statute itself or to any of the twenty-one listed treaties" (Alston 2014, p. 205). This is incorrect as Article 8 of the draft Statute vests this power in the WCHR and not in the ICJ. His criticism that this power "contrasts strongly with the existing situation, under which only specified UN organs and agencies may request advisory opinions" (Alston 2014, p. 205) is therefore equally incorrect. In fact, Article 8 of the draft Statute is inspired by Article 64 of the American Convention on Human Rights, as explained in the Commentary to the draft Statute (Kozma et al. 2010, p. 37). Nevertheless, Philip Alston concludes by asserting that "the statute opts for a maximalist position and indeed leaves no controversial stone unturned in order to ensure the creation of a truly powerful international court" (Alston 2014, p. 205).

Concerns of Vision

After having advanced a range of concerns relating to the political feasibility, magnitude, and expensiveness of the proposed WCHR, Philip Alston concedes that these concerns could be dealt with by, e.g., eliminating on-site investigations, reducing the range of standards or treaties, making interim measures optional, and making the judgments nonbinding. However, his concerns of scale and power only prepare the ground for his more fundamental objections:

> My critique is, however, more deeply-rooted. I consider the basic assumptions underlying the statute to be problematic and misconceived. In my view, the very act of putting forward a WCHR as a major stand-alone initiative skews and distorts the debate, and pursuing such a vision distracts attention, resources, and energy from more pressing endeavors. (Alston 2014, p. 205)

He divides his concerns of vision into the following four arguments around legalism, hierarchy, the role of "Entities," and universalism.

Legalism

Alston argues that "[t]he proposal privileges justiciability over all other means by which to uphold human rights .... Judges and lawyers are effectively seen as the frontline of global human rights protection ... vision in which courts in general, let alone a single World Court, offer the best hope of resolving complex and contested problems ..." (Alston 2014, p. 205–206). These and similar arguments show that Philip Alston fundamentally misunderstands the purpose of the proposed WCHR. Its proponents never assumed that the WCHR should replace other mechanisms and would solve all human rights problems. On the contrary, it was made clear that the proposed WCHR should complement the existing mechanisms for the protection of human rights, whether at the regional or universal level, whether Charter-based or treaty-based. The existing UN human rights treaty bodies should remain in existence and would only gradually cede one of their functions (i.e., the examination of individual complaints) to the future Court and thereby would free time for their main function, i.e., the examination of State reports. The WCHR would not function as an appeal court to regional human rights courts in Europe, the Americas, and Africa. On the contrary, applicants would have to choose whether to apply to regional courts, if applicable, or to the WCHR. It is fully recognized that gross and systematic human rights violations can more effectively be dealt with by political bodies, such as the UN Human Rights Council, the General Assembly, or, in exceptional cases, the Security Council. However, in the opinion of the proponents of the WCHR, independent judges and courts are best qualified to decide about individual complaints.

Hierarchy

In his more journalistic critique of the WCHR, Philip Alston is even blunter in his mistrust and disrespect of any judicial protection of human rights. He argues that:

> [t]he proposal is both remarkable and troubling for its hierarchical nature . . . the notion that a single court would be given the authority to issue determinative interpretations on every issue of human rights on a global basis defies any understandings of systematic pluralism, diversity, or separation of powers . . . It is, in short, difficult to understand how and why human rights proponents would wish to vouchsafe such vast powers to a handful of judges . . . the resulting jurisprudence would be potentially disastrous for human rights. (Alston 2014, p. 206)

He goes on to suggest that "the proposal is highly elitist since it would vest ultimate power in the hands of a tiny coterie of judges . . . Such a vision is barely compatible with the values underlying the ideal of an international regime governed by the rule of law and democratic institutions" (Alston 2013, p. 2). This seems a puzzling statement from one of the most eminent and respected human rights lawyers of our time. Would he make the same accusations against the ICJ, the ICC, the European Court of Human Rights, the Inter-American Court of Human Rights, or the Supreme Court of the United States? Why is a system in which States draft, adopt, and ratify binding human rights treaties and then agree to entrust independent courts with the power to decide in a legally binding manner on individual complaints lodged by alleged victims of human rights violations incompatible with the notions of separation of powers, the rule of law, and democracy? Is the idea of separation of powers, as developed by John Locke or Montesquieu and for the first time enshrined in the Constitution of the United States, not based on the conviction that laws shall be made by the legislative power, which represents the sovereignty of the people which allows that these laws shall be implemented by the executive power and the supervision and monitoring of the execution of the laws shall be entrusted to independent courts? Are independent courts not the best guarantee for the implementation of the rule of law? Why should the jurisprudence of a WCHR, composed of the best human rights lawyers and judges from the different regions of the world, be "potentially disastrous for human rights"? Does the performance of the ICJ or the UN Human Rights Committee support these arguments? There seems to be no evidence to justify such blunt and sweeping allegations.

Entities

Article 51 of the draft Statute of the WCHR authorizes any "Entity" to recognize the competence of the WCHR to examine complaints from any person, NGO, or group of individuals claiming to be the victim of a human rights violation by the respective "Entity." Article 4(1) defines the term Entity as "any inter-governmental organization or non-State actor, including any business corporation, which has recognized the jurisdiction of the Court in accordance with Article 51."

Philip Alston agrees that the inability of present international law to hold transnational corporations and other non-State actors accountable for their human rights violations is one of the most important gaps in the current international human rights regime. Nevertheless, he criticizes the radical implications of the proposed WCHR which seem, in his opinion, "not to have been thought through or even considered" (Alston 2014, p. 207). For example, he criticizes that organized crime groups are excluded from the examples of "Entities" listed in the Commentary the draft Statute (Kozma et al. 2010, p. 33). It is, however, doubtful whether organized criminal groups would be among the first organizations to recognize the jurisdiction of the Court. Nevertheless, one can agree that it is not easy to draw a clear line between non-State actors and decide which should be invited to accept the jurisdiction of the Court and which that should not. "Entities" are thus defined in a broad manner which leaves the decision to recognize the jurisdiction of the Court to the "Entities" themselves. The same is true for the range of human rights to be applied to "Entities." Finally, it will be up to the Court to decide whether certain human rights can be applied to intergovernmental organizations or non-State actors and which domestic remedies will have to be exhausted before lodging a complaint with the Court. However, one can certainly agree with Philip Alston that we are entering unchartered waters with this provision.

Universality

Philip Alston also finds the draft Statute's approach to the question of universality as another "problematic aspect of the vision of the court" (Alston 2014, p. 208). He finds the reassurance that the WCHR should complement rather than duplicate existing regional courts "not convincing" (Alston 2014, p. 209) and asserts that the principle of complementarity mentioned in the Preamble of the draft Statute "finds no direct expression in the operative provisions of the statute, in contrast to the approach of the ICC" (Alston 2014, p. 209). As outlined above, the principle of complementarity is reflected most visibly in Article 9, which deals with the exhaustion of domestic remedies and the corresponding obligation of States parties to provide an effective domestic judicial remedy. Whether it is true that the three existing regional courts of human rights in Europe, the Americas, and Africa "would be gradually marginalized" by the WCHR (Alston 2014, p. 209) remains to be seen. But the broad range of human rights to be adjudicated by the WCHR might provide an incentive to the regional organizations to also broaden the respective jurisdiction of regional courts, by, e.g., including economic, social, and cultural rights.

Philip Alston's Conclusions

In conclusion, Philip Alston deplores the "absence of any plausible theory of change that would explain how such a dramatic leap could be achieved at the world level" (Alston 2014, 210). He also alleges that the proposal to create a WCHR would distract resources and attention away from the far more pressing and important issues that challenge the evolution of the human rights regime (Alston 2013, p. 2, 2014a, p. 211, 2014b, p. 2). To him, these issues include:

> the need to nurture a culture of human rights at all levels of society, the creation of tailored national accountability mechanisms, the strengthening of regional systems (not just courts) especially in Asia and the Pacific and in the Arab World, the building of means by which corporations as well as international organizations can be held to account, far-reaching reform of the treaty body system, and refinement of the UN Human Rights Council's Universal Periodic Review process to make it more targeted and demanding. ... These complex challenges cannot be dealt with in a meaningful way by seeking to bypass them all and create a WCHR as if it were some magical panacea. (Alston 2013, p. 2, 2014a, p. 210–211, 2014b, p. 2)

Again, these seem to be sweeping allegations. On the one hand, the proposal of a WCHR only addresses one shortcoming of the present international human rights regime, namely, the fact that individual human rights complaints are entrusted by the United Nations to quasi-judicial human rights committees rather than to a judicial body, as in Europe, Africa, and the Americas. Consequently, some of the human rights challenges mentioned by Philip Alston, such as the refinement of the Human Rights Council's Universal Periodic Review, cannot be addressed by the WCHR. However, this does not mean that the proposal is distracting the resources and attention away from these other challenges. More important, however, is that most of the challenges mentioned by Philip Alston are in fact addressed by the proposal. The experience with regional human rights courts illustrates that their existence and jurisprudence in fact did nurture a culture of human rights in the respective regions. The creation of tailored national accountability mechanisms would be the direct result of States' obligations under Article 9(1) of the draft Statute, supported by the trust fund provided for in Article 39 of the draft Statute. The establishment of a WCHR would also provide an incentive to create further regional human rights courts, especially in the Asia-Pacific and the Arab regions. The proposed jurisdiction over "Entities" as defined in Article 4 is so far the most advanced proposal to hold international organizations and transnational corporations accountable to international human rights standards. Similarly, the establishment of a WCHR constitutes the most far-reaching proposal of reforming the UN treaty body system without any need to amend existing treaties, as it would create a more effective system for dealing with individual complaints and at the same time would free time for the existing treaty monitoring bodies to examine State reports. Why the proposal would bypass these challenges, as Philip Alston deplores, is difficult to understand.

Final Remarks

One can certainly agree with Philip Alston that the project of establishing a WCHR is a very ambitious one. The proposal presents a solution to various problems in the field of human rights protection mechanisms. It should be seen as a contribution to the current debate about UN treaty body reform; it aims at giving more weight to individual complaints before UN bodies as a supplement (not as an alternative) to the State reporting procedures and political mechanisms; it presents a possible solution for holding intergovernmental organizations and non-State actors accountable for their human rights violations; and it provides a tool for enforcing the UN Basic Guidelines and Principles on the right of victims to an effective remedy and adequate reparation. In this sense, it is "maximalist," and some of its components, such as broad powers of fact-finding in situ or the right to render advisory opinions, could be taken out of our proposal during a political drafting process without damaging the overall objective of the Court.

As this rebuttal of Philip Alston's comprehensive attack on the WCHR has tried to show, most of his more fundamental and principled arguments are far from convincing. Some of the arguments are not based on scientific arguments. This is true not only for the estimate of the resources needed for a WCHR but also for the suggestion that a WCHR should be stripped of the legally binding effect of its judgments. What is certainly not correct is that a future WCHR would vest ultimate power in the hands of a tiny coterie of judges, which would be barely compatible with the values of the rule of law, democracy, and separation of powers. The opposite is true. After careful analysis of Philip Alston's arguments, the conviction remains that in the end a WCHR is a truly excellent idea, even if our time of global human rights crises seems not yet ripe for such a fundamental reform.

References

Alston P (2013) A world court for human rights is not a good idea. Available at http://justsecurity. org/2796/world-court-human-rights-good-idea. Accessed 28 Jan 2018

Alston P (2014a) Against a world court of human rights, working paper no 31–71 of October 2013 at the New York University School of Law. Reprinted in Ethics & International Affairs 28(2):197–212

Alston P (2014b) A truly bad idea: a world court for human rights. Available at https://www. opendemocracy.net/openglobalrights-blog/philip-alston/truly-bad-idea-world-court-for-human-rights. Accessed 28 Jan 2018

Alston P, Tessitore J (2014) Interview with Philip Alston on a world court for human rights. Available at https://www.ethicsandinternationalaffairs.org/2014/eia-interview-with-philip-alston-on-a-world-court-for-human-rights. Accessed 28 Jan 2018

BBC News (2012) Prisoners will not get the vote, says David Cameron. Available at http://www. bbc.com/news/uk-politics-20053244. Accessed 22 Feb 2018

Cassese A (2012) Realizing utopia: the future of international law. Oxford University Press, Oxford

Devereux A (2002) Australia and the international scrutiny of civil and political rights: an analysis of Australia's negotiating policies 1946–1966. Aust Yearb Int Law 22:47–52

European Court of Human Rights (2005) Hirst v UK, No. 74025/01, Judgement of the Grand Chamber of 6 October 2005

Frowein J (2002) Provisional measures by the international court of justice, the La Grand case. ZAÖRVR 62(1–2):55–60

International Commission of Jurists (2011) Towards a world court of human rights: questions and answers, supporting paper to the 2011 report of the panel on human dignity, Geneva

International Court of Justice (1993) Genocide case (Bosnia and Herzegovina v Yugoslavia), provisional measures, order of 13 Sept 1993, I.C.J. Reports 1993, at 325

International Court of Justice (2001) La Grand case (Germany v United States), judgment of 27 June 2001, I.C.J. Reports 2001, at 466

International Court of Justice (2016). Annual report. UN Doc. A/71/4 of 11 Aug 2016

Kirkpatrick J (2014) A modest proposal: a global court of human rights. J Hum Rights 13(2):230–248. https://doi.org/10.1080/14754835.2013.824288

Kozma J, Nowak M, Scheinin M (2010) A world court of human rights: consolidated statute and commentary. NWV, Wien

Leach P, Paraskeva C, Uzelak G (2009) International human rights & fact finding: an analysis of the fact-finding missions conducted by the European Commission and European Court of Human Rights. London Metropolitan University, London

Li T (2017) The establishment of a world court of human rights and the design of its complementarity jurisdiction. Doctoral Thesis at Vienna University

Nowak M (2007) The need for a world court of human rights. IIRLR 7(1):251–259

Nowak M (2009) Eight reasons why we need a world court of human rights. In: Alfredsson G, Grimheden J, Ramacharan B, de Zayas A (eds) International human rights monitoring mechanisms – essays in honour of Jakob Th. Möller, vol 2. Brill, Leiden, pp 695–706

Nowak M (2012a) It's time for a world court of human rights. In: Bassiouni C, Schabas W (eds) New challenges to the UN human rights machinery – what future for the UN treaty body system and the human rights council procedures? Intersentia, Cambridge, pp 17–34

Nowak M (2012b) On the creation of a world court of human rights. Nat Taiwan Univ Law Rev 7(1):257–291

Nowak M (2013a) A new world court of human rights: a role for international humanitarian law? In: Kolb R, Gaggioli G (eds) Research handbook on human rights and humanitarian law. Edward Elgar, Cheltenham, pp 531–539

Nowak M (2013b) Comments on the UN high commissioner's proposals aimed at strengthening the UN human rights treaty body system. NQHR 31(1):3–8

Nowak M (2014) The right of victims of human rights violations to a remedy: the need for a world
    court of human rights. NJHR 32(1):3–17
Panel of Eminent Persons. Protecting dignity: an agenda for human rights, www.UDHR60.ch.
    Accessed 28 Jan 2018
Ssenyonjo M (2016) Economic, social and cultural rights in international law, 2nd edn.
    Oxford, Hart
Trechsel S (2004) A world court for human rights? Northwest J Int Hum Rights 1. Available at
    https://scholarlycommons.law.northwestern.edu/cgi/viewcontent.cgi?article=1002&context=njihr.
    Accessed 28 Jan 2018
UN Commission on Human Rights, Draft resolution for an International Court on Human Rights /
    submitted by the representative of Australia, UN Doc. E/CN.4/15, UN 5 Feb 1947
UN General Assembly Resolution 60/147 of 16 Dec 2005

National Human Rights Institutions

Kirsten Roberts Lyer

Contents

Introduction 292
NHRI Terminology and Typology 293
Origins, Mandate, and Functions of NHRIs 295
The Paris Principles and the Sub-Committee on Accreditation 296
International Engagement 300
Regional Organizations 304
Achievements and Challenges 306
Azerbaijan 306
Venezuela 307
Burundi 308
Conclusion 311
References 313

Abstract

Improving the national implementation of international human rights standards has long been a goal of the UN human rights system. This chapter discusses the potential and challenges of National Human Rights Institutions (NHRI) as an institutional connection between the national level and international human rights mechanisms. Established under the UN Paris Principles (1993) and encouraged by the UN as promoters and protectors of human rights, NHRIs' prominence has been increasing since the adoption of the Paris Principles. NHRIs have shown that they have great potential as partners in the domestic implementation of international human rights norms, because of their independent access to a wide range of UN and regional human rights mechanisms, coupled with national expertise and a broad mandate to improve human rights domestically. Yet, as state-established

K. Roberts Lyer (✉)
School of Public Policy, Central European University, Budapest, Hungary
e-mail: robertsk@spp.ceu.edu

© Springer Nature Singapore Pte Ltd. 2018
G. Oberleitner (ed.), *International Human Rights Institutions, Tribunals, and Courts*,
International Human Rights, https://doi.org/10.1007/978-981-10-5206-4_24

bodies, they are often approached with a level of cynicism regarding their independence and commitment to human rights. This chapter introduces the origins, roles, and functions of NHRIs and sets out the extent of their engagement with UN human rights mechanisms. Through examples of NHRI practice, it discusses what can go wrong with these institutions as international partners and what tools are available where this happens, particularly focusing on the role of the NHRI peer review process of the Global Alliance of NHRIs' Sub-Committee on Accreditation. Finally, it examines the value of NHRIs as human rights actors and considers some of the challenges they face into the future.

Keywords
National Human Rights Institutions · Paris Principles · Domestic implementation of international human rights standards · Human Rights Council

Introduction

It may at first seem out of place to have a chapter on national institutions in a publication focusing, inter alia, on United Nations (UN) human rights bodies Yet, the UN human rights system relies on the engagement of national-level actors to ensure the viability of its monitoring and oversight as well as the implementation of international human rights standards. The UN cannot rely solely on the reports provided by states on their own compliance, given the possibility for inaccuracy. Neither does it posess the resources to have its own personnel on the ground in every country monitoring human rights implementation. Rather, it relies on local actors to provide it with reliable information on the human rights situation and act as implementing partners. Since the adoption of the Principles relating to the status of national institutions (the "Paris Principles") by the UN General Assembly in 1993, National Human Rights Institutions (NHRIs) have become an accepted part of this international-national human rights cooperation. Importantly, NHRIs can work as a "two-way street," as they have the ability not only to be information providers to the UN human rights system, but they can also actively promote the implementation of international rights norms and recommendations at the national level through their mandated functions.

Having national-level, state-established human rights bodies with a mandate to interact at the international level has been conceptualized and promoted by the UN since its foundation. But it is only since 1993 that NHRIs have come to be seen as a requirement for the domestic human rights architecture. By way of illustration, in the Human Rights Council's Universal Periodic Review (UPR) process, the establishment or strengthening of NHRIs has been mentioned in the review of 190 states out of 193 (UPR Info 2017). The phenomenon of these institutions is now widespread globally. At the time of writing, over 120 countries have an NHRI, 78 of which have been assessed as being in compliance with the Paris Principles (GANHRI 2017a), meaning that they are independent institutions for the promotion and protection of human rights. Given the aforementioned expectation on states to have an NHRI, their prominence and prevalence is likely to increase into the future.

This chapter focuses on the potential and challenges for NHRIs from the perspective of these institutions as a national connection to the international level. The examination in this chapter originates both from research and personal experience working in an NHRI. First, the chapter sets out what NHRIs are and why they were established, as well as how their mandate and functions enable them to be useful partners with the international system. It examines the unique peer-accreditation process undertaken by the international network of NHRIs, which acts as both a developer and a check on these institutions. It also examines some of the formal and practical ways in which NHRIs engage with the international human rights system, demonstrating the extent of their interaction. The chapter then considers some of the main challenges for these institutions and the potential for NHRIs where they work at their best.

NHRI Terminology and Typology

In this chapter, the term NHRIs refers to domestic human rights institutions established by states on the basis of the UN Paris Principles. It necessarily results in generalization to speak about NHRIs as a homogenous group when there are over 120 institutions across almost as many countries (the one NHRI per country rule has the exception of the United Kingdom, which has separate NHRIs for Northern Ireland and Scotland). However, approaching NHRIs as a homogenous group is justifiable, particularly when considering their interaction at the international level, for the reasons that NHRIs are based on a set of standards that set out their specific roles and functions and are assessed by their own international network for compliance with these standards. They also tend to undertake broadly similar activities. Furthermore, NHRIs operate through relatively formally structured networks both regionally and internationally, and are approached by the UN and regional human rights bodies as a homogenous group. Nonetheless, there remains some disagreement over what constitutes an "NHRI." Goodman and Pegram, for example, contended that in 2012, the number of NHRIs globally ranged from 120 to 178 (Goodman and Pegram 2012). In comparison, at this time the Global Alliance of National Human Rights Institutions (GANHRI, formerly the International Coordinating Committee of National Human Rights Institutions) comprised 99 "A," "B," and "C-Status" NHRIs. Sonia Cardenas in her 2003 work on the UN and NHRIs identified 300–500 institutions (Cardenas 2003). This disparity between the numbers of institutions labeled as an NHRI is mainly a result of a lack of agreement on whether or not to classify an institution that meets some but not all of the requirements of the Paris Principles in this way. This chapter focuses on those institutions that have sought and received the highest level of accreditation from GANHRI for their compliance with the Paris Principles, that is, "A-Status" accreditation. Importantly, this designation of "A-Status" for an NHRI is recognized by the UN human rights mechanisms as a verification that the institution is independent of government and acts for the promotion and protection of human rights. These institutions are given a particularly high level of access to UN mechanisms. "A-Status" therefore acts as a mark of legitimacy both internationally and nationally for an NHRI.

Adding to the complexity in identifying what is an NHRI is the different forms they take. Using the Paris Principles as guidelines, governments choose the type of institutions that they will set up. At least in principle, they establish the one that is most closely aligned with the national legal and institutional structure. In reality, governments are likely to also choose a design that fits their political interests rather than exclusively the needs of human rights in the country. In this regard, Linos and Pegram's study of the mandates of NHRIs is a particularly useful source on the different mandates and state choices on NHRI type (Linos and Pegram 2015).

The Paris Principles set out the powers and functions for NHRIs without detailing the form the institution should take. The discretion given to states as to the form of NHRI they set up has resulted in a wide range of different NHRI types. A broad classification of the four main NHRI types is set out in the following table:

Institution type	Examples of countries with "A-Status" NHRI (2017)	Mandate and powers
Human Rights Commissions	Australia, Canada, India, Ireland, New Zealand, Nigeria, Northern Ireland, Scotland, South Africa, Uganda	Multimember board. Broad mandate that includes protection, promotion, and monitoring, through, e.g., reports and inquiries, legislative reviews, awareness, and education
Ombuds Institutions/ Defensor del Pueblo	Argentina, Bolivia, Ecuador, Peru, Poland, Portugal, Spain	Usually single-member leadership (e.g., ombudsperson). Traditionally focusing on handling individual complaints
Human Rights Institutes	Denmark, Germany, Netherlands	Focusing on research, education, and advisory functions, often with a more limited protection mandate
Advisory/ Consultative Committees	France, Greece, Luxembourg, Morocco	Often have a large number of commissioners/board members with an advisory council. Greater emphasis on advisory functions

Even within each of these categories, there are considerable differences in size, mandate, powers, structure, functions, and role in the national and international context among individual NHRIs. Nonetheless, the overall purpose of all Paris Principle-compliant NHRIs is intended to be the promotion and protection of human rights.

As well as diverse forms of NHRIs, the global spread of these institutions means that they operate across a diverse range of state types. To give an example using one measure, the 2012 Economist Intelligence Unit's Democracy Index, it can be seen that in 2014, 48% of states labeled as "full democracies" had an "A-Status" NHRI, as well as 48% of "flawed democracies," 49% of "hybrid regimes," and 22% of "authoritarian regimes." The different state types in which NHRIs operate will inevitably have an impact on their ability to fully exercise their mandate. Yet, while NHRIs operate in a wide range of different national contexts, their basic functions and role remain similar. Furthermore, as will be seen in the final section of this chapter, state type and a challenging national context do not prevent the awarding of "A-Status" nor the undertaking of human rights promotion and protection activities.

It is worth noting here that within NHRI scholarship, there is also a deeper debate about what NHRIs primary function is. Several scholars classify NHRIs as "regulatory agencies" (e.g., Linos and Pegram 2016, Hafner-Burton 2013, Cardenas 2014). While it is the case that the Paris Principles identify an almost regulatory function for NHRIs: "[a]ffirming that priority should be accorded to the development of appropriate arrangements at the national level to *ensure the effective implementation of international human rights standards*" (emphasis added), a designation of NHRIs as purely regulatory bodies is overly restrictive. NHRIs are institutions that should seek to make real improvements for people in their country. They are not merely supervisory, oversight, or monitoring bodies, but have a clear role in *actively* making changes and advancing human rights.

Origins, Mandate, and Functions of NHRIs

While NHRIs in their modern form have been established primarily since 1993, the concept of setting up a national level body to engage with international human rights mechanisms has existed since 1946 (OHCHR 1995). From the earliest stages of the development of the modern human rights framework, it was recognized that more would be needed than the official information from states on their human rights compliance. A proposal was made at the Economic and Social Council (ECOSOC) in 1946, for the Council to suggest to member nations that they would set up information groups or local human rights committees to "transmit periodical information to the Commission on Human Rights on the observance of human rights in their countries, both in their legal systems and their jurisdictional and administrative practice" (ECOSOC 1946). The subsequent ECOSOC Resolution 9 (II) (1946) encouraged states to "consider the desirability" of establishing such bodies for information provision, yet progress on establishing national committees was markedly slow, with evidence of both a lack of interest and of pushback by states against information being transmitted outside the formal channels of government.

Several further proposals were made between 1946 and 1960, including that local or national committees might have a role in making recommendations on compliance with the Universal Declaration of Human Rights. However, the idea did not gain any serious traction within the UN, and there was almost no discernible progress from the early 1960s through the 1970s. It was not until 1978 that a UN resolution was adopted reviving the concept and providing more detail on the idea of national human rights bodies. General Assembly Resolution 33/46 (1978) on "national institutions for the promotion and protection of human rights" was adopted following a conference held in September 1978 that had produced a set of guidelines on the functions and structure of national institutions (UN General Assembly 1979). These guidelines, which are clear forerunners to the Paris Principles and contain many of the same proposals for functions and structure, resulted in the early adoption by some states of NHRI-type institutions and saw the concept of national-level human rights bodies return to the UN's agenda, where it has remained ever since.

The Paris Principles and the Sub-Committee on Accreditation

While annual resolutions on NHRIs were adopted at the General Assembly after the 1978 guidelines, it was not until 1991 that a more concerted effort toward shaping national institutions was made. As is clear from reading these resolutions and the reports of the secretary general between 1979 and 1991, what constituted a national institution for the protection of human rights was still very much a subject of debate. In October 1991, a workshop on National Institutions for the Promotion and Protection of Human Rights was held in Paris (ECOSOC 1991). This workshop adopted a series of recommendations and a list of principles – the Paris Principles – which were eventually adopted without amendment by the UN General Assembly. As described by the GANHRI Sub-Committee on Accreditation, the Paris Principles provide "a broad normative framework for the status, structure, mandate, composition, power and methods of operation of the principal domestic human rights mechanism" (SCA 2017a).

The content of the Paris Principles has been criticized by NHRI scholars and practitioners for many years. Linos and Pegram undertook a review of the drafting of the Principles that provides some explanation as to why this is the case. They concluded that "a handful of participants – who did not represent states – made decisions about what to include and exclude in three days and with very limited information" (Linos and Pegram 2016). The lack of attention paid by states to the subsequent adoption of the Paris Principles is evident even from their text, which includes a typographical error. Moreover, the text of the Principles is lacking in detail that would sufficiently indicate what these institutions should be in practice, and the Principles leave a wide margin to states in terms of what form the institution should take. Murray's 2007 assessment of NHRIs perhaps best sums up the view taken by most NHRI scholars and practitioners: "while [the Paris Principles] are an appropriate starting point, they focus more on factors relevant to the establishment of such bodies, rather than how they perform once created and how they are perceived by others" (Murray 2007). In recognition of the shortcomings of the Paris Principles, considerable effort has been made by NHRIs themselves to elaborate on their contents. It is worth discussing in some detail here the role of the peer review process for accrediting NHRIs for their compliance with the Paris Principles, which has shaped the development of NHRIs as well as the understanding of the content of the Principles.

Following the adoption of the Paris Principles in 1993, the then-existing NHRIs created a network, the International Coordinating Committee of NHRIs, incorporating regional networks in Africa, the Asia-Pacific, the Americas, and Europe. The International Coordinating Committee became a legal entity under Swiss law in 2008, when it also adopted a written statute (Roberts 2013). In 2016, it changed its name to GANHRI. Pursuant to its statute, this international network acts as a coordinating body, including for NHRI interaction and cooperation with the UN, and promotes the establishment and strengthening of NHRIs (GANHRI 2017b).

The GANHRI Sub-Committee on Accreditation is arguably the most important feature of the international NHRI coordinating body. This Sub-Committee acts as a guarantor and overseer of NHRIs' compliance with the Paris Principles. The Sub-Committee is made up of a rotating panel of members of four "A-Status"

NHRIs – one from each of the four NHRI regional groups – and assesses and 'grades" NHRIs for their compliance with the Paris Principles. NHRIs can be given either "A-Status," meaning that that they are fully compliant with the Paris Principles, or "B-Status" meaning that they are partially compliant (GANHRI 2017c). A "non-compliant," or "C-Status," was used at one time but is no longer actively applied.

This peer review system does not operate in isolation among NHRIs, however. Illustrating the close connection between the UN and these institutions, the Sub-Committee's assessment that an NHRI is fully in compliance with the Paris Principles brings with it a higher level of access for that NHRI within the UN system, including the right, for example, to make statements before the Human Rights Council. The Sub-Committee's recommendations have also been used by international bodies such as UN treaty bodies and the Human Rights Council as a basis on which to call on member states to strengthen their NHRIs. "A-Status" therefore brings with it a particular level of access and recognition at the international level to independently engage with UN human rights system, as well as an internationally recognized stamp of approval.

Regular periodic accreditation by the Sub-Committee takes place once every 5 years. The NHRI must submit a copy of its establishing instrument, an outline of its organizational structure including staff and annual budget, and its most recently published annual report, and fill out "a detailed statement showing how it complies with the Paris Principles as well as any respects in which it does not so comply and any proposals to ensure compliance" (GANHRI 2017b). A hearing is then held at the premesis of the Office of the High Commissioner for Human Rights (OHCHR) in Geneva, where the NHRI under review discusses its application with the Sub-Committee, usually via teleconference. In addition to hearing the NHRI under review, the Sub-Committee routinely hears from the relevant OHCHR desk officer regarding the activities of the NHRI. The Sub-Committee may also receive written submissions from NGOs and civil society organizations. Following this hearing, a recommendation regarding the NHRI's accreditation status is sent to the 16-member GANHRI bureau, which comprises four "A-Status" NHRIs from each of the four regional groups, and then ultimately to the plenary meeting held annually, usually in Geneva, where all "A-Status" NHRIs have a vote on the adoption of the Sub-Committee's report (GANHRI 2017c). Article 16.2 of the GANHRI Statute also allows for special reviews of NHRI accreditation in cases where the circumstances of the NHRI have changed in such a way as to impact its continued compliance with the Paris Principles. Examples of this are given later in this chapter.

When the Sub-Committee provides its assessment of an NHRI, it is important to note that while the recommendations are addressed to the NHRI, they are often issues that the government must rectify. The accreditation process is thus somewhat unusual, given that the NHRI has not been responsible for its own establishment nor for many of the issues that the Sub-Committee highlights as concerns, such as its basis in national legislation, the procedure for the appointment of members and staff, and size of its budget. The Sub-Committee recognizes that NHRIs are generally reliant on the government to make changes in formal areas such as its mandate or budget. However, the Sub-Committee expects that its recommendations will be used by the NHRI to lobby the government or parliament for changes or improvements. Indeed, the Sub-Committee uses the level of effort put in by the NHRI to improve its own situation as a benchmark for the NHRI's legitimacy, as it shows the NHRIs desire to be a properly functioning institution. Overall, the peer review process as an elaboration of the Paris Principles thus operates as an important interpreter of the Principles and a regular check on their implementation by states.

The Sub-Committee's application of the Paris Principles to NHRIs over the course of many years has resulted in the development of a set of General Observations, which interpret and elaborate on the requirements of the Principles. The Sub-Committee has also categorized the requirements of the Paris Principles into two levels: "essential requirements" and "practices that directly promote…compliance." The essential requirements are:

1.1. The establishment of NHRIs
1.2. Human rights mandate
1.3. Encouraging ratification or accession to international human rights instruments
1.4. Interaction with the international human rights system
1.5. Cooperation with other human rights bodies
1.6. Recommendations by NHRIs
1.7. Ensuring pluralism of the NHRI
1.8. Selection and appointment of the decision-making body of NHRIs
1.9. Political representatives on NHRIs
1.10. Adequate funding of NHRIs
1.11. Annual reports of NHRIs (SCA 2017a)

Practices considered as directly promoting compliance with the Paris Principles, but not essential, are:

2.1. Guarantee of tenure for members of the NHRI decision-making body
2.2. Full-time members of a NHRI
2.3. Guarantee of functional immunity
2.4. Recruitment and retention of NHRI staff
2.5. Staffing of the NHRI by secondment
2.6. NHRIs during the situation of a coup d'état or a state of emergency
2.7. Limitation of power of NHRIs due to national security
2.8. Administrative regulation of NHRIs
2.9. Assessing NHRIs as National Preventive and National Monitoring Mechanisms
2.10. The quasi-judicial competency of NHRIs (complaints handling) (SCA 2017a)

In its assessment of NHRIs over the past 10 years, the Sub-Committee has shown itself to be most concerned with issues around the establishment, mandate, board, staffing, budget, and external engagement of NHRIs. The following table illustrates what an NHRI should look like in terms of its structure and functions, by summarizing the Sub-Committee's main areas of concern and the requirements for each area, as elaborated through its General Observations.

Element	Requirement
Establishment	In legislation or the national constitution (not by an executive instrument) with sufficient detail specifying "role, functions, powers, funding, and lines of accountability, as well as the appointment mechanism for, and terms of office of, its members" (SCA 2017a)
Mandate	Should be broad, covering the promotion and protection of all human rights and with freedom to consider any human rights issue
Functions	Promotion of human rights, through education, outreach, media, publications, training, and capacity building activities, as well as by advising and assisting the government and state bodies on human rights compliance. Protection of human rights, through the prevention of human rights abuses, including through "monitoring, inquiring, investigating, and reporting on human rights violations and may include individual complaint handling" (SCA 2017a)
Members and head of institution	The appointment process should include the following: "(a) Publicize vacancies broadly (b) Maximize the number of potential candidates from a wide range of societal groups (c) Promote broad consultation and/or participation in the application, screening, selection, and appointment process (d) Assess applicants on the basis of predetermined, objective, and publicly available criteria (e) Select members to serve in their own individual capacity rather than on behalf of the organization they represent" (SCA 2017a) The board must have security of tenure; it should have fixed terms, and any dismissal or forced resignation may be cause for review of accreditation status
Staffing	The institution should have the ability to appoint its own staff, not seconded from government departments or ministries, through an open and transparent process. The NHRI should determine its staffing structure and the skills needed. Where there are seconded staff, senior-level posts should not be filled by secondees, and the number of seconded staff should not exceed 25% of the total workforce of the NHRI barring "exceptional or relevant" circumstances
Budget	Resources must be sufficient to allow the institution to undertake its mandated functions, the budget should be separate and secure and one over which the NHRI has management and control. The Sub-Committee on Accreditation has determined that this as a minimum should include the allocation of funds for adequate premises (at least its head office), salaries and benefits awarded to its staff comparable to civil service salaries and conditions, remuneration of members of the decision-making body (where appropriate), and the establishment of well-functioning communications systems including telephone and the Internet (SCA 2017a)
Broad engagement	The NHRI should actively engage with a broad range of national stakeholders including relevant human rights bodies and with the international human rights system

In practice, the type of activities undertaken by NHRIs includes individual complaint handling, legislative review, monitoring and making recommendations on human rights issues in the country, education and training, reporting to UN treaty bodies and other international and regional human rights mechanisms, and visiting places of detention (OHCHR 2009). The extent to which an NHRI undertakes these activities will differ depending on its mandate and the decisions of its leadership in respect of national human rights priorities.

International Engagement

Since the adoption of the Paris Principles, the UN has not just encouraged the establishment of NHRIs by member states but has promoted NHRIs as independent partners and stakeholders in a range of UN mechanisms, including with the Human Rights Council, treaty bodies, and special procedures mandate holders. This role has been gradually increasing, and as Pegram puts it, "NHRIs have been granted unprecedented access to a growing set of UN venues and contexts within which they inform decision-making and about human rights policy" (Pegram 2015). This level of access is in part a recognition of the potential of NHRIs to both input into the international monitoring system and to promote the implementation of international recommendations and standards at the national level. To understand the extent to which NHRIs engage with the international human rights system, particularly at the UN, this section details some of the practical involvement of NHRIs, including the active engagement of NHRIs in expanding their own role. In this regard, Sidoti has described the emergence of a "bottom-up" relationship between NHRIs and the UN as part of the maturation of NHRIs and their work (Sidoti 2012).

The Paris Principles list four separate requirements in relation to the international engagement of NHRIs, including that they should promote the harmonization of national legislation and practice with international human rights standards, encourage the ratification of international instruments, contribute to the UN and regional human rights reporting process, and cooperate with the UN and regional human rights organizations. The Sub-Committee on Accreditation considers interaction with the international human rights system as essential for NHRIs and encourages NHRIs to seek an explicit reference to international engagement in its legislation. For example, in the Sub-Committee's examination of the NHRI of Bosnia and Herzegovina in November 2016, it called for the NHRI "to advocate for changes in its enabling law to explicitly allow the institution to interact with the regional and international human rights system." The Sub-Committee also specified the particular means for effective engagement with the international system including submitting parallel reports, making statements at the Human Rights Council, assisting and participating in visits of UN experts, and monitoring and promoting the implementation of international recommendations (SCA November 2016, see SCA 2017b). The NHRI networks actively encourage independent interaction with UN mechanisms, both via GANHRI and through the regional networks' secretariats, particularly in Africa, Europe, and the Asia-Pacific. The Sub-Committee on Accreditation also plays an important role in advising NHRIs on, and regulating the activities of NHRIs in relation to, the international human rights system. For example, in its November 2016 review of Costa Rica, the Sub-Committee noted that it had received "concerning correspondence from the Special Rapporteur on extreme poverty and human rights alleging that the [NHRI] has not fully engaged and cooperated with some United Nations mechanisms and bodies." While the NHRI disputed the allegation, the Sub-Committee nonetheless reiterated the role of NHRIs should have in its interaction with international mechanisms:

> While it is appropriate for governments to consult with NHRIs in the preparation of a state's reports to human rights mechanisms, NHRIs should neither prepare the country report nor should they report on behalf of the government. NHRIs must maintain their independence and, where they have the capacity to provide information to human rights mechanisms, do so in their own right. NHRIs should not participate as part of a government delegation during the Universal Periodic Review, during reviews before the Treaty Bodies, or in other international mechanisms where independent participation rights for NHRIs exist. Where independent participation rights for NHRIs do not exist in a particular fora and an NHRI chooses to participate as part of a state delegation, the manner of their participation must clearly distinguish them as an independent NHRI. (SCA November 2016, see SCA 2017b)

Promoting interaction with the international system is a common area for recommendations by the Sub-Committee to NHRIs, whether through encouraging the NHRI to participate, criticizing it for not submitting shadow reports, or challenging it for failing to sufficiently differentiate and distance itself from its government's engagement.

Within UN human rights fora, there has been a clear interest in promoting NHRI involvement. This is particularly the case in Geneva, likely aided by the presence of the OHCHR, which has been the chief institutional promoter of NHRIs. The OHCHR has a specific unit that works with NHRIs, and it supports the presence of the GANHRI Geneva representative and annual plenary meetings, as well as acting as the secretariat for the Sub-Committee on Accreditation. In a 2015 evaluation of the work of the OHCHR with NHRIs, the following forms of institutional engagement were identified: supporting the creation of NHRIs, monitoring and advising to promote compliance with the Paris Principles, capacity building, facilitating the intervention of NHRIs with the international human rights system, and strengthening partnerships within UN agencies and programs, supporting GANHRI and regional mechanisms (Jessup and Kounte 2015).

At the UN General Assembly, NHRIs are recognized through the adoption of regular resolutions, which reaffirm the importance of NHRIs, albeit often in rather vague terms. Illustrating how NHRIs act as promoters of their own institutions, and gain international institutional support for their mandates and functioning, GANHRI has been active in lobbying for support for these resolutions. In 2011, for example, the General Assembly adopted Resolution 66/169 on NHRIs, co-sponsored by more than 80 countries, reaffirming the importance of developing such institutions and the contribution they make to promoting and protecting human rights. GANHRI (then the International Coordinating Committee) undertook advocacy to support both the content and adoption of the resolution. In particular, it was invited to submit its preliminary comments and objectives to the main sponsor of the resolution (International Coordinating Committee 2011). NHRIs also supported the adoption of the resolution through interaction with their own ministries of foreign affairs, calling on them to support the resolution.

It is at the Human Rights Council, however, where NHRIs have been perhaps the most prominent. Sidoti describes NHRI engagement with the Human Rights Council as "full and broad," noting the success NHRIs have had in gaining access to the mechanism (Sidoti 2012). In its Resolution 60/251 (2006) establishing the Council, the UN General Assembly specifically urged the Council to work in close cooperation with NHRIs, a requirement reflected in Human Rights Council Resolution 5/1 (2007) (Human Rights Council 2007) and this engagement has been increasing since that time. "A-Status" NHRIs are entitled to submit documents and make oral and written statements to the Council on any matter on its agenda. NHRIs have a designated physical seating space in the Council chamber, separate from NGOs and governments. They are also able to, and regularly do, hold parallel events on the margins of the Council meetings.

GANHRI, as well as individual NHRIs, have used this access to make submissions and statements on a wide range of substantive topics such as human rights education and training, transitional justice, the rights of persons with disabilities, human rights and countering terrorism, violence against women, internally displaced persons, and sexual orientation and gender identity. These statements often highlight the role of NHRIs can play in relation the particular thematic issue under discussion – something that is not always well known either nationally or internationally. Their statements also generally include proposals for enhancing the role of NHRIs at the national level and the possibilities for NHRIs to contribute to the improvement of the implementation of the relevant international standards. For example, in its 2016 statement to the high-level panel discussion on the 5th Anniversary of the United Nations Declaration on Human Rights Education and Training, GANHRI welcomed the recognition of the "enhanced strategic role of NHRIs" in the resolution, "which includes working structurally for the advancement of effective policies on human rights education." Specifically, it noted "the potential of NHRIs to work across their mandates, including: coordination and cooperation among [human rights education] stakeholders, giving advice to parliamentarians and responsible education authorities as well as monitoring of human rights education." The statement also underlines the potential for NHRIs to "have an eminent and far more sustainable impact on the integration of human rights education in the formal education sector than is currently the case in many States." Its three proposals encouraged states to invite NHRIs to support the implementation of human rights education in the formal sector, including monitoring human rights education; providing advice to parliament; coordinating and consulting of training programs, "serving as independent advisers to Parliaments and responsible educational authorities on human rights education, formal, non-formal and informal," and monitoring and data collection related to target 4.7 of the Sustainable Development Goals (GANHRI 2016). This statement is representative of the type of intervention regularly made by GANHRI. In terms of the added value of NHRIs, it is worth emphasizing that because GANHRI statements represent national-level knowledge and expertise from almost 80 countries from every region of the world, their pronouncements can have substantial weight. NHRIs have significant potential to further develop their prominence as a collective voice for human rights at the international level through this kind of engagement.

As well as this type of specific intervention highlighting the role that NHRIs can and do play, NHRIs have intervened on issues regarding the relationship between NHRIs and the UN human rights mechanisms – including the role and functions of NHRIs and the need to strengthen international mechanisms such as the treaty bodies and the special procedures of the Council (International Coordinating Committee 2007, 2012, Meuwissen 2013). NHRIs have also sought to both support and develop international human rights standards at the Council. For example, GANHRI was particularly active on the issue of standards on business and human rights. It set up a Working Group on the topic in 2009 and made a number of submissions to the development of the Framework for Business and Human Rights (the "Ruggie Framework"), as well as advocating for the role of NHRIs within the Framework, resulting in the Human Rights Council explicitly recognizing NHRIs in Resolution 17/4 (2011b) on human rights and transnational corporations and other business enterprises. The NHRI engagement on the business and human rights agenda illustrates NHRIs' potential as developers of new international human rights standards, particularly given the global reach of the GANHRI network and NHRIs value in implementation of new standards domestically.

NHRIs have also been successful at promoting a greater role for their institutions at the Human Rights Council. During the 2011 review of the work of the Council, their advocacy efforts resulted in increased prominence for NHRIs in the Universal Periodic Review (UPR) process, the main human rights review undertaken by the Council, with the inclusion of a specific section in the UPR OHCHR stakeholder's information document for the submissions of "A-Status" NHRIs. This was an important change for NHRIs as it differentiates them from society organizations and increases their prominence, as the summary of the NHRI submission is the first section in the document. NHRIs also became entitled under Resolution 16/21 (2011a Human Rights Council), to speak directly after the state under review, during the adoption of the UPR outcome report by the Council. And a procedure for facilitating NHRIs to make statements by video link or video statement was introduced. These changes have increased the visibility of "A-Status" NHRIs in the UPR process. Generally, NHRI engagement with the UPR sees them providing a critical assessment of their state's compliance with the relevant international human rights standards. Importantly, however, NHRIs also have the function of monitoring and promoting the implementation of the UPR recommendations domestically, meaning that their engagement with the UPR is not limited to the provision of information.

Another particularly active area of international engagement for NHRIs is in relation to the UN treaty bodies. NHRIs directly contribute information to the treaty body process through the submission of "parallel" or "shadow" reports on compliance with the treaty in their country. An evaluation of OHCHR support to NHRIs found that in 2010, of 80 countries examined that had an NHRI, 49 NHRI shadow reports were submitted (Jessup and Kounte 2015). NHRIs also have the opportunity to meet directly with the treaty body to express their concerns and propose their recommendations. Many of the treaty bodies for their part have formalized interaction with NHRIs. The Committee on the Elimination of Racial Discrimination includes NHRIs in the hearing process, allowing NHRIs to speak during the state hearing (CERD working methods 2017) and has promoted state engagement with NHRIs (CERD 2009). The Committee on the Rights of the Child has elaborated working methods specifically encouraging NHRIs to provide reports, and the Committee can meet in private with NHRIs at their request (CRC working methods 2017 see also CRC 2002). The Human Rights Committee has also invited NHRIs to submit reports on the ICCPR, and NHRIs may make oral statements to the Committee during the first morning meeting of every plenary session (HRC working methods 2017). And the Committee on the Elimination of Discrimination against Women has issued a statement on its relationship with NHRIs and the roles of NHRIs in monitoring and protecting the rights of women (CEDAW 2008) and promoted the establishment of NHRIs (CEDAW 2010). Since 2006, GANHRI has also participated in the annual inter-committee meeting of the treaty bodies and special procedure mandate holders. As with the UPR process, NHRI engagement with the treaty bodies is more than just information provision. Their mandates task them with promoting and protecting the rights contained in the UN conventions, including through proposals for legislative amendments, training and education programs, as well as using their protection mandates to prevent abuses.

Meeting with the NHRI has also become a regular feature of the in-country visits of the UN special procedure mandate holders. NHRIs provide independent information on the national situation separate from the state and civil society. "A-Status" NHRIs are also entitled to intervene immediately after the state under consideration by a report of a mandate holder. Furthermore, "A-Status" NHRIs are able to nominate candidates to these positions, and several NHRI leaders have become mandate holders themselves.

While it is not possible to go into detail on every example of UN-NHRI engagement in this chapter, it is worth finally also noting that the UN Development Programme (UNDP) undertakes extensive work with NHRIs both on the ground through its field presences and strategically at a policy level. For example, it has produced a number of materials jointly with the Asia-Pacific Forum of NHRIs, the Asia-Pacific regional NHRI network's secretariat, including a capacity assessment manual (Asia Pacific Forum and UNDP 2014), and at the time of writing, there is an ongoing 18-month partnership agreement between the Forum and the UNDP Asia-Pacific Regional Hub, with outcomes including training and an international conference on issues of sexual orientation and gender identity (Asia-Pacific Forum 2017).

Regional Organizations

It is important to at least briefly note here that there is also considerable interaction between NHRIs and regional human rights bodies. In Europe, the Council of Europe gives a broader definition to national institutions for the promotion and protection of human rights, working with "National Human Rights Structures" that include national thematic ombudspersons, administrative ombudspersons, and equality bodies that may or may not be based on the requirements of the Paris Principles. The Council of Europe Commissioner for Human Rights interacts with NHRIs and ombudsmen that "comply with the Paris Principles and abide by the Council of Europe's values" (CoE Commissioner 2017). The Commissioner supports NHRI independence where they exist and offers technical assistance in their establishment. The Parliamentary Assembly of the Council of Europe has issued a number of resolutions in support of NHRIs both institutionally and on thematic issues. The Committee of Ministers overseeing the execution of judgments of the European Court of Human Rights has also identified NHRIs as important partners in the implementation of judgments and in improving the human rights situation nationally, with the aim of reducing the volume of judgments. The Organization for Security and Co-operation in Europe (OSCE), the EU's Fundamental Rights Agency, and the European Commission also all have engagement with NHRIs, including involving them in research and human rights monitoring.

In the Americas, the Organization of American States has issued regular resolutions on NHRIs, actively promoting their establishment and granting speaking and participation rights to "A-Status" institutions (OAS 2009). Article 26 of the African Charter on Human and Peoples' Rights explicitly recognizes that states parties have a duty to "allow the establishment and improvement of appropriate national institutions entrusted with the promotion and protection of the rights and freedoms guaranteed by the present Charter" (ACHPR 1982). In furtherance of this provision, NHRIs have had observer status at the African Commission on Human and Peoples' Rights since 1998 pursuant to Resolution 31/XXIV.

While the above survey cannot cover all of the ways in which NHRIs engage with the international human rights system, it nonetheless provides a sense of the breadth and depth of their interaction. It also illustrates how the formalization of NHRI interaction with UN mechanisms means that "A-Status" equals a high degree of international acceptance. The credibility of NHRIs within the UN context rests on "A-Status" being a meaningful reflection of the legitimacy of the institution. Overall, the UN views NHRIs as a means of improving its own human rights monitoring mechanisms, through providing alternative, authoritative, national-level information and improving the connection between the state and the UN on human rights issues and domestic implementation. For NHRIs, it is an opportunity to enlist the support of the international human rights mechanisms to make positive changes to the human rights situation in their country. Yet there is a paradoxical aspect to this engagement. On the one hand, the information from and involvement of NHRIs can be a significant boost to the awareness and understanding of the human rights situation on the ground, thus increasing the likelihood of positive change through effective and targeted international recommendations. On the other hand, the level of access given to NHRIs and reliance on them as an independent national human rights body means that where they are not fulfilling their duties toward the promotion and protection of human rights, for example, by denying the existence of human rights abuses, they can potentially lessen the likelihood of action at the international level.

In terms of the existence of NHRIs, this latter issue is a significant one, as it may undermine the entire concept of these institutions as independent voices on human rights.

Achievements and Challenges

NHRIs face many challenges individually and collectively. One of the most significant challenges arises from the state-NHRI relationship. While their position as a state body gives them the legitimacy and ability to promote and protect human rights, it also means that NHRIs are highly dependent upon the state in which they operate and particularly on the government of the day. This dependency arises in particular because the state, either through parliament or the executive, determines the legal mandate, selects the members and leadership, and sets the budget of the institution. This control over NHRIs can have a devastating impact on the proper functioning of the institution, with a knock-on effect on human rights protections in the country.

The problematic aspect of the state-NHRI relationship can manifest itself in a number of ways that are particularly relevant for NHRI engagement at the international level. The NHRI can be censored by a state that does not wish it to act independently. This can happen through the NHRI avoiding challenging or contentious issues from concerns about the government's response (self-censorship) or through the state "punishing" the NHRI by cutting its funding or changing its leadership or mandate where it does not like the activities of the institution (state censorship). State censorship can also involve the government and/or parliament moving slowly in the implementation of recommendations of the institution, or choosing to ignore them altogether, severely undermining the NHRIs' authority. Another challenge that arises is where the NHRI is a human rights promoter and protector on paper only, undertaking few activities. This can occur where the NHRI has been established in technical compliance with the Paris Principles, but given insufficient powers, budget, or staff (in numbers, expertise, or both), or where the leadership of the NHRI is de facto loyal to the government and unwilling to challenge it. A combination of these elements can result in institutions that fail to act for the promotion and protection of human rights and support a repressive regime. The three examples below, of the NHRIs in Azerbaijan, Burundi, and Venezuela, demonstrate instances of where these situations have arisen and highlight how this causes problems for NHRI engagement at the international level.

Azerbaijan

In the past number of years, there has been a serious crackdown against human rights and human rights defenders in Azerbaijan, which has been widely criticized by the international community. Since 2009, concerns had been expressed about the independence of the "A-Status" Azerbaijan NHRI, the Human Rights Commissioner of the Republic of Azerbaijan, with the UN Committee Against Torture questioning whether the institution had sufficient independence to be the National Preventive Mechanism under the Optional Protocol to the Convention Against Torture. Despite reviews by the Sub-Committee on Accreditation in 2011 and 2012, the NHRI kept its "A-Status" and retained it even through international concerns regarding its low level of engagement during a serious deterioration in the human rights situation from 2014. In 2017, the Sub-Committee recommended downgrading the institution due to information received on its "unwillingness to effectively engage on serious human rights violations, including those relating to torture and conditions of detention, arbitrary detention, freedom of expression, and the protection of human rights defenders." The Sub-Committee noted that the Committee Against Torture had again expressed concern in 2015 that the NHRI had not been effective in addressing issues of ill-treatment and human rights abuses in places of detention and that the Human Rights Committee had expressed similar concerns in 2016. In addition, civil society organizations reported to the Sub-Committee on the NHRI's "failure to respond to gross human rights violations, including by remaining silent in relation to government crackdowns on civil society, the jailing of leading human rights defenders." The Sub-Committee was of the view that the NHRI "has not spoken out in a manner that promotes protection for human rights in response to credible allegations of serious human rights violation having been committed by government authorities." At the time of writing, the NHRI has challenged this decision and the outcome is awaited in late 2017 (SCA March 2017, see SCA 2017b).

Venezuela

In May 2013, the Venezuela NHRI, the Defensoría del Pueblo, was reaccredited with "A-Status," despite the Sub-Committee on Accreditation noting that the NHRI had not taken a strong position on major human rights issues. One year later, in March 2014, the Sub-Committee indicated its intention to undertake a special review of the NHRI because of "actions taken or not taken, and statements made or not made" by the NHRI and tweets made by the NHRI. These tweets included a statement by the then head of the NHRI that she was the "daughter of Commander Chavez" (SCA March 2015, see SCA 2017b). The NHRI had also supported legislation that had been criticized by human rights groups, such as laws allowing the use of deadly force at demonstrations, which the NHRI said were in place to protect human rights at demonstrations. Some NGOs in Venezuela were highly critical of the NHRI, and a coalition of NGOs wrote to the Sub-Committee requesting the downgrading of the NHRI and highlighting issues they contended evidenced the lack of independence and impartiality of the NHRI (Mama Tierra 2014). The UN Human Rights Committee and Committee Against Torture both also questioned the independence of the NHRI. In March 2015, the Sub-Committee recommended that the NHRI be downgraded to "B-Status" because the NHRI had remained silent on serious human rights issues, including trials of civilians in military courts and threats by the president against trade union leaders, the withdrawal of Venezuela from the American Convention on Human Rights, and the continued arbitrary detention of a judge. The Sub-Committee's report details numerous instances of the NHRI acting as a supporter for the actions of the government, rather than as an independent human rights body. Despite the appointment of a new head of the NHRI, the Sub-Committee in May 2016 found more indications of inaction by the NHRI and determined that the NHRI was "not prepared to speak out in a manner that promotes respect for human rights in response to credible allegations of serious human rights abuses having been committed by government authorities" (SCA May 2016, see SCA 2017b). Because of this failure to demonstrate independence, the NHRI was downgraded to "B-Status" at the end of 2016.

Burundi

In November 2016, the Sub-Committee reviewed the "A-Status" NHRI of Burundi, the *Commission Nationale Indépendante des Droits de l'Homme*, pursuant to Article 16.2 of the GANHRI Statute. In its report, the Sub-Committee noted that it had received information that "raised concerns that the [NHRI] may no longer be operating in full compliance with the Paris Principles," including "actions taken or not taken…since June 2015, in the aftermath of the election in Burundi, and statements made or not made …regarding gross human rights violations in the country." Specifically, the Sub-Committee stated it had received allegations that the NHRI "is perceived as having taken positions that do not demonstrate independence from government; has not taken a position vis-a-vis abuses by security forces and militias in respect of certain gross human rights violations, including arbitrary detention and extrajudicial executions; and has underreported instances of serious human rights violations, including with respect to incidences of torture and the existence of mass graves" (SCA November 2016, see SCA 2017b).

Furthermore, according to a report of the United Nations Independent Investigation on Burundi, the NHRI had also issued only one report since the crisis and that "downplays gross human rights violations by indicating only minimal numbers" (SCA November 2016, see SCA 2017b). Examples of non-compliant activity included a statement by the NHRI urging the International Criminal Court to stop its preliminary examination of alleged human rights violations in Burundi. The chairman of the NHRI was also reported in the media as stating that no international crimes occurred in Burundi between 2015 and 2017. The Sub-Committee concluded that:

> In view of all of the material before it, the SCA is of the view that [the NHRI] has not spoken out in a manner that promotes protection for human rights in response to credible allegations of gross human rights violations having been committed by government authorities. The failure to do so demonstrates a lack of its independence. Therefore, the SCA is of the view that [the NHRI] is acting in a way that has seriously compromised its compliance with the Paris Principles. (SCA November 2016, see SCA 2017b)

The NHRI was scheduled to be downgraded from "A-Status" to "B-Status" in November 2017, failing a demonstration of its compliance with the Paris Principles.

The above examples from Azerbaijan, Venezuela, and Burundi indicate what can go wrong with an NHRI. These types of situations pose a number of challenges for NHRIs individually and collectively, including putting at risk their level of access and engagement with international human rights mechanisms. Instances like these must bring the "A-Status" accreditation into question for members of international expert committees and other observers, as evidenced by the concerns raised by treaty bodies noted above. It also has potentially serious consequences for international scrutiny of the domestic human rights situation, because, particularly in countries with restricted civil society, "A-Status' institutions may be one of the only bodies apart from the government that is able to provide an external assessment. Where that assessment is flawed, it risks giving a false view of the human rights situation in the country, potentially enabling continued human rights abuses, undermining civil society, and giving the international community the impression that little or no action is needed. These examples also highlight a flaw in the NHRI accreditation process, which is that under the GANHRI Statute, NHRIs retain their "A-Status" for a year at least after a proposal to downgrade them, in order to give the NHRI time to evidence their continued compliance with the Paris Principles. The Sub-Committee on Accreditation may extend this 1-year period if it defers consideration of the NHRI's accreditation. In the situation of Venezuela, this meant that from May 2013 to the end of 2016, the NHRI retained its "A-Status" and the privileges that went with it. This included having their submission placed in the first section of the stakeholder's summary for the UPR process on Venezuela in November 2016. Illustrating how problematic this situation can be, the summary of the NHRI's submission gives a largely positive review of the conditions in the country, particularly when compared with the information about serious human rights abuses raised by NGOs in the remainder of the summary. Such situations, where an "A-Status" NHRI is demonstrably unreliable, risk severely undermining the concept of NHRIs as independent human rights bodies.

Yet these three examples also illustrate the remedy that is available where NHRIs fail to promote and protect human rights. They underscore the importance of the peer review process as a means of ensuring that any institution designated as an "NHRI" meets certain standards. The existence of the peer review is evidence of the under-standing that a state-established human rights body would need some independent oversight to ensure that the NHRI was not rubber-stamping the human rights-abusing actions of the state. And the responses by the Sub-Committee on Accred-itation to the above situations demonstrate how that system operates to regulate NHRIs that are not behaving as independent human rights bodies. It is also welcome evidence of the Sub-Committee on Accreditation's attention to the human rights *practice* of NHRIs, which has been increasing in recent years, where previously it focused on a more formalistic compliance by NHRIs with the roles and functions set out in the Paris Principles.

While the three above NHRIs may give a rather gloomy picture of this type of institution, there are on the contrary many examples of NHRIs doing excellent work. Many, if not the vast majority of "A-Status" NHRIs, work for the implementation of international human rights standards, frequently in challenging and at times danger-ous national situations.

The "A-Status" Afghan Independent Human Rights Commission (AIHRC), for example, operates in a country where there is an ongoing conflict, as well as serious human rights issues. In 2015, a bus carrying staff from the Commission struck an explosive device, and two members were killed and six injured (OHCHR 2015). Despite the challenges faced by the NHRI, it has spoken out on the impact of terrorism on human rights as well as the rule of law, education, and access to justice. The Amnesty International in its Annual Report 2016/2017 notes that the NHRI has reported on "thousands of cases in the first six months of [2016], including beatings, killings and acid attacks" (Amnesty International 2016/2017). The NHRI reports that its human rights educational programs were attended by over half a million people, more than 44% of whom were women, in the 13 years prior to the year 1394 (corresponding to the year starting 21 March 2015 in the Gregorian calendar). In the same period, it also presented over 240,000 hours of radio and television and circulated over four million copies of materials. It registered and addressed 32,629 cases of violence against women and 28,184 complaints of human rights violations. It also made 17,489 visits and monitoring missions to detention centers and identified 92 mass graves of war victims (AIHRC 2016). The Special Rapporteur on violence against women commended the Commission for its "commitment and leading role in addressing the issue of violence against women in the country, despite the constraints and challenges it faces" (UN Human Rights Council 2015). The AIHRC has not been without its problems arising from its relationship with the state. In 2013, the government appointed five new commissioners through a process that was considered nontransparent. Furthermore, and unusually for an NHRI, it is almost exclusively reliant on donor funding. Nonetheless, it remains an example of how an NHRI can take action to improve human rights even under severely challenging circumstances.

There are many other examples of positive contributions from NHRIs. The Ukraine NHRI has been active in engaging with the NHRI of the Russian Federation, despite the ongoing conflict between the two countries. This engagement has worked on finding solutions for human rights issues, including identifying solutions such as the transfer of Ukrainian citizens from prisons in Russia-controlled Crimea, as well as issues of arbitrary detention of Ukrainian citizens in Russia. The heads of the two NHRIs have also undertaken joint visits to detention centers in Crimea (Ukrainian Parliament Commissioner 2017). This is a particularly interesting example of NHRIs' potential to facilitate direct contact across borders for the promotion and protection of human rights at a semi-official level and illustrates how NHRIs can act as "human rights diplomats" in conflict situations (Roberts 2011). The Kenya NHRI has been active in promoting equal rights for LGBTI people in a country where 90% of the population believed homosexuality should not be accepted by society (Pew Research 2013) and same-sex sexual activity is illegal (KNCHR 2012). This is just one example of how NHRIs work in promoting international human rights standards at the national level and positively contextualizing international norms. The Philippines NHRI continues to actively promote human rights in the country and condemn the methods used by the government despite the serious threats faced by human rights defenders in the country, following President Duterte's crackdown on drugs in the country since 2016. The Philippine NHRI's state-established status gives additional weight to their voiced concerns and provides a degree of "protection" from government retaliation that NGOs may not have.

These examples can only give a brief sense of the work that NHRIs do; nonetheless, they provide an indication of the positive nature of NHRI activities where they are engaging as independent human rights promoters and protectors. The four examples above highlight how NHRIs promote and protect international human rights standards at the national level. Coupled with the examples of NHRI engagement at the international level described above, they also further demonstrate the value and potential of these institutions as partners for international human rights mechanisms.

Conclusion

NHRIs occupy a unique position in the human rights framework. Although they are state-established institutions, they are nonetheless expected to interact independently with the international human rights system. This role for them was foreseen from the earliest days of the UN, and in 1993, the concept was formalized with the adoption of the Paris Principles. Since then, over 120 countries have established an NHRI. With this increase in numbers has come a rise in prominence and the creation of formal paths for NHRIs to interact with UN institutions.

The potential for NHRIs to be important partners for international human rights mechanisms clearly exists. They provide independent expert information on the human rights situation in a given country; work to improve law, policy, and practice in line with international human rights norms; highlight and challenge abuses; and raise awareness of rights through training and education. They can also be a vital supporter of civil society and NGOs, which are increasingly seeing their space to operate shrink in countries around the world. Their national-level knowledge and expertise enables NHRIs to contextualize international standards at the national level and thus also offers something of a solution to the perceived problem of international organizations and human rights standards as being "imposed" on states from the international level. NHRIs also work, particularly through their networks, to enhance their own role within the international system. Individually and collectively, NHRIs support the operation of the international human rights system.

There is another side to NHRI involvement, however, where the institutions are not acting as independent human rights bodies. As was seen in the examples of the NHRIs of Venezuela, Burundi, and Azerbaijan, poorly functioning institutions can act as a rubber stamp for the human rights non-compliance of the state, distract from serious issues, diminish the role of civil society, and give their expertise to the misapplication of human rights norms. It is thus vital that institutions calling themselves NHRIs are indeed acting in the best interests of human rights for the people in their country.

A major challenge for NHRIs is that they are dependent on the state in which they operate and may be subject to the whims of the government of the day. This means that they can change significantly over time in terms of their leadership, mandate, budget, and functions. Maintaining the legitimacy of the Sub-Committee on Accreditation's process is highly important to ensuring NHRIs retain their access to human rights mechanisms at international level. That the Sub-Committee system is a peer review has both a positive and a negative side. On the positive side, peer institutions are ideally placed to understand the abilities and limitations of NHRIs and have an intimate knowledge of NHRI functioning. On the negative side, there is the potential for colleagues to be unduly lenient on failing institutions out of personal or professional loyalties. The designation of "A-Status" must represent NHRIs that are independently and actively promoting and protecting human rights in their country, and where they are not, the designation needs to be promptly removed. Ensuring that institutions under the NHRI label are in fact independent human rights promotion and protection bodies is critical both to the legitimacy of NHRIs as a group and for human rights protections at the national level. It may be that in the future, the Sub-Committee will need to consider the use of a suspension of status in particularly egregious cases in order to avoid non-compliant NHRIs retaining the legitimating "A-Status" designation.

From the perspective of future research, the overall study of NHRIs has been relatively limited to date. However, this is changing, with more detailed studies emerging in the past few years. These studies, such as those carried out by Linos and Pegram, will allow for an evidence-based understanding of what makes NHRIs effective and what can be done to strengthen them as bodies promoting and protecting human rights. In the broader picture of independent state-based institutions, the Paris Principles' model is an increasingly relied on form: two of the newest international human rights instruments, the Optional Protocol to the Convention Against Torture and the Convention on the Rights of Persons with Disabilities, contain requirements for the establishment of Paris Principle-style mechanisms. The Paris Principles are also increasingly cited for the design of data protection bodies, specialized ombudsman, equality bodies, and other oversight bodies such as judicial councils. This places additional importance on the work of the Sub-Committee on Accreditation in assessing NHRIs and developing the Paris Principles through its General Observations. NHRIs have recognized the inherent weaknesses of the Principles and made considerable efforts to remedy them, and this should be taken into account by institutions seeking to base themselves on the Principles. The NHRI peer assessment model is also one that is worth consideration in the context of other independent oversight and monitoring bodies.

Going forward, it is clear that there is considerable potential from NHRIs that remains untapped, particularly in their collective action at the international level. Their regional and international networks represent a broad cross-regional global consensus, giving their engagement on human rights issues significant weight and credibility. If NHRIs can enhance their collective engagement, they can continue to grow as a strong international voice on human rights.

The main challenge and opportunity for NHRIs going forward is to guard, enhance, and develop their legitimacy as human rights actors. No NHRI does everything right, and some do significant wrongs, but while there is no "silver bullet" that can ensure the fulfillment of human rights at the national level, NHRIs that are committed to improving the human rights situation on the ground have shown themselves to be an important actor in the international and domestic human rights frameworks.

References

Afghanistan Independent Human Rights Commission (2016) Annual report 1394. http://www.aihrc. org.af/media/files/Reports/Annual%20Reports/English/Annual-Report-94-Eng-for-website.pdf. Accessed 1 Sept 2017

African Charter on Human and Peoples' Rights (1982) 21 ILM 58 (African Charter)

African Commission on Human and People's Rights (1998) Resolution on the granting of observer status to national human rights institutions in Africa (1998) ACHPR/Res 31(XXIV)98

Amnesty International (2017) Annual Report 2016/2017, London

Asia Pacific Forum of National Human Rights Institutions (2017) APF-UNDP partnership to strengthen NHRIs. http://www.asiapacificforum.net/human-rights/sogisc/apf-undp-partnership-strengthen-nhris/. Accessed 30 Aug 2017

Asia Pacific Forum of National Human Rights Institutions and UNDP (2014) Capacity assessment manual for national human rights institutions. Asia Pacific Forum of National Human Rights Institutions and the United Nations Development Programme Asia-Pacific Regional Centre, Bangkok/Sydney

Cardenas S (2003) Emerging global actors: the United nations and national human rights institutions. Glob Gov 9:23–42

Cardenas S (2014) Chains of justice: the global rise of state institutions for human rights. University of Pennsylvania Press, Philadelphia

Council of Europe Commissioner for Human Rights (2017) Cooperation with national human rights structures. http://www.coe.int/en/web/commissioner/co-operation-with-national-human-rights-structures. Accessed 20 Aug 2017

GANHRI (2016) GANHRI statement on the unique role of NHRIs in promoting effective polices for human rights education, Geneva, 14 Sept 2016

GANHRI (2017a) Chart of the status of national human rights institutions, 26 May 2017

GANHRI (2017b) Statute, Version Adopted 6 Mar 2017

GANHRI (2017c) Sub-Committee on accreditation rules of procedure, Version Adopted 6 Mar 2017

Global Alliance of NHRIs (GANHRI) documents. Available at: http://nhri.ohchr.org/EN/Pages/default.aspx. Accessed 21 Aug 2017

Goodman R, Pegram T (eds) (2012) Human rights, state compliance and social change: assessing national human rights institutions. Cambridge University Press, New York

Hafner-Burton EM (2013) Making human rights a reality. Princeton University Press, Princeton

International Coordinating Committee of NHRIs (2007) Conclusions of the international roundtable on the role of national human rights institutions and treaty bodies, Berlin, 23 and 24 Nov 2006

International Coordinating Committee of NHRIs (2011) Recommended objectives by the ICC, 66th session of the general assembly resolution on national human rights institutions, presented at the ICC Bureau meeting

International Coordinating Committee of NHRIs (2012) Position paper: the treaty body strengthening process: effective participation of national human rights institutions

Jessup and Kounte (2015) Evaluation of OHCHR support to national human rights institutions – final report

Kenya National Commission on Human Rights (2012) Realising sexual and reproductive health rights in Kenya: a myth or reality? a report of the public inquiry into violations of sexual and reproductive health rights in Kenya. Kenya National Commission on Human Rights, Nairobi

Linos K, Pegram T (2015) Interrogating form and function: designing effective national human rights institutions. Danish Institute for Human Rights, Copenhagen

Linos K, Pegram T (2016) The language of compromise in international agreements. Int Organ 70:587–621

Mama Tiera (2014) Request for the withdrawal of the accreditation of the Venezuelan People's Defender – submission of reports, Geneva, 19 Mar 2014. https://www.mama-tierra.org/with drawal-of-the-accreditation-of-thevenezuelan-peoples-defender/. Accessed 1 Sept 2017

Meuwissen K (2013) NHRI participation in United Nations human rights procedures: international promotion versus institutional consolidation. In: Wouters J, Meuwissen K (eds) National human rights institutions in Europe: comparative, European and international perspectives. Intersentia, Cambridge

Murray R (2007) National human rights institutions: criteria and factors for assessing their effectiveness. NQHR 25:189

OHCHR (1995) A handbook on the establishment and strengthening of national human rights institutions for the promotion and protection of human rights. United Nations, New York/Geneva

OHCHR (2009) Survey on national human rights institutions. United Nations, Geneva

OHCHR (2015) Zeid deplores deadly attack on Afghanistan's human rights commission, Geneva, 26 Oct 2015. http://www.ohchr.org/EN/NewsEvents/Pages/DisplayNews.aspx?NewsID=16648&LangID=E. Accessed 31 Aug 2017

Organization of American States (2009) Resolution AG/RES. 2448 (XXXI X-O/09) on strengthening the role of national institutions for the promotion and protection of human rights in the organization of American states

Pegram T (2015) Global human rights governance and orchestration: national human rights institutions as intermediaries. EJIR 21:595

Pew Research Centre Global Attitudes Project (2013) The global divide on homosexuality. Greater acceptance in more secular and affluent countries

Roberts K (2011) National human rights institutions as diplomacy actors. In: O'Flaherty M (ed) Human rights diplomacy: contemporary perspectives. Nijhoff, Leiden

Roberts K (2013) The role and functioning of the international coordinating committee of national human rights institutions in international human rights bodies. In: Wouters J, Meuwissen K (eds) National human rights institutions in Europe: comparative, European and international perspectives. Intersentia, Cambridge

SCA (2017a) General observations of the GANHRI sub-committee on accreditation, Version Adopted 6 Mar 2017

SCA (2017b) Accreditation reports – GANHRI sub-committee on accreditation reports since 2006. Available at: http://nhri.ohchr.org/EN/Pages/default.aspx. Accessed 21 Aug 2017

Sidoti C (2012) National human rights institutions and the international human rights system. In: Goodman R, Pegram T (eds) Human rights, state compliance and social change: assessing national human rights institutions. Cambridge University Press, New York

Ukrainian Parliament Commissioner (2017) Statement of the Ukrainian Parliament Commissioner for Human Rights Ms. Valeriya Lutkovska at the 34th regular session of the United Nations Human Rights Council during adoption of the report on Ukraine. http://www.ombudsman.gov.ua/en/all-news/pr/22317-df-statement-of-the-ukrainian-parliament-commissioner-for-human-rights-ms/. Accessed 5 March 2018

UN Committee on the Elimination of All Forms of Discrimination against Women (2008) Statement by the committee on the elimination of discrimination against women on its relationship with national human rights institutions UN Doc E/CN.6/2008/CR 1, Annex II

UN Committee on the Elimination of All Forms of Discrimination Against Women (2010) General recommendation No. 28 on the core obligations of states parties under article 2 of the convention on the elimination of all forms of discrimination against women (19 Oct 2010) UN Doc CEDAW/C/2010/47/GC.2

UN Committee on the Elimination of Racial Discrimination (2009) General recommendation No. 33, Follow-up to the Durban review conference (29 Sept 2009) UN Doc CERD/C/GC/33

UN Committee on the Elimination of Racial Discrimination, Working methods. http://www.ohchr.org/EN/HRBodies/CERD/Pages/WorkingMethods.aspx. Accessed 22 Aug 2017

UN Committee on the Rights of the Child (2002) General comment No. 2 (2002) The role of independent national human rights institutions in the promotion and protection of the rights of the child (15 Nov 2002) UN Doc CRC/GC/2002/2

UN Committee on the Rights of the Child, Working Methods. http://www.ohchr.org/EN/HRBodies/CRC/Pages/WorkingMethods.aspx. Accessed 22 Aug 2017

UN ECOSOC Commission on Human Rights (1946) Report of the commission on human rights to the second session of the economic and social council (21 May 1946) UN Doc E/38/Rev 1

UN ECOSOC Commission on Human Rights (1991) Report of the international workshop on national institutions for the promotion and protection of human rights (Paris 7–9 Oct 1991) (16 Dec 1991) UN Doc E/CN.4/1992/43

UN General Assembly (1979) Guidelines on the structure and functioning of national and local institutions for the promotion and protection of human rights (18 Dec 1978) UN Doc A/RES/33/46

UN General Assembly (1993) Principles relating to the status of national institutions. Resolution 48/134 of 20 Dec 1993, UNGA Res A/RES/48/134 (20 Dec 1993)

UN General Assembly (2006) Resolution 60/251 human rights council (15 Mar 2006)

UN General Assembly (2007) Resolution 5/1 Institution-building of the United Nations human rights council (7 Aug 2007)

UN Human Rights Committee, Working Methods. http://www.ohchr.org/EN/HRBodies/CCPR/Pages/WorkingMethods.aspx. Accessed 22 Aug 2017

UN Human Rights Council (2011a) Resolution 16/21 review of the work and functioning of the human rights council (12 Apr 2011)

UN Human Rights Council (2011b) Resolution 17/4 human rights and transnational corporations and other business enterprises (6 July 2011)

UN Human Rights Council (2015) Report of the special rapporteur on violence against women, its causes and consequences, on her mission to Afghanistan (4–12 Nov 2014) UN Doc A/HRC/29/27/Add.3 (12 May 2015)

UPR Info (2017) Statistics of recommendations. https://www.upr-info.org/database/statistics/index_issues.php?fk_issue=34&cycle. Accessed 18 Aug 2017

Part II

Human Rights Violations as Crimes: International Courts and Tribunals

Human Rights: The Nuremberg Legacy

Miriam Cohen

Contents

Introduction 320
International Crimes and the Nuremberg and Tokyo Trials: A Historical Overview 321
The Norms and Limitations of International Law before Nuremberg 322
A Court of International Justice: The Legacy of Nuremberg 325
Nuremberg and the Shaping of International Human Rights Law 327
The Gap of the Nuremberg and Tokyo Legacies: Victims' Reparations 328
Conclusion 330
References 331

Abstract

The trials in Nuremberg and Tokyo in the aftermath of the Second World War represented a milestone in international law and human rights. While mass atrocities were committed during the War, a system of human rights protection had not yet been conceived. In the aftermath of the War, the concept of accountability took the shape of criminal prosecutions of international crimes that were committed during the War. The trials focused on violations of human rights that amounted to international crimes. The Nuremberg trials marked the beginning of an era where mass atrocities are accounted for. This chapter dwells upon the development of the Nuremberg and Tokyo trials, including their legacy. It then addresses one major gap in their trials: albeit a major historical step forward in accountability, the Nuremberg and Tokyo trials focused on the offenders and their punishment and thus left a gap in relation to reparations for victims. Human rights institutions were later formed to fill in this gap, from a State responsibility perspective.

M. Cohen (✉)
Université de Montréal, Montreal, QC, Canada
e-mail: mcohen@lakeheadu.ca

© Springer Nature Singapore Pte Ltd. 2018
G. Oberleitner (ed.), *International Human Rights Institutions, Tribunals, and Courts*,
International Human Rights, https://doi.org/10.1007/978-981-10-5206-4_11

Keywords
Nuremberg · Tokyo · IMT · International crimes · Accountability · Second World
War

Introduction

Human rights violations are not a recent phenomenon. Yet, accountability for those
violations has a shorter history. During the Second World War, widespread mass
atrocities were committed, but a system of human rights protection had not yet been
developed. In the aftermath of the War, the concept of accountability took the shape
of criminal prosecutions of international crimes that were committed during the War.
The trials focused on violations of human rights that amounted to international
crimes. The Nuremberg trials marked the beginning of an era where mass atrocities
are accounted for. This is one of the major legacies of the trials that followed to the
World War: individual perpetrators can be held accountable for international crimes.

The suffering of victims during the War was often referred to as a justification for
the creation of the tribunals and prosecution of those responsible before international
fora (Moffett 2014). While the American Chief Prosecutor Robert Jackson stated
that a finding of guilt against the defendants meant that "justice may be done to these
individuals as to their countless victims" (IMT Transcripts), justice was achieved
through the punishment of Nazi and Japanese perpetrators (Garkawe 2006). Victim
reparations for crimes which they had suffered were not part of the justice system
that was created to prosecute perpetrators of international crimes. The building
blocks of modern international criminal law, by these historical trials, conceived
"justice for victims" through a criminal dimension – the trial and punishment of
perpetrators – which provided victims a symbolic sense of justice. At its inception,
international criminal justice had no space for a dimension that included reparations
for victims.

Other more recent international and hybrid criminal tribunals have followed this
model: they delivered justice for victims through the prosecution and punishment of
individual perpetrators, thus limiting international justice to a criminal dimension, as
will be further discussed below. It stems from the legacy of the Nuremberg trials and
ad hoc international criminal tribunals that trial and accountability of perpetrators
were their primary goals.

More recent developments in international criminal law not only mean that
victims play a more active role in the proceedings (Vasiliev 2015; Trumbull 2007;
Mekjian and Varughese 2005; McGonigle 2009; Chung 2007) but also include the
possibility of the award of reparations, by imposing a legal duty on individual
perpetrators. One of the main innovations of the ICC as compared to other precursor
international criminal tribunals was to incorporate victims' rights within the framework of an international criminal tribunal. This change in the dynamics of international criminal law however brings about many questions, challenges, and critiques.

In this light, this chapter dwells upon the development of the Nuremberg and
Tokyo trials, including their legacy. It then addresses one major gap in their trials:

albeit a major historical step forward in accountability, the Nuremberg and Tokyo trials focused on the offenders and their punishment and thus left a gap in relation to reparations for victims. Human rights institutions were later formed to fill in this gap, from a State responsibility perspective.

International Crimes and the Nuremberg and Tokyo Trials: A Historical Overview

Following the end of the Second World War, the Allied Powers (primarily Britain, the United States, France, and the Soviet Union) (hereinafter the "Allies") were forced to decide what to do with the German war criminals they had captured (McKeown 2014). The Allies decision to prosecute Nazi and Japanese war criminals before military tribunals, rather than summarily execute them, represented a major change to the previous norms of international law (Leyh 2016).

The London Charter, also known as the Agreement for the Prosecution and Punishment of the Major War Criminals of the European Axis Powers, was signed by the Allies on August 8, 1945 (McKeown 2014). Article 1 of the London Charter called for the establishment of the International Military Tribunal (hereinafter the "IMT" or "Nuremberg Tribunal") in order to prosecute German war criminals (Matas 2006). The Nuremberg Tribunals represented Allied hopes for a new effective and impartial international criminal process which would serve to restrain international conflict and govern the resolution of interstate disputes (Venkata Raman 1994). The trials at the IMT began November 14, 1945 (Novak 2015; Kyriakides and Weinstein 2005). The IMT delivered its judgment on October 1, 1946 (Sadat 2016).

Modeled upon the IMT, the International Military Tribunal of the Far East (the hereinafter "Tokyo Tribunal") was first mentioned in the Potsdam Agreement signed with the Japanese on August 14, 1946 following their surrender. The Agreement placed General Douglas MacArthur in the position of the Supreme Commander for the Allied Powers in Japan (Pritchard 1995; Novak 2015). In this position, General MacArthur issued the Charter of the International Military Tribunal of the Far East on January 19, 1946 which formally established the Tokyo Tribunals. The eleven prosecutors issued an indictment on April 29, 1946, and opening statements were delivered on May 3, 1946 (Kaufman 2013). The Tokyo Tribunals lasted approximately 2.5 years, and judgments were delivered between November 4 and 12, 1948 (Kaufman 2013).

A United Nations General Assembly resolution adopted in December 1948 requested the International Law Commission to prepare a statute for an "international penal tribunal" (Schabas 2001). Despite this resolution, no general system of international criminal justice was developed until 1998 (Matas 2006). Nuremberg, which was described by a US prosecutor Telford Taylor as a twin effort to the United Nations, represented the last major effort between the Allies and the Soviet Union prior to the fall of the iron curtain (Kyriakides and Weinstein 2005). As a result, Nuremberg's lessons were largely forgotten by the international community through the duration of the Cold War.

While the Cold War slowed the international development of what are now known as the "Nuremberg Principles," these principles continued to be integrated in domestic criminal justice systems. The collapse of the USSR and the normalization of relations with the West facilitated the establishment of the International Criminal Tribunal for the Former Yugoslavia (hereinafter the "ICTY") and Rwanda (hereinafter the "ICTR") (Leyh 2016). These ad hoc Tribunals relied heavily on the principles of international criminal law articulated by the Nuremberg Tribunal (Leyh 2016).

The Nuremberg and Tokyo Tribunals reflected a paradigm shift in international criminal law during the mid-twentieth century. As the earliest expressions of this new paradigm, the London Charter, the Nuremberg Principles, and the IMT's final judgment have become indispensable features of modern international law and have helped shape the current international criminal justice system (Sadat 2016; Leyh 2016). Often overshadowed by the Nuremberg trials, the Tokyo trials, based on the Nuremberg model, built upon the lessons learned in Nuremberg.

The Norms and Limitations of International Law before Nuremberg

To understand the significant change the London Charter and the IMT represented to the international legal order, it is necessary to investigate the order it sought to replace. International disputes before Nuremberg were generally governed by the principles established through the Peace of Westphalia ("Westphalia"), a series of treaties signed in 1648 (Morrison 1995).

Before 1648, the pope and emperor claimed jurisdiction over political power (Morrison 1995). Following the Peace of Westphalia, nobody had jurisdiction over the local sovereign (Morrison 1995). This change ushered in the age of State sovereignty (Morrison 1995). Under the Westphalian world order, the State was the ultimate authority. Customary international law at the time accepted wars of colonial conquest, wars of aggression, and wars among "civilized" States (Morrison 1995). The international legal norms of time were well illustrated by this statement:

> It always lies within the power of a state to endeavor to obtain redress for wrongs, or to gain political or other advantages over another, not merely by the employment of force, but also by direct recourse to war. (Morrison 1995)

At the time, no State could impose laws on another without their expressed agreement through an international treaty or similar instrument. Examples of such instruments were the Covenant of the League of Nations, which provided temporary and procedural relief from hostility, and the Kellog-Briand Pact, which banned aggressive war and was only binding on signatories (Morrison 1995; Borgwardt 2008).

While the Westphalian system regulated some aspects of interstate relationships, it left a nation's relationship with its own citizen completely unregulated.

International law only regulated the treatment of aliens by foreign governments (Morrison 1995). In 1905, Oppenheim noted that: "Owing to its personal supremacy over them, a State may treat its subject according to its discretion" (Oppenheim 1905). This sentiment was echoed by Hyde after the Second World War who stated that "[a] state enjoys the right normally to accord such treatment as it may seem for its own nationals within places subject to its control" (Hyde 1922). Hyde also believed that any interference with that right would impair a State's political independence (Morrison 1995).

International law permitted a State to try members of the armed forces of an enemy State who had committed war crimes; however no actual cases had occurred where the political leadership of a defeated country had been put on trial (Tomuschat 2006). Wars were a natural feature of interstate relationships, and the general consensus was that there was nothing to be gained by pursing criminal prosecutions (Tomuschat 2006). This may be attributable to the monarchial structure of Europe's past which was characterized by its interrelated network of royal families. These relationships encouraged reconciliation and discouraged a victor from trying an opposing State's leadership in order to avoid creating obstacles to peace (Tomuschat 2006).

The Allied attempts at justice following the First World War illustrate the system which prevailed prior to the Nuremberg and Tokyo trials. Britain, France, and Russia declared their intention to hold members of the Turkish government and the officials who had participated in the massacre of Armenians, responsible for their atrocities (Matas 1989). At the 1919 Preliminary Peace Conference following First World War, the Allies pushed for the prosecution of Kaiser Wilhelm II (the "Kaiser"), along with German war criminals, and Turkish officials. These discussions ultimately culminated in the Treaty of Versailles, signed June 28, 1919.

Prior to the signing of the Treaty of Versailles, the Commission on the Responsibility of the Authors of the War and on Enforcement of Penalties (the "Commission of Fifteen") was asked to investigate and ultimately report on the individuals who had initiated the war and violated the laws and customs of war (Matas 1989; Bassiouni 1997). This Commission created a report published on March 29, 1919. It cited the *Martens* Clause found in the preamble of the Hague Convention of 1907 when concluding that Germany and the Ottoman empire had "carried on the war by barbarous or illegitimate methods in violation of the elementary laws of humanity" (Bassiouni 1997). The report called for the criminal prosecution of all persons belonging to enemy countries who had committed offenses against the laws of humanity (Matas 1989; Bassiouni 1997). The report then listed the crimes which had been committed by Germany against its allies and crimes the Ottomans had committed against its own people (Matas 1989).

The Americans and the Japanese wrote dissenting comments on the Commission of Fifteen's report (Matas 1989), which opposed the Commission as they felt it had gone beyond the boundaries of its mandate (Bassiouni 1997). The Japanese and Americans felt the Commission's job was to investigate violations of the laws and customs of war, and not the uncodified "laws of humanity" (Bassiouni 1997). The Americans argued that "laws of humanity" did not exist (Matas 1989). The United

States felt laws of humanity depended upon notions of morality, that they were too vague to have the character of law and that they were not legal norms (Matas 1989). This disagreement meant that the Treaty of Versailles neglected to reference "crimes against humanity" as there was no agreement on what those crimes entailed (Matas 1989).

Therefore, the Treaty of Versailles included Article 227 which provided for an ad hoc international criminal tribunal established to prosecute the Kaiser along with Article 228 and 229 which provided for the prosecution of German military personnel. However, none of these clauses were actually implemented (Matas 1989).

The Allies were not willing to set a new international precedent by prosecuting a Head of State for an international crime (Bassiouni 1997). Article 227, authored primarily by Great Britain, was drafted very carefully (Bassiouni 1997). The "indictment" of the Kaiser did not allege that the Kaiser had committed any crimes known to international law (Bassiouni 1997; Tomuschat 2006). The crime of aggression mentioned in Article 227 was characterized as a "political" crime (Bassiouni 1997).

As there was only a "political" crime alleged, the Dutch could decline to extradite the Kaiser on the basis that no international law had been violated (Bassiouni 1997). However, the Allied request never came. The Allies discussed the possibility of extradition with the Netherlands through diplomatic channels, but since the Kaiser cousin was a sitting monarch in the Netherlands, these discussions never progressed (Tomuschat 2006). As such, the Allies never formally requested the Kaiser's extradition (Bassiouni 1997).

The Allies also never created a tribunal to prosecute the Kaiser, nor did they ever hold a judicial process through which the Kaiser's extradition could be formally denied (Bassiouni 1997). Article 227 was likely inserted in order to support Article 231 which held Germany responsible for the costs of the war and cleared the Allies of contributory responsibility (Tomuschat 2006). It is possible that Article 227 was never meant to be fully implemented and was included as a concession to those seeking to further humiliate Germany following the First World War (Bassiouni 1997).

In the aftermath of First World War, the Allies also failed to implement Article 228 and 229 of the Treaty of Versailles. An international tribunal was not established; instead Germany passed national legislation which adopted Articles 228 and 229. This meant these prosecutions, known as the Leipzig trials, relied on Germany's own national laws. Thus, the German Procurator General of the Supreme Court (the "German Procurator") had prosecutorial discretion over which cases would be tried, while the Allies were responsible for forwarding the names and evidence. Of the 895 individuals named in the Commission's report, only 45 files were filed with the German Procurator. Only twelve were convicted (Bassiouni 1997).

By the time the Leipzig trials had commenced in 1921, the political will to prosecute those accused of crimes had evaporated. The major powers sought to maintain peace rather than pursue justice (Bassiouni 1997). Articles 227, 228, and 229 are said to be early manifestations of international criminal law (Tomuschat 2006). The Allied failure to implement these articles, however, represented a missed opportunity to establish a politically independent international justice system (Bassiouni 1997).

The prosecution of officials of the Turkish Government responsible for atrocities committed against Greek and Armenian populations was not authorized pursuant to the Treaty of Versailles but instead the Treaty of Sèvres. The Treaty of Sèvres was a peace treaty between the Allies and Turkey signed August 10, 1920 (Matas 1989; Bassiouni 1997). The Treaty provided for war crimes trials and contemplated not only the prosecution of those responsible for killing allied soldiers and civilians but also contemplated the prosecution of those who had committed crimes against Ottoman subjects as well (Schabas 2001). The Allies insisted that the Treaty contains particular language which is now viewed as the earliest conception of what is now known as crimes against humanity (Matas 1989).

While the Treaty of Sèvres offered hope for a new international legal order, like the Treaty of Versailles, the Treaty of Sèvres was never implemented (Schabas 2001). The Allies reserved the right to designate the forum where the accused would be tried, and the Turkish government undertook to recognize the Allies choice of forum (Matas 1989). The Treaty also contemplated the possibility that a tribunal of competent jurisdiction could be created by the League of Nations (Matas 1989). The League of Nations never created such a tribunal, and the Allies failed to designate a tribunal (Matas 1989). The Treaty of Sèvres depended upon Turkey recognizing the Allied choice of tribunal, which demonstrates the extent to which the Treaty of Sèvres relied upon Turkey's internal jurisdiction to prosecute its own subjects, rather than the nascent rules of international criminal law of the time.

As mentioned above, the Treaty of Sèvres was never ratified. It was replaced 3 years later in 1923 by the Treaty of Lausanne which extended amnesty for all offenses committed between August 1, 1914, and November 20, 1922 (Matas 1989). This leads to the inference that there were crimes to be amnestied, but these crimes were never defined (Matas 1989). The amnesty was likely extended in order to prevent the spread of Bolshevism to Turkey (Matas 1989).

The Treaty of Versailles and the Treaty of Sèvres demonstrate the Allies intention to prosecute those who had committed atrocities during the First World War. However, the Allies actions demonstrate how politics, the monarchial history of Europe, the embryonic State of international criminal law, and the lack of an independent international tribunal are able to impartially adjudicate the alleged crimes, all conspired to prevent the criminal prosecution of war criminals following First World War.

A Court of International Justice: The Legacy of Nuremberg

Between the First and Second World Wars, little progress was made at establishing "a court of international justice." In 1937, the League of Nations adopted a treaty contemplating the creation of an international court, but it never came into force (Schabas 2001).

The international community's failure to create an international court of justice following the First World War stimulated international interest in the matter (Schabas 2001). Nuremberg, like the Peace of Westphalia, was a defining moment in history. Nuremberg codified and confirmed changes that had already occurred and was the catalyst for changes to come (Morrison 1995). While Nuremberg did not completely replace the Westphalian system, it attempted to place limits on the unrestricted sovereignty of States and restrain the use of physical power to assert political superiority (Morrison 1995).

The larger goal of Nuremberg was to shape the postwar order (Borgwardt 2008). Initial discussions which would lead to the Nuremberg Tribunals initially took place at the San Francisco Conference of 1945 where the United Nations Declaration was signed (Borgwardt 2008). On August 8, 1945, the United States, the United Kingdom, France, and the Soviet Union formally adopted the Agreement for the Prosecution and Punishment of Major War Criminals of the European Axis, establishing the Charter of the International Military Tribunal, also known as the London Agreement (Schabas 2001; Bassiouni 1997). The London Agreement was adopted by 19 other states, making 23 in total (Schabas 2001).

The Charter of the International Military Tribunal (hereinafter the "Charter") was annexed to this agreement (Schabas 2001; Bassiouni 1997). According to Article 2 of the London Agreement, the Charter determined the constitution, jurisdiction, and sentencing power of the IMT (Jescheck 2004).

Article 6 of the Charter enumerated three substantive crimes: (1) crimes against peace; (2) war crimes; and (3) crimes against humanity (Bassiouni 1997). As mentioned above, crimes against peace or the waging of aggressive war was not prohibited under international law (Morrison 1995; Jescheck 2004). A primary argument advanced by the defense was that no leader had ever been convicted for waging war (Tomuschat 2006). Crimes against humanity was also poorly defined by international law prior to the Charter, as it only protected aliens at the hands of foreign governments and did not protect a State's citizens from their own government (Morrison 1995). War crimes had been better defined by the Hague Conventions and the Geneva Convention Relative to the Treatment of Prisoners of War, but prior to Nuremberg only signatories were bound by these conventions (Morrison 1995). To overcome these deficiencies, the IMT noted that, as a signatory to the Kellog-Briand Pact of 1928, Germany had recognized that aggressive wars were illegal and were not conducted by States as abstract entities, but by human beings (Borgwardt 2008). If aggressive war was illegal then the individuals responsible for the war should face consequences (Tomuschat 2006). Additionally, the Charter had the legal quality of occupation law. The final judgment of the IMT stated that the Charter was a legitimate "exercise of the sovereign legislative power by the countries to which the German Reich unconditionally surrendered" and was "the expression of international law existing at the time of its creation" (Jescheck 2004). Prosecutors also decided to include the controversial fourth charge of "Conspiracy."

One of the major legacies of the Nuremberg and Tokyo trials is the understanding and general acceptance of the notion that individuals are subjects of international law and should be held criminally responsible for perpetrating war crimes, crimes against humanity, and (later) genocide (Leyh 2016).

Nuremberg thus represents a visible symbol of the transition from a Westphalian system of State sovereignty to an international system that took place in the middle of this century (Morrison 1995). It is the foundation of modern thinking about international law with an emphasis on the maintenance of peace, responsibility of the State, and accountability of its officers to international standards (Morrison 1995).

The Peace of Westphalia was the defining event for international law for three centuries, and the judgment at Nuremberg is one of the formative events for the international law of our day (Morrison 1995). Unabashed claims of national sovereignty – prompted by the recognition of the nation-state system at Westphalia – was modified by the universalist claims for peace, human rights, and limitations on the use of force articulated in the Nuremberg and Tokyo trials as well as individual accountability for international crimes (Morrison 1995). Nuremberg confirmed and proclaimed changes that had been occurring during the preceding half century and stands as the precursor of those of the next period (Morrison 1995). However, this was not yet fully absorbed by the time of the Nuremberg proceedings (Morrison 1995). The decision to hold a trial and the accomplishment of the task to a high level of professionalism and distinction represented an extraordinary achievement for international justice (Sadat 2016).

Nuremberg and the Shaping of International Human Rights Law

The trials held at Nuremberg and Tokyo marked a change in the world as it had existed before (Leyh 2016). It gave "rise to a new vision of moral responsibility among nations" (Sadat 2016). Nuremberg changed international norms and expectations of accountability for atrocities and massive human rights violations. Nuremberg planted the seed for the adoption of the Genocide Convention and the Universal Declaration of Human Rights (Morrison 1995).

Nuremberg marks a special place in international relations: as the creation of an international criminal tribunal reflected and contributed to the restoration of order in Europe following the destruction generated by so many years of warfare (Kyriakides and Weinstein 2005). The Nuremberg Tribunal and the United Nations Organization "were virtually twin offspring" of the allied negotiations and agreements intended to secure peace (Morrison 1995). The Tribunal represented last major episode of cooperation between the West and the Soviet Union before a demise of their wartime "marriage of convenience" (Morrison 1995). It represented a significant milestone in the development of international law, and the trial at Nuremberg proved to be the foundation of what has now become a permanent feature of modern international justice (Morrison 1995).

Concerning contributions to substantive human rights law, the establishment of the Tribunal was critical to the evolution of genocide as a legal concept, even though it was not included in the Charter (Morrison 1995). The word had just been coined in 1944, by Dr. Raphael Lemkin, who served as an adviser to the US legal team at the Tribunal (Morrison 1995). The Tribunal paved the way for the subsequent drafting of the Convention on the Prevention or Punishment of the Crime of Genocide (Morrison 1995), one of the major human rights conventions of our days.

Modern human rights law rests upon the Nuremberg foundation (Sadat 2016). The trial, together with the United Nations Charter of 1945, was the center of the incipient human rights movement until the adoption of the Universal Declaration of

Human Rights in 1948. Corollary to the notion that individuals have duties under international law is that they may also acquire rights there under international law.

Furthermore, the "Nuremberg Principles" were prepared by the International Law Commission and presented to the General Assembly after the war (Sadat 2016). At least some of the "law" enshrined in the Charter and the Nuremberg Judgment found its way into new and crucial international human rights instruments on apartheid, genocide, the laws of war, and torture. The "Nuremberg Principles" eschew collective responsibility in favor of individual criminal responsibility (Sadat 2016). They provide that no human being is above the law with respect to the most serious crimes of concern to humanity as a whole. Reliance upon domestic law is no defense to crime for which an individual may have responsibility under international law.

In terms of institutional design, the structure and approach of the Nuremburg and Tokyo trials paved the way for and heavily influenced the shape of future international courts and domestic responses to serious human rights violations (Leyh 2016). Jurisprudence that emerged also aided in the further development of international norms (Leyh 2016). The understanding and general acceptance of the notion that individuals are subject of international law and should be held criminally responsible for perpetrating war crimes, crimes against humanity, and genocide were finally solidified.

Prior to the proliferation of international and hybrid criminal courts, criminal prosecutions remained the sole prerogative of States, and there was no general agreement over the extent of States' duty to prosecute serious human rights or humanitarian law violations (Leyh 2016). Following military tribunals in Nuremberg and Tokyo, the United Nations sought to codify the Nuremberg Principles and looked into the establishment of a permeant international criminal court (Leyh 2016). It took decades for the creation of a Court due to the Cold War.

During the hiatus between the Nuremberg trials and the establishment of a permanent international criminal court, 50 years after Nuremburg, the UN Security Council established the international criminal tribunals for the former Yugoslavia and Rwanda (Leyh 2016). These were ad hoc tribunals with specific mandates and of a temporary nature. It is widely recognized the connection between Nuremberg and these tribunals (Leyh 2016). The establishment of the ICC on July 1, 2002, was "undoubtedly part of the legacy of Nuremberg" (Leyh 2016). The developing case law of the court continues to underscore the Nuremberg principles in practice.

The Nuremberg principles have also found their way into international human rights law jurisprudence (Leyh 2016). The European and Inter-American courts of human rights have developed a broad jurisprudence relating to international atrocities.

The Gap of the Nuremberg and Tokyo Legacies: Victims' Reparations

The legacy of the Nuremberg and Tokyo trials to human rights and to the building blocks of a global human rights system is undeniable. As already discussed, the Nuremberg and Tokyo trials did not provide for a possibility of victim reparation

(Danieli 2005; Pross 1998; Ferencz 1998). As a consequence, since victims of Nazi crimes were not able to claim civil redress against the perpetrators during the international criminal trial proceedings, they obtained reparation through other means, mainly through lump-sum agreements (Colonomos and Armstrong 2006; Authers 2006).

The main point of interest of the precedent of the Nuremberg and Tokyo trials and reparations after the Second World War is that civil redress in relation to those crimes was mainly based on State responsibility (Colonomos and Armstrong 2006; Authers 2006). These trials did not set up a regime for civil redress or individual civil responsibility at the international criminal level for the victims of Second World War crimes (international crimes). Thus, under this regime, to obtain reparation, State responsibility was a prerequisite. Fast forwarding to recent conflicts, the problem is when State responsibility is not engaged, that is, when the State (machinery) is not necessarily involved in the international crime. In this scenario, civil redress is not an option (Ingadottir 2000).

It seems paradoxical that while the main point of international criminal justice at its inception was to hold *individuals* criminally accountable for the crimes they committed, thus departing from a system based purely on State responsibility as "crimes are committed by men, not by abstract entities" (Atwater 1947), there is a visible reliance on States for civil redress at the international level (Bonafè 2009; Dupuy 2002; Nollkaemper 2003).

Modern international criminal law developed as a response to the atrocities committed during the Second World War. In the war's aftermath, it became clear that the atrocities committed during the Second World War needed to be addressed by the international community. However, holding an abstract entity such as a State solely responsible, without punishing those who individually perpetrated the atrocities, was no longer acceptable, or desirable, and often failed to reflect domestic criminal justice systems. Therefore, the punishment of individual perpetrators was seen as a necessary step toward the reestablishment of an international legal order.

The advent of modern international criminal law represents a turning point in the conceptual framework of international law. This paradigm shift is well illustrated in a statement made by the International Military Tribunal at Nuremberg which noted that "crimes against international law are committed by men, not by abstract entities, and only by punishing individuals who commit such crimes can the provisions of international law be enforced" (*Trial of Major War Criminals* 1947). This statement also demonstrates that, since its inception, international criminal law was premised on a narrow definition of justice which focused primarily on the trial and punishment of individuals who perpetrated atrocities in order to achieve international criminal law objectives.

Hersch Lauterpacht warned of the risks of continuing to hold a purely State-centered approach stating that "[t]here is little hope for international law if an individual, acting as an organ of the state, can in violation of international law, effectively shelter behind the abstract and artificial notion of the state" (Lauterpacht 1937). The idea that individuals who bear responsibility for certain acts should not be shielded by the State was necessary to shift international criminal law from a State orientated system to one that included individual accountability for international crimes, thus creating a system of concurrent State and individual liability for certain international acts (Nollkaemper 2003). The focus on retribution and punishment of the perpetrator, in contrast with reparations, during this early stage of the development of international criminal law, can be explained by the idea that "[individual] punishment, in contrast to [interstate] reparation, satisfies . . . the need for guarantees against future infractions of the law" (Lauterpacht 1937).

Focusing solely on punishing individual perpetrators, as opposed to developing a framework that included redress for victims alongside criminal sanctions, can be better understood by considering the position of the individual as a subject of the State during the early development of international criminal law. The battle of that time was to pierce the veil of the State in order to be able to put on trial the individuals responsible for the atrocities of the Second World War (Westlake 1914). Thus, justice for victims encompassed solely a criminal dimension, that is, holding the criminal perpetrators accountable.

However, a State-based framework was not completely dismantled. State sovereignty remained as far as reparations for victims were concerned: if there was any claim for reparations by an individual victim, it was for the sovereign State to "represent" their interests, and reparations for international crimes were to be sought by States rather than by individuals (Colonomos and Armstrong 2006; Authers 2006). In other words, redress for victims of international crimes remained centered around a State-based approach (Colonomos and Armstrong 2006; Authers 2006). The development of international human rights law mechanisms began to fill some of the gaps concerning redress for mass human rights violations.

Conclusion

The Nuremberg and Tokyo trials changed the course of history. They set the path for the development of human rights law and accountability for human rights violations. The trials highlighted the significance of human life and denounced to the world human rights violations. The trials at Nuremberg and Tokyo were not simply trials in the aftermath of a war; they were truly the first international trial where mass human rights violations were accounted for and perpetrators held responsible. The trials were a watershed moment in international law surpassing the dichotomy between State sovereignty and individual accountability.

The Nuremberg principles were as bold as they were significant for the future development of international law. They promoted express individual accountability, marking a shift in international law; they defined international crimes and, in particular, the new "crimes against humanity"; they held leaders accountable through legal proceedings. It was remarkable, in that print of history, that the trials actually took place and that judgments were rendered. The model of Nuremberg led the way to future international criminal tribunals and laid the conceptual foundation for the progressive development of treaties that focus on human rights, in or out of war. The horrors of the Second World War made Nuremberg and Tokyo necessary; the principle and legacies they have set made human rights law possible.

References

Authers J (2006) Making good again: German compensation for forced and slave laborers. In: Greiff P (ed) The handbook of reparations. Oxford University Press, Oxford, pp 420–450

Atwater E (1947) Judgment of the tribunal. Am J Int Law 41:172

Bassiouni MC (1997) Seventy-five years: the need to establish a permanent international criminal court. Harvard Hum Rights J 10:11–62

Bonafè B (2009) The relationship between state and individual responsibility for international crimes. Brill, The Hague

Borgwardt E (2008) A new deal for the Nuremburg trial: the limits of law in generating human rights norms. Law Hist Rev 26(3):679–705

Chung C (2007) Victim's participation at the international criminal court: are concessions if the court clouding promise. Northwestern J Int Hum Rights 6:459

Colonomos A, Armstrong A (2006) German reparations to the Jews after world war II: a turning point in the history of reparations. In: Greiff P (ed) The handbook of reparations. Oxford University Press, Oxford, pp 390–419

Danieli Y (2005) Reappraising the Nuremberg trials and their legacy: the role of victims in international law. Cardozo Law Rev 27:1633

Dupuy PM (2002) International criminal responsibility of the individual and international responsibility of the state. In: Cassese A et al (eds) International criminal court: a commentary. Oxford University Press, Oxford

Ferencz BB (1998) International criminal courts: the legacy of Nuremberg. Pace Int Law Rev 10:203

Garkawe SB (2006) The role and rights of victims at the Nuremberg international military tribunal. In: Reginbogin HR, Stafferling C. The Nuremberg trials: international criminal law since, vol 1945. De Gruyter, Munich, pp 86–94

Hyde CC (1922) International law as chiefly interpreted and applied by the United States. Little, Brown and Company, Boston, pp 87–88

IMT Transcripts, vol. XIX. In: Moffett L (2014) Justice for Victims before the International Criminal Court. Routledge, New York, p 434

Ingadottir T (2000) The trust fund of the ICC. In: Shelton D (ed) International crimes, peace, and human rights: the role of the international criminal court. Transnational Publishers, Leiden, p 159

Jescheck H (2004) The general principles of international criminal law set out in Nuremberg, as mirrored in the ICC statute. J Int Crim Justice 2:38–55

Kaufman Z (2013) Transitional justice for Tojo's Japan: the United States role in the establishment of the international military Tribunal for the far East and Other Transitional Justice Mechanisms for Japan after world war II. Emory Int Law Rev 27:755–798

Kyriakides K, Weinstein S (2005) Nuremberg in retrospect. Int Crim Law Rev 5:373–386

Lauterpacht H (1937) Règles générales du droit de la paix. Recueil des Cours 62:351. (translation)

Leyh BM (2016) Nuremberg's legacy within transitional justice: prosecutions are here to stay. Washington Univ Global Stud Law Rev 15:559–574

Matas D (1989) Prosecuting crimes against humanity: the lessons of world war I. Forham Int Law J 13:86–104

Matas D (2006) From Nuremberg to Rome: tracing the legacy of the Nuremburg trials. Gonzaga J Int Law 10:17

McGonigle BN (2009) Bridging the divides in international criminal proceedings: an examination into the victim participation endeavor of the international criminal court. Florida J Int Law 21:93

McKeown T (2014) The Nuremberg trial: procedural due process at the international military tribunal. Victoria Univ Wellington Law Rev 45(1):109–132

Mekjian GJ, Varughese MC (2005) Hearing the Victim's voice: analysis of victims' advocate participation in the trial proceeding of the international criminal court. Pace Int Law Rev 17:1–413

Moffett L (2014) Justice for victims before the international criminal court. Routledge, New York

Morrison FL (1995) The significance of Nuremberg for modern international law. Military Law Rev 149:207–215

Nollkaemper A (2003) Concurrence between individual responsibility and state responsibility in international law. Int Comp Law Q 52:615–640

Novak A (2015) Chapter 2: origins of international criminal justice. In: Novak A (ed) The International Criminal Court. Springer, Geneva, pp 7–9

Oppenheim L (1905) International law: a treatise. Longmans, Green, and Co, London, p 172

Pritchard J (1995) The international military Tribunal for the far East and its contemporary resonances. Mil Law Rev 149:27

Pross C (1998) Paying for the past: the struggle over reparations for surviving victims of the Nazi terror. Johns Hopkins University Press, London

Sadat LN (2016) The Nuremberg trial, seventy years later. Washington Univ Global Stud Law Rev 15:575–592

Schabas W (2001) An introduction to the international criminal court. Cambridge University Press, Cambridge, pp 4–8

Tomuschat C (2006) The legacy of Nuremberg. J Int Crim Justice 4:830–844

Trial of Major War Criminals before the International Military Tribunal, 14 November 1945–1 October 1946, (Nuremberg: International Military Tribunal, 1947), at 223

Trumbull CP (2007) The victims of victim participation in international criminal proceedings. Michigan J Int Law 29:777

Vasiliev S (2015) Victim participation revisited: what the ICC is learning about itself. In: Stahn C (ed) The law and the practice of the international criminal court. Oxford University Press, Oxford

Venkata Raman K (1994) The Future of the Nuremberg Promise Criminal Reports 28 CR-ART 392

Westlake J (1914) In: Oppenheim L (ed) The collected papers of John Westlake on public international law. Cambridge University Press, Cambridge, p 411

Human Rights: Future of Ad Hoc Tribunals

Milena Sterio

Contents

Introduction 334
The Human Rights Legacy of (Past) Ad Hoc Tribunals 335
The Future of Ad Hoc Tribunals: Continuing to Protect Human Rights? 343
Special Tribunal for Lebanon 343
Kosovo Specialist Chambers 346
Syria Mechanism 348
Conclusion 350
References 351

Abstract

The Nuremberg and Tokyo tribunals, in the wake of World War II, created the precedent that individuals, including state leaders, could be held criminally accountable for war crimes and crimes against humanity. The Nuremberg experience in particular set in motion the idea that individuals responsible for massive human rights violations should face criminal responsibility. This idea remained somewhat dormant until the early 1990s, when two new ad hoc tribunals for the former Yugoslavia and for Rwanda were created by the United Nations Security Council. Over the past two decades, the international community has witnessed a proliferation of international and hybrid tribunals tasked with prosecuting those responsible for human rights violations: the International Criminal Court was created in the late 1990s and began its work in 2002; and several ad hoc tribunals have been created to investigate and prosecute cases in East Timor, Cambodia, Sierra Leone, Lebanon, Kosovo, and Bosnia. Most recently, the United Nations General Assembly established a Mechanism for Syria, tasked with collecting and

M. Sterio (✉)
Cleveland-Marshall College of Law, Cleveland, OH, USA
e-mail: m.sterio@csuohio.edu

© Springer Nature Singapore Pte Ltd. 2018
G. Oberleitner (ed.), *International Human Rights Institutions, Tribunals, and Courts*,
International Human Rights, https://doi.org/10.1007/978-981-10-5206-4_12

storing evidence of massive human rights violations in Syria, such as genocide, crimes against humanity, and war crimes. The Mechanism is expected to share this type of evidence and information with future tribunals prosecuting those responsible for such violations of human rights in Syria – with national jurisdictions as well as with a future ad hoc tribunal for Syria (should one be established). These tribunals, starting with the Yugoslavia and Rwanda courts and leading to the Syrian Mechanism, have significantly contributed toward the protection of human rights, by fine-tuning existing substantive human rights norms and by developing elaborate procedures aimed at protecting defense rights and the impartiality and fairness of judicial processes. This chapter will examine the human rights legacy and contribution of the Yugoslavia and Rwanda tribunals, before turning to a discussion of current and future ad hoc tribunals. Thus, this chapter will focus on the Special Tribunal for Lebanon, the Kosovo Specialist Chambers, and the Syria Mechanism. For each of these ad hoc tribunals and mechanisms, this chapter will analyze their substantive and procedural focus on the protection of human rights. It will conclude that it is likely that current and future ad hoc tribunals (for Syria, perhaps) will continue to build upon the Yugoslavia and the Rwanda tribunals' legacy in the field of human rights and that they will continue to contribute toward the elaboration of human rights norms.

Keywords
International criminal law · International criminal tribunals · International Criminal Tribunal for the former Yugoslavia · International Criminal Tribunal for Rwanda · Special Tribunal for Lebanon · Kosovo Specialist Chambers · Syria Mechanism

Introduction

"Violations of human rights cannot stand as legitimate acts of state. Therefore, they must be considered as criminal acts, committed by individuals who can and should be prosecuted in criminal proceedings" (Human Rights Advocacy and the History of International Human Rights Standards 2017).

The Nuremberg and Tokyo tribunals, in the wake of World War II, created the precedent that individuals, including state leaders, could be held criminally accountable for war crimes and crimes against humanity. The Nuremberg experience in particular set in motion the idea that individuals responsible for massive human rights violations should face criminal responsibility. This idea remained somewhat dormant until the early 1990s, when two new ad hoc tribunals for the former Yugoslavia and for Rwanda were created by the United Nations Security Council. Over the past two decades, the international community has witnessed a proliferation of international and hybrid tribunals tasked with prosecuting those responsible for human rights violations: the International Criminal Court was created in the late 1990s and began its work in 2002; and several ad hoc tribunals have been created to investigate and prosecute cases in East Timor, Cambodia, Sierra Leone, Lebanon, Kosovo, and Bosnia. Most recently, the United Nations General Assembly established a Mechanism for Syria, tasked with collecting and storing evidence of massive human rights violations in Syria, such as genocide, crimes against humanity, and war crimes. The Mechanism is expected to share this type of evidence and information with future tribunals prosecuting those responsible for such violations of human rights in Syria – with national jurisdictions as well as with a future ad hoc tribunal for Syria (should one be established). These tribunals, starting with the Yugoslavia and Rwanda courts and leading to the Syrian Mechanism, have significantly contributed toward the protection of human rights, by fine-tuning existing substantive human rights norms and by developing elaborate procedures aimed at protecting defense rights and the impartiality and fairness of judicial processes.

This chapter will examine the human rights legacy and contribution of the Yugoslavia and Rwanda tribunals, before turning to a discussion of current and future ad hoc tribunals. Thus, this chapter will focus on the Special Tribunal for Lebanon, the Kosovo Specialist Chambers, and the Syria Mechanism. For each of these ad hoc tribunals and mechanisms, this chapter will analyze their substantive and procedural focus on the protection of human rights. This chapter will conclude that it is likely that current and future ad hoc tribunals (for Syria, perhaps) will continue to build upon the Yugoslavia and the Rwanda tribunals' legacy in the field of human rights and that they will continue to contribute toward the elaboration of human rights norms.

The Human Rights Legacy of (Past) Ad Hoc Tribunals

The International Criminal Tribunal for Rwanda (ICTR) officially closed, having completed all of its trial and appellate-level work, at the end of 2015 (United Nations Mechanism for International Criminal Tribunals 2017). The International Criminal Tribunal for the former Yugoslavia (ICTY) is nearing completion: the tribunal is currently finishing its last trial in the Mladic case, with judgment expected in November 2017; and in the last appellate case, Prlic et al., judgment is also expected in November 2017 (Mechanism for International Criminal Tribunals. Cases). Remaining proceedings in the cases of Karadžić, Šešelj, and Stanišić and Simatović are under the jurisdiction of the so-called Mechanism for International Criminal Tribunals (Mechanism or the Mechanism) (United Nations Mechanism for International Criminal Tribunals 2017). The Mechanism has been mandated to perform a number of essential functions previously carried out by the ICTY and the ICTR and has assumed responsibility for, inter alia, the enforcement of sentences, administrative review, assignment of cases and counsel, review, contempt and appellate proceedings, issues regarding the referral of cases to national jurisdictions, witness protection measures, as well as various evidentiary and documentary issues (United Nations Mechanism for International Criminal Tribunals 2017). In carrying out these multiple functions, the Mechanism maintains the legacies of these two pioneering ad hoc international criminal courts and strives to reflect best practices in the field of international criminal justice and international human rights.

With the closing of the ICTR and the upcoming closing of the ICTY, an important chapter in international human rights law has come to an end. The ICTY and the ICTR played crucial roles in the development of international criminal law four decades post-Nuremberg, and they contributed toward the solidification of several human rights norms. They reignited the development of international human rights law in general, and their case law contributed toward the fine-tuning of complex legal doctrines, such as genocide and superior or command responsibility, the definition of international armed conflict, the prosecution of crimes of sexual violence, as well as the crystallization of norms protecting human rights. The section below will discuss the general legacies of the Yugoslavia and Rwanda tribunals, before turning to a more specific discussion of the tribunals' human rights legacy.

In the context of international criminal tribunals, scholars have defined "legacy" to mean a lasting impact, most notably on bolstering the rule of law in a particular society by conducting effective trials while also strengthening domestic capacity to do so. Legacy, in this context, implies the extent to which a particular court has had a significant effect by modeling best practices in handling the individual cases and compiling a historical record of the conflict (Pocar 2008, p. 655; O'Keefe 2015, pp. 483–491). Legacy also means laying the groundwork for future efforts to prevent a recurrence of crimes by offering precedents for legal reform, building faith in judicial processes, and promoting greater civic engagement on issues of accountability and justice. This type of legacy is supposed to be long-lasting and continue to have an impact even after the work of the tribunal is completed. According to the United Nations Office of the High Commissioner for Human Rights, "legacy" signifies not just the lasting impact of an ad hoc tribunal on promoting the rule of law in a particular society, which can be achieved by conducting effective trials in order to end impunity while also strengthening domestic judicial capacity. A report on maximizing the legacy of hybrid courts asserted that the need for such tribunals to leave a legacy is firmly accepted as part of United Nations' policy (Office of the UN High Commissioner for Human Rights 2008). In addition to the above view of legal legacy and impact, tribunals can have other types of roles which can meaningfully affect the pursuit of justice and human rights. King and Meernik have described the core missions of the ICTY's mandate (to bring to justice those responsible for serious violations of international humanitarian law) as follows: (1) developing the tribunals' functional and institutional capacities; (2) interpreting, applying, and developing international humanitarian and criminal law; (3) attending to and interacting with the various stakeholders who have vested interests; and (4) promoting deterrence and fostering peace-building to prevent future aggression and conflict (King Kimi and Meernik 2011, pp. 7–8). This framework is also applicable to the ICTR, as this tribunal was charged with the same mandate as the ICTY, with the addition of promoting national reconciliation in Rwanda. In light of the above, "legacy" can be defined more broadly as the enduring influence of the tribunals' work and processes on the ideals, conceptions, and instrumentalities of international criminal law, justice, and human rights.

While the tribunals' legacy is equally important in the development of domestic justice and international criminal law more broadly, the focus of this chapter is on the field of international human rights and international humanitarian law – what is the significance, impact, and legacy of the ad hoc tribunals through this particular lens? The hope is that the legacy of ad hoc tribunals in the fields of international human rights and international humanitarian law will be of particular assistance to those who work with the International Criminal Court (ICC), as much of the ad hoc tribunals' case law has served and will serve as important precedent within the ICC and as the ICC will most likely continue to enhance the same international law principles and doctrines which the ad hoc tribunals have developed. The hope is also that the ICTY and the ICTR will serve as models for future ad hoc tribunals and that such future tribunals will continue to build upon the ICTY's and the ICTR's legacy in the field of human rights law.

First, the ad hoc tribunals have contributed to the protection of universal human rights by successfully charging and convicting defendants of genocidal offenses and by establishing that the violation of the most basic human rights standard – the protection of human life – should never remain unpunished (Robinson and MacNeil 2016, pp. 193–196).

The ICTR in the Akayesu case became the first international tribunal to enter a judgment for genocide as well as the first to interpret the definition of genocide set forth in the 1948 Geneva Conventions. In the Kambanda case, also before the Rwanda tribunal, the defendant pled guilty to genocide, marking the first time in history of international criminal law that an accused person admitted responsibility to for genocide and conspiracy to commit genocide. And by accepting this guilty plea in the Kambanda case, the Rwanda tribunal became the first international tribunal since Nuremberg to issue a judgment against a former head of state. In another case (Bosco Barayagwiza, Nahimana, and Ngeze), the ICTR convicted members of the Rwandan media by holding them responsible for broadcasts intended to inflame the public to commit acts of genocide (Kendall and Nouwen 2016, p. 219; United Nations Mechanism for International Criminal Tribunals 2017).

The ICTY was the first international criminal tribunal to enter a genocide conviction in Europe. In April 2004, in the case of Radislav Krstić, the Appeals Chamber determined that genocide was committed in Srebrenica in 1995, through the execution of more than 7000 Bosnian Muslim men and boys following the take-over of the town by Bosnian Serb forces in the case of Krstić (ICTY Prosecutor v. Krstić 2004). Several other completed ICTY cases relating to the Srebrenica events have ensured that the genocide has been well documented and, in the words of ICTY President Theodor Meron, "consigned to infamy" (Meron 2004). And according to the appellate judgment in the Krstić case "[t]hose who devise and implement genocide seek to deprive humanity of the manifold richness its national-ities, races, ethnicities and religions provide. This is a crime against all humankind, its harm being felt not only by the group targeted for destruction, but by all of humanity" (ICTY Prosecutor v. Krstić 2004, para. 36).

In sum, these ad hoc tribunals, the ICTY and the ICTR, have significantly contributed toward the prosecution of the crime of genocide and toward the notion that genocide is a crime against all that will never again be tolerated by the international community. According to Robinson and MacNeil, "[t]he Tribunals have done much to make the law of genocide workable" (Robinson and MacNeil 2016, p. 196). By focusing on the crime of genocide, which entails the intentional destruction of a specific group within a larger population, the ICTY and the ICTR have established that violations of basic human rights norms, such as the right to life, impose individual criminal responsibility on the offenders (an outcome which human rights tribunals are unable to reach because of their non-penal nature).

Second, the ICTY and the ICTR have contributed to the development of international human rights law by developing case law on crimes of sexual violence and by focusing on specific gender issues. In the Akayesu case, the Rwanda tribunal for the first time defined the crime of rape in international criminal law and recognized rape as a means of perpetrating genocide (ICTR Prosecutor v. Akayesu 1998, paras. 732–733). The Rwanda tribunal created a special unit for gender issues and assistance to victims of genocide, choosing to focus on gender issues and to provide support and care to the victims of genocide. In this manner, the tribunals have, in addition to developing case law on crimes of sexual violence, created a participatory legacy – the idea that victims of serious crimes have a voice within international criminal prosecutions of such crimes (United Nations Mechanism for International Criminal Tribunals 2017). This idea, for better or for worse, is squarely present within the Rome Statute of the ICC. This idea contributes toward the overall protection of human rights, by creating a specific participatory role for victims of human rights violations and by placing on emphasis on victims within international criminal law.

The ICTY has also played a historic role in the prosecution of wartime sexual violence in the former Yugoslavia and has paved the way for a more robust adjudication of such crimes worldwide. From the first days of the tribunal's mandate, investigations were conducted into reports of systematic detention and rape of women, men, and children. More than a third of those convicted by the ICTY have been found guilty of crimes involving sexual violence. Such convictions are one of the tribunal's pioneering achievements. They have ensured that treaties and conventions which have existed on paper throughout the twentieth century have finally been put in practice and violations punished (Sexual Violence and the Triumph of Justice 2017).

The ICTY took groundbreaking steps to respond to the imperative of prosecuting wartime sexual violence. Together with its sister tribunal for Rwanda, the tribunal was among the first courts of its kind to bring explicit charges of wartime sexual violence and to define gender crimes such as rape and sexual enslavement under customary law (ICTY Timeline 2017).

The ICTY was also the first international criminal tribunal to enter convictions for rape as a form of torture and for sexual enslavement as crime against humanity, as well as the first international tribunal based in Europe to pass convictions for rape as a crime against humanity, following a previous case adjudicated by the ICTR. The ICTY proved that effective prosecution of wartime sexual violence is feasible and provided a platform for the survivors to talk about their suffering. That ultimately helped to break the silence and the culture of impunity surrounding these terrible acts. According to Robinson and MacNeil, "the Tribunals have recognized many other forms of sexual and gender-based violence, including sexual slavery, enforced prostitution, enforced sterilization, sexual mutilation, and public humiliation of a sexual nature. Related significant developments lie not in the definition of crimes but in the much needed judicial interventions to ensure that sexual violence is suitably prioritized, properly investigated, and responsibly handled" (Robinson and MacNeil 2016, p. 202).

In addition, the ICTY established a robust Victims and Witnesses Section (VWS), which provided the witnesses with assistance prior to, during, and after their testimony, ranging from practical issues to psychological counseling during their stay in The Hague (ICTY Witnesses 2017). In this manner, the Yugoslavia tribunal, like the Rwanda tribunal, has contributed significantly to the legacy of developing and prosecuting gender-specific crimes and crimes of sexual violence and to ensuring meaningful victim participation in the adjudication process. The two tribunals have thus contributed toward the protection of human rights norms, by ensuring that those who violate such norms, including specific norms on women's rights, will face criminal accountability.

Third, both ad hoc tribunals have contributed toward the development of the doctrine of superior responsibility, by holding that superior responsibility applies to civilians in leadership positions and that it is not confined to purely military leaders (Robinson and MacNeil 2016, pp. 204–209; ICTY Prosecutor v. Delalic 2001, paras. 56–84). This contribution by the ad hoc tribunals is particularly relevant in light of modern-day warfare where conflicts are often fought outside of well-defined militaries and where orders and policies are often crafted by nonmilitary leaders. In this manner, the tribunals have contributed toward upholding and protecting basic human rights norms of protection of life and protection from torture and violence, by holding all leaders, including nonmilitary ones, responsible for possible violations of such norms.

Fourth, the ad hoc tribunals have established a legacy of cooperation and impact on domestic jurisdictions between international tribunals and national authorities. Multiple countries have signed agreements on the enforcement of ICTR's sentences (Mali, Benin, France, Italy, Mali, Rwanda, Senegal, Swaziland, and Sweden). "These agreements illustrate the important role national authorities play in ensuring that those convicted of serious violations of international law serve their sentences in compliance with international detention standards" (United Nations Mechanism for International Criminal Tribunals, ICTR Milestones 2017). In addition, the Rwanda tribunal upheld the first referral of an international criminal indictment to Rwandan national authorities for trial, in the case against Jean-Bosco Uwinkindi. A total of eight ICTR cases have now been referred to Rwanda. Two additional cases have been referred to France for trial. Monitoring in all referred cases is presently being conducted by the Mechanism (United Nations Mechanism for International Criminal Tribunals, ICTR Milestones 2017). By establishing lasting cooperation between the ICTR and national authorities, as well as by providing monitoring schemes, this tribunal has contributed toward ensuring that national jurisdictions and authorities protect and respect human rights in their own ongoing and future trials and proceedings. According to Kendall and Nouwen, "[i]t has been widely claimed that the

ICTR has shaped the Rwandan criminal justice system," by influencing national authorities to abolish the death penalty, to ensure better witness protection programs, and to improve prison conditions (Kendall and Nouwen 2016, p. 212).

Throughout its existence, the ICTY Office of the Prosecutor (OTP) has worked closely with the new states and territories that emerged from the former Yugoslavia on their domestic prosecutions. In the aftermath of the war in Bosnia and Herzegovina (BiH), returning displaced persons and refugees voiced fears about arbitrary arrests on suspicion of war crimes. To protect against this, the OTP agreed to operate a "Rules of the Road" scheme under which local prosecutors were obliged to submit case files to The Hague for review. The Rules of the Road procedure, established under the Rome Agreement of 18 February 1996, regulated the arrest and indictment of alleged perpetrators of war crimes by national authorities. As part of the tribunal's contribution to the reestablishment of peace and security in the region, the ICTY prosecutor agreed to provide an independent review of all local war crimes cases. If a person was already indicted by the OTP, he could be arrested by the national police. If the national police wished to make an arrest where there was no prior indictment, they had to send their evidence to the OTP. Under the Rome Agreement, decisions of the OTP became binding on local prosecutors. In this manner, the ICTY OTP ensured that national authorities within the former Yugoslavia engaged in legitimate prosecutions only without harassing individuals who had not committed any wrongdoing (for political or other nonlegal purposes) (ICTY Working with the Region 2017). Thus, the ICTY OTP contributed toward the protection of basic human rights norms of individuals living in the former Yugoslavia, by ensuring that they were free of arbitrary arrest and unwarranted legal proceedings.

To ensure that as many persons as possible suspected of war crimes are brought to justice, the OTP has provided assistance to national bodies in the region by passing on evidence that may have been of use in local investigations and by transferring whole cases for prosecution locally. A dedicated transition team within the OTP was tasked with handing over to national courts cases involving intermediate- and lower-ranking accused. Such cases have included case files of suspects investigated by the OTP but where no indictments were ever issued, which has resulted in the referral of some files with investigative material to authorities in Serbia, Croatia, and Bosnia, which have then pursued these cases. Secondly, despite indictments issued by the ICTY, a total of 8 cases involving 13 accused have been referred to courts in the former Yugoslavia, mostly to Bosnia and Herzegovina, pursuant to Rule 11bis of the Rules of Procedure and Evidence. On the basis of an ICTY indictment and the supporting evidence provided by the tribunal's prosecution, these cases are then tried in accordance with the national laws of the state in question (ICTY Working with the Region 2017). Thus, the ICTY has contributed toward the protection of human rights norms by ensuring that many of those accused of horrific human rights violations are brought to justice – within national jurisdictions – and by ensuring that national jurisdictions have the tools necessary in order to conduct successful prosecutions while respecting the defendants' rights.

Finally, the OTP has promoted regional cooperation among national prosecutors. The ICTY prosecution has strongly supported efforts to enhance cooperation in criminal matters between states of the former Yugoslavia, as it is an essential step toward rebuilding trust and justice in the region. Successful trials before national courts require that prosecutors in the neighboring countries can collaborate in the collection of evidence and securing witnesses. OTP officials have taken part in several regional meetings, facilitating the creation of good working relationships between the prosecutors in the different states (ICTY Working with the Region 2017). Thus, the Rwanda and the Yugoslavia tribunals have created a significant legacy of cooperation with national authorities and have developed specific models of cooperation that have contributed toward the rebuilding of national justice systems. In this manner, the tribunals have contributed toward the protection of human rights by ensuring that many defendants are prosecuted by the ad hoc tribunals and by national jurisdictions and by promoting adequate due process and judicial standards within national jurisdictions.

Fifth, the ad hoc tribunals have created a significant legacy in the operational sense – by establishing specific case management strategies for the prosecution of complex international crimes and by establishing particular evidentiary procedures resulting in the long-term preservation of evidence which will enable national jurisdictions to prosecute additional cases in the future. For example, the ICTR has held special deposition proceedings in the case of Félicien Kabuga to preserve evidence for use at trial once he is arrested. Similar proceedings were later held in the cases of two other fugitives: Augustin Bizimana and Protais Mpiranya (United Nations Mechanism for International Criminal Tribunals, ICTR Milestones 2017). By holding these proceedings, the ICTR has ensured that the passage of time does not jeopardize the international community's ability to bring these suspects to trial when they are finally apprehended. And the ICTY has established specific evidentiary standards regarding victims of crimes of sexual violence, by allowing them to testify anonymously – witnesses have been able to testify under a pseudonym, with face and voice distortion in video feeds, or in closed session. Through the development of its rules of procedure, the ICTY has also sought to protect the victims of sexual violence from abusive lines of questioning during testimony. "These efforts have led to improved procedural rules, improved protection of victims and witnesses, and the inclusion of relevant advisers on the Tribunals' staffs" (Robinson and MacNeil 2016, p. 202). The ad hoc tribunals have thus left behind an operational legacy, which will undoubtedly serve as a model for future international criminal prosecutions. They have contributed toward the protection of human rights of victims of crimes of sexual violence and have ensured, in at least three cases, that future tribunals will be able to prosecute perpetrators of human rights violations by preserving evidence for potential future prosecutorial use.

Sixth, the ICTR and the ICTY have established a significant legacy regarding due process rights for the accused. According to Michael Karnavas, former President of the Association of Defence Counsel Practicing before the ICTY, "[t]he results at the end of a trial will be meaningless unless a robust defence is afforded to the accused" (ICTY Defence 2017). Despite some shortcomings, it may be argued that the ICTY and the ICTR have established a powerful legacy of the protection of defendants' rights.

The ICTY Statute established that every defendant had the right to counsel of his or her own choosing and that indigent defendants would be provided with defense counsel. In accordance with Article 21 of the ICTY Statute, an accused person may elect to represent himself in person (Updated Statute of the ICTY Article 21 2017). While this right is not unlimited, several ICTY cases have recognized the right to self-representation and allowed the accused to conduct their own defense. Slobodan Milosevic was allowed to conduct his own defense and to self-represent, and defendants Radovan Karadzic and Vojislav Seselj also conducted their defense pro se (Temminck Tuinstra 2011, pp. 346, 353). In Krajisnik, the ICTY Appeals Chamber held that the defendant "nonetheless has a 'cornerstone' right to make his own case to the Tribunal" (ICTY Decision on Mocilo Krajisnik's Request to Self-represent 2007). In such cases of self-representation, the tribunal, through the registrar, has ensured the provision of adequate facilities to the self-represented accused, including the assignment of legal advisers and other support staff to assist the self-represented accused in the preparation of his case, privileged communication with certain categories of defense team members, photocopying, and storage facilities. Furthermore, the ICTY Registrar adopted a special remuneration scheme for persons assisting indigent self-represented accused. A provision was also made for the assignment of an investigator, a case manager, and a language assistant where necessary, to assist with translation (Trechsel 2011, pp. 182–183). It should be noted that many have criticized the ICTY's struggle with the right to self-representation and have highlighted the tribunal's ambiguous approach to this issue, the fact remains that the ICTY did allow several high-profile defendants to represent themselves and did establish this general defense right (Temminck Tuinstra 2011, p. 346). The ICTR, however, has granted the right to self-representation to only one accused, Akayesu, and solely during the sentencing phase of his trial (Temminck Tuinstra 2011, p. 345).

In addition to the defendant's right to self-represent, the ICTY established other important rights for the defendant, such as the right to obtain information upon arrest, the right to be brought before a judge, as well as the right to be tried within a reasonable time (Trechsel 2011, pp. 160–173). Although the ICTR has been criticized on some of these accounts, it adopted virtually identical Rule of Procedure and Evidence as the ICTY, and its judges demonstrated a willingness to protect some of these defense rights. For example, in the case of Jean-Bosco Barayagwiza, the ICTR Appeals Chamber found such fundamental violations of the right to be brought promptly before a judge and to habeas corpus proceedings that it dismissed the indictment and ordered that the defendant be immediately released (ICTR Jean-Bosco Barayagwiza v. The Prosecutor 1999). Thus, both tribunals have contributed toward the legacy of defense rights – by establishing, through case law as well as through elaborate Rules of Procedure and Evidence, that even those accused of the most serious crimes are entitled to the protection of their due process rights.

In sum, the ICTY and the ICTR have significantly contributed toward the development of the field of international criminal law and toward the protection of human rights, by sending a message of impunity and holding those responsible for serious human rights violations criminally accountable, as well as by protecting defense rights on an individual level. The general protection of human rights can be perceived as part of the tribunals' legacy, and future ad hoc tribunals will undoubtedly continue to examine the ICTY and ICTR case law and procedures as relevant models. "The solutions implemented after the ICTY's and ICTR's closure will undoubtedly become part and parcel of the international criminal justice landscape, shaping the normative environment of other ad hoc tribunals and similar experiences in the decades to come" (Acquaviva 2011, p. 536).

The Future of Ad Hoc Tribunals: Continuing to Protect Human Rights?

In light of the ICTY and ICTR precedent and legacy with respect to the protection of human rights, it is interesting to review present and future ad hoc tribunals, in order to assess how these may additionally contribute toward protecting human rights. The following section will discuss the existing Special Tribunal for Lebanon, the recently created Kosovo Special Mechanism, as well as the proposal for a Syria accountability mechanism. For each of these ad hoc tribunals, this section will focus on the goal of protecting human rights and will assess how and whether these tribunals are likely to contribute toward the protectionist narrative, as the ICTY and the ICTR had done.

Special Tribunal for Lebanon

The Special Tribunal for Lebanon (STL) was established in the wake of the assassination of Rafik Hariri, the former Prime Minister of Lebanon, on 14 February 2005. Hariri was assassinated in a large explosion that killed 21 others and injured 226 more people in downtown Beirut. The attack was immediately denounced by the international community and then-United Nations Secretary-General Kofi Annan, who "condemn[ed] in the strongest terms those who instigated, planned and executed this callous political assassination" (Special Tribunal for Lebanon, STL Timeline of Events 2017).

Following additional killings and bombings in Lebanon, in December 2005, the Lebanese government requested that the United Nations create a tribunal of an "international character" to prosecute those responsible for the Hariri assassination and attack, as well as to expand the existing United Nations' mandate to investigate assassinations, assassination attempts, and explosions in Lebanon. The United Nations Security Council adopted Resolution 1644 on December 15, 2005, in which it reaffirmed its condemnation of the February 14, 2005, attack and requested the Secretary-General "to help the Lebanese government identify the assistance needed to try those eventually charged with perpetrating the attack" (Security Council Resolution 1644 2005). In a subsequent Resolution 1664, on March 29, 2006, the Security Council requested that the United Nations Secretary-General consult with the Lebanese government on the establishment of an international tribunal to prosecute those responsible for the February 14, 2005, attack (Security Council Resolution 1664 2006).

In January and February 2007, the Lebanese government and the United Nations signed an agreement for the Special Tribunal for Lebanon. The agreement was never adopted by the Lebanese Parliament, but in April 2007, a majority of Lebanese Members of Parliament called for a Security Council resolution under Chap. VII of the United Nations Charter in order to establish a special tribunal (Special Tribunal for Lebanon, STL Timeline of Events 2017). The United Nations Security Council adopted Resolution 1757 on May 30, 2007, authorizing the establishment of the Special Tribunal for Lebanon (under Chap. VII of the United Nations Charter) (Security Council Resolution 1757 2007). In August 2007, the Netherlands agreed to host the tribunal, and STL officially opened on March 1, 2009, in Leidschendam (near The Hague) (Special Tribunal for Lebanon, STL Timeline of Events 2017).

STL has contributed toward an evolution in the development of international criminal justice with a number of unique features, which do not exist in other international tribunals or courts. First, STL is the first international tribunal to try crimes under national law. STL has been prosecuting, under the Lebanese criminal code, crimes relating to terrorism and "offences against life and personal integrity, illicit associations and failure to report crimes and offences" (Special Tribunal for Lebanon, STL Timeline of Events 2017). STL is the first tribunal of its kind to deal with terrorism as a distinct crime; although terrorism has been described by the United Nations Security Council as a "threat to international peace and security," it has not been within the subject matter of any other international criminal tribunals and has been viewed as a purely domestic offense. STL Appeals Chamber has defined terrorism as an international crime, contributing therefor to the conceptualization of terrorism as an international crime and to ensuring that perpetrators of terrorism offenses will face international justice (Flash 2011).

Although the STL is mandated to apply Lebanese law in its proceedings, the Appeals Chamber of the STL issued an interlocutory decision in which it held that the STL could apply international law related to the definition of terrorism to which Lebanon is bound. The Appeals Chamber referenced the Arab Convention for the Suppression of Terrorism (Convention), articulated a customary international definition of terrorism, and explained how the STL is not limited by Lebanese case law as it applies the Lebanese Criminal Code related to terrorism. This is the first internationalized tribunal to try crimes of terrorism. Thus, *the decisions regarding what constitutes a crime of terrorism could impact how other countries prosecute individuals accused of committing acts of terrorism* (Flash 2011, emphasis added). STL has thus contributed to the protection of human rights, by ensuring that terrorism is prosecuted as an international crime and by allowing victims of terrorist attacks to have their claims heard in an international forum.

Second, STL has adopted a particular participation regime for victims. Under the STL procedures, victims who have suffered harm in the relevant attacks may participate in the trial to present their views and concerns. In fact, victims may become involved in the STL proceedings as soon as the investigation phase is over and the indictments have been confirmed. Although STL Statute does not allow victims to seek compensation at the tribunal, such victims are free to pursue their claims through national courts on the basis of a pronounced STL judgment.

According to the Tribunal's official website, "[t]he STL statute aims to balance the rights of victims to participate in proceedings with the rights of the accused and the Office of the Prosecutor's strategy" (Special Tribunal for Lebanon, Unique features 2017). Through the adoption of a victim participation regime, STL has contributed toward the protection of victims' right – a "trend" in international criminal justice which has also been espoused by the ICC and which may be adopted by future ad hoc tribunals (Trumbull IV 2008, p. 277).

Third, STL Statute has provisions which allow for trials in absentia – without the accused being present or in the custody of the tribunal (Special Tribunal for Lebanon, Unique features 2017). The intent behind this provision is to ensure that justice is pursued and that international criminal prosecutions should not be thwarted by fleeting defendants or states unwilling to extradite such defendants. In order to balance the needs of international criminal justice with the defendants' due process rights, STL Statute allows for trial in absentia under strict conditions: if the accused has waived the right to be present, if the accused has fled or cannot be found, or if the state concerned has not handed the accused over to the tribunal. An absent defendant, according to the STL Statute, must be represented by defense counsel before the tribunal, and such a defendant retains the right to appear in court once the trial has started as well as the right to ask for a retrial once the case is over (Special Tribunal for Lebanon, Unique features 2017). By allowing trials in absentia, STL has contributed toward the protection of human rights by ensuring that relevant cases involving serious crimes are pursued despite the defendant's absence, as well as by respecting due process rights of absent defendants, including allowing such defendants to ask for a retrial.

Fourth, STL has made a significant contribution toward the protection of defense rights. It is the first international tribunal to have established an independent Defence Office with a status equal to that of the Office of the Prosecutor. The Defence Office's mandate is to protect the rights of the accused at all stages of the proceedings, in order to ensure that each accused gets a fair trial. In this manner, STL has contributed toward the protection of due process rights in the international arena, by ensuring that those rights are equally protected and taken into account during international criminal prosecutions (Jalloh 2014, p. 765).

Last, STL has been lauded as contributing to the safeguard of procedural rights, by adopting civil law features which enhance the role of the judge and protect the parties from the dangers of an overzealously conducted adversarial process, as well as by having a standing pretrial judge who ensures that pretrial proceedings are conducted in an efficient manner. Jalloh has argued that these procedural features of STL are beneficial, because "[t]he trial, instead of being shaped to reflect the position most favorable to the parties' particular interests, becomes primarily concerned with discerning the truth and dispensing evenhanded justice" (Jalloh 2014, p. 771).

In sum, following the ICTY and the ICTR models, STL has been established as an ad hoc tribunal that will continue to contribute toward the protection of human rights norms, through its mandate to prosecute terrorist offenses as an international crime and through its unique features aimed at ensuring that international justice is pursued while protecting due process rights of the accused.

Kosovo Specialist Chambers

The Kosovo Specialist Chambers (KSC) and Specialist Prosecutor's Office (KSPO) were established in August 2015. They have jurisdiction over crimes against humanity, war crimes, and other crimes under Kosovo law, and, like the ICTY and STL, they are located at The Hague (Kosovo Specialist Chambers and Specialist Prosecutor's Office, Background 2017). In the wake of the publication of a Council of Europe Parliamentary Assembly Report in January 2011, the European Union decided to create a Special Investigative Task Force (SITF) in September 2011, to conduct a criminal investigation into some of the allegations contained in the report, as well as into other crimes related to such allegations. SITF determined, by summer of 2014, that the evidence investigated was sufficient to support an indictment; however, questions arose as to the adequate judicial forum where such allegations could be investigated and potentially prosecuted. The European Union consulted with Kosovar authorities, through an exchange of letters, regarding the best modality for dealing with these serious allegations. On August 3, 2015, the Kosovo Assembly adopted Article 162 of the Kosovo Constitution and the Law on Specialist Chambers and Specialist Prosecutor's Office (Kosovo Specialist Chambers and Specialist Prosecutor's Office, Background 2017).

KSC is comprised of two organs, the Chambers and the Registry. The Chambers are attached to each level of the court system in Kosovo: the Basic Court, Court of Appeals, Supreme Court, and Constitutional Court. The Chambers will apply Kosovo laws as well as customary international law and international human rights law. KSPO is an independent office for the investigation and prosecution of the crimes within the jurisdiction of the Specialist Chambers. Both KSC and KSPO are staffed with international judges, prosecutors, and officers (Kosovo Specialist Chambers and Specialist Prosecutor's Office, Background 2017).

It is premature to assess whether KSC and KSPO have contributed toward the protection of human rights in general, but it is possible to ascertain the types of protections that may be available under these two mechanisms in light of their governing law and their rules of procedure and evidence. First, it is notable that the Law on Specialist Chambers and Specialist Prosecutor's Office (Governing Law) specifies that the Chambers shall apply, in addition to Kosovo law and customary international law, "international human rights law which sets criminal justice standards including the European Convention on Human Rights and Fundamental Freedoms and the International Covenant on Civil and Political Rights, as given superiority over domestic laws by Article 22 of the Constitution" (Law on Specialist Chambers and Specialist Prosecutor's Office 2017). This explicit reference to human rights law, which will take precedence over Kosovo domestic law, may indicate that the new Kosovo tribunal will pay particular attention to the protection of human rights and that its proceedings will take place in accordance with specific human rights standards. In addition, the Governing Law contains additional references to human rights law (the European Convention on Human Rights and Fundamental Freedoms and the International Covenant on Civil and Political Rights) in Article 12, Applicable Law, and the Governing Law provides explicit definitions of crimes against humanity and war crimes, in Articles 13 and 14, which are consistent with the same definitions as used by other ad hoc tribunals, including the ICTY and the ICTR (Law on Specialist Chambers and Specialist Prosecutor's Office 2017).

In this manner, the KSC may continue building upon the ICTY and ICTR legacies with respect to prosecuting those responsible of most heinous human rights violations and may add on to such legacies by applying specific human rights standards found in fundamental human rights treaties. Article 16 of the Governing Law equally builds upon accomplishments of the Yugoslavia and Rwanda tribunals, by excluding head-of-state immunity, by providing that superior orders will not be a complete defense, and by establishing individual liability based on command responsibility. By embracing these provisions, KSC may ensure that those who commit human rights violations will not be able to escape liability if they did not directly commit the relevant offenses. The Governing Law also incorporates human rights standard into procedure: Article 19 specifies that "[t]he Rules of Procedure and Evidence shall reflect the highest standards of international human rights law including the ECHR and ICCPR with a view to ensuring a fair and expeditious trial taking into account the nature, location and specificities of the proceedings to be heard by the Specialist Chambers" (Law on Specialist Chambers and Specialist Prosecutor's Office 2017). KSC will thus be governed by procedural rights which are consistent with basic human rights standards, and it will conduct fair and efficient trials, thereby ensuring that defense rights are adequately protected (Law on Specialist Chambers and Specialist Prosecutor's Office 2017). Article 21 further elaborates on defense rights, by holding that the accused shall have basic rights, such as the right to be informed of charges pending against him or her, the right to counsel, the right to a fair and expeditious trial, as well as the right not to be compelled to testify against him or herself (Law on Specialist Chambers and Specialist Prosecutor's Office 2017).

Finally, Article 44 on punishments specifically incorporates human rights standards, by holding that KSC should, when determining an appropriate sentence for a convicted defendant, take into account Article 7(2) of the European Convention on Human Rights and Fundamental Freedoms and Article 15(2) of the International Covenant on Civil and Political Rights (Law on Specialist Chambers and Specialist Prosecutor's Office 2017). By embracing specific defense rights and sentencing considerations consistent with international human rights standards, KSC may build on the accomplishments of the ICTY and the ICTR in this area and may on its own contribute further to this field. Similar to the ICC, KSC adopts a victim participation regime – Article 22 of the Governing Law provides that victims are entitled to officially participate in KSC proceedings and to be officially represented by Victims' Counsel (Law on Specialist Chambers and Specialist Prosecutor's Office 2017). Finally, Article 23 creates a victim and witness protection regime, by specifying that KSC's Rules of Procedure and Evidence "shall provide for the protection of victims and witnesses including their safety, physical and psychological well-being, dignity and privacy" (Law on Specialist Chambers and Specialist Prosecutor's Office 2017). KSC thus goes further than the ICTY and the ICTR in terms of its victim participation regime and, like the ICTY and the ICTR, attempts to create adequate protectionist mechanism to encourage victim and witness safety during and after the proceedings. It is likely that KSC will thus contribute to the protection of victims' rights by ensuring that they have a voice in future criminal proceedings and by paying particular attention to their safety and well-being.

In addition to the Governing Law detailed above, which contains multiple specific references to international human rights standards, it should be noted that KSC's Rules of Procedure and Evidence, adopted in August 2017, contain elaborate procedural safeguards which are consistent with ICTY's and ICTR's procedural rules and which will likely ensure that KSC's proceedings function in uniformity with relevant international procedural standards (Rules of Procedure and Evidence before the Kosovo Specialist Chambers 2017). KSC's Rules of Procedure and Evidence specifically refer to the European Convention on Human Rights, which "is remarkable in many regards: the preference to refer to the ECHR rather than 'internationally recognized human rights' (Article 21(3) ICC-Statute) has the potential of strengthening the rights of the defendant" (Heinze 2017). "In principle, the primary desired impact from the Kosovo Specialist Chambers is to bring justice to the victims, to hold perpetrators accountable for their crimes, and end the cycle of impunity in the hope that it will leave a positive legacy for peace and justice in Kosovo and the wider region" (Visoka 2017). If KSC were to actually accomplish this, most would agree that it would contribute significantly to the protection of human rights on the individual level and to the strengthening of human rights norms at the normative and institutional levels.

Syria Mechanism

Since 2011, the conflict in Syria has caused the death of hundreds of thousands of individuals and the displacement of millions. Efforts to refer the Syrian situation to the ICC have consistently failed despite well-documented reports about the commission of serious crimes in Syria, including the use of chemical weapons against civilians, torture, the use of child soldiers, and crimes of sexual violence. Only a handful of situations have been investigated thus far, mostly within national jurisdictions of Western European nations. While the Security Council has been deadlocked with respect to Syria, General Assembly passed a resolution in December 2016, establishing the International, Impartial and Independent Mechanism to Assist in the Investigation and Prosecution of Persons Responsible for the Most Serious Crimes Under International Law Committed in the Syrian Arab Republic since March 2011 (Mechanism) (Hohler and Pederson 2017).

The Mechanism is not a tribunal, and its purpose instead is to collect and preserve evidence, which will later be shared with relevant international and national tribunals that may in the future prosecute those responsible for crimes committed in Syria. The Mechanism's mandate is to focus on the most serious crimes: genocide, crimes against humanity, and war crimes. The Mechanism will be located in Geneva, and it will be staffed with an international judge or prosecutor and renowned experts in international criminal law. The Mechanism's primary purpose will be to collect and organize evidence (both inculpatory and exculpatory), which will in the future be shared with competent tribunals and which will contribute toward future prosecutions of perpetrators of Syrian atrocities. The Mechanism, however, will not share information with jurisdictions and authorities which impose the death penalty and/or which do not abide by basic international human rights standards, such as the right to a fair trial (Hohler and Pederson 2017). According to one set of commentators, "[t]he Mechanism is an important addition to the international justice landscape" which may "provide a bridge between the contemporaneous collection of evidence and its use in trials that may take place years or even decades later" (Hohler and Pederson 2017). Overall, the Mechanism's ultimate goal is to "ensure justice for the victims of these crimes and for all the Syrian people affected by the violence" (Love 2017).

For now, according to Kenneth Roth, executive director of Human Rights Watch, the Mechanism is a "prosecutor without a tribunal," and it remains to be seen how the evidence it collects may be used in the future and whether the Mechanism will ultimately contribute toward the protection of human rights (Reini 2017). Because of Russian veto, Security Council has been deadlocked, and it is unlikely that the Syrian situation will be referred to the ICC in the near future. Thus, it appears more likely that the Mechanism will share evidence and information with national jurisdictions, prosecuting perpetrators of Syrian atrocities under a universal jurisdiction model. According to Amnesty International, investigations into Syria are already occurring in France, Germany, the Netherlands, Norway, Sweden, and Switzerland. In Sweden, two rebels have been separately tried and jailed for crimes in Syria's war after they left the country and traveled to Sweden. In addition, Spanish authorities have initiated proceedings against nine Syrian government officials over claims of the torture and execution of a detained man; this case has been brought by the alleged victim's sister, who is a Spanish woman of Syrian origin (Reini 2017). More investigations and cases of this sort could take place in the future, and it is human rights defenders' hope that the Mechanism will continue to assist with such prosecutions and cases. While prosecuting perpetrators of Syrian atrocities in national courts under universal jurisdiction constitutes imperfect justice (because such cases are often piecemeal, unlikely to satisfy all victims, result in trials in absentia, and may result in dismissals), slow and imperfect justice may be beneficial to no justice at all. According to war crimes prosecutor Stephen Rapp, "the slow-moving wheels of justice eventually caught up with Chile's Augusto Pinochet and Slobodan Milosevic of the former Yugoslavia" (Reini 2017).

With respect to Syria, it may be that the war ends in regime transition and that members of the Assad leadership face accountability, either in the ICC (assuming no Russian veto) or in an ad hoc tribunal, set up by the General Assembly or negotiated by the new Syrian leadership and the international community. In the United States, a group of senator recently introduced a bipartisan bill – Syrian War Crimes Accountability Act – aimed at investigating war crimes, crimes against humanity, and genocide in Syria and at imposing accountability on Syrian President Assad. In this bill, the senators called on the United States Secretary of State to assist in creating a hybrid tribunal to investigate and prosecute those responsible for most heinous abuses in Syria, as part of "credible transitional justice efforts" (US Senators call for 'hybrid' tribunal for Syrian war crimes 2017).

In sum, it may be argued that the Mechanism is the first step necessary toward protecting human rights in Syria, by collecting evidence necessary toward successful future prosecutions and by initiating the accountability conversation regarding Syria within the international community. As mentioned above, in light of the Russian veto, it is unlikely that the Security Council will refer the Syrian situation to the ICC in the near future. It is more likely that the Syrian situation will be investigated either within national jurisdictions or that a new ad hoc tribunal will be created. A new ad hoc tribunal on Syria could build upon the legacy of the ICTY and the ICTR and could contribute further toward the protection of human rights in the international community.

Conclusion

As discussed above, the ICTY and the ICTR have contributed significantly toward the elaboration of human rights norms on both the substantive and procedural levels. These ad hoc tribunals have contributed toward the development of specific international criminal law norms, aimed at imposing liability on those most responsible for heinous human rights violations. As discussed above, the ICTY and the ICTR were the first tribunals ever to prosecute and convict individuals of genocide; they were pioneers in terms of prosecuting crimes of sexual violence; they confirmed the idea that civilian leaders can face criminal responsibility in almost the same manner as military commanders; and they established specific protective procedures for victims, in order to ensure their safe participation within criminal proceedings involving their aggressors. In addition, these ad hoc tribunals have solidified due process rights for all defendants, including those accused of the most serious crimes and human rights violations. Finally, these ad hoc tribunals have developed extensive procedural and evidentiary rules, which have contributed further toward safeguarding defendants' due process rights and toward protecting the fairness and impartiality of international judicial processes.

Other ad hoc tribunals have built upon the ICTY's and the ICTR's legacy, by adopting similar substantive and procedural norms aimed at protecting human rights in general. The Special Tribunal for Lebanon is a prime example of a more recent ad hoc tribunal which has embraced the Yugoslavia and Rwanda tribunals' models while also adding unique features, such as prosecuting the crime of terrorism as an international offense, establishing a victim participation regime, providing for trials in absentia, solidifying defense rights, and creating elaborate procedural rules which encompass common and civil law features. STL's unique features can be viewed as enhancing the tribunal's ability to protect human rights. In addition, two new accountability mechanisms may further contribute toward the protection of human rights: the newly established Kosovo Specialist Chambers and the International, Impartial, and Independent Mechanism for Syria. The Kosovo Specialist Chambers have followed the ICTY's and ICTR's model in some ways, by choosing to prosecute offenders for the same heinous international criminal law violations as the ICTY and the ICTR (genocide, crimes against humanity, and war crimes). KSC however goes a step further than the ICTY and the ICTR in terms of protecting human rights: it embraces a victim participation regime, and it specifically references and incorporates basic human rights treaties, such as the International Covenant on Civil and Political Rights and the European Convention, into its constitutive documents. The Mechanism for Syria is for now an evidence-collecting organ, but many in the international community are hopeful that it will someday share such evidence with a future ad hoc tribunal prosecuting perpetrators of human rights violation in Syria. Current and future ad hoc tribunals have benefitted tremendously from the ICTY and ICTR models, and they will hopefully continue the excellent work completed by the Yugoslavia and the Rwanda tribunals in the field of human rights law. Human rights norms will likely continue to evolve through the work of current and future ad hoc tribunals.

References

Acquaviva G (2011) 'Best before date shown': residual mechanisms at the ICTY. In: Swart B, Zaharand A, Sluiter G (eds) The legacy of the international criminal tribunal for the former Yugoslavia. Oxford University Press, Oxford, pp 507–537

Flash M (2011) Special tribunal for Lebanon defines terrorism, human rights brief 10 Oct 2011. http://hrbrief.org/hearings/the-special-tribunal-for-lebanon-defines-terrorism. Accessed 10 Sept 2017

Heinze A (2017) The Kosovo Specialist Chamber's rules of procedure and evidence, EjilTalk! 17 Aug 2017. https://www.ejiltalk.org/the-kosovo-specialist-chambers-rules-of-procedure-and-evidence/. Accessed 5 Sept 2017

Hohler B, Pederson E (2017) The Syria mechanism: bridge to prosecutions or evidentiary limbo? E-International Relations 26 May 2017. http://www.e-ir.info/2017/05/26/the-syria-mechanism-bridge-to-prosecutions-or-evidentiary-limbo/. Accessed 12 Sept 2017

http://www.icty.org/en/about/registry/witnesses International Criminal Tribunal for the former Yugoslavia, Witnesses (2017) http://www.icty.org/en/about/registry/witnesses. Accessed 5 Sept 2017

Human Rights Advocacy and the History of International Human Rights Standards (2017) Individual criminal accountability. http://humanrightshistory.umich.edu/accountability/individual-criminal-accountability. Accessed 10 Sept 2017

International Criminal Court for the Former Yugoslavia, Prosecutor v. Delalic (2001) Case No. IT-96-21-A, Appeals judgment, 20 Feb 2001

International Criminal Tribunal for Former Yugoslavia, ICTY Timeline (2017) http://www.icty.org/en/in-focus/timeline. Accessed 5 Sept 2017

International Criminal Tribunal for Rwanda Jean-Bosco Barayagwiza v. The Prosecutor (1999) Case No ICTR-97-19-AR73, Decision of the Appeals Chamber, 3 Nov 1999

International Criminal Tribunal for the Former Yugoslavia Decision on Mocilo Krajisnik's Request to Self-represent (2007) On Counsel's motions in relation to appointment of amicus curiae, and on the prosecution motion of 16 February 2007, Krajisnik, IT-00-39-A, ICTY App Ch., 11 May 2007

International Criminal Tribunal for the Former Yugoslavia, Defence (2017). http://www.icty.org/en/about/defence. Accessed 1 Sept 2017

International Criminal Tribunal for the Former Yugoslavia Prosecutor v. Krstić (2004) Case No. IT-98-33-A, Appeals judgment, 19 Apr 2004

International Criminal Tribunal for the former Yugoslavia, Working with the Region (2017) http://www.icty.org/en/about/office-of-the-prosecutor/working-with-the-region. Accessed 6 Sept 2017

Jalloh CC (2014) The special tribunal for Lebanon: a defense perspective. Vanderbilt J Transnat'l Law 47:765–842

Kendall S, Nouwen SMH (2016) Speaking of legacy: toward an ethos of modesty at the international criminal tribunal for Rwanda. American J Int'l L 110:212–232

King Kimi L, Meernik JD (2011) Assessing the impact of the international criminal tribunal for the former Yugoslavia: balancing international and local interests while doing justice. In: Swart B et al (eds) The legacy of the international criminal tribunal for the former Yugoslavia. Oxford University Press, Oxford, pp 7–54

Kosovo Specialist Chambers and Specialist Prosecutor's Office, Background (2017) https://www.scp-ks.org/en/background. Accessed 11 Sept 2017

Law on Specialist Chambers and Specialist Prosecutor's Office (2017) http://www.kuvendikosoves.org/common/docs/ligjet/05-L-053%20a.pdf. Accessed 12 Sept 2017

Love K (2017) Will U.N.'s accountability mechanism provide justice in Syria?, Washington Report on Middle East Affairs 5 April 2017. https://www.washingtonreport.me/jordan/lebanon/syria/will-u.n.s-accountability-mechanism-provide-justice-in-syria.html. Accessed 13 Sept 2017

Meron T (2004) Address by the ICTY President, 23 June 2004. http://www.icty.org/en/press/address-icty-president-theodor-meron-potocari-memorial-cemetery. Accessed 7 Sept 2017

O'Keefe R (2015) International criminal law. Oxford University Press, Oxford

Office of the UN High Commissioner for Human Rights (2008) Rule of law tools for Postconflict States, maximizing the legacy of hybrid courts, UN Sales No. HR/PUB/08/2

Pocar F (2008) Completion or continuation strategy? Appraising problems and possible developments in building the legacy of the ICTY. J Int'l Crim Justice 6(6):655–665

Reini J (2017) Could Syria's 'prosecutor without a tribunal' work? Aljazeera 31 May 2017. http://www.aljazeera.com/indepth/features/2017/05/syria-prosecutor-tribunal-work-170529110910869.html. Accessed 13 Sept 2017

Robinson D, MacNeil G (2016) The tribunals and the renaissance of international criminal law: three themes. American J Int'l L 110:191–211

Rules of Procedure and Evidence before the Kosovo Specialist Chambers (2017), KSC-BD-03/Rev1/2017/1 of 127. https://www.scp-ks.org/en/documents/rules-procedure-and-evidence-kosovo-specialist-chambers-including-rules-procedure. Accessed 13 Sept 2017

Security Council Resolution 1644. UN Doc. S/RES/1644 (2005)

Security Council Resolution 1664. UN Doc. S/RES/1664 (2006)

Security Council Resolution 1757. UN Doc. S/RES/1757 (2007)

Sexual Violence and the Triumph of Justice Documentary. (2017) http://www.icty.org/en/in-focus/timeline. Accessed 10 Sept 2017

Special Tribunal for Lebanon, STL Timeline of Events. (2017) https://www.stl-tsl.org/en/about-the-stl/636-creation-of-the-stl. Accessed 6 Sept 2017

Special Tribunal for Lebanon, Unique features (2017) – The participation of victims. https://www.stl-tsl.org/en/about-the-stl/unique-features/628-the-participation-of-victims. Accessed 9 Sept 2017

Temminck Tuinstra J (2011) The ICTY's continuing struggle with the right to self-representation. In: Swart B, Zaharand A, Sluiter G (eds) The legacy of the international criminal tribunal for the former Yugoslavia. Oxford University Press, Oxford, pp 345–376

Trechsel S (2011) Rights in criminal proceedings under the ECHR and the ICTY statute – a precarious comparison. In: Swart B, Zaharand A, Sluiter G (eds) The legacy of the international criminal tribunal for the former Yugoslavia. Oxford University Press, Oxford, pp 149–189

Trumbull CP IV (2008) The victims of victim participation in international criminal proceedings. Mich J Int'l L 29(4):777–826

United Nations Mechanism for International Criminal Tribunals, A Compendium on the Legacy of the ICTR and the Development of International Law. http://unictr.unmict.org/en/compendium-legacy-ictr-and-development-international-law. Accessed 5 Sept 2017

United Nations Mechanism for International Criminal Tribunals (2017) Cases, Akayesu, Jean-Paul. http://www.unmict.org/en/cases/mict-13-30. Accessed 5 Sept 2017

United Nations Mechanism for International Criminal Tribunals, ICTR Milestones (2017) http://unictr.unmict.org/en/ictr-milestones. Accessed 10 Sept 2017

Updated Statute of the International Criminal Tribunal for the Former Yugoslavia (2017) http://www.icty.org/x/file/Legal%20Library/Statute/statute_sept09_en.pdf. Accessed 31 Aug 2017

US Senators call for 'hybrid' tribunal for Syrian war crimes. rt.com 7 April 2017. https://www.rt.com/usa/384024-hybrid-tribunal-syria-bill/. Accessed 13 Sept 2017

Visoka G (2017) Righting justice: can the Kosovo Specialist Chambers make a positive societal impact? Prishtina Insight 25 Aug 2017. http://prishtinainsight.com/righting-justice-can-kosovo-specialist-chambers-make-positive-societal-impact/. Accessed 5 Sept 2017

The International Criminal Court between Human Rights and Realpolitik

Luigi Daniele

Contents

Introduction: The Road to the International Criminal Court 356
Structure of the International Criminal Court 358
Crimes "of concern to the international community as a whole" 360
   Genocide 361
   Crimes Against Humanity 362
   War Crimes 364
   The Crime of Aggression 367
"Trigger Mechanisms" and the Jurisdiction of the International Criminal Court 367
Admissibility Issues 369
Conclusion: The Unfulfilled Promises of the International Criminal Court 371
References 374

Abstract

This chapter provides a general overview on the law and practice of the International Criminal Court (ICC). The introductive section presents an account of the early modern attempts to establish a permanent international criminal tribunal. Section two describes the structure of the Court and the role of its different organs. The third section examines the main legal features of the crimes defined in the Rome Statute, that is, genocide, crimes against humanity, war crimes, and the crime of aggression. Section four describes the jurisdiction of the Court and its trigger mechanisms. Section five, after outlining the notion of complementarity, debates the issues of admissibility of situation and cases before the Court itself. Section six places into question whether and to what extent the Court can be considered a human rights institution, taking into account the different, complex,

L. Daniele (✉)
Nottingham Trent University, Nottingham, UK

University of the Studies of Naples Federico II, Naples, Italy
e-mail: luigi.daniele@ntu.ac.uk

© Springer Nature Singapore Pte Ltd. 2018
G. Oberleitner (ed.), *International Human Rights Institutions, Tribunals, and Courts*,
International Human Rights, https://doi.org/10.1007/978-981-10-5206-4_13

and sometimes conflicting goals declared in the Statute and conceptualized by the scholarship. It also offers an overview of the main problems surrounding role and practice of the ICC, with a focus on the Court's unwillingness or inability to investigate and sanction serious violations committed by agents of powerful states in the international arena.

Keywords
International Criminal Court · ICC · International criminal law · Genocide · Crimes against humanity · War crimes · Crime of aggression

Introduction: The Road to the International Criminal Court

The creation of a permanent international criminal tribunal as the International Criminal Court (ICC) , with potentially worldwide jurisdiction, is one of the most significant developments not only in international criminal law in the last decades, but possibly in the institutional and legal history of contemporaneity (Bergsmo et al. 2014). By signing and ratifying the 1998 Rome Statute, in fact, for the first time States have voluntarily accepted to limit their sovereignty and to confer (complementary) jurisdiction over international crimes to a supranational institution. This profile constitutes a breakthrough in the international legal landscape, in particular considering that criminal law has historically been the most self-contained part of domestic justice systems, as direct expression of the criminal policy options and of the sociocultural identity of the countries. Until a few decades ago, this achievement would have been regarded as utopic and unlikely. Several proposals for a supranational criminal court, had in fact, been advanced since the late 1800s (Hall 1998) and different attempts to establish an international criminal tribunal had failed in the past.

After World War I, the extent of violence and destruction brought about by the transgressions of the laws and customs of war prompted the Allied governments, during the Paris Peace Conference of 1919, to establish a Commission on the Responsibility of the Authors of the War and on Enforcement of Penalties. It was tasked with formulating recommendations to identify and try suspected war criminals of the defeated powers. Following the Commission's report, the Versailles Treaty included provisions affirming the right of the Allies "to bring before military tribunals persons accused of having committed acts in violation of the laws and customs of war." As a result, William II of Hohenzollern was arraigned for a "supreme offence against international morality and the sanctity of treaties." Alongside the former emperor, the list of war crimes suspects included hundreds of individuals sought for extradition by the Allies. The offences were mostly related to the killing of civilians during the invasion of Belgium and France, while other major categories included crimes against prisoners of war, and deportations. After the establishment of the war crimes tribunal in Leipzig, in the end, only 12 trials were held, while Wilhelm fled to The Netherlands, where he was granted asylum.

After the failure of the Leipzig war crime tribunal, in the Third Committee of the First Assembly of the League of Nations, and against the proposal to establish a High

Court of Justice competent to try crimes constituting a "breach of international public order or against the universal law of nations," it was acknowledged that "[t]here [was] not yet any international penal law recognised by all nations" (Records of the First Assembly of the League of Nations 1920). Delegates recognized that the boundaries of criminal law were still coincident with those of the nation-state, both theoretically and politically.

Another failed attempt occurred in 1937, at the International Conference on the Repression of Terrorism. Two draft conventions were discussed. The first draft convention, considered and adopted by the Conference, dealt with the prevention and punishment of terrorism, and qualified as criminal various terrorist acts. The second was a draft convention for the creation of an international criminal tribunal, which would have exercised its jurisdiction over "persons accused of any offence dealt with in the Convention for the Prevention and Punishment of Terrorism." The contracting parties, thus, instead of proceeding in their own courts, were entitled to commit for trial to the international criminal court persons charged with different acts referred to in the Terrorism Convention. It was intended that this international criminal court would have been a permanent body, which would have sat only when seized of an offence within its jurisdiction.

A significant step was taken following the conclusion of World War II with the establishment of the International Military Tribunal of Nuremberg and the International Military Tribunal of Tokyo (IMT), which represented an extraordinary advance in the path of international criminal justice. However, the Nuremberg IMT was established by the Allies to adjudicate the crimes of the major war criminals of the Axis, therefore with a special focus on a category of perpetrators, rather than on the conducts themselves, and, most importantly, ex post facto, with several points of attrition with the legality principle (Kelsen 1947). Furthermore, even if the principles affirmed in the Charter and in the Judgement of the Nuremberg Tribunal were recognized to be part of International Law, no other international criminal tribunals were created until half a century later.

Meanwhile, in 1948 the question of an international criminal jurisdiction re-emerged during the negotiations for the Genocide Convention. However, the Convention only mentioned the possibility of a future international penal tribunal to try persons charged with genocide, upon acceptance of the jurisdiction by the contracting parties. In occasion of the approval of the Convention, the UN General Assembly commissioned the ILC to conduct a study on the possibility of establishing an international judicial mechanism for the prosecution of international crimes, with particular concern to the crime of genocide. The idea of a permanent tribunal, however, had not gathered enough support in the international community, and the mounting tensions, which would have culminated in the Cold War, generated a stall in the relevant institutional debate.

In line with the studies that – in countertrend to the ample attention directed at euro-centrism and the colonial mind-set behind the rise of modern international law – illustrate the importance of the decolonization and of the endeavors of politicians, jurists, and diplomats of the Global South in setting the human rights agenda after 1948 (Jensen 2016), it can be noted that it was a proposal by Trinidad and Tobago (leading a coalition of 16 Caribbean and African States) to the UN General Assembly, in 1989, that fostered new attention around the possibility to create a permanent supranational criminal tribunal. The General Assembly, in response, requested that to the ILC to draft a statute for the new court, which was finalized in 1994 (Bassiouni 1998). The draft proposed that the jurisdiction of the new court should have included several crimes, between which the grave breaches listed in the 1977 Additional Protocol I to the Geneva Conventions: offences under six terrorism instruments, offences contained in the Apartheid Convention, and the offences contained in the UN Drug Convention.

Around the same period, international criminal justice regained centrality and support in the international community, in response to mass atrocities and human rights violations that – for the first time under extensive mass media coverage – were disclosed to the world public (Simmons 2009). This climate prompted the creation of the ad hoc International Criminal Tribunals for Rwanda and Former Yugoslavia. These tribunals, however, were established by the United Nation Security Council, through Security Council resolutions 827 (1993) and 955 (1994), and even if behind these initiatives there had been multilateral efforts, it was argued by some that the Security Council had no power – not even under Chap. VII of the UN Charter – to establish jurisdictional institutions.

Despite the controversies, these developments increased the belief in the necessity of a permanent international criminal tribunal. This, together with the growing mobilization from civil society and NGOs demanding accountability for the most serious human rights violations (Pace and Schense 2002), paved the way for the establishment of the International Criminal Court. A Preparatory Committee was entrusted with composing a draft convention on the basis of the text completed by the ILC in 1994. The Committee made significant progresses, putting together a draft statute with hundreds of alternative proposals. It was on the basis of this document that the 1998 Rome Conference on the Establishment of an International Criminal Court commenced its works, with participation of delegations from 160 States and a number of NGOs. The negotiations lasted 5 weeks and included delicate compromises over a plethora of highly controversial and debated issues of legal, political, and linguistic nature (Lee 1999). The Rome Statute, approved by 120 States on 17 July 1998, reflects these compromises in its law and transposes them in the structure and working mechanisms of the ICC. Before looking at the substantive law of the Court and at the crime within its jurisdiction, it is important to understand its structure and composition.

Structure of the International Criminal Court

The Court is composed of four organs: the Chambers, the Office of the Prosecutor, the Presidency, and the Registry. Each of these organs carries out specific functions. Chambers are organized into three divisions: Pre-Trial Chambers (each composed of one or three judges), Trial Chambers (each composed by three judges), and Appeals Chamber (composed of five judges). The Pre-Trial Chambers decide over all the issues arising before the trial phase. They have a crucial role in supervising how the Office of the Prosecutor carries out its investigations and prosecutorial activities. These Chambers safeguards the rights of suspects, victims, and witnesses during the investigatory phase, and ensure legality and integrity of the proceedings. The Pre-Trial Chambers decide whether or not to issue arrest warrants (in case there are reasonable grounds to believe that the person has committed a crime within the Court's jurisdiction and that he or she will not appear voluntarily before the Court, or will endanger the proceedings or investigation, or will continue committing crimes if not arrested) or summons to appear at the Office of the Prosecutor's request (if there are grounds to believe that the person will cooperate and appear before to the Court voluntarily). These Chambers also decide whether or not to confirm the charges formulated by the Office of the Prosecutor against a suspect, if there is sufficient evidence to establish substantial grounds to believe that the person committed the crimes charged. Finally, they decide on the admissibility of situations and cases.

Once a Pre-Trial Chamber confirms the charges against an alleged perpetrator, the Presidency constitutes a Trial Chamber (composed of three judges) to try the case. The Trial Chamber rules on the admissibility or relevance of evidence, and decides on the merit of the case, that is whether an accused is innocent or guilty of the charges. If the accused is found guilty, these Chambers can impose a sentence (for a maximum of 30 years or life imprisonment). Financial penalties, or restitutions and compensations, may also be imposed. Trial Chambers, in addition, ensure that trials are fair and expeditious, and conducted in full respect of the rights of the accused and due regard for the protection of victims and witnesses.

Following the acquittal or the conviction of the accused, both the Defense and the Prosecutor have right to appeal a Trial Chamber's verdict before the Appeal Chamber. The Prosecutor can appeal on the basis of an error of fact, an error of law, or a procedural error. The Defense can appeal on the same bases, but also on the basis of other ground that affects the fairness or reliability of the proceedings or decision. Sentences passed by the Chamber may also be appealed, on the ground of disproportion between the crime and the sentence. If the Appeals Chamber finds that the proceedings were unfair, to the point of affecting the reliability of the decision or of the sentence, or that the decision or sentence was affected by error of fact, of law, or procedural error, it can amend the sentence or even reverse the decision. In this case, this will be the final judgement of the case, unless, on the same grounds, the Appeals Chamber orders a new trial before a different Trial Chamber. The Appeal Chamber is composed of five judges. They are never the same as those who gave the original verdict.

All the judges of the ICC need to have established competence in criminal law and relevant areas of international law. The Statute requires the judges to be chosen from "among persons of high moral character, impartiality and integrity." Art. 36 of the Statute, in addition, requires the States Parties to take into account, for the selection of the judges, representation of the principal legal systems of the world, equitable geographical representation, and fair representation of female and male judges.

It is the Assembly of States Parties that proceeds to the elections of the 18 judges of the Court, by secret ballot, and for a mandate of 9 years.

The Office of the Prosecutor (OTP), an independent and separate organ of the ICC, has a mandate to examine situations in which one or more crimes within the jurisdiction of the Court appear to have been committed. The purpose of these examinations is to determine whether there is a reasonable basis to initiate an investigation and then to prosecute those who are allegedly most responsible for those crimes. As the ICC itself declares, it is "for the first time in history that an international Prosecutor has been given the mandate, by an ever-growing number of States, to independently and impartiality select situations for investigation where atrocity crimes are or have been committed on their territories or by their nationals."

Three division compose the OTP which work together to fulfil its mandate. Firstly, there is the Investigation Division, responsible for gathering and examining evidence, questioning individuals under investigation, victims, and witnesses. Importantly, in this respect, the Statute requires the OPT to investigate both incriminating and exonerating circumstances. The OTP therefore has a duty both to act in the interests of justice, and at the same time, safeguard the interests of those being investigated. Secondly, the Office has a Prosecution Division, whose main duty is to litigate cases before the various Chambers of the Court. Thirdly, there is the Jurisdiction, Complementarity, and Cooperation Division, which, supported by the Investigation Division, assesses information received and the situations referred to the Court, in order to determine their admissibility.

The Presidency (composed of a President and two Vice-Presidents elected by an absolute majority of the judges) has responsibility for the administration of the Court, with the exception of the Office of the Prosecutor. The Presidency constitutes the Chambers and assigns the cases. In addition, it represents the Court in external relations and activities, both with States and other entities. As for the Registry, its mandate is to provide for the nonjudicial aspects of the administration and servicing of the Court. It provides administrative support to the Chambers and the Office of the Prosecutor. The Registry is the Court's channel of communication, and therefore has responsibility for the ICC's public information and outreach activities.

Crimes "of concern to the international community as a whole"

The ICC has jurisdiction over those crimes described by the Preamble of the Rome Statute as "most serious crimes of concern to the international community as a whole." Literature debates what are the distinctive legal features of international crimes generally considered (Heller 2017). Bassiouni identifies in this respect five criteria applicable to the

> policy of international criminalization: (a) the prohibited conduct affects a significant international interest, in particular, if it constitutes a threat to international peace and security; (b) the prohibited conduct constitutes egregious conduct deemed offensive to the commonly shared values of the world community, including what has historically been referred to as conduct shocking to the conscience of humanity; (c) the prohibited conduct has transnational implications in that it involves or effects more than one state in its planning, preparation, or commission, either through the diversity of nationality of its perpetrators or

victims, or because the means employed transcend national boundaries; (d) the conduct is harmful to an internationally protected person or interest; and (e) the conduct violates an internationally protected interest but it does not rise to the level required by (a) or (b), however, because of its nature, it can best be prevented and suppressed by international criminalization (Bassiouni 2012).

On the basis of an empirical analysis of 281 conventions, the same author classified 27 international crimes. However, only four of these crimes fall within the jurisdiction of the ICC. They are often referred to as international "core crimes," namely: genocide, crimes against humanity, war crimes, and – from July 2018 – the crime of aggression.

The main common features of these crimes, in relation to their objective elements, are their scale and systematic nature. They are in fact usually characterized by a degree of "systemic criminality" (Röling 1960), involving ideological, political or ethnic elements, a connection with a state or state-like organization policy or plan, or a large-scale commission. Furthermore, whether they are committed by state officials, leaders of non-state armed groups, or other individuals, these crimes usually involve many actors and patterns of actions violating the most fundamental human rights of their victims, from physical integrity to dignity. It is this systematic nature and heinousness that bring these offences to be – as declared by the Preamble – of concern to the international community as a whole, as if the conduct to be adjudicated had the capacity of violating not only the basic rights of the victims, but also of negating a sort of minimum, common moral ground of mankind – of Kantian ascendance – by dehumanizing the victims themselves.

Genocide

The first crime mentioned in the Rome Statute constitutes a preeminent example of this. It is the crime of genocide. The term "genocide" was coined in 1943 by the Polish Jurist Raphael Lemkin, whose family was killed during the Nazi occupation of Poland. The term appeared for the first time in papers in 1944, in Lemkin's text "Axis Rule in Occupied Europe." With this concept, the jurist meant to designate not only the immediate destruction of a group, but also a coordinated plan, involving different conducts, aimed at destroying the fundamental premises for the life of a group, including political and social institutions, culture, language, freedom, and dignity. The legal concept is today narrower than that outlined in this original version. Art. 6 of the Statute, reproducing Art. II of the Genocide Convention of 1948 and the definition adopted in the Statutes of the ad hoc tribunals, states:

> [. . .] 'genocide' means any of the following acts committed with intent to destroy, in whole or in part, a national, ethnical, racial or religious group, as such: (a) Killing members of the group; (b) Causing serious bodily or mental harm to members of the group; (c) Deliberately inflicting on the group conditions of life calculated to bring about its physical destruction in whole or in part; (d) Imposing measures intended to prevent births within the group; (e) Forcibly transferring children of the group to another group.

As stated in the General Assembly Res. 96(1) of 1946, genocide "is the denial of the right of existence of entire human groups, as homicide is the denial of the right to live of individual human beings." This crime is therefore simultaneously aimed at eliminating individuals, as members of a group, at destroying the group itself, and – ultimately – at eliminating, by so doing, a segment of human diversity. The distinctive element of this crime, thus, is the special intent "to destroy, in whole or in part, a national, ethnical, racial or religious group, as such," which has to sustain the intention to commit the specific prohibited acts listed in art. 6 (a) to (e). Intuitively, the most problematic aspect of this formulation of the offence is the proof of the special intent behind the prohibited conducts.

When direct evidence is not available, international criminal jurisprudence has admitted the possibility to infer this intent from circumstantial evidence, such as the actions or the words of the perpetrator, or from nature, scale, and systematic nature of the actions against the victim-group, included – arguably – those committed by other perpetrators.

In the past, a widely debated issue was the possibility of considering this mental element to be met by the actions of an isolated individual perpetrator motivated by the unrealistic aim of eliminating a national, ethnical, racial or religious group (Akhavan 2012; Behrens and Henham 2013; Schabas 2000). Except in some early decisions of the ad hoc tribunals, this possibility is not sustained by other case law or doctrine.

In addition, for what concern more closely the offence in the Rome Statute, it can be noted the Elements of Crimes clarify the necessity of a specific "contextual element." The presence of this contextual element was not explicitly mentioned in the Genocide Convention. It is the requirement that each prohibited act "took place in the contest of a manifest pattern of similar conduct directed against that group or was conduct that could itself effect such destruction." As argued in the literature, the contextual element should not be seen as an addition to the crime's *actus reus* but as an objective point of reference for the determination of a realistic genocidal intent (Kreß 2009).

In sum, as stated by the ICC Pre-Trial Chamber in the Al Bashir case,

> the crime of genocide is only completed when the relevant conduct presents a concrete threat to the existence of the targeted group, or a part thereof. In other words, the protection offered by the penal norm defining the crime of genocide - as an ultima ratio mechanism to preserve the highest values of the international community - is only triggered when the threat against the existence of the targeted group, or part thereof, becomes concrete and real, as opposed to just being latent or hypothetical (ICC, Prosecutor v. Omar Hassan Ahmad Al Bashir 2009).

Crimes Against Humanity

The jurisdiction of the ICC also includes crimes against humanity. These crimes "are particularly odious offences in that they constitute a serious attack on human dignity or a grave humiliation or degradation for one or more persons" (Cassese 2008). Art. 7 of the Rome Statute lists several conducts – such as murder, extermination, enslavement, deportation or forcible transfer of population, torture, rape, sexual slavery and enforced prostitution, persecution, and apartheid – and qualifies them as crimes against humanity when "committed as part of a widespread or systematic attack directed against any civilian population, with knowledge of the attack."

Two aspects of Art. 7 distinguish the provision from previous legal definitions of these crimes. Firstly, the Nuremberg and Tokyo Charters, when defining crimes against humanity, required them to be "in execution of or in connection with any crime within the jurisdiction of the Tribunal," that is, war crimes and aggression (in its original formulation of "crimes against peace"). In other words, the international military tribunals, in order to have jurisdiction over crimes against humanity, required a nexus with an armed conflict. The same nexus was contemplated by art. 6 of the ICTY Statute, restraining its power to prosecute the prohibited conducts "when committed in armed conflict, whether international or internal in character." Secondly, art. 5 of the ICTR required a so-called "discriminatory *animus*," by placing the prohibited conducts in the frame of an attack "against any civilian population on national, political, ethnic, racial or religious grounds."

The ICC Statute, from this point of view, makes a significant step forward, by severing both the war nexus and the required link with discriminatory grounds. Crimes against humanity are therefore prohibited and punishable whether they are committed in time of war or peace. The contextual element underlined in art. 7, however, is particularly significant. This provision, by requiring a widespread and systematic attack against the civilian population, makes clear that crimes against humanity cannot be isolated or sporadic events. In the Element of Crimes, it is clarified that "attack directed against a civilian population" means "a course of conduct involving the multiple commission of acts referred to in article 7, paragraph 1, of the Statute against any civilian population, pursuant to or in furtherance of a State or organizational policy to commit such attack." In other words, the offences have to be part of, or be condoned or tolerated by, a government's or a de facto authority's policy.

As for the "widespread" or "systematic" character of the attack, the first term is generally understood as denoting the large scale of the violence, and the high number of victims. The second, instead, indicates the organized nature of the acts of violence constituting the attack and the improbability of their random occurrence. During the Rome Conference, the disjunctive nature of the "widespread *or* systematic" test attracted debate and opposition, on the basis of the objection that it would have included crimes committed on a large scale, but unconnected, not part of a plan (e.g., a wave of crimes after a natural disaster). The compromise reached was to maintain the disjunctive nature of the test, while including the "policy element" in the definition of "attack."

The policy element still constitutes the most controversial aspect of the Rome Statute's definition of crimes against humanity, raising concerns about the difficulty to prove it, as well as for contradicting the disjunctive nature of the "widespread or systematic" test. On the one hand, the Rome Statute requires the policy element. On the other hand, jurisprudence of other international criminal tribunals negates the necessity of this element. In sum, both jurisprudence and doctrine remain divided on this issue (Mettraux 2011).

Lastly, regarding the mental element, in relation to the different prohibited acts listed in art. 7(1)(a) to (k), the Elements of Crimes – assisting the Court in the interpretation and application of the offences within its jurisdiction – specify that each of these conducts has to be committed as part of a widespread or systematic attack directed against a civilian population, reinforcing in this way the required nexus between the conduct and the overall attack. In addition, it is required that the perpetrator knew that the conduct was part of or intended the conduct to be part of the attack. The same document, however, specifies that this clause should not be interpreted as requiring proof that the perpetrator had detailed knowledge of the attack or precise knowledge of the plan or policy.

War Crimes

Unlike crimes against humanity, the third category of crimes falling within the jurisdiction of the ICC, namely war crimes, can only be prosecuted if committed during an armed conflict. Art. 8(1) of the Rome Statute states "the Court shall have jurisdiction in respect of war crimes in particular when committed as part of a plan or policy or as part of a large-scale commission of such crimes." Therefore, it has to be noted that the formulation of the paragraph, especially the use of term "in particular," suggests that, for war crimes, the existence of a policy or a large-scale commission does not constitute a necessary component of the crime. As it has been underlined, "plan, policy and large-scale commission" are by no means required elements of war crimes. A single and isolated act, such as the rape or killing of a single person by a single perpetrator, can amount to a war crime (Cottier 2016). The majority of the scholarship shares the view that this paragraph offers a practical guideline for the Court, indicating factors the Prosecutor should take into account when determining whether to commence an investigation with regard to alleged commission of war crimes (Ambos 2014).

The existence of an armed conflict, instead, constitutes a prerequisite for the commission of a war crime. In this area, international criminal law and international humanitarian law (IHL) overlap. It is IHL, in fact, mainly through the four 1949 Geneva Conventions and their two 1977 Additional Protocols, that dictates under what conditions an armed conflict can be deemed to exist, and, if there is one, how it has to be classified, if of international, or noninternational character. However, it should be noted that this dichotomy does not capture all the possible typologies of armed conflicts occurring in the world, which can present both international and noninternational elements (Vité 2009).

When interpreting the IHL provisions about the existence of armed conflicts, the landmark jurisprudence is still represented by the ICTY decision in the Tadić case, in which the judges stated that "an armed conflict exists whenever there is a resort to armed force between States or protracted armed violence between governmental authorities and organized armed groups or between such groups within a State. International humanitarian law applies from the initiation of such armed conflicts and extends beyond the cessation of hostilities until a general conclusion of peace is reached; or, in the case of internal conflicts, a peaceful settlement is achieved." Therefore, when an armed conflict exists, IHL automatically applies, and its serious violations criminalized at the international level can be prosecuted.

Following the structure of Art. 8 of the Rome Statute, its para. 2(a) states that war crimes are firstly the "grave breaches of the Geneva Conventions of 12 August 1949," which include willful killing, torture or inhumane treatment, extensive destruction and appropriation of property not justified by military necessity and carried out unlawfully and wantonly, deprivation of the rights of fair and regular trial for a prisoner of war, unlawful deportation or transfer or unlawful confinement, and taking of hostages. However, even if these grave breaches are criminalized in the Rome Statute, it is important to understand the differences between "war crimes" under international criminal law and the "grave breaches" regime of the Geneva Conventions (and their Additional Protocols) under IHL. Although the dividing line between the two concepts has been blurred over the last decades, originally, war crimes and grave breaches were distinct concepts in international law. War crimes were certain acts or omissions carried out in times of armed conflicts and criminalized in international legal instruments. Grave breaches were a limited set of particularly serious violations of the Geneva Conventions of 1949 that gave rise to special obligations of the States Parties for the enactment and enforcement of domestic criminal law. As explained by Divac Öberg,

> [w]ar crimes, on the one hand, are acts and omissions that violate international humanitarian law and are criminalized in international criminal law. [. . .] The Geneva Conventions did not provide for any international criminal liability for grave breaches. Rather, grave breaches constituted a category of violations of those conventions considered so serious that states agreed to enact domestic penal legislation, search for suspects, and judge them or hand them over to another state for trial. (Divac Öberg 2009).

Grave breaches, therefore, originally attracted national jurisdiction, and the duty of the State Parties to the Geneva Conventions to extradite or prosecute those suspected of their commission. With their criminalization under the Rome Statute, if a State party is unwilling or unable to investigate or prosecute these crimes, the Court can activate and exercise its jurisdiction, therefore enforcing the grave breaches prohibitions at the international level.

Beyond the grave breaches, Art. 8(2) of the Statute lists 45 other offences. These offences are classified by art. 8, respectively, as "[o]ther serious violations of the laws and customs applicable in international armed conflict, within the established framework of international law" (lit. b); then, within an armed conflict not of an international character, "serious violations of article 3 common to the four Geneva Conventions of 12 August 1949, committed against persons taking no active part in the hostilities, including members of armed forces who have laid down their arms and those placed hors de combat by sickness, wounds, detention or any other cause" (lit. c); finally, "[o]ther serious violations of the laws and customs applicable in armed conflicts not of an international character, within the established framework of international law" (lit. e).

An analysis of all the prohibited war crimes would be beyond the ambits of this chapter. However, it can be summarized that these offences transpose into international criminal law an enforcement regime for many IHL prohibitions protecting civilians, combatants *hors de combat* and prisoners of war in armed conflicts. In particular, the ICC Statute offences related more closely to combat situations and the targeting procedures that are linked with the three core IHL principles regulating the conduct of hostilities, that is: the principle of distinction; which imposes an obligation on a party to an armed conflict to distinguish at all times between civilians and combatants, and between military objectives and civilian objects, and accordingly to direct attacks only against legitimate military objectives; the principle of proportionality, which prohibits a party to an armed conflict from launching attacks that may be expected to cause incidental loss of civilian life, injury to civilians, damage to civilian objects, or a combination thereof, which would be excessive in relation to the concrete and direct military advantage anticipated; the principle of precaution, which requires those in charge of an attacking decision to take all the feasible precautions to (1) verify that the objectives to be attacked are neither civilians nor civilian objects, and (2) in choosing a means and methods of attack with a view to avoiding, and in any event to minimizing, incidental loss of civilian life, injury to civilians and damage to civilian objects.

The prohibited conduct span from intentionally directing attacks against the civilian population as such, civilian objects, or against individual civilians not taking direct part in hostilities, to intentionally launching attacks in the knowledge that the losses or injury between civilians, or damage to civilian objects, will be clearly excessive in relation to the concrete and direct overall military advantage anticipated, to employing poison or poisoned weapons, poisonous or other gases, or bullets which expand or flatten easily in the human body, and to employing weapons, projectiles, and material which are of a nature to cause superfluous injury or unnecessary suffering or which are inherently indiscriminate.

It should be noted that in addition to the 45 offences of this section of Art. 8, the Sixteenth Assembly of the State Parties, held in New York in December 2017, has adopted three amendments adding to the list of war crimes within the jurisdiction of the Court. These are "employing weapons, which use microbial or other biological agents, or toxins, whatever their origin or method of production; employing weapons the primary effect of which is to injure by fragments which in the human body escape detection by X-rays, employing laser weapons specifically designed, as their sole combat function or as one of their combat functions, to cause permanent blindness to unenhanced vision, that is to the naked eye or to the eye with corrective eyesight devices."

Importantly, in order to constitute war crimes, all these conducts have not only to be committed during an armed conflict, but they also have to be linked with it. In other words, in order to qualify as a war crime, criminal conduct must be closely related to the hostilities. It is necessary, in other words, to identify a so-called "nexus," or "link," between the prohibited actions and the conflict. For each of the prohibited act, the Elements of Crime require that "[t]he conduct took place in the context of and was associated with an international armed conflict," and that "[t]he perpetrator was aware of factual circumstances that established the existence of an armed conflict."

The nexus between armed conflict and prohibited conduct is crucial to distinguish between, on the one hand, war crimes and generic criminal offences falling under the relevant domestic law committed during an armed conflict, but unrelated to it, on the other hand. As explained by Cassese, "to be labelled as a war crime [. . .] the offence must be committed to pursue the aims of the conflict or, alternatively, it must be carried out with a view to somehow contributing to attain the ultimate goals of a military campaign or, at a minimum, in unison with the military campaign." (Cassese and Gaeta 2013).

The Crime of Aggression

During the 2010 Kampala Review Conference of the Rome Statute, State parties for the first time agreed on a definition of the crime of aggression (Bassiouni and Ferencz 2008; Kreß and von Holtzendorff 2010; McDougall 2013). The crime of aggression is now contained in Art. 8 bis of the ICC Statute which states

> crime of aggression means the planning, preparation, initiation or execution, by a person in a position effectively to exercise control over or to direct the political or military action of a State, of an act of aggression which, by its character, gravity and scale, constitutes a manifest violation of the Charter of the United Nations.

Art. 8 bis adds that "act of aggression means the use of armed force by a State against the sovereignty, territorial integrity or political independence of another State, or in any other manner inconsistent with the Charter of the United Nations." Given these premises, the Article sets out different actions that can amount to acts of aggression: from the invasion or attack by the armed forces, to military occupation and annexation, from the blockade of the ports or coasts, to the sending by or on behalf of a State of armed bands, groups, irregulars, or mercenaries, carrying out acts of armed force against another State of such gravity as to amount to one of the actions mentioned.

The resolution amending the Statute (Resolution RC/ Res.6) also introduced the new articles 15 bis and 15 ter which contain complex provisions on the conditions for the exercise of jurisdiction on the crime of aggression. Inter alia, it was agreed that the Court may exercise jurisdiction only with respect to crimes of aggression committed 1 year after the ratification or acceptance of the amendments by 30 States Parties, and that the effective exercise of the jurisdiction over this crime was subject to a decision to be taken after 1 January 2017. To date, 35 States have ratified the Kampala amendments on the crime of aggression. Most importantly, the Sixteenth Assembly of the State Parties, in December 2017, finally adopted a resolution which activates the jurisdiction of the Court over the crime of aggression, starting on 17 July 2018.

"Trigger Mechanisms" and the Jurisdiction of the International Criminal Court

As stated above, the ICC has potentially world-wide jurisdiction. Ideally, for this "global" authority to be fully developed, all the States should become parties to the Rome Statute. Essentially, being a treaty-based institution, the Court's rules are binding only on its states parties. However, the fact the Court is based on a treaty does not mean that its jurisdiction is strictly limited to State parties with no exceptions. The first exception is provided by Art. 12(3), which grants to States that are not parties to the State possibility to declare their acceptance of the jurisdiction of the Court with respect to a crime.

The second exception is contained in Art. 13(b) which affirms that the Security Council of the UN, acting under Chap. VII of the UN Charter, can refer to the Prosecutor a situation in which one or more of such crimes appear to have been committed. In this case, the Court will have jurisdiction even if none of the States involved has consented. Examples of this referral can be found in 2005, when the situation in Darfur and Sudan were referred to the ICC by the UN Security Council, and in 2011, when the same happened regarding the situation in Libya (Cryer 2006).

Conversely, and problematically, Art. 16 of the Statute affirms that "no investigation or prosecution may be commenced or proceeded with under this Statute for a period of 12 months after the Security Council, in a resolution adopted under Chap. VII of the Charter of the United Nations, has requested the Court to that effect." This provision clearly raises concerns over the extent of independence and autonomy of the Court, in particular considering its last sentence, affirming "that request may be renewed by the Council under the same conditions." The "deferral" of the investigation or prosecution, therefore, seems renewable sine die (Bergsmo et al. 2016; Condorelli and Villalpando 2002).

Beyond the specific situations mentioned, however, only State parties can refer to the Prosecutor situations in which core crimes appear to have been committed. In the early years following 2002, when the ICC began to function, different states on the territory of which crimes potentially under the Court jurisdiction were being committed made "self-referrals." These states included Uganda, Democratic Republic of Congo, Central African Republic, and Mali. Authors have doubted that the Statute contemplated such types of referrals, while others had warned that, in divided countries, self-referrals could have become tools to seek interventions of the ICC as a means of political struggle against oppositions (Kreß 2004; Robinson 2011; Schabas 2006). In the literature, however, it has been noted that the drafting history of the Statute shows that self-referrals were considered and approved (Cryer et al. 2007).

Alongside these "trigger mechanisms" – and without need for a referral by a State party, the Security Council, or a declaration under Art. 12(3) by a non-State party – Art. 15 of the Statute establish the possibility for the Prosecutor to open investigations on her/his own initiative (the *proprio motu* investigation). This could be done on the basis of information received about crimes within the jurisdiction of the Court. It is duty of the Prosecutor to assess the "seriousness" of these information and, if he or she concludes that there is a reasonable basis to proceed with an investigation, to submit a request along with supporting material to the Pre-Trial Chamber.

The decision of the Pre-Trial Chamber to authorize the investigation is necessary to proceed to the trial stage, but does not preclude subsequent determinations of the Court in respect to jurisdiction and admissibility and, if negative, does not impede the presentation of another request by the Prosecutor based on new facts or evidence.

In order to gather the material supporting the request and to make better evaluations, the Prosecutor may seek additional information from states, organs of the United Nations, intergovernmental, or nongovernmental organizations, and receive written or oral testimony. The Rules of Procedure and Evidence also permit victims to make representations before the Pre-Trial Chamber.

But what are the criteria establishing the jurisdiction of the Court? Art. 12 of the Statute provides:

> the Court may exercise its jurisdiction if one or more of the following States are Parties to this Statute or have accepted the jurisdiction of the Court in accordance with paragraph 3: (a) The State on the territory of which the conduct in question occurred or, if the crime was committed on board a vessel or aircraft, the State of registration of that vessel or aircraft; (b) The State of which the person accused of the crime is a national.

The territory where the alleged conduct took place and nationality of the accused constitute the two main links to activate the jurisdiction of the ICC. The Court's jurisdiction is limited to persons who were 18 at the time the alleged offence was committed. Temporally, the jurisdiction of the Court is limited to offences committed before the entry into force of the Statute, i.e., 1 July 2002. If a State becomes a Party to this Statute after its entry into force, the Court may exercise its jurisdiction only with respect to crimes committed after the entry into force of this Statute for that State. Any State, through a declaration under Art. 12(3), can accept retroactively the jurisdiction of the Court until the original entry into force of the Statute. In no cases, however, the Court can adjudicate alleged crimes committed before 1 July 2002.

Admissibility Issues

Complementarity is the fundamental principle upon which the jurisdiction of the ICC is based, governing the relationship between the Court itself and the national legal orders. The Court is intended as an instrument of last resort, since – as stated in the Preamble of the Rome Statute – it is "duty of every State to exercise its criminal jurisdiction over those responsible for international crimes." States remain therefore the main actors in the prevention and control of international core crimes.

In order to respect the principle of complementarity and establish that a case is admissible, a two-fold test has to be considered. Firstly, it is necessary to assess whether the same case is being investigated or prosecuted at national level. To affirm that a "case" is "the same" as that subject to proceedings at national level, "national investigations must cover the same individual and substantially the same conduct as alleged in the proceedings before the Court" (Ruto et al. 2011). Especially, the notion of conduct has to be considered factually. In other words, if the conduct is legally characterized in a different way between State's proceedings and ICC's proceedings, but the episodes investigated are the same, complementarity has to be respected. Secondly, it has to be evaluated if the competent State is unwilling or unable to *genuinely* investigate and prosecute the crimes. More specifically, the existence of national investigation or prosecution will render the case inadmissible unless the ICC Prosecutor demonstrate unwillingness or inability of the state.

"Unwillingness" can be determined, according to Art. 17(2), in light of the principles of due process recognized by international law, when: (a) proceedings and national decisions have been made "for the purpose of shielding the person concerned from criminal responsibility" for crimes within the jurisdiction of the Court; (b) there has been unjustified delay in the proceedings; and (c) the proceedings have not been conducted independently and impartially, or have been conducted in a manner inconsistent with the intent to bring the person to justice. Many authors have proposed that the wording of this article of the Statute suggests that a case will be admissible if the Court determines that the State asserting jurisdiction will not provide the defendant with due process (Ellis 2002; Kleffner 2003), thus identifying in the ICC elements typical of a human rights court. Other scholars assert that Art. 17 permits the Court to find a State "unwilling or unable" only if its proceedings are designed to make the defendant's conviction less likely, irrespective of how unfair those proceedings may be (Heller 2006).

In this matter, the Pre-Trial Chamber, in the Al Sanussi decision of 2013, for the first time affirmed that alleged violations of the accused's procedural rights are not sufficient grounds for a finding of unwillingness or inability. The alleged breaches of the suspect's procedural rights are relevant only "when the manner in which the proceedings are being conducted, together with indicating a lack of independence and impartiality, is to be considered, in the circumstances, inconsistent with the intent to bring the person to justice." It can be argued, therefore, that other violations of the accused's rights do not prevent a State to exercise its jurisdiction.

As for "inability," the criteria to identify it are somehow more objective than those established for the unwillingness test. According to Art. 17(3), in order to determine inability, the Court shall consider whether, due to a total or substantial collapse or unavailability of its national judicial system, the State is unable to obtain the accused or the necessary evidence and testimony. Even absence of necessary legislation may constitute ground for a finding of inability. Another ground for inadmissibility is the respect of the *ne bis in idem* principle, protecting individuals from being tried twice for the same conduct. The Court shall not try anyone if the case has been investigated by a State with jurisdiction over it and the State decided not to prosecute the person concerned. However, if this decision is the result of unwillingness or inability of the State genuinely to prosecute the suspect, the case will be admissible nonetheless.

The final and more problematic ground for inadmissibility provided by the Statute is when a case "is not of sufficient gravity to justify further action by the Court." It is the Prosecutor that has to consider gravity, both when selecting situations to investigate and at the later stage of the selection of cases (deGuzman 2008).

In 2003, after receiving 240 communications concerning the situation in Iraq, the former Prosecutor stated that gravity constitutes "an additional threshold [. . .] even where the subject-matter jurisdiction is satisfied" adding that "the Office considers various factors in assessing gravity. A key consideration is the number of victims of particularly serious crimes" (ICC, Office of the Prosecutor, Letter concerning communication on the situation in Iraq 2006). However, judges in more recent decisions have affirmed that "gravity of a given case should not be assessed only from a quantitative perspective, i.e. by considering the number of victims; rather, the qualitative dimension of the crime should also be taken into consideration when assessing the gravity of a given case" (ICC, Abu Garda, PTC I, 8 February 2013, para. 31).

In the Ntaganda case, gravity was object of debate between the Appeals Chamber and the Pre-Trial Chamber. The latter emphasized the importance of several factors in relation to gravity, such as the systematic nature and large scale of the conduct, and social harm caused, or senior leadership of the suspect. The Appeals Chamber, on the contrary, stressed that there was no basis in the Statute to consider these factors as criteria to be met when considering gravity (ICC, Situation in the DRC, A. Ch., 13 July 2006, para. 82).

In 2014, the Prosecutor declined to open the investigation on the Israeli Defence Forces' (IDF) attack on the Mavi Marmara ships sailing towards Gaza. The OTP found that the alleged war crimes potentially committed on board the ships were of insufficient gravity. The Prosecutor's evaluation of gravity took into account: "(i) whether the individuals or groups of persons that are likely to be the object of an investigation, include those who may bear the greatest responsibility for the alleged crimes committed; and (ii) the gravity of the crimes committed within the incidents which are likely to be the focus of an investigation" (ICC, Office of the Prosecutor, Comoros Decision 2014, para. 150).

The OTP has also recently restated that "gravity includes an assessment of the scale, nature, manner of commission of the crimes, and their impact, bearing in mind the potential cases that would likely arise from an investigation of the situation" (ICC, Office of the Prosecutor, Report on Preliminary Examination Activities 2016). Conclusively, however, the Rome Statute does not provide clarifications on the constitutive elements of the gravity test. This lack of specific indications about the content of gravity in the Statute attracts a great deal of academic debate, since it entails, at different stages of the proceedings, ample margins of discretion of judges and the Prosecutor in this matter (Knoops 2004). Particularly the Prosecutor is afforded with substantial discretion in deciding whether situations and cases deserve international adjudication, generating the risk of abuses of discretionary powers and double standards (Azarova and Mariniello 2017; Gallavin 2006; Coté 2005; Brubacher 2004).

Conclusion: The Unfulfilled Promises of the International Criminal Court

As already mentioned, the debate around the nexus between admissibility of situation and cases before the ICC and due process of the accused in national proceedings raises the issue of the institutional nature of the Court. Is it a human rights tribunal, whose task is bringing justice and reparations to victims of massive human rights violations? Or is it a purely criminal tribunal, which can only aim to impose individual criminal sanctions to perpetrators of crimes? The ICC seems to escape the classic conceptual and normative frameworks defining the boundaries of supranational jurisdictions. The Preamble to the Rome Statute well represents the momentous expectations placed on the ICC, giving rise to many "promises." Much beyond the objectives of national criminal justice systems, in fact, the ICC professes to propagate human rights values and reinforce global civil conscience around them, to provide a forum for the voice of victims of international core crimes, to produce a reliable historical record of the crimes perpetrated and the context in which they were committed, to strengthen peace and security of the world.

Moreover, particular fortune has encountered in the last year the concept of "positive complementarity," implicating that, on the one hand, the Court will initiate prosecutions against persons who bear the most responsibility for the crimes under investigation, and, on the other hand, it will encourage national trials for the lower-ranking perpetrators. This adds another task to the ones mentioned, since the ICC is expected in this way to reinforce States' ability to investigate and prosecute international crimes. Therefore, as it has been noted,

> the Court appears as a single body with a multiplicity of identities: a criminal court dealing with individual criminal responsibility; a form of restorative justice, which – as a forum for victims to express their views and concerns – contributes to reconciliation; a pedagogic institution strengthening the public sense of accountability for human rights violations; in cases of referrals by the Security Council, an organ of international security with the duty to restore peace between nation-states; a human rights court with the main purpose to protect human dignity; a historian vested with the authority to make an objective record of events; an agency engaging in activities which enhance the effectiveness of national jurisdiction capacity to prosecute serious crimes (Mariniello 2014).

As efficaciously synthetized by Damaška, "the task of fulfilling all these self-imposed demands is truly gargantuan. Unlike Atlas, international criminal courts are not bodies of titanic strength, capable of carrying on their shoulders the burden of so many tasks. Even national systems of criminal justice, with their far greater enforcement powers and institutional support, would stagger under this load" (Damaška 2008). This overload of goals also generates internal teleological tensions. Trials of political and military leaders, for example, do not necessarily assist de-escalations in armed conflicts. On the contrary, the perspective of being prosecuted might prompt leaders to obstinately continue to fight, rather than agreeing a ceasefire with the enemy. Moreover, the idea of producing an accurate historiographical record of the context in which core crimes were committed does not fit, and rather seems to conflict, with the normative tools and procedural equipment of the Court, which remains a criminal court which is called to adjudicate individual criminal responsibilities. Additionally, it has to be considered the tension between the pursuit of individual criminal liability and crimes usually characterized by a huge collective dimension, in which main perpetrators, aiders, and abettors can be thousands (Drumbl 2004).

Overload of goals and overload of expectations have inevitably led to gradual disenchantment regarding the role of the ICC as a new global civilizing institution

(Jessberger and Geneuss 2013). Almost two decades after the entry into force of the Rome Statute, the ICC has attracted strong criticism.

The Court has encountered significant difficulties in regard to State cooperation. Collection of evidence, security of witnesses, forfeiture of assets, execution of arrest warrants, are all actions on which the Court is dependent upon domestic authorities. An example of this friction is the lack of cooperation from domestic authorities in the Al Bashir Case, which resulted in the failure to implement the arrest warrant issued by the OTP, seriously undermining the credibility of the system.

Furthermore, the length of proceedings has raised concerns. The detention of Thomas Lubanga lasted 6 years before he was convicted (ICC, Prosecutor v Thomas Lubanga Dyilo 2012). Germain Katanga was sentenced 7 years after he was surrendered to the Court (ICC, Prosecutor v. Katanga and Ngudjolo 2014). In some cases, the judges took 3 years just to confirm charges (ICC, Prosecutor v. Laurent Gbagbo 2014). Proportion and difficulty of international criminal proceedings is obviously hardly comparable to that of domestic justice systems. But reducing the length of trials is paramount in order to respect the right to a fair trial of the accused.

Most of all, however, the Court seems entangled in a strident contradiction between the resounding goals mentioned and the selectivity of its practice (Schabas 2011). Recently, the Court has been under severe critique for its focus on African States, which prompted tensions between the African Union and the Court (Schabas 2013). Scholars have also criticized the motivations provided by the Prosecutor not to commence investigations in some specific contexts. As it has been seen in relation to Iraq, despite the number of communications to the OTP concerning crimes committed in the conflict, the Prosecutor decided to not open an investigation, holding that the crimes potentially committed did not meet the gravity threshold of Art. 17 of the Statute. Moreover, for the alleged war crimes committed during the Israeli military offensive in Gaza in 2014, after 3 years and many communications, the Prosecutor issued a meagre two-page decision (OTP, Situation in Palestine, 2012) stating that it was competence to the Assembly of State Parties or UN General Assembly, to clarify whether Palestine could have been considered a State (Dugard 2013).

In sum, ever since the beginning of ICC activities, all the ongoing inquiries, and the judgments passed, concerned citizens of nonpowerful states, while none action has been taken to contrast the serious violations committed by agents of hegemonic nations. This discriminatory selectivity has prompted many scholars to develop a radical critique of international criminal justice, articulated in many positions and studies culminating in questioning the desirability itself of institutions such as the ICC. This jurisdiction has often been depicted as an instrument of colonial domination, reproducing the hegemonic equilibrium of the international legal sphere (Schuerch 2017). There is also who accuses this institution to entail a model of "criminal law of the enemy" *par excellence* (Pastor 2006), or that tracks down in it simply a symbolic gesture (Rothe and Mullins 2006). While many critical remarks of this literature are agreeable, its risk is the avoidance of any efforts to improve the concrete chances of this legal framework to achieve its general-preventive functions. Conceiving modern international criminal law as a "construction" shaped by power politics should constitute a premise. The real challenge is not to merely point out power's "footprint" on the substantive development of this legal field, but rather to identify how power relations have adversely affected its normativity, and consequently to develop technical devices to restore substantial equality in relation to core crimes committed by the powerful.

References

Akhavan P (2012) Reducing genocide to law. Cambridge University Press, Cambridge

Ambos K (2014) Treaties on international criminal law Vol. II: the crimes and sentencing. Oxford University Press, Oxford

Azarova V, Mariniello T (2017) Why the ICC needs a 'Palestine situation' (more than Palestine needs the ICC): on the Court's potential role(s) in the Israeli-Palestinian context. Diritti umani e diritto internazionale 1:115–150

Bassiouni C (1998) The statute of the international criminal court: a documentary history. Transnational Publishers, Ardsley

Bassiouni C (ed) (2012) Introduction to international criminal law, 2nd edn. Brill, Leiden

Bassiouni C, Ferencz B (2008) The crime against peace and aggression: from its origins to the ICC. In: Bassiouni C (ed) International criminal law. Vol. 1. Sources, subjects, and contents, 3rd edn. Nijhoff, Leiden, pp 207–242

Behrens P, Henham R (2013) Elements of genocide. Routledge, London

Bergsmo M, Pejic J, Zhu W (2016) Art. 16. Deferral of investigation or prosecution. In: Trifterer O, Ambos K (eds) The Rome statute of the international criminal court. A commentary, 3rd edn. C.H. Beck/Hart/Nomos, Munich

Bergsmo M, Wui Ling C, Tianying S, Ping Y (eds) (2014) Historical origins of international criminal law. Vol I-V. Torkel Opsahl Academic EPublisher, Brussels

Brubacher MR (2004) Prosecutorial discretion within the international criminal court. Journal of International Criminal Justice 2(1):71–95

Cassese A (2008) International Criminal Law, 2nd edn., Oxford University Press, NY, p. 98

Cassese A and Gaeta P (rev) (2013) Cassese's international criminal law, 3rd ed. Oxford University Press, Oxford

Condorelli L, Villalpando S (2002) Referral and deferral by the Security Council. In: Cassese A, Gaeta P, JRWD J (eds) The Rome statute of the international criminal court: a commentary, vol 1. Oxford University Press, Oxford, pp 627–655

Coté L (2005) Reflections on the exercise of prosecutorial discretion in international criminal law. Journal of International Criminal Justice 3(1):162–186

Cottier M (2016) War crimes. Art. 8 para. 1. In: Ambos K, Trifterer O (eds) The Rome statute of the international criminal court. A commentary, 3rd edn. C.H. Beck/Hart/Nomos, Munich, pp 295–323

Cryer R (2006) Sudan, resolution 1593, and international criminal justice. Leiden Journal of International Law 19(1):195–222

Cryer R, Friman H, Robinson D, Wilmshurt E (eds) (2007) An Introduction to international criminal law and procedure. Cambridge University Press, Cambridge

Damaška M (2008) What is the point of international criminal justice? Chicago-Kent Law Review 83:329–365

deGuzman MM (2008) Gravity and the legitimacy of the international criminal court. Fordham International Law Journal 32(5):1400–1465

Divac Öberg M (2009) The absorption of grave breaches into war crimes law. International Review of the Red Cross 91(873):163–183

Drumbl MA (2004) Collective violence and individual punishment: the criminality of mass atrocity. Northwest Univ Law Rev 99(2):539–610

Dugard J (2013) Palestine and international criminal court: institutional failure or bias? Journal of International Criminal Justice 11(3):563–570

Ellis MS (2002) The international criminal court and its implication for domestic law and national capacity building. Florida Journal of International Law 15:215–241

Gallavin C (2006) Prosecutorial discretion within the ICC: under the pressure of justice. Crim Law Forum 17(1):43–58

Hall CK (1998) The first proposal for a permanent international criminal court. International Review of the Red Cross 38(322):57–74

Heller KJ (2006) The shadow side of complementarity: the effect of article 17 of the Rome statute on national due process. Crim Law Forum 17(3):255–280

Heller KJ (2017) What is an international crime? (a revisionist history). Harvard International Law Journal 58(2):1–8

ICC, Office of the Prosecutor, Comoros Decision 2014, report, Annex A, 6 November 2014

ICC, Office of the Prosecutor, Letter concerning communication on the situation in Iraq, 9 February 2006

ICC, Office of the Prosecutor, Report on Preliminary Examination Activities 2016, 14 November 2016

ICC, Office of the Prosecutor, Situation in Palestine, 3 April 2012

ICC, Office of the Prosecutor, Situation on Registered Vessels of Comoros, Greece and Cambodia, Article 53(1)

ICC, Prosecutor v. Katanga and Ngudjolo, ICC-01/04-01/07-3484, Décision relative à la peine (article 76 du Statut), Trial Chamber II, 23 May 2014

ICC, Prosecutor v. Laurent Gbagbo, ICC-02/11-01/11-656-Red, Decision on the confirmation of charges against Laurent Gbagbo, Pre-Trial Chamber I, 12 June 2014

ICC, Prosecutor v. Thomas Lubanga Dyilo, ICC-01/04-01/06-2842, Judgment pursuant to Article 74 of the Statute, Trial Chamber (Lubanga Judgment), 14 March 2012

ICC, Prosecutor v. Omar Hassan Ahmad Al Bashir, Decision on the Prosecution's Application for a Warrant of Arrest against Omar Hassan Ahmad Al Bashir, ICC-02/05-01/09-3, PTC I, 4 March 2009

ICC, The Prosecutor v. William Samoei Ruto and Joshua Arap Sang, ICC-01/09-01/11-1, Decision on the Prosecutor's Application for Summons to Appear for William Samoei Ruto, Henry Kiprono Kosgey and Joshua Arap Sang, Pre-Trial Chamber II, 8 March 2011

Jensen SLB (2016) The making of international human rights. The 1960s, decolonization, and the reconstruction of global values. Oxford University Press, Oxford

Jessberger F, Geneuss S (2013) Down the drain or down to earth? International criminal justice under pressure. Journal of International Criminal Justice 11(3):501–503

Kelsen H (1947) Will the judgment in the Nuremberg trial constitute a precedent in international law? International Law Quarterly 1(1):153–171

Kleffner J (2003) The impact of complementarity on national implementation of substantive international criminal law. Journal of International Criminal Justice 1(1):86–113

Knoops A (2004) Challenging the legitimacy of initiating contemporary international criminal proceedings: rethinking prosecutorial discretionary powers from a legal, ethical and political perspective. Crim Law Forum 15(4):365–390

Kreß C (2004) Self-referrals and waivers of complementarity – some considerations in law and policy. Journal of International Criminal Justice 2(4):944–948

Kreß C (2009) The crime of genocide and contextual elements: a comment on the ICC pre-trial Chamber's decision in the Al Bashir case. Journal of International Criminal Justice 7(2):297–306

Kreß C, von Holtzendorff L (2010) The Kampala compromise on the crime of aggression. Journal of International Criminal Justice 8(5):1179–1217

Lee RSK (1999) The international criminal court: the making of the Rome statute. Kluwer International, The Hague

Mariniello T (ed) (2014) The international criminal court in search of its purpose and identity. Routledge, London

McDougall C (2013) The crime of aggression under the Rome statute of the international criminal court. Cambridge University Press, Cambridge

Mettraux G (2011) The definition of crimes against humanity and the question of a policy element. In: Sadat L (ed) Forging a convention for crimes against humanity. Cambridge University Press, Cambridge, pp 142–176

Pace WR, Schense J (2002) The role of non-governmental organisations. In: Cassese A, Gaeta P, JRWD J (eds) The Rome statute of the international criminal court: a commentary. Oxford University Press, Oxford, pp 105–118

Pastor D (2006) El derecho penal del enemigo en el espero del poder punitivo internacional. In: Cancio Melia M, Jara Dìez CG (eds) Derecho penal del enemigo: el discurso penal de la exclusión. Edisofer, Montevide, Madrid-Buenos Aires, pp 475–522

Robinson D (2011) The controversy over territorial state referrals and reflections on ICL discourse. Journal of International Criminal Justice 9(2):355–384

Röling BVA (1960) The law of war and the national jurisdiction since 1945. In: The Hague Academy of International Law (ed) Collected courses of the Hague Academy of International Law. The Hague Academy of International Law, The Hague, pp 323–456

Rothe D, Mullins CW (2006) Symbolic gestures and the generation of global social control: the international criminal court. Lexington Books, Plymouth

Schabas W (2000) Genocide in international law: the crimes of crimes. Cambridge University Press, Cambridge

Schabas W (2006) First prosecutions at the international criminal court. Human Rights Law Journal 27(1/4):25–40

Schabas W (2011) The international criminal court at ten. Crim Law Forum 22(4):493–509

Schabas W (2013) The banality of international justice. Journal of International Criminal Justice 11(3):545–551

Schuerch R (2017) The International Criminal Court at the mercy of powerful states: an assessment of the neo-Colonialism claim made by African stakeholders. Springer/Asser Press, Berlin/The Hague

Shahabudeen M (2004) Does the principle of legality stand in the way of progressive development of law? Journal of International Criminal Justice 2(4):1007–1017

Simmons M (2009) International criminal tribunals and the media. Journal of International Criminal Justice 7(1):83–88

Vité S (2009) Typology of armed conflicts in international humanitarian law: legal concepts and actual situations. International Review of the Red Cross 91(873):69–94

Enforcement of International Humanitarian Law

Gentian Zyberi

Contents

Introduction 378
Some Factors Inducing Compliance with IHL 380
Enforcing IHL 380
Enforcement at the Domestic Level 381
Enforcement at the Regional Level 384
The European Court of Human Rights 384
The Inter-American Court and Commission on Human Rights 385
The African Court and Commission on Human and Peoples' Rights 386
Enforcement at the International Level 388
Enforcement Mechanisms Included in IHL Treaties 388
Enforcement Through the United Nations System 389
Enforcement Through the Security Council 390
Enforcement Through the General Assembly 391
Enforcement Through the International Court of Justice 393
Enforcement of IHL Through International Criminal Law Mechanisms 393
Enforcement by Non-State Actors 394
Concluding Remarks 395
References 396

Abstract

This chapter provides a critical assessment of the enforcement system of international humanitarian law (IHL), also referred to as the law of armed conflict (LOAC) or *jus in bello*. The notion of enforcement should be distinguished from that of implementation, which is much broader, in that enforcement involves at least some degree of sanctioning for violations of IHL, which could encompass individual criminal responsibility or State responsibility and liability

G. Zyberi (✉)
Norwegian Centre for Human Rights, University of Oslo, Oslo, Norway
e-mail: Gentian.Zyberi@nchr.uio.no

© Springer Nature Singapore Pte Ltd. 2018
G. Oberleitner (ed.), *International Human Rights Institutions, Tribunals, and Courts*,
International Human Rights, https://doi.org/10.1007/978-981-10-5206-4_14

for reparations. After briefly discussing several factors that induce compliance with IHL, this chapter focuses on IHL enforcement at the three possible levels. At the domestic level, the chapter starts from the obligations imposed on States under the 1949 Geneva Conventions (GCs) and their two Additional Protocols of 1977 (AP1 and AP2), including the obligation to investigate and prosecute war crimes amounting to grave breaches. At the regional level, the chapter addresses the enforcement of IHL through the regional human rights systems, focusing on the three regional human rights courts, but also including relevant findings by the Inter-American Commission on Human Rights and the African Commission on Human and Peoples' Rights. At the international level, the chapter analyzes the enforcement of IHL by discussing briefly the mechanisms included under IHL treaties, including Protecting Powers, the ad hoc and the standing International Fact-Finding Commission (established through Article 90 of AP1), and the ICRC. The focus then shifts onto the main UN organs, including the Security Council, the General Assembly (and its subsidiary bodies, the Human Rights Council and the International Law Commission), and the International Court of Justice (ICJ). Another type of enforcement mechanisms addressed here includes international criminal courts and tribunals. Finally, the chapter addresses briefly the role of non-State actors, focusing on non-State armed groups (NSAGs) and nongovernmental organizations (NGOs).

Keywords

International humanitarian law · IHL · Law of armed conflict · Jus in bello · Enforcement · United Nations · Geneva Conventions and Additional Protocols · International Committee of the Red Cross

Introduction

This chapter provides a critical assessment of the enforcement system of international humanitarian law (IHL), also referred to as the law of armed conflict (LOAC) or *jus in bello* (Kalshoven 2007, p. 593–620; Schmitt and von Heinegg 2012; Schabas 2001, p. 439–459; Green 2003, p. 101–131; Vöneky 2013, p. 647–700; Crawford and Pert 2015, p. 235–266; Melzer 2016, p. 263–308). Enforcement involves a variety of measures aimed at ensuring observance of IHL through international monitoring, to assigning responsibility for serious violations through courts or other mechanisms, to providing reparations for serious IHL violations to affected individuals or States. The UK Manual of the Law of Armed Conflict provides a long list of actions aimed at the effective enforcement of IHL, which includes, among others, disseminating knowledge within the armed forces, international legal adjudication, good offices and mediation, media publicity, penal and disciplinary measures, demands for reparations in respect of violations, and reprisals by the aggrieved State (UK Ministry of Defence 2004, p. 412–413). The notion of enforcement should be distinguished from that of implementation, which is much broader, in that enforcement involves at least some degree or type of sanctioning for violations of IHL, which ranges from public condemnation of violations to individual criminal responsibility or State responsibility (Sassòli 2002, p. 401–434) and liability for reparations. Section VI of the 2005 ICRC study on customary IHL is entitled "Implementation" and includes five chapters, namely, Chap. 40 "Compliance with International Humanitarian Law," Chap. 41 "Enforcement of International Humanitarian Law," Chap. 42 "Responsibility and Reparation," Chap. 43 "Individual Responsibility," and Chap. 44 "War Crimes" (Henckaerts and Doswald-Beck 2005). The notion of sanctioning adopted here is quite broad, including also public statements by State officials, by staff of international organizations, or reports by NGOs that address serious IHL violations.

The assessment of the IHL enforcement system involves a two-step approach: *first*, an introduction of the extant enforcement mechanisms, at the respective levels, namely, the domestic (Blank 2011, p. 205–224; Weill 2014a; ICRC database on national implementation), the regional (de Wet and Kleffner 2014, Chaps. 13, 14, and 15), and the international level (Schmitt and von Heinegg 2012; Darcy 2014). *Second*, an analysis of the enforcement efforts of each mechanism is provided, highlighting the main achievements and persisting challenges. This analysis covers the system of enforcement of IHL for both international (IACs) and non-international armed conflicts (NIACs). When considering the enforcement process, it is possible to categorize that in terms of judicial and nonjudicial enforcement; in terms of the law of international responsibility, as responsibility of States, international organizations, individuals, or non-State actors; and, in terms of the levels or layers of enforcement, the domestic, the regional, and the international levels. After briefly discussing several factors that induce compliance with IHL, this chapter focuses on IHL enforcement at each of the three levels.

At the domestic level, the chapter focuses on the obligations imposed on States under the 1949 Geneva Conventions (GCs) and their two Additional Protocols of 1977 (AP1 and AP2), including the obligation to investigate and prosecute war crimes amounting to grave breaches. At the regional level, the analysis focuses on the three regional human rights courts while including relevant findings by the Inter-American and the African Commission on Human Rights. At the international level, the analysis includes the mechanisms established under the main IHL treaties, including Protecting Powers, the ad hoc commissions and the standing International Fact-Finding Commission (established under Article 90 of AP1), and the ICRC. The focus then shifts onto the main UN organs, including the Security Council, the General Assembly (and its two subsidiary bodies, the Human Rights Council and the International Law Commission), and the International Court of Justice (ICJ). A discussion of international enforcement mechanisms would not be complete without analyzing the work of international criminal courts and tribunals. Finally, the chapter addresses briefly the role of non-State armed groups (NSAGs) and nongovernmental organizations (NGOs) in enforcing IHL.

Some Factors Inducing Compliance with IHL

There are several considerations and factors built into the fabric of IHL, which are aimed at ensuring compliance by warrying parties and others affected. Some of these measures relate to the general implementation of IHL during peacetime, including dissemination of IHL, education and awareness-raising among the general public, adequate training of the military forces, and other national implementing measures, aimed at ensuring conditions furthering compliance with IHL. Other measures, directly aimed at the enforcement of IHL during armed conflict, include activities by a range of actors, including those of Protecting Powers, the ICRC, the main UN organs, good offices and related diplomatic activities at the international and the regional level, international fact-finding commissions, penal and disciplinary measures, and activities of NGOs. Besides relevant legal considerations, the personal conviction and sense of moral responsibility of the individuals involved, expressed in the form of the principle of chivalry, are quite important for ensuring compliance with IHL (Gill 2013, p. 33–51). As Gill has noted, chivalry and martial honor have always been part of the "code of the warrior" and have played a significant role in the development of the law of war, notwithstanding undeniable obstacles and challenges to their application (Gill 2013, p. 49). Disregard for this ethical and moral code has become more prevalent in recent armed conflicts between States and NSAGs.

The success of the measures and activities carried out by different actors aimed at ensuring compliance with IHL depends on a range of factors, internal and external, which influence the behavior of the parties to an armed conflict. Several general weaknesses and challenges to the enforcement of IHL have been identified, including a lack of incentives on the part of NSAGs to comply with IHL, use of new technologies, inability or unwillingness on the part of warrying parties to fulfil the needs of civilians and prohibition of access to humanitarian assistance, use of explosive weapons in densely populated areas, tendency of States to label as "terrorist" all acts of warfare committed by NSAGs against them especially in NIACs, and so on (ICRC 2015, p. 1427–1502; Sassòli 2007, p. 45–73). Generating respect for IHL remains a troublesome endeavor, despite continued and sustained efforts by different stakeholders. However, as the following sections will show, major progress has been done in the course of the last 150 years, both in terms of substantive law and in terms of enforcement mechanisms and practices.

Enforcing IHL

Article 1 common to the 1949 Geneva Conventions provides that States and other parties to an armed conflict have an obligation to "respect and ensure respect for" IHL "in all circumstances." As Melzer has noted, this duty has several aspects, including (1) a negative duty to abstain from any deliberate violation of IHL, (2) a positive internal duty to ensure the national implementation and application of IHL, and (3) a positive external duty of States to exert bilateral or multilateral pressure on other States or belligerent parties to comply with IHL (Melzer 2016, p. 268). These duties are part of the law of international responsibility.

Treaty and customary IHL have codified five types of war crimes, which eventually would trigger international responsibility, for States, individuals, international organizations, as well as for non-State actors more generally (Jørgensen 2003; Bonafè 2009; Crawford et al. 2010; van Sliedregt 2012). These five categories are as follows: war crimes against persons requiring particular protection, war crimes against property and other rights, prohibited methods of warfare (attacks on non-military targets and other prohibited methods), prohibited means of warfare, crimes against humanitarian assistance, and crimes against peacekeeping operations (Nerlich 2009, p. 566–570). This is a topical characterization of war crimes, based on the protection included under both treaty and customary IHL. The typology generally employed by the international criminal courts and tribunals is based on that of armed conflicts, namely, war crimes in IACs and in NIACs. This is the case in the ICTY Statute (Article 2 on "grave breaches of the Geneva Conventions of 1949" and Article 3 on "violations of the laws or customs of war"), the ICTR Statute (Article 4 on "violations of Article 3 Common to the Geneva Conventions and of Additional Protocol II"), and in the ICC Statute (Article 8 on "war crimes") (Vité 2009, p. 69–94). Notably, although formally preserving the distinction between war crimes in IACs and NIACs, the case law of these international courts has helped bridge the protection gap between the two types of armed conflict.

The enforcement of IHL happens at three levels, domestic, regional, and international, and involves different types of mechanisms. The chapter devotes significant attention to judicial enforcement, but also other types of mechanisms are included. Despite operating at different levels, the activity of the courts is connected, since in order to bring a case before a regional court it usually is necessary to exhaust available domestic remedies. Similarly, the permanent International Criminal Court (ICC), that has jurisdiction over war crimes, operates on the basis of the principle of complementarity and will investigate a situation and start cases if a State is unable or unwilling to do so by itself through its own domestic courts (ICC Statute, Articles 17 and 19; El Zeidy 2008; Kleffner 2008; Stahn and El Zeidy 2011; Nouwen 2013). The following sections explain and analyze the different mechanisms available at the three levels, highlighting their main achievements and shortcomings.

Enforcement at the Domestic Level

The domestic mechanisms provide the first level of enforcement of IHL. As mentioned above, Article 1 common to the Geneva Conventions imposes an obligation on States to respect and ensure respect for IHL. This has been confirmed by the International Court of Justice as applicable to both international and non-international armed conflicts (ICJ, Nicaragua 1986, paras. 115, 216, 255, and 256; ICJ, Legal Consequences of the Construction of a Wall in the Occupied Palestinian Territory 2004, paras. 158–9). Moreover, the ICJ has found that "a great many rules of humanitarian law applicable in armed conflict are so fundamental to the respect of the human person and elementary considerations of humanity . . . that they are to be observed by all States whether or not they have ratified the conventions that contain them, because they constitute intransgressible principles of international customary law" (ICJ, Legality of the Threat or Use of Nuclear Weapons 1996, para. 79). While there is more clarity about a State's own obligation to respect IHL (ICRC Commentary to Geneva Convention IV, p. 15–17; Boisson de Chazournes and Condorelli 2000, p. 67–87; Focarelli 2010, p. 125–171; Dörmann and Serralvo 2014, p. 707–736; ICJ, Legal Consequences of the Construction of a Wall in the Occupied Palestinian Territory 2004, paras. 149–153), what a State can and should do to ensure respect for IHL by another State or non-State actors remains debatable. Besides calling on other States to stay within the confines of IHL, publicly condemning violations, and recalling diplomatic staff or severing diplomatic relations, States must ensure they do not become complicit in committing war crimes by supplying weapons used to commit war crimes (Arms Trade Treaty, Article 6(3)). This last issue has been raised in recent armed conflicts, such as that in Syria and Yemen.

Given that IHL rules incorporate obligations which are essentially of an *erga omnes* character (ICJ, Legal Consequences of the Construction of a Wall in the Occupied Palestinian Territory 2004, para. 157) under Article 48 of the International Law Commission's (ILC) Articles on State Responsibility, a State other than an injured State can ask cessation of the internationally wrongful act and assurances and guarantees of non-repetition and performance of the obligation of reparation, in the interest of the injured State or of the beneficiaries of the obligation breached. More generally, from the perspective of the law on international responsibility, a State must not recognize an illegal situation or render aid or assistance in its maintenance.

Given that the international legal system is State-centered, States play a primary role in the enforcement of IHL. As Melzer has noted, the duty to respect and ensure respect may involve a broad range of preventive, supervisory, and punitive measures, including (a) domestic legislation and regulations; (b) instructions, military orders, and legal advice; (c) training and the dissemination of all pertinent information; (d) the establishment of national IHL committees; (e) technical preparation; and (f) criminal repression (Melzer 2016, p. 268–269). The universally ratified 1949 Geneva Conventions, as well as the 1977 Additional Protocol I, impose on States an obligation to incorporate IHL into domestic law, especially with regard to penalizing conduct which has been described as grave breaches of the Geneva Conventions (GC1, Article 49; GC2, Article 50; GC3, Article 129; and GC4, Article 146; AP1, Article 85(1)). Some of the main war crimes falling under the grave breaches system include willful killing, torture or inhuman treatment, biological experiments, willfully causing great suffering, causing serious injury to body or heath, unlawful and wanton extensive destruction, and appropriation of property not justified by military necessity. Other protections under IHL that need to be included into domestic legislation include those relating to the protection of the Red Cross emblem, the protection of cultural property, and the prohibition of certain weapons. The obligation to criminalize war crimes is further strengthened through the statutes of the two ad hoc international criminal tribunals for the former Yugoslavia and Rwanda (ICTY and ICTR) and that of the permanent ICC.

National courts play an essential role in enforcing IHL (Weill 2014b, p. 859–879; International Crimes Database, T.M.C. Asser Institute). The national military codes and the military justice system, as well as the military chain of command, play an equally important role. In dealing with the structural aspects of ensuring enforcement of IHL by national courts, Weill has pointed out that these include the existence of domestic legislation that allows for (1) the independence and impartiality of the judiciary, (2) the application and enforcement of IHL rules by national judges (either through a direct application of IHL rules into the national legal system or through their endorsement through national laws), (3) access to courts in cases of IHL violations, and (4) the equal and effective application of the law by the judiciary (Weill 2014b, p. 860). A problematic development has been the effort of US authorities to exclude from the protection of the law the so-called unlawful combatants, by detaining them in the Guantanamo Bay military base or through the extraordinary renditions program (ECtHR, El-Masri v. "The former Yugoslav Republic of Macedonia" 2012a; Al Nashiri v. Poland 2014a; and Husayn (Abu Zubaydah) v. Poland 2014b). The US Supreme Court has countered this effort in several of its decisions (US Supreme Court, Hamdan v. Rumsfeld 2006; Boumediene v. Bush 2008). However, serious challenges remain with regard to access to courts and the equal and effective application of the law in many countries.

The criminal prosecution of serious IHL violations can occur through courts martial or domestic courts, depending on the choice of the domestic legislator. Several armies have their own justice system that deals with military offences, including war crimes. The 1949 Geneva Conventions have created a system of universal jurisdiction (GC1, Article 49; GC2, Article 50; GC3, Article 129; GC4, Article 146), whereby every State has an obligation to search for persons alleged to have committed, or to have ordered to be committed, such grave breaches and bring such persons, regardless of their nationality, before its own courts. A State may also, if it prefers, and in accordance with the provisions of its own legislation, hand such persons over for trial to another High Contracting Party concerned, provided such High Contracting Party has made out a "prima facie" case.

The universal jurisdiction concerning violations amounting to grave breaches is accompanied by the principle of extradite or prosecute (*aut dedere aut judicare*) (Final Report of the International Law Commission 2014). Although included in the 1949 Geneva Conventions, and incorporated in the domestic jurisdiction of States parties to these treaties, applying the principle of universal jurisdiction is not without problems, because of limitations imposed by diplomatic immunity and other problems of a more practical nature. There have been several high profile cases brought before domestic courts on charges of war crimes where the issue of immunity has been invoked (ICJ, Arrest Warrant 2002, paras. 56–61, at 58; Inazumi 2005; Macedo 2006; van Alebeek 2008; Seibert-Fohr 2009; Orakhelashvili 2015; Kwakwa 2004, p. 407–430; Princeton Project on Universal Jurisdiction 2001). The International Law Commission is currently working on this topic. It seems unlikely that domestic courts will be granted jurisdiction to try incumbent senior foreign State officials that enjoy immunity under international law.

Enforcement at the Regional Level

The enforcement of IHL at the regional level happens through different mechanisms of a judicial or nonjudicial nature. Some of the main regional organizations include the Organization of American States (OAS), the Council of Europe (CoE), the European Union (EU), the African Union (AU), and the Organization for Security and Co-operation in Europe (OSCE). Ensuring respect for human rights in armed conflict is part of the mandate of these regional organizations. Given the close relationship between human rights and humanitarian law (Oberleitner 2015) and the resurgence of armed conflicts in different parts of the world, the activity of regional organizations has increasingly addressed situations of armed conflict. Although regional human rights courts are not properly equipped to deal with mass atrocity crimes, including war crimes, their case law is important for the enforcement of IHL, especially in terms of clarifying State obligations in situations of armed conflicts at home and armed forces operating abroad. This section focuses on enforcement of IHL through the three regional human rights courts, the European, the Inter-American, and the African, while also taking into account relevant work of the Inter-American and the African human rights' commissions.

The European Court of Human Rights

The ECtHR plays a significant role in the enforcement of IHL, despite the fact that IHL violations as such do not fall into the scope of the European Convention on Human Rights (ECHR) (Gioia 2011, p. 201–249; Oellers-Frahm 2014, p. 333–364; Hartridge 2014, p. 257–287). The enforcement of IHL through the case law of the ECtHR involves both individual applications under Article 34, as well as inter-State cases under Article 33. Some of the inter-State cases relating to armed conflict are Cyprus v. Turkey, Georgia v. Russian Federation, and Ukraine v. Russian Federation. Individual applications have covered violations related to the conflict between Turkish security forces and the PKK (Workers' Party of Kurdistan), the Armenian-Azerbaijani conflict over Nagorno-Karabakh, the war in Croatia and in Bosnia and Herzegovina, the 1999 NATO operation in the former Yugoslavia, and the conflict in Chechnya. There have been also a number of cases relating to the activity of European States' military forces abroad, including cases concerning the ISAF operation in Afghanistan and the international military operations in Iraq. Most of the violations relate to the right to life (Article 2) (ECtHR, McCann and Others v. the United Kingdom 1995), the prohibition of torture and inhuman or degrading treatment (Article 3) (ECtHR, Aksoy v. Turkey 1996; Öcalan v. Turkey 2005), the right to liberty and security (Article 5) (ECtHR, A. and Others v. the United Kingdom 2009), and the right to a fair trial (Article 6) (ECtHR, Cyprus v. Turkey 2001; Marguš v. Croatia 2012b; Stichting Mothers of Srebrenica and Others v. the Netherlands 2013). However, several cases also relate to respect for the home and property of displaced persons and violation of the right to an effective remedy (Article 13).

The cases that consider the right to life and the freedom from arbitrary detention demonstrate the difficulty that the Court is faced with when dealing with situations of armed conflict (Hartridge 2014, p. 285). The ECtHR has been reluctant to engage with IHL, unless the State concerned has declared martial law or a state of emergency. So far, nine States have had recourse to this right, namely, Albania, Armenia, France, Georgia, Greece, Ireland, Turkey, the United Kingdom, and Ukraine. Article 15(2) lists as non-derogable the right to life (Article 2), except in respect of deaths resulting from lawful acts of war, the prohibition of torture and inhuman or degrading treatment or punishment (Article 3), the prohibition of slavery and servitude (Article 4), and no punishment without law (Article 7). The notice of derogation under Article 15(3) of the ECHR amounts to the consent of the State concerned to accept the special or extended power of the Court to apply not only the law enshrined in the ECHR but also IHL (Oellers-Frahm 2014, p. 342). Oellers-Frahm has noted that particularly in cases concerning the right to life the ECtHR, although applying Article 2 of the ECHR, has used the vocabulary of humanitarian law such as "incidental loss of civilian life," "choice of means and methods," "legitimate military targets," and "disproportionality in the weapons used" and resorted to the cardinal principles of IHL, namely, limitations of means and methods of combat, the principle of distinction, and the principle of proportionality (Oellers-Frahm 2014, p. 350). Some of the shortcomings identified are the reluctance to apply and the inconsistent application of IHL, ECtHR's jurisdictional limitation to cases where rights are violated by a State, and the issue of immunity of international organizations. That said, overall, the case law of the ECtHR has helped clarify certain substantive and procedural aspects of State obligations under the ECHR in situations of armed conflict.

The Inter-American Court and Commission on Human Rights

The Inter-American system of human rights protection is quite comprehensive in terms of substantive human rights, as well as the mechanisms it includes for their enforcement, including both the Commission and the Court (IACtHR and IACmHR, or just Court and Commission). As Shelton has noted, this system has become a forum for the enforcement of IHL due to the number of cases presented and reports prepared that concern States in which internal armed conflicts exist (Shelton 2014, p. 392). Similar to Article 15 of the ECHR, Article 27 of the Inter-American Convention on Human Rights (IACHR) allows for derogations in time of war, public danger, or other emergency that threatens the independence or security of a State party. Article 27(2) provides a list of non-derogable rights, including the right to juridical personality (Article 3), the right to life (Article 4), the right to humane treatment (Article 5), and freedom from slavery (Article 6). The Court has found that "essential" judicial guarantees which are not subject to derogation, according to Article 27(2) of the Convention, include habeas corpus (Art. 7(6)), amparo, and any other effective remedy before judges or competent tribunals (Art. 25(1)), which is designed to guarantee the respect of the rights and freedoms whose suspension is not authorized by the Convention (Judicial Guarantees in States of Emergency (Arts. 27(2), 25, and 8 American Convention on Human Rights) 1987b, para. 41(1); Habeas Corpus in Emergency Situations (Arts. 27(2), 25(1), and 7(6) American Convention on Human Rights 1987a). The Commission has a broader scope of jurisdiction that covers all OAS States and a dual function which includes a monitoring function, besides accepting individual complaints. Some of the main cases the Commission has dealt with include serious human rights violations (massacres committed by the military juntas), specific issues as terrorism and human rights, and the closure of the notorious Guantanamo prison. The Commission and the Court appear to have wavered at times in their views about the direct applicability of IHL, although they are in agreement that alleged violations of the Declaration or Convention must be assessed during armed conflicts in the light of IHL norms as *lex specialis* (Shelton 2014, p. 377). Nevertheless, both mechanisms have provided an important contribution to IHL enforcement, through the emphasis placed on the right to truth, the protection of the civilian population, and reparations for war crimes (Bámaca-Velásquez v Guatemala 2000; Case of the Pueblo Bello Massacre v Colombia 2006; Buis 2008, p. 269–293; Cerna 2011, p. 3–52; Shelton 2014, p. 365–394; Tabak 2016, p. 661–715). Shelton has noted that the use of IHL experts in presenting the cases could benefit the tribunals in achieving this goal, since more commissioners and judges are not specialists in IHL (Shelton 2014, p. 392). Heeding this specific concern, also valid for proceedings before the other regional courts, would help the Inter-American Court and the Commission avoid fragmentation or contradictory findings, as well as potentially increase the acceptability of their decisions by the States concerned.

The African Court and Commission on Human and Peoples' Rights

The two-tiered African system of human rights protection with the Commission and the Court (ACmHPR and ACtHPR) is potentially very important for the enforcement of IHL in the African continent. Despite the currently limited case law, the ongoing consolidation of the African regional human rights system and the existence of several NIACs means that both the Commission and the Court will be increasingly involved in cases and situations where IHL is applicable (ACmHPR, Commission Nationale des Droits de l'Homme et des Libertés v Chad 2000 (Chad Mass Violations case); Amnesty International and Others v Sudan 2007a; Democratic Republic of Congo v Burundi, Rwanda and Uganda 2003; Article 19 v Eritrea 2007b; Viljoen 2014, p. 303–332; Krieger 2015). Interestingly, the African Charter on Human and Peoples Rights (ACHPR or African Charter) does not contain a clause allowing for derogations, and the African Commission has held that derogations are not allowed (ACmHPR, Commission Nationale des Droits de l'Homme et des Libertés v Chad 2000, para 21). While the African Charter entitles the African Commission to make findings of massive and serious violations of human rights, under Article 58(1) the Commission is only competent to "draw the attention" of the AU Assembly of Heads of State and Government to the existence of these violations and must await a request by the Assembly mandating it to undertake "an in-depth study" and report back to the Assembly (Viljoen 2014, p. 311–312). As Viljoen has noted, despite a number of such referrals by the Commission, the Assembly has never authorized an in-depth study under Article 58, which to some extent explains the Commission's apparent reluctance to explicitly find "massive or serious violations" of Charter provisions (Viljoen 2014, p. 312).

Violations of IHL may be raised before the Commission or the Court. At the Commission such issues may be raised through individual cases, as well as part of the State reporting process, either by the State in the report itself or by the African Commission in its Concluding Observations on the report (Viljoen 2014, p. 320). The Commission has dealt with several serious IHL violations, including rape, dumping of bodies and mass burials, forced displacement, destruction of property, and extrajudicial executions (ACmHPR, Sudan Human Rights Organisation & Centre on Housing Rights and Evictions (COHRE) v Sudan 2009). The subject-matter jurisdiction of the Commission can be expanded through Articles 60 and 61 of the African Charter. Under Article 60, the Commission can refer to treaties adopted under the African Union framework, which make specific references to IHL, such as the 2003 Protocol to the African Charter on the Rights of Women in Africa (Women's Protocol) and the 2009 AU Convention for the Protection and Assistance of Internally Displaced Persons in Africa (IDP Convention) (Viljoen 2014, p. 321–322). Additionally, by finding that the six main humanitarian law treaties fall within the scope of Article 61 of the African Charter, the Commission can use relevant IHL provisions in the determination of the case at hand (Viljoen 2014, p. 315). However, the Commission has not been consistent in taking this approach and making use of IHL treaty provisions or rules of customary IHL.

The ACtHPR has been vested with broad jurisdiction under Article 3(1), which extends to all cases and disputes submitted to it concerning the interpretation and application of the African Charter, the Protocol, and any other relevant human rights instrument ratified by the States concerned. Both the contentious and the advisory function of the Court are relevant. In a case relating to the armed conflict in Libya, the Court acting proprio motu ordered the Libyan government to refrain from any action that would result in loss of life or violation of physical integrity of persons, which could be a breach of the provisions of the Charter or of other human rights instruments to which Libya is a party (ACtHPR, African Commission on Human and Peoples' Rights v. Great Socialist People's Libyan Arab Jamahiriya 2011, para. 25(1); case discontinued in March 2013). Given the dearth of cases, it remains to be seen to what extent parties to proceedings before the Court will rely on IHL. The advisory jurisdiction of the Court might be quite important in terms of clarifying the relationship between human rights and humanitarian law within the African system of human rights protection, as well as concerning specific issues that have arisen in the context of armed conflicts in African countries. The established practice of the Inter-American and the European human rights mechanisms could eventually assist the African human rights organs when dealing with similar issues.

Enforcement at the International Level

The international level of enforcement of IHL is quite complex, in that it includes a variety of mechanisms of a political, judicial, fact-finding, and good offices nature, which are aimed at ensuring better enforcement of IHL by warrying parties in both IACs and NIACs. This section will cover first the traditional enforcement mechanisms included under IHL treaties themselves. Then, the focus shall turn on the enforcement through the UN system, starting with the UN main organs, namely, the Security Council, the General Assembly, and the International Court of Justice. The activity of the International Law Commission and the Human Rights Council is briefly discussed, in the context of the work of the General Assembly. Finally, the subsequent section will analyze IHL enforcement through international criminal courts and tribunals.

Enforcement Mechanisms Included in IHL Treaties

International humanitarian law treaties have established four mechanisms for the enforcement of IHL, namely, the Protecting Powers (GCs 1–3, Common Article 8; GC4, Article 9; and AP1, Article 5), the ICRC, the ad hoc fact-finding commissions under the GCs (GC1, Article 52; GC2, Article 53; GC3, Article 132; and GC4, Article 149), and a standing International Fact-finding Commission (AP1, Article 90). The Protecting Powers system has been used only five times (Crawford and Pert 2015, p. 240), the ad hoc fact-finding commissions have never been used (Crawford and Pert 2015, p. 243), and the standing International Fact-Finding Commission has only been used once so far (OSCE request in 2017). This situation provides a very bleak picture of the practical relevance of these three potentially important IHL treaty-based mechanisms.

Protecting Powers have a number of responsibilities for enforcing IHL, including visiting protected persons in detention and providing assistance in judicial proceedings against protected persons. The reasons behind the limited use of Protecting Powers are related to the substantive duties such a position entails, the need for agreement on such appointments by the warring parties, and political motives, including reluctance of States to submit to supervision by a third State during an armed conflict (Pfanner 2009, 287). Given the prominent role played by the ICRC in covering similar functions, it is unlikely that the mechanism of Protecting Powers will be used with increased frequency than it has been the case so far.

The four Geneva Conventions allow for the establishment of ad hoc fact-finding commissions. The relevant provisions state that, "[a]t the request of a Party to the conflict, an enquiry shall be instituted, in a manner to be decided between the interested Parties, concerning any alleged violation of the Convention" (GC1, Article 52; GC2, Article 53; GC3, Article 132; and GC4, Article 149). Given that initiating this enquiry procedure depends on the consent of the warring parties, it is unlikely that the mechanism will ever be used. Given the lack of requests for making use of this ad hoc procedure, the international community decided to establish a standing International Fact-Finding Commission (IFFC). Under Article 90(2)(c) of AP1, the IFFC is competent to (i) enquire into any facts alleged to be a grave breach as defined in the Conventions and this Protocol or other serious violation of the Conventions or of this Protocol and (ii) facilitate, through its good offices, the restoration of an attitude of respect for the Conventions and this Protocol.

While potentially quite important, the fact that since its establishment in 1991 this mechanism has only been used once shows that States are reluctant to accept the IFFC's authority or consent to its investigation of serious violations of IHL. However, the first use of this mechanism to investigate an explosion involving personnel and a vehicle of the OSCE's Special Monitoring Mission (SMM) in Eastern Ukraine shows that the Commission can be used effectively to enquire into situations potentially involving IHL violations (Azzarello and Niederhauser 2018).

The ICRC's role in enforcing IHL is manifold, embedded in the IHL treaties, and further developed through its institutional practice over time. This institution is enjoined "to undertake the tasks incumbent upon it under the Geneva Conventions, to work for the faithful application of international humanitarian law applicable in armed conflicts and to take cognizance of any complaints based on alleged breaches of that law" and "to endeavour at all times – as a neutral institution whose humanitarian work is carried out particularly in time of international and other armed conflicts or internal strife – to ensure the protection of and assistance to military and civilian victims of such events and of their direct results" (Pfanner 2009, p. 290). As a general guardian of IHL, the ICRC has played an important role in enforcing IHL.

Enforcement Through the United Nations System

The main UN organs play an important role in the enforcement of IHL (Office of the High Commissioner on Human Rights 2011, p. 92–116). Other relevant UN entities include the Offices of the United Nations High Commissioner for Refugees (UNHCR) and of the United Nations High Commissioner for Human Rights (OHCHR), as well as UN agencies such as the World Food Programme (WFP), the United Nations Development Programme (UNDP), and the United Nations Children's Fund (UNICEF), which often deal with, and provide assistance to, persons affected by armed conflict, including victims of IHL violations (Melzer 2016, p. 276). This section analyzes the role of the Security Council (UNSC), the General Assembly (UNGA), and the International Court of Justice (ICJ). The Security Council has primary responsibility under the UN Charter to maintain and restore international peace and security, hence its inherent role with regard to the enforcement of IHL. Under Chap. VII of the UN Charter, the UNSC is entrusted with powers to indicate measures to respond to threats to and breaches of the peace through a range of measures, from those that do not involve the use of force (Article 41) to military action (Article 42). The General Assembly plays an important normative and enforcement role, including through two of its subsidiary organs, namely, the International Law Commission and the Human Rights Council. The ICJ has contributed to the enforcement of IHL through its advisory and contentious jurisdiction, as well as through provisional measures indicated in situations of armed conflict (Zyberi 2008; Zyberi 2010, p. 571–584). ICJ's decisions are very important in laying down standards of conduct under the law of international responsibility that eventually are conducive to better compliance with IHL.

Enforcement Through the Security Council

The UNSC is quite important in enforcing IHL, given its authority under Chap. VII of the UN Charter, to respond to threats to and breaches of the peace (Repertoire of the Practice of the Security Council; Lowe et al. 2010). Under Article 41, the UNSC can undertake different measures not involving the use of force, whereas under Article 42 it can authorize military action (Resolutions 1970 (2011) and 1973 (2011) on the situation in Libya). The activity of the UNSC has been important for the enforcement of IHL, through mandating international peacekeeping operations; indicating sanctions, including travel bans, freezing of assets, and arms embargoes; establishing accountability and inquiry mechanisms; and emphasizing the protection of civilians, children, and women. In the framework of peacekeeping missions, the UNSC has established the doctrine of protection of civilians (POC) (S/RES/1265/ 1999, para. 4), which obliges peacekeepers to protect civilians from serious violations of human rights and humanitarian law (S/RES/1674/2006 on the protection of civilians in armed conflict; S/RES/1325/2000 on women, peace, and security; S/RES/1612/2005 on children and armed conflict).

The contribution of the UNSC to the enforcement of IHL involves both normative and operational aspects. In terms of normative aspects, it is important to highlight UNSC's attention toward the protection of women, children, and the doctrine of protection of civilians (Foley 2017). In terms of operational aspects, it is important to highlight mandating peacekeeping missions under Chap. VII of the UN Charter to use force to protect civilians from serious violations of human rights and humanitarian law, the authorization of the use of force to prevent serious violations of human rights and humanitarian law which threaten international peace and security in the case of Libya in 2011, and the establishment of mechanisms to ensure individual criminal accountability or to investigate serious violations. The Security Council has also condemned serious violations of humanitarian law in different armed conflicts and has called for accountability, including for non-State armed groups.

The UNSC enforces IHL through its peacekeeping missions in different parts of the world (Koops et al. 2015; Larsen 2012; Genser and Stagno Ugarte 2014). According to the UN Department of Peacekeeping Operations (DPKO), there are about 110,000 peacekeepers in 14 missions (2018). An important part of the mandate of these missions is the use of force for the protection of civilians (Willmot and Sheeran 2013, p. 517–538). The lack of appreciation of the *inherent* normative basis for UN peacekeepers to protect civilians irrespective of an express mandate has resulted in the failure to recognize that UN peacekeepers will always have the authority to intervene in order to protect civilians under imminent threat of violence where the host State cannot act (Willmot and Sheeran 2013, p. 537). A recent UN report has shown that although an inherent part of their mandate, peacekeepers have hesitated to use force to protect civilians (Howard and Dayal 2018, p. 71–103; Findlay 2002). At the same time, it must be noted that the UN blue helmet does not offer the expected protection from acts of violence, as peacekeepers have been increasingly targeted in recent years.

The UNSC has powers that allow it to pursue a degree of individual accountability for serious violations of IHL. Thus, in 1993 and 1994, respectively, acting under Chap. VII of the UN Charter, the UNSC established the ad hoc tribunals for the former Yugoslavia and for Rwanda, in order to investigate and prosecute serious violations of IHL (S/RES/808/1993 and 827/1993; S/RES/955/1994). The authority of the UNSC under Article 13(b) of the ICC Statute to refer to the International Criminal Court (ICC) situations where serious violations of IHL are being committed is quite important. So far, there have been two Security Council referrals, namely, Sudan (Darfur) in 2005 and Libya in 2011. Regrettably, the UNSC does not seem diligent enough in supporting the work of the ICC in investigating those crimes, as well as in ensuring that those persons charged with war crimes are brought before the ICC. Moreover, although the war in Syria has been raging for several years, the UNSC has been unable to refer the situation to the ICC due to the use of veto power by a permanent member.

As Roscini has noted, the privileged position of the Security Council, which has exclusive competence to take coercive measures involving the use of armed force and whose decisions are binding on all UN Member States, makes it potentially a formidable instrument against serious violations of IHL, which can at least partly remedy the lack of enforcing mechanisms in the treaties on the laws of war, where compliance is mainly based on the goodwill of the States parties (Roscini 2010, p. 358). The selectivity of the UNSC, however, means that at times this international body can only play a limited role with regard to IHL enforcement.

Enforcement Through the General Assembly

The contribution of the General Assembly to the enforcement of IHL has both a normative, as well as an operational aspect, based, respectively, on Articles 10, 11, 12, 13, and 15 of the UN Charter, as well as the "Uniting for Peace" Resolution (A/RES/377(V) 1950). The normative aspect is carried out through resolutions adopted by the UNGA itself or through the work of its subsidiary bodies, especially the International Law Commission and the Human Rights Council. Starting with the 1968 Proclamation of Teheran, the UNGA has reminded parties to an armed conflict of their IHL obligations, issuing several resolutions on "Respect for Human Rights in Armed Conflict" (A/RES/2444(XXIII) 1968). An important example of normative resolutions adopted by the UNGA is the "United Nations Basic Principles and Guidelines on the Right to a Remedy and Reparation for Victims of Gross Violations of International Human Rights Law and Serious Violations of International Humanitarian Law" (A/RES/60/147 2005, especially paras. 15–23). More recently, in 2005, the UNGA has adopted the responsibility to protect doctrine (RtoP) which requires

States to protect their populations from mass atrocity crimes, including war crimes (A/RES/60/1 2005, paras. 138–140). This doctrine is based on the primary responsibility of States to protect their populations from mass atrocity crimes, including war crimes, and a subsidiary responsibility on the part of the organized international community to assist States in this duty (Ryngaert and Cuyckens 2013, p. 109–129). The three pillars of the RtoP doctrine are Pillar one, the protection responsibilities of the State; Pillar two, International assistance and capacity-building; and Pillar three, timely and decisive response.

The normative contribution of the General Assembly comes also through the work of its subsidiary body, the International Law Commission, mandated with the codification and progressive development of international law. The ILC has worked on several issues relevant to the enforcement of IHL, including "Formulation of the Nürnberg Principles," "Draft code of offences against the peace and security of mankind (Part I)," "Draft code of crimes against the peace and security of mankind (Part II) — including the draft statute for an international criminal court," "Effects of armed conflicts on treaties," "Obligation to extradite or prosecute (*aut dedere, aut judicare*)," "Articles on responsibility of States for internationally wrongful acts," "Articles on the responsibility of international organizations for internationally wrongful acts," "Immunity of State officials from foreign criminal jurisdiction," "Peremptory norms of general international law (*Jus cogens*)," and "Protection of the environment in relation to armed conflicts."

The operational aspect of the mandate of the UNGA is carried out mainly through its subsidiary organ, the Human Rights Council, an intergovernmental body within the United Nations system responsible for strengthening the promotion and protection of human rights and for addressing situations of human rights violations and making recommendations on them (Zhu 2014, p. 186–212). As mentioned above, another possibility is available through the UNGA's 1950 "Uniting for Peace" Resolution. The work of the Human Rights Council includes both the Universal Periodic Review (UPR), as well as the work of the special procedures, through the various Special Rapporteurs, expert groups, and agencies established or mandated within the UN framework to express their concerns, views, and recommendations with regard to IHL violations. Some of the relevant thematic Special Rapporteurs include the Special Rapporteur on extrajudicial, summary, or arbitrary executions; the Special Rapporteur on the promotion and protection of human rights and fundamental freedoms while countering terrorism; Special Rapporteur on torture and other cruel, inhuman, or degrading treatment or punishment; and the Special Rapporteur on the promotion of truth, justice, reparation, and guarantees of non-recurrence. By interpreting the terms "human rights obligations and commitments" in Operative paragraph 5(e) of General Assembly Resolution 60/251 to cover IHL, the UPR Mechanism of 18 June 2007, as a part of the Institution-building of the new Council, clearly incorporated IHL into the UPR machinery, the most innovative creation of the new Council (Zhu 2014, p. 211). Depending on the expertise of States and the efforts and attention paid to IHL, the review of compliance with IHL under the UPR mechanism could become more comprehensive, adding another opportunity to address shortcomings concerning IHL enforcement on the part of States.

Enforcement Through the International Court of Justice

The ICJ's position as one of the main organs of the UN and its principal judicial organ makes its role quite important (Gardam 2001, p. 349–365; Chetail 2003, p. 235–268; Raimondo 2007, p. 593–611; Kress 2013, p. 263–298). This institutional role is reflected also in requests for advisory opinions on IHL-related issues by the General Assembly. Some of the aspects of the work of the Court which are relevant to the enforcement of IHL are State responsibility for violations of IHL; reparations due to States, legal entities, and individuals; and indication of provisional measures of protection in armed conflict situations (ICJ, Application of the Convention on the Prevention and Punishment of the Crime of Genocide 1993; Armed Activities on the Territory of the Congo 2000; Application of the International Convention on the Elimination of All Forms of Racial Discrimination 2008). As Chetail has pointed out, the Court's case law as a whole has certainly helped to strengthen and clarify the normative basis of international humanitarian law by highlighting its relationships with general international law and by setting out the basic principles governing the conduct of hostilities and the protection of victims of war (Chetail 2003, p. 268). This author has pointed out the threefold function of the ICJ with regard to developing IHL, namely, (1) first and foremost, the ICJ clarifies and develops rules and principles of IHL through deciding cases brought before it, (2) it integrates international humanitarian law concepts and principles within the wider framework of international law, and (3) it contributes to maintaining the unity of international humanitarian law and its uniform application by international judicial bodies operating in this field (Zyberi 2008, p. 332).

Reparations for IHL violations are important (Zegveld 2003, p. 497–527; Gillard 2003, p. 529–553). In the "Armed Activities" case, the ICJ made an explicit finding in the *dispositif* of its judgment about a State having violated its obligations under international humanitarian law and being under obligation to make reparation for the injury caused (ICJ, Armed Activities on the Territory of the Congo 2005, para. 345(3) and (5)). In the *Wall* Advisory Opinion, the ICJ found that Israel was under an obligation to make reparation for the damage caused to all the natural or legal persons affected by the construction of the wall in the occupied Palestinian territory (ICJ, Legal Consequences of the Construction of a Wall in the Occupied Palestinian Territory 2004, para. 152). The contribution of the ICJ to the enforcement of IHL is relevant in terms of the law of international responsibility, as well as concerning the awarding of reparations for serious violations of IHL.

Enforcement of IHL Through International Criminal Law Mechanisms

The enforcement of IHL is furthered by pursuing individual criminal responsibility for serious violations of IHL through international criminal courts and tribunals (Pejić 2002, p. 13–33; Darcy and Powderly 2010). Some of the most prominent courts and tribunals are the ICTY, the ICTR, and the ICC. The two ad hoc tribunals established by the UNSC continued in the footsteps of the Nuremberg and the Tokyo tribunals while addressing important questions which had not been addressed before, including the existence of war crimes in NIACs. The ICTY has played an important role in enforcing IHL by indicting 161 persons for war crimes, crimes against humanity, and genocide committed in the former Yugoslavia in the 1990s (Quéguiner 2003, p. 271–311). Some of the main contributions of the ICTY include the development of the grave breaches regime and of individual criminal responsibility, including command responsibility; bridging the protection gap between IACs and NIACs; firmly establishing the prohibition of torture under international law as a *jus cogens* norm; finding that most norms of international humanitarian law, in particular those prohibiting war crimes, crimes against humanity, and genocide, are also peremptory norms of international law or *jus cogens* (Wagner 2003, p. 351–383; Williamson 2008, p. 303–317; Zyberi 2014a, p. 395–416). The ICTR has led the way by prosecuting rape as a war crime, clarifying the law on superior responsibility, as well as by further developing the law on war crimes in NIACs (van den Herik 2005). The ICC has further developed the law on modes of individual criminal liability, as well as the law on reparations for serious violations of IHL. The reach of international criminal justice is still small though, focusing mainly on those most responsible, hence necessitating the support of domestic authorities and criminal investigation and prosecution of alleged perpetrators of war crimes before domestic courts.

Enforcement by Non-State Actors

Although States are crucial for ensuring the enforcement of IHL, non-State actors (NSAs) and especially non-State armed groups (NSAGs) have become increasingly important (Zyberi 2014b, p. 53–74; Clapham 2014, p. 766–810). Most of the ongoing armed conflicts are of a non-international nature, which further emphasizes the role for NSAGs in enforcing IHL. By now, it is commonly accepted that IHL binds all parties to an armed conflict, including NSAGs. Clapham has suggested a number of options that can be used to address violations of IHL by NSAs, including criminal accountability, sanctions, monitoring and reporting, encouraging codes of conduct and deeds of commitment, and initiatives aimed at the underlying causes of the conflict (Clapham 2014, p. 809–810). Other relevant actors for the enforcement of IHL are nongovernmental organizations (NGOs). Many international (and local) NGOs are involved in fact-finding, publication of their findings, "naming and shaming" those who violate IHL, and lobbying relevant actors to prevent and stop IHL violations. Other relevant activities by NGOs include education and awareness-raising campaigns aimed at the broader public, as well as engagement with NSAGs in order to train or to encourage them to comply with IHL.

Concluding Remarks

War crimes are serious violations of IHL that can trigger individual criminal responsibility, State responsibility, or the responsibility of international organizations. The resurgence of NIACs and the clashes of State armed forces with NSAGs that control large parts of territory, or operate cross-border, have contributed to an increase in the number of war crimes and other violations of IHL affecting large parts of the population. While the grave breaches system only applies in IACs, customary IHL and the practice of international courts and tribunals has largely bridged the protection gap between IACs and NIACs. Over the last 150 years, different mechanisms have been established and entrusted with the enforcement of IHL at the three levels, namely, domestic, regional, and international levels. These mechanisms can have a judicial or a nonjudicial nature. The IHL enforcement system is based on the foundational obligation of States to respect and ensure respect for IHL under common Article 1 to the 1949 Geneva Conventions. The measures that States can take to enforce IHL are of a preventive, punitive, and supervisory or monitoring nature. Besides enforcement at the domestic level through domestic courts, or other relevant mechanisms, the regional human rights system is also important in ensuring respect for IHL. Although IHL per se does not fall under the purview of their jurisdiction, the regional human rights systems through the courts or commissions have managed to enforce IHL and develop relevant standards of conduct for States and other parties to armed conflicts.

Some treaty-based enforcement mechanisms such as Protecting Powers, ad hoc inquiry commissions and the International Fact-Finding Comisssion have barely been used, whereas other enforcement mechanisms focusing on individual criminal responsibility such as international criminal courts and tribunals have taken on important functions in terms of ensuring accountability, reparations, and reconciliation. As Green has pointed out with regard to the future, the jurisprudence of both the tribunals for the former Yugoslavia and Rwanda might serve as a deterrent against breaches of humanitarian law, although it is more likely that what will happen is that similar ad hoc tribunals or the International Criminal Court will be called upon to enforce the law by way of post facto process and punishment (Green 2003, p. 130). The work of international criminal justice mechanisms needs to be supported and further expanded through a functioning domestic criminal justice system.

The UN main organs play an important role in enforcing IHL, although their work is occasionally permeated by selectivity and power-politics calculations, as well as jurisdictional and other practical limitations. This situation has caused serious mass violations committed in armed conflicts in different parts of the world to go unstopped or unpunished. While the enforcement of IHL remains a challenge, the combination of the work of existing IHL mechanisms with those established with a primary function of enforcing human rights has improved the chances of having serious violations of IHL adjudicated or otherwise raised and considered at different levels and forums.

References

ACmHPR (2000) Commission Nationale des Droits de l'Homme et des Libertés v. Chad, AHRLR 66
ACmHPR (2003) Democratic Republic of Congo v. Burundi, Rwanda and Uganda, AHRLR 19
ACmHPR (2007a) Amnesty International and others v. Sudan, AHRLR 297
ACmHPR (2007b) Article 19 v. Eritrea, AHRLR 73
ACmHPR (2009) Sudan Human Rights Organisation & Centre on Housing Rights and Evictions (COHRE) v. Sudan, AHRLR 153
ACtHR (2011) African Commission on Human and Peoples' Rights v. Great Socialist People's Libyan Arab Jamahiriya
Additional Protocol (I) to the Geneva Conventions 1977
Additional Protocol (II) to the Geneva Conventions 1977
Azzarello C and Niederhauser M (2018) The independent humanitarian fact-finding commission: has the 'sleeping beauty' awoken?, 9 January 2018. Available at http://blogs.icrc.org/law-and-policy/2018/01/09/the-independent-humanitarian-fact-finding-commission-has-the-sleeping-beauty-awoken. Accessed 27 Mar 2018
Blank LR (2011) Understanding when and how domestic courts apply IHL. Case Western Reserve Journal of International Law 44:205–224
Boisson de Chazournes L, Condorelli L (2000) Common article 1 of the Geneva conventions revisited: protecting collective interests. International Review of the Red Cross 82(837):67–87
Bonafè B (2009) The relationship between state and individual responsibility for international crimes. Brill, Leiden
Buis EJ (2008) The implementation of international humanitarian law by human rights courts: the example of the inter-American human rights system. In: Arnold R, Quénivet N (eds) International humanitarian law and human rights law: towards a new merger in international law. Martinus Nijhoff Publishers, Leiden, pp 269–293
Cerna C (2011) The history of the inter-American system's jurisprudence as regards situations of armed conflict. Journal of International Humanitarian Legal Studies 2(1):3–52
Chetail V (2003) The contribution of the international court of justice to international humanitarian law. International Review of the Red Cross 85(850):235–268
Clapham A (2014) Focusing on armed non-state actors. In: Clapham A, Gaeta P (eds) The Oxford handbook of international law in armed conflict. Oxford University Press, Oxford, pp 766–810
Crawford E, Pert A (2015) International humanitarian law. Cambridge University Press, Cambridge
Crawford J, Pellet A, Olleson S (eds) (2010) The law of international responsibility. Oxford University Press, Oxford
Darcy S (2014) Judges, law and war: the judicial development of international humanitarian law. Cambridge University Press, Cambridge
Darcy S, Powderly J (eds) (2010) Judicial creativity at the international criminal tribunals. Oxford University Press, Oxford
de Wet E, Kleffner J (eds) (2014) Convergence and conflicts of human rights and international humanitarian law in military operations. Pretoria University Law Press, Pretoria
Dörmann K, Serralvo J (2014) Common article 1 to the Geneva conventions and the obligation to prevent international humanitarian law violations. International Review of the Red Cross 96 (895/896):707–736
ECtHR (1995) McCann and others v. the United Kingdom (Application no. 18984/91)
ECtHR (1996) Aksoy v. Turkey (Application no. 37546/08)
ECtHR (2001) Cyprus v. Turkey (Application no. 25781/94)
ECtHR (2005) Öcalan v. Turkey (Application no. 46221/99)
ECtHR (2009) A. and others v. the United Kingdom (Application no. 3455/05)
ECtHR (2012a) El-Masri v. "The former Yugoslav Republic of Macedonia" (Application no. 39630/09)
ECtHR (2012b) Marguš v. Croatia (Application no. 4455/10)

ECtHR (2013) Stichting mothers of Srebrenica and others v. the Netherlands (Application no. 65542/12)

ECtHR (2014a) Al Nashiri v. Poland (Application no. 28761/11)

ECtHR (2014b) Husayn (Abu Zubaydah) v. Poland (Application no. 7511/13)

El Zeidy M (2008) The principle of complementarity in international criminal law: origin, development and practice. Brill, Leiden

Findlay T (2002) The use of force in UN peace operations. Oxford University Press, Oxford

Focarelli C (2010) Common article 1 of the 1949 Geneva conventions: a soap bubble? EJIL 21(1):125–171

Foley C (2017) UN peacekeeping operations and the protection of civilians: saving succeeding generations. Cambridge University Press, Cambridge

Gardam J (2001) The contribution of the international court of justice to international humanitarian law. Leiden Journal of International Law 14:349–365

Geneva Convention (I) on wounded and sick in armed forces in the field 1949

Geneva Convention (II) on wounded, sick and shipwrecked of armed forces at sea 1949

Geneva Convention (III) on prisoners of war 1949

Geneva Convention (IV) on civilians 1949

Genser J, Stagno Ugarte B (eds) (2014) The United Nations Security Council in the age of human rights. Cambridge University Press, Cambridge

Gill T (2013) Chivalry: a principle of the law of armed conflict? In: Matthee M, Toebes B, Brus M (eds) Armed conflict and international law: in search of the human face – liber Amicorum in memory of Avril McDonald. Springer, Heidelberg, pp 33–51

Gillard E-C (2003) Reparation for violations of international humanitarian law. International Review of the Red Cross 85(851):529–553

Gioia A (2011) The role of the European court of human rights in monitoring compliance with humanitarian law in armed conflict. In: Ben-Naftali O (ed) International humanitarian law and international human rights law. Oxford University Press, Oxford, pp 201–249

Green LC (2003) Enforcement of international humanitarian law and threats to National Sovereignty. Journal of Conflict and Security Law 8(1):101–131

Hartridge S (2014) The European court of human Right's engagement with international humanitarian law. In: Jinks D, Maogoto JN, Solomon S (eds) Applying international humanitarian law in judicial and quasi-judicial bodies. Springer, Heidelberg, pp 257–287

Henckaerts J-M, Doswald-Beck L (eds) (2005) Customary international humanitarian law: volume I, rules; volume II, practice: part 1 and part 2. Cambridge University Press, Cambridge

IACtHR (1987a) Habeas Corpus in emergency situations (Arts. 27 (2), 25 (I) and 7 (6) American Convention on Human Rights) (advisory opinion) Ser A No 8 (30 Jan 1987)

IACtHR (1987b) Judicial Guarantees in States of Emergency (Arts. 27(2), 25 and 8 American Convention on Human Rights) (Advisory Opinion) Ser A No 9 (6 Oct 1987)

IACtHR (2000) Bámaca-Velásquez v. Guatemala (Merits and Judgment) Ser C No 70 IACHR (25 Nov 2000)

IACtHR (2006) Case of the Pueblo Bello massacre v. Colombia (Merits, Reparations and Costs) Ser C No 140 IACHR (31 Jan 2006)

ICJ (1986) Military and Paramilitary Activities in and against Nicaragua (Nicaragua v. United States of America), Merits, ICJ Reports 1986, p. 14

ICJ (1993) Application of the Convention on the Prevention and Punishment of the Crime of Genocide (Bosnia and Herzegovina v. Serbia and Montenegro), ICJ Reports 1993, p. 3

ICJ (1996) Legality of the threat or use of nuclear weapons, ICJ Reports 1996, p. 226

ICJ (2000) Armed Activities on the Territory of the Congo (Democratic Republic of the Congo v. Uganda), ICJ Reports 2000, p. 111

ICJ (2002) Arrest Warrant of 11 April 2000 (Democratic Republic of the Congo v. Belgium), ICJ Reports 2002, p. 3

ICJ (2004) Legal consequences of the construction of a wall in the occupied Palestinian territory, advisory opinion, ICJ Reports 2004, p. 136

ICJ (2005) Armed activities on the territory of the Congo (Democratic Republic of the Congo v. Uganda, ICJ Reports 2005, p. 168

ICJ (2008) Application of the International Convention on the Elimination of All Forms of Racial Discrimination (Georgia v. Russian Federation), ICJ Reports 2008, p. 353

ICRC (2015) International humanitarian law and the challenges of contemporary armed conflicts: document prepared by the international committee of the red cross for the 32nd international conference of the red cross and red crescent, Geneva, Switzerland, 8–10 December 2015. International Review of the Red Cross 900:1427–1502

ICRC Database on National Implementation. https://ihl-databases.icrc.org/ihl-nat

ICTR (2008, 2011) Bagosora et al. (Military I) (ICTR-98-41)

ICTR (1998, 2000) Jean Kambanda (ICTR-97-23)

ICTR (1998, 2001) Jean Paul Akayesu (ICTR-96-4)

ICTY (2016) Radovan Karadžić (IT-95-5/18)

ICTY (2017) Ratko Mladić (IT-09-92)

ICTY (1995) Duško Tadić (IT-94-1-AR72)

ICTY (2001, 2002) Kunarac et al. (IT-96-23 & IT-96-23/1)

ICTY (2013, 2017) Prlić et al. (IT-04-74)

ICTY (2009, 2014) Šainović et al. (IT-05-87)

ICTY (2005, 2007) Limaj et al. (IT-03-66)

Inazumi M (2005) Universal jurisdiction in modern international law: expansion of national jurisdiction for prosecuting serious crimes under international law. Intersentia, Cambridge

International Crimes Database, T.M.C. Asser Institute. www.internationalcrimesdatabase.org

Jørgensen N (2003) The responsibility of states for international crimes. Oxford University Press, Oxford

Kalshoven F (2007) Implementation and enforcement of international humanitarian law. In: Kalshoven F (ed) Reflections on the law of war: collected essays. Brill, Leiden, pp 593–620

Kleffner J (2008) Complementarity in the Rome statute and national criminal jurisdictions. Oxford University Press, Oxford

Koops J, MacQueen N, Tardy T, Williams PD (eds) (2015) The Oxford handbook of United Nations peacekeeping operations. Oxford University Press, Oxford

Kress C (2013) The international court of justice and the law of armed conflicts. In: Tams C, Sloan J (eds) The development of international law by the international court of justice. Oxford University Press, Oxford, pp 263–298

Krieger H (ed) (2015) Inducing compliance with international humanitarian law: lessons from the African Great Lakes region. Cambridge University Press, Cambridge

Kwakwa E (2004) The Cairo-Arusha principles on universal jurisdiction in respect of gross human rights offenses: an African perspective. In: Yusuf A (ed) African yearbook of international law/Annuaire Africain de Droit International, volume 10 (2002). Nijhoff, The Hague, pp 407–430

Larsen KM (2012) The human rights treaty obligations of peacekeepers. Cambridge University Press, Cambridge

Lowe V, Roberts A, Welsh J, Zaum D (eds) (2010) The United Nations security council and war: the evolution of thought and practice since 1945. Oxford University Press, Oxford

Macedo S (2006) Universal jurisdiction: national courts and the prosecution of serious crimes under international law. University of Pennsylvania Press, Philadelphia

Melzer N (2016) International humanitarian law: a comprehensive introduction. ICRC, Geneva

Morjé Howard L, Dayal AK (2018) The use of force in UN peacekeeping. Int Organ 72(1):71–103

Nerlich V (2009) War crimes. In: Cassese A (ed) The Oxford companion to international criminal justice. Oxford University Press, Oxford, pp 566–570

Nouwen S (2013) Complementarity in the line of fire: the catalysing effect of the international criminal court in Uganda and Sudan. Cambridge University Press, Cambridge

Oberleitner G (2015) Human rights in armed conflict. Cambridge University Press, Cambridge

Oellers-Frahm K (2014) A regional perspective on the convergence and conflicts of human rights and international humanitarian law in military operations: the European court of human rights.

In: de Wet E, Kleffner J (eds) Convergence and conflicts of human rights and international humanitarian law in military operations. Pretoria University Law Press, Pretoria, pp 333–364

Office of the High Commissioner on Human Rights (2011) International legal protection of human rights in armed conflict. United Nations, Geneva

Orakhelashvili A (ed) (2015) Research handbook on jurisdiction and immunities in international law. Edward Elgar Publishing, London

Pejić J (2002) Accountability for international crimes: from conjecture to reality. International Review of the Red Cross 84(845):13–33

Pfanner T (2009) Various mechanisms and approaches for implementing international humanitarian law and protecting and assisting war victims. International Review of the Red Cross 91(874):279–328

Princeton Project on Universal Jurisdiction (2001) The Princeton principles on universal jurisdiction. Program in law and public affairs. Princeton University, Princeton

Quéguiner J-F (2003) Dix ans après la création du Tribunal penal international pour l'ex-Yougoslavie: évaluation de l'apport de sa jurisprudence au droit international humanitaire. International Review of the Red Cross 85(850):271–311

Raimondo F (2007) The international court of justice as a guardian of the unity of humanitarian law. Leiden Journal of International Law 20:593–611

Roscini M (2010) The United Nations security council and the enforcement of international humanitarian law. Israel Law Review 43(2):330–359

Ryngaert C, Cuyckens H (2013) The general assembly. In: Zyberi G (ed) An institutional approach to the responsibility to protect. Cambridge University Press, Cambridge, pp 109–129

Sassòli M (2002) State responsibility for violations of international humanitarian law. International Review of the Red Cross 84(846):401–434

Sassòli M (2007) The implementation of international humanitarian law: current and inherent challenges. Yearbook of International Humanitarian Law 10:45–73

Schabas WA (2001) Enforcing international humanitarian law: catching the accomplices. International Review of the Red Cross 83:439–459

Schmitt M, von Heinegg WH (eds) (2012) The implementation and enforcement of international humanitarian law. Ashgate, Aldershot

Seibert-Fohr A (2009) Prosecuting serious human rights violations. Oxford University Press, Oxford

Shelton D (2014) Humanitarian law in the inter-American human rights system. In: de Wet E, Kleffner J (eds) Convergence and conflicts of human rights and international humanitarian law in military operations. Pretoria University Law Press, Pretoria, pp 365–394

Stahn K, El Zeidy M (eds) (2011) The international criminal court and complementarity: from theory to practice. Cambridge University Press, Cambridge

Tabak S (2016) Ambivalent enforcement: international humanitarian law at human rights tribunals. Michigan Journal of International Law 37.661–715

UK Ministry of Defence (2004) The manual of the law of armed conflict. Oxford University Press, Oxford

US Supreme Court (2006) Hamdan v. Rumsfeld, 548 U.S. 557

US Supreme Court (2008) Boumediene v. Bush, 553 U.S. 723

van Alebeek R (2008) The immunity of states and their officials in international criminal law and international human rights law. Oxford University Press, Oxford

van den Herik L (2005) The contribution of the Rwanda tribunal to the development of international law. Martinus Nijhoff Publishers, Leiden/Boston

van Sliedregt E (2012) Individual criminal responsibility in international law. Oxford University Press, Oxford

Viljoen F (2014) The relationship between international human rights and humanitarian law in the African human rights system: an institutional approach. In: de Wet E, Kleffner J (eds) Convergence and conflicts of human rights and international humanitarian law in military operations. Pretoria University Law Press, Pretoria, pp 303–332

Vité S (2009) Typology of armed conflicts in international humanitarian law: legal concepts and actual situations. International Review of the Red Cross 91(873):69–94

Vöneky S (2013) Implementation and enforcement of international humanitarian law. In: Fleck D (ed) The handbook of international humanitarian law, 3rd edn. Oxford University Press, Oxford, pp 647–700

Wagner N (2003) The development of the grave breaches regime and of individual criminal responsibility by the international criminal tribunal for the former Yugoslavia. International Review of the Red Cross 85(850):351–383

Weill S (2014a) The role of national courts in applying international humanitarian law. Oxford University Press, Oxford

Weill S (2014b) Building respect for IHL through national courts. International Review of the Red Cross 96(895/896):859–879

Williamson JA (2008) Some considerations on command responsibility and criminal liability. International Review of the Red Cross 90(870):303–317

Willmot H, Sheeran S (2013) The protection of civilians mandate in UN peacekeeping operations: reconciling protection concepts and practices. International Review of the Red Cross 95(891/892):517–538

Zegveld L (2003) Remedies for victims of violations of international humanitarian law. International Review of the Red Cross 85(851):497–527

Zhu L (2014) International humanitarian law in the universal periodic review of the UN human rights council: an empirical survey. Journal of International Humanitarian Legal Studies 5:186–212

Zyberi G (2008) The humanitarian face of the international court of justice: its contribution to interpreting and developing international human rights and humanitarian law rules and principles. Intersentia, Cambridge

Zyberi G (2010) Provisional measures of the international court of justice in armed conflict situations. Leiden Journal of International Law 23:571–584

Zyberi G (2014a) The jurisprudence of the international court of justice and international criminal courts and tribunals. In: de Wet E, Kleffner J (eds) Convergence and conflicts of human rights and international humanitarian law in military operations. Pretoria University Law Press, Pretoria, pp 395–416

Zyberi G (2014b) The role of non-state actors in implementing the responsibility to protect. In: Ryngaert C, Noortmann M (eds) Human security and international law: the challenge of non-state actors. Intersentia, Cambridge, pp 53–74

Transitional Justice for Human Rights: The Legacy and Future of Truth and Reconciliation Commissions

Elin Skaar

Contents

Introduction 402
What Is a Truth Commission? And What Is It Not? 403
The Malleable Universe of Truth Commissions 405
The Multiple Objectives of Truth Commissions 406
The Functions and Mandates of Truth Commissions 407
Truth Commissions in a Transitional Justice Context 408
What Truth Commissions Are Meant to Achieve: Claims and Evidence 409
Claims and Evidence for the Impact of Truth Commissions on Democracy 410
Evidence on the Impact of Truth Commissions on Democracy 410
Claims and Evidence for the Impact of Truth Commissions on Peace 411
Evidence for the Impact of Truth Commissions on Peace 412
Claims and Evidence for the Impact of Truth Commissions on Reconciliation 413
Evidence on the Impact of Truth Commissions on Reconciliation 414
Alternatives to Examining Truth Commission Impact 417
Truth Commission Reports and Recommendations 417
Some Reflections on the Future of Truth Commissions 418
References 419

Abstract

Truth commissions are an integral component of transitional justice, that is, formal and informal mechanisms set up by the state or civil society to address human rights violations committed in the past. This chapter examines the claims related to how truth commissions may contribute to peace, democracy, and

This chapter draws on previous work on truth commissions published in Skaar 2013; Skaar et al. 2015, 2016a.

E. Skaar (✉)
Chr. Michelsen Institute (CMI), Bergen, Norway
e-mail: elin.skaar@cmi.no

reconciliation and takes stock of the legacy of truth commissions by examining the impact literature related to these three chief objectives. Finally, the chapter offers some reflections on the potential importance of truth commissions in the future.

Keywords
Truth commission · Transitional justice · Human rights · Peace · Democracy · Reconciliation · Impact

Introduction

Unlike the other institutions discussed in this volume, truth commissions are fact-finding bodies with no prosecutorial powers. Truth commissions have over the past four decades become an increasingly important form of confronting past human rights abuses committed by the military, state agents, paramilitaries, or opposition forces during repressive regimes or periods of armed conflict – a practice that has come to be known as transitional justice (TJ). The prime function of truth commissions is to unveil and document human rights violations – and thereby to prevent atrocities of taking place in the future.

Although the predecessor of truth commissions – commissions of inquiry – has a history dating back to the eleventh-century England (Prasser 2017), truth commissions, as we know them today, have a relatively short history. The first truth commission in the world was set up in Uganda in the 1970s under the brutal regime of Idi Amin, followed by the truth commission in Bolivia in the early 1980s (Hayner 1994, pp. 611–14). The South African Truth and Reconciliation Commission is arguably the world's best known. However, the idea and model of a truth commission were developed and perfected in Latin America. This region has, as of 2017, seen 11 official and 5 alternative/nonofficial truth commissions in 13 different countries since the 1980s (Skaar et al. forthcoming). There are somewhere between 50 and 100 truth commissions in the world – depending on what definition one uses and on how one counts. Among the most well-known truth commissions, we find South Africa's Truth and Reconciliation Commission, Argentina's Commission on the Disappearance of Persons (CONADEP), and Chile's Rettig Commission. On the list of obscurer, less-studied, and therefore less-known commissions, we find the truth commissions of Panama, Haiti, and Ecuador. Latecomers on the truth commission scene include those set up in Afghanistan, Burundi, Benin, Brazil, Lebanon, Liberia, and Nepal. More commissions are currently underway in, among other countries, Bolivia and Colombia. There is thus no reason to believe that this growing list is about to exhaust itself any time soon. As more countries emerge from war and conflict, truth commissions are one of several likely responses to how states deal with the violence committed by one or more parties to the conflict. Adding to the universe of truth commissions set down in times of political transition, there is also a recent and growing trend of governments in well-established democracies of setting down commissions mandated to investigate patterns of abuse committed against certain minority groups in a distant past under democratic rule. This trend poses challenges to the conceptual, temporal and investigative functions of truth commissions.

This chapter explores the legacy of truth commissions. It is organized in six parts. Following this short introduction, the next part offers several definitions of a truth commission and sketches the universe of truth commissions according to different definitions. The third part situates truth commissions within the larger scholarly field of transitional justice. The fourth part examines the claims related to what truth commissions are expected to achieve with respect to peace, democracy, and reconciliation and brings to the table the patchy evidence on the impact of truth commissions. The fifth part summarizes the legacy of truth commissions and poses some reflections on the future potential contributions of truth commissions.

What Is a Truth Commission? And What Is It Not?

There is no single, widely accepted definition of what a truth commission is. However, there are some central definitions that dominate the growing literature on truth commission, which I will spell out below. In addition to trying to establish what a truth commission is or should be, these definitions also have implications for what a truth commission *is not*.

The earliest coined, and perhaps still most widely used, truth commission definition comes from transitional justice expert Priscilla Hayner. She describes truth commissions as "bodies set up to investigate a past history of violations of human rights in a particular country – which can include violations by the military or other government forces or armed opposition forces," and which have four primary elements:

> First, a truth commission focuses on the *past*. Second, a truth commission is *not focused on a specific event*, but attempts to paint the overall picture of certain human rights abuses, or violations of international humanitarian law, *over a period of time*. Third, a truth commission usually exists *temporarily* and for a pre-defined period of time, ceasing to exist with the submission of a report of its findings. Finally, a truth commission is always vested with some sort of *authority*, by way of its sponsor, that allows it greater access to information, greater security or protection to dig into sensitive issues, and a greater impact with its *report*. (Hayner 1994, p. 604) (italics by the author)

What types of commissions should be defined as truth commissions was an issue from the very start. As Hayner points out, "[t]here have been a number of national nongovernmental projects that have served truth commission-like functions investigating the record of violence and publishing a report – but which have not operated with the authority or typical structure of a truth commission" (Hayner 1994, p. 604). Seeing that her own definition had "some limitations" by simply being too broad in scope and hence "potentially including so many commissions of inquiry – .... that the very meaning begins to be lost" (Hayner 2010, p. 11), Hayner coined a slightly revised definition that significantly narrowed the universe of truth commission by insisting that they should be state-sponsored or authorized:

> A truth commission (1) is focused on the past, rather than ongoing, events; (2) investigates a pattern of events that took place over a period of time; (3) engages directly and broadly with the affected population, gathering information on their experience; (4) is a temporary body, *with the aim of concluding with a final report*; and (5) is *officially authorized or empowered by the state* under review. (Hayner 2010, pp. 11–12) (italics by the author)

One of the central points for Hayner was to easily distinguish a truth commission from a government standing human rights body or from a judicial commission of inquiry (such as various international investigative bodies established by the United Nations) that aims to clarify the facts of one narrow event (Hayner, p. 12). The new element of a truth commission having to be *officially authorized or empowered by the state* is inspired by Mark Freeman's definition of truth commission:

> an ad hoc, autonomous, and *victim-centered* commission of inquiry set up in and *authorized by a state* for the primary purposes of (1) investigating and reporting on the principal causes and consequences of broad and relatively recent patterns of severe violence or repression that occurred in the state during *determinate periods of abusive rule or conflict*, and (2) *making recommendations* for their redress and future prevention. (Freeman 2006, p. 18) (italics by the author)

Mark Freeman's definition also singles out yet a new central element in the scholarly debates on what a truth commission should be: they should not only document abuses but also have a focus on victims. This reflects the trend toward more focus on victims of human rights violations around the turn of the century (García-Godos 2016).

These three definitions provide the basis for most scholarly work on truth commissions, although different scholars operate with slightly modified versions of one or more of the definitions above (see Bakiner 2016, p. 24; Ferrara 2015, p. 4; Wiebelhaus-Brahm 2010, pp. 3–4). Building closely on Hayner's (2010) and Wiebelhaus-Brahm's (2010) definitions, Tricia Olsen, Andrew Reiter, and Leigh Payne in their much-cited work based on their Transitional Justice Database (TJDB) bring back in the element of non-state commissions when launching a fourth definition:

> "The TJDB defines truth commissions as newly established, temporary bodies officially sanctioned by the state *or an international governmental organization* to investigate a pattern of human rights abuses".…. "We exclude pre-existing government institutions that investigate past human rights violations as part of their official duties. We further exclude commissions created to investigate corruption, embezzlement, fraud, and similar crimes." Furthermore, "We exclude non-state, independent projects that investigate and uncover the truth about past violations since they do not represent official decisions on behalf of state actors." (Olsen et al. 2010a, p. 992, including fn. 58) (italics by the author)

In sum, there are at least four key differences between the various established definitions of truth commissions: (1) whether they are formal or informal fact-finding bodies, that is, set up or sponsored and authorized by the state or not, (2) whether they are established in a post-conflict setting or not, (3) whether they are victims centered or not, and (4) whether they have produced a report and made recommendations to be followed up by the government or not.

The more defining elements a truth commission should have, the more restrictive the definition, and the narrower the universe of commissions. To sum up, Freeman's (2006) definition is a more restrictive definition than Hayner's seminal (1994) definition. It is also much more restrictive than the more expansive definition used in recent statistical work on truth commissions by Olsen et al. (2010b). The most expansive definition of all is held by the International Center for Transitional Justice (ICTJ), a trendsetting New York-based international organization that has lent much technical and monetary assistance to truth commissions set up all over the world after the ICTJ was established in 2002. Including a greater international focus on social and economic rights in recent years, the ICTJ defines truth commissions as follows:

> Truth commissions are non-judicial inquiries established to determine the facts, *root causes, and societal consequences of past human rights violations.* Through their focus on the testimony of victims of atrocity, truth commissions provide acknowledgement and recognition of suffering and survival to those most affected. . . . Truth commissions are evolving institutions: *their focus is expanding to cover more types of violations, going beyond crimes against physical integrity to examine violations of economic, social, and cultural rights.* They are also becoming more adept at capturing and addressing the experiences of different sectors of the population, including those of women, children, and indigenous peoples. (ICTJ 2017) (italics by the author)

The boundaries for what a truth commissions is and what a truth commission should do are continuously being pushed. Current scholarly as well as policy debates include tensions over the contextual limits of truth commissions. For instance, some argue that truth commissions should not only address violations committed during political authoritarianism but also under democratic rule. Nicola Henry makes the case that "a broader conceptualization of transitional justice is instrumental not only for examining the past wrongdoings of established democracies, but also for giving coherence to diverse and competing discourses on colonial injustices" (Henry 2015, p. 199). Furthermore, arguments have also been made for including corruption as a central aim of truth commissions (Robinson 2015). This general tendency toward broader definitions allows us to include more and more truth commissions in our analysis. However, I would caution strongly against diluting the definition so much that the core functions of truth commissions (namely, addressing human rights violations) disappear among too many other broad aims and visions and that we end up comparing apples and pears.

In summary, definitions of what a truth commission is – or is not – or what they should focus their work on has changed over the years. The universe of truth commissions has changed accordingly.

The Malleable Universe of Truth Commissions

As Eric Wiebelhaus-Brahm, one of the world's foremost experts on truth commissions, pointed out almost a decade ago, the scholars who launched the various definitions of truth commissions outlined above were not necessarily concerned with comparative analysis (Wiebelhaus-Brahm 2009). Nevertheless, a number of scholars have used one or more of these definitions to try to get a grasp of the universe of truth commissions and to assess their importance and impact. As in all forms of social science research, the definition you use defines the universe that you get.

When Hayner carried out her pioneer study of truth commissions worldwide established between 1974 and 1994, she identified 15 truth commissions, 11 of which were government sponsored (Hayner 1994). Applying her revised definition of a truth commission, Hayner a decade and a half later documented 40 such commissions (Hayner, Appendix 2). By contrast, using Freeman's definition, we in previous research recorded 33 truth commissions worldwide during the period 1982–2014 (Skaar et al. 2015, Appendix 1, pp. 199–200) – three of which were in the making. This finding contrasts also with Olsen et al. (2010) comparative work identifying more than 70 commissions at the same time as we published our work. This point is important (particularly in statistical analysis) because the objectives and expected contributions of truth commissions necessarily reflect the definition used. Two of the defining points are whether the commission is state-sponsored/authorized or not and whether the commission has published a report or not. If we further expand the definition of truth commissions to include commissions in established democracies that investigate wrongdoings in a colonial or non-colonial past, the extended universe of truth commissions would include, among others, the Greensboro Truth and Reconciliation Commission (USA), the Truth and Reconciliation Commission of Canada, and the National Inquiry into the Separation of Aboriginal and Torres Strait Islander Children from Their Families (Australia).

The Multiple Objectives of Truth Commissions

Revealing, documenting, and recording the "truth" are the key objectives of truth commissions. Nevertheless, truth commissions are generically assumed to also promote a wide range of stated objectives. Professed aims, drawn from truth commission mandates, the widely cited article by Tristan Anne Borer (2006) and a range of other sources, make an impressive list of objectives, including (in alphabetical order) accountability, acknowledgment, amnesty, apology, coexistence, confession, dignity, forgiveness, healing, human rights culture, justice, mental health, mercy, national unity, *nunca más* or "never again," peace, political impact, (nonprosecutorial) punishment, reconciliation, reconstruction, remorse, reparations, repentance, responsibility, restoration, retribution, rule of law, and, finally, truth.

Although truth commissions have widely varying mandates, a fair share have *reconciliation* as a specific end goal: the National Commission for Truth and Reconciliation (Chile); Commission for Reception, Truth, and Reconciliation (East Timor); National Reconciliation Commission (Ghana); Truth and Reconciliation Commission (Peru); Truth and Reconciliation Commission (Sierra Leone); Truth and Reconciliation Commission (South Africa); Truth and Reconciliation Commission for Serbia and Montenegro (former Yugoslavia); Equity and Reconciliation Commission (Morocco); Truth and Reconciliation Commission (Nepal); and Truth and Reconciliation Commission (Liberia), to list but a few. Other truth commissions have stressed their link to *justice*, such as the National Commission for Truth and Justice (Haiti), Truth and Justice Commission (Mauritius), Truth and Justice Commission (Paraguay), and Truth, Justice, and Reconciliation Commission (Kenya). Yet other commissions have various other expressed goals or ambitions, such as *friendship* as the Indonesia-Timor Leste Commission on Truth and Friendship, or *dignity*, such as the Truth and Dignity Commission (Tunisia).

Apart from their main goals – as frequently, but far from always, signaled in the name of the truth commission or in the report of the commission – most truth commissions share some fundamental functions.

The Functions and Mandates of Truth Commissions

The three most fundamental undertakings of truth commissions are (i) to investigate human rights abuses, (ii) to document human rights abuses, and (iii) to make recommendations that both address these abuses and make similar abuses less likely to be repeated in the future. These three undertakings are usually specified in the mandate of the truth commission. The mandate spells out what kinds of violations, committed by what agents (state actors, non-state actors, particular groups, etc.), and during what period should be subject to investigation. The mandate will also usually state if a report is anticipated/mandatory or not. Finally, in some cases, the mandate also specifies what types of recommendations the commissioners should make in the final report.

Victims of human rights violations may play different roles in all three stages of the truth commission's work. Some truth commissions, though far from all, receive testimonies from victims during the investigation stage. Arguably, commissions may have more of an effect on society if they conduct public hearings and/or more purposefully engage with the media and civil society. The documentation of truth commissions generally in part relies on victims' testimonies and in part on documentation collected by victims' organizations and other nongovernmental and intergovernmental human rights organizations during the period of conflict/violations. What a commission actually reports on may vary from the systematic recollection of facts and data to the historical interpretation of events and processes. Victims usually do not have a central role in the reporting function, as only very few commissions (like the one in Ecuador and the current truth commission that is underway in Colombia) include victims among their commissioners.

It is hoped that truth commission reports potentially make similar abuses less likely in the future. The transformative potential of truth commissions arguably lies most directly in the body of recommendations put forward in their final reports. Already more than 20 years ago, Hayner advised that "[w]hen possible, it should be agreed in advance that a truth commission's recommendations are obligatory" (Hayner 1994, p. 653). Nevertheless, the recommendations of truth commissions were until very recently a severely under-researched topic. Only in recent years, have more scholars emphasized the potential importance of the recommendations made by truth commissions in their reports (Skaar et al. forthcoming). Yet recommendations usually include proposals to reform legal, security, political, and social institutions. They also frequently recommend reparations of various kinds and other sorts of measures to further address past violations. The list of recommendations is often extensive, raising questions about expectations and the possibility of implementation. Since this remains an underexplored area in the transitional justice field, there is much room for more systematic and thorough analysis here.

Truth Commissions in a Transitional Justice Context

Truth commissions do not operate in a vacuum. They are frequently preceded by, or operate alongside, other institutional and noninstitutional measures established to address past human rights abuses committed during repressive regimes or periods of armed conflict. Together, these measures are constitutive of what we call transitional justice (TJ), which include prosecutions, truth commissions, amnesties, reparations, lustration, institutional reform, and local justice processes (Roht-Arriaza and Mariezcurrena 2006; Teitel 2000). Truth commissions appear most frequently with amnesty laws, in context where truth commissions are set up during or soon after the political transition or peace agreement. When truth commissions are set down several years, sometimes even decades, after the human rights violations have taken place (as in the case of Brazil or Colombia) – forming what we call post-transition commissions – other TJ mechanisms (such as typically reparations) may already be in place (Skaar et al. 2016b). We have to take this complexity into account when we try to assess the importance or contributions of truth commissions.

There has been plenty of wishful thinking over the years with respect to what transitional justice processes can and should achieve. The overall assumption in the literature is that transitional justice broadly understood plays an important role in transitions from authoritarian rule to democracy or from situations of armed conflict to peace. However, the dominant views on the impact of these processes have changed over time. These changes reflect important shifts in international factors such as prevalent human rights norms and practices and an expansion of the so-called transitional justice toolbox. Ruti Teitel in a seminal article usefully refers to three phases of transitional justice (Teitel 2003). Phase I, between the end of World War II and the onset of the Cold War, was characterized by interstate cooperation, war crimes trials, and sanctions, as seen in the Nuremberg and Tokyo trials – but no truth commissions. Then came an intermittent period of almost four decades with little or no transitional justice at all. Phase II, the post-Cold War phase, coincided with the "third wave of democratization" (Huntington 1991). From an almost exclusive focus on legal responses, intended primarily to ensure the rule of law, the transitional justice discourse in the post-Cold War phase proceeded to expand to a more diverse focus on "truth" and "justice," with "reconciliation" as a desired outcome. This period saw diversification of the formal mechanisms employed to bring about justice for past human rights violations, including a series of nonlegal mechanisms such as truth commissions.

In Phase III, the current phase, transitional justice has become an established component of post-conflict processes. Discussions of transitional justice frequently begin even before a conflict has ended – as in the case of Colombia's recent peace process (García-Godos and Lid 2010). A particular feature of this phase is an increased interest in local or traditional processes of justice and reconciliation (McEvoy and McGregor 2008; Shaw et al. 2010). Another feature of the third phase is diversification of actors: in addition to local actors, including ordinary citizens at the grassroots level, there has been a proliferation of donors and international donors eager to contribute to a "justice cascade" (Sikkink 2011).

The transitional justice literature, which initially was dominated by legal scholars and political scientists, has become truly interdisciplinary. The scholarly debates have also shifted from a principal focus on normative claims to an increasing concern with their empirical verification. Which TJ mechanisms work, how, and why questions are raised by academics as well as by practitioners and donors. As more and more money pours into transitional justice, and as more and more actors enter the field – including nongovernmental organizations, transitional justice programs, and activist networks – the concern with measurement and usefulness of transitional justice has grown.

Accordingly, there has in recent years been a steadily growing literature trying to assess the virtues (and increasingly also vices) of transitional justice. The three meta-goals of truth, justice, and reconciliation – aptly referred to as the "triumvirate" of transitional justice (Gready 2010) – still dominate the literature. Claims regarding the relationships between these three overarching goals have shifted over time, as have the claims about the links (and possible tensions) between the immediate goals of "truth and justice," on one hand, and the long-term goals of "peace and democracy," on the other (Leebaw 2008). The next section narrows the focus to expectations tied to truth commissions specifically.

What Truth Commissions Are Meant to Achieve: Claims and Evidence

Periods of state repression or internal armed conflict typically are accompanied by disagreement and confusion regarding the extent of human rights violations and who is responsible for these violations. Establishing the relevant facts is therefore a main challenge. "Truth-telling" or "truth-seeking" regarding past violations is achieved principally through truth commissions, though human rights violations may also be exposed in court trials (Orentlicher 1991).

The most important objective of truth commissions is obviously to investigate and document past violations, hence contribute to establishing the facts about violations. But as suggested above, truth commissions are associated with a number of objectives, including clarifying and acknowledging past abuses, meeting the needs of victims, contributing to justice and accountability, delineating institutional responsibility for past abuses and promoting reform, and promoting reconciliation and a reduction in tensions over the past (Hayner 2010, p. 11). This is a tall order.

Consequently, the establishment of truth commissions in countries around the world has often generated broad expectations among academics, activists, policymakers, victims, and mass publics that they will lead to peace and justice, more democracy, and reconciliation, objectives that typically are cited to justify their creation. The rest of this section examines the claims made for the impact of truth commissions on democracy, peace, and reconciliation, as well as the evidence that supports, or negates, the various claims. It will draw on a selection of statistical analysis, medium-sized comparative analysis, and a small selection of single-case in-depth studies, the latter constituting the largest category.

Claims and Evidence for the Impact of Truth Commissions on Democracy

Truth commissions may advance democracy by strengthening the rule of law (Freeman and Hayner 2003); promoting and strengthening democratic institutions, practices, and values in war-torn societies (Mendeloff 2004, p. 361); settling disputes over history (Mendeloff 2004, p. 361); contributing to a more democratic, inclusive, and responsible government (Chapman and Merwe 2008); and preempting and deterring future atrocities (Meernik et al. 2010). The core argument here is that a viable democratic society based on civic trust and respect for state institutions cannot be built on a historical lie. By bringing the facts of repression into the public sphere, one can establish culpability, which is particularly important where the state is the abuser. As a result, argues Wiebelhaus-Brahm, "commissions may contribute to political stability by both (re)building a sense of shared destiny among groups by giving them a stake in the 'national project,' and through de-legitimizing the non-democratic exercise of authority" (Wiebelhaus-Brahm 2010, p. 24).

However, truth commissions do not always have a positive impact. As Wiebelhaus-Brahm notes, they have occasionally jeopardized democracy in cases where victims, unsatisfied with the limited accountability provided by the process, have resorted to vigilante behavior, taking the law into their own hands. What have truth commissions across the world actually achieved?

Evidence on the Impact of Truth Commissions on Democracy

Evidence is at best mixed. To start with the overall view, broader, cross-national research has reached inconsistent findings with respect to the effects of truth commissions on a variety of professed goals. Wiebelhaus-Brahm's analysis of truth commissions in 78 countries from 1980 to 2003 reaches no convincing conclusions regarding their impact on human rights protection and democratic practice (Brahm 2007). His more in-depth cross-national research also does not find a consistent relationship between truth commissions and democracy (Wiebelhaus-Brahm 2010).

Some of these seemingly contradicting findings are also reflected in medium-sized comparative analysis. I will here refer briefly to a systematic in-depth analysis of the major truth-seeking attempts in four countries, two of which had truth commissions (Uruguay and Peru) and two of which had not (Angola and Rwanda). Our findings suggest that in Uruguay and Peru the truth commission processes helped strengthen democracy – or at least did not harm it (Skaar et al. 2015). In Uruguay there have been several attempts at truth-seeking that jointly have shed light on past violations and created a record that most Uruguayans can agree on. In particular, the Comisión para la Paz established in 2003 had broad government support and issued a report and recommendations that were followed up by succeeding governments. However, torture, the most widespread form of abuse during the military dictatorship, was disregarded by all the Uruguayan commissions. This demonstrates the governments' unwillingness to open an uncomfortable public discussion of egregious state practices. Even though the government of Uruguay has taken several legal measures to combat torture, abuses and ill treatment, especially of prisoners in detention, are still reported in Uruguay today. We can thus make an argument for the possible connection between an unresolved problem from the authoritarian era and the failure of current democratic state institutions to end this practice.

The impact of the Peruvian truth commission (CVR), which started its work in 2001, is arguably also mixed. The CVR experience has to some extent perpetuated dominant narratives that have casted "victims" and "perpetrators" as distinct, homogeneous, and mutually exclusive groups. This narrative of victims and terrorists is still current in Peru and used by the government to justify criminalization of social protest. For all its shortcomings, though, the CVR can be credited with having demanded recognition and respect for the victims of violence – mainly indigenous, rural people who have been marginalized throughout modern history. In that sense the CVR has contributed to the democratic elements of inclusion, rights, and equality, though there is still a long way to go in Peru before indigenous people enjoy equal citizenship.

In sum, at least in the case of the two truth commissions examined in Uruguay and Peru, respectively, they have contributed to documenting at least part of the "truth" regarding human rights violations. However, it is hard to clearly distinguish between their (potential) impacts on democracy.

Claims and Evidence for the Impact of Truth Commissions on Peace

Many persuasive reasons have been offered to explain why truth commissions may be good for peace: truth-seeking promotes justice, social and psychological healing, and reconciliation, all of which help consolidate peace in war-torn societies. It may also deter future crimes through public shaming of wrongdoers. Truth commissions contribute to nation building, as exposing the details of past crimes helps usher in a new democratic era and advances the cause of human rights through peaceful

coexistence. In short, truth-telling is considered one of several mechanisms necessary to achieve reconciliation and, ultimately, lasting peace after conflict.

There are numerous claims as to why and how truth-seeking carried out by truth
commissions should promote peace: truth-seeking ensures justice, promotes social
and psychological healing, fosters reconciliation, and deters future crimes, "all of
which help consolidate peace in war-torn societies" (Mendeloff 2004, p. 356).
Overall, it is claimed that truth-telling positively influences peace (building) by
addressing grievances derived from human rights violations in armed conflict,
by addressing the presumed causes of violence, and by promoting non-violent
ways of dealing with social conflict in the future. Official truth-telling is also
expected "to create a historical transcript of past events that can be useful in avoiding
manipulation of history by both supporters of the perpetrators and vengeful victims
groups" (Subotic 2009, p. 106).

While scholars generally assume truth commissions to have a positive impact on
conflict-torn societies by promoting reconciliation and peaceful coexistence, some
authors caution against overoptimism. Mendeloff argues that "the impact of truth-
telling mechanisms in the short-term consolidation of peace is almost certainly
negligible, if not irrelevant" (Mendeloff 2004, p. 356). Some scholars take this
critique even a step further and argue that truth commissions may in certain cases
have a detrimental impact on peace. For instance, referring to the experience of the
Balkans, Subotic claims that truth commissions can potentially inflame preexisting
ethnic prejudices and exacerbate social divisions, thereby threatening the peace
(Subotic 2009, p. 55). Based on their analysis of the Peruvian truth commission,
Laplante and Theidon argue that because truth commissions are usually held in
polarized political contexts marked by strong group identities, the commissions are
structurally inclined to overlook the gray zone in which the lines between perpetrators and victims are blurred (Laplante and Theidon 2010). A similar argument has
been made by Amy Rothschild, who shows that the truth commission in East Timor
has – unintendedly – exacerbated the negative relationship between victims and
combatants (Rothschild 2017). Indeed, truth commissions typically construct a
discourse that presents two distinct homogenous groups as mutually exclusive:
perpetrators versus victims or combatants versus victims. By ignoring the political
agency of the perpetrators and also the victims, one may overlook effective strategies
for preventing future violence and for addressing structural factors that may have
contributed to the violence.

Evidence for the Impact of Truth Commissions on Peace

A range of studies has tried to assess whether or not truth commissions indeed have a
peace-promoting function. Statistical work supports the claim that truth commissions promote human rights (Kim and Sikkink 2010). Other scholars, using other
data, find that human rights worsen in the wake of truth commissions (Olsen et al.
2010b) but that truth commissions are more likely to have a positive outcome if
balanced by amnesties (Olsen et al. 2010b).

Contradictory findings are not only a problem in statistical work. Here I cite some details from a comparative study of the Comisión de la Verdad y Reconciliación (CVR) in Peru (which had "reconciliation" in its official name) and Comisión para la Paz in Uruguay (which highlighted "peace" in its name), simply to illustrate how difficult it is to assess the impact on peace, even in qualitative studies. In this particular study, we arrived at the following conclusions: first, it is clear that none of these two truth commission processes sparked renewed violence that would threaten the peace. There has been no significant violence in Uruguay since the return to democracy. Peru has seen several violent episodes in recent years, with many deaths, but this violence is not related to the CVR; it has stemmed from other causes, such as the struggle for control over natural resources. The fact that indigenous groups as well as former military participated in the CVR process in Peru could be interpreted as a contribution to national reconciliation. However, the military rejected the truth commission's final report. Victims, for their part, claim that without justice there will be no reconciliation. Hence, the CVR's impact on national reconciliation is marginal. In Uruguay, the contributions to peace of the Comisión para la Paz are not entirely clear. The fact that the armed forces in Uruguay were invited to testify before the commission in exchange for a promise of impunity may to some degree have enhanced dialogue among former warring factions.

In sum, evidence is inconclusive when it comes to what the contribution of truth commissions to larger societal goals like peace might be.

Claims and Evidence for the Impact of Truth Commissions on Reconciliation

The explicit aim of many truth commissions is to foster reconciliation at the individual, group, and national level. Hayner's pioneer study on truth commissions cautioned that, "[e]stablishing a truth commission is only one of the steps necessary in order to move a nation towards peaceful reconciliation and respect for human rights. A truth commission should go hand in hand with institutional changes – judicial, political, or military reform, for example – that can reduce the likelihood of repetition of such abuses in the future, as well as official measures to promote reconciliation and reparation, as appropriate" (Hayner 1994, p. 655).

Yet, the scholarly literature has tried to isolate the impact of truth commissions on a series of social phenomenon and – not surprisingly – has arrived at widely disparate conclusions. For instance, scholarly opinions have shifted as to whether or not truth commissions promote reconciliation. Some have seen revealing the truth about gross human rights violations as an obstacle to reconciliation in that it could promote animosity, reopen old wounds, and increase political instability. However, "the idea that a durable peace requires countries to address past violence is now widely held and promoted by influential leaders and institutions under the broad heading of 'transitional justice'" (Leebaw 2008, p. 96). One of the primary claims of the post-conflict and peace-building literatures is that truth-telling contributes to psychological healing of individual victims and thus promotes social healing and group reconciliation (Mendeloff 2004, p. 358). Some claim that "truth telling demanded by victims is essential for reconciliation" (Prager 2003, p. 12).

Truth commissions have also been seen as a way to promote political reconciliation by fostering dialogue across lines of political and social conflict (Osiel 1997). Truth commissions can foster deliberative democracy, and in turn reconciliation, by encouraging "accommodation to conflicting views that fall within the range of reasonable disagreement" (Gutman and Thompson 2000, p. 41). Akhavan asserts that "truth-telling promotes interethnic reconciliation through the individualisation of guilt in hate-mongering leaders and by disabusing the people of the myth that adversary ethnic groups bear collective responsibility for crimes" (Akhavan 1998, p. 766).

In addition, the reports issued by truth commissions may also have an effect on reconciliation: "if reconciliation in any . . . sense is to take place, there must be some agreement about what happened and why" (Crocker 2003). The official, authoritative historical record provided by truth commissions may establish a "new shared history," thus fostering group reconciliation.

Not all scholars view truth commissions favorably, though. More generally, Mendeloff argues that many of the claims for the relationship between truth-telling and reconciliation in a context of peace building are flawed or at least questionable, thus raising critical questions regarding the utility of truth commissions (Mendeloff 2004, p. 362). Other authors agree that truth does not always promote reconciliation. Truth commissions must be managed in a sensitive way if they are to have positive effects. While truth-telling can be considered a cornerstone of transitional justice, it is also essential to recognize that too much truth-telling can be counterproductive and instead of healing social cleavages can generate more (Verwoerd 2003). Another criticism against truth commissions is that their mandates are too limited to allow them to contribute effectively to the consolidation of democratic regimes. Citing research that shows a correlation between citizens' experiences of corruption and low public legitimacy of their governments, Cavallaro and Albuja argue that it is necessary to address economic crimes as well as civil and political ones in order to strengthen prospects for reconciliation (Cavallaro and Albuja 2008). These issues are generally perceived to lie outside the realm of truth commissions.

Evidence on the Impact of Truth Commissions on Reconciliation

Surprisingly few scholarly studies have examined the impact of truth commissions on reconciliation – even in cases where the truth commissions openly have had reconciliation as one of their main goals. As I have argued in previous work, there are several reasons for this. First, many truth commissions have been set up only in the last few years, so that not enough time has passed to effectively measure or assess their impact. Second, many of the studies of truth commissions are based on moral conviction and rely primarily on anecdotal evidence. Third, and most important, much of the literature on truth commissions is limited to descriptive narrative and lacks an analytical focus on results. Studies that do attempt to gauge success or failure often stop with the immediate reception of the commission's report, rather than assessing the long-term impact on goals such as reconciliation. The few analytical impact studies that exist are limited to a handful of cases, which are unlikely to be representative (Skaar 2013). Finally, "reconciliation" (even more than "peace" and "democracy") is inherently hard to define and measure, making comparative analysis virtually impossible.

Here is therefore a short comment on the reconciliation process in South Africa, which is the country that has by far the most abundant data on the impact of its truth commission. Of all truth commissions to date, it is the South African Truth and Reconciliation Commission (TRC) that has most effectively captured world public attention as well as provided a model for many subsequent commissions – possibly also inspired other commissions to include "reconciliation" in its name. The literature on the TRC, by both South African and international scholars, is extensive. However, assessments of the TRC's "success" in terms of achieving reconciliation for postapartheid South Africa are contradictory. Two comprehensive studies that use complementary methodologies to evaluate to what extent the South African TRC actually contributed to reconciliation come to very different conclusions.

Reconciliation was a central part of the TRC's mandate, but in fact, the TRC had a far more expansive mandate than most other truth commissions: it was to promote national unity and reconciliation across social divisions. The TCR was also mandated to facilitate the granting of amnesty to those who made full factual disclosure, restore the human and civil dignity of victims by providing them an opportunity to tell their own stories, and make recommendations to the president on measures to prevent future human rights violations (Chapman and van der Merwe 2008, p. 4).

The TRC recognized multiple types of truth – narrative, forensic, historical, and social or dialogic. It also recognized and made use of multiple understandings of reconciliation. Evaluating the impact of the TRC on reconciliation has thus proved a complicated task for scholars, who have arrived at strikingly different answers to the question of whether the TRC produced truth that has contributed to reconciliation.

Based on rigorous analysis of individual-level data collected in an extensive survey of 3700 individual respondents, beginning in 2001, James L. Gibson concluded that truth had contributed to reconciliation in South Africa. In his words, "The truth and reconciliation effort was successful at exposing human rights abuses by all sides in the struggle over apartheid – thereby contributing to the country's collective memory about its apartheid past" (Gibson 2004, p. 207). He added, however, that different racial groups assess the truth generated by the TRC differently. A majority of white, Asian, and colored South Africans surveyed said that the truth contributed to interracial reconciliation. Among black South Africans, however, truth seemed to contribute little to reconciliation. Even though this may be a disappointing finding, he writes, "in no instance is truth associated with *irreconciliation*" (Gibson 2004, p. 214). Gibson, however, in a later study explicitly questions whether lessons from the South African TRC apply elsewhere, given the particular circumstances of apartheid (Gibson 2006, p. 82, 105).

A second in-depth study of the TRC, by Audrey Chapman and Hugo van der Merwe, provides a comprehensive evaluation of the TRC process and its impact on South African society. Drawing on an extensive analysis of the victim hearings, amnesty hearings, institutional hearings, and public opinion survey data, as well as on extensive interviews with a range of TRC staff, people who worked with the commission, and members of different communities affected by it, the authors raise fundamental questions about the TRC (and indeed about all truth commissions). They question the capacity of such bodies to carry out the mandates assigned to them and particularly to achieve the difficult balance between truth finding and reconciliation. At best, they argue, the South African TRC established only "an incomplete truth." Part of the problem rested with the failure of the commissioners to agree on what they meant by the "truth" or whose "truth" should be documented and made public. In addition, the TRC never defined precisely what it meant by the term "reconciliation," making any evaluation of impact very difficult.

These authors also conclude that the TRC "effectively put a hold on attempts to secure justice by survivors of human rights abuses," and thus the process "robbed survivors of justice for over 1000 incidents of abuse" (Chapman and van der Merwe 2008, p. 284). They ask whether the work of a truth commission may in fact deepen rather than close the wounds of victims and survivors of gross human rights violations, at least in the short term. And they stress the need to distinguish between short-term and long-term effects on society, including reconciliation. In short, evaluations of the model TRC in South Africa point to sharply different conclusions on whether or not its net impacts contribute to reconciliation.

To sum up, truth commissions have often been perceived as less threatening than trials because they do not have prosecutorial power. Therefore, truth commissions have been assumed to have a positive effect on democracy and on conflict-torn societies by promoting reconciliation and peaceful coexistence. However, as this section has shown, evidence is at best inconclusive. One obvious challenge in this kind of research is that it is extremely difficult to establish causal connections. Another problem, particularly in quantitative research, is that it does not adequately account for qualitative differences in truth commissions. Truth commissions vary considerably in terms of how they were constructed and the powers granted them. Some commissions have been fraught processes that intentionally were made to fail; they could simply be the result of cynical politics on the part of state officials. Even the most exemplary commissions have limited powers and insufficient resources. In statistical research, all kinds of truth commissions, small and large, well organized or not, and resourceful or not, are lumped together, making it difficult to draw general conclusions. Glimpses of qualitative research given in the above section show that although qualitative studies can pay more attention to context, they too have problems drawing firm conclusions. This makes it hard to synthesize what the legacy of truth commissions is on the ground, across time, countries, and regional experiences. Since the links between truth commissions and their contributions to overarching societal goals like peace, democracy, and reconciliation are, at best, tenuous, it might be more useful to look at the more concrete impacts of truth commissions.

Alternatives to Examining Truth Commission Impact

Several recent studies of truth commissions have narrowed their impact to more immediate goals. For instance, Onur Bakiner's thorough comparative work examines several causal mechanisms through which commissions are expected to influence politics and society. More specifically, he looks at direct political impact through the implementation of recommendations and indirect political impact through civil society mobilization. He finds that truth commissions may also have positive judicial impact by contributing to human rights accountability and negative judicial impact by promoting impunity – especially when human rights and victims' groups pressure governments for policy implementation (Bakiner 2014).

In an attempt to address some of the shortcomings of statistical research, we in a comparative structured analysis of the transitional justice processes of nine Latin American countries explored the impact of truth commission on its immediate goal, namely, accountability for past human rights violations. We found that over time truth commissions have had a positive effect in all of the countries we included in the study, although there were substantial variations among them due to the particular qualities of each truth commission (Skaar et al. 2016a). Not surprisingly, we also found that whether truth commissions "succeed" depends on a range of factors, which may be very context specific. One such important factor (which statistical work certainly fails to take into account) is the expectations tied to truth commissions. Where public expectations are high, the "success" of truth commissions is harder to achieve than in contexts where public expectations are low – simply because there is a mismatch between expectations and delivered results. While truth commissions generate mixed expectations, our research shows that the most effective at securing legitimacy are likely those commissions that produce a final report that sets the agenda for further measures to address the past and to instigate reforms (Skaar et al. 2016b).

Truth Commission Reports and Recommendations

One of the legacies of truth commissions is the reports with follow-up recommendations to the government. Very little work has been done on the implementation record of the recommendations made by truth commissions. In fact, most of the abundant scholarly work on truth commissions does not refer to recommendations at all. As preliminary findings from an ongoing study of the implementation rate across 13 Latin American truth commissions show, in general, there are many obstacles to implementing truth commission recommendations (Skaar et al. forthcoming). Political will or resources are often lacking, as governments may have other priorities. Powerful interests who are threatened by the recommendations – such as the military or other actors involved in the abuses – may create roadblocks. Yet, when successfully implemented, recommendations may have societal impact way beyond the truth commission itself. This is thus an important legacy of truth commissions that remains largely unexplored.

Some Reflections on the Future of Truth Commissions

Truth commissions have become an integral part of transitional justice since the early 1980s. Some commissions are vested with expansive mandates, beyond their immediate main goal of being fact-finding bodies. A critical examination of the literature examining the influence, contributions, or impact of truth commissions shows that it is extremely difficult to draw firm conclusions on what the overall contributions of truth commissions are. Some commissions have been highly respected and left deep marks in the societies where they were created, such as Argentina's Commission on the Disappearance of Persons and the South African Truth and Reconciliation Commission. Other commissions, such as the National Commission for Truth and Justice in Haiti, are largely unknown or forgotten, although the recommendations made by the commission are mirrored in ongoing civil society claims for reparations to victims and more justice.

From my own comparative work on truth commissions over many years, I tentatively conclude that truth commissions have often succeeded in documenting the violations that have been committed during authoritarianism and internal armed conflict – however imperfect and however contested the "truth" brought to the table is. This rudimentary sketching of a common narrative, I think, is one of such commissions' most important contributions. And it is a first important step toward holding the government accountable for these abuses. I am more skeptical toward the potential of truth commissions to bring about "democracy," "peace," or "reconciliation." At best, truth commissions are one of many mechanisms or processes that may in best-case scenarios contribute in a positive manner toward making societies more democratic and more respectful of human rights. The recommendations made by truth commissions upon concluding their work, if implemented well, may identify such measures that enhance democratic institutions and practices. Hence, recommendations may in the future prove to be one of the most important legacies of truth commissions.

However, there are many obstacles to the effective operation of truth commissions, as well as to the implementation of the recommendations made by such commissions in their reports. Nevertheless, the efforts made by truth commissions are, overall, a significant push in the direction of more respect for human rights. A signal that they are a phenomenon to be counted on also in the future is that there are more commissions in the making. The most recent truth commission is that launched by the government in Bolivia in August 2017 to investigate military dictatorships' crimes. More than three decades have passed since the Bolivian government set down its first truth commission in 1983 to investigate the same abuses, but in a political environment so volatile that the commission never made public its report. In Spanish, the saying "*la justicia tarda, pero llega*" (justice comes late, but it comes) could thus be rephrased as "*la verdad tarda, pero llega*." Late truth may well be partial or imperfect truth, but I am willing to argue that it is better than no truth at all. Where systematic and widespread human rights abuses remain unrecorded and undocumented, the multiple narratives of what the "truth" of violations is are likely to continue and to get in the way of positive, complex, long-term societal processes like fostering democracy, peace building, or reconciliation.

References

Akhavan P (1998) Justice in the Hague, peace in the former Yugoslavia? A commentary on the United Nations War Crimes Tribunal. Hum Rights Q 20:737–816

Bakiner O (2014) Truth commission impact: an assessment of how commissions influence politics and society. Int J Transit Justice 8(1):6–30

Bakiner O (2016) Truth commissions: memory, power, and legitimacy. University of Pennsylvania Press, Philadelphia

Borer TA (2006) Truth telling as a peace-building activity: a theoretical overview. In: Tristan AB (ed) Telling the truths: truth telling and peace building in post-conflict societies. University of Notre Dame Press, South Bend, pp 1–57

Brahm E (2007) Uncovering the truth: examining truth commission success and impact. Int Stud Perspect 8(1):16–35

Cavallaro JL, Albuja S (2008) The lost agenda: economic crimes and truth commissions in Latin America and beyond. In: McEvoy K, McGregor L (eds) Transitional justice from below: grassroots activism and the struggle for change. Hart, Portland, pp 121–141

Chapman AR, van der Merwe H (2008) Truth and reconciliation in South Africa: did the TRC deliver? University of Pennsylvania Press, Philadelphia

Crocker DA (2003) Reckoning with past wrongs: a normative framework. In: Prager CAL, Govier T (eds) Dilemmas of reconciliation: cases and concepts. Wilfrid Laurier University Press, Waterloo, pp 39–63

Ferrara A (2015) Assessing the long-term impact of truth commissions: the Chilean truth and reconciliation commission in historical perspective, Transitional justice series. Routledge, London

Freeman M (2006) Truth commissions and procedural fairness. Cambridge University Press, New York

Freeman M, Hayner PB (2003) Truth-telling. In: Bloomfield D, Barnes T, Huyse L (eds) Reconciliation after violent conflict: a handbook. International Institute for Democracy and Electoral Assistance (IDEA), Halmstad, pp 133–144

García-Godos J (2016) Victims in focus. Int J Transit Justice 10(2):350–358. https://doi.org/10.1 093/ijtj/ijv038

García-Godos J, Lid KAO (2010) Transitional justice and victims' rights before the end of a conflict: the unusual case of Colombia. J Lat Am Stud 42(3):487–516

Gibson JL (2004) Does truth lead to reconciliation? Testing the causal assumptions of the south African truth and reconciliation process. Am J Polit Sci 48(2):201–217

Gibson JL (2006) Overcoming apartheid: can truth reconcile a divided nation? Ann Am Acad Pol Soc Sci 603:82–110

Gready P (2010) The era of transitional justice: the aftermath of the truth and reconciliation commission in South Africa and beyond. Routledge, New York

Gutman A, Thompson D (2000) The moral foundations of truth commissions. In: Rotberg RI, Thompson D (eds) Truth V. Justice: the morality of truth commissions. Princeton University Press, Princeton, pp 22–44

Hayner PB (1994) Fifteen truth commissions – 1974 to 1994: a comparative study. Hum Rights Q 16(4):597–655

Hayner PB (2010) Unspeakable truths: transitional justice and the challenge of truth commissions, 2nd edn. Routledge, London

Henry N (2015) From reconciliation to transitional justice: the contours of redress politics in established democracies. Int J Transit Justice 9(2):199–218. https://doi.org/10.1093/ijtj/ijv001

Huntington SP (1991) The third wave: democratization in the late twentieth century. Cambridge University Press, New York

International Center for Transitional Justice (ICTJ) (2017) Can we handle the truth? https://www.ictj.org/gallery-items/truth-commissions. Accessed 23 Nov 2017

Kim H, Sikkink K (2010) Explaining the deterrence effect of human rights prosecutions for transitional countries. Int Stud Q 54(4):939–963

Laplante LJ, Theidon K (2010) Commissioning truth, constructing silences. The Peruvian truth commission and the others truths of "Terrorists". In: Clarke KM, Goodale M (eds) Mirrors of justice. Law and power in the post-cold war era. Cambridge University Press, New York, pp 291–315

Leebaw BA (2008) The irreconcilable goals of transitional justice. Hum Rights Q 30(1):95–118

McEvoy K, McGregor L (2008) Transitional justice from below: grassroots activism and the struggle for change. Hart, Oxford

Meernik JD, Nichols A, King KL (2010) The impact of international tribunals and domestic trials on peace and human rights after civil war. Int Stud Perspect 11(4):309–334

Mendeloff D (2004) Truth-seeking, truth-telling, and postconflict peacebuilding: curb the enthusiasm? Int Stud Rev 6(3):355–380

Olsen TD, Payne LA, Reiter AG (2010a) The justice balance: when transitional justice improves human rights and democracy. Hum Rights Q 32(4):980–1007

Olsen TD, Payne LA, Reiter AG (2010b) Transitional justice in balance: comparing processes, weighing efficacy. United States Institute of Peace Press, Washington, DC

Orentlicher DF (1991) Settling accounts: the duty to prosecute human rights violations of a prior regime. Symposium: international law. Yale Law J 100(8):2537–2615

Osiel M (1997) Mass atrocity, collective memory, and the law. Transaction, New Brunswick

Prager CAL (2003) Introduction. In: Prager CAL, Govier T (eds) Dilemmas of reconciliation: cases and concepts. Wilfrid Laurier University Press, Waterloo, pp 1–26

Prasser S (2017) Public inquiries. http://www.publicinquiries.com.au/history.htm. Accessed 23 Nov 2017

Robinson I (2015) Truth commissions and anti-corruption: towards a complementary framework? Int J Transit Justice 9(1):33–50. https://doi.org/10.1093/ijtj/iju022

Roht-Arriaza N, Mariezcurrena J (2006) Transitional justice in the twenty-first century. Beyond truth versus justice. Cambridge University Press, Cambridge

Rothschild A (2017) Victims versus veterans: agency, resistance and legacies of Timor-Leste's truth commission. Int J Transit Justice 11(3):443–462. https://doi.org/10.1093/ijtj/ijx018

Shaw R, Waldorf L, Hazan P (2010) Localizing transitional justice: justice interventions and priorities after mass violence. Stanford University Press, Stanford

Sikkink K (2011) The justice cascade: how human rights prosecutions are changing world politics. W. W. Norton & Co, New York

Skaar E (2013) Reconciliation in a transitional justice perspective. Transit Justice Rev 1(1, Article 10):53–103

Skaar E, Malca CG, Eide T (2015) After violence: transitional justice, peace and democracy. Routledge, London

Skaar E, Collins C, García-Godos J (2016a) Conclusions: the uneven road towards accountability in Latin America. In: Skaar E, García-Godos J, Collins C (eds) Transitional justice in Latin America: the uneven road from impunity towards accountability. Routledge, London, pp 275–298

Skaar E, García-Godos J, Collins C (2016b) Transitional justice in Latin America: the uneven road from impunity towards accountability. Routledge, London

Skaar E, Wiebelhaus-Brahm E, García-Godos J (forthcoming) Beyond words. Implementing Latin American truth commission recommendation. Book manuscript in progress

Subotic J (2009) Hijacked justice: dealing with the past in the Balkans. Cornell University Press, Ithaca

Teitel R (2000) Transitional justice. Oxford University Press, New York

Teitel R (2003) Transitional justice genealogy. Harv Hum Rights J 16(Spring):69–94

Verwoerd W (2003) Toward a response to criticisms of the South African truth and reconciliation commission. In: Prager CAL, Govier T (eds) Dilemmas of reconciliation: cases and concepts. Wilfrid Laurier University Press, Waterloo, pp 245–278

Wiebelhaus-Brahm E (2009) What is a truth commission and why does it matter? Peace Confl Rev 3(2 Spring):1–14

Wiebelhaus-Brahm E (2010) Truth commissions and transitional societies: the impact on human rights and democracy. Routledge, New York

Part III

Regional Human Rights Systems

The European Court of Human Rights: Achievements and Prospects

Philip Leach

Contents

Introduction 424
Mandate and Functioning 424
Assessing the European Court's Achievements 426
State Participation 427
The Court's Jurisprudence 428
Human Rights in Conflict and Post-Conflict Situations 432
Practice and Procedure: An Accessible System 432
Redress and Systemic Violations 435
The Election of Judges 436
Impact: The Implementation of Judgments 437
The Future Potential and the Challenges Ahead 439
References 441

Abstract

This chapter discusses and analyses the origins, workings, and future prospects of the most significant human rights mechanism that Europe has seen – the European Court of Human Rights. Created by European governments in the immediate aftermath of the atrocities experienced during World War II, over the ensuing decades, the Court has laid down a remarkably comprehensive set of standards for states in upholding core civil and political rights, notably the right to a fair trial, the prohibition of torture, and the right to freedom of expression. As state accession to the Council of Europe increased following the breakup of the former Yugoslavia and the dissolution of the Soviet Union, the Court has been faced with increasing numbers of large-scale systemic cases which have necessitated

P. Leach (✉)
European Human Rights Advocacy Centre (EHRAC), Middlesex University, London, UK
e-mail: p.leach@mdx.ac.uk

© Springer Nature Singapore Pte Ltd. 2018   423
G. Oberleitner (ed.), *International Human Rights Institutions, Tribunals, and Courts*,
International Human Rights, https://doi.org/10.1007/978-981-10-5206-4_16

changes in its practice and procedure and a more creative, incisive approach to providing redress. The Court has succeeded in setting credible standards for the continent (and beyond) but has been weighed down with a huge back load of cases for several decades. Within a regional polity that has become less receptive and indeed increasingly hostile, toward the very concept of human rights, the future challenges for the Court are to maintain its independence, its legitimacy, and its potency as a safety net for victims of human rights violations across the continent.

Keywords

European Court of Human Rights · Council of Europe · European Convention on Human Rights · Jurisprudence · Redress · Implementation

Introduction

Across the continent of Europe, it is the European Court of Human Rights (the European Court) and its application of the European Convention on Human Rights (the European Convention or ECHR), which have undoubtedly had the most significant impact in upholding human rights standards and principles. The European Convention was drafted in the immediate aftermath of the World War II, in response to grave and widespread human rights atrocities. Its development and that of the Court reflected an aspiration for greater European unity and enhanced democracy and the need to establish an early warning system to prevent a descent into totalitarianism ever happening on the continent again. The Convention and Court were the creations of the Council of Europe, an interstate body established in 1949 to promote peace and solidarity in Europe (an organization that is entirely separate from the European Union).

Mandate and Functioning

The European Convention represented, for Europe, a significant step in the enforcement of particular aspects of the 1948 United Nations Universal Declaration of Human Rights. It was primarily intended to protect civil and political rights rather than economic, social, or cultural rights. It established a right of individual petition – the right of individuals (and organizations) to challenge their governments by taking cases to the European Commission of Human Rights (established in 1954) and then to the European Court (established in 1959). To permit such a right of individual petition was at the time of the creation of the Convention system a revolutionary development, given the strength of notions of the independent sovereignty of the state. In other ways, however, the process involved undeniably political aspects: the system was to be supervised by a political body, the Committee of Ministers; the European Commission initially had a majority of serving or former ministers and civil servants or MPs rather than legal professionals; and the procedure before the Commission was kept confidential. This two-tier system (embodying both a Commission and Court) is mirrored by the regional human rights mechanisms in the Americas and Africa, but in Europe the first tier (the European Commission on Human Rights) was abolished in 1998, a step which was primarily taken in order to speed up the litigation process, as these bodies became inundated with many thousands of cases.

The European Convention on Human Rights was adopted in 1950; it embodies a series of civil and political rights, the core of which are reflected in other comparable international and regional human rights standards established in the second half of the twentieth century. Its rights include the right to life; freedom from torture; freedom from slavery and forced labour; the right to liberty of the person; the right to a fair trial; the right to privacy; the rights to freedom of thought, conscience and religion, freedom of expression, and peaceful assembly and association; the right to marry; and the prohibition of discrimination. These Convention rights have not been amended, but they have been supplemented, between 1952 and 2002, by additional protocols to the Convention covering rights including the following: the protection of property, right to education, and right to free elections (Protocol No. 1), the right to freedom of movement and the prohibition of expulsion of nationals and the collective expulsion of aliens (Protocol No. 4), the abolition of the death penalty both at times of war and of peace (Protocols No. 6 and No. 13), and the right not to be tried or punished twice (Protocol No. 7).

The Court sits in a single-judge formation, in committees of three judges, in chambers of seven judges, or in a Grand Chamber of 17 judges. It also comprises a court registry of more than 640 lawyers and other staff. Its two official languages are English and French – although in practice litigating parties are frequently permitted to use national languages in their written or oral pleadings. All cases must pass the Court's admissibility criteria, the most important of which in practice are the requirement first to exhaust any available and effective domestic remedies and then to introduce an application at the Court strictly within a period of 6 months after the final domestic decision in the case was taken. The vast majority of cases are dealt with purely by way of written pleadings. It will hold a hearing in some cases – such hearings involve legal argument only and take up less than 3 hours (they are webcast by the Court on the same day). Very exceptionally, the Court may hold a separate fact-finding hearing (in-country or in Strasbourg).

The most significant cases are decided by the Grand Chamber – either such cases are routed directly to the Grand Chamber or once a chamber has issued a judgment, any of the parties involved can request its referral to the Grand Chamber. This is not a *right* of appeal, as only a small number of such requests are accepted – those raising the most important issues. Judges may append separate opinions to the judgments, either concurring with or dissenting from the majority stance – a facet of the system which has provided a rich source of "alternative views," some of which then form the basis of the majority view in later decisions.

Exceptionally, states are permitted to opt out of ("derogate" from) certain aspects of the Convention where there is a "public emergency threatening the life of the nation" (Article 15) – this right of derogation was considered in the Court's very first judgment, Lawless v Ireland in 1961, concerning powers of detention without trial in the late 1950s. The UK government used this provision in order to be able to detain terrorist suspects for extended periods without charge in Northern Ireland in the 1980s, but when it invoked Article 15 again after the terrorist attacks on the United States in 2001, in order to detain foreign nationals who were suspected of involvement in international terrorism, the measure was struck down by the Court because it discriminated unjustifiably between national and non-nationals (A and others v United Kingdom 2009). There have been a spate of recent derogations, which are yet to be tested before the Court: Ukraine derogated in 2015 as a result of the conflict in eastern Ukraine; France did so in the same year after the terrorist attacks in Paris; and Turkey declared a state of emergency and issued a notice of derogation following the attempted coup in July 2016.

Assessing the European Court's Achievements

There can be little doubt that it is the European Convention on Human Rights which has exerted the most influence on the development of legislation and policy in the human rights field throughout Europe; one former President of the European Court, Rolv Ryssdal, described it as "the basic law of Europe." It has sought not to harmonize laws but rather to set out common standards for the continent – to prescribe a level in the areas it covers below which states should not fall. Indeed, the Convention is considered to represent one of the most successful human rights systems in the world. The Strasbourg Court's effectiveness has been grounded on the high level of state take-up, the periodic addition of new substantive rights, the incorporation of the Convention into domestic law by the Council of Europe states, the depth of the Court's case law in particular areas, and the extent to which its judgments have led to changes in domestic laws and practice (PACE 2016). Beyond Europe, the Court has established itself as a key pillar in the universal system of human rights protection, its decisions being continually cited by international, regional, and national courts.

Arguably pivotal to the Court's influence was its development in the early years of the foundational principles as to how human rights standards should be appropriately applied in a democratic order – above all the concepts of legality and proportionality which were laid out initially in seminal cases such as Handyside v United Kingdom (concerning the banning of a book for schoolchildren on sex education, on grounds of obscenity) and Sunday Times v United Kingdom (concerning an injunction issued to prevent the Sunday Times newspaper from publishing an article about the litigation relating to children affected by the drug thalidomide). These are fundamental principles which have subsequently become embedded in the national laws (and indeed legal cultures) of most Council of Europe states. The Court's scrutiny of the proportionality of state interferences into the "qualified" Convention rights (such as respect for private life, freedom of expression, and freedom of religion) is, however, subject to the notion of subsidiarity – that the Court's supervisory role is subsidiary to that played by national bodies (governments, parliaments, and courts) which should take the lead in upholding human rights standards at the national level. Furthermore, in assessing the proportionality of an interference with a Convention right, the Court established its "margin of appreci-ation" doctrine that national bodies are in principle in a better position than the European Court to judge the necessity of restrictions on rights. This has allowed for a limited extent of variation in national standards, arguably without unacceptably lowering Convention standards to accommodate "national or local differences," which are sometimes cited by states (globally) in order to try to avoid liability for transgressing human rights. These qualifications of the Court's role and powers have been critical to its widespread acceptance by domestic legal jurisdictions across the European continent. They have led to an unprecedented level of acceptance of the Court by states – which is remarkable in view of the need to overlay these European standards across 47 domestic legal systems (based on common law or civil law or the legal systems established in the former socialist/communist states of central and eastern Europe) embodying their own diverse legal cultures, traditions and practices. It is also no mean feat given that the granting of the right of individual petition (the direct right of individuals to challenge states at the Court) was such a novel development in public international law.

State Participation

Since ten states came together in 1949 to adopt the Statute of the Council of Europe and then ratify the European Convention on Human Rights in the early 1950s, accession has increased the number of state parties almost fivefold, including, in the 1990s, many of the states which had formerly been part of the Soviet Union. With membership at 47 since 2006, just Belarus remains out in the cold. Although the admission of certain states into the Council of Europe at particular junctures has been criticized (notably as regards Russia in the late 1990s at a time when it was embroiled in the second conflict in Chechnya), the fact that virtually all European states have proved willing to join it and accordingly to be subject to the resulting obligations – at least in principle, if not always in practice – is itself significant and lends the organization further credibility and gravitas in the pursuit of achieving common minimum standards applicable across the continent.

It should be acknowledged that the significant increase in state accession to the Convention, especially since the 1990s, has meant an evolution in the Court's role. It continues to perform the vital function of enhancing standards of rights protection as regards states where compliance with the Convention is relatively strong, but it has also increasingly been required to adjudicate on cases of egregious human rights violations and on large numbers of systemic or widespread violations (both of which are discussed further below), which in the main (although not exclusively) concern newer member states from central and eastern Europe.

It is notable, however, that the high level of state accession has not led to a concomitant rise in the use of the interstate application process, which allows member states to challenge other states at the European Court. There is no need for applicant states to have a direct "interest" in a particular case in the sense that one or more of its citizens need to have been victims of Convention violations, and therefore this procedure could enable the Council of Europe states to provide a wider policing or monitoring role. For example, states could have challenged the systematic abuses committed over many years by the Russian security forces in the north Caucasus region. Aside from a challenge launched by Denmark, Norway, Sweden, and the Netherlands to the abuses committed by the Greek military junta in the late 1960s, the interstate process has not been used in this way. Only 20 such cases have ever been instigated, and most have been brought by states with a direct interest in the matter at hand: Cyprus challenging Turkey as a consequence of its occupation of northern Cyprus since the mid-1970s, Georgia litigating against Russia following the 2008 armed conflict in South Ossetia, and Ukraine bringing several cases against Russia in 2014 due to the occupation of Crimea and conflict in eastern Ukraine. A case brought by Ireland against the United Kingdom led to a Court judgment in 1978, holding that the interrogation techniques employed by the British Army in Northern Ireland constituted inhuman and degrading treatment (in violation of Article 3 of the Convention) but that they did *not* amount to torture. This decision was challenged afresh by the Irish Government in 2014 when new evidence was unearthed at the national archives in Kew – but the request for revision was rejected by the Court in 2018 on the basis that the new evidence would not have had a decisive effect on the original judgment.

The Court's Jurisprudence

There are a number of areas of particular strength and depth in the Court's jurisprudence, which have been developed over decades. As the oldest of the regional human rights courts, it is perhaps unsurprising that the weight and extent of its case law in distinct areas have enabled the Court to engage in gradations and nuances of its case law, the equivalent of which cannot be found elsewhere. One such area is the field of criminal justice – reflecting the fact that the majority of decided cases have concerned Article 5 (the right to liberty and security of the person) and 6 (the right to a fair trial) of the Convention. The Court has been required to elucidate how principles such as the right of access to court, the privilege against self-incrimination, the equality of arms, and the right to an independent and impartial tribunal should be applied in numerous situations which have arisen across 47 European states. It has clarified the "overall fairness" test (under Article 6), including where there is evidence that criminal proceedings were manifestly arbitrary, and it has refined its approach as to the fairness in criminal proceedings of admitting statements by absent witnesses. Its case law has been refined in relation to the right of access to a lawyer for suspects held in police custody, to detention on grounds of mental health, to the need to conduct reviews into the detention of life sentence prisoners, and as regards prison conditions (and the treatment of people with disabilities in detention). In recent years, the Court has had to adjudicate on a number of high-profile cases of "political prosecutions" – where prosecuting authorities have found to have unjustifiably targeted opposition politicians (Merabishvili v Georgia 2017) or human rights activists (Rasul Jafarov v Azerbaijan 2016) – leading to violations of Article 5 together with Article 18.

The Court has applied a rigorous and searching scrutiny of cases in which state agents have used lethal force – which is only permitted where it can be shown to have been "absolutely necessary." Another area of focus has concerned the duty on the state to carry out effective investigations into fatal incidents, which was developed in particular in the case law relating to the actions of the British security forces in Northern Ireland and subsequently the cases in the 1990s concerning Convention violations committed by the security forces in south-east Turkey (from the Kurdish regions) and by the Russian security forces in Chechnya (in the 2000s).

In spite of mounting international political pressure resulting in particular from international terrorism, the Court has held firm in maintaining the absolute prohibition on torture (Article 3), even in the face of direct challenges from states such as Italy and the United Kingdom (Saadi v Italy 2008). The Court has also upheld the absolute nature of Article 3 in the context of the "migration crisis." In M.S.S. v Belgium and Greece (2011), the applicant claimed asylum in Greece and complained that the conditions in which he was detained at Athens airport were inhuman and degrading. The Court acknowledged the pressures on states created by increasing numbers of migrants and asylum-seekers (which was exacerbated by the transfers of asylum-seekers by other member states under the Dublin Regulation) but found that this could not absolve Greece from its Article 3 obligations. Furthermore, the Court has maintained the principle that although the EU's Dublin asylum system may allow one Council of Europe state to transfer an asylum-seeker to another Council of Europe state, the transferring state must still make sure that the intermediary country's asylum procedure affords sufficient guarantees to ensure that Article 3 will not be violated. On that basis Belgium was also held to have breached Article 3 by transferring the applicant to Greece, because of its deemed knowledge of how poorly asylum-seekers were being treated there. In the same decision, the Grand Chamber additionally found that extreme material poverty may breach Article 3 – in this case, because the applicant asylum-seeker was homeless in Greece and was unable to cater for his most basic needs: food, hygiene, and a place to live.

In the Abu Qatada judgment (Othman v United Kingdom 2012), the Court for the first time held that an applicant's deportation (from the United Kingdom to Jordan) would violate the right to a fair hearing and amount to a "flagrant denial of justice," because of the real risk of the admission at his Jordanian trial of evidence obtained by torturing witnesses. However, in the same decision, the Court also concluded that there would be no violation of Article 3 on the basis that assurances made by the Jordanian government in a memorandum of understanding (backed up by independent monitoring) removed any real risk of ill-treatment. A series of landmark judgments (such as El-Masri v former Yugoslav Republic of Macedonia 2012) exposed the practice of "extraordinary rendition" – with states including Macedonia, Italy, and Poland being found responsible for the torture and secret transfer of terrorist suspects into US custody, when they were then severely ill-treated by the

CIA, and some transferred to the US naval base at Guantánamo Bay. Causing no little controversy in 2015, the Grand Chamber decided that Article 3 had been violated when a Belgian police officer slapped a 17-year old once in the face (Bouyid v Belgium 2015).

The Court has also proved resolute in seeking to uphold fundamental democratic principles in a myriad of circumstances, for example, taking a stand over the dissolution of political parties (especially prevalent in Turkey), election irregularities, restrictions imposed on minority rights associations, and the banning of marches or demonstrations. What is more, the Court has repeatedly emphasized the central importance of freedom of speech (particularly political speech) in democratic societies, including statements that may be offensive, shocking, or disturbing to some. It has upheld the right of the media and civil society to scrutinize and criticize political leaders, bolstered pluralistic and independent public broadcasting services, sought to protect the confidentiality of journalistic sources, and closely probed instances of prior restraint of the media and the application of heavy-handed defamation laws. The Court has fought against the unjustifiable severity of sanctions imposed on journalists (especially imprisonment) and has found against states for failing to provide adequate protection of journalists under threat. The European Convention does not, however, provide absolute protection to free speech – accordingly, steps taken by national authorities in response to the incitement of racial hatred, hate speech, and the glorification of violence have been upheld.

State surveillance techniques have repeatedly been raised before the Court, its findings in the 1980s leading to legislative control of phone tapping by the police in the United Kingdom (Malone v United Kingdom 1984), and in 2015 the Grand Chamber found the legal framework governing secret surveillance of mobile telephone communications by the security services in Russia to be wholly inadequate (Roman Zakharov v Russia 2015).

In this necessarily brief and selective overview of the Court's case law, it is important to recognize that the Court's more recent decisions have highlighted discrimination on the basis of gender, ethnicity, nationality, sexual orientation, and disability (including discrimination against people with HIV). There have been decisions concerning the failure to give legal recognition to same-sex partnerships, restrictions on the right to freedom of religion in the workplace, the right of conscientious objection to military service, the balancing of rights under Articles 8 (respect for private and family life) and 10 (freedom of expression), and cases upholding freedom of expression via the Internet. Additionally, there is jurisprudence on the right to receive information, the right to demonstrate peacefully and for political purposes, trade union rights, and the duty to contain violent, homophobic counter-demonstrators. Other cases have addressed restrictions on in vitro fertilization and surrogacy, the spate of "missing babies" in Serbia, the treatment of migrants traveling by sea (including collective expulsions), and structural deficiencies in asylum procedures.

There are, inevitably, a number of substantive areas where the Court's jurisprudence has been the subject of forceful criticism. Such critiques have concerned, for example, its disregard for the rights of minorities, its cautious interpretation of the prohibition of discrimination, its approach to the right to freedom of religion (notably in relation to Islam), its inconsistency as to the parameters of extraterritorial jurisdiction (where a state acts beyond its boundaries), and the application of the Court's "margin of appreciation" doctrine. The Court is sometimes taken to task for the lack of clarity of its reasoning or the inconsistencies in its case law as between different sections of the Court. Another area of criticism from applicants and their advisers has been the relatively low levels of damages awards issued by the Court and the lack of specificity in its case law to explain how such awards are calculated.

The substantive limitations of the European Convention certainly need to be acknowledged. As a treaty concerned only with civil and political rights, it lacks even the limited range of socioeconomic rights that were written into the equivalent treaties in the Inter-American and African systems. Nor does it incorporate third-generation rights or the broader range of civil and political rights that have been reflected in later human rights treaties, such as children's rights. These (important) limitations aside, there are two principles of interpretation which, above all else, have been applied by the Court in a progressive way to ensure that the Convention and its case law have not become outdated or irrelevant. The first is the teleological notion that the Convention represents a "living instrument." Thus its standards must be assessed through conceptions that are of the present day – not historical. In this way the Convention continues to evolve and enables the Court to take account of, for example, changes in societal attitudes and perceptions of scientific and technological developments and indeed refinements in related fields of international law. This evolutive approach to the law is an essential feature of an international human rights court and arguably indeed of any domestic court (Hale 2011).

The second interpretative principle is the notion of "positive obligations" – including those which are not explicitly referred to in the Convention itself but which have been implied by the Court through its case law. For example, by applying an expansive interpretation of the right to life and of physical integrity and of the prohibition of torture and inhuman or degrading treatment, the Court has considerably strengthened the protection of some of the most vulnerable people on the continent. Grounded on the positive obligations to prevent and protect, the Court has upheld complaints that national authorities have failed to take adequate steps to protect individuals against foreseeable threats by others, including victims of domestic violence and trafficking. The Court has also highlighted legislative deficiencies which have led to the inadequate protection of victims of rape and domestic servitude. As a result, the "horizontal effect" of the Court's jurisprudence has had a profound impact in upholding the rights of victims of human rights violations committed by other individuals (or organizations).

For some politicians and commentators, the European Court's expansive and evolutive approach means it has strayed into the realm of judicial lawmaking – indeed the Court is periodically criticized (as are all international human rights bodies) by those who perceive unjustifiable incursions into state sovereignty. One particular target has been the breadth of the Court's application of Article 8 – the right to respect for private and family life, home, and correspondence. However, as noted above, one of the Court's central jurisprudential principles in interpreting

Convention rights is to allow states a discretion (the "margin of appreciation"), the breadth of which is variable, depending on the particular context. Thus, where a particularly important facet of an individual's existence or identity is at stake, the margin allowed to the state will be more restricted, but where cases are considered to raise sensitive moral or ethical issues, the margin will be wider.

Human Rights in Conflict and Post-Conflict Situations

The European Court has been required to adjudicate on egregious violations of the Convention in the context of situations of armed conflict, notably by the security forces in south-east Turkey in the 1990s and the Russian armed forces in Chechnya in the 2000s. In respect of both of these regions and also in relation to northern Cyprus, the Court has tackled the phenomenon of enforced disappearances, building on the earlier case law of the Inter-American Court of Human Rights. In these regions of conflict, the Court has played a very important role in casting a spotlight on the nature and extent of human rights violations, often in the absence of effective prevention or monitoring work by other regional or international human rights mechanisms. There are, however, real limitations in the Court's oversight. It would be right to acknowledge, for example, that there has been a remarkably high rate of findings of substantive violations of the right to life in the Chechen cases (in other words, that state agents were found to be directly responsible). However, in many of the disappearance cases, the Court's processes have not enabled the victim's relatives to find out, for example, whether in fact the victim has died (rather than being presumed dead) or how, when, or where they died or which identifiable state agency or agents were responsible (Leach 2008).

Elsewhere, the Court has had selective success in securing the release of individuals unlawfully detained by separatist groups in Georgia and Moldova. Moreover, the Court has confirmed that the extraterritorial jurisdiction of the Convention does extend to human rights violations perpetrated by member states' armed forces acting beyond the boundaries of the Council of Europe, such as the operations of the British army in Iraq. There have been important developments in the case law concerning detention during occupation or armed conflict, involving the application of international humanitarian law concurrently with international human rights law (Hassan v United Kingdom 2014). Victims of conflict who have been displaced from their homes and land over many years have successfully sought acknowledgment of their lost property rights, such as those affected by the Nagorno-Karabakh armed conflict between Armenia and Azerbaijan (Chiragov v Armenia 2015; Sargsyan v Azerbaijan 2015).

Practice and Procedure: An Accessible System

One of the notable features of the European Court system is its relative accessibility. Some have argued that this is a weakness, as it means that vast numbers of cases are submitted which have caused an enduring backlog of several tens of thousands of cases, rising to a height of 160,000 pending cases in 2011. However, it is the Court's role in genuinely providing access to justice to individual applicants who have been let down in some way by their national authorities, which should remain a preeminent factor in influencing how the Court functions. In the twenty-first century, Europe continues to produce applicants to the Court who are illiterate; who have been institutionalized (for example, in prisons, psychiatric hospitals, or children's "care homes"); who are profoundly vulnerable having been the victims of trafficking, domestic violence, or armed conflict; or who suffer debilitating discrimination on a daily basis as members of minority groups. In some regions, fundamental human rights are systematically violated by state security forces, with approval at the highest political levels. Those who are the victims of such abuses need no further impediments to the struggle to achieve some measure of access to justice – this is vital to the Strasbourg process.

It is still the case that there is no court fee at all and that applicants can initiate cases at the European Court themselves, without necessarily engaging a lawyer. The fact that, in practice, applicants will not have legal costs awarded against them, even if their cases are unsuccessful, is also a critical aspect of the Court's accessibility. Furthermore, legal aid is available to applicants – in practice this provides only a limited contribution toward the actual costs likely to be incurred, but it will cover the costs of attending a hearing at the Court. In 2010 an additional admissibility criterion was introduced, with the aim of stemming the flow of de minimis cases, by ruling out cases in which applicants had not suffered a "significant disadvantage." This development raised concerns that cases could be unreasonably blocked on the basis of this vague criterion: however, in practice, the Court has applied this new test reasonably, acknowledging that important matters of principle may be raised by cases which have less serious consequences for the applicant's personal situation. In order to tighten up the Court's application procedure, in 2014, the Court for the first time required all applicants to lodge their initial petitions using a prescribed form available online. As the Court's practice has been to scrutinize such forms very closely – and to reject applications which are not correctly completed throughout – this meant that initially, nearly a quarter of new applications were dismissed by the Court for a failure to comply with these formal criteria. However, such teething problems have leveled off, and the Court has explicitly accepted that not every applicant will be in a position to get access to the form – including prisoners and applicants from regions of ongoing conflict (such as eastern Ukraine) where there is disruption of public services. The Court's increasing use of electronic filing (for applicants as well as governments) is also to be welcomed as making communications quicker and simpler.

In 2010 the Court for the first time formalized a priority policy, so that urgent cases can be fast-tracked, giving precedence in particular to cases involving a risk to the applicant's life or health, cases concerning the deprivation of liberty and those in which the well-being of a child is at risk. In very urgent cases, the Court may act speedily (sometimes in a matter of hours) to direct a state to take particular steps to protect an applicant in a pending case (the "interim measures" procedure). This has most commonly been applied where an applicant faces the risk of ill-treatment or death because of their expulsion to another state, in which case the Court will step in to order the state not to expel the person in question while the case is pending before the Court – which it did in its first such decision, in the case of Soering v United Kingdom (1989), to prevent the applicant's extradition to the United States on a charge carrying the death penalty. This urgent mechanism (which is legally binding) has also been applied in a range of other situations, especially to direct the authorities to ensure that sick prisoners receive the requisite medical treatment but also to direct state authorities to obtain relevant evidence (Diri v Turkey 2007), to ensure the safety of litigants and family members (R.R. v Hungary 2012), to prevent housing evictions (Yordanova v Bulgaria 2012), to preserve embryos (Evans v United Kingdom 2007), and even to protect the plurality of the media (Rustavi 2 v Georgia 2017).

The Court's "victim status" requirement means that applicants must be able to show that they themselves have been victims of the breach of the Convention which they are raising – preventing, for example, NGOs from bringing "representative" cases on behalf of applicants, as is possible in the African system. However, very exceptionally, the Court will allow an NGO to stand in the place of an applicant, as it did in the case of Câmpeanu v Romania (2014), permitting the Centre for Legal Resources to bring an application against Romania on behalf of an 18-year-old mentally disabled, HIV-positive Roma man who had died in an orphanage. The Court will also admit cases brought by potential victims, such as people who are at risk of being prosecuted under legislation criminalizing homosexual acts (Dudgeon v United Kingdom 1981) or journalists who may be the subject of the untrammeled powers of the state security forces to intercept communications (Roman Zakharov v Russia 2015). Furthermore, the Court has recently started to group cases together which are factually unrelated but which raise similar legal questions, in order to lay down broadly applicable standards (Lashmankin v Russia 2017). It has not, however, gone as far as permitting wider, class actions and abolishing the requirement of victim status, as some commentators have advocated.

Another area of distinction of the Strasbourg Court is its relatively progressive approach to obtaining and considering evidence. Evidential problems inevitably arise in the context of the work of an international court with a remit covering 47 states and have resulted in the Court itself dispatching its judges to hear witnesses in order to establish the facts, in reversing the burden of proof in relation to ill-treatment and deaths in custody and in the Court drawing inferences from a respondent state's failure to disclose key domestic documents. The high point of the Court's practice of holding fact-finding hearings was a period in the 1990s when panels of judges regularly held witness hearings in Turkey – in cases brought by the Kurdish minority concerning Convention violations committed by the Turkish security forces (including enforced disappearances, extrajudicial executions, the torture of detainees, and village destruction cases) (Leach et al. 2009). This was considered necessary because there was, in practice, no domestic court fact-finding process. When, however, comparable cases in Chechnya began to surface in the early 2000s, the Court declined to carry out a similar fact-finding role.

The litigation process is also accessible to third-party intervenors, which has enabled civil society organizations to have a discernible impact on the development of the Court's jurisprudence in certain areas – such as the NGO Interights' intervention in

Opuz v Turkey (2009), the groundbreaking case laying down obligations as to the prevention and investigation of cases of domestic violence (applicable in respect of the police, prosecutors and the courts, and as regards legislation). Governments will also take up this opportunity from time to time – for example, ten states intervened in Lautsi v Italy (2011), a case challenging the practice of displaying crucifixes in classrooms in Italian state schools (which was upheld by the Grand Chamber). Reflecting the increasing pressures on human rights defenders in various European states (notably Azerbaijan and Russia), the Council of Europe's former Commissioner for Human Rights, Nils Muižnieks, developed a practice since 2015 of submitting third-party interventions to the Court setting out how international standards should be applied by states so as to protect human rights defenders themselves and uphold their work.

Nevertheless, aside from these positive facets of the Court's accessibility, the greatest disincentive for applicants remains the length of time which is involved in resolving cases. Even the introduction in 2010 of the priority policy has not had a particularly discernible impact, primarily because the Court's total backlog of cases has remained consistently high: although case numbers have reduced since the 2011 high of over 160,000, they rose again in 2016 to a figure of just over 80,000, due in particular to cases concerning poor prison conditions in Hungary and Romania and large numbers emanating from the conflict zones of eastern Ukraine and from Turkey as a result of repressive measures being taken by the state authorities following the attempted coup d'état in 2016.

Another significant obstacle has been the inaccessibility of the Court's decisions in national languages: its judgments and other decisions are published in either English or French (occasionally both). Much effort has been made very recently to provide access through the Court's official search engine (the HUDOC system) to "unofficial translations" of the Court's decisions in a variety of languages, but this remains a significant problem for lawyers and applicants (not to mention domestic judges and officials) who use any of the 30–40 or so other European languages but are not sufficiently conversant with the Council of Europe's two official languages.

Redress and Systemic Violations

The European Court has traditionally been cautious and tentative in its consideration of redress, applying during its first four decades an essentially declaratory approach in its judgments and limiting itself to awarding damages. As a result it has been left behind by the Inter-American Court, which although it was established 20 years after the European Court, has already developed a rich and progressive jurisprudence on reparations, taking account of the victim's life plan (proyecto de vida) and encompassing symbolic and collective remedies. However, in more recent years, the European Court has proved to be rather more progressive and indeed interventionist, by including in its judgments binding obligations on governments to take particular measures, such as returning property, holding rehearings of trials deemed to be unfair, requiring detainees held unlawfully to be released, and ordering the reinstatement of a judge who was unfairly dismissed.

Of even greater significance has been the European Court's development of a new approach to systemic human rights violations – those which relate to widespread or structural issues affecting thousands. Since 2004, by invoking its "pilot-judgment procedure," the Court has developed an approach of explicitly identifying the source of large-scale structural problems (usually malfunctioning legislation or a defective legal system) and establishing a binding obligation on the government to resolve the issue (without, however, specifying how it should be done). This may include an obligation to legislate – and to do so within a specified time period. The majority of pilot judgments to date have concerned disputes over property – particularly arising from the non-enforcement of domestic court judgments and the excessive length of legal proceedings. Initially, the respondents in such cases were predominantly states from eastern Europe and the former Soviet bloc, but western and central European states have also been targeted by pilot judgments, as a consequence of various systemic failings, such as overly lengthy legal proceedings, inhuman prison conditions, the disenfranchisement of convicted prisoners (the United Kingdom), and issues arising from the breakup of Yugoslavia: lost foreign currency savings (in various states) and the denial of the rights of the "erased" who lost their permanent residence status after Slovenia attained independence.

These innovations have been introduced, at least in part, because of the massive backlog of cases pending at the European Court, many of which are "repeat violation" cases. Where states and their respective national authorities fail to resolve at the national level issues which are adjudicated upon by the Court, more cases raising exactly the same problem (sometimes in their thousands) pile up in Strasbourg. The Court's more prescriptive position is therefore justified, and in some cases, states have responded reasonably swiftly to pilot judgments by introducing legislative changes aimed at the resolving the problems. However, the Court's increasing interventionism has also been met with growing recalcitrance in some quarters – both from and within states. One example concerns the issue of prisoner voting in the United Kingdom. As the UK authorities had failed to alter the ban (enshrined in legislation) on convicted prisoners voting while they remain in prison, following a Grand Chamber judgment on the issue in 2005, the European Court issued a pilot judgment in 2010, requiring remedial legislation to be brought forward within 6 months (Greens and M.T. v United Kingdom 2010). That an international court could intervene on such a question met with strong domestic ministerial and parliamentary disapproval, and, as a result, it was only at the end of 2017 that the UK government finally put forward proposals to resolve this issue (by granting the franchise to a very small number of prisoners released on licence).

The Election of Judges

European Court judges are elected (one per state) by the Parliamentary Assembly of the Council of Europe, a body which is made up of members of the national parliaments of the 47 states. They are elected for a single of term of 9 years, which cannot be renewed. The majority of Strasbourg judges have substantial domestic judicial experience, although it is another strength of the system that some judges have differing backgrounds – as former prosecutors, academics, practising lawyers, and having worked for NGOs.

The makeup of the judicial cohort has been the subject of criticism from time to time. A good deal of this is simply "xenophobic fury" (Bratza 2011), but there is undoubtedly still a need to improve national processes for the selection of Strasbourg judges, to ensure that only those suitable for the highest judicial office are elected to the Court. As it is the states which put forward a list of three candidates to the Parliamentary Assembly, this is primarily a matter of ensuring there are rigorous, objective national selection procedures (certainly to ensure that they are non-politicized), backed up by close, objective scrutiny at the European level, which enables the rejection of states' lists where this proves necessary. In recent years, the processes have been criticized because of the continuing under-representation of women on the Strasbourg bench (former Judge Elisabet Fura decried the "dominantly male" leadership of the Court (Council of Europe 2010)) and because of nepotism and the extensive efforts made by some states to ensure that a particular ("pro-government") candidate is elected. To its credit, the Parliamentary Assembly has shown itself to be increasingly willing to reject states' lists where such problems become evident. At the time of writing, 16 of the Court's 47 judges were women, so there is clearly some way still to go to achieve gender balance.

One distinctive feature of the Court's judicial practice is that it includes in its composition to hear individual cases the judge who is the national of the defendant state (as does the International Court of Justice but not the African Court on Human and Peoples' Rights). This has proven to be a strength of the system supporting its perceived legitimacy because the "national judge" in practice plays a significant role in elucidating the domestic law context. However, on occasions this aspect of the Court's procedure has been controversial where "national judges" are seen to consistently dissent (on their own) against findings of violations of the Convention made against "their" states.

Impact: The Implementation of Judgments

There can be no question that the decisions of the European Court over the last five decades have been remarkably impactful. The Court's judgments have led to numerous instances of redress being provided to individual litigants, not only in the form of the payment of damages but also, for example, by the reopening of domestic proceedings, the withdrawal of expulsion orders, the withdrawal of arrest warrants, and the release from custody. Of ever-greater consequence have been the myriad ways in which domestic legislation and case law have been changed (PACE 2016), policies amended, and public officials been newly trained to understand and apply new standards. One study of the impact of the Convention on national systems within 18 Council of Europe states referred to thousands of discrete legal and policy outcomes which have been altered as a result of the influence of Convention rights (Keller et al. 2008). The study also argued that even the original contracting states had no real conception as to how the Convention would influence their national legal orders and concluded that the Court's impact, admittedly variable across states, has increased over the years.

By dint of states' ratification of the European Convention, the Court's judgments are legally binding as a matter of international law. The supervision of the implementation of the European Court judgments is carried out by the Committee of Ministers, which holds four meetings a year (involving state diplomats) to consider and debate the most pressing cases, leading to the publication of decisions and interim resolutions encouraging and cajoling state compliance and final resolutions where a case is considered to have been fully implemented.

Nevertheless, the question of the implementation of the European Court's judgments – whether states comply with its rulings and whether adequate steps are taken at the national level as a consequence – has become one of the most dominant and recurring issues affecting debates about the validity and legitimacy of the European human rights system. In far too many cases, state authorities are failing to respond adequately to the Court's judgments, which require legislative amendments, changes in policy or practice, or a much more significant domestic political investment to tackle large-scale systemic problems. As a consequence, the Committee of Ministers' caseload has risen in recent years to a figure consistently around 10,000–11,000. There has also been an increase in the number of cases pending for more than 5 years: by 2015, these amounted to 55% of the pending cases.

The question of implementation is in some cases inextricably linked to the nature of the redress which the Court grants – the more specific the nature of the redress stipulated, the easier it is to assess whether or not compliance has been achieved. In a case brought against Azerbaijan concerning criminal proceedings instigated against the activist and opposition blogger Ilgar Mammadov, the Court found in its 2014 judgment that the criminal proceedings brought against him had in fact been intended to punish him for criticising the government, and the Committee of Ministers subsequently called for his release. As he nevertheless remained in custody, the Secretary General of the Council of Europe, Thorbjørn Jagland, weighed in by opening an inquiry into the implementation of the judgment under Article 52 of the Convention. At the time of writing, however, Mr. Mammadov still languishes in prison.

One new mechanism – "infringement proceedings" – was recently adopted by the Council of Europe states as an additional means to improve levels of implementation. Where a state fails to comply with a judgment, the Committee of Ministers may refer the case back to the Court. It does not incorporate a "sanction" as such, but such a process would reflect the strong disapproval of the Council of Europe and would represent a significant diplomatic embarrassment for recalcitrant states and could therefore exert enough pressure to leverage change. However, since it was introduced in 2010, the mechanism has only ever been invoked once (at the end of 2017 in relation to the Ilgar Mammadov case). Given the high rate of non-implementation of the European Court judgments, this is inexplicable, unless one is resigned to the fact that the Committee of Ministers' process is a relatively toothless system based on peer pressure, with states' primary objectives being to avoid being identified themselves as violators of the Convention.

The Future Potential and the Challenges Ahead

The principal challenges for the European Court in the coming years are likely to be questions about its legitimacy, the weight of its caseload, and the extent to which there is state compliance and effective implementation of its judgments. Although the Court's reasoning and its practices in particular circumstances can of course be criticized (and indeed the system undoubtedly benefits from close external scrutiny), the primary drivers of debates about the Court's "legitimacy" have been governments and politicians (and sometimes domestic judges) who object to being thwarted from carrying through measures which would breach the European human rights standards. To protect the rights of minorities by pointing out the errors of majoritarian ways, will often not be popular. However, this does not mean that the Court can be described as having no "legitimacy," in order to undermine its practices and decisions. On the contrary, it retains its legitimacy through, among other things, the level of voluntary state accession (47 states), the fact that its judges are elected by national parliamentarians from those states and, above all, through its (usually) carefully reasoned jurisprudence and its judicial self-restraint.

Be that as it may, hostility toward the Court remains a political reality, which has led in recent years, in states such as Russia and the United Kingdom, to calls at the highest levels for withdrawal from the jurisdiction of the Court. Yet, the only country to have done so was Greece under the control of a military junta in the late 1960s – it remains the case that no democratic state has ever done so. Almost on a par is the challenge of states seeking to water down their obligations arising from the Court's judgments, exemplified by the law introduced in Russia in 2015 which, in effect, allows its Constitutional Court to pick and choose which European Court judgments to implement. Such developments must be resisted in order to maintain a viable human rights system with binding legal force.

The vast number of cases which have been, and continue to be, submitted to the Court from across Europe arguably reflect contradictory influences – both the level of respect and trust which leads applicants to petition the Court and the extent to which states have failed to resolve repeat violations. However, the vast majority of cases submitted continue to be declared inadmissible by the Court (more than 90%), which means that too much of the Court's time is taken up with disposing of clearly unmeritorious cases and that the meritorious cases take far too long to be processed. This issue seems to indicate a continuing need for better training of the legal profession across the continent.

More fundamentally, the backlog is also indicative of an underlying "crisis of implementation" – state authorities (governments, parliaments, the courts, and other bodies) are failing to respond adequately to address the shortcomings which the Court has highlighted (in some cases, again and again and again). This is the other side of the subsidiarity principle – that the Convention should be effectively applied and enforced at the national level. A new protocol to the Convention (Protocol No. 16) adopted in 2013 will, once it enters into force, enable the European Court to issue advisory opinions on the application of the Convention at the request of the highest domestic courts. This could, in theory, provide states with an "early warning system" which highlights problematic areas before they arise and are litigated at the Strasbourg Court. However, its efficacy will depend on the extent to which national authorities prove to be willing and able to respond to the European Court's guidance by amending its law and practice appropriately and in good time. In any event, the Court's newer strategies for tackling systemic violations through a more collective approach (including pilot judgments) will need to be developed further, and a variety of means found of assisting states in devising and implementing the reforms which are needed to resolve the most widespread, endemic breaches. The Council of Europe states need to take the erga omnes principle seriously, by carefully scrutinizing each of the Court's significant judgments of principle (notably Grand Chamber decisions) in order to consider their application within the particular national context and to maintain rigorous systems of auditing of draft legislation (involving parliamentarians supported by expert legal advice) to ensure Convention compliance. Law students, lawyers, and national judges need access to, and thorough training in, the Court's case law, and the training of all public officials should inculcate an understanding of the essential principles and standards (which are most relevant to their roles) which the Convention lays down.

One question which has been debated for decades, but which still remains unresolved, is the accession of the European Union to the European Convention. This is intended to improve the harmonization of human rights standards in Europe and in particular to ensure that the acts of EU institutions are subject to the scrutiny of the European Court of Human Rights. The process was stalled in 2014 when the Court of Justice of the European Union (CJEU) issued a critical opinion on the draft agreement for accession. There is no sign of any recent political desire to reactivate the accession process, and it has no doubt been further sidelined by the ongoing negotiations concerning "Brexit" (the process of the United Kingdom leaving the European Union, following the referendum in 2016).

The debate about the need to reform the Strasbourg Court has continued for several decades, driven predominantly by the problems created by the excessive caseload. At the heart of this debate has been, or should be, a fundamental question about the role of the Court. Although the Convention's preamble envisages a collective obligation on the European states to ensure compliance with the Convention, the reality is that the Court's work over the last six decades has been concerned with thousands of individual applications. In recent years, there has been a tendency for the debate to be polarized between those who emphasize the importance of the right of individual petition and the principle of access to justice and those who argue that the Court should only deal with the most "important" cases, acting akin to a constitutional court for the region and setting standards for the continent as a whole. Through the adoption of a prioritization policy and the development of the pilot-judgment procedure since the mid-2000s, the Court has already taken important steps in developing a more focused and collective approach, which could still be taken further. There needs to be a rather more nuanced recognition of the various distinctive tasks which the Court can and should carry out, encompassing Grand Chamber decisions on significant legal questions which set standards for the continent as a whole and upholding the right of individual petition, particularly in developing areas of law and in relation to egregious or systemic human rights violations. This is an approach which acknowledges the Convention system as "an authoritative, dynamic, and transnational source of law'" (Keller and Stone Sweet 2008) for the continent of Europe but also one which is predicated on truly effective implementation at the national level.

References

Bates E (2010) The evolution of the European Convention on Human Rights: from its inception to the creation of a permanent court of human rights. Oxford University Press, Oxford

Blackburn R, Polakiewicz J (eds) (2001) Fundamental rights in Europe: the ECHR and its member states, 1950–2000. Oxford University Press, Oxford

Bratza N (2011) The relationship between the UK courts and Strasbourg. Eur Hum Rights Law Rev 5:505–512

Buckley C, Donald A, Leach P (eds) (2016) Towards coherence in international human rights law: approaches of regional and international systems. Brill (Martinus Nijhoff), Leiden

Council of Europe (2010) The conscience of Europe – 50 years of the European Court of Human Rights. Third Millennium Publishing Limited, London

Donald A, Leach P (2016) Parliaments and the European Court of Human Rights. Oxford University Press, Oxford

Early L, Austin A, Ovey C, Chernishova O (eds) (2016) The right to life under article 2 of the European Convention on Human Rights – twenty years of legal developments since McCann v. the United Kingdom. Will-Jan van der Wolf, Oisterwijk

Føllesdal A, Schlütter B, Ulfstein G (eds) (2013) Constituting Europe – the European Court of Human Rights in a National, European and global context. Cambridge University Press, Cambridge

Goldhaber M (2009) A people's history of the European Court of Human Rights. Rutgers University Press, New Brunswick

Hale B (2011) Common law and convention law: the limits to interpretation. Eur Hum Rights Law Rev 5:534–543

Keller H, Stone Sweet A (eds) (2008) A Europe of rights – the impact of the ECHR on national legal systems. Oxford University Press, Oxford

Lambert Abdelgawad E (ed) (2011) Preventing and sanctioning hindrances to the right of individual petition before the European Court of Human Rights. Intersentia, Cambridge

Leach P (2008) The Chechen conflict: analysing the oversight of the European Court of Human Rights. European Human Rights Law Review 6:732–761

Leach P (2013) The European system and approach. In: Sheeran S, Rodley N (eds) Routledge handbook of international human rights law. Routledge, Abingdon

Leach P (2017) Taking a case to the European Court of Human Rights. Oxford University Press, Oxford

Leach P, Paraskeva C, Uzelac G (2009) International human rights and fact-finding – an analysis of the fact-finding missions conducted by the European Commission and Court of Human Rights. London Metropolitan University, London

Leach P, Hardman H, Stephenson S, Blitz B (2010) Responding to systemic human rights violations – an analysis of pilot judgments of the European Court of Human Rights and their impact at national level. Intersentia, Antwerp

Parliamentary Assembly of the Council of Europe (2016) Impact of the European Convention on Human Rights in states parties: Selected examples, AS/Jur/Inf (2016) 04. Council of Europe, Strasbourg

Schmahl S, Breuer M (eds) (2017) The council of Europe – its law and policies. Oxford University Press, Oxford

European Court of Human Rights Jurisprudence

A and others v. United Kingdom, Application No. 3455/05, Judgment of 19 February 2009

A, B & C v. Ireland, Application No. 25579/05, Judgment of 16 December 2010

Alekseyev v. Russia, Application Nos. 4916/07, 25924/08 & 14599/09, Judgment of 22 October 2010

Al-Skeini v. United Kingdom, Application No. 55721/07, Judgment of 7 July 2011

Aslakhanova and Others v. Russia, Application Nos. 2944/06 et al, Judgment of 18 December 2012

Bouyid v. Belgium, Application No. 23380/09, Judgment of 28 September 2015

Broniowski v. Poland, Application No. 31443/96, Judgment of 22 June 2004

Castells v. Spain, Application No. 11798/85, Judgment of 23 April 1992

Centre for Legal Resources on behalf of Valentin Câmpeanu v. Romania, Application No. 47848/08, Judgment of 17 July 2014

Chiragov and Others v. Armenia, Application No. 13216/05, Judgment of 16 June 2015

Diri v. Turkey, Application No. 68351/01, Judgment of 31 July 2007

Dudgeon v. United Kingdom, Application No. 7525/76, Judgment of 23 September 1981

El-Masri v. the Former Yugoslav Republic of Macedonia, Application No. 39630/09, Judgment of 13 December 2012

Evans v. United Kingdom, Application No. 6399/05, Judgment of 10 April 2007

Gäfgen v. Germany, Application No. 22978/05, Judgment of 1 June 2010

Greens and M.T. v. United Kingdom, Application Nos. 60041/08 and 60054/08, Judgment of 23 November 2010

Handyside v. United Kingdom, Application No. 5493/72, Judgment of 7 December 1976

Hassan v. United Kingdom, Application No. 29750/09, Judgment of 16 September 2014

Ilgar Mammadov v. Azerbaijan, Application No. 15172/13, Judgment of 22 May 2014

Ireland v. United Kingdom, Application, No. 5310/71, Judgment of 18 January 1978

Lashmankin v. Russia, Application No. 57818/09, Judgment of 7 February 2017

Lautsi and Others v. Italy, Application No. 30814/06, Judgment of 18 March 2011

Leyla Sahin v Turkey, Application No. 44774/98, Judgment of 10 November 2005

M.C. v. Bulgaria, Application No. 39272/98, Judgment of 4 December 2003

M.S.S. v Belgium and Greece, Application No. 30696/09, Judgment of 21 January 2011

Malone v. United Kingdom, Application No. 8691/79, Judgment of 2 August 1984

Merabishvili v. Georgia, Application No. 72508/13, Judgment of 28 November 2017

Observer and Guardian v. United Kingdom, Application No. 13585/88, Judgment of 26 November 1991

Oleksandr Volkov v. Ukraine, Application No. 21722/11, Judgment of 9 January 2013

Opuz v. Turkey, Application No. 33401/02, Judgment of 9 June 2009

Othman (Abu Qatada) v. United Kingdom, Application No. 8139/09, Judgment of 17 January 2012

R.R. v. Hungary, Application No. 8139/09, Judgment of 4 December 2012

Rantsev v. Cyprus and Russia, Application No. 25965/04, Judgment of 7 January 2010

Rasul Jafarov v. Azerbaijan, Application No. 69981/14, Judgment of 17 March 2016

Roman Zakharov v. Russia, Application No. 47143/06, Judgment of 4 December 2015

Rustavi 2 Broadcasting Company v. Georgia, Application No. 16812/17 (pending) 2017

Saadi v. Italy, Application No. 37201/06, Judgment of 28 February 2008

Sargsyan v. Azerbaijan, Application No. 40167/06, Judgment of 16 June 2015

Siliadin v. France, Application No. 73316/01, Judgment of 26 July 2005

Soering v. United Kingdom, Application No. 14038/88, Judgment of 7 July 1989

Sunday Times v. United Kingdom (No. 1), Application No. 6538/74, Judgment of 26 April 1979

Sürek v. Turkey (No. 1), Application No. 26682/95, Judgment of 8 July 1999

United Communist Party of Turkey and others v. Turkey, Application No. 19392/92, Judgment of 30 January 1998

Yordanova v. Bulgaria, Application No. 25446/06, Judgment of 24 April 2012

The European Union Fundamental Rights Agency

Gabriel N. Toggenburg

Contents

The European Human Rights Landscape and the EU Fundamental Rights Agency 444
The Agency's Institutional Setup: The Four Bodies of the Agency 446
The Networks of the Agency 448
The Staff and Resources of the Agency 449
The Agency's Mandate: Objective and Substantive Purview 449
The Policy Areas Covered by the Agency's Work 451
The Territorial Scope of the Agency 452
The Agency as a Provider of a Solid Evidence Base (Data Collection) 452
The Agency as a Consultative Center of Expertise (Policy Advice) 454
The Agency as a Communication Tool ("Multilogue" with Civil Society) 455
Challenges Ahead 457
References 458

Abstract

The European Union Agency for Fundamental Rights (FRA) is the European Union's independent expert body providing fundamental rights expertise and assistance to the EU institutions and the EU member states. It is mandated to deal with the fundamental rights situation in the EU territory and publishes large-scale surveys, research reports, and legal opinions. Whereas it was created to provide evidence-based policy advice, it increasingly also assumed more operational tasks, including, for instance, consultative tasks in the hotspots in Greece. Founded in 2007 it has over the years developed into a renowned center of expertise that complements the institutional human rights landscape in Europe.

This article reflects the author's personal views and cannot be attributed to the Agency.

G. N. Toggenburg (✉)
Office of the Director of the European Union Agency for Fundamental Rights (FRA), Vienna, Austria
e-mail: gtoggenburg@gmail.com

Whereas it is not mandated to deal with individual rights violations, it has contributed – next to the entry into force of the Lisbon treaty and the Charter of Fundamental Rights – to boost the EU's development toward a human rights organization. At the end of 2018, an independent external evaluation of the agency concluded that it has substantially added value and that its mandate should be extended.

Keywords

European Union · Fundamental Rights Agency · FRA · EU Charter of Fundamental Rights · EU agency · Evidence-based advise · Treaty of Lisbon · European Union law

The European Human Rights Landscape and the EU Fundamental Rights Agency

Europe is well known for its densely developed net of human rights actors. This is true not only for the national but also for the intergovernmental level. Both the Organization for Security and Co-operation in Europe (OSCE) and the Council of Europe are equipped with institutions and mechanisms specialized in the protection of these rights. Already more than half a century ago, the Council of Europe provided for a European Convention on Human Rights (ECHR) and the European Court of Human Rights (ECtHR) in Strasbourg. The fall of the iron curtain brought the protection of human and minority rights to the fore of international attention and allowed for a political climate favoring the establishment of new institutions and mechanisms. In 1991, the OSCE established the Office for Democratic Institutions and Human Rights (ODIHR) in Warsaw. In 1993 the Council of Europe introduced the European Commission against Racism and Intolerance (ECRI) in Strasbourg. The year 1993 gave birth to a minority-specific institution, namely, the Office of the High Commissioner on National Minorities (HCNM) of the OSCE in The Hague. Finally, in 1999, the Council of Europe established the Commissioner for Human Rights (CHR). Also at the national level, the 1990s stands for a dynamic period in the institutionalization of human rights concerns – countless national human rights institutions (NHRIs) had been established during that period, following in particular from the commitment to do so in the 1993 Vienna Declaration and Program of Action (Vienna Declaration and Programme of Action 1993). There is another layer of governance which might be considered a latecomer in the area of human rights but who has over the recent decades with increasing speed and visibility conquered its share in the European landscape: the European Union (EU) (Alston 1999; Toggenburg 2004).

Human rights were soon a prominent topic in the EU's external relations vis-à-vis third countries. Internally, fundamental rights were confined to the case law as prominently (for lawyers at least) developed by the Court of Justice of the European Union (then European Court of Justice). At the institutional level, it was first and foremost the European Parliament that showed an early interest in human rights, including minority rights. Its Committee on Civil Liberties, Justice and Home Affairs (LIBE Committee) is explicitly responsible for these issues. Since 1992, the EU has been equipped with an ombudsman to investigate complaints about maladministration in the EU institutions. Between 1997 and 2007, the EU had a European Monitoring Center on Racism and Xenophobia (EUMC), based in Vienna which was collecting data and coordinating research in the area of ethnic discrimination and racism within the EU (established by Council Regulation (EC) No. 1035/97 of 1997). Since 2004 the EU has a European Data Protection Supervisor who safeguards the right to data protection. In late 2009, FREMP (the Working Party on Fundamental Rights, Citizens' Rights and Free Movement of Persons) became a permanent working party within the Council structures. In 2010 a member of the European Commission, Viviane Reding, became explicitly and prominently responsible (also) for fundamental rights. However, it was already under her predecessor Franco Frattini that the EU had negotiated and agreed upon the establishment of a specialized and independent EU institution that would deal with all fundamental rights. In March 2007 the European Union Agency for Fundamental Rights (FRA) was established.

The genesis of the Agency was not the outcome of any concerted long-term political strategy. The very idea of an Agency to safeguard human rights arose in academic circles in the second half of the 1990s (Alston and Weiler 1999, pp. 55–59). It received serious attention at the international political level only when the three so-called wise men ended the "Austrian crisis" in 2000 (when the far-right party FPÖ entered the Austrian government, the other, then 14, EU member states had imposed sanctions against Austria) (Toggenburg 2001, pp. 735–756). However, neither the Council nor the European Commission responded positively to the suggestions to create such an agency. On the contrary, both institutions underlined their disagreement with the establishment of a human rights agency, at least as regards the foreign policy of the EU (European Commission 2001, p. 23; Council 2001). When discussing the reform of the EUMC, the Commission reached the general conclusion that the EUMC "should continue to concentrate on racism and that an extension to other fields would be an unwelcome distraction within the limits of the resources likely to be available to the Centre" (European Commission COM (2003) 483 final of 5 August 2003). Given this background, it came as a considerable surprise when representatives of the member states announced on 13 December 2003 their intent to establish a human rights agency (Toggenburg 2007).

From the beginning, it seemed natural to think of a future EU human rights body as being based upon the already existing EUMC in Vienna. Because the prime objective of the latter was the provision of reliable and comparable data, this was perceived as a core task of any future agency in the field of human rights. Moreover, for obvious legal reasons, it was already clear that, should the EU ever be equipped with its own human rights institution, the latter would not be a court-like institution. In light of the established typology of NHRIs (Aichele 2003, pp. 101, 110, 203) which distinguishes between an advisory committee model (to be found, e.g., in France, Greece, or Luxembourg), an institute model (Denmark and Germany), an ombudsman model (Portugal, Spain, and Sweden), and a commission model

(Ireland), one could have predicted that an EU agency dealing with fundamental rights will be a mixture of the committee model and the institute model. However, the very particular mandate of the Agency and the fact that this new institution is not a national entity but part of the structure of the EU made soon clear that a hitherto unknown type of actor was created in the global family of human rights actors.

The Agency's Institutional Setup: The Four Bodies of the Agency

The Agency's Founding Regulation establishes that the Agency has four bodies: a Management Board, an Executive Board, a Scientific Committee, and a Director (Founding Regulation). The Management Board comprises 31 experts: one independent person appointed by each member state "having high level responsibilities in an independent national human rights institution or other public or private sector organisation," two representatives of the European Commission, and one independent person appointed by the Council of Europe (Art. 12 Founding Regulation). It is important to note that different from other agencies, the Founding Regulation stresses that the composition of the board "should ensure the Agency's independence from both Community institutions and Member State governments and assemble the broadest possible expertise in the field of fundamental rights" (Consideration No. 20 Founding Regulation). The Management does thus not represent the interest of Member States but brings together expert views as well as the interests of the European Commission and the Council of Europe.

The Management Board is the planning and monitoring body of the Agency. It adopts the Annual Work Program, the annual Fundamental Rights Report, and the Agency's draft and final budgets. The board exercises disciplinary authority over the director and appoints and, if necessary, dismisses the latter. It also appoints and revokes the members of the Scientific Committee. The Management Board is furthermore responsible for more technical issues like the adoption of the Agency's rules of procedure (on the basis of a draft submitted by the director), the financial rules applicable to the Agency, all the necessary measures to implement the staff regulations, the arrangements on transparency and access to documents, or the administrative arrangements on the cooperation with other (inter)national players. The board has to convene at least twice a year.

The Executive Board assists the Management Board, and the latter may delegate some of its responsibilities to the Executive Board (Art. 12(7) Founding Regulation). The Executive Board meets four times a year and consists of the chairperson and the vice-chairperson of the Management Board, two other members of the Management Board elected by the Management Board, and one of the representatives of the European Commission in the Management Board. The person appointed by the Council of Europe in the Management Board may participate in the meetings of the Executive Board. The director takes part in the meetings of the Executive Board but has no voting rights. The board is convened by the chairperson whenever necessary to prepare decisions of the Management Board and to advise the director. It decides by simple majority.

The Scientific Committee – not foreseen in the initial proposal of the Founding Regulation as presented by the European Commission in 2005 – is the "guarantor of the scientific quality of the Agency's work, guiding the work to that effect." In this sense, the Scientific Committee is more than a mere scientific council that looks into the Agency's functioning once a year. On the other hand, scientific "guidance" is not meant to do away with the fact that the committee is a consultative organ. Its pronouncements are not legally binding for other bodies of the Agency. Rather, it seems that the Founding Regulation looks at the committee as a semipermanent partner of the operational services of the Agency providing them with input and controlling their output. For this purpose, the director shall involve the Scientific Committee "as early as appropriate in the preparation" of all documents drawn up in the Agency's work" (Art. 14(5) Founding Regulation). The Scientific Committee comprises 11 independent persons "highly qualified in the field of fundamental rights" (Art. 14(1) Founding Regulation). Like in the case of the other bodies, the term of office of the board members is 5 years and is not renewable. The Scientific Committee elects its chairperson and vice-chairperson for a term of office of 1 year. They are allowed to attend the meetings of the Management Board as observers (Art. 12(10) Founding Regulation). The Scientific Committee has the right to submit its opinion concerning the draft Annual Work Program before it is adopted by the Management Board (Art. 12(6)(a) Founding Regulation). The same applies to the adoption of the Agency's rules of procedure (Art. 12(6)(g) Founding Regulation). The committee has furthermore to be consulted before the Management Board adopts the annual report (Art. 12(6)(b) Founding Regulation). The committee decides by two-thirds majority and shall be convened by its chairperson four times per year. The members of the current Committee include present and former members of European Courts, the United National Human Rights Committee, monitoring bodies of the Council of Europe or national human rights monitoring bodies. For instance, it includes an acting judge at the European Court of Human Rights, the first United Nations Special Rapporteur on human rights and counter-terrorism or the former United Nations Special Rapporteur on the Human Rights of Migrants.

The Director of the Agency is responsible for the Agency's general tasks and the preparation and publication of its various reports and studies, the preparation and implementation of the Agency's Annual Work Programme, all staff matters, all matters of day-to-day administration, the implementation of the Agency's budget, the implementation of "effective monitoring and evaluation procedures relating to the performance of the Agency against its objectives according to professionally recognized standards," the cooperation with National Liaison Officers, and the cooperation with civil society, including the coordination of the Fundamental Rights Platform (Art. 15(4) Founding Regulation). The Director is also the person representing the Agency in its relations with third parties. The selection procedure for the position of the Director is highly complex. No other Agency applies a comparable procedure. In this procedure, the parliament, the Commission, and the Council of the EU are involved (Art. 15(2) Founding Regulation). On 7 March 2007, Morten Kjaerum was appointed as the Agency's first director. The second director of the Agency, Michael O'Flaherty, took office in December 2015. Just as the founding director he is not a former politician but a widely recognised independent expert: Michael O'Flaherty was Established Professor of Human Rights Law and Director of the Irish Centre for Human Rights at the National University of Ireland, Galway. He has served as Chief Commissioner of the Northern Ireland Human Rights Commission. From 2004–2012, he was a member of the United Nations Human Rights Committee, latterly as a Vice-Chairperson.

The Networks of the Agency

The Agency is more than an EU body with a seat in Vienna. It is a network of networks reaching out to the different national environments. The Founding Regulation establishes that every member states nominates a "National Liaison Officer" (NLO). In practice, these are civil servants working in ministries of interior and external affairs or in the office of the prime minister. They make sure that a permanent information channel between the Agency and the individual member states is maintained. The NLOs meet once a year at the venue of the Agency to discuss the Agency's work and exchange views on relevant developments at national level. In the institutional practice, this network is complemented by national parliamentary focal points. They are the Agency's principal partners in the parliamentary administrations of member states. The Founding Regulation mentions the creation of networks as one of the Agency's working methods (Art. 6(1) Founding Regulation). And indeed much of the work of the Agency is network-based or at least builds on networks in order to establish efficient relations among relevant human rights actors. The comparative studies drafted by the Agency's staff build on national reports that are drafted under the guidance of the Agency's experts by national contractors in the 28 member states (universities or expert NGOs) who build the Agency's multidisciplinary research network called "FRANET." As laid down in its Founding Regulation, the Agency also cooperates with and links up with national equality bodies, ombudsmen, and national human rights institutions in order to allow for an exchange of promising practices and experiences and transfer of human rights knowledge and information across national boundaries. The Agency keeps regular contact with these crucial partners which build the "fundamental rights landscape" at the national level.

The Agency also works with group of member states on specific topics. By way of illustration, one can point to a working group in which the agency develops together with EU member states methods and indicators how best to measure progress on the integration of Roma across the EU. Another example is the Agency's role in a high-level expert group to combat racism, xenophobia, and other forms of intolerance, which serves to foster the further exchange and dissemination of best practices between national authorities and aims to fill existing gaps and better prevent and combat hate crime and hate speech.

Finally, the Agency has been pioneering new ways for international organizations to work with civil society. According to the Founding Regulation, the Agency "shall closely cooperate with non-governmental organisations and with institutions of civil society, active in the field of fundamental rights" (Art. 10(1) Founding Regulation). For this purpose, the Agency has to run a Fundamental Rights Platform which shall constitute "a mechanism for the exchange of information and pooling of knowledge ... ensure[ing] close cooperation between the Agency and relevant stakeholders" (Art. 10(2) Founding Regulation).

The Staff and Resources of the Agency

The Agency employs close to 120 persons out of which over 70 are the so-called temporary agents, around 30 are "contract agents," and less than 10 are Seconded National Experts. Close to 80 persons of the staff are providing operational tasks; the rest are in support functions. The experts working at FRA have different backgrounds and include lawyers, statisticians, social and political scientists. Every year around 30 new interns join FRA to assist the Agency in all the different departments for 12 months. Next to the Director and his Advisors, the Agency has five units: Research and Data; Institutional Cooperation and Networks; Technical Assistance and Capacity Building; Communication and Events; Corporate Services (revised internal structure as of November 2018).

The budget of the Agency was in 2017 close to € 23 million of which around € 7 million were allocated to specific projects. Compared to the budget of FRONTEX, the EU's Border and Coast Guard Agency, which disposed in 2017 a budget of € 305 million and a staff of 655 persons, FRA is a rather small entity. Admittedly, given the different tasks, the two bodies are not comparable. But comparing FRA with all the nearly ten EU agencies active in the area of Justice and Home Affairs reveals that the policy context of recent years (migration, security) led to an increase in staff and resources in these agencies but much less so at FRA.

The Agency's Mandate: Objective and Substantive Purview

According to Article 2 of the Founding Regulation, the Agency's objective is to provide assistance and expertise in the field of fundamental rights to institutions and bodies of the EU as well as to member states when the latter are acting within the scope of EU law. The Agency was thereby established as a consultative body. It has neither quasi-judicial functions nor does it deal with individual violations of rights. Its purpose is that of a center of excellence that provides evidence-based advice to key actors at EU and national levels.

The Founding Regulation is ambitious as it wants to make sure that the EU and its member states are "fully respecting" rights, including the promotion of these rights. The impact of the Agency is every 5 years assessed in an external evaluation (Art. 30(3) Founding Regulation, see last section of this contribution). In order to deliver such advice, the Agency may deal with fundamental rights along three dimensions: upstream, downstream, and besides the legislative stream. Upon request, the Agency provides legal opinions on legislative drafts discussed at EU level (upstream).

For instance, in 2016, the Agency delivered such opinions on six different legislative proposals, mainly in the areas of migration and asylum. Secondly, the Agency may provide practical advice to national actors when these are implementing EU legislation at national level. This type of advice can take a plethora of forms ranging from comparative reports to surveys or very practical "do's and don'ts." By way of illustration for the latter category, one can point to "Twelve operational fundamental rights considerations for law enforcement when processing Passenger Name Record (PNR) data" which FRA has identified (Fundamental Rights Agency 2014). Another very practical form of advice is provided in the Agency's small field presence in the so-called hotspots in Greece (hotspots are specifically assigned areas in Greece and Italy where incoming migrants are identified and registered). Finally, the Agency is not only looking at proposed EU legislation and the implementation of existing legislation but is also mandated to have views on "where legislative improvements [at the EU level] would be most welcome" in order to close eventual protection gaps (European Parliament resolution 2005, para. 43).

The Agency's substantive purview is confined to the competence areas of the EU as prescribed in the EU treaties. In fact, the wording of the Founding Regulation is more restrictive and hopelessly outdated as it states that the Agency shall carry out its task "within the competencies of the Community as laid down in the Treaty establishing the European Community" (Art. 3(1) Founding Regulation). However, with the entry into force of the treaty of Lisbon in December 2009, this very Community ceased to exist and was replaced by the European Union. Whereas the European Union is competent for all former "pillars," this was different with the former "Community." The latter was confined to "first pillar issues," thereby excluding the EU's common foreign and security policy (second pillar) and the judicial and police cooperation in criminal matters (third pillar). Whereas back in 2005 the European Commission had proposed a council decision empowering the Agency to also pursue activities in the area of police and judicial cooperation in criminal matters (European Commission COM (2005) 280), this decision was never adopted. However, the Council adopted a declaration that it is up to the EU institutions to consult the Agency on a voluntary basis within the range of the third pillar (Council of the European Union document 6166/07, 4).

It is submitted that once the Lisbon treaty entered into force, the Agency's Founding Regulation was automatically extended to all areas of EU law given the fact that the Lisbon treaty abolished the distinction between the former pillars and ordered that in all legal documents, "European Union" is replacing the former "European Community." However, the fact that the Agency's Founding Regulation is still phrased in pre-Lisbon language is confusing and should be changed (Toggenburg 2014).

In terms of fundamental rights standards, the Agency is required to apply in its work fundamental rights "as defined in Article 6(2) of the Treaty on European Union" (Art. 3(2) Founding Regulation). This provision imports fundamental rights standards from the European Convention on Human Rights in the EU system and draws on the member states' constitutional traditions. Whereas the Founding Regulation speaks of a "close connection between the Charter" and the Agency

(Consideration No. 9 Founding Regulation), the Charter of fundamental rights of the European Union is not referred to as a core standard of the Agency's work.

This is another expression of the outdated phrasing of the regulation which predates the entry into force of the Lisbon treaty (and hence also the Charter). Indeed, the Agency is mandated to deal with fundamental rights as they have been developed in the case law of the Court of Justice of the European Union and as they are reflected in the EU's Charter of Fundamental Rights. In the institutional practice of the Agency, the Charter is given core importance throughout all activities, with countless references also being made to relevant human rights standards as they developed in the Council of Europe and the UN system.

The Policy Areas Covered by the Agency's Work

Whereas the Agency's mandate covers all policy areas in which the EU holds a competence, the Agency's autonomy to deal with policy areas of its own choice is limited. This is because the Founding Regulation introduced a "Multi-annual Framework" (MAF) which explicitly lists those areas in which the Agency can become active on its own. Activities that fall squarely outside the policy areas listed in the MAF need an explicit request by the European Parliament, the European Commission, or the Council of the European Union to the Agency for delivering work in that very area.

The MAF is adopted by the Council of the European Union in a unanimous decision that is valid for 5 years. The thematic areas listed in the MAF must be "in line with the Union's priorities, taking due account of the orientations resulting from the European Parliament resolutions and Council conclusions in the field of fundamental rights" (Art. 5(2)(c) Founding Regulation). The Founding Regulation establishes that the fight against racism, xenophobia, and related intolerance is a permanent thematic area of the Agency, which is therefore immune to any change from one MAF to another (Art. 5(2)(b) Founding Regulation). The fact that the MAF limits the Agency's autonomy to deal with all policy areas it might consider relevant was criticized in the past. A more specific point of criticism was the noninclusion of the area of judicial and police cooperation in criminal matters.

The current MAF which runs from 2018 to 2022 was adopted at the end of 2017. It largely reflects the thematic areas that were already contained in the first two MAFs of the Agency: (a) victims of crime and access to justice; (b) equality and discrimination based on any ground such as sex, race, color, ethnic or social origin, genetic features, language, religion or belief, political or any other opinion, membership of a national minority, property, birth, disability, age, or sexual orientation or on the grounds of nationality; (c) information society and, in particular, respect for private life and protection of personal data; (d) judicial cooperation, except in criminal matters; (e) migration, borders, asylum, and integration of refugees and migrants; (f) racism, xenophobia, and related intolerance; (g) rights of the child; (h) integration and social inclusion of Roma (Council of the European Union decision 2017/2269, Art. 2).

The Territorial Scope of the Agency

The Agency's mandate is limited to EU member states. It is worthwhile to recall that during the creation of the Agency, there were voices arguing for its wide responsibility for the fundamental rights performance in third states – an idea that raised concerns in the Council of Europe as it feared overlaps and unnecessary competition. The initial proposal of the European Commission enshrined at least the possibility for the Agency to collect information on countries with which the European Union (then European Community) is planning to conclude association agreements, in particular on countries covered by the European Neighbourhood Policy. In contrast to this, the Founding Regulation allows for only very limited possibilities to extend the Agency's territorial scope to third countries. Such participation in the Agency's work is only open for EU candidate countries or countries that have concluded a Stabilisation and Association Agreement with the EU.

The only examples so far of third countries participating in the FRA were Croatia from April 2011 until the country' accession to the EU in July 2013 and Macedonia which became part of the agency's work in October 2017. Progress with regard to the participation of Serbia and Albania is ongoing. A future revision of the Founding Regulation could look into this and allow for a more flexible provision which would make it possible for additional states – for instance, those that are part of the European Economic Area (but not the EU) – to profit from FRA activities and services.

The Agency as a Provider of a Solid Evidence Base (Data Collection)

The Founding Regulation identifies eight tasks that the Agency is set to fulfill (Art. 4(1)(a-g) Founding Regulation). By way of (over)simplification these are here subsumed under three major functions, namely, the provision of solid evidence, policy advice (including technical assistance, capacity building and expert opinions), and the communication of rights (including the building and maintainance of networks).

The function the Agency has focused on its first years was to collect, analyze, and disseminate relevant, objective, and comparable information in the field of fundamental rights and to develop methods and standards to improve the comparability, objectivity, and reliability of such data at the European level (Art. 4(1)(a) and (b) Founding Regulation; Consideration No. 4 Founding Regulation). The large-scale surveys carried out by the Agency over the last decade in all 28 EU member states are prime examples of these activities. They allowed applying the very same sound methodology across all countries covered and thereby provided a snapshot of the situation across the EU. These surveys concerned women or minority populations such as migrant communities, religious communities, and LGTBI persons. Some of these surveys were repeated so as to identify trends over time.

The survey on violence against women may serve as an example to explain the survey work of the Agency and the sort of results and political impact it may generate. While it is acknowledged that violence against women involves serious and widespread fundamental rights violations, until recently little comprehensive data on the extent of the problem were available. In 2009, this prompted the European Parliament and subsequently the Council of the EU to call on FRA to collect comparative data on violence against women within the EU. The Agency responded by launching the first EU-wide survey to record women's experiences with violence. The survey encompassed different types of physical, sexual, and psychological violence experienced by women since the age of 15 as well as women's childhood experiences with violence (by an adult) before the age of 15. The survey included face-to-face interviews with 42,000 women in the 28 EU member states. Based on a representative sample of women in the general population, it presents a comprehensive picture of women's experiences with violence. The survey found that an estimated 13 million women in the EU had experienced physical violence in the 12-month period preceding the survey and that an estimated 3.7 million women had experienced sexual violence in the same period. Overall, 1 in 3 women (33%) indicated that they had been a victim of physical and/or sexual violence at least once since the age of 15, and 1 in 20 women indicated that they had been raped. The survey also captured experiences of sexual harassment. Depending on the forms or examples of sexual harassment asked about in the survey, between 45% and 55% of women indicated that they had experienced at least one form of sexual harassment since the age of 15. Many women had experienced multiple incidents. According to the survey, only 14% of women reported the most serious incident of physical and/or sexual violence to the police in cases where the perpetrator was an intimate partner. Against the background of this new evidence base, the discussion on whether the EU should accede to the Council of Europe's Convention on preventing and combating violence against women and domestic violence (the Istanbul Convention) gained momentum, and on 11 May 2017, the EU decided to sign the Convention.

The Agency is also working on a general Fundamental Rights Survey which will collect information on people's experiences of and views on fundamental rights issues. Looking at everyday issues such as access to justice, consumer rights, and good administration from a fundamental rights perspective, the survey will identify gaps in the realization of rights and service provision across a broad range of areas. In general, the Agency has shifted the focus from the law in the books to the experiences in the street. By applying the UN's "structure–process–outcome" model, the Agency not only looks at existing laws and institutions (the "structure" dimension) but equally analyzes existing policies (the "process" dimension) and, maybe most innovatively, the concrete results on the ground (the "outcome" dimension). This last dimension is least covered by existing monitoring bodies. There is a huge amount of data and analysis available as to whether the legislation of states is human rights proof (structure dimension), but there is a disturbing absence of information as to how the situation is in the real lives of real people (the outcome dimension).

FRA data and analysis are complementary to the monitoring reports of other actors at the national level, in the Council of Europe, or at the level of the UN of the 28 EU member states. The Agency recently decided to make the data and analysis of these other actors more accessible and hence more prominent. A "European Fundamental Rights Information System" is being developed that has the ambition to bring all existing human rights information on all EU member states delivered by international and European actors together in one easily accessible one-stop shop. This online tool would complement other online tools such as the Charterpedia (http://fra. europa.eu/de/charterpedia), a database that brings together information related to the EU Fundamental Rights Charter, including case law by the Court of Justice of the European Union, the European Court of Human rights, and national courts.

The Agency as a Consultative Center of Expertise (Policy Advice)

According to Article 4 of the Founding Regulation, the Agency has to carry out, cooperate with, and encourage scientific research, surveys, and studies. It should also publish thematic reports and formulate conclusions and opinions on specific topics. Whereas these forms and formats are used to deliver on the overall objective of the Agency, namely, to provide to the key actors assistance and expertise, the Agency also applies more informal and practical formats to cooperate with its stakeholders. The spectrum ranges from informal email exchanges, expert meetings, the participation in Schengen evaluations, and the drafting of "do's and don'ts" for practitioners working in specific fields to tecnical assistance such as the establishment of a small field presence in Greece in 2016. All these activities are conceptualized and carried out by FRA staff. Even where the drafting of studies is outsourced, the drafting of the "opinions" of the resulting reports is drafted in-house and is discussed within the Agency by an internal body composed of the Director, the management, and senior experts so as to guarantee full consistency with earlier opinions and ensure full ownership by the institution.

A specific form of advice is the provision of legal (or socio-legal) opinions on legislative drafts that are discussed within the EU institutions. According to Article 4(2) of the Founding Regulation, conclusions, opinions, and reports that "concern" legislative proposals from the commission (or positions taken by the EU institutions in the course of the legislative procedure) can be formulated by the Agency only if it is requested by one of the EU institutions to do so. Six of them were published in 2016 alone, commenting on the revisions of key pieces of EU legislation in the field of migration (including legislation on the so-called Dublin system or an EU list of safe countries of origin). Such legal opinions from an independent expert body can supplement internal impact assessments and legal scrutiny by the legal services of the EU institutions. One expert assessed various legislative files where the FRA has delivered opinions and stated that "[q]uite naturally, it has taken some time to consider the contributions of the FRA and possible other stakeholders, such as the EDPS (the European Data Protection Supervisor), but this has not led to delays. If we consider the "costs" and "benefits" of the ex ante processes, we can easily come to the conclusion that benefits outnumber and outweigh the costs. It is the quality of the legal text that is the winner of this process." The expert concluded that FRA could be given "a more effective role in ex ante review functions by extending its mandate and allocating it adequate resources to fulfil its increased tasks" (Fyhr 2016).

Although FRA's legal expertise is not yet requested systematically during the preparation of EU legislation, the Agency is increasingly invited to participate in hearings at the European Parliament and meetings of Council working groups. Whereas so far mainly but not exclusively the European Parliament requested the Agency to deliver such opinions, the EU institutions acknowledge the added value of FRA's input when discussing measures that affect fundamental rights. Even the European Council stressed that the EU institutions should "make full use of" FRA's expertise in devising the EU's actions in the area of freedom, security, and justice and invited them "to consult, where appropriate, with the Agency, in line with its mandate, on the development of policies and legislation with implications for fundamental rights, and to use it for the communication to citizens of human rights issues affecting them in their everyday life" (Council of the European Union 2009, p. 12). This underlines the importance of sound evidence to inform the EU legislators and policymakers.

Just as the funding regulation explicitly requires for the Agency's annual Fundamental Rights Report, other FRA reports tend to highlight examples of good practice across all member states. Highlighting such examples is only possible after a process of horizontal monitoring among the EU member states. FRA reports normally cover all or most EU member states. So far, the Agency did not see any added value in providing country-by-country reports as is done by other actors (even if, admittedly, these reports tend to cover only a selection of states at a given moment of time). Only in exceptional cases of major fundamental rights, incident reports on a single country or two countries were published. This was, for instance, the case in 2013 when a report on Hungary and Greece was published (Fundamental Rights Agency 2013). The motivation was that at the time the two countries showed not only serious manifestations of violent racism and other forms of intolerance but also a substantial parliamentary representation of parties that used paramilitary tactics or were closely associated with paramilitary groups and used extremist rhetoric to target irregular migrants in Greece and the Roma and Jews in Hungary.

The Agency as a Communication Tool ("Multilogue" with Civil Society)

The Agency is to develop a communication strategy and promote dialogue with civil society. These tasks have the twofold aim of raising public awareness of fundamental rights and actively disseminating information about the Agency's work (Art. 4(1)(h) Founding Regulation). The Founding Regulation underlines that greater knowledge and broader awareness of fundamental rights issues are conducive to ensuring full respect for fundamental rights (Consideration No. 4 Founding Regulation). It is therefore the task of the Agency to raise awareness about fundamental rights mechanisms in broad terms (Consideration No. 15 Founding Regulation).

The Founding Regulation recognizes the important role of civil society in the protection of fundamental rights. It is therefore the task of the Agency to promote dialogue and work closely with nongovernmental organizations (NGOs). A permanent "structured and fruitful" dialogue is guaranteed through the creation of the Fundamental Rights Platform (FRP), allowing for close cooperation with all relevant stakeholders (Consideration No. 19 and Art. 10 Founding Regulation). The Founding Regulation enters innovative territory by underlining that one-way communication with civil society is not enough. In fact, the platform is an institutional expression of the Agency's need to obtain (at least) three types of input from civil society: first, planning input required to draft the Annual Work Program (Art. 10(4)(a) Founding Regulation); second, evaluation input required to gain feedback (Art. 10(4)(b) Founding Regulation) and thereby enabling the director (Art. 15(4)(f) and Art. 30(1) Founding Regulation) and the Management Board (Art. 12(6)(f) Founding Regulations) to ensure that the Agency performs the tasks entrusted to it; and third, information input, which allows the Agency to track the various developments on the ground (i.e., court decisions, employment situation, development in the social sector, news in academia, etc.) (Art. 10(4)(c) Founding Regulation).

With regard to the composition of the Fundamental Rights Platform, the Founding Regulation says that it should be composed of "non-governmental organisations dealing with human rights, trade unions and employers' organisations, relevant social and professional organisations, churches, religious, philosophical and non-confessional organisations, universities and other qualified experts of European and international bodies and organisations" (Art. 10(1) Founding Regulation). The platform should be inclusive and open to all these organizations that are "interested and qualified" (Art. 10(3) Founding Regulation). The regulation does not specify the selection process for participants nor the duration of their terms of participation. It leaves these decisions to the Agency's institutional practice which is characterized by openness. Whereas the Agency developed a code of conduct in the platform, membership remained open to all having a genuine interest in a constructive and fruitful dialogue. Only once an application to participate in the platform led to an exchange of arguments before the European Ombudsman with the latter concluding that the Agency had appropriate procedures in place and enjoyed a wide margin of appreciation. The Ombudsman confirmed that in carrying out the selection process the agency "acted lawfully, in accordance with principles of good administration, and did not commit a manifest error of appreciation" (European Ombudsman 2012, para 28).

The Agency reacts on feedback it receives and is currently reforming its engagement with civil society in order to make it more concrete and sector-specific. In 2017, it launched a call to civil society organizations to register in a database which will in the future allow for such cooperation. Over 500 organizations reacted to the call. Based on interviews with the respective civil society partners, the Fundamental Rights Platform was described as "the first semi-institutionalised civil society platform integrated into the work of EU governance institutions [which] undoubtedly changed the way participating CSOs interact with the Union, network with and learn from each other, and coordinate their input in cross-sectoral ways" (Thiel 2017, p. 159). The inspiring potential of the Agency's approach is also confirmed by the fact that the revision of the Founding Regulation of FRONTEX came along with the establishment of a "Consultative Forum" (Council Regulation (EC) No 2007/2004, p. 1) open to civil society organizations "promoting the respect of fundamental rights in the fields of border and migration management" (FRONTEX Management Board decision 2012). The European Asylum Support Office (EASO) also followed up and established a Consultative Forum aimed at maintaining "a close dialogue with relevant civil society organisations and relevant competent bodies operating in the field of asylum policy at local, regional, national, European or international level" (Art. 51 Regulation (EU) No 439/2010 of the European Parliament and of the Council of 19 May 2010 establishing a European Asylum Support Office).

Challenges Ahead

The Agency exists for over a decade. Its creation ended a situation where the EU was not equipped with an independent expert center dedicated to the protection and promotion of fundamental rights within the EU. External actors have acknowledged that the FRA became a relevant actor applying innovative methodologies and approaches in its largely appreciated work. The second independent external evaluation of the agency concluded on the basis of over 250 interviews with stakeholders that the agency's work adds value to the EU's fundamental rights landscape and that the quality of its outputs is undisputed (Optimity 2017).

But there is no room for complacency. The current fundamental rights situation within the European Union speaks for itself (Fundamental Rights Agency 2017): the need for an independent EU expert body to provide assistance and expertise to the EU and its member states persists. Data collection and analysis should continue to build on a socio-legal approach. The Agency should also continue to not only look at the duty bearer (the states and their laws and institutions) but also the rights holder (the individuals and their experiences on the ground). The Agency is hence likely to repeat past surveys among minority populations and launch a new Fundamental Rights Survey targeting the general population.

The Agency will also expand on its experience in developing indicators (especially in the areas of children rights, Roma integration, and the protection of persons with disabilities). The further development of indicators can help measuring the "outcome dimension" of human rights policies. This is increasingly important as progress on the UN Sustainable Development Goals or goals and policy cycles that are established in the framework of the EU's economic governance (such as the European Semester and Europe 2020) can only be properly assessed if appropriate indicators are available.

The experience of the first 10 years of the Agency's existence shows that rights-related challenges may arise at short notice. The recent migration situation put EU member states under unexpected levels of pressure. FRA provided hands-on assistance and expertise to relevant actors on the ground by engaging in the hotspots in

Greece. By focusing on practical issues such as how to apply child protection safeguards in guardianship systems for unaccompanied children (Fundamental Rights Agency 2017) and steps to reduce the risk of refoulement in external border management (Fundamental Rights Agency 2016a), FRA provided practical guidance to national actors on how to address fundamental rights issues in migration management. It will hence be important that the Agency preserves its ability to react at short notice and guarantees sufficient flexibility in its planning so to reshuffle resources where new needs arise.

The EU will continue to be very engaged in areas that are of utmost relevance for human rights such as criminal law or migration and asylum law. This speaks in favor of increasing the role of the Agency in the context of EU legislation so to allow the Agency to contribute more systematically to better lawmaking and the implementation of laws in the EU – in complete independence from the EU's political institutions and the EU member states. Currently, the area of data protection holds a privileged standing in this regard as the European Data Protection Officer is examining all relevant EU legislation, whereas the FRA, as the EU's expert body for all fundamental rights, is invited only on an ad hoc basis to examine legislative drafts in this area.

In terms of how best to promote and communicate rights, new challenges have arisen. Anti-human rights rhetoric is emerging, and rights are often misread as "political correctness" rather than legal obligations. If left unchecked, intolerant rhetoric in political discourse, disseminated through the media, can incite discrimination, hatred, or violence, as recent FRA contributions show (Fundamental Rights Agency 2016b). Human rights actors such as FRA have to address the mistrust of public institutions and perceived threats deriving from phenomena such as immigration or globalization. The Agency and others will have to more efficiently communicate the role of fundamental rights for everyone in the EU. A closer and more targeted cooperation with local institutions and civil society organizations will be helpful. The same goes for national actors in order for FRA to discuss and address specific human rights issues of particular national relevance, as the Agency has done, for example, regarding hate crime and Roma integration.

References

Aichele V (2003) Nationale Menschenrechtsinstitutionen: Ein Beitrag zur nationalen Implementierung der Menschenrechte. Peter Lang, Frankfurt
Alston P (1999) The EU and human rights. Oxford University Press, Oxford
Alston P, Weiler JHH (1999) An 'ever closer union' in need of a human rights policy: the European Union and human rights. In: Alston P (ed) The EU and human rights. Oxford University Press, Oxford, pp 3–66
Council of the European Union (2001) Conclusions of the 2362nd council meeting, 25 June 2001
Council of the European Union (2007) Regulation (EC) no 168/2007 of 15 February 2007 establishing a European Union agency for fundamental rights (founding regulation)
Council of the European Union (2009) The Stockholm programme – an open and secure Europe serving and protecting the citizens, 17024/09, 2 December 2009

Council of the European Union decision (EU) 2017/2269 of 7 December 2017 establishing a multiannual framework for the European Union agency for fundamental rights for 2018–2022

Council of the European Union document 6166/07

Council Regulation (EC) No. 1035/97 establishing a European monitoring centre on Racism and Xenophobia, OJ 1997 L 151, 10 June 1997

Council Regulation (EC) No 2007/2004 of 26 October 2004 establishing a European agency for the management of operation cooperation at the external borders of the Member States of the European Union OJ L 349, 25.11.2004, as last amended

European Commission COM (2001) 252 final as of 8 May 2001

European Commission COM (2003) 483 final of 5 August 2003

European Commission COM (2005) 280, Proposal for a council decision empowering the Agency "to pursue its activities in areas referred to in Title VI of the Treaty on the European Union"

European Ombudsman (2012) Decision closing the inquiry into complaint 565/2012/ER against the European Union agency for fundamental rights

European Parliament recommendation (2017) of the LIBE-committee on the draft council decision establishing a multiannual framework for the European Union agency for fundamental rights for 2018–2022, 2 May 2017

European Parliament resolution (2005) Promotion and protection of fundamental rights, 26 May 2005

European Parliament resolution (2009) on the situation of fundamental rights in the European Union 2004–2008, 14 January 2009

FRONTEX Management Board decision no 12/2012 of 23 May 2012

Fundamental Rights Agency (2013) Racism, discrimination, intolerance and extremism: learning from experiences in Greece and Hungary. Available at http://fra.europa.eu/en/publication/2013/racism-discrimination-intolerance-and-extremism-learning-experiences-greece-and. Accessed 17 Apr 2018

Fundamental Rights Agency (2014) Twelve operational fundamental rights considerations for law enforcement when processing passenger name records. Available at http://fra.europa.eu/en/news/2014/fra-provides-guidance-member-states-setting-national-pnr-systems. Accessed 17 Apr 2018

Fundamental Rights Agency (2016a) Guidance on how to reduce the risk of refoulement in external border management when working in or together with third countries. Available at http://fraeuropaeu/en/publication/2016/guidance-how-reduce-risk-refoulement-external-border-management-when-working-or Accessed 17 Apr 208

Fundamental Rights Agency (2016b) Incitement in media content and political discourse in EU member states. Contribution to the second annual colloquium on fundamental rights. Available at http://fra.europa.eu/en/publication/2016/incitement-media-content-and-political-discourse-member-states-european-union. Accessed 17 Apr 2018

Fundamental Rights Agency (2017) Between promise and delivery. Available at http://fra.europa.eu/en/publication/2017/between-promise-and-delivery 10-years-fundamental-rights-eu. Accessed 17 Apr 2018

Fyhr K (2016) Making fundamental rights a reality in EU legislative process. Dissertation at the University of Helsinki. Available at https://helda.helsinki.fi/bitstream/handle/10138/168098/MAKINGFU.pdf?sequence=1. Accessed 17 Apr 2018

Optimity (2017) 2nd independent external evaluation of the European Union agency for fundamental rights. http://ec.europa.eu/newsroom/just/document.cfm?doc_id=49324. Accessed 17 Apr 2018

Regulation (EU) No 439/2010 of the European Parliament and of the council of 19 May 2010 establishing a European Asylum Support Office, in OJ 2010 L 132, 29 May 2010

Thiel M (2017) European civil society and human rights advocacy. University of Pennsylvania Press, Philadelphia

Toggenburg G (2001) La crisi austriaca: delicati equilibrismi sospesi tra molte dimensioni. Diritto pubblico comparato ed europeo 2:735–756

Toggenburg G (2004) Minority protection and the enlarged European Union: the way forward. Open Society Institute, Budapest

Toggenburg G (2007) The EU fundamental rights agency: satellite or guiding star? SWP Comments 5. Available at http://www.swp-berlin.org/en/common/get_document.php?asset_id=3820. Accessed 17 Apr 2018

Toggenburg G (2008) The role of the new EU fundamental rights agency: debating the 'sex of angels' or improving Europe's human rights performance? ELR 3:385–398

Toggenburg G (2014) The EU fundamental rights agency and the fundamental rights charter: how fundamental is the link between them?. Peers St et al (eds) The EU Charter of Fundamental Rights, Hart Publishing Oxford: 1613–1626

Vienna Declaration and Programme of Action, Adopted 25 June 1993. Available at http://www.ohchr.org/EN/ProfessionalInterest/Pages/Vienna.aspx. Accessed 17 Apr 2018

The Inter-American Commission and Court of Human Rights

Veronica Gomez

Contents

A Long Look Back 462
Protective Measures and the Prevention of Serious Human Rights Violations 471
Local Review and Enforcement of States' Legal Obligations: Conventionality Control 472
A Brief Look Forward 474
References 476

Abstract

During six decades of regional supervision, the Inter/American Commission and Court of Human Rights have exercised their role as interpreters of the human rights instruments adopted by the member states of the Organization of American States, with some degree of healthy controversy. There has been much discussion on their understanding of the states' duty to prevent harm to individuals and communities at risk: the extent of reparations for material and nonmaterial damage caused by human rights violations including the obligation to investigate such violations, carry out prosecutions exhaustively and ensure non-repetition; and the extensive legal obligation of the judiciary and other domestic authorities to implement legal standards as interpreted by the Inter-American Court. With its idiosyncratic traditions and perspectives, the protection of human rights in the Americas is challenged by structural poverty, inequality, discrimination, violence, and weakness in the rule of law and by the remaining question on whether organs such as the Commission and Court are truly called or equipped to play a significant role in overcoming them.

V. Gomez (✉)
Centro Internacional de Estudios Politicos, Universidad Nacional de San Martin, Buenos Aires, Argentina
e-mail: vgomez@ciep.unsam.edu.ar

© Springer Nature Singapore Pte Ltd. 2018   461
G. Oberleitner (ed.), *International Human Rights Institutions, Tribunals, and Courts*,
International Human Rights, https://doi.org/10.1007/978-981-10-5206-4_17

Keywords

Organization of American States · Inter-American Commission on Human Rights · Inter-American Court of Human Rights · American Convention on Human Rights · Inter-American human rights instruments · Precautionary measures · Conventionality control · Reparations

A Long Look Back

It has been said that the history of a person starts before she or he is born. Likewise, an organ's purpose and principles are influenced by the aims and aspirations of pre-existing institutions and – in the world of international law and multilateralism – by those of the states that have created them. The current shape of regional promotion and protection of human rights in the Americas and its legacy and future challenges come into focus when considered in light of historic events and alliances.

As generally acknowledged, the course of destiny for the indigenous populations of what we now call the Americas was traumatically changed by discovery, conquest, and colonization by various European powers between the late fifteenth and eighteenth centuries. During approximately 300 years, extraneous political, social, and economic interests were imposed on them by force. The original inhabitants were subject to foreign legal systems and religious beliefs; their ancestral land was taken and used for the extraction of precious stones and metals, and the development of crops (sugarcane, among others, at that time) coveted by European consumers; and profits for the colonial powers and those acting on their behalf thanks to gracious concessions were maximized by the use of slave labor. As a consequence, in some portions of the continent, indigenous populations were either exterminated or subjugated, and in others African population was selectively introduced, discarded, and replaced through a vast machinery of slave trade.

In time, the ideals of the Enlightenment, the French revolution, and above all the geopolitical consequences of conflict in Europe led to the emergence of an independence movement, promoted in many cases by the population of European descent, born in the continent. Spearheaded by the US Declaration of Independence and Constitution in the late eighteenth century, this wave continued notably with the success of the 1804 Haitian slave revolt. The colonies of South America followed suit with a decade long war of independence against Spain that came to a close in 1820. A few years later, Portugal granted independence to its own large colony in the region.

Once independence was achieved in South America, disagreements in connection with the adoption of particular forms of political organization and government in many of the new states engendered internal conflicts that raged intermittently during the first half of the nineteenth century. In the second half of the century, a fairly solid agreement between the predominant social forces leads to the adoption of national constitutions mostly intended to consolidate economic development through national organization and republican models with executive power concentration in a normative pattern that for the most part has survived into the twenty-first century (Gargarella 2013, p. 6).

Also during the nineteenth century, Andrés Bello and Carlos Calvo emerged as two foundational figures of international law. In fact, Carlos Calvo was one of the first writers to use the term "Latin America" to highlight the new states' identification with the classic civilisations and the cultural influence of France while distancing them from the United States' aggressive interventionist policies (Obregon 2009, p. 94). These internationalists ignited a legal tradition with a distinctively regional point of view on the role of the law in balancing inequalities of power and wealth in international relations. In their view the foreign policy of the Latin American States should strategically rely on international law as a counterforce to the United States' imperialist streak in the region (Obregon 2004, p. 154). By the end of that century, in an era signalled by threats to political and economic independence of weaker postcolonial national states through gunboat diplomacy, Latin American countries took decisive steps toward promoting multilateralism and the development of international law. In particular, they championed a regional discourse on the international recognition of equality of jurisdiction over nationals and aliens (Obregon 2009, p. 95) in order to supersede military interventions frequently carried out by powerful states over peripheral ones on the pretext of the international protection of nationals abroad.

One of the earliest and more significant steps was taken in 1889 when Argentina, Bolivia, Brazil, Chile, Colombia, Costa Rica, Ecuador, El Salvador, Guatemala, Haiti, Honduras, Mexico, Nicaragua, Paraguay, Peru, Uruguay, and Venezuela accepted an invitation to gather with the United States in Washington DC. This so-called First Conference of American Republics became an opportunity to balance the terms of dialogue with the neighboring emerging global power. Its most enduring outcome was the creation of the so-called Commercial Bureau of American Republics, renamed as "International Bureau" in 1902, as "Union of American Republics" in 1910, and later as "Pan American Union." This organization – in time joined also by Cuba, Dominican Republic, and Panama – became a platform for the promotion of the codification and development of public and private international law and the establishment of institutions such as the enduring Inter-American Commission of Women that in 1928 catalyzed the first regional debates on women's political representation.

By the end of WWII, these states – receptors of millions of migrants fleeing conflict in Europe and also North Africa during the first half of the century – were at the forefront of the debate on the recognition of human rights in international law. In early 1945 they held an Inter-American Conference on Problems of War and Peace in Mexico, where they decided to draft a human rights treaty. This regional agenda on human rights – held in parallel with the Dumbarton Oaks drafting of the UN Charter – had a direct impact on the discussions at the San Francisco Conference where the Latin American States became the single largest regional group with 20 delegations out of 50. The documented outcome of their thrust is the inclusion of human rights protection as one of the purposes of the organization of the United Nations (Sikkink 2015, p. 210). Later, in December 1948, they would greatly influence the UN Universal Declaration on Human Rights by contributing two of the main drafts – prepared by Panama and Chile – and achieving the insertion of the rights to nondiscrimination and access to effective legal remedies, among other substantive contributions to the final text (Carozza 2003, p. 284).

Earlier, in April 1948, the Latin American States and the United States had already gathered in Bogota to hold the Ninth International Conference of American States where they transformed the previous Pan American arrangement into the regional political organization known today as the Organization of American States (OAS). The OAS Charter reflects the Latin American postcolonial ideals of an international order based on the respect of state sovereignty, territorial integrity, and independence, nonintervention in the affairs of other states, solidarity, the conduct of reciprocal relations pursuant to international law, and the protection of the fundamental rights of the individual without distinction as to race, nationality, creed, or gender. For its governance, the OAS chose to rely on a system of equal voting for all member states paired with a tradition of consensus decision-making. The Bogota Conference also adopted the American Declaration on the Rights and Duties of Man, the first international instrument of its kind to enshrine the recognition of civil, political, economic, social, and cultural rights.

After the adoption of the American Declaration, the Latin American impetus to further the development of international law in general and of international human rights law in particular declined in a geopolitical context increasingly dominated by the Cold War. Some states of the continent took sides in an ideological dispute ruled by alignments and nonalignments that at times made multilateral dialogue at the OAS irrelevant. As a consequence, the post WWII project of a regional system of protection based on a treaty – that had already come to fruition in Europe with the Convention for the Protection of Human Rights and Fundamental Freedoms – was de facto shelved for two decades.

Instead, progress was made through the flexible development of the cornerstone institution of human rights in the Americas: the Inter-American Commission on Human Rights (IACHR). The IACHR was established not by a treaty but by a precarious Resolution of the Fifth Meeting of Consultation of Ministers of Foreign Affairs, held in 1959 in Santiago de Chile, as a seven-member part-time body based at the headquarters of the OAS in Washington DC (OAS 1960, p. 5). The IACHR's 1960 Statute – drafted by the then OAS Council (today's General Assembly) – provided for a retrenching mandate: to make recommendations to member states "within the framework of their domestic law," verify information, prepare studies, and furnish advisory services to the OAS.

The IACHR was initially conceived and created as a follow-up mechanism on the situation in Cuba and therefore as a potential pawn in the vernacular version of the Cold War. Although it actively sought to initiate its on-site activities in that Island, the regime never granted permission for the visit. Soon in 1962 the Eighth Meeting of Consultation of Ministers of Foreign Affairs held in Montevideo excluded the Government of Cuba from participating in the political organs of the OAS. Despite this, Cuba was considered a member state subject to compliance with the standards in the American Declaration and to the IACHR's periodic reporting. After many decades of questionable ostracism, Cuba's exclusion from the OAS was finally lifted in 2009 (AG/RES. 2438 [XXXIX-O/09]), but the "too little, too late" multilateral gesture was snubbed with vocal disinterest in a return to the political organs of the Organization. Cuba is still a nonresponsive member of the OAS, and although the IACHR continues to monitor and report, its ambition to conduct an *in loco* observation in that country remains unfulfilled.

Instead of Cuba, the IACHR initiated its activities with a number of on-site observations in the Dominican Republic, starting in 1961, and it had a role overseeing the human rights situation during the 1965 revolution at the request of both the Government of National Reconstruction and the Constitutional Government (Reque 1973, p. 229). It also monitored the situation in Haiti, Guatemala, and Chile, among others. On the basis of these and other experiences in connection with on-site observations, the reception of spontaneous petitions from individuals, the mediation in conflicts, and the drafting of outcome reports on human rights situations, the IACHR fashioned early on a number of tools to conduct fact-finding missions, process individual complaints, reach friendly settlements, and publish country reports that today we take for granted. These were reflected in its 1965 Statute, explicitly providing for the functions of scrutinizing the observance of the American Declaration, of examining individual communications and to that effect requesting information from states and issuing recommendations, and of submitting reports to the political organs of the OAS. Another important milestone in the IACHR development was reached in 1967 with its inclusion in the OAS Charter as one of the main organs of the Organization, through the Protocol of Buenos Aires. This amendment, in force as from 1970, crystalized the mandate of the IACHR to promote and protect human rights *vis-à-vis* all member states of the OAS on the basis of the American Declaration as well as its role within the Organization itself.

In 1969 the OAS member states finally reached an agreement on a treaty-based human rights system. The Inter-American Human Rights Conference held in San Jose, Costa Rica, adopted the text of the American Convention on Human Rights with a catalogue of civil and political rights and a two-tier supervision mechanism – to some extent inspired in the European system of that time – involving the pre-existing IACHR as a quasi-judicial organ and an Inter-American Court of Human Rights (IACourtHR) as ultimate interpreter of the Convention with contentious and advisory jurisdiction. The adoption of the text, however, was not matched by the collective political will to realize the immediate entry into force of the Treaty that was delayed for another decade.

During the 1960s and 1970s, poverty, inequality, and political polarization lead to the emergence of revolutionary movements and guerrilla warfare in several countries of the region. With communism identified as a threat to national and regional security, the advent of the National Security Doctrine provided a framework for the intervention of the Armed Forces at all levels of society to preserve "Western civilization" values and consider groups or individuals who did not conform to this interpretation as enemies of the state. Among the countries of the region ruled either by military dictatorships or repressive regimes during that period were Paraguay (Alfredo Stroessner 1954–1989), Bolivia (Hugo Banzer 1971–1978), Chile

(Augusto Pinochet 1973–1990), Uruguay (Juan Maria Bordaberry 1973–1985), Argentina (National Reorganization Process 1976–1983), Nicaragua (the Somoza dynasty), El Salvador, Honduras, and Guatemala. With the suppression of democratic institutions, the fight against subversion both through military and clandestine methods – with collateral excuses for the repression of trade unions and other social expressions of dissent – turned into one of the most violent and darkest chapters in the history of the region involving extrajudicial executions, forced disappearances, indefinite detention, and torture (in many cases in secret locations) of political and social leaders and other individuals suspected of having a connection with them; the suppression of identity of children born in detention and given away to other families; acts of violence against entire rural or indigenous communities; permanent derogation of the rights to freedom of expression, information, and reunion and political participation; and the absence or limitation of due process guarantees.

It has been argued that this was one of the late 1970s regional contexts leading to the emergence of human rights activism both at the local and the international level that ignited the previously lethargic international supervision of human rights (Moyn 2010, p. 121). With domestic constitutional rights and guarantees suppressed and a judiciary either complicit or under threat, a growing number of organizations were created by the victims' family members and by individual members of the Catholic Church across the region, seeking to be heard beyond borders. Their call was amplified by the emerging international nongovernmental organizations – some of them based in the United States – that in turn galvanized the attention of the international community.

During the early seventies, there was little incentive for repressive regimes to consent to treaties establishing the obligation to respect and ensure the rights to life, physical integrity, reunion, expression, and effective judicial protection, among others. During 1977 and 1978, however, an important number of states ratified the American Convention due to international pressure. First among those exerting pressure was the Carter Administration in the United States. Although the military regimes in Argentina, Brazil, Chile, Paraguay, and Uruguay resisted international pressure, by 1978 the treaty finally entered into force prompting the birth of the IACourtHR, as a part-time seven-member body based in San José, Costa Rica.

As with other newly established courts, the IACourtHR would only yield judgments in later years. A number of states had chosen not to deposit the optional clause on acceptance of its contentious jurisdiction, and those who had consented to it were for some time exempt on a case-by-case basis due to the intricacies of jurisdiction *ratione temporis*. Thus, at the time, the Regional Protection System relied more than ever on the IACHR for whom the OAS member states adopted a new Statute in 1979. The Statute equipped the IACHR with a double mandate in connection with the member states that had ratified the American Convention and with those that had not, on the basis of the same procedure for the study of individual petitions and monitoring of general situations and the same outcome in terms of recommendations, reporting, publicity, and follow-up. The only distinction between the two mandates was – and still is – the possibility of referring to the IACourtHR cases on the responsibility of states that have ratified the Convention and deposited the optional clause whenever they fail to comply with the recommendations issued by the IACHR.

The IACHR mandate became particularly relevant in connection with the large number of states ratifying the OAS Charter between the late 1960s and the early 1990s, including 11 newly independent English-speaking nations from the Caribbean (Antigua and Barbuda, Bahamas, Barbados, Belize, Dominica, Grenada, Jamaica, Saint Lucia, Saint Kitts and Nevis, Saint Vincent and the Grenadines, and Trinidad and Tobago), Suriname, Guyana, and Canada. These ratifications largely expanded the membership of the Organization from the original 21 member states to 35, although recently Venezuela – that had previously denounced the American Convention – in the midst of a serious political crisis took steps to denounce the OAS Charter as well. The expansion in membership enriched the Organization's cultural, legal, and diplomatic diversity while undeniably modifying the subregional balance of the one country one vote decision-making that is relevant – for instance – for the election of commissioners and judges. The expansion also balanced the faded Latin American idealism on the positive influence of international law with the new members' strong skepticism over the value of regional protection of human rights. Only Barbados, Dominica, Jamaica, Suriname, and Trinidad and Tobago would eventually ratify the American Convention, and in the case of Trinidad and Tobago, ratification was followed by denunciation in 1998 as soon as the IACHR and the IACourtHR scrutinized the mandatory application of the death penalty in that country in light of international standards (Tittemore 2004, p. 474; I/A Court H.R. 2002). For these states, including the United States and Canada, the 1948 American Declaration – in conjunction with the Charter of the Organization – remained as the only source of legal obligations (I/A Court H.R. 1989, para. 43), under the scrutiny of the IACHR on the basis of the 1979 Statute.

During the late 1970s and the 1980s, the IACHR fulfilled an important role documenting serious human rights violations in the Southern Cone and Central America, receiving and processing complaints filed by individuals and organizations, and bringing attention to the situation and the responsibility of oppressive regimes. In addition to the double mandate to process complaints under the Declaration and the Convention, the 1979 Statute and the 1980 Regulations included invaluable tools for the task at hand, such as a tried and tested protocol on the conduction of on-site observations; the competence to receive and process complaints filed by individuals, groups of individuals, and organizations on their own behalf or on behalf of other persons, victims many times disappeared or held in incommunicado detention; the competence to initiate the processing of a petition motu proprio (in cases where expecting a petition was unrealistic due to death, disappearance, and insecurity for any survivors); and the competence to issue precautionary measures in urgent cases involving risk of irreparable harm to persons. During this period, the IACHR conducted several visits – during which it received thousands of complaints – and issued historic reports on the situation in Argentina, Bolivia, Colombia, Cuba, Chile, El Salvador, Guatemala, Haiti, Paraguay, Panama, Suriname, and Uruguay, among others.

With the slow reemergence of the rule of law in the region as from the mid-1980s, the IACHR accompanied the process of transition to democracy. It eloquently stressed the relationship between the effective exercise of democracy and the full observance of human rights in its reports (IACHR 1986). At this time, the OAS member states strengthened this principle in the OAS Charter – from then on establishing a mechanism for the suspension of member states with nondemocratic governments – and further reinforced it by adopting the 2001 Inter-American Democratic Charter.

In the early 1980s, the IACHR referred the first group of individual cases relating to forced disappearances in Honduras to the jurisdiction of the IACourtHR. In its first judgment on the merits in the *Velásquez Rodríguez Case v. Honduras* (I/A Court H.R. 1988), the IACourtHR defined forced disappearance as a continuous violation of various rights, including personal liberty, humane treatment, life, and the recognition as a person before the law. It explained that victims' disappearances begin with their deprivation of liberty and the subsequent failure to provide information as to their whereabouts and continues for so long as their whereabouts have not been established or the remains identified. The judgment established that states have the duty to conduct investigations ex officio to establish the whereabouts of forcibly disappeared victims, in order to establish the truth of what happened. It acknowledged the victims' families right to know the truth of what happened to their loved ones and the state's obligation to provide simple and effective remedies to ensure compliance with its duty. These findings on the extent of state responsibility – for a conduct that, due to its complexity, at the time was not contemplated in domestic legislations – were momentous for the development of the regional protection of human rights. They would become the basis for the 1994 Inter-American Convention on Forced Disappearance of Persons, and eventually they would inform changes in domestic legislation in several states of the region.

In parallel with its vision of democracy and human rights, during the 1980s and 1990s, the IACHR supported the victims' demands for justice for the serious crimes perpetrated during the years of the dictatorships and the authoritarian regimes. The IACHR did so by drawing principles on truth, justice, and reparations both in its general and country reports and in its growing number of individual cases. The emphasis on the incompatibility of Amnesty Laws and Military Justice with the American Declaration and Convention when used to impede the investigation of human rights violations became a significant contribution to transitional justice worldwide. These arguments were first tested before the IACourtHR in the *Barrios Altos Case v. Peru* (I/A Court H.R. 2001a) in connection with crimes perpetrated during the government of Alberto Fujimori. The judgment states that amnesty provisions, statutes of limitations, and the exclusion of responsibility seeking to impede the investigation and punishment of serious human rights violations such as torture, summary executions, and forced disappearances – contravening non-derogable rights recognized by the international law of human rights – are incompatible with the American Convention and therefore are prohibited. The IACourtHR found that due to this incompatibility the self-amnesty adopted to impede criminal investigations in the case lacked legal effect and could not pose an obstacle to the prosecution of those responsible for perpetrating crimes. This decision became the legal basis for the judicial decisions that eventually made possible the extradition, prosecution, and conviction in Peru of former President Alberto Fujimori, in 2009.

During the 1990s, the examination of cases involving Suriname, Peru, Colombia, Nicaragua, and Venezuela before the IACourtHR exposed shortcomings in the language and mechanism established in the American Convention for the referral and litigation of contentious cases. The IACHR's conventional role in the selection of cases for referral and its mandatory appearance in Costa Rica on behalf of the victims – instead of the victims appearing on their own behalf – came into focus as a legal deficiency in terms of due process guarantees for the victims and their families. Instead of pushing for the amendment of the American Convention, the IACHR and the IACourtHR addressed these issues by amending their respective Rules of Procedure in 2001. These amendments ensured the referral to the IACourtHR of all cases where states failed to comply with the recommendations issued by the IACHR and secured the *locus standi* of the victims and their families during all procedural stages before the Court.

In the late 1990s and the years that followed, the IACHR concentrated on the processing of individual cases. The monitoring of the effects of the internal armed conflict in Colombia in the civilian population – in particular in connection with internal displacement and the situation of indigenous communities, Afro-descendant populations, and human rights defenders – was followed by a large number of protective measures and a set of important judgments on state responsibility for the crimes of paramilitary groups (I/A Court H.R. 2006a). During this period, the IACHR further developed its interpretation on the violation of the American Declaration due to the application of the death penalty in the United States, and also an important number of cases on the mandatory application of the death penalty in the Caribbean were referred to the IACourtHR (Tittemore 2004; IACHR 2011). It was also at this time that the IACourtHR heard its first case on indigenous rights (I/A Court H.R. 2001b).

The entry into force of the Convention on the Prevention, Punishment and Eradication of Violence against Women (Belem do Para) in 1995 and the San Salvador Protocol on Economic, Social and Cultural Rights in 1999 enhanced the available tools to promote and protect equality through litigation and monitoring. At that time, the IACHR turned its attention to standard setting through thematic Rapporteurships. The first Rapporteurships were mandated to promote standards on gender equality (notably with Commissioner Claudio Grossman as its first Expert), indigenous peoples, and freedom of expression. Member states – now represented by democratic governments that clamored for an emphasis on human rights promotion rather than on human rights scrutiny though individual cases – favored this trend. In response, the IACHR was emphatic about a human rights promotion strategy that far from relegating litigation of individual cases relied on a holistic view of the advisory and the quasi-judicial mandates as complementary. In any case, the new Rapporteurships required material support for their functioning.

Since its inception, the IACHR was funded from the budget of the OAS, but the incremental growth in its work was not accompanied by a proportional provision of human and material resources. The thematic expansion further exposed the material challenges faced by the part-time and ill resourced IACHR to carry out its ever-increasing mandates. As from the late 1990s, the IACHR – as other human rights governmental and nongovernmental bodies – chose to rely on international cooperation to supplement the resources needed for observation and dissemination. Thanks to that support, thematic Rapporteurships continued to expand significantly during the following decades to cover the rights of children; migrants; Afro-descendants; persons deprived of their liberty; human rights defenders; lesbian, gay, bisexual, trans, and intersex persons; as well as economic, social, cultural, and environmental rights. In some cases, the sustainability of the thematic threads has occasionally been in financial peril; in others, the member states themselves have questioned the fundraising agenda of the IACHR as well as the donors' and the consequent emphasis on certain themes (IIDH 2012). Despite these challenges, the IACHR has continued with its sui generis mandate, and in 2017 the OAS General Assembly decided to double the budget of both organs of human rights protection in an unequivocal gesture of support.

It has been noted that in recent years, the system – without neglecting its follow-up on accountability and reparations of massive human rights violations of non-derogable rights – is shifting its interest toward structural inequality and its impact on the enjoyment of rights (Abramovich 2009, p. 12). Arguably, the shift is palpable not only in the IACHR agenda but also in that of the IACourtHR with the – long awaited – diversification of its portfolio in the direction of nondiscrimination (I/A Court H.R. 2012), indigenous rights (I/A Court H.R. 2007), gender issues (I/A Court H.R. 2009), and access to health (I/A Court H.R. 2015), with a focus on economic, social, and cultural rights in connection with previously marginalized groups (I/A Court H.R. 2006b).

It is indeed appropriate that after an infancy threatened and distracted by the Cold War and the growing pains of the violent authoritarianism of the seventies and eighties, these organs finally engage the true face of the continent and its complex vital needs, born out of a history of inequality, that will not be resolved on the basis of the mere redistribution of rights (Beloff and Clerico 2016, p. 169). Centuries later, the early protagonists of the story – indigenous peoples and Afro-descendants – are once more center stage in a debate involving economic, social, cultural, and environmental tensions and contradictions.

Among the contributions made by the IACHR and the IACourtHR through their resolutions, reports, judgments, and advisory opinions during six decades of work, there are two legal vehicles of interest as special developments in the international protection of human rights: the mechanism for prevention of imminent human rights violations and the doctrine on local review and enforcement of states' legal obligations in light of regional instruments and their authorized interpretation. These strategies appear as idiosyncratic responses to current threats to basic rights and to structural deficiencies, and – although their intensity may vary in light of composition and context – they tend to defy the conventional (without capital) legal tools of international protection of human rights.

Protective Measures and the Prevention of Serious Human Rights Violations

One of the more audacious tools developed in the Inter-American System is the broad interpretation of the mandate to request or order measures to prevent imminent irreparable harm to persons through precautionary measures granted by the IACHR and provisional measures ordered by the IACourtHR.

In 1980 the IACHR decided to introduce the request of precautionary measures in situations of imminent danger of irreparable harm to persons in its new Rules of Procedure as a solution to the absence of mechanisms to prevent the consummation of violations of the rights to life and physical integrity that could not be adequately addressed through the study of individual complaints, on-site visits, or general recommendations. The idea of measures for cases of "extreme gravity and urgency...necessary to avoid irreparable damage to persons" had been introduced in Article 63.2 of the American Convention in the shape of provisional measures issued by the IACourtHR in pending cases or at the request of the IACHR. Thus, the entry into force of the Convention and the somewhat vague language of Article 63.2 provided a cue for the development of a flexible protective mechanism that the IACHR had been considering on the basis of its experience with human rights monitoring on the ground and its contact with the incipient community of human rights organizations in the region.

As is the case with other international treaty bodies, precautionary and provisional measures may be invoked as injunctions to preserve either the Commission's or the Court's jurisdiction *vis-à-vis* an imminent change of circumstance that might affect a claim pending before them. But precautionary measures can also be invoked as urgent protective measures to prevent irreparable harm to persons under the jurisdiction of any OAS member state where a violation of the American Convention, the Declaration, or other Inter-American instrument might be imminent, and there is still no claim pending before the organs of the system.

The mechanism is frequently invoked to protect the lives of human rights defenders in the broadest sense (activists, trade union leaders, victims or their families pursing a claim for justice) who are under threat. There are also numerous examples of members of the judiciary and civil servants requesting precautionary measures as protection from retaliation in response of their human rights-related work.

In other areas precautionary and provisional measures have been invoked, *inter alia*, to ensure access to humanitarian aid by indigenous and Afro-descendant communities suffering the impact of forced displacement from their ancestral lands or communal territories (I/A Court H.R. 2005). They have also been invoked to protect communities afflicted by environmental hazards and to ensure access to health services (IACHR 2004, para. 44). Between 1999 and 2002, the IACHR granted precautionary measures to ensure that states that did not offer universal diagnosis and/or treatment to patients infected with HIV/AIDS through their respective national health services (Chile, El Salvador, Bolivia, Ecuador, Guatemala,

Honduras, Nicaragua, Peru, Dominican Republic, and Venezuela) adopt positive measures to provide medical attention and access to antiretroviral medications to patients pursuant to the standards established by the Pan American Health Organization.

These measures have also been granted to ensure that states comply with their duty to provide medical treatment to persons in custody, whenever their condition – if untreated – could generate irreparable harm to health. The Commission and the Court have also ordered the adoption of measures to improve sanitation in penitentiaries, detention centers for adults, rehabilitation centers for children, and police stations whenever conditions of detention could cause harm to the health of the detainees (I/A Court H.R. 2004). They have also been issued in connection with the situation of patients at mental health facilities where children were held together with adults; individuals were held for years in solitary confinement; and poor sanitation posed a threat to health (IACHR 2003, para. 60). Precautionary measures have also been used to follow up on the right to physical integrity and due process of persons held in *incommunicado* detention, as it was the case with the detainees in the United States military base at Guantanamo Bay (IACHR 2015).

The IACHR has justified the legal validity of precautionary measures on the basis of the general duty of the states to respect and ensure human rights, to adopt legislative or other measures necessary for the effective observance of human rights, and to carry out their obligations under the American Convention and the OAS Charter in good faith (IACHR 2006, para 241). Over time, the mechanism has gained institutional recognition at the governmental, judicial, and legislative levels. For instance, the Constitutional Court of Colombia and other lower courts issued a number of decisions ordering sanctions against officials for failing to comply with precautionary and provisional measures, on the basis of the state's obligation to ensure respect for the rights protected in Article 1.1 of the American Convention (Corte Constitucional – Colombia 2003). At the legislative level, Law No. 23506 "On Habeas Corpus and *Amparo*" adopted in Peru acknowledges the right to appeal to the IACHR to seek remedies in cases of a threat to constitutional rights (Articles 2 and 39).

Since the mechanism was first incorporated into the Rules of Procedure in 1980, the Commission has issued over a thousand precautionary measures. Although in statistical terms the number of measures granted per year is much lower than in previous decades *vis-à-vis* the significant increase in the number of requests, these protective measures remain a viable mechanism for the prevention of harm to individuals and communities at risk in the entire region.

Local Review and Enforcement of States' Legal Obligations: Conventionality Control

The return of many countries of the region to democracy in the 1980s and 1990s marked a propitious moment for constitutional amendments ensuring the integration of human rights treaties into domestic legal orders – in several cases at the same level as the constitution itself – in an era that saw the expansion and strengthening of international supervision. At the time, supreme and constitutional courts were receptive to this integration between international and domestic law (Corte Suprema de Justicia de la Nación – Argentina 2004).

In this context, the IACourtHR called upon national judges and other authorities to adjust the interpretation of domestic law on a case-by-case basis to make it compatible with international obligations. This appeal was first articulated in the judgment *Almonacid Arellano v. Chile* establishing that domestic judges and courts are bound to apply the provisions in force within the legal system, including the American Convention, and that they must exercise a "conventionality control" of domestic legal provisions applied to specific cases, in light of the Convention and the interpretation thereof as issued by the IACourtHR as ultimate interpreter of the Treaty (I/A Court H. R. 2006c, para. 124).

Since then, the IACourtHR has refined the content and scope of the concept of conventionality control. It has clarified that its purpose consists of verifying the compatibility of domestic norms and practices with the American Convention, other applicable Inter-American treaties, and the IACourtHR's judgments; that this control is an obligation that must be discharged ex officio by all public authorities when exercising their competence; and that the control may involve either the suppression or the reinterpretation of norms and practices incompatible with the Inter-American treaties, subject to the competences of each public authority. In other words, conventionality control does not necessarily involve legislative amendment. In theory, it could be satisfied through substantive reinterpretation of constitutional, legal, or infra-legal standards in light of Inter-American human rights treaties and decisions (I/A Court H.R. 2012).

Since its initial articulation in 2006 and further development, conventionality control has been introduced as an expectation on domestic authorities. The expected outcome being that "unconventional" norms or practices will be disregarded or repealed in a manner that will avoid international responsibility for actions or omissions of the branches of government while ensuring the protection of the minimum standards enshrined in Inter-American human rights instruments.

It has been pointed out that there is no universally accepted conception of conventionality control, its consequences, the manner of exercise by the subjects empowered to apply it, or the circumstances in which it should be exercised (Garcia Ramirez 2015, p. 149). There is no denying that the IACourtHR's appeal for conventionality control by domestic institutions is ambitious in the decentralization of its scope and challenging in the potential (dis)harmoniousness of its effect. But despite this, it is a vote of trust and an acknowledgment that ultimately, beyond the minimum core in human rights treaties, the fundamental rights of the individual are dependent on the domestic legal order and authority (Nogueira 2013, p. 547).

Conventionality control is a paradox of subsidiarity, where the empowerment of local judges and authorities is alternatively loosely knotted to the tides of interpretation in supranational shores or uncomfortably linked to ill-tempered disagreements on legal alternatives for compliance with judgments in specific cases (I/A Court

H.R. 2011 and *Corte Suprema* – Argentina 2017). Still, conventionality control has been for the most part embraced as part of what the IACourtHR has called the "judicial dialogue" with the administrations of justice in the countries of the region. There is little doubt that the dialogue on standards and obligations is essential for the engagement of domestic legal orders as an avenue for access to justice for the individuals protected under the system.

A Brief Look Forward

The organs of protection of the Inter-American System face a number of substantive and institutional challenges. The main substantive human rights challenges faced by the region are structural inequalities and deficiencies in access to justice. Both of them are connected by the cross-cutting theme of poverty.

In 2016 there were 186 million poor in Latin America, representing 30.7% of the population, with 61 million people – 10% of the population – living in extreme poverty. These figures reflect a reversal of the previous trend – experienced between 2002 and 2014 – where poverty and extreme poverty had decreased (ECLAC 2017, p. 80). The so-called vulnerable sector – the sector most likely to fall into poverty – continues to be the largest population group in Latin American and the Caribbean, with the middle class no longer projected to become the largest group in the near future (World Bank 2016).

Poverty seems to hold the keys of the past and the future. For a very long time, it enabled structural inequality – the second challenge of the region – and made vulnerable and historically marginalized groups invisible to society, politics, economy, and international relations. As to the future, children are overrepresented in the total number of people living in poverty: 47 out of every 100 children under 15 are poor, and 17 of them live in extreme poverty (ECLAC 2017, p. 90), a situation that compromises their personal development and in the long run the chances of development of the region itself.

The human rights system is no longer neutral to this scenario and to the fact that poverty has a negative impact in the enjoyment of all human rights. Recently, the IACHR started addressing poverty with a human rights approach as a thematic thread (IACHR 2017), and it established a full-time Special Rapporteur for Economic, Social, Cultural and Environmental Rights. It also works together with the Working Group on the Protocol of San Salvador in the design of indicators, data collection, and more recently in the national progress reports on economic, social, and cultural rights. The question is whether these assessments might eventually yield a fresh approach to address the responsibility of states and private actors and their constructive role in the sustainable improvement of the living conditions in the region for an important part of the population and their right to a dignified existence (I/A Court H.R. 1999, para.144).

A third challenge – also interconnected with poverty and inequality – is that of access to justice in a context of serious deficiencies in the administration of justice, impunity, corruption, and violence. The IACHR and the IACourtHR have already conceptualized this challenges as well as the differentiated obstacles that some collectives face when seeking redress for their rights or facing scrutiny.

During the last decades, the most frequent type of supervision that the IACHR and the IACourtHR have been called to make is that of reviewing the actions and omissions of the organs in charge of the administration of justice at the domestic level. In a large majority of cases, their international review has not focused on the final outcome of the domestic judicial activity – the compatibility of a final decision with the American Declaration, Convention, or other Inter-American treaty – but rather on the absence of results in the judicial investigation of serious violations of the rights to life, physical integrity, and liberty, among others, directly or indirectly attributable to state agents or to private parties. Those claims have tended to be admissible via the exceptions to the rule on prior exhaustion of domestic remedies, and the findings on the merits have tended to gravitate toward the incompatibility of the means used in the criminal investigation or civil and administrative proceedings with the obligations to ensure access to an effective remedy and due process of law.

Merits of each case aside, it has been argued that the IACHR and the IACourtHR have hesitated to defer to domestic judicial institutions due to the limited capacities of these agencies to protect human rights at the local level, and that the tendency places the Inter-American organs at risk of substituting domestic authorities in their appreciation of the more material aspects of individual claims, in tension with the principle of subsidiarity (Duhaime 2014, p. 314). It is clear that while domestic agencies in Latin America and the Caribbean may be ill equipped to arbitrate the necessary means to ensure access to justice pursuant to due process in individual cases at the local level, the Inter-American System has limited means at its disposal to ensure access to redress to all affected individuals, at the regional level. A fresh approach on the part of the IACHR, the IACourtHR, and the OAS member states is probably due in order to reinfuse the responsiveness of regional supervision in the Americas in accordance with the needs of the individuals and communities under its protection, with an emphasis on a greater impact on policy making.

As far as institutional challenges are concerned, the IACHR and the IACourtHR are not immune to a certain climate of social skepticism surrounding human rights, felt also at the global level. This sort of climate can sometimes permeate national institutions and have an impact in their conduct at the international level. There is also the unprecedented denunciation of the American Convention and the OAS Charter by Venezuela – a founding member of the 1889 Bureau of American Republics and the OAS. The denunciation is probably a metaphor for the current isolation of one of the historical pillars of the regional community.

Despite this, the IACHR and the IACourtHR seem resolute to enhance their dialogue with civil society – in particular with groups and collectives historically excluded (IACHR 2017b) – and with domestic institutions in order to draw an agenda that is relevant to the structural challenges faced in the Americas.

References

Abramovich V (2009) De las violaciones masivas a los patrones estructurales: nuevos enfoques y clásicas tensiones en el. Sistema Interamericano de Derechos Humanos Sur 6(11):7–39

Beloff M, Clérico L (2016) Derecho a condiciones de existencia digna y situación de vulnerabilidad en la jurisprudencia de la Corte Interamericana. Estudios Constitucionales 14(1):139–178

Carozza P (2003) From conquest to constitutions: retrieving a Latin American tradition of the idea of human rights. Hum Rights Q 25(2):281–313

Corte Constitucional – Colombia (2003) Decision T-558/03 (Caso T-719935) Tutela Matilde Velásquez Restrepo c. Ministerio de Relaciones Exteriores y Ministerio del Interior, 10 de juio de 2003

Corte Suprema de Justicia de la Nación – Argentina (2004), (Expediente 224. XXXIX), "Espósito, Miguel Angel s/incidente de prescripción de la acción penal promovido por su defensa", 23 de diciembre de 2004, considerando 6

Corte Suprema de Justicia de la Nacion – Argentina (2017) SJ368/1998(34-M)/CS1 Ministerio de Relaciones Exteriores y Culto s/informe sentencia dictada en el caso Fontevecchia y D'Amico vs. Argentina por la Corte Interamericana de Derechos Humanos, febrero 2017

Duhaime B (2014) Subsidiarity in the Americas. What room is there for deference in the inter-America system? In: Gruszczynsky L, Werner W (eds) Deference in international courts and tribunals. Oxford University Press, Oxford

ECLAC (2017) Social panorama of Latin America 2017. ECLAC, Santiago de Chile

García Ramírez S (2015) The relationship between inter-American jurisdiction and states (national systems): some pertinent questions. Notre Dame J Int Comp Law 5(1):115–152

Gargarella R (2013) Latin American constitutionalism 1810–2010: the engine room of the constitution. Oxford University Press, New York

I/A Court H.R. (1988) Case of Velásquez Rodríguez v. Honduras. Merits. Judgment of July 29, 1988. Series C no. 4

I/A Court H.R. (1989) Interpretation of the American declaration of the rights and duties of man within the framework of article 64 of the American convention on human rights, advisory opinion OC10/89, opinion of July 14, 1898. Series A no 10

I/A Court H.R. (1999) Case of the street children (Villagran Morales et al.) v. Guatemala. Merits. Judgment November 19, 1999. Series C no. 63

I/A Court H.R. (2001a) Case of Barrios Altos v. Peru. Merits. Judgment March 14, 2001. Series C no. 75

I/A Court H.R. (2001b) Case of the Mayagna (sumo) Awas Tingni community v. Nicaragua. Merits, reparations and costs. Judgment of August 31, 2001. Series C no. 79

I/A Court H.R. (2002) Case of Hilaire, Constantine and Benjamin et al. v. Trinidad and Tobago. Merits, reparations and costs. Judgment of June 21, 2002. Series C no. 94

I/A Court H.R. (2004) Matter of the Mendoza prisons regarding Argentina. Provisional measures. Order of the inter-American court of human rights of November 22, 2004 (only in Spanish)

I/A Court H.R. (2005) Matter of the communities of Jiguamiandó and Curvaradó regarding Colombia. Provisional measures. Order of the inter-American court of human rights of march 15, 2005 (only in Spanish)

I/A Court H.R. (2006a) Case of the pueblo Bello massacre v. Colombia. Merits, reparations and costs. Judgment of January 31, 2006. Series C no. 140

I/A Court H.R. (2006b) Case of the Sawhoyamaxa indigenous community v. Paraguay. Merits, reparations and costs. Judgment of March 29, 2006. Series C no. 146

I/A Court H.R. (2006c) Case of Almonacid Arellano et al. v. Chile. Preliminary objections, merits, reparations and costs. Judgment of September 26, 2006. Series C no. 154

I/A Court H.R. (2007) Case of the Saramaka people. v. Suriname. Preliminary objections, merits, reparations, and costs. Judgment of November 28, 2007 Series C no. 172

I/A Court H.R. (2009) Case of González et al. ("cotton field") v. Mexico. Preliminary objection, merits, reparations and costs. Judgment of November 16, 2009. Series C no. 205

I/A Court H.R. (2011) Case of Fontevecchia and D'Amico v. Argentina. Merits, reparations and costs. Judgment of November 29, 2011. Series C no. 238

I/A Court H.R. (2012) Case of Atala Riffo and daughters v. Chile. Merits, reparations and costs. Judgment of February 24, 2012. Series C no. 239

I/A Court H.R. (2015) Case of Gonzales Lluy et al. v. Ecuador. Preliminary objections, merits, reparations and costs. Judgment of September 1, 2015. Series C no. 298

IACHR (1986) IACHR, annual report of the inter-American commission on human rights 1985–1986, OEA/SerL/V/II68, Doc 8 rev 1, 26 September 1986, Chapter V

IACHR (2003) Annual report of the IACHR 2003 OEA/Ser.L/V/II. 118 Doc. 5 rev. 2, 29 December 2003, Chapter III, section C.1

IACHR (2004) Annual report of the IACHR 2004 OEA/Ser.L/V/II.122 Doc. 5 rev. 1, 23 February 2005, Chapter III, section C.1

IACHR (2006) Report on the situation of human rights defenders in the Americas, OEA/Ser.L/V/II.124 Doc. 5 rev.1

IACHR (2011) The death penalty in the inter-American human rights system: from restrictions to abolition OEA/Ser.L/V/II. Doc. 68 31 December 2011

IACHR (2015) Towards the closure of Guantanamo Bay OAS/Ser.L/V/II. Doc. 20/15 3 June 2015

IACHR (2017a) Report on poverty and human rights in the Americas OEA/Ser.L/V/II.164 Doc, 7 September 2017

IACHR (2017b) IACHR strategic plan 2017–2021 OEA/Ser.L/V/II.161Doc. 27/17 20 March 2017

IIDH (2012) Proceso de Fortalecimiento del Sistema Interamericano de Derechos Humanos Contexto histórico y politico. Available at http://www.oas.org/es/cidh/consulta/docs/contexto_historico_y_politico_del_sidh_2012_cidh.pdf. Accessed 12 Apr 2018

Moyn S (2010) The last utopia. Harvard University Press, Cambridge, MA

Nogueira H (2013) El Control del Convencionalidad y el dialogo interjurisdiccional entre tribunales nacionales y la Corte Interamericana de Derechos Humanos. Anuario de Derecho Constitucional Latinoamericano XIX:511–553

OAS (1960) Final act of the fifth meeting of consultation of ministers of foreign affairs, Santiago, Chile, August 12–18, 1959. OAS official records, OEA/SerC/II5:11

Obregon L (2004) The colluding worlds of the lawyer, the scholar and the policymaker: a view of international law from Latin America. Wisconsin Int Law J 23(1):145–172

Obregon L (2009) The universal declaration of human rights and Latin America. Md J Int'l L 24:94–98

Reque L (1973) The Organization of American States and the protection of human rights. In: Inter-American yearbook on human rights 1968. OAS General Secretariat, Washington, DC, pp 220–234

Sikkink K (2015) Latin America's protagonist role in human rights. Sur Int J Hum Rights 12 (22):207–219

Tittemore B (2004) The mandatory death penalty in the commonwealth Caribbean and the inter-American human rights system: an evolution in the development and implementation of international human rights protections. William Mary Bill Rights J 13(2):445–520

World Bank (2016) Poverty and inequality and monitoring Latin America and the Caribbean: a slowdown on social gains. Available at http://pubdocs.worldbank.org/en/797001460055022577/A-Slowdown-in-Social-Gains-LAC-Poverty-Inequality-Monitoring-April-2016.pdf. Accessed 12 Apr 2018

The African Commission and Court on Human and Peoples' Rights

Manisuli Ssenyonjo

Contents

Introduction 480
African Commission on Human and Peoples' Rights: Background and Context 482
Decisions on the Exhaustion of Domestic Remedies 483
Decisions on Communications on Merits 485
Adoption of Resolutions, Principles/Guidelines, General Comments, Model Laws, and
Advisory Opinions 493
Special Rapporteurs, Working Groups, and Committees 497
Consideration of State Reports 498
African Court on Human and Peoples' Rights 498
Direct Access to the African Court by Individuals and NGOs 500
Indirect Access to the African Court Through the African Commission's Referral of
Communications to the African Court 504
Referral of Noncompliance or Unwillingness to Comply with the Commission's
Recommendations 504
Referral of Noncompliance with the Commission's Request for Provisional (Interim)
Measures 505
Referral of Serious or Massive Violations of Human Rights 506
Referral at "Any Stage of the Examination of a Communication" 506
Conclusion 506
References 508

Abstract

This chapter examines the contribution of the African Commission on Human
and Peoples' Rights (1987–2018) and the African Court on Human and Peoples'
Rights (2006–2018) to the protection of human rights and the development of
international human rights law. The focus of the chapter is limited to the

M. Ssenyonjo (✉)
Brunel Law School, Brunel University London, London, UK
e-mail: manisuli.ssenyonjo@brunel.ac.uk

© Springer Nature Singapore Pte Ltd. 2018
G. Oberleitner (ed.), *International Human Rights Institutions, Tribunals, and Courts*,
International Human Rights, https://doi.org/10.1007/978-981-10-5206-4_18

consideration of the Commission's contribution with respect to: decisions on admissibility of communications concerning mainly exhaustion of domestic remedies; decisions on merits of communications; adoption of resolutions, principles/guidelines, general comments, model laws, and advisory opinions; special rapporteurs and working groups dealing with thematic human rights issues; consideration of State reports and conducting on-site visits; and referral of communications to the African Court involving unimplemented interim measures, serious or massive violations of human rights, or the Commission's findings on admissibility and merits. It also considers some difficulties faced by the African Commission and Court.

Keywords
African Charter on Human and Peoples' Rights · African Commission on Human and Peoples' Rights · African Court on Human and Peoples' Rights · African Union – exhaustion of domestic remedies, communications, special rapporteurs

Introduction

The African Commission on Human and Peoples' Rights (African Commission) and the African Court on Human and Peoples' Rights (African Court) have developed procedures and frameworks which could enable them to protect human rights in Africa, the world's second largest and second-most populous continent with a population of over 1.2 billion. Africa has historically been a region with widespread human rights violations manifested in several forms including slavery, (neo)-colonialism, apartheid, multidimensional (extreme) poverty, genocide in Rwanda in 1994, as well as armed conflicts in several States including Somalia, Sierra Leone, Côte d'Ivoire, and Liberia. During colonialism, Africa's human and material resources were "largely exploited for the benefit of outside powers" (African Commission on Human and Peoples' Rights, *Social and Economic Rights Action Centre and the Centre for Economic and Social Rights v Nigeria (SERAC v Nigeria)*, Communication 155/96, para. 56). This left Africa in poverty which reflects an acute "deprivation of the resources, capabilities, choices, security and power necessary for the enjoyment of an adequate standard of living" (Committee on Economic, Social and Cultural Rights 2001, para. 10).

Thus, in 1963 the Charter of the Organisation of African Unity (OAU) was adopted to, among others, "achieve a better life for the peoples of Africa" and to "eradicate all forms of colonialism from Africa" (Charter of the Organisation of African Unity 1963). Although the preamble to the OAU Charter reaffirmed adherence to the Charter of the United Nations of 1945 and the Universal Declaration of Human Rights of 1948, the main focus of the OAU was to eliminate colonialism in African states. This required a regional system to respect, protect, and fulfill human rights. The African Charter on Human and Peoples' Rights (African Charter) was adopted by the 18th Assembly of Heads of State and Government of the OAU in June 1981 and entered into force on 21 October 1986. After achieving its main objective of the liberation of Africa from colonialism and apartheid, the OAU was replaced by the African Union (AU) in 2000. One of the AU objectives is to "promote and protect human and peoples' rights in accordance with the African Charter and 'other relevant human rights instruments'" (Constitutive Act of the African Union 2000, Art. 3(h)). The African Charter, which has been ratified by 54 AU member States, except the Kingdom of Morocco (which re-joined the AU in January 2017), marked the birth of the African regional human rights system (Ssenyonjo 2012). Over the years, several other human rights treaties have been adopted in Africa to strengthen the protection of rights of vulnerable groups including refugees, children, women, youth, internally displaced persons, and older persons (African Union, OAU/AU Treaties, Conventions, Protocols & Charters 2018). In 1987 the OAU Assembly elected 11 members of the African Commission on Human and Peoples' Rights (the African Commission), which remains the main and oldest African regional quasi-judicial supervisory body for the protection of human rights in Africa. The Commission, among others, receives and considers cases (called "communications") alleging human rights violations by any State party to the African Charter and makes quasi-judicial "recommendations." The jurisdiction of the Commission is compulsory and automatic as it extends to all States parties to the African Charter. The African Court on Human and Peoples' Rights (African Court) complements the protective mandate of the African Commission by providing legally binding judicial decisions since the Court became operational in July 2006 through the adoption of the Protocol to the African Charter on Human and Peoples' Rights on the Establishment of an African Court on Human and Peoples' Rights 1998 (African Court Protocol). The Court has jurisdiction to determine "all cases and disputes" submitted to it concerning the interpretation and application of the African Charter and "any other human rights instrument" (including UN instruments) ratified by the States concerned (African Court Protocol, Art. 3). The future court intended to replace the existing African Court, the "African Court of Justice and Human Rights," yet to be established is not discussed in this chapter since it is not operational (Protocol on the Statute of the African Court of Justice and Human Rights, and Statute of the African Court of Justice and Human Rights 2008). For the same reason, the chapter does not examine the yet-to-be-established "African Court of Justice and Human and Peoples Rights" with jurisdiction, inter alia, over international and transnational crimes (Protocol on Amendments to the Protocol on the Statute of the African Court of Justice and Human Rights, and Statute of the African Court of Justice and Human Rights 2014).

In 2018 the African Charter had marked 37 years since its adoption (in 1981) and 32 years since its entry into force (in 1986). In 2018 Africa's quasi-judicial supervisory body, the African Commission, marked 31 years since it became operational in 1987 and its judicial body, the African Court, had been in existence for 12 years since it became operational in 2006. Against the above background, this chapter examines the main achievements and challenges of the African Commission between 1987 and 2018 and the African Court in the first 12 years of its operation from 2006 to 2018. These are the two main bodies established to ensure the implementation of human rights in Africa. Due to space constraint, the third body, the African Committee of Experts on the Rights and Welfare of the Child, is outside the scope of this chapter. The Committee is not among the entities that can refer cases to the African Court. Similarly, the scope of the chapter does not extend to subregional courts in Africa, envisaged under Article 56(7) of the African Charter, e.g., the Economic Community of West African States *(ECOWAS)* Community Court of Justice, and the East African Court of Justice, which exercise some human rights jurisdiction. The chapter ends with concluding observations.

African Commission on Human and Peoples' Rights: Background and Context

The African Commission was established in 1987 following the entry into force of the African Charter in 1986. Its headquarters are based in Banjul, The Gambia. The Commission consists of "eleven members chosen from amongst African personalities of the highest reputation, known for their high morality, integrity, impartiality and competence in matters of human and peoples' rights; particular consideration being given to persons having legal experience" (African Charter, Art. 31(1)). Commissioners are nominated by States parties to the African Charter and elected by the AU Assembly of Heads of State and Government, but they are required to "serve in their personal capacity" on a part-time basis (African Charter, Art. 31(2)). However, in the past the independence of some individual commissioners has been questionable on the basis that they were senior civil servants and diplomatic representatives. For example, in 2003 a commissioner from Mauritania was appointed as a cabinet minister shortly after being elected to the Commission. Furthermore, the Commission is largely subservient to the primary political organ of the AU, the Assembly of Heads of State and Government (African Charter, Art. 58(1) and 59).

The Commission meets twice a year in regular sessions for a period of up to 2 weeks. The functions of the African Commission include the promotion of human rights through research "on African problems in the field of human and peoples' rights," dissemination of information, and co-operation with "other African and international institutions concerned with the promotion and protection of human and peoples' rights" (African Charter, Art. 45(1)). It is also empowered to "ensure the protection of human and peoples' rights" under conditions laid down by the African Charter (African Charter, Art. 45(2)). In addition, the Commission has the mandate to "interpret" all the provisions of the African Charter at the request of a State party, an institution of the AU or an African organization recognized by the AU (African Charter, Art. 45(3)). It also considers interstate communications (complaints) by which one State brings a complaint alleging violations of human rights in another State (African Charter, Art. 47–59).

However, interstate complaints have been rare. By 2018, the only inter-State complaint decided by the African Commission was Democratic Republic of the Congo v Burundi, Rwanda, and Uganda (Communication 227/99). Similar procedures for interstate complaints under United Nations human rights treaty bodies have never been used. This is mainly due to the perception that interstate complaints are "a hostile and quite drastic response by a state desiring to address human rights questions in another state" (Leckie 1988). Furthermore, the Commission considers periodic State reports on the domestic implementation of the African Charter and its Protocol on the Rights of women followed by the adoption of concluding observations (African Charter, Art. 62; Protocol to the African Charter on Human and Peoples' Rights on the Rights of Women in Africa (Maputo Protocol) 2003, Art. 26). In addition, the Commission considers communications or complaints lodged by individuals and nongovernmental organizations (NGOs) under Articles 55–58 of the African Charter, subject to meeting the admissibility criteria (African Charter, Art. 56), without requiring the complainant to be a victim or a family member of the victim (African Commission on Human and Peoples' Rights, *SERAC v Nigeria*, para. 49).

The main achievements of the Commission include the development of standards on the various provisions of the African Charter through: (i) decisions on admissibility of communications mainly concerning exhaustion of domestic remedies; (ii) decisions on merits of communications; (iii) adoption of resolutions, principles/ guidelines, general comments, model laws and advisory opinions; (iv) special rapporteurs and working groups to deal with thematic human rights issues; (v) consideration of State reports and conducting on-site visits; and (vi) referral of communications (unimplemented interim measures, serious or massive human rights violations, or Commission's admissibility and merits finding) to the African Court.

Decisions on the Exhaustion of Domestic Remedies

The Commission has encouraged African States to develop effective judicial domestic remedies. This is consistent with the fact that the machinery of protection of human rights established by the African Charter is subsidiary to the national systems protecting human rights. Therefore, one of the "most important" criteria for admissibility of communications before the African Commission, like in other regional human rights systems in America and Europe, is the exhaustion of domestic (local) remedies according to the generally recognized rules/principles of international law. Under Article 56(5) of the African Charter, applicants are under an obligation to use the remedies provided by national law, which are sufficient to afford redress in respect of the violations of human rights alleged. The Commission considers on merits communications sent "after exhausting local remedies, if any, unless it is obvious that this procedure is unduly prolonged." In its established jurisprudence, the African Court applies the same admissibility criteria in the case of *Lohe Issa Konate v Burkina Faso*, Application 4/13, 5 December 2014, para. 77, and *Kijiji Isiaga v United Republic of Tanzania*, Application 032/2015, 21 March 2018, para. 45. Determining whether, or not, an applicant has exhausted domestic remedies requires careful consideration of the personal circumstances of the applicant, as well as the general legal and political context in which the remedies operate.

In order to exhaust available domestic remedies, a victim must generally demonstrate that a final decision from the competent domestic highest court was obtained as regards the particular complaint they wish to make before the Commission. This is significant because the requirement for exhaustion of available domestic remedies gives the first opportunity to the respondent State to remedy or redress an alleged violation of human rights within the framework of its own domestic legal system before being called before an international body (African Commission on Human and Peoples' Rights, *SERAC v Nigeria,* para. 37–39; *World Organisation against Torture and Others v Zaire*, Communications 25/89, 47/90, 56/91 & 100/93, para. 36; *Rencontre Africaine pour la Défense des Droits de l'Homme v Zambia*, Communication 71/92, para. 11).

Thus, communications have been declared inadmissible on account of failure of applicants to indicate that domestic remedies were exhausted or ineffective (African Commission on Human and Peoples' Rights, *Association Que. Choisir Bénin v Benin*, Communication 264/02, paras. 21–32; *Filimao Pedro Tivane (represented by Dr. Simeao Cuamba) v Mozambique*, Communication 434/12, paras. 51–54; *Sana Dumbaya v The Gambia*, Communication 127/94, paras. 2 and 3; *Ousman Manjang v The Gambia*, Communication 131/94, para. 1; *International Pen (in respect of Kemal al-Jazouli) v Sudan*, Communication 92/93, para. 3; *Mohamed L. Diakité v Gabon*, Communication 73/92, para. 17; *MS Ceesay v The Gambia*, Communication 86/93, para. 4). This "prevents the Commission from acting as a court [or a quasi-judicial body] of first instance rather than a body of last resort" (African Commission on Human and Peoples' Rights, *Sir Dawda K. Jawara v The Gambia*, Communication 147/95 and 149/96, para. 31), in line with the principle that postnational norms and institutions are subsidiary to and supplement rather than replace national norms and institutions. The Commission requires that local remedies to be exhausted must be "available, effective and sufficient" (African Commission on Human and Peoples' Rights, *Sir Dawda K. Jawara v The Gambia*, Communication 147/95 and 149/96, paras. 31 and 35) as well as "realistic" or "sufficiently certain" (reasonably accessible, capable of providing redress in respect of the complaint with reasonable prospects of success) not only in theory but also in practice (African Commission on Human and Peoples' Rights, *Purohit and Moore v The Gambia*, Communication 241/01, paras. 37 and 38; The Nubian Community in *Kenya v The Republic of Kenya*, Communication 317/2006, paras. 45–51). It follows that there is no obligation to attempt to use a remedy which is ineffective or inadequate, for example, if national law shows that a remedy, such as an appeal, has no reasonable chances of success.

In Sir Dawda K. Jawara v The Gambia, the complainant was the former Head of State of the Republic of The Gambia. He was overthrown by the military in a coup of July 1994 and tried in absentia. Former Ministers and Members of Parliament of his government were detained and there was terror and fear for lives in the country. The complainant alleged violation of several provisions of the African Charter. In considering whether he had exhausted local remedies, the Commission stated in paragraph 32 that: "A remedy is considered available if the petitioner can pursue it without impediment, it is deemed effective if it offers a prospect of success, and it is found sufficient if it is capable of redressing the complaint." The Commission considered that in a situation where the jurisdiction of the courts have been ousted by decrees whose validity cannot be challenged or questioned, as was the position in this case, local remedies are deemed to be both "unavailable" as well as "nonexistent" (para. 34).

Similarly complainants who are unable to pursue domestic remedies (when outside a State's territory and fear to return for life on account of persecution) are deemed to have constructively exhausted domestic remedies (African Commission on Human and Peoples' Rights, *Alhassan Abubakar v Ghana*, Communication 103/93, para. 6; *John D. Ouko v Kenya*, Communication 232/99, para 19; *Kazeem Aminu v Nigeria*, Communication 205/97, para. 13). It is essential to note that remedies to be exhausted must be of a "judicial" nature sought from independent sources and "not subordinated to the discretionary power of public authorities" (*Amnesty international and Others v Sudan*, Communication 48/90, 50/91, 52/91 & 89/93, para. 31; *Alfred B. Cudjoe v Ghana*, Communication 221/98, para. 14; *Romy Goornah (represented by Dev Hurnam) v The Republic of Mauritius*, Communication 596/16, para. 58). As the Commission noted: "It would be improper to insist on the complainants seeking remedies from sources which do not operate impartially and have no obligation to decide according to legal principles" (African Commission on Human and Peoples' Rights, *Constitutional Rights Project (in respect of Akamu and Others) v Nigeria*, Communication 60/91, paras. 9–11; *Constitutional Rights Project (in respect of Lekwot & Others) v Nigeria*, Communication 87/93, paras. 6–9; *Civil Liberties Organisation v Nigeria*, Communication 151/96, paras. 11–16). Consequently, States have to put in place effective and adequate domestic remedies granted by fully independent courts not only in theory but also in practice.

Decisions on Communications on Merits

In the period 1987 to 2017, i.e., in 30 decades of the African Commission, the Commission had received well over 400 communications, nearly all from individuals, organizations, or groups alleging violations of human rights in the African Charter. It handed down about 228 decisions on communications on merits and admissibility including communications declared inadmissible or discontinued due to withdrawal or loss of contact with the complainant. With the exception of one interstate complaint only (African Commission on Human and Peoples' Rights, *Democratic Republic of the Congo v Burundi, Rwanda and Uganda*, Communication 227/99), all other complaints have been submitted by individuals and NGOs. Although the African Commission has determined fewer complaints in its first 30 years than other comparable regional human rights mechanisms, the Commission's jurisprudence has contributed to the development of human rights in several ways.

First, the Commission has developed progressive jurisprudence concerning the meaning of vague (civil and political, economic, social, and cultural) rights protected by the African Charter through its decisions on communications, resolutions, principles and guidelines, and general comments. While the legal status of the

Commission's recommendations is debatable, the Commission considers them to be legally binding (African Commission on Human and Peoples' Rights, Legal Resources Foundation v Zambia, Communication 211/98, paras. 61–62; International Pen, Constitutional Rights Project, Civil Liberties Organisations and Interights (on behalf of Ken Saro-Wira) v Nigeria, Communications 137/94, 139/94, 154/96, 161/97, paras. 113 and 116). With the exception of Botswana which asserted that "it is not bound by the decision of the Commission" (Combined 32nd and 33rd Activity Report of the African Commission on Human and Peoples' Rights 2013, para. 24), many States have never questioned or challenged the legal status of the African Commission's recommendations.

Second, the Commission has clarified that some rights not explicitly protected by the African Charter are implied in other rights protected in the Charter. For example, although the African Charter does not contain an explicit protection of the right to adequate housing, the Commission noted that the combined effect of Articles 14 (the right to property), 16 (the right to enjoy the best attainable state of mental and physical health), and 18(1) (the protection accorded to the family) of the African Charter "reads into the African Charter a right to shelter or housing" and the right to food (African Commission on Human and Peoples' Rights, *SERAC v Nigeria*, Communication 155/96, paras. 60 and 64–67). Under this approach, several internationally recognized human rights not explicitly protected by the African Charter (e.g., privacy, adequate food, water, sanitation, housing, and social security) can be read into the Charter.

Third, the Commission has clarified the scope of State obligations under the African Charter to respect, protect, and fulfill human rights in accordance with Articles 60 and 61 of the African Charter or "international human rights instruments and practices" (African Commission on Human and Peoples' Rights, *Scanlen and Holdreness v Zimbabwe*, Communication 297/05, para. 115). Significantly, the Commission has limited the potential negative impact of the "clawback clauses" in the African Charter by consistently holding in its jurisprudence that the clause, in Articles 8–14 of the African Charter, "subject to law," "within the law," "abides by the law," "provided for by law," "in accordance with the law," or "appropriate laws" does not provide a blanket approval of any domestic law regardless of its effect on human rights. Rather the clause constitutes a reference to "international law, meaning that only restrictions on rights which are consistent with the Charter and with States Parties' international obligations should be enacted by the relevant national authorities" (African Commission on Human and Peoples' Rights, *Patrick Okiring and Agupio Samson (represented by Human Rights Network and ISIS-WICCE) v Republic of Uganda*, Communication 339/2007, para. 108; *Article 19 v Eritrea*, Communication 275/03, paras. 91,92). Accordingly, the Commission has contributed to respect for international human rights law by holding that domestic law in African States (including the application of Islamic Shari'a) must comply with other State obligations including international human rights standards (African Commission on Human and Peoples' Rights, *Amnesty International, Comité Loosli Bachelard, Lawyers' Committee for Human Rights, Association of Members of the Episcopal Conference of East Africa v Sudan*, Communications 48/90, 50/91, 52/91,

89/93, para. 73). Thus, State sovereignty and noninterference in "internal affairs" cannot justify violations of human rights.

The African Charter provides in Article 1 that States parties shall "recognize the rights, duties and freedoms" enshrined in the Charter and "shall undertake to adopt legislative or other measures to give effect to them." On this basis, the Commission's jurisprudence has confirmed that States are obliged to protect individuals and groups against violations by non-State (private) actors (African Commission on Human and Peoples' Rights, *Scanlen and Holdreness v Zimbabwe*, Communication 297/05, paras. 57–58). This requires adopting and enforcing appropriate legislation and policy protecting rights recognized in the African Charter. Thus, a State's failure to ensure that the rights in the Charter are not violated constitutes a violation "even if the state or its agents are not the immediate cause of the violation" (African Commission on Human and Peoples' Rights, *Commission Nationale des Droits de L'Homme et des libertés v Chad*, Communication 74/92, para. 20). The Commission has also clarified the responsibility of nonstate actors not to violate human rights. For instance, with respect to the right to adequate food, the Commission has called on "non-state actors involved in conflicts to allow unhindered access to humanitarian organisations to provide relief food and assistance to affected populations" (African Commission on Human and Peoples' Rights, Resolution on the Right to Food and Food Insecurity in Africa 2017, para. 4).

Fourth, despite the lack of an express mandate on remedies in the African Charter, the Commission has made significant improvements in awarding remedies to victims of human rights violations. It should be noted that the Commission for many years placed overemphasis on promoting a "positive dialogue" leading to amicable resolution of disputes in relation to individual communications. It was reluctant to award effective reparation (such as restitution, monetary compensation for loss suffered, rehabilitation, satisfaction, and guarantees of nonrepetition) proportional to the gravity of human rights violations. After finding (serious or massive) violations of the African Charter, the Commission, in many communications, did not require any specific actions or measures to be taken by States to provide any remedy (African Commission on Human and Peoples' Rights, *Krischna Achutan (on behalf of Aleke Banda), Amnesty International on behalf of Orton and Vera Chirwa* and *Amnesty International on behalf of Orton and Vera Chirwa v Malawi*, Communication 64/92, 68/92, 78/92; Free Legal Assistance Group, Lawyers' Committee for Human Rights, Union interafricaine des droits de l'Homme, Les témoins de Jehovah v Zaire, Communications 25/89, 47/90, 56/91, 100/93 (joined); Commission Nationale des Droits de L'Homme et des libertés v Chad, Communication 74/92; *Civil Liberties Organization v Nigeria*, Communication 129/94; *Amnesty International v Zambia*, Communication 212/98; *Rights International v Nigeria*, Communication 215/98; *Forum of Conscience v Sierra Leone*, Communication 223/98; and *Huri-Laws v Nigeria*, Communication 225/98).

In some communications, the Commission made vague "requests" to violating States to "take the necessary steps to bring [domestic] law into conformity with the Charter" (African Commission on Human and Peoples' Rights, *Media Rights Agenda, Constitutional Rights Project, Media Rights Agenda and Constitutional*

Rights Project v Nigeria, Communication 105/93–128/94–130/94–152/96 (joined); *Constitutional Rights Project and Civil Liberties Organisation v Nigeria*, Communications 143/95, 150/96; *Media Rights Agenda v Nigeria*, Communication 224/98); to "take the appropriate measures to remedy the situation" (*Mouvement Ivoirien Des droits Humains (MIDH) v Côte d'Ivoire*, Communication 246/02); simply "invites" the violating State to "take all necessary steps to comply with its obligations under the Charter" (*Constitutional Rights Project, Civil Liberties Organisation and Media Rights Agenda v Nigeria*, Communication 140/94, 141/94, 145/95), or it deferred to the States concerned to arrive at an "amicable solution" (*Rencontre Africaine pour la Défence des droits de l'Homme (RADDHO) v Zambia*, Communication 71/92; John K Modise v Botswana (No 1), Communication 97/93).

For example, after deciding that the administrative detention of 517 nationals of West African States from Zambia for a period of over 2 months, the deprivation of their property and their subsequent detention constituted a violation of Articles 2, 7(1)(a), and 12(5) of the African Charter, the Commission resolved to "continue efforts to pursue an amicable resolution in this case" instead of awarding compensation (African Commission on Human and Peoples' Rights, *RADDHO v Zambia*, Communication 71/92). Victims were not afforded an adequate remedy. In some limited communications in which the Commission accepted that victims suffered damages, it did not quantify the amount of damages but instead decided that damages be determined under relevant domestic law. For example, in *Embga Mekongo Louis v Cameroon*, Communication 59/91, Mekongo, a citizen of Cameroon claimed damages in the sum of $105 m for alleged false imprisonment and miscarriage of justice. The Commission found that the author had been denied due process, contrary to Article 7 of African Charter, and had in fact suffered damages. However, the Commission stated that it was "unable to determine the amount of damages" and thus recommended that "the quantum should be determined under the law of Cameroon."

Although the Commission has not been consistent in its approach to remedies for human rights violations, in recent years (at least from 2003 onwards), the Commission has made some notable nonmonetary recommendations. These include recommendations that complainants under detention, or civilians/journalists tried, convicted and sentenced by military tribunals, be released (African Commission on Human and Peoples' Rights, *Centre for Free Speech v Nigeria*, Communication 206/97; *Constitutional Rights Project v Nigeria*, Communication 148/96), or afforded a fair trial including access to family and legal representatives (African Commission on Human and Peoples' Rights, *Article 19 v Eritrea*, Communication 275/2003; *Dawit Isaak v Republic of Eritrea*, Communication 428/12); annulment of government decrees ousting of judicial jurisdiction (African Commission on Human and Peoples' Rights, *Civil Liberties Organisation (in respect of the Nigerian Bar Association) v Nigeria*, Communication 101/93); amendment, repeal or adoption of domestic legislation and policy in conformity with a State's human rights "obligations under the African Charter and other relevant international human rights instruments" (African Commission on Human and Peoples' Rights, *Curtis Francis Doebbler v Sudan*, Communication 236/2000; *Law Offices of Ghazi Suleiman v Sudan*, Communication 228/99).

The Commission has also ordered States to ensure that immigration policies, measures, and legislations do not have the effect of discriminating against persons on the basis of any prohibited ground (including race, color, descent, national, ethnic origin, or any other status) and particularly take into account the vulnerability of women, children, and asylum seekers (African Commission on Human and Peoples' Rights, *Institute for Human Rights and Development in Africa (on behalf of Esmaila Connateh & 13 Others) v Republic of Angola*, Communication 292/2004, para. 87); ensure that individuals are not deported/expelled to countries where they might face torture or their lives could be at risk; reinstatement of complainants "unduly dismissed and/or forcibly retired workers" in former employment (African Commission on Human and Peoples' Rights, *Annette Pagnoulle (on behalf of Abdoulaye Mazou) v Cameroon*, Communication 39/90; *Malawi Africa Association, Amnesty International, Ms. Sarr Diop, Union interafricaine des droits de l'Homme and RADDHO, Collectif des veuves et ayantsDroit, Association mauritanienne des droits de l'Homme v Mauritania*, Communications 54/91, 61/91, 96/93, 98/93, 164/97,196/97, and 210/98); rescission of deportation orders incompatible with the African Charter (African Commission on Human and Peoples' Rights, *Zimbabwe Lawyers for Human Rights and Institute for Human Rights and Development in Africa (on behalf of Andrew Barclay Meldrum) v Zimbabwe*, Communication 294/04); restoration of property rights (African Commission on Human and Peoples' Rights, *Mouvement Ivoirien de droits de l'Homme (MIDH) [Ivorian Human Rights Movement] v Côte d'Ivoire*, Communication 262/02); and provision of "adequate medical care and material care for persons suffering from mental health problems" (African Commission on Human and Peoples' Rights, *Purohit and Moore v The Gambia*, Communication 241/2001).

Other recommendations made by the Commission include equitable allocation of national projects (African Commission on Human and Peoples' Rights, *Kevin Mgwanga Gunme* et al. *v Cameroon*, Communication 266/2003, para. 215(4)); lifting press bans (African Commission on Human and Peoples' Rights, *Article 19 v Eritrea*, Communication 275/2003); abolition of corporal punishments such as the penalty of lashes (African Commission on Human and Peoples' Rights, *Curtis Francis Doebbler v Sudan*, Communication 236/2000); conduct prompt, impartial, and effective official investigations into abuses of human rights, identify and prosecute those responsible for the human rights violations (African Commission on Human and Peoples' Rights, Movement Burkinabé des Droits de l'Homme et des Peuples v Burkina Faso, Communication 204/97; *Sudan Human Rights Organisation & Centre on Housing Rights and Evictions (COHRE) v Sudan*, Communication 279/2003 and 296/2005, para 229); the rehabilitation of a State's economic and social infrastructure such as education, health, water, and agricultural services (African Commission on Human and Peoples' Rights, *Sudan Human Rights Organisation & Centre on Housing Rights and Evictions (COHRE) v Sudan*, Communication 279/2003 and 296/2005); establish "objective, transparent and nondiscriminatory criteria" for determining citizenship; and take measures to ensure that evictions are carried out in accordance with international human rights standards (African Commission on Human and Peoples' Rights, *The Nubian Community in Kenya v The Republic of Kenya*, Communication 317/2006, para. 171).

In addition, the Commission has acknowledged the significance of monetary awards, acknowledging the need for "just and adequate" or "fair and equitable" compensation, to victims of human rights violations against several violating States including Benin, Botswana, Cameroon, Congo, Democratic Republic of Congo (DRC), Eritrea, Guinea, Kenya, Mauritania, Sudan, Zimbabwe, and Uganda (African Commission on Human and Peoples' Rights, *Odjouoriby Cossi Paul v Benin*, Communication 199/97; *Kenneth Good v Republic of Botswana*, Communication 313/05; *Antoine Bissangou v Republic of Congo*, Communication 253/2002; *Kevin Mgwanga Gunme* et al. *v Cameroon*, Communication 266/2003; *Antoine Bissangou v Republic of Congo*, Communication 253/2002; *Marcel Wetsh'okonda Koso and others v Democratic Republic of Congo*, Communication 281/2003; *Liesbeth Zegveld and Mussie Ephrem v Eritrea*, Communication 250/2002; *African Institute for Human Rights and Development (on behalf of Sierra Leonean Refugees in Guinea) v Republic of Guinea*, Communication 249/2002; *Centre for Minority Rights Development (Kenya) and Minority Rights Group International on behalf of Endorois Welfare Council v Kenya*, Communication 276/2003; *Interights, Institute for Human Rights and Development in Africa, and Association Mauritanienne des Droits de l'Homme v Mauritania*, Communication 373/2006; *Sudan Human Rights Organisation & Centre for Housing Rights and Evictions v Sudan*, Communication 279/2003 and 296/2005, para 229(4); *Zimbabwe Human Rights NGO Forum v Zimbabwe*, Communication 245/2002; *Patrick Okiring and Agupio Samson (represented by Human Rights Network and ISIS-WICCE) v Republic of Uganda*, Communication 339/2007, (2017), para 139(iii)).

These examples provide a basis to develop a coherent approach to remedies. However, the Commission has been inconsistent in its approach to monetary damages. While in some communications it has specified the quantum of monetary damages awarded (African Commission on Human and Peoples' Rights, *Hossam Ezzat & Rania Enayet (represented by Egyptian Initiative for Personal Rights & Interrights) v The Arab Republic of Egypt*, Communication 355/07, (2016), para. 185(e)), it has avoided quantifying "adequate compensation" in some communications leaving it to respondent States to assess "the manner and mode of payment of compensation" guided by unspecified international norms and practices relating to payment of compensatory damages (African Commission on Human and Peoples' Rights, *Patrick Okiring and Agupio Samson (represented by Human Rights Network and ISIS-WICCE) v Republic of Uganda*, Communication 339/2007, (2017), para. 139(iii)). This has left States with a very wide margin of discretion making it difficult to monitor whether the Commission's recommendations have been implemented or not. In some communications, the Commission has recommended that respondent States report to the Commission on the measures taken and/or obstacles faced in the implementation of the Commission's recommendations. This is required within a certain period of time depending on the nature of violations found and remedies awarded (e.g., 90 days or 3 months, 180 days or 6 months, or during the presentation of a State's "next periodic report" in terms of Article 62 of the African Charter) from the date of notification. However, compliance remains low and there are no effective mechanisms to follow up the implementation of the Commission's (open-ended) monetary remedies.

Article 1 of the African Charter requires States Parties to "recognize the rights, duties, and freedoms enshrined in the Charter" and to "undertake to adopt legislative or other measures to give effect to them." This includes undertaking measures to give effect to the recommendations of the supervisory mechanisms of the African Charter including the African Commission. Do States implement adverse decisions or recommendations made by the African Commission in order to ensure that States are in compliance with their obligations under the African Charter? In other words, do States undertake legislative or other appropriate measures (e.g., through judicial decisions, administrative actions, or executive decrees) to give effect to the Commission's recommendations?

There are examples showing the influence of the African Charter and the African Commission's case law on African judiciaries as a guide to the interpretation and application of national law. This is partly because "there is a *prima facie* presumption that the legislature does not intend to act in breach of international law, including treaty provisions" as interpreted by relevant bodies (African Commission on Human and Peoples' Rights, *Molefi Ts'epe v The Independent Electoral Commission and Others*, Civ No 11/05, Court of Appeal of Lesotho, 30 June 2005) para. 16). Some domestic courts have relied on the African Charter and African Commission's case law to find violations of human rights. Examples include cases of discrimination on the basis sexual orientation or sex. In 2015 the High Court of Kenya in *Eric Gitari v Non-governmental Organisation Coordination Board and four others* (Petition 440 of 2013, [2015] eKLR, High Court of Kenya at Nairobi, 24 April 2015), extensively relied, inter alia, on the Article 10 of the African Charter, decisions of the African Commission on freedom of association and the Commission's resolution on the Right to Freedom of Association to protect "sexual minorities" in Kenya from nondiscrimination on the basis of their actual or perceived sexual orientation or gender-identity. The Court found that nonregistration of a NGO that promoted rights of lesbian, gay, bisexual, transgender/transsexual, and intersex (LGBTI) persons living in Kenya violated the right to freedom of association guaranteed under Article 36 of the Constitution of Kenya (2010). Other domestic courts have relied on the African Charter to protect women's rights to equality and nondiscrimination, for example, in inheritance on the grounds of sex (*Mary Rono v Jane and William Rono, Court of Appeal Civil Appeal 66 of 2002*, Kenya Court of Appeal at Eldoret, 29 April 2005; *Molefi Ts'epe v The Independent Electoral Commission and Others*, Civ No 11/05, Court of Appeal of Lesotho, 30 June 2005, para. 16).

The African Charter and the Commission's case law has also been relied on by domestic courts to protect the right of access to an independent and impartial court (*Ousman Sabally v Inspector General of Police and Others*, Civil Reference 2/2001, Supreme Court of The Gambia, 5 December 2001), and the right to liberty and security of the person due to detention beyond constitutionally prescribed limit of 72 h (*Ajaratou Mariam Denton v Director General of National Intelligence Agency and Others*, Civil HC 241/06/MF/087/F1, High Court of The Gambia, 24 July 2006). At a national level, civil society has used either the fact of submission of communications to the Commission or the Commission's findings to campaign for legal reform culminating in the repeal of decrees in violations of rights protected in the African Charter such as the right to a fair trial (African Commission on Human and Peoples' Rights, *The Constitutional Rights Project (in respect of Zamani Lekwot and Six Others) v Nigeria*, Communication 87/93) and freedom from arbitrary arrest (African Commission on Human and Peoples' Rights, *International PEN, Constitutional Rights Project, Civil Liberties Organisation and Interights (on behalf of Ken Saro-Wiwa Jnr.) v Nigeria*, Communications 137/94,139/94,154/96,161/97).

However, it should be noted that the implementation of, or State compliance with, the recommendations has generally remained very low. This is due to the lack of political will to implement the Commission's recommendations and inadequate "follow-up" or monitoring of the implementation of the Commission's recommendations, in terms of reporting, information-gathering, assessment, and enforcement. Unsatisfactory follow-up has been caused, at least in part, by the lack of a reliable mechanism to assess compliance and data on the implementation of all decisions, as well as insufficient funding to develop such a mechanism or data base. In 2017, the Commission observed:

> The insufficient funding of the Commission from the member state budget also impedes the Commission's capacity to follow-up on implementation as it prevents the Commission from developing effective follow up of its findings during country visits, and recommendations arising from its findings, resulting in the overall weakening of the effectiveness of the Commission (42nd Activity Report of the African Commission on Human and Peoples' Rights, para. 45).

Despite the absence of a provision in the African Charter on interim or provisional measures, the Commission Rules of Procedure (2010) grant the Commission power to grant provisional measures under Rule 111. Rule 98(4) requires States to report to the African Commission on measures taken to implement provisional measures. Importantly, the Commission has granted provisional measures (especially in the form of letters of appeal to the Heads of State urging their intervention pending the outcome of complaints before the Commission) in several cases, including *Shereen Said Hamd Bakhet v Arab Republic of Egypt*, Communication 658/17; *Ahmed Mustafa & 5 Others (Represented by Justice for Human Rights & AMAN Organisation) v Arab Republic of Egypt*, Communication 659/17; *Franck Diongo Shamba (represented by All4Rights) v Democratic Republic of Congo*, Communication 652/17; *Ahmed Abdul Wahab Al Khateeb v Arab Republic of Egypt*, Communication 654/17; *Les femmes de Lieke Lesole parties civiles dans l'affaire Basele Lututula, alias colonel Thom's et autres (représentées par Action Contre l'Impunité pour les Droits Humains) v République Démocratique du Congo*, Communication 655/17; *Anas Ahmed Khalifa v Arab Republic of Egypt*, Communication 656/17; *Andargachew Tsege and Others (Represented by Reprieve and REDRESS) v The Federal Democratic Republic of Ethiopia*, Communication 507/15). These include cases when an execution has been imminent (African Commission on Human and Peoples' Rights, *Interights (on behalf of Safia Yakubu Husaini and Others) v Nigeria*, Communication 269/2003), cases of arrest and detention of individuals without trial such as journalists (African Commission on Human and Peoples' Rights, *Samuel Kofi*

Woods, II and Kabineh M. Ja'neh v Liberia, Communication 256/2002) and former governmental officials (African Commission on Human and Peoples' Rights, *Liesbeth Zegveld and Mussie Ephrem v Eritrea*, Communication 250/2002), and to prevent irreparable harm being caused to victims of alleged human rights violations (African Commission on Human and Peoples' Rights, *The Indigenous Peoples of the Lower Omo (Represented by Survival International Charitable Trust) v Ethiopia*, Communication 419/2012).

Although the Commission has held that the refusal to comply with provisional measures violates State parties' obligation under Article 1 of the African Charter to "undertake measures to give effect" to the provisions of the Charter, States have rarely complied with the Commission's requests for provisional measures or letters of urgent appeal regarding allegations of human rights violations in States. For example, executions have been carried out by governments in violation of provisional measures to stay execution (African Commission on Human and Peoples' Rights, *International PEN, Constitutional Rights Project, Civil Liberties Organisation and Interights (on behalf of Ken Saro-Wiwa Jnr.) v Nigeria*, Communication 137/94, 139/94, 154/96 and 161/97) and using hanging, as a method of execution (which is "inhuman and degrading") in violation of Article 5 of the African Charter (African Commission on Human and Peoples' Rights, *Interights & Ditshwanelo v The Republic of Botswana*, Communication 319/06).

Adoption of Resolutions, Principles/Guidelines, General Comments, Model Laws, and Advisory Opinions

Article 45(1)(b) of the African Charter mandates the Commission to "formulate and lay down, principles and rules aimed at solving legal problems relating to human and peoples' rights and fundamental freedoms upon which African Governments may base their legislations" (emphasis added). Under this provision, the Commission (in collaboration with civil society including NGOs) has adopted significant resolutions, declarations, principles/guidelines, and general comments to guide the interpretation and application of specific rights under the African Charter and other relevant human rights instruments in Africa and to ensure their coherent application to a range of situations, including their implementation at the domestic level. The Commission's resolutions could generally be classified into three categories, namely, thematic, administrative, and country-specific resolutions.

First, thematic resolutions elaborate in greater detail specific human right themes or particular substantive rights protected explicitly or implicitly protected in the Charter. Generally, they define obligations of states parties to the Charter in greater detail similar to the general comments of the UN treaty bodies. The Commission has passed a number of thematic resolutions and declarations covering a wide range of themes including the death penalty, indigenous peoples, the situation of women and children, the situation of human rights defenders in Africa, Economic, Social and Cultural Rights in Africa, right to education, maternal mortality, HIV/AIDS, the right to food and food insecurity in Africa, electoral process and good governance, prisons in Africa, torture, independence of the judiciary, contemporary forms of slavery, freedom of association, freedom of expression, fair trial, protection against human rights violations on the basis of one's real or imputed sexual orientation or gender identity, situation of Internally Displaced Persons in Africa, and the Importance of the Implementation of the Recommendations of the African Commission. The Commission has subsequently relied on its resolutions in its case law.

For example, in Interights v Botswana, the Commission relied on its resolution on the death penalty to urge "all states party to the African Charter on Human and Peoples' Rights to take all measures to refrain from exercising the death penalty" (African Commission on Human and Peoples' Rights, Interights et al. (on behalf of Mariette Sonjaleen Bosch) v Botswana, Communication 240/2001, para. 52). Later, in November 2015, the Commission specifically urged Botswana "to take all measures to comply with the Resolution urging State Parties to observe a Moratorium on the Death Penalty" and "to take steps to abolish the death penalty" (African Commission on Human and Peoples' Rights, *Interights & Ditshwanelo v The Republic of Botswana*, Communication 319/06, para. 99). Although several African States have not formally abolished the death penalty (including hanging as a method of execution), the application of the death penalty in practice has increasingly been restricted.

For example, under various laws of Uganda a broad array of crimes (including murder, aggravated robbery, treason, and terrorism resulting in the death of a person) were punishable by a mandatory death penalty. In 2009 the Supreme Court of Uganda held that the various provisions of the laws of Uganda which prescribe a mandatory death sentence were unconstitutional (*Attorney General v Susan Kigula & 417 Others*, Constitutional Appeal No 03 of 2006, 21 January 2009). It further decided that the mandatorily imposed death sentences received by the vast majority of more than 400 appellants in this case should be commuted to life imprisonment. Several other African States (including Tanzania, Nigeria, Mauritania and Sudan) have commuted death sentences to life imprisonments (43rd Activity Report of the African Commission on Human and Peoples' Rights, para. 35(xiii)). The judiciary in other African States is increasingly against the application of the death penalty for all crimes. This is clearly demonstrated in two decisions of the Constitutional Court of Benin. The first one was delivered on 4 August 2012 declaring that, due to Benin's accession to the Second Optional Protocol to the International Covenant on Civil and Political Rights, aiming at the abolition of the death penalty, "no legal provision can now mention the death penalty" in Benin (Benin Constitutional Court Decision DCC 12–153, 4 August 2012). The second one was delivered on 21 January 2016 stating that the entry into force of ICCPR-OP2, and its accession by the Republic of Benin, "now renders inoperative all legal provisions stipulating the death penalty as a punishment" and that "no one can now be sentenced to capital punishment in Benin" (Benin Constitutional Court Decision DCC 16–020, 21 January 2016). Accordingly, the government of Benin commuted death sentences to life imprisonment.

In addition, the Commission has adopted several guidelines on various human rights issues including reporting; torture; fair trial and legal assistance in Africa;

economic, social, and cultural rights; arrest; terrorism; policing of assemblies; freedom of association and assembly; sexual violence; and access to information and decriminalization of petty offences. It has also adopted model laws, such as Model Law on Access to Information for Africa of 2011, and general comments on some human rights issues including rights of women; the right to life; the right to redress for victims of torture; and ending child marriage. Through such documents, the Commission has clarified the scope of State parties' obligations to respect, protect, and fulfill human rights within a State's jurisdiction or otherwise where a State exercises effective authority, power, or control over either the perpetrator or the victim or exercises effective control over the territory on which the victim's rights are affected. The jurisprudence of the Commission developed in the guidelines has subsequently been applied in the Commission's case law (African Commission on Human and Peoples' Rights, *Patrick Okiring and Agupio Samson (represented by Human Rights Network and ISIS-WICCE) v Republic of Uganda*, Communication 339/2007, (2017), paras 104–106, 115, 126, 132, and 139(vi)).

The Commission has also interpreted civil and political rights to contain aspects of economic, social, and cultural rights. For example, with respect to the right to life under Article 4 of the African Charter, the Commission stated in General Comment No. 3 that the African Charter envisages "the protection not only of life in a narrow sense, but of dignified life" (African Commission on Human and Peoples' Rights, General Comment No. 3 2015, para. 3). It observed that this requires the "realization of all human rights" recognized in the African Charter, including civil, political, economic, social, and cultural rights and peoples' rights, particularly the right to peace (para. 6). It follows that in certain circumstances violations of economic, social, and cultural rights (death resulting, for example, from the arbitrary denial of available healthcare, food, water or housing) may entail violations of the right to life (para. 43).

This broad understanding of the right to life imposes on States obligations to "respect, protect, promote, and fulfill" the right to life (para. 7). First, States are obliged to "prevent arbitrary deprivations of life" caused by State agents (para. 2). Second, States are obliged to protect individuals and groups from real and immediate risks to their lives caused either by actions or inactions of third parties and other private individuals or entities, including corporations (paras. 2, 3, and 21). The obligation to protect life entails both actions to preventive steps to "preserve and protect the natural environment and humanitarian responses to natural disasters, famines, outbreaks of infectious diseases, or other emergencies" (paras. 3 and 41). It also includes State responsibility to "address more chronic yet pervasive threats to life, for example with respect to preventable maternal mortality, by establishing functioning health systems" and eliminating discriminatory laws and practices which impact on individuals' and groups' ability to seek healthcare (para. 42). The third obligation requires States to "conduct prompt, impartial, thorough and transparent investigations' into any killings or deprivations of life that may have occurred, holding those responsible to account and providing for an effective remedy and reparation for the victim or victims, including, where appropriate, their immediate family and dependents" (para. 7). It follows from the foregoing that a "State can be held responsible for killings by non-State actors if it approves, supports or acquiesces in those acts or if it fails to exercise due diligence to prevent such killings or to ensure proper investigation and accountability" (para. 9).

Second, administrative resolutions deal with the Commission's procedures, internal mechanisms, and relationship between the Commission and other organs of the AU, intergovernmental organizations, National Human Rights Institutions (NHRIs), and NGOs. Some of the Commission's administrative resolutions include resolutions on the appointment and mandate of special rapporteurs and working groups, resolutions on the criteria for grant of observer status to NGOs and affiliate status to NHRIs, and the resolution on the protection of the name, acronym, and logo of the Commission.

Third, country-specific resolutions address pertinent human rights concerns in member states. This category of resolution has proven very useful whenever there are widespread violations in a member state, but no individual has submitted any communications to the Commission in respect of those violations. The Commission has passed specific resolutions to address the human rights situation in many African States including Sudan, Uganda, Zimbabwe, Ethiopia, Eritrea, Somalia, Kenya, DRC, Côte d'Ivoire, Comoros, Libya, Tunisia, Guinea Bissau, Liberia, Burundi, and Rwanda.

Finally, the African Charter grants mandate to the African Commission to give its "views or make recommendations to the Governments" (African Charter, Art. 45(1)(a)) and to "interpret all the provisions of the [African] Charter" at the request of a State party, an institution of the AU or an African organization recognized by the AU (African Charter, Art. 45(3)). On this basis, the Commission can provide advisory opinions on human rights issues in Africa. While the Commission has not issued several advisory opinions, it issued an important advisory opinion on the United Nations Declaration on the Rights of Indigenous Peoples of 2007. This alleviated concerns African States had about the "political, economic, social, and constitutional implications" of the adoption of the UN Declaration on the Rights of Indigenous Peoples on the African continent. Following the African Commission's opinion, no African State voted against the adoption of the Declaration. The Declaration was adopted by the UN General Assembly by a majority of 143 States in favor, 4 votes against (Australia, Canada, New Zealand, and the United States), and 11 abstentions (Azerbaijan, Bangladesh, Bhutan, Burundi, Colombia, Georgia, Kenya, Nigeria, Russian Federation, Samoa, and Ukraine).

Since then there has been increased recognition of indigenous peoples' rights in Africa. This is partly reflected in litigation and emerging African jurisprudence by the African Commission and national courts on issues that are essential to indigenous peoples rights in Africa such as nondiscrimination, self-identification, land rights, and development (African Commission on Human and Peoples' Rights, *Centre for Minority Rights Development (Kenya) and Minority Rights Group International on behalf of Endorois Welfare Council v Kenya*, Communication 276/2003; *Roy Sesana, Keiwa Setlhobogwa and 241 others v the Attorney General of the*

Republic of Botswana, Misca. No. 52 of 2002 (High Court of Botswana, 13 December 2006); *Matsipane Mosetlhanyene and Gakenyatsiwe Matsipane v the Attorney General*, Civil Appeal No. CACLB-074-10 (High Court of Botswana, 27 January 2011); *Alexkor Ltd. and Another v Richtersveld Community and Others* 2004 (5) SA 460 (Constitutional Court of South Africa, 14 October 2003); *Uganda Land Alliance, Ltd. v Uganda Wildlife Authority*, Misc Cause No 0001 of 2004 (High Court of Uganda at Mbale, Consent Judgment and Decree)).

Special Rapporteurs, Working Groups, and Committees

Rule 23 (1) of the Commission's Rules of Procedure provides that: "The Commission may create subsidiary mechanisms such as special rapporteurs, committees, and working groups." From mid-1990s the Commission has appointed various Special Rapporteurs (normally members of the Commission) and working groups (some of which include members outside the Commission) to deal with thematic human rights issues. These include the Special Rapporteur on Death Penalty, Extrajudicial, Summary, or Arbitrary Killings in Africa; Freedom of Expression and Access to Information in Africa; the Rights of Women in Africa; Human Rights Defenders in Africa; Prisons, Conditions of Detention and Policing in Africa; the Protection of the Rights of People Living with HIV and those at Risk, Vulnerable to and Affected by HIV; Communications; Indigenous Populations/Communities in Africa; Refugees, Asylum Seekers, Internally Displaced Persons and Migrants in Africa; Extractive Industries, Environment and Human Rights Violations in Africa; and the Prevention of Torture in Africa. Rule 112(4) of the African Commission's 2010 Rules of Procedure empowered rapporteurs to "monitor the measures taken by the State Party to give effect to the Commission's recommendations on each Communication."

The Commission has also established Working Groups on various human rights issues including Indigenous Populations or Communities; Economic, Social and Cultural Rights in Africa; the Death Penalty; the Rights of Older Persons and Persons with Disabilities in Africa; and Extractive Industries, Environment and Human Rights Violations. Furthermore, the Commission has established committees on issues such as the Prevention of Torture in Africa; the Protection of the Rights of People Living with HIV (PLHIV) and Those at Risk, Vulnerable to and Affected by HIV; and a Committee on Resolutions. The special rapporteurs, committees, and working groups examine developments in areas covered by their mandates, undertake on-site visits, and produce reports with recommendations to improve the protection of human rights in Africa. Some general comments were developed by the working groups. For example, General Comment 3 on the right to life, which clarifies the scope of the right to life under the African Charter, was developed by the Working Group on the Death Penalty and Extrajudicial, Summary or Arbitrary Killings in Africa.

Consideration of State Reports

Under Article 62 of the African Charter, each state party undertakes to submit every 2 years "a report on the legislative or other measures" taken to give effect to the rights guaranteed by the African Charter. The Commission examines the report, conducts a "constructive dialogue" with State representative concerned, and adopts concluding observations since 2001. Through concluding observations, the Commission has highlighted positive aspects and identified the factors/challenges restricting the enjoyment of human rights in many African States. Such factors include widespread poverty and unemployment; harmful cultural practices and deeply entrenched prejudices, in particular against women, minorities and indigenous peoples; lack of human rights awareness; and conflict and political crises. The Commission has also made recommendations to States regarding the measures required to strengthen the enjoyment of human rights guaranteed by the African Charter, as well as other relevant regional and international human rights instruments.

For example, the Commission has recommended that States take the "necessary steps" to amend national Constitution to incorporate economic, social, cultural, and environmental rights, ratify international human rights treaties such as the International Covenant on Economic, Social and Cultural Rights, consider withdrawing reservations to human rights treaties, and institute a moratorium on the death penalty (African Commission on Human and Peoples' Rights, Concluding Observations and Recommendations on the Initial Periodic Report of the Republic of Botswana, 12–26 May 2010, paras. 53–57). Recent recommendations, for example, Concluding Observations and Recommendations on the 5th Periodic Report of the Federal Republic of Nigeria, 4–18 November 2015, are more detailed commenting on specific rights and groups. The Commission requires States to inform it in the next periodic report, of the "measures taken" to address issues of concern, and to "ensure the effective implementation of the recommendations."

However, the ability of the African Commission to monitor State compliance with human rights obligations under the African Charter has been largely limited by the fact that most States have not taken their reporting obligations seriously. As a result, most reports have not been submitted on time. By the end of 2017, some States (Comoros, Equatorial Guinea, Guinea Bissau, Sao Tome and Principe, Somalia, and South Sudan) had never submitted any report. Only a few States (Burkina Faso, DRC, Malawi, Nigeria, Namibia, Mauritania, Rwanda, Senegal, and South Africa) had complied with reporting obligations under Article 26 of the Protocol on the Rights of Women in Africa.

African Court on Human and Peoples' Rights

In 2006 the protective mandate of the African Commission was complemented by the African Court on Human and Peoples' Rights. Significantly, under Article 3(1) of the Protocol to the African Charter on Human and Peoples' Rights on the

Establishment of an African Court on Human and Peoples' Rights, the material jurisdiction of the African Court extends to all "human rights instrument[s]" ratified by relevant States. The Protocol on the Establishment of an African Court has not yet been ratified by all States parties to the African Charter.

By Article 5 of the Protocol, cases may be submitted to the Court directly by individuals and NGOs or indirectly through the African Commission. If the Court finds a violation of a human right, it is empowered to "make appropriate orders to remedy the violation." A remedy may be considered "appropriate" if it is "adequate, effective, promptly attributed, holistic and proportional to the gravity of the harm suffered" (Committee on the Elimination of all Forms of Discrimination against Women, General Recommendation No. 33 on Women's Access to Justice 2015, para. 19(b)). This includes, under Article 27(1) of the Protocol to the African Charter on Human and Peoples' Rights on the Establishment of an African Court on Human and Peoples' Rights, the payment of "fair compensation" (whether provided in the form of money, goods or services) or adequate "reparation" (restitution, reinstatement). Other possible remedies the Court may grant, based on the practice of other human rights bodies, include rehabilitation (medical and psychological care and other social services); orders of investigations and prosecutions of perpetrators when human rights violations occur in conflict or postconflict contexts; and mandate institutional reforms, repeal discriminatory legislation, and enact legislation providing for adequate sanctions, guarantees of nonrepetition.

Judgments and orders of the Court in contentious proceedings are legally binding. Thus, States parties are required by Article 30 of the Protocol to "comply with the judgment in any case to which they are parties within the time stipulated by the Court and to guarantee its execution." Execution of judgments, under Articles 29(2) and 31 of the Protocol, is monitored by the Executive Council of the AU on behalf of the AU Assembly. The Assembly is empowered to impose sanctions or take "other measures of a political or economic nature" against States that do not comply with the AU "decisions" (Constitutive Act of the African Union 2000, Art. 23(2)). Such decisions include the Court's judgments and orders of provisional measures.

Article 4 of the Protocol grants the Court jurisdiction to provide advisory opinions on "any legal matter" relating to the African Charter or "any other relevant human rights instruments" (e.g., other AU human rights treaties and UN human rights treaties) provided the matter does not relate to an application pending before the African Commission (African Court of Human and Peoples' Rights, *The Pan African Lawyers' Union (PALU) and Southern African Litigation Centre (SALC)*, Request 2/2012, Order Striking Out Request (Similar Request at the African Commission, 15 March 2013)). The substantive scope of the Court's advisory opinions is limited to "human rights instruments" only as opposed to instruments on other areas of "public international law" such as instruments dealing with individual criminal responsibility for international crimes (African Court of Human and Peoples' Rights, *Coalition for the International Criminal Court, Legal Defence & Assistance Project (LEDAP), Civil Resource Development & Documentation Center and Women Advocates Documentation Center*, Request 1/2015 (Order Striking Out the Request, 29 November 2015), para. 18).

Such opinions are provided under Article 4 of the Protocol at the request of a member State of the AU, the AU, any of its organs, or any "African organization" (either intergovernmental or non-governmental) recognized by the AU. This recognition is achieved through the granting of observer status with the AU or the signing of any Memorandum of Understanding between the AU and the NGOs. The Court has declined to give Advisory Opinions requested by African Organisations which do not meet this requirement (African Court of Human and Peoples' Rights, Request for Advisory Opinion by 1. The Centre for Human Rights, University of Pretoria 2. Federation of Women Lawyers, Kenya 3. Women's Legal Centre 4. Women Advocates Research and Documentation Centre 5. Zimbabwe Women Lawyers Association, Request No 001/2016, Advisory Opinion 28 September 2017, para. 48).

Direct Access to the African Court by Individuals and NGOs

This is the easiest way to access the Court without delays associated with the process of going through the Commission. The Court has received numerous cases mainly brought directly to it by individuals and NGOs after exhaustion of domestic remedies. In March 2018, out of 161 applications filed before Court, 147 were brought by individuals, 11 by NGOs, and 3 by the African Commission. The Court handed down its first decision on jurisdiction ("judgment") in 2009 in the case of *Michelot Yogogombaye v The Republic of Senegal*, Application 001/2008 (15 December 2009).

It has since handed down some judgments on merits in which it found violations of the African Charter (African Court of Human and Peoples' Rights, *Konaté v Burkina Faso*, Application 4/13 (Judgment, 5 December 2014); *Abdoulaye Nikiema, Ernest Zongo, Blaise Ilboudo & Burkinabe Human and Peoples' Rights Movement v Burkina Faso*, Application 13/11 (Judgment, 28 March 2014); *Onyango Nganyi v Tanzania*, Application 6/2013, (Judgment, 18 March 2016); *Jonas v Tanzania*, Application 11/2015 (Judgment, 28 September 2017); *Onyachi and Others v Tanzania*, Application 3/2015 (Judgment, 28 September 2017); *African Commission on Human and Peoples' Rights v Kenya*, Application 6/2012 (Judgment, 26 May 2017); *Actions pour la protection des droits de l'homme (APDH) v Côte d'Ivoire*, Application 1/2014 (Judgment, 18 November 2016); *Christopher Jonas v United Republic of Tanzania*, Application 011/2015 (Judgment, 28 September 2017); *Kijiji Isiaga v United Republic of Tanzania*, Application 032/2015 (Judgment, 21 March 2018); *Anudo Ochieng Anudo v The United Republic of Tanzania*, Application 012/2015 (Judgment, 22 March 2018); *Nguza Viking (Babu Seya) and Johnson Nguza (Papi Kocha) v United Republic of Tanzania*, Application 006/2015 (Judgment, 23 March 2018)), or no violations (Mtikila v Tanzania, Application 11/2011, (Judgment, 14 June 2013); *Thomas v Tanzania*, Application 5/2013, (Judgment, 20 November 2015); *Onyango Nganyi v Tanzania*, Application 6/2013, (Judgment, 18 March 2016); *Abubakari v Tanzania*, Application 7/2013, (Judgment, 3 June 2016)).

The Court has also found violations of other human rights instruments including the Universal Declaration of Human Rights and the International Covenant on Civil and Political Rights. For example, in *Konaté v Burkina Faso,* Application 4/13, the Court found, inter alia, a violation of Article 19 ICCPR. In *Anudo Ochieng Anudo v The United Republic of Tanzania*, Application 012/2015 (Judgment 22 March 2018) Tanzania annulled the applicant's passport (who was of Tanzanian nationality), which he had, until then enjoyed, declared him an "illegal immigrant" and expelled him from Tanzania, without the possibility of an appeal before a national court. The Court found that this constituted the violation of the applicant's right not to be arbitrarily deprived of his nationality in violation of Article 15(2) of the Universal Declaration of Human Rights; the right not to be arbitrarily expelled from a State and violation of the right to judicial remedy (the right to have his cause heard by a judge) contrary to Article 7 of the African Charter and Article 14 of the International Covenant on Civil and Political Rights. It ordered Tanzania to take all the necessary steps to restore the applicant's rights, by allowing him to return to the national territory, ensure his protection and ordered Tanzania to amend its legislation to provide individuals with judicial remedies in the event of dispute over their citizenship.

In addition, the Court has also issued orders mainly dismissing applications for failure to comply with the admissibility requirements under Article 56 of the African Charter. These include the failure to exhaust domestic (local) remedies before commencing proceedings under Rule 34(4) of the African Court of Human and Peoples' Rights (African Court of Human and Peoples' Rights, *Fidèle Mulindahabi v Republic of Rwanda*, Application 008/2017 (order, 28 September 2017); *Diakitè Couple v Republic of Mali*, Application 009/2016 (Judgment, 28 September 2017)), or the failure to submit cases within a reasonable period from the time local remedies are exhausted under Rule 34(4) (African Court of Human and Peoples' Rights, *Fidèle Mulindahabi v Republic of Rwanda*, Application 008/2017 (order, 28 September 2017); *Diakitè Couple v Republic of Mali*, Application 009/2016 (Judgment, 28 September 2017)). At the request of States concerned, the Court has clarified aspects of its orders to enable States to implement the Court's rulings (African Court of Human and Peoples' Rights, *Urban Mkandawire v The Republic of Malawi*, Application 3/2011, (Ruling on Application for Interpretation of Judgment, 28 March 2014); and *Alex Thomas v United Republic of Tanzania*, Application 001/2017 for Interpretation of Judgment of 20 November 2015 (Judgment, 28 September 2017); *Mohamed Abubakari v United Republic of Tanzania*, Application 002/2017 for Interpretation of Judgment of 3 June 2016 (Judgment, 28 September 2017); *Mariam Kouma and Ousmane Diabatè v Republic of Mali*, Application 040/2016 (Judgment, 21 March 2018)).

It is important to note that in its first decade of operation, the Court decided more contentious cases than other regional human rights courts during the corresponding period. However, in most cases it found that it lacked jurisdiction mainly because of the limitations placed on direct access to the Court by individuals and NGOs. It should be noted that the Court's personal jurisdiction (jurisdiction *ratione personae*) is limited to States parties to the African Charter and the African Court Protocol. However, the Protocol is yet to be ratified by all African States. By March 2018, 30 States (Algeria, Benin, Burkina Faso, Burundi, Cameroon, Chad, Côte d'Ivoire, Comoros, Congo,

Gabon, Gambia, Ghana, Kenya, Libya, Lesotho, Mali, Malawi, Mozambique, Mauritania, Mauritius, Nigeria, Niger, Rwanda, Sahrawi Arab Democratic Republic, South Africa, Senegal, Tanzania, Togo, Tunisia and Uganda) out of 55 AU member States had ratified the African Court Protocol. Thus, cases brought against non-State parties to the African Charter and African Court's Protocol were unsuccessful (African Court of Human and Peoples' Rights, *Femi Falana v African Union*, Application 1/2011, (Judgment of 26 June 2012); *Atabong Denis Atemnkeng v African Union*, Application 14/2011 (Judgment, 15 March 2013); *Youssef Ababou v Kingdom of Morocco*, Application 7/2011, (Decision on Jurisdiction, 2 September 2011)).

Another significant limitation is that direct access to the Court by individuals and NGOs (to obtain a remedy or to be represented as a victim in a contentious case or to solicit an advisory opinion) is limited by the requirement under Articles 5(3) and 34(6) of the Protocol for an optional declaration made by State concerned recognizing the competence of the Court to receive cases from individuals and NGOs (with observer status before the African Commission). Since it is optional to submit such a declaration, a State may unilaterally withdraw it. Consequently, "states retain discretion to withdraw their commitments" without providing any reason (African Court of Human and Peoples' Rights, *Inbabire Victoire Umuhoza v Rwanda*, App 3/2014, Ruling on the Effects of the Withdrawal of the Declaration under Article 34(6) of the Protocol (3 June 2016), para. 58). In March 2018, only 8 of the 30 States Parties to the Protocol had made the declaration recognizing the competence of the Court to receive cases from individuals and NGOs (in alphabetical order): Benin (2016), Burkina Faso (1998), Côte d'Ivoire (2013), Ghana (2011), Mali (2010), Malawi (2008), Tanzania (2010), and Tunisia (2017). Since most States have not deposited this optional declaration, the Court lacks jurisdiction to "receive any petition" from individuals and NGOs involving any State Party which has not made such a declaration.

For this reason, several cases brought against States (e.g., Algeria, Cameroon, Côte d'Ivoire, Gabon, Mozambique, Nigeria, Senegal, South Africa, Sudan, and Tunisia) that had not made the optional declaration at the relevant time failed (African Court of Human and Peoples' Rights, *Soufiane Ababou v Algeria*, Application 2/2011; *Ekollo v Cameroon and Nigeria*, Application 8/2011; *Association Juristes d'Afrique pour la Bonne Gouvernance v Côte d'Ivoire*, Application 6/2011; *National Convention of Teachers Trade Union v Gabon*, Application 12/2011; *Daniel Amare and Mulugeta Amare v Mozambique and Mozambique Airlines*, Application 5/2011; *Ekollo M. Alexandre v Cameroon and Nigeria*, Application 8/2011; *Michelot Yogogombaye v Senegal*, Application 1/2008; *Delta International investments (SA), AGL De Lange and M. De Lange v South Africa*, Application 2/2012; *Emmanuel Joseph Uko and others v South Africa*, Application 4/2012; *Amir Adam Timan v Sudan*, Application 5/2012; *Baghdadi Ali Mahmoudi v Tunisia*, Application 7/2012).

In accordance with Article 27(2) of the African Court Protocol, and Rule 51(1) of the Rules of Court (2010), the Court has since 2011 delivered several orders for provisional measures in cases of "extreme gravity and urgency" and "when necessary to avoid irreparable harm to persons" and "necessary to adopt in the interest of the parties or of justice." The cases in which provisional measures were issued were brought against Burkina Faso, Kenya, Libya, Ghana, Rwanda, and Tanzania (African Court of Human and Peoples' Rights, *African Commission v Lybia (Bengazi)*, Application 4/2011, Order for Provisional Measures (25 March 2011); *African Commission v Lybia (Saif Al-Islam Kadhafi)*, Application 2/2013, Order for Provisional Measures (15 March 2013); *African Commission v Kenya (Ogiek)*, Application 6/2012, Order for Provisional Measures (15 March 2013); *Konate v Burkina Faso*, Application 4/2013, Order for Provisional Measures (4 October 2013); *Guehi v Tanzania*, Application 1/2015, Order for Provisional Measures (18 March 2016); *Rajabu and 4 others v Tanzania*, Application 7/2015, Order for Provisional Measures (8 March 2016); *Alfred Agbesi Woyome v Republic of Ghana*, Application 001/2017 (24 November 2017); *Lèon Mugesera v Republic of Rwanda*, Application 012/2017 (28 September 2017); and *Dexter Eddie Johnson v Republic of Ghana*, Application 016/2017 (28 September 2017)). Significantly, most orders of provisional measurers in the period 2015–2016 related to cases brought by individuals (convicted prisoners on death row) against Tanzania to refrain from executing the death penalty confirmed by relevant domestic courts pending the determination of their applications.

Orders for Provisional Measures were granted in the following cases: *Armand Guehi v The United Republic of Tanzania*, Application 001/2015 (18 March 2016); *Ally Rajabu and 4 Others v The United Republic of Tanzania*, Application 007/2015 (18 March 2016); *John Lazaro v The United Republic of Tanzania*, Application 003/2016 (18 March 2016); *Evodius Rutechura v The United Republic of Tanzania*, Application 004/2016 (18 March 2016); *Habiyalimana Augustino and Mburo Abdulkarim v The United Republic of Tanzania*, Application 015/2016 (3 June 2016); *Deogratius Nicholaus Jeshi v The United Republic of Tanzania*, Application 017/2016 (3 June 2016); *Cosma Faustine v The United Republic of Tanzania*, Application 018/2016 (3 June 2016); *Joseph Mukwano v The United Republic of Tanzania*, Application 021/2016 (3 June 2016); *Amini Juma v The United Republic of Tanzania*, Application 024/2016 (3 June 2016); *Dominick Damian v The United Republic of Tanzania*, Application 048/2016 (18 November 2016); *Chrizant John v The United Republic of Tanzania*, Application 049/2016 (18 November 2016); *Crospery Gabriel & Ernest Mutakyawa v The United Republic of Tanzania*, Application 050/2016 (18 November 2016); *Nzigiyimana Zabron v The United Republic of Tanzania*, Application 051/2016 (18 November 2016); *Marthine Chistian Msuguri v The United Republic of Tanzania*, Application 052/2016 (18 November 2016); *Oscar Josiah v The United Republic of Tanzania*, Application 053/2016 (18 November 2016); *Gozbert Henerico v The United Republic of Tanzania*, Application 056/2016; *Mulokozi Anatori v The United Republic of Tanzania*, Application 057/2016 (18 November 2016). The Court took the view that the risk of execution of the death penalty will jeopardize the enjoyment of the rights to life, fair trial, and freedom from inhuman or degrading treatment or punishment under Articles 3(2), 4, and 7(1)(c) of the African Charter (*Crospery Gabriel & Ernest Mutakyawa v United Republic of Tanzania*, Application 050/2016 (18 November 2016), para 16), Article 14 of the ICCPR (*Evodius Rutechura v The United Republic of Tanzania*,

Application 004/2016 (18 March 2016), paras 16–17; *Ally Rajabu and 4 Others v The United Republic of Tanzania*, Application 007/2015 (18 March 2016), paras 18–19; *Armand Guehi v The United Republic of Tanzania*, Application 001/2015 (18 March 2016), para 19–20), and Articles 3 and 5 of the UDHR (*Dexter Eddie Johnson v Republic of Ghana*, Application 016/2017 (28 September 2017), para 17).

In 2017 the Court granted provisional measures ordering a respondent State to allow a person in custody access to his lawyers visit by his family members and access to medical care (African Court of Human and Peoples' Rights, *Lèon Mugesera v Republic of Rwanda*, Application 012/2017 (28 September 2017)). It also granted provisional measures ordering a respondent State to stay the attachment and sale of the applicant's property until his application is heard and determined (African Court of Human and Peoples' Rights, *Alfred Agbesi Woyome v Republic of Ghana*, Application 001/2017 (24 November 2017). Thus, provisional measures have been used to protect not only civil and political rights but also economic, social, and cultural rights including ordering a State to provide a detained journalist with the "medication and health care required" (African Court of Human and Peoples' Rights, *Konate v Burkina Faso*, Application 4/2013, Order for Provisional Measures (4 October 2013), para 23(ii)).

Indirect Access to the African Court Through the African Commission's Referral of Communications to the African Court

Rule 118 of the 2010 Commission's Rules of Procedure allows the Commission to submit cases to the African Court in respect of all States parties to the African Court Protocol under four circumstances: (i) where a State has not complied or is unwilling to comply with the Commission's recommendations; (ii) where a State has not complied with the Commission's request for provisional (interim/precautionary) measures; (iii) situations involving serious or massive violations of human rights; and (iv) if the Commission "deems necessary" to refer a communication to the Court at any stage (Commission's admissibility and merits finding). In all these situations, the Commission represents the interest of one party to the dispute (the applicant) before the Court. However, the Court has discretion to hear "any person" including the original complainants before the Commission (victims) and their representatives as well as amici curiae (African Court of Human and Peoples' Rights, *African Commission v Kenya (Ogiek)*, Application 6/2012, paras. 27–29).

Referral of Noncompliance or Unwillingness to Comply with the Commission's Recommendations

The African Commission "may," at its discretion, submit a case to the African Court, where it "considers that the State [party to the African Court Protocol] has not complied or is unwilling to comply with its recommendations in respect of the communication" within the period specified (Commission's Rules of Procedure, Rule 112(2)). The aim is to enable the African Court to give legally binding judicial "enforcement" to the quasi-judicial decisions of the African Commission where the State has failed or is unwilling to implement recommendations made by a quasi-judicial body (the Commission) in communications decided by the Commission on the merits. As at the time of writing in 2018, the African Commission had not yet referred to the Court cases decided on merits of alleged noncompliance with its recommendations. It is desirable to refer all cases of noncompliance to the Court, "unless there is a reasoned decision by an absolute majority of members of the Commission to the contrary" (See Rules of Procedure of the Inter-American Commission (2009), Rule 45(1)). The Commission did not refer States to the Court because most noncomplying States in cases finalized by the Commission (Angola, Botswana, DRC, Ethiopia, Eritrea, Sudan, and Zimbabwe) in the period 2010–2018 had not accepted the jurisdiction of the African Court. In addition, the Commission was reluctant to make referrals to the Court in appropriate cases in which there was noncompliance, possibly to avoid a possibility of conflicting findings on the merits by the Court after reconsideration of the facts.

Referral of Noncompliance with the Commission's Request for Provisional (Interim) Measures

Under Rule 98 of the African Commission's Rules of Procedure (2010), the Commission may, on its initiative or at the request of a party to the communication, "request" that the State concerned adopt provisional measures to prevent irreparable harm to the victim or victims of the alleged violation as urgently as the situation demands. This may be done at any time after the receipt of a communication and before a determination on the merits. If the Commission considers that the State has not complied with the provisional measures requested, the Commission may refer the communication to the Court and inform the complainant and the State concerned (Rule 118(2)). The referral is intended to transform the Commission's "requests" for provisional measures into legally binding Court "orders" of provisional measures. In a few cases of noncompliance with the Commission's "requests" for provisional measures referred to the African Court, the Court ordered provisional measures of its own (African Court of Human and Peoples' Rights, *African Commission (Saif Al-Islam Kadhafi) v Lybia*, Application 2/2013, Order of Provisional Measures (15 March 2013); *African Commission (Ogiek) v Kenya*, Application 6/2012, Order for Provisional Measures (15 March 2013)), and subsequently considered cases referred to it on the merits finding human rights violations (*African Commission (Saif Al-Islam Gaddafi) v Lybia*, Application 2/2013, Judgment (3 June 2015), the Court found that Libya had violated the fair trial rights of the detainee; *African Commission v Kenya (Ogiek)*, Application 6/2012 (26 May 2017)).

Referral of Serious or Massive Violations of Human Rights

The Commission may submit a communication (already pending before it) to the Court against a State party if in its view a "situation" has come to its attention which constitutes "one of serious or massive violations of human rights" (Rule 118(3) and Rule 84(2) of the Rules of Procedure of the African Court on Human and Peoples' Rights; African Charter, Art. 58). The referral of Libya to the Court in 2011 represents an example of such a situation. The UN Security Council deplored "the gross and systematic violation of human rights" in Libya particularly the widespread and systematic attacks against the civilian population in UN Security Council Resolution 1970 of 26 February 2011 (UN Doc. S/RES/1970 (2011)). As noted above, since the AU Assembly of Heads of State and Government has failed to take action in any of the cases revealing the existence of a series of "serious or massive violations" of human rights referred to it by the Commission under Article 58(1) of the African Charter, it is desirable to refer all situations of "serious or massive" violations of human rights to the Court in the future.

Referral at "Any Stage of the Examination of a Communication"

Finally, the Commission may "seize" the Court "at any stage of the examination of a communication if it deems necessary" (Rule 118(4) of the Rules of Procedure of the African Commission). This means that the Commission may refer cases to the Court before deciding communications before it on the merits. The referral may be made at "any stage" even before deciding on the admissibility of the communication before the Commission. Such referrals should be made only if it is "necessary" to do so, meaning that there must be pressing need for a binding order or judgment in response to a situation of extreme gravity and urgency (African Court on Human and Peoples' Rights, *Benghazi v Libya*, Application 4/2011, Order for Provisional Measures (25 March 2011)).

Conclusion

While there is much progress still to be made, the African Commission has greatly contributed to the regional protection of human rights in Africa. The Commission has exposed human rights violations in most authoritarian African States. Through its decisions on communications, it has developed progressive human rights jurisprudence in Africa on several aspects, consistent with the jurisprudence of other human rights bodies such as the UN Human Rights Committee, the European Court of Human Rights, the Inter-American-Commission on Human Rights, and the Inter-American-Court of Human Rights. These include jurisprudence on exhaustion of local remedies, State obligations concerning civil and political rights, economic, social, and cultural rights as well as group rights such indigenous peoples' rights and the right to development. Nevertheless, the African

Commission has only received and decided very few communications related to economic, social, and cultural rights.

Initially, it was thought the Commission would be unable to hold States accountable for violations of human rights and to provide reparations to victims. However, over the years the Commission has confronted human rights violations through its decisions on communications; adoption of resolutions, principles/guidelines, general comments, model laws and advisory opinions; special rapporteurs and working groups to deal with thematic human rights issues; conducting on-site visits; consideration of State reports and adoption of concluding observations; as well as the referral of communications to the African Court. Despite delays in timely submission of reports, the State reporting mechanism has provided an opportunity for constructive dialogue and review. It has also helped most States to keep stock of their human rights achievements and challenges.

Nevertheless, compliance with the Commission's "requests" for provisional measures/letters of urgent appeals, decisions and recommendations of the Commission, as set out in the Communications and concluding observations on State reports, have been low. The insufficient funding of the Commission from the member States budget and human crisis at the Commission's Secretariat impedes the Commission's capacity to follow up on implementation as it prevents the Commission from developing effective follow-up of its findings during country visits, and recommendations arising from its findings, resulting in the overall weakening of the effectiveness of the Commission (42nd Activity Report of the African Commission on Human and Peoples' Rights, paras. 45 and 52).

Although the contribution of the African Court is still modest, it is noteworthy that between 2006 and March 2018, it has handed down judgments in 11 contentious cases (excluding admissibility decisions), finding violations in all of them. The Court has shown willingness to achieve harmonization of international and regional human rights standards by drawing inspiration from the case law of other human rights bodies including the African Commission, the European Court of Human Rights and the Inter-American Court of Human Rights as well as the Human Rights Committee (African Commission on Human and Peoples' Rights, *Consolidated Matter of 1. Tanganyika Law Society 2. The Legal and Human Rights Centre v The United Republic of Tanzania, Application 009/2011 and Reverend Christopher R. Mtikila v The United Republic of Tanzania*, 011/2011, (14 June 2013) paras. 82 and 106–109). It also adopted one advisory opinion during the same period. Three main challenges to the Court limit its effectiveness.

First, the limited direct access by individuals and NGOs to the Court due to a limited number of States that have accepted the Court's jurisdiction and allowed individuals and NGOs direct access to the Court. Thus, there is a need for more States to ratify the Court's Protocol and to allow individuals and NGOs direct access to the Court. This will help to consolidate a pan-African judicial system for the protection of human rights which applies to over 1.2 billion people in Africa. In addition, an amendment of Article 34(6) the African Court Protocol by a decision of the AU Assembly of Heads of State and Government to allow individuals and NGOs direct access to the Court would make the Court more accessible to victims of human rights violations in Africa. Until this is achieved, the African Commission should submit more cases to the Court in accordance with Rule 118 discussed above, particularly those cases in which States have failed to implement the Commission's decisions.

Second, the nonimplementation of the Court's decisions, including refusals to implement, failure to inform the Court of what measures have been taken, and the slow-pace or "reluctance" to comply limits the Court's effectiveness (African Court, Mid-Term Activity Report 2017, paras. 45–46; AU Executive Council, Report on the Activities of the African Court to the Executive Council 2017, para. 57). In 2013, for example, the Court adopted an Interim Report noting that "Libya has failed to comply with a judgment of the Court" (African Court, Interim Report of the African Court notifying the Executive Council of non-compliance by a State (Interim Report on Libya) 2013, para. 8). It called on the AU Assembly of Heads of State to take such other measures as it deems appropriate to ensure that Libya fully complies with the Court Order. However, the Assembly did not take any action. This shows that noncompliance and nonenforcement applies to both the Commission's recommendations and the Court's orders. Thus, the ability of the AU organs to impose sanctions consistently on noncomplying States is necessary in order to strengthen the credibility of the African Court's orders and judgments.

Third, a lack of awareness about the African human rights system, the AU human rights treaties and institutions including the African Commission and Court by aggrieved individuals/groups, and limited knowledge about the system by domestic lawyers limits potential applications to the Commission and the Court. Therefore, States and other actors including educational institutions should through human rights education raise awareness about the African Commission and Court among public and government officials and other actors including religious leaders, judges, lawyers, and law enforcement officials throughout Africa.

Finally, given the limited resources of the Commission and the Court, subsidiarity (as reflected in the requirement to exhaust domestic remedies) must be strengthened. Effective and accessible remedies before domestic and subregional courts will decrease the workload of the Commission and the Court. In the longer term, both the Commission and the Court must continue to examine ways to maintain their effectiveness and legitimacy in order to discharge their respective mandates.

References

42nd Activity Report of the African Commission on Human and Peoples' Rights. Available at http://www.achpr.org/activity-reports/42. Accessed 14 May 2018

43rd Activity Report of the African Commission on Human and Peoples' Rights. Available at http://www.achpr.org/activity-reports/43. Accessed 14 May 2018

African Commission on Human and Peoples' Rights, General Comment No. 3 on the African Charter on Human and Peoples' Rights: the right to life (Article 4), adopted during the 57th Ordinary Session of the African Commission on Human and Peoples' Rights, 4 to 18 November 2015. Available at http://www.achpr.org/instruments/general-comments-right-to-life. Accessed 14 May 2018

African Commission on Human and Peoples' Rights. Available at http://www.achpr.org. Accessed 14 May 2018

African Commission, Resolution on the Right to Food and Food Insecurity in Africa, ACHPR/Res. 374 (LX) 2017, 22 May 2017

African Committee of Experts on the Rights and Welfare of the Child. Available at http://www. acerwc.org. Accessed 14 May 2018

African Court on Human and Peoples' Rights. Available at http://www.african-court.org. Accessed 14 May 2018

African Court, Interim Report of the African Court notifying the Executive Council of non-compliance by a State (Interim Report on Libya), 17 May 2013

African Court, Mid-Term Activity Report 1 January – 30 June 2017

African Human Rights Case Law Analyser. https://www.ihrda.org/african-human-rights-case-law-analyzer. Accessed 14 May 2018

African Union, OAU/AU Treaties, Conventions, Protocols & Charters. Available at https://au.int/en/treaties. Accessed 15 May 2018

AU Executive Council, Report on the Activities of the African Court to the Executive Council, 22–27 January 2017

Charter of the Organisation of African Unity 1963

Combined 32nd and 33rd Activity Report of the African Commission on Human and Peoples' Rights. EX.CL/782(XXII) Rev.2, 2013

Committee on Economic, Social and Cultural Rights (2001) Statement adopted by the Committee on economic, social and cultural rights, 4 May 2011, UN Doc. E/C.12/2001/10, 10 May 2001

Committee on the Elimination of all Forms of Discrimination against Women, General Recommendation No. 33 on Women's Access to Justice, UN Doc. CEDAW/C/GC/33, 3 August 2015

Constitutive Act of the African Union 2000

Leckie S (1988) The inter-state complaint procedure in international human rights law: hopeful prospects or wishful thinking? Hum Rights Q 10(2):249–303

Murray R, Long D (2015) The implementation of the findings of the African Commission on Human and Peoples Rights. Cambridge University Press, Cambridge, MA

Protocol on Amendments to the Protocol on the Statute of the African Court of Justice and Human Rights, and Statute of the African Court of Justice and Human Rights 2014

Protocol on the Statute of the African Court of Justice and Human Rights, and Statute of the African Court of Justice and Human Rights 2008

Protocol to the African Charter on Human and Peoples' Rights on the Establishment of an African Court on Human and Peoples' Rights 1998

Protocol to the African Charter on Human and Peoples' Rights on the Rights of Women in Africa (the Maputo Protocol) 2003

Ssenyonjo M (ed) (2012) The African regional human rights system. Nijhoff, Leiden

Viljoen F (2018) Understanding and overcoming challenges in accessing the African Court on Human and Peoples' Rights. ICLQ 67:63–98

Human Rights Mechanisms in the Arab World: Politics and Protection

Zaid Eyadat and Hani Okasheh

Contents

Introduction 512
The League of Arab States' Human Rights General Framework 513
The Arab Charter on Human Rights 514
The Arab Human Rights Committee 515
The Arab Court of Human Rights 516
Critical Review of the ACHR 519
The Exclusive Process of Drafting the ACHR's Statute 519
Subject Matter Jurisdiction of the ACHR 520
Execution of ACHR Rulings 521
Access to the ACHR and Admissibility of Cases 522
Independence and Impartiality of the Court and Its Judges 523
Conclusion 524
References 525

Abstract

This chapter provides a historical overview of the evolution of human rights mechanisms in the MENA region, starting with the initial process of drafting an Arab Charter on Human Rights and its subsequent adoption 10 years after the emergence of the first draft. It also provides an overview of the functions and mandate of multiple organs tasked with ensuring the promotion and respect of human rights in the MENA, primarily the Arab Human Rights Committee which came into existence upon the ratification of the Arab Charter on Human Rights. With a mandate to promote and strengthen the respect of human rights in the

Z. Eyadat (✉)
Human Rights Centre, University of Connecticut, Storrs, Connecticut, USA
e-mail: zaid.eyadat@uconn.edu

H. Okasheh
University of Jordan, Amman, Jordan
e-mail: hani_okasheh@hotmail.co.uk

© Springer Nature Singapore Pte Ltd. 2018   511
G. Oberleitner (ed.), *International Human Rights Institutions, Tribunals, and Courts*,
International Human Rights, https://doi.org/10.1007/978-981-10-5206-4_19

MENA, the chapter reviews one of the Arab Human Rights Committee's most important functions, which is to consider reports of the state parties to the Charter, in which each signatory state must indicate measures undertaken to enforce the rights and freedoms enshrined in the Charter. The chapter then provides a critical account of the Arab Court of Human Rights, highlighting the Court's Statute and the impediments inhibiting the Court's function as an effective mechanism to address human rights violations in the region by redressing victims of rights violations and holding perpetrators of these violations accountable for their actions. Finally, the chapter concludes with recommendations to enhance the aforementioned human rights frameworks, emphasizing the role of civil society in any effort that aims at promoting and strengthening the respect of human rights in the MENA.

Keywords

Arab Charter on Human Rights · Arab Court of Human Rights · League of Arab States · Arab Human Rights Committee · Statute of the Arab Court of Human Rights

Introduction

Human rights in the Middle East is not the smoothest task for any writer to take up; however, a viable starting point for this chapter can be the Arab Spring. Whether it has been a sincere, spontaneous expression of popular discontent with social, political, and economic injustice or an allegedly orchestrated act of "constructive chaos," human rights were at the core of popular demands among those who took to the streets their frustration of successive governments failing to deliver on their promises of social, economic, and political reform across countries in the Middle East.

The impacts of the Arab Spring varied from one Arab State to another. For example, while peaceful protests in Tunisia lead to overthrowing the autocratic Ben Ali regime, the peaceful protests which started in Southern Syrian provinces lead to a full-blown civil war between the Syrian regime and countless military factions, each fighting to advance the agenda of whatever external power that is funding its military operations, ultimately resulting in an estimated death toll of about 475,000 people and the displacement of about 11 million people.

In similar fashion, civil wars broke out in Libya and Yemen, resulting in protracted refugee crises that further undermined the rights of the peoples of Arab States. In the context of the Syrian refugee crisis, the human rights of both refugee and host communities, especially in countries that bore the brunt of the refugee crises such as Jordan and Lebanon, were compromised. This was mainly due to the limited resources, fragile economies, and absence of effective domestic policies to cater to the needs of both citizens and refugee populations in these countries.

For decades, the human rights discourse in the Middle East was riddled with superficiality and detachment from reality. A perfect depiction of this detachment can be observed in Arab States' periodic report to treaty bodies, but an example of superficiality could be the functions of institutions tasked with the enforcements of human rights standards and norms.

To this end, this chapter seeks to provide an account of the human rights mechanisms and processes in the Middle East and North Africa (MENA) region, thus explaining its development and progress on the multiple legislative and procedural aspects. The chapter will provide a comprehensive review of the efforts of the League of Arab States to establish a framework for safeguarding the human rights of people in the MENA region on the level of member states, primarily the Arab Charter on Human Rights, the Arab Human Rights Committee, and the Arab Court of Human Rights.

The chapter will also feature a critical assessment of these human rights frameworks and mechanisms, where it will compile various views from experts and civil society organizations on their perception of these mechanisms, ultimately seeking to inform the reader of the status of human rights in the Arab region as well as the institutions and tribunals tasked with ensuring the protection and promotion of these rights, highlighting their progress, shortcomings, and the ways forward.

The League of Arab States' Human Rights General Framework

The Charter of the League of the Arab States did not provide for mechanisms of enhancement and protection of human rights. To address this shortcoming, the Human Rights Department was established in 2001 under the oversight of the General Secretariat and tasked with coordinating the positions of Arab countries in regional and international forums on issues relating to the promotion of human rights. This department acted as the technical secretariat for the Standing Committee on Human Rights (established in 1968).

Among the most important achievements of this Committee is the drafting of the Arab Charter on Human Rights in 1994. The Arab Charter on Human Rights was amended in 2004 and entered force on 16 March 2008, which has subsequently been declared Arab Human Rights Day. Responding to the endeavors, Arab States adopted the Arab Plan of Action for Human Rights Education in 2008, its Guiding Manual in 2010, as well as the Arab Plan for Enhancing the Culture of Human Rights in 2010.

In the same context and with the purpose of activating the role of national institutions and non-governmental organization concerned with human rights, the General Secretariat of the Arab League offered many of these organizations the status of observer in the Standing Arab Human Rights Committee. To date, the number of these institutions and organizations has reached 23 from 12 Arab countries. The Arab League also established cooperation frameworks with multiple international human rights institutions including the Office of the High Commissioner for Human Rights (OHCHR), the United Nations High Commissioner for Refugee (UNHCR), and the European Union. This cooperation took many forms including holding capacity building seminars and workshops to enhance the capacity of governmental and national institutions in addition to non-governmental organizations working in the field of human rights.

The Arab Charter on Human Rights

The Arab Charter on Human Rights (ACHR) was adopted in the 16th ordinary session of the Council of the Arab League of Arab States at the Summit Level by resolution no. 270 of 23 May 2004. The ACHR entered into force on 15 March 2008 after seven states – Jordan, the United Arab Emirates, Bahrain, Syrian, Palestine, Libya, and Algeria – ratified it as per paragraph 2 of Article 49 of the Charter. The actual Charter consists of a preamble and four sections that include a total of 53 articles covering all civil, political, economic, social, and cultural rights. The Charter also provides for the establishment of its mechanism, the Arab Human Rights Committee (AHRC).

In 1994, the League of Arab States created a first version of the Arab Charter on Human Rights at its 50-year anniversary. By doing so, the League of Arab States attempted to signal the growing importance and recognition of human rights among its members as well as the need to establish a regional instrument for human rights in the Arab region, especially given that many regional organizations had already adopted instruments for the protection and promotion of human rights such as the European Convention on Human Rights (1950), the American Convention on Human Rights (1969), and the African Charter on Human and Peoples' Rights (1981).

The initial version of the Charter consisted of 43 articles following its preamble, which reaffirms the principles of the Universal Declaration of Human Rights, as well as the International Covenants on Civil and Political Rights and on Economic, Social, and Cultural Rights and the Cairo Declaration on Human Rights in Islam despite the unsettled tensions between the latter and the Universal Declaration on Human Rights. Despite this, the Charter, to a degree, enshrines the essential rights contained in other international and regional human right instruments (Al-Midani 2005).

Despite the creation of the Arab Charter on Human Rights of 1994, no state ratified it. There was also a fair share of criticism of the initial version of the Charter. Many experts in the Arab region and outside regarded the Charter as lacking an effective enforcement mechanism, especially if compared to other international and regional instruments of human rights. The Charter's only enforcement mechanism were the reports submitted by state parties to the experts committee, while the Charter lacked individual complaints or state petitions to this committee in the event of significant violation of an article of the Charter by a state party (Al-Midani 2005).

Given the amount of criticism which the initial version of the Charter faced, the Arab League acknowledged the need to amend the Charter. In January 2003, the Arab Human Rights Committee extended an invitation to Arab States to present proposals to improve the Charter with an outlook to introduce amendments in 2004.

In the same prism, the UN High Commissioner on Human Rights held a meeting of Arab experts in December 2003 in Cairo with the purpose of collecting observations and proposals to improve the Charter (Al-Midani 2005).

These efforts ultimately resulted in the issuance of a new version of the Charter in May 2003 during the Arab Summit in Tunisia. The new version of the Charter contained 53 articles, following the preamble which remained the same despite criticism regarding its incompatibility with the Universal Declaration on Human Rights (Al-Midani 2005).

Perhaps the most significant improvements in the 2004 version of the Charter are the open affirmation of equality between men and women in the Arab World, the introduction of provisions on children's rights, and the acknowledgment of the rights of persons with disabilities. However, the Charter fell short of providing an effective enforcement and monitoring mechanism (Al-Midani 2005).

Building on this, the provisions of the new version of the Charter can be broken down into four main categories. The first category provides articles related to individual rights: the right to life (Articles 5, 6, and 7), the right not to be subjected to torture or inhuman or degrading treatment (Articles 8, 9, 18, and 20), the right to be free from slavery (Article 10), and the right to security of the person (Articles 14 and 18). The second category concerns rules of justice: the right of all persons to be equal before the law (Article 12) and the rights to due process and fair trial (Articles 13, 15, 16, 17, and 19).

The third category concerns civil and political rights: the right to freedom of movement (Articles 24, 26, and 27); the right to respect for private and family life (Article 21); the rights of minorities (Article 25); the right of political asylum (Article 28); the right to acquire a nationality (Article 29); the right to liberty of thought and religion (Article 30); the right to private property (Article 31); the right to information and liberty of opinion, expression, and research (Article 32); and the right to marriage (Article 33). The fourth category concerns economic, social, and cultural rights: the right to work (Article 34), the right to form trade unions (Article 35), the right to social protection (Article 36), the right to development (Article 37), the right to education (Article 41), and the right to participate in cultural life (Article 42) (Al-Midani 2005).

The Arab Human Rights Committee

Article 45 of the ACHR provides for the establishment of the Arab Human Rights Committee (referred to hereafter as the Committee), making it the first Arab regional mechanism for enhancing and promoting human rights. According to the Charter, the newly established Committee is tasked with considering reports of the state parties to the Charter, in which each signatory state has to indicate measures undertaken to enforce the rights and freedoms enshrined in the Charter. The Committee consists of seven members who are independently elected through secret ballot by state parties and function in their personal capacity. The elected members must be highly experienced in the field of human rights and should be impartial and unbiased. They must be nationals of a state party. No state party may have more than one national in the Committee. Members of the Committee can be re-elected only once, each for a 4-year term. However, the mandates for three members of the Committee of those who were elected the first time expire after 2 years; these are selected by lot. The Charter provides guarantees that members of the Committee enjoy immunity in performing their tasks. This is important to protect them against any form of pressure or prosecution especially because of their statements or positions they take while exercising their mandates as members of the Committee (League of Arab States 2008).

State parties are obliged to submit periodic reports every 3 years (except for the first report where states had to submit 1 year after the Charter went into force). The Charter also stipulates that states must comply with the requests of the Committee which can require further information pursuant to commitments made under the Charter. To ensure that the reporting process is unified, the Committee provides state parties with reporting guidelines on the form and structure of the content of the report. The purpose of that is to ensure that States can convey the situation of human rights in their respective contexts in a comprehensive manner to showcase their progress against obligations set out in the Charter.

After submitting the reports to the Secretary-General of the Arab League, the reports are referred to the Committee for examination. In turn, the Committee provides its observations ahead of its discussion with the State party. The discussion is held with the official delegation of the state party where the Committee delivers its observations and recommendations in accordance with the provisions and goals of the Charter. These reports, along with concluding observations and recommendations, are then made public documents and disseminated by the Committee. The Committee is also tasked with submitting an annual report detailing its observations and recommendations to the Council of the Arab League (League of Arab States 2008). The Committee holds its meetings periodically to follow up the situation of human rights in state parties in addition to considering their reports. The Committee is also able to hold extraordinary meetings to discuss developments and urgencies if required.

The Arab Court of Human Rights

On 7 September 2014, the Council of the League of Arab States on the level of Ministers of Foreign Affairs adopted during its 142nd session the Statute of the Arab Court of Human Rights by its resolution no. 7790, E.A (142) C 3. Establishing the Arab Court of Human Rights was an important step to promote and protect human rights among member states. Al Manama, the capital of Bahrain, was selected to be home for the court. The Statute will enter into force after seven-member states have ratified it.

Given that one of the main critiques of the Arab Charter on Human Rights was not providing for mechanisms to protect and promote the human rights, the decision of the Foreign Ministers of the Arab League came to fill the gap in the mechanism of the Charter. Thus, the Arab Human Rights Court came into existence with the task of ensuring the respect of human rights and fundamental freedoms in the member states of the Arab League.

According to its Statute, the Arab Court of Human Rights is to be established within the framework of the League of Arab States as an independent Arab judicial organ to reinforce the desire of the state parties to implement their obligation regarding human rights freedom (Arab Court of Human Rights Statute 2013).

The Statute of the Court also provides for the establishment of the Court's Assembly which is comprised of representatives of State parties. The Assembly is tasked with handling the core administrative and functional tasks of the Court. Firstly, the Assembly must lay down its internal regulations which include determining the dates of its meetings (at least once annually) as well as preparing its budget and the basis of its annual reporting. Secondly, the Assembly must define its mandate including the election of judges, as well as identifying a mechanism to ensure the execution of the Court's rulings. States which are not parties to the Statute of the Court can attend the meetings of the Assembly; however, they do not have the right to vote (Arab Court of Human Rights Statute 2013).

The Court is comprised of seven judges who are citizens of state parties to the Statute. The number of judges can be increased to 11 upon request of the Court and by discretion of the Assembly under the condition of not electing more than one judge from the same nationality.

Judges are elected through secret ballot from a list of candidates. Based on the request from the Secretary-General of the League of Arab States, each state party can nominate two of its citizens within 90 days of the Statute entering into force. Candidates with the highest votes are selected as primary judges. In the event of more than one candidate getting the same number of votes, the voting procedure must be repeated to eliminate candidates who get the least number of votes at every round. In addition to the list of primary judges, the Assembly must establish a list of reserve judges from the candidates who were not elected as primary judges in accordance with the number of votes they received, respectively.

Each of the elected judges remains in their position for a 4-year term, with the possibility of being elected for a second, nonrenewable tenure. The tenure of three of the primary judges who were elected in the first elections shall conclude after 2 years. This is determined through the drawing of lots by the President of the Assembly right after the completion of the elections. During their tenure, judges are expected to exercise their duties in an impartial and unbiased manner while remaining at the Court's service in all times. Judges' duties conclude with the end of their tenure.

The Court must elect a President and a Vice-President from among of its members for a term of 2 years; they are eligible for re-election for one more term only. The President's main duties include managing the Courts' work as well as representing it before the judicial authorities or third parties. The President also presides over the Court's sessions, in addition to other tasks articulated in the Rules of the Court. The President must also exercise his or her duties on a full-time basis and to this end must reside in the country hosting the seat of the court. The Vice-President replaces the

President in cases of contingencies or absence, and in the event of a vacancy of the President's office, the Court must elect a new President to replace him or her for the remainder term of office. Also in the event of absence of the President and Vice-President, other judges replace them in accordance with the rules of seniority articulated in Article 12 of the Court's Statute.

The Statute of the Court guarantees the immunity of judges and members of the court. Article 15 of the Statute states that judges may in no circumstances or at any time even after the end of their tenure be held accountable for the opinions they have expressed or decisions they have taken during their time in service of the Court. To this end, the same Article forbids judges from performing any work or activities which might interfere or affect their impartiality. Judges are also not allowed to hear a case that they were previously involved with, whether as an agent, attorney, or consultant for one of the parties or as a member of an internal or international court, of an investigation or arbitration commission, or in any other capacity.

Article 15 also provides for the non-dismissal of a judge or the termination of his or her tenure except with the consent of the rest of the judges maintaining that one of them no longer meets the requirements necessary to presuming their position or does not meet the standards for which they were selected anymore. Article 16 of the Statute states that the Court has jurisdiction over all lawsuits and conflicts resulting from the interpretation or implementation of the Arab Charter on Human Rights or other (Arab) human rights conventions involving a member state. Hence, the Court is given the power to decide any dispute related to its jurisdiction where it shall examine the lawsuits, petitions, or cases at hand. Article 18 provides for the jurisdiction of the Court being complementary to the national judiciary of member states and does in no way attempt to supersede or replace it. To this end, the Article stipulates that the Court cannot hear a case that has not exhausted all local remedies in the respondent state by a final and definitive judgment according to the national legal system. The Court also does not hear a case that is pending before another regional human rights court. Finally, the Court does not hear a case that has been filed 6 months after the claimant's reception of the definitive judgment.

Article 19 of the Statute provides that for a citizen of a state party to file a case on a human rights violation, the claimant state and the defendant state must be parties to the Statute or have accepted the jurisdiction of the Court as determined in Article 20 of the Statute. Article 19 also provides that state parties can accept that one or more NGOs which are recognized by the state party and are acknowledged for their work and experience in the field of human rights can provide the facility for victims of human rights violations to access the court.

Article 20 of the Statute provides that member states of the Arab League who are not parties to the Court's Statute are able to declare at any time their acceptance of the jurisdiction of the Court in a specific case or in general. This declaration can be based on the reciprocity, or it can be unconditional or for a limited period. Declarations of this nature must be submitted to the Secretary-General while also sending copes to state parties to the Statute.

Critical Review of the ACHR

The events of the "Arab Spring" raised the alarm on the state of human rights in the MENA. Many voices were raised across the political and civic spectrums calling for reform and ensuring more respect and protection of human rights in the region. The League of Arab States recognized that it is imperative to take measures to promote the respect of human rights in the region, in response to the public outcries for an enhanced framework of human rights in the region. One of the primary reform initiatives undertaken by the League of Arab States is the establishment of the Arab Court of Human Rights. Indeed, the idea of establishing an impartial and effective regional mechanism to safeguard the rights of the people in the MENA has garnered a great deal of support and was met with enthusiasm among human rights advocates and civil society organizations across the MENA. However, as soon as the final draft of the Court's Statute made it to the public, many were disappointed as it was deemed by many as falling short of international standards.

Although many have initially welcomed the introduction of the ACHR, the process of establishing the court, drafting, and adopting its Statute has been marred with challenges and critique. The following sections will provide a critical review of the primary points of contention surrounding the Arab Human Rights Court and its statute, as well as establish a comparison between the Arab Human Rights Court and another key regional human rights mechanism. They will outline the key points of contention surrounding the ACHR and its statute: the exclusive procedure of establishing the Court and drafting its Statute, the jurisdiction of the court, access to the Court and the admissibility of cases, the execution of rulings rendered by the court, and finally the independence and impartiality of the Court and its judges. When relevant, a comparison will be established between the ACHR and the African Court of Human and Peoples' Rights, which came into existence when the African Union adopted the Protocol to the African Charter on Human and Peoples' Rights on the Establishment of the African Court on Human and Peoples' Rights in 1998, which is annexed to the African Charter on Human and Peoples' Rights adopted in 1981. This comparison can be helpful to highlight how another regional mechanism with a mandate like the ACHR addresses the identified shortcomings of the ACHR and its mandate.

The Exclusive Process of Drafting the ACHR's Statute

To reform the human rights system in the MENA, especially as it relates to the establishment of the ACHR, it would have been crucial to adopt a participatory approach in the process of establishing the Court as well as drafting its Statute where relevant stakeholders are meaningfully engaged in the process. However, drafting the ACHR's Statute was widely criticized as lacking meaningful partici-pation of relevant stakeholders, especially civil society actors such as non-govern-mental organizations, bar associations, human rights lawyers, activists, or direct and indirect representation of victims of human rights violations (International Commission of Jurists 2015).

To draft the ACHR's Statute, the Secretariat of the League of Arab States resorted to the appointment of an expert committee. The identities of appointed experts remained concealed, as were the results and details about their meetings (Stork 2014). The process also saw little to no engagement or active consultations with civil society. In a statement by the International Commission of Jurists, the process of drafting the Statute of the Court as being "opaque and conducted behind closed doors, thus contravening basic principles of inclusive participation and transparency" (International Commission of Jurists 2015). Ultimately, the result of this lack of engagement and transparency was successive drafts of the Statute that witnessed a gradual shedding of important provisions and aspects of the Court's mandate (Stork 2014).

Although a number of civil society organization were eventually invited by the Bahrain Human Rights Institution to a conference discussing the ACHR and its Statute on 25 and 26 May 2015 in Bahrain, the conference had little to contribute to the ACHR or its Statute's drafting process as the Secretary-General of the League of Arab States announced that the expert committee had concluded its work on the draft, which was already adopted by the Ministerial Council on 15 May, 2 weeks before the Bahrain conference (International Commission of Jurists 2015).

Ultimately, the outcome was a Statute of an Arab Court of Human Rights that does not comply with international standards of human rights and is thus unable to provide effective remedy and redress for victims of violation of human rights.

Subject Matter Jurisdiction of the ACHR

The ACHR's Statute grants the Court jurisdiction over "all cases and litigation arising from the application and interpretation of the Arab Charter on Human Rights or any other Arab treaty in the field of human rights to which the disputing States are party" (Article 16). Furthermore, the Preamble of the Statute states that "the Arab Court of human Rights will contribute to the realization of the purposes and objectives of the Arab Charter on Human Rights." To achieve this, the ACHR seeks to provide the facility for an effective judicial remedy for violation of rights under the Arab Charter, which is the essential purpose of any human rights court. Although the Arab Charter appears quite progressive and in harmony with universal standards of human rights in certain respects, it falls in direct contradiction with International Conventions on Human Rights in various other respects (International Commission of Jurists 2015).

An example of the above is Article 3 of the Charter which states "men and women are equal in respect of human dignity, rights and obligations within the framework of the positive discrimination established in favour of women by the Islamic Shari'a, other divine laws and by applicable laws and legal instruments." This provision is problematic because it falls short of realizing the international standards for equality between men and women enshrined in the International Convention on Civil and

Political Rights (ICCPR) and the Convention on the Elimination of all Forms of Discrimination against Women (CEDAW) to which most Arab States are signatory. Thus, off-putting equality between men and women from the framework offered by international human rights standards to that set by Shari'a and other divine laws potentially nullifies the recognition, enjoyment, and exercise of human rights by women, especially within matters of personal status such as marriage, inheritance, and divorce (International Commission of Jurists 2015).

Another example where the subject matter of jurisdiction of the Court comes into conflict with universal human rights standards is the issue of imposing the death sentence of individuals under the age of 18 which the Arab Charter on Human Rights permits (Article 7). This comes into direct contradiction with the UN Convention on the Rights of the Child (CRC) to which all Arab States are signatory and which ultimately prohibit the imposition of the death sentence of life imprisonment for crimes committed by individuals under the age of 18 (Article 37(a) CRC). The same is also clearly articulated in Article 6 of the ICCPR stating that a "sentence of death shall not be imposed for crimes committed by persons below eighteen years of age" (International Commission of Jurists 2015).

Another instance where the Arab Charter comes short is in its failure to define what constitutes an act of torture or ill-treatment, although it provides for the prohibition of subjecting any individual to "physical or psychological torture or to cruel, degrading, humiliating or inhuman treatment" (Article 8). However, the Charter does not clearly prohibit cruel, inhuman, or degrading punishment. Thus, the Charter is rendered inconsistent with international standards including the Convention against Torture and Other Cruel, Inhuman or Degrading Treatment or Punishment (CAT) and the ICCPR (International Commission of Jurists 2015).

For comparison's sake, the mandate of the African Court of Human and Peoples' Rights surpasses that of the Arab Court. The African Court can decide on cases and disputes concerning the interpretation and application of the African Charter, the Protocol of the Court, and any human rights treaty ratified by the State concerned. But the Court may also issue an advisory opinion on any matter within its jurisdiction. An advisory opinion may be sought by the African Union member states, African Union institutions, and any African organization recognized by the African Union. The Court is also empowered to promote the amicable settlement of the cases before it and the Court can also interpret its judgment.

Execution of ACHR Rulings

Article 26 of the ACHR's Statute provides that the rulings rendered by the Court are executable. According to the Statute, the Court must deliver the judgment within 60 days of the conclusion of the Court's deliberations. The Statute also provides facility for petitions for reconsideration to be made: (a) If the judgment includes a breach of an essential procedural rule; (b) If a fact with a decisive impact on the judgment emerges that was unknown at the time of the decision by both the Court and the petitioning party, provided that the party's ignorance of the fact was not a result of negligence on his part; (c) If the judgment does not clarify the reasons on which it is based; (d) If the Court flagrantly exceeds its jurisdiction; (e) If a deceit, fraud or falsification liable to influence the judgment took place; [or] (f) In the event of an influence over a member of the Court that led him to change his opinion in the case (Article 27(2)).

Although the Statute affirms that the ACHR's rulings are final and executable, it lacks a monitoring mechanism to ensure the execution of the Court's rulings; neither does it contain any provision for enforcement measures in the event of non-compliance. The only provision relating to monitoring and enforcement that exists is a requirement for the Arab Court to prepare an annual report listing cases of non-compliance with its judgments, which is to be submitted to the Assembly of States Parties. However, the Statute is silent as to how the Court will obtain the information required for this report and what options are available to the Assembly of States Parties upon receipt of the report (Article 29). Further, although the Statute requires the elaboration of a bylaw by the Assembly of States Parties, which must include a mechanism for the execution of judgments, there is nothing to guarantee the effectiveness of this mechanism.

Access to the ACHR and Admissibility of Cases

Access to the ACHR, as articulated in the Statute, has been a subject of wide criticism, especially as individuals' ability to file complaints directly to the Court is a basic requirement for a human rights system that seeks to remedy violations of individual rights. Thus, limiting the ability to file complaints to state parties could undercut the very purpose a human rights court should seek to serve (Stork 2014). In a similar fashion, the Statute of the ACHR does not provide the possibility for NGOs to petition the Court on behalf of individuals (Bassiouni 2014).

Article 19 of the Statute restricts access to the Arab Court to "[a] State party, whose subject claims to be a victim of a human rights violation." It also provides that "State parties can accept, when ratifying or acceding to the Statute or at any time later, that one or more NGOs that are accredited and working in the field of human rights in the State whose subject claims to be a victim of a human rights violation have access to the Court." No access to the Court is granted to individuals.

Article 19 is likely to impede the effectiveness of the Court, mainly because, as previously mentioned, States tend to avoid making interstate human rights-related complaints procedures for diplomatic and political reasons. Decades of experience with existing regional human rights courts and UN human rights treaty bodies have proven this. No interstate complaint has even been lodged before any of the UN treaty bodies. Hence, it is very unlikely that the situation will be different in the case of the ACHR (International Commission of Jurists 2015).

The right of individual access is critical to any human rights court that seeks to redress victims of human rights violations. An earlier version of the draft Statute contained provisions allowing individuals the right to access the court. However, these provisions allowing individual access were omitted in the final version. This omission will certainly bear an impact on the effectiveness of the ACHR of delivering justice to victims of human rights violations.

In comparison, the entities authorized to submit communications to the African Court are the African Commission, State Parties to the Protocol of the Court, and African organizations composed of States and non-governmental organizations that have observer status before the Committee as well as individuals. Articles 6 and 34(6) of the Protocol establishing the African Court provide for the following admission requirements for NGOs and individuals: in addition to the seven requirements accepted under Article 56 of the African Charter, cases brought directly before the Court by individuals and organizations are accepted only when the State against which the complaint is lodged has made a declaration under Article 5(3) of the Protocol of the Court to accept the Court's jurisdiction to receive such complaints (Shammout 2016).

Independence and Impartiality of the Court and Its Judges

Although the ACHR's Statutes stress the independence of the Court and its judges, the selection, tenure, and dismissal of judges do not meet international standards, thus compromising the independence of the Court and its judges (International Commission of Jurists 2015).

The Statute provides that persons of "recognised integrity and commitment to high moral values" can be candidates for the position of judges (Article 17). In addition to being competent and experienced in legal or judicial office, judges must also possess the required qualification for appointment in the highest judicial or legal office in their countries, with preference given to judges with more experience in the field of human rights. The last point is perhaps the most contentious as the Statute provides that experience in the field of human rights law is preferable as opposed to being required, something that is in line with international standards despite an earlier draft of the Statute requiring that judges have at least 10 years of experience in the field of human rights, a condition which was later omitted. In addition to this, the ACHR's Statute does not require the equal representation of gender, geographic region, or legal systems among judges. Again, an earlier draft of the Statute contained provisions establishing these parameters; however they were omitted from the final draft. All of these are guaranteed by other similar regional courts including the European and African Courts, both of which clearly provide for equitable gender representation and geographic representation in their Statutes (Articles 12(2), 14 (3), and 14(2) Protocol to the African Charter on Human and Peoples' Rights on the Establishment of an African Court on Human and Peoples' Rights 2004; Committee of Ministers of the Council of Europe 2012).

The nomination and election procedures are other aspects where the Statute falls short of international standards. This is mainly because it provides for States to nominate two judges and does not clearly hold states accountable to ensuring transparency and accountability in their selection of nominees. For example, there is no clear provision in the Statute that requires States to make nomination procedures public and open, allowing all qualified candidates to apply for nomination (International Commission of Jurists 2015).

Moreover, Article 15(5) of the ACHR's Statute addresses the suspension of judges and provides that for a judge's tenure to be terminated it is required that the rest of the judges agree that a judge no longer meets the requirement of his office. The Statute, however, does not clarify or establish an established procedure according to which judges may be dismissed from office or have their tenure terminated which, again, falls short of international standards where allegations of judicial misconduct must be subject to an independent, thorough, and impartial investigation and where as a result consequent fair and proportionate disciplinary measures to be taken (International Commission of Jurists 2015).

Finally, the last point to be tackled with regard to the independence of the ACHR and its judges is the rules of procedures of the Court. The Statute, in Article 28, establishes that the Court must set its rules of procedure and submit them to the Assembly of States Parties for adoption. This is an important aspect where the Statute falls short as the rules and procedures have to be submitted to States for revision and adoption which greatly undermines the Court's independence and impartiality (International Commission of Jurists 2015). In comparison, Article 33 of the Protocol to the African Charter on Human and Peoples' Rights on the Establishment of an African Court on Human and Peoples' Rights provides that "[t]he Court shall draw up its Rules and determine its own procedures. The Court shall consult the Commission as appropriate." Furthermore, the Burgh House Principles on the independence of the international judiciary (drafted by the Study Group of the International Law Association on the Practice and Procedure of International Courts and Tribunals in association with the Project on International Courts and Tribunals) instruct that if a Court is established as an organ within an international organization, both the Court and their judges must exercise their judicial functions without interference from other organs or authorities (Burgh House Principles 2004, principle 1.2).

Conclusion

To dismiss all the efforts of the League of Arab States for the creation of frameworks for human rights in the region is neither productive nor practical at this stage. Indeed though, in their current state, these frameworks, including the draft Statute of the ACHR, need drastic revisions to make them comply with international human rights standards and practices, and its the responsibility of the LAS and its members to do so. (Amman Centre for Human Rights Studies 2014). It is also evident that the adoption of human rights frameworks and agreements consumes lengthy amounts of time on the level of Arab States, and when they eventually get ratified and enter into force, these mechanisms remain largely at States level and are minimally integrated in interstate processes.

Therefore, for these regional human rights mechanisms in the MENA region to be effective and able to sustain their mandate of promoting and protecting the human rights of the peoples of the Arab region, there are several issues that should be addressed. First and foremost, it is necessary that all Arab States ratify the Arab Charter on Human Rights. Also, it is necessary to amend the Arab Charter on Human Rights so that it becomes compliant with international human rights standards. These amendments should also be reflected in the Statute of the Arab Court of Human Rights. This should not be viewed as a farfetched idea, especially given that many Arab States are signatories to other international human rights conventions, which indicates that the political will exists at least on individual states' level.

As for the Statute of the Arab Court of Human Rights, there is a need to allow for individuals, groups of individuals, as well as non-governmental organization to petition this Court. In its current format, the Statute only allows States or State-approved non-governmental organizations to do so. This clearly limits the core function of a human rights court.

The other issue that must be addressed is the limited jurisdiction of the Arab Court of Human Rights. In its current format, the Statute does not hold state parties accountable under other international human rights conventions to which they are signatory, where it clearly states in Article 16 that "[t]he Court shall have jurisdiction over all suits and conflicts resulting from the implementation and interpretation of the Arab Charter of Human Rights, or any other Arab convention in the field of Human Rights involving a member State." Returning to the example of the African Court, the jurisdiction of this Court expands to include all conventions ratified by state parties against which a case is lodged, hence not limiting it to the African Charter on Human and Peoples' Rights.

Furthermore, there is a need to effectively engage civil society and create real partnerships, especially in the process of formulating, revising, and amending human rights mechanisms in the Arab region. Many civil society organizations have expressed their dissatisfaction with the opaqueness and lack of transparency that has characterized the processes of drafting and formulating human rights conventions and documents by the League of Arab States.

Finally, if the purpose was to establish a functional and effective mechanism for the protection and promotion of human rights in the Arab region, it is very important for the League of Arab States to open channels of dialogue with international entities tasked with the protection and promotion of human rights, especially the Office of the High Commissioner for Human Rights and relevant Special Rapporteurs of the Human Rights Council.

References

Al-Midani MA (2005) The league of Arab states and the Arab charter on human rights. Available at https://www.acihl.org/articles.htm?article_id=6. Accessed 4 Apr 2018

Amman Centre for Human Rights Studies (2014) Proposed Arab court of human rights: an empty vessel without substantial changes to the draft statute. Available at http://www.achrs.org/english/index.php/arab-and-international-mainmenu-46/international-news-mainmenu-47/392-proposed-arab-court-of-human-rights-an-empty-vessel-without-substantial-changes-to-the-draft-statute.html. Accessed 4 Apr 2018

Bassiouni MC (2014) New Arab court for human rights is fake 'Potemkin tribunal'. Available at https://www.ibanet.org/Article/NewDetail.aspx?ArticleUid=c64f9646-15a5-4624-8c07-bae9d9ac42df. Accessed 4 Apr 2018

Burgh House Principles on the independence of the international judiciary (2004) Available at http://www.pict-pcti.org/FINAL%2025%20November%202004%20ILA%20Study%20Group%20Principles.doc. Accessed 4 Apr 2018

Committee of Ministers of the Council of Europe (2012) Guidelines on the selection of candidates for the post of judge at the European Court of Human Rights, Adopted 29 Mar 2012, CM(2012)40

International Commission of Jurists (2015) The Arab court of human rights: a flawed statute for an ineffective court. International Commission of Jurists, Geneva

League of Arab States (2008) Background on the Arab charter on human rights and the Arab human rights committee, 16 Mar 2008. Available at http://www.lasportal.org/ar/humanrights/Committee/Documents/%D9%86%D8%A8%D8%B0%D8%A9%20%D8%AA%D8%B9%D8%B1%D9%8A%D9%81%D9%8A%D8%A9%20%D8%B9%D9%86%20%D9%84%D8%AC%D9%86%D8%A9%20%D8%AD%D9%82%D9%88%D9%82%20%D8%A7%D9%84%D8%A5%D9%86%D8%B3%D8%A7%D9%86%20%D8%A7%D9. Accessed 4 Apr 2018

Protocol to the African Charter on Human and Peoples' Rights on the Establishment of the African Court on Human and Peoples' Rights (2004) Adopted 25 Jan 2004. Available at http://www.achpr.org/files/instruments/court-establishment/achpr_instr_proto_court_eng.pdf. Accessed 3 Apr 2018

Shammout A (2016) استشراف واقع ..الانسان لحقوق العربيه المحكمه. Al Naher, 22 June 2016. Available at http://alnahernews.com/News.aspx?id=81468#.WdsR-LpuJC8. Accessed 4 Apr 2018

Stork J (2014) New Arab human rights court is doomed from the start. Available at https://www.hrw.org/news/2014/11/26/new-arab-human-rights-court-doomed-start. Accessed 4 Apr 2018

The Arab Charter for Human Rights (2014) Adopted 23 May 2014. Available at http://www.lasportal.org/ar/legalnetwork/Documents/%D8%A7%D9%84%D9%85%D9%8A%D8%AB%D8%A7%D9%82%20%D8%A7%D9%84%D8%B9%D8%B1%D8%A8%D9%89%20%D9%84%D8%AD%D9%82%D9%88%D9%82%20%D8%A7%D9%84%D8%A3%D9%86%D8%B3%D8%A7%D9%86.pdf. Accessed 4 Apr 2018

The Arab Court of Human Rights Statute (2013) Adopted 26 March 2013. Available at http://www.lasportal.org/ar/humanrights/Committee/Documents/محكمةللحم20%يساسأال20%ماظننلا%١% الإنسان20%قوقحل20%ةيبرعلا.pdf. Accessed 4 Apr 2018

ASEAN Human Rights Mechanisms

Sriprapha Petcharamesree

Contents

Introduction 528
The Association of Southeast Asian Nations (ASEAN) and Human Rights 529
Turning Point in ASEAN? 530
Toward an ASEAN Human Rights Regime 533
The ASEAN Intergovernmental Commission on Human Rights (AICHR) 537
Mandate and Functions of the AICHR 538
The ASEAN Commission on the Promotion and Protection of the Rights of
Women and Children (ACWC) 541
Mandate and Functions of the ACWC 542
The ASEAN Human Rights Commissions and Their Challenges 544
Conclusions: The Future of the ASEAN Human Rights System 546
References 548

Abstract

Asia and the Pacific is the only region in the world without a region-wide intergovernmental human rights system to promote and protect human rights. However, there exists a few subregional human rights regimes; the most established subregional human rights system in the region is found in Southeast Asia. Since 2009, the Association of Southeast Asian Nations (ASEAN) has established two ASEAN intergovernmental commissions on human rights – the ASEAN Intergovernmental Commission on Human Rights (AICHR) and the ASEAN Commission on the Promotion and Protection of the Rights of Women and Children (ACWC). ASEAN has also adopted various non-binding human rights and human rights-related documents especially the ASEAN Human Rights Declaration. However, after almost a decade of existence, the ASEAN Human

S. Petcharamesree (✉)
Institute of Human Rights and Peace Studies, Mahidol University, Salaya, Thailand
e-mail: sripraphapet@gmail.com

© Springer Nature Singapore Pte Ltd. 2018

527

G. Oberleitner (ed.), *International Human Rights Institutions, Tribunals, and Courts*,
International Human Rights, https://doi.org/10.1007/978-981-10-5206-4_20

Rights Commissions have been facing criticisms and challenges. They have been constrained both by structural design, a limited protection mandate and functions, and by the prevailing perceptions of human rights of the ASEAN Member States. Even though the future may not be bright for better protection of human rights, some opportunities are there as ASEAN is more engaged with the international community. The ASEAN Vision 2025 which has committed to build an ASEAN that is people-oriented and people-centered may contribute to consolidating and strengthening the ASEAN Human Rights Mechanisms.

Keywords

Association of Southeast Asian Nations · ASEAN · ASEAN human rights system · ASEAN Intergovernmental Commission on Human Rights · AICHR · ASEAN Commission on the Promotion and Protection of the Rights of Women and Children · ACWC

Introduction

Asia and the Pacific is the only region in the world without a region-wide intergovernmental human rights system to promote and protect human rights. However, there exist a few subregional human rights regimes. The Arab Human Rights system was established under the League of Arab States and comprises the Arab Charter on Human Rights and the Arab Human Rights Committee. In South Asia, the South Asian Association for Regional Cooperation or SAARC has adopted a number of legally binding documents pertaining to the promotion and protection of human rights including the Convention on Preventing and Combating Trafficking in Women and Children for Prostitution (2002), the Convention on the Promotion of Child Welfare in South Asia (2002), the Social Charter (2004), and the Charter on Democracy (2011). Nevertheless, no human rights body was put in place in order to monitor the human rights situation in South Asia as yet. In addition, Pacific Island nations are actively exploring strategies to develop human rights bodies that best meet their specific needs and circumstances (Asia Pacific Forum on National Human Rights Institutions 2018). In Northeast Asia which is comprised of China, Japan, the two Koreas, and Mongolia, historical and political tension has been too high for any subregional cooperation to be realized.

The most established subregional human rights system in Asia and the Pacific is found in Southeast Asia. The Association of Southeast Asian Nations or ASEAN is a regional intergovernmental organization comprising ten Southeast Asian states. Since the adoption of the ASEAN Charter in 2007 and its entry into force in December 2008, two subregional human rights commissions have been set up, namely, the ASEAN Intergovernmental Commission on Human Rights (AICHR) and the ASEAN Commission on the Promotion and Protection of the Rights of Women and Children (ACWC). ASEAN has also adopted various human rights and human rights-related documents, especially the ASEAN Human Rights Declaration.

This chapter aims at first studying the pathway toward establishing (sub-)regional human rights regime in ASEAN. It also examines the mandate and functions of the two commissions. It will also critically assess their achievements and discuss the challenges they face as well as the future potential for the promotion and protection of human rights.

The chapter begins with a brief introduction of ASEAN and human rights in the region. This section will be followed by an account of the long process it took to establish the AICHR and the ACWC. An explanation and discussion on mandates and functions of the two Commissions will follow. In the next section, the major challenges shall be identified and analyzed. The chapter will conclude by looking at the future of the ASEAN Human Rights Mechanisms.

The Association of Southeast Asian Nations (ASEAN) and Human Rights

The Association of Southeast Asian Nations or ASEAN was established in August 1967. The Bangkok Declaration, signed by the five founding members Indonesia, Malaysia, the Philippines, Singapore, and Thailand, declared the establishment of an Association for Regional Cooperation among countries of Southeast Asia known as the Association of Southeast Asian Nations (ASEAN). In 1999, ASEAN had ten member states as Brunei Darussalam joined on 7 January 1984, followed by Vietnam on 28 July 1995, Lao People's Democratic Republic (Lao PDR) and Myanmar on 23 July 1997, and Cambodia on 30 April 1999. Today, ASEAN has ten member states. In 2007, ASEAN adopted the ASEAN Charter, which entered into force on 15 December 2008 once all ASEAN Member States (AMS) had ratified it. The ASEAN Charter provides the legal status and institutional framework for ASEAN. It serves as "a firm commitment in achieving ASEAN Community" (ASEAN Secretariat 2008a) based on three pillars – Political-Security, Economic, and Socio-Cultural. It also "codifies ASEAN norms, rules and values; sets clear targets for ASEAN; and presents accountability and compliance" (ASEAN Secretariat 2008b). For ASEAN, the ASEAN Charter has become a legally binding agreement among the ten AMS.

The 1967 ASEAN Declaration (ASEAN Bangkok Declaration) set seven aims and purposes, none of which referred to human rights or fundamental freedoms. Only point 2 of the Declaration which says "to promote regional peace and stability through abiding respect for justice and the rule of law in the relationship among countries of the region and adherence to the principles of the United Nations Charter" could be interpreted to embrace human rights, as it includes peace, respect for justice and rule of law, and adherence to the principles of the UN Charter. Indeed, the UN Charter "reaffirms faith in fundamental human rights, in the dignity and worth of the human person, in the equal rights of men and women and of nations large and small, and to establish conditions under which justice and respect for the obligations arising from treaties and other sources of international law can be maintained, and to promote social progress and better standards of life in larger freedom." Article 1 of the UN Charter sets out the organization's purposes and principles including "promoting and encouraging respect for human rights and for fundamental freedoms for all without distinction as to race, sex, language, or religion." The purposes and principles were further reiterated by Article 55: "the United Nations shall promote: (c) universal respect for, and observance of, human rights and fundamental freedoms for all without distinction as to race, sex, language, or religion." Article 56 affirms that "[a]ll Members pledge themselves to take joint and separate action in cooperation with the Organization for the achievement of the purposes set forth in Article 55." A complex human rights system was created at the UN level comprising both international human rights standards and monitoring bodies including Charter-based and treaty-based bodies.

However, "from its creation in 1967 through to the mid-1990s, ASEAN was an association little troubled by human rights concerns. While it is true that ASEAN has always had some sort of declaratory commitment to economic and social welfare, and since 1975 has had a sub-committee on the role of women, it has steered clear of any engagement with either the language or the substance of human rights, especially those of a civil and political nature" (Matthew 2014 p.110). Admittedly, ASEAN has been much better known for its success in economic development and in keeping peace and stability in the region than for the promotion and protection of human rights. It is worth noting that the term "human rights" appears in an ASEAN document for the first time in the Joint Declaration of the First ASEAN-EC Ministerial Meeting in Brussels adopted on 21 November 1978. Paragraph 11 of the Joint Declaration says that "[t]he Foreign Ministers of the Member States of the European Community and ASEAN ... agreed that this cooperation should serve their people by promoting greater prosperity, social justice and human rights" (ASEAN Joint Declaration of the First ASEAN-EC Ministerial Meeting 1978). While this reference to human rights has been taken seriously by the European Community (EC), subsequently known as European Union (EU), there were no concrete policies or actions regarding the promotion and protection of human rights between the two organizations until the advent of the ASEAN Charter.

Turning Point in ASEAN?

The turning point took place in the early 1990s amidst radical transformation at the global level – the collapse of the Berlin Wall and the democratization of Eastern Europe – coined the "end of the Cold War," which culminated in the World Conference on Human Rights held in Vienna in June 1993 which, for many, marked "a key moment in the history of human rights movement" (O'Flaherty 2013). It is noteworthy that this conference was preceded by a world conference organized by the UN General Assembly in 1989 to assess what progress had been made since the adoption of the Universal Declaration of Human Rights (UDHR) (Feeney 2013).

Within ASEAN, a cautious reference to human rights in an ASEAN Ministerial Meeting was registered in 1991. The 1991 Joint Communique of the 24th ASEAN

Ministerial Meeting issued in Kuala Lumpur, Malaysia, on 20 July 1991 stated "the Ministers noted with concern the increasing tendencies to link the issues of environmental protection and human rights to development and commercial cooperation. They stressed that these issues should not be used as conditionality for aid and development financing" (ASEAN Ministerial Meeting 1991, para 59). This statement was repeated and further elaborated in the 1992 Joint Communique of the 25th ASEAN Ministerial Meeting issued in Manila, the Philippines, on 22 July 1992 noting that:

[t]he Foreign Ministers maintained that environmental and human rights concerns should not be made as conditionality in economic and development cooperation. They noted that basic human rights while universal in character, are governed by the distinct culture and history and socioeconomic conditions in each country. Their expression and application in the national context are within the competence and responsibility of each country. (ASEAN Ministerial Meeting 1992, para.18)

The inclusion of human rights language in the AMM Joint Communiques reflects the concerns of ASEAN on the use of human rights by a third party for political and economic purposes rather than the promotion and protection of the rights of ASEAN people.

However, the human rights discourse in ASEAN slightly changed in 1993. For the first time in ASEAN history, human rights were mentioned in a separate heading, occupying three long paragraphs in the Joint Communique, issued in the 26th ASEAN Ministerial Meeting held in Singapore from 23 to 24 July 1993:

16. The Foreign Ministers welcomed the international consensus achieved during the World Conference on Human Rights in Vienna, 14-25 June 1993, and reaffirmed ASEAN's commitment to and respect for human rights and fundamental freedoms as set out in the Vienna Declaration of 25 June 1993.They stressed that human rights are interrelated and indivisible comprising civil, political, economic, social and cultural rights. These rights are of equal importance. They should be addressed in a balanced and integrated manner and protected and promoted with due regard for specific cultural, social, economic and political circumstances. They emphasized that the promotion and protection of human rights should not be politicized.

17. The Foreign Ministers agreed that ASEAN should coordinate a common approach on human rights and actively participate and contribute to the application, promotion and protection of human rights. They noted that the UN Charter had placed the question of universal observance and promotion of human rights within the context of international cooperation. They stressed that development is an inalienable right and that the use of human rights as a conditionality for economic cooperation and development assistance is detrimental to international cooperation and could undermine an international consensus on human rights. They emphasized that the protection and promotion of human rights in the international community should take cognizance of the principles of respect for national sovereignty, territorial integrity and non-interference in the internal affairs of states. They were convinced that freedom, progress and national stability are promoted by a balance between the rights of the individual and those of the community, through which many individual rights are realized, as provided for in the Universal Declaration of Human Rights.

18. The Foreign Ministers reviewed with satisfaction the considerable and continuing progress of ASEAN in freeing its peoples from fear and want, enabling them to live in dignity. They stressed that the violations of basic human rights must be redressed and should not be tolerated under any pretext. They further stressed the importance of strengthening international cooperation on all aspects of human rights and that all governments should uphold humane standards and respect human dignity. In this regard and in support of the Vienna Declaration and Programme of Action of 25 June 1993, they agreed that ASEAN should also consider the establishment of an appropriate regional mechanism on human rights. (ASEAN Ministerial Meeting 1993)

It can be seen in the above paragraphs that the Communique not only made reference to the World Conference on Human Rights in Vienna, 14–25 June 1993, and the Vienna Declaration and Plan of Action (VDPA) adopted on 25 June 1993 but also made some promises. In the first two paragraphs, the Communique continues to caution against the use of human rights as a conditionality for economic cooperation and development. The Ministers also emphasized the principles of respect for national sovereignty, territorial integrity and noninterference in the internal affairs of states as applied by ASEAN, and a balance between the rights of the individual and those of the community. However, to certain extent, they committed to consider the establishment of an appropriate regional mechanism on human rights.

One will have to put such a commitment made by the six AMS which back then made up ASEAN (i.e., the five founding members and Brunei) into the context of the time. The 1993 Joint Communique was issued 1 month after the 1993 World Conference on Human Rights in Vienna in which all AMS had actively participated. Paragraph 37 of the VDPA recognized the fundamental roles played by the regional human rights arrangements. It reiterated "the need to consider the possibility of establishing regional and sub-regional arrangements for the promotion and protection of human rights where they do not exist" (Vienna Declaration and Programme of Action 1993). In response to such a call, ASEAN committed, as already mentioned earlier, to consider an establishment of "appropriate" regional mechanism on human rights.

It is important to note here that in the lead up of the World Conference on Human Rights in Vienna, three regions have convened the preparatory meetings including one in Bangkok, Thailand. In Asia, the Ministers and representatives of Asian states met in Bangkok from 29 March to 2 April 1993 during which the Declaration of the Regional Meeting for Asia of the World Conference on Human Rights was adopted. The document reiterated "the need to explore the possibilities of establishing regional arrangements for the promotion and protection of human rights in Asia" (Final Declaration of the Regional Meeting for Asia of the World Conference on Human Rights 1993). On the eve of the government meeting, a gathering was organized in Bangkok between 24 and 28 March 1993 by more than 110 NGOs, the outcome of which was the Bangkok NGO Declaration on Human Rights. One of the points made in the Declaration stated that NGOs welcomed "the initiative by governments to set up a regional mechanism for the protection and promotion of human rights in the Asia-Pacific" (United Nations Bangkok NGO Declaration on Human Rights 1993). The Declaration, nevertheless, added "conditions" if a "regional commission" was to be established. Out of 11 conditions listed, a number of them focused on full investigative powers and individual complaints, public disclosure, and a public reporting system as well as the composition of the Commission (United Nations Bangkok NGO Declaration on Human Rights 1993). The Declaration further recommended a separate body to be set up to adjudicate complaints. We will see in the later section that none of this was included in the terms of reference (TOR) of the two ASEAN Human Rights Commissions. The region-wide human rights system has hardly been discussed after 1993 except in a few initiatives by Australia and South Korea. Even though ASEAN did not meet all commitments made and did not respond to the demands advanced by NGOs in 1993, the move could still be considered as a turning point for ASEAN.

Toward an ASEAN Human Rights Regime

After 1993, there have been changes in ASEAN. First is the expansion of membership to include states which, by that time, if not known for human rights violations, were certainly not known for being human rights friendly. These are Vietnam, Lao PDR, Myanmar, and Cambodia. One could recall that the admission of Myanmar as a member state of ASEAN has created serious concerns by the international community, especially the EU and some of its members as well as the United States, and has attracted criticism by civil society groups. In 1997, when Myanmar was admitted to ASEAN, the 13th ASEAN-EC Joint Cooperation Committee Meeting scheduled for November 1997 in Bangkok was postponed for the second time (tni 2005). However, the project of an "ASEAN 10" was finally completed in 1999 when Cambodia was admitted as the tenth member of ASEAN.

Second, most countries in ASEAN and especially Thailand, Malaysia, the Philippines, and Indonesia faced a financial crisis in 1997–1998. These countries experienced rapid devaluation and capital outflows, and the political ramifications of the economic crisis were felt in various countries. Indonesia is a case in point as the country was hit hard by the economic crisis with widespread impact on the life of Indonesian people. Its attendant social affects pushed ordinary Indonesians to join the movements of protest against their government which turned out to have a major impact on the course of Indonesian politics, the collapse of the Suharto regime, and the beginning of democratization process in Indonesia (Sherlock 1998). In 1997, Thailand enjoyed democratic liberalization despite the economic crisis and adopted the democratic "People's Constitution."

Third, the economic and political crisis or transformation in ASEAN countries put the region in the international spotlight. Reports of human rights violations and oppression in some AMS attracted serious international criticisms. At the same time, the democratization processes in some states, such as Malaysia, the Philippines, Thailand, and Indonesia, allowed space not only for issues regarding human rights and fundamental freedoms to be discussed but also for civil society to be more engaged. Amidst the economic and political transformation, one civil society group

– the Working Group for an ASEAN Human Rights Mechanism – was established to advocate for the setting up of an ASEAN human rights system.

As mentioned earlier, ASEAN committed in 1993 to consider the establishment of an appropriate mechanism on human rights. However, from 1993 to 1997, no progress was made and there was no mentioning of such a commitment in subsequent ASEAN Ministerial Meetings' Joint Communiques. The idea and discourse about a human rights body in ASEAN was missing from ASEAN main documents. In 1995, under the Human Rights Committee of LAWASIA (the Law Association for Asia and the Pacific) and with the support of a group of academics and NGOs as well as other like-minded individuals, the Working Group for an ASEAN Human Rights Mechanism was created. Its main objective was to push for the creation of an intergovernmental human rights body (Working Group for an ASEAN Human Rights Mechanism 2018). The Working Group began to engage with ASEAN senior officials of foreign affairs as well as ASEAN Foreign Ministers, both as a group and as individual Ministers. A formal dialogue was initiated, and in 1998, the Working Group was recognized by the ASEAN Foreign Ministers. The AMM Joint Communique of 1998 "noted the establishment of the Informal Non-Governmental Working Group for an ASEAN Human Rights Mechanism," "recognized the importance of continuing these dialogues" and "took note of the proposal made by the Working Group during its latest dialogue with ASEAN held in Manila on 22 July 1998" (ASEAN Ministerial Meeting 1998, para 28). More or less the same statement was repeated in the 1999 AMM Joint Communique (ASEAN Ministerial Meeting 1999).

Again, the move made by ASEAN coincided with an international event. The world, not least the UN, was celebrating the 50th anniversary of the Universal Declaration of Human Rights. In addition, in 1997, during the 5th ASEAN Summit held in Kuala Lumpur in December, ASEAN adopted the ASEAN Vision 2020 which envisioned:

> a socially cohesive and caring ASEAN where hunger, malnutrition, deprivation and poverty are no longer basic problems, where strong families as the basic units of society tend to their members particularly the children, youth, women and elderly; and where the civil society is empowered and gives special attention to the disadvantaged, disabled and marginalized and where social justice and the rule of law reign. (ASEAN Vision 2020 1997)

A cohesive and caring ASEAN could not be realized without human rights especially for groups such as children, youth, women, and the elderly as stated in paragraph 29 of the 1998 AMM Joint Communique (ASEAN Vision 2020 1997):

> The Foreign Ministers noted that the world will celebrate in December 1998, the 50th anniversary of the Declaration of Human Rights. Considering that two-thirds of the ASEAN population consist of women and children, they recognized the importance of international conventions and declarations relating to the promotion of human rights, such as the Convention on the Rights of the Child (CRC) and the UN Convention on the Elimination of all Forms of Discrimination Against Women (CEDAW). The Foreign Ministers took cognizance of the fact that steps are being taken to bring to fruition the

creation of a community of caring societies, as enshrined in the ASEAN Vision 2020, which gives particular emphasis to children, youth, women and the elderly. (ASEAN Vision 2020 1997, para. 29)

In 2000, the Working Group for an ASEAN Human Rights Mechanism submitted a Draft Agreement for the Establishment of the ASEAN Human Rights Commission to ASEAN senior officials. Working Group meetings with senior officials began and were "noted with appreciation" by the Foreign Ministers in Joint Communiqués (Working Group for an ASEAN Human Rights Mechanism 2018). The Draft Agreement was based on the ASEAN commitment made in 1993, the 1998 Hanoi Declaration and Plan of Action, and the Vision 2020. The draft of a legally binding document proposed the setting up of a permanent and independent ASEAN Human Rights Commission composed of seven members with recognized competence in the field of human rights serving in his/her personal capacity for a 5-year term. The main functions and powers as stipulated in Article 11 of the Draft Agreement included both protection and promotion of human rights with investigative power to address individual communications and possible investigation on its own initiatives (Working Group for an ASEAN Human Rights Mechanism 2000). It was envisaged that the instrument would enter into force upon the third ratification and no reservations were to be allowed. Even though the ASEAN Foreign Ministers took note of this Draft Agreement, there was unfortunately no formal answer to nor action taken on the submission of the document despite the continued engagement between the Working Group for an ASEAN Human Rights Mechanism and the AMM/ASEAN Senior Officials Meeting (SOM) through regular meetings, workshops, and round tables jointly organized between 2001 and 2008.

Another turning point regarding the setting up of ASEAN human rights body was recorded in 2004 when the Vientiane Action Program (VAP) was adopted by the ASEAN leaders who "recognize the need to strengthen ASEAN and shall work towards the development of an ASEAN Charter" (Vientiane Action Program 2004). The promotion of human rights and obligations was prescribed under the ASEAN Security Community (Political Development) section (ASEAN Vientiane Action Program 2004). The Programme Areas and Measures included the promotion of human rights through seven measures, one of which was the establishment of an ASEAN Commission on the Promotion and Protection of the Rights of Women and Children (ASEAN Vientiane Action Program 2004). It is worth noting that most of the measures specified were based on recommendations made by the Working Group for an ASEAN Human Rights Mechanism through their engagement and activities since 1997.

The VAP set the time line as "conceivably achievable by 2010" (ASEAN Vientiane Action Program 2004). In 2005, the ASEAN leaders adopted the Kuala Lumpur Declaration on the Establishment of the ASEAN Charter, which established an Eminent Persons Group (EPG) with the mandate to examine and provide practical recommendations on the directions and nature of the ASEAN Charter. The report of the EPG on the ASEAN Charter recommended "a new ASEAN" with objectives which included "the strengthening of democratic values, ensuring good governance, upholding the rule of law, respect for human rights and international humanitarian law, and achieving sustainable development" (ASEAN Report of Eminent Persons Group on the ASEAN Charter 2006). Indeed, these elements were included in the basic principles and purposes of the Charter. The report also recommended ASEAN to promote an ASEAN People-Centred Organisation by continuing to develop democracy, promote good governance, and uphold human rights and the rule of law. The report stated that:

[t]he EPG discussed the possibility of setting up of an ASEAN human rights mechanism, and noted that this worthy idea should be pursued further, especially in clarifying how such a regional mechanism can contribute to ensuring the respect for and protection of human rights of every individual in every Member State. (ASEAN Report of Eminent Persons Group on the ASEAN Charter 2006, para 47)

The same report also "recommended that the ASEAN Charter should provide channels at different levels for regular consultations through appropriate mechanisms that may be established for this purpose" (ASEAN Report of Eminent Persons Group on the ASEAN Charter 2006 para 47). As a result, the establishment of an ASEAN human rights body was stipulated in Article 14 of the ASEAN Charter.

Indeed, the ASEAN Charter put in the preamble the "adherence to the principles of democracy, the rule of law and good governance, respect for and protection of human rights and fundamental freedoms." This was reiterated in Article 1 on the purposes of the Charter: "to strengthen democracy, enhance good governance and the rule of law, and to promote and protect human rights and fundamental freedoms, with due regard to the rights and responsibilities of the Member States of ASEAN." It can be seen that for ASEAN, rights of individuals have to be balanced by the rights and responsibilities of the AMS. "Respect for fundamental freedoms, the promotion and protection of human rights, and the promotion of social justice" was also included as part of Article 2 of the Charter, but this provision continues by setting forth the principles of "respect for the independence, sovereignty, equality, territorial integrity and national identity of all ASEAN Member States" and "non-interference in the internal affairs of ASEAN Member States." As already stated earlier, Article 14 of the Charter provides for the setting up of ASEAN human rights body. It stipulates as follows: "1. In conformity with the purposes and principles of the ASEAN Charter relating to the promotion and protection of human rights and fundamental freedoms, ASEAN shall establish an ASEAN human rights body. 2. This ASEAN human rights body shall operate in accordance with the terms of reference to be determined by the ASEAN Foreign Ministers Meeting."

In fact, even before the entry into force of the ASEAN Charter, the High Level Panel on an ASEAN human rights body was established to draft the TOR of such an ASEAN human rights body in July 2008. The High Level Panel was composed of one representative from each AMS and was expected to finalize and present the draft TOR of the ASEAN human rights body to the ASEAN Foreign Ministers in 2009. The High Level Panel also included one academic, Prof. Vitit Muntarbhorn, a law professor from Thailand and former special rapporteur on sales of the child and child pornography and on the situation of human rights in North Korea and active in various UN capacities. He was appointed an alternate to the Thai representative who was the Chair of the High Level Panel. His contribution was significant but was considered too progressive for the Panel to adopt his ideas especially on the protection mandate of the Commission. A few consultations with civil society groups including the Working Group for an ASEAN Human Rights Mechanism were organized by the High Level Panel. The finalized TOR were presented and approved by the ASEAN Foreign Ministers during the 42nd AMM under the chairmanship of Thailand. The "body" was named in the TOR as the "ASEAN Intergovernmental Commission on Human Rights (AICHR)" and was officially inaugurated at the 15th ASEAN Summit on 23 October 2009.

The ASEAN Intergovernmental Commission on Human Rights (AICHR)

Since its establishment and inauguration in October 2009, the AICHR has been performing a number of activities. However, more and more criticism has been heard as the human rights situation in ASEAN is deteriorating in most of the countries in the region. Human rights violations range from political oppression against civil society and political oppositions in Cambodia to the discrimination and violence against Rohingya in Myanmar, extrajudicial killings in the Philippines, and lack of freedom of expression in Thailand, to name but a few. The AICHR does not meet expectations so far. This section analyzes why and what are the challenges faced by the body. It carefully examines the TOR of the AICHR including mandates and functions.

To understand the current TOR of the AICHR and the way it has been performing, one will have to look at the background of the inclusion of the ASEAN human rights body in the Charter and the debates in the process. It is to be remembered that ASEAN is comprised of a diverse group of states from all aspects. Politically, one country is under absolute monarchy rule, two still call themselves socialist states, while some others, such as Cambodia, Indonesia, Malaysia, Myanmar, the Philippines, and Singapore, are considered "electoral democracies" with a variety of internal political challenges and "democratic openness," ranging from very limited political space to more open to political participation. Thailand is currently under a military regime with limited freedom. Economically, ASEAN comprises some of the richest countries in the world, such as Singapore and (to a certain extent) Brunei. Half of the AMS are classified as middle income countries, while a few others, namely, Cambodia, Lao PDR, Myanmar, and Vietnam, are less developed in terms of their economy. Culturally, half of the population are Muslim, and the rest are Buddhist or Catholic or adhere to other religions. More important is the difference in the perceptions toward human rights. These differences translate into different levels of "comfort" and different attitudes toward human rights which have impacts on the way the AICHR performs because the functions and implementation have to be comfortable hence acceptable to all.

As was reflected in the previous section, ASEAN still does not accept certain concepts of human rights. The inclusion of human rights and fundamental freedoms in the Charter was heatedly debated and was considered the most contentious issues during negotiations. Consensus was reached with compromises, one of which was the lack of specification of the nature of the human rights body to be established. The prescription for the establishment of an ASEAN human rights body in Article 14 was not specific as it should have been as it was subjected to the TOR which were determined at an ASEAN Foreign Ministers Meeting level and were accordingly the result of negotiations and compromises (Petcharamesree 2013). As noted earlier, the "body" is now called the "Intergovernmental Commission" and not just the "Commission" as commonly used in other regions. "By adding the term 'Intergovernmental' the Commission has to be conscious that it is accountable to the government. This fact has been repeatedly emphasized by a number of representatives of the AICHR" (Petcharamesree 2013, p. 50).

As a result, the body was established as a consultative body. The TOR provide that "[e]ach ASEAN Member State shall appoint a Representative to the AICHR who shall be accountable to the appointing Government." As such, the members of the AICHR are called "representatives" not "commissioners," and they are appointed by their respective governments. So far, only representatives of Indonesia and Thailand were selected through open and participatory process, and none of their representatives is a government official. The rest were handpicked by their government, and most of them are either retired officials or active officers (the list of current and past representatives is available at http://aichr.org/documents). According to the TOR of AICHR, governments were only recommended to "consult, if required by their respective internal process, with appropriate stakeholders in their appointment of their representatives to the AICHR." In addition, despite the fact that the TOR prescribes the "competence in the field of human rights," only some have extensive human rights background. Each representative serves for a term of 3 years and may be consecutively reappointed for only one more term, and the government has discretion to replace its representative as they see fit.

Mandate and Functions of the AICHR

What was examined earlier has implications on how the mandate and functions were designed and how the AICHR has been performing. Article 4 of the TOR of AICHR prescribes for a broad mandate of promotion and protection of human rights and fundamental freedoms with 14 functions which the AICHR has to perform, including "any other tasks as may be assigned to it by the ASEAN Foreign Ministers Meeting" (TOR of AICHR). This open-ended mandate gives power to the AMM to assign the AICHR to deal with human rights issues if it wishes. Unfortunately, the AMM has never used this power so far.

Although the main mandate of the AICHR is to promote and protect human rights, it tends to focus on a more promotional mandate of the body, except for a few which could be translated into protection functions, provided the AICHR would interpret them creatively and progressively, which, unfortunately, has not been the case yet. Article 4.10 of the TOR says that the AICHR has function "to obtain information from ASEAN Member States on the promotion and protection of human rights." If used innovatively, the AICHR could seek for information about situations of human rights abuses from the AMS and try to address them. This is also the case for Article 4.12 of the TOR which prescribes the AICHR "to prepare studies on thematic issues of human rights in ASEAN." In fact, the AICHR has identified a number of thematic issues for studies such as corporate social responsibility, migration, trafficking in person (particularly women and children), child soldiers, women and children in conflicts and disasters, juvenile justice, right to health, right to education, and right to life (AICHR Five Year Work Plan 2010–2015). As of the end of 2017, only one thematic study – the Thematic Study on CSR and Human Rights in ASEAN – was completed. The study was coined a "baseline study" and had the objective to identify state practices and practices of corporate social responsibility of ASEAN-based businesses, explore activities of actors involved in promoting corporate social responsibility, identify various mechanisms that contribute to engagement among different actors, and formulate recommendations (AICHR 2014). In spite of many complaints petitioned by NGOs in the region, no cases of human rights violations committed by business companies in the region were examined in the study. The thematic study on migration began in 2010 but no progress has been made until today. There are a number of studies which are ongoing such as the study on the right to peace (led by the Lao representative), right to education (led jointly by the representatives of Cambodia and Lao), and the right to life (led by the Thai representative). The potential for thematic studies as a tool to perform the AICHR's protection mandate is high but has not been exploited.

In addition, a few other functions as prescribed by the TOR could serve the obligations of the Commission to protect human rights. Article 4.13 of the TOR requires the AICHR to submit an annual report on its activities, or other reports if deemed necessary, to the ASEAN Foreign Ministers Meeting. Article 4.6 requires it to promote the full implementation of ASEAN instruments related to human rights. If combined, these two functions could be used by the AICHR to prepare reports on the national implementation of international human rights treaties that the AMS have already ratified. Initiatives could have been taken to require reports from the AMS on the submission of their country reports to the three international human rights conventions of which all AMS are party, namely, CRC, CEDAW, and the Convention on the Elimination of Racial Discrimination (CERD). Again, this did not happen, as the AICHR did not deem it necessary. The AICHR is concerned about the interference in internal affairs of other member states, one of the principles specified in the TOR. As such, the proposal to the AICHR to prepare the "ASEAN UPR" by the first Thai representative to the AICHR was perceived as "too progressive" and therefore was not accepted. The basic idea of such proposal was based on the fact that all ASEAN Member States are required to submit the Universal Periodic Report – UPR – to the UN Human Rights Council every 4 years and most if not all have been investing efforts to produce the report as required. They seemed fine to be reviewed by other members of the United Nations, why not by their peer in ASEAN.

Out of the 14 mandate and functions of the AICHR, the first few seem to be fully or almost fully implemented. The strategies and plan for the promotion and protection of human rights and fundamental freedoms (Article 4.1 TOR) have been developed. The Commission is currently implementing their second Five-Year Work Plan from 2016 to 2020. Interestingly, the current work plan identifies additional themes for studies, namely, right to information in criminal justice, legal aid, and freedom of religion and belief. It is hard to know how these studies will be conducted. Activities to promote the rights of persons with disabilities have been actively organized by the AICHR (especially by the current Thai representative). The Commission also plans to assess its work and submit recommendations for the possible review of its TOR.

As for the Article 4.2 which asks the AICHR to "develop an ASEAN Human Rights Declaration with a view to establishing a framework for human rights cooperation through various ASEAN conventions and other instruments dealing with human rights," the AICHR has given priority to implement this function in the first 3 years of its existence. The process of drafting the ASEAN Human Rights Declaration (AHRD) was completed, and the Declaration, together with the Phnom Penh Statement on the Adoption of the ASEAN Human Rights Declaration, was adopted in November 2012 in Phnom Penh under the chairmanship of Cambodia. Prime Minister Hun Sen wanted it to be the highlight of his turn as the Chair of ASEAN. Nevertheless, the discussions on possible "various ASEAN conventions and other instruments dealing with human rights" have not been initiated yet because having any legally binding human rights instruments will inevitably require the AICHR to perform the monitoring function which is important for protection mandate. However, one human rights-related legally binding document, the ASEAN Convention Against Trafficking in Persons, Especially Women and Children, was adopted in 2015.

The AICHR has started to "engage in dialogue and consultation with other ASEAN bodies and entities associated with ASEAN, including civil society organisations and other stakeholders, as provided for in Chap. V of the ASEAN Charter" (TOR of AICHR). Meetings with "other ASEAN bodies" have become more frequent than during the first 4 years of the establishment of the AICHR. As for "entities associated with ASEAN, including civil society organisations and other stakeholders," the AICHR has been meeting with the Working Group for an ASEAN Human Rights Mechanism which is the only human rights "entity associated with ASEAN" included in the Annex II of the ASEAN Charter. In February 2015, the AICHR adopted the Guidelines on the AICHR's Relations with Civil Society Organizations, which allows the body to register civil society groups desiring to engage with the AICHR. The modalities of engagement include consultations, seminars, workshops, regular reporting and briefings, the implementation of specific studies upon request of the AICHR, project implementation, and any other format determined by the AICHR (AICHR Guidelines 2015). According to the list established by the AICHR, 22 organizations were registered and given "consultative relation status" by the AICHR. This excludes the Working Group for an ASEAN Human Rights Mechanism which is an entity associated with ASEAN recognized by the ASEAN Charter.

After more than 8 years of existence, the AICHR has indeed been active in organizing meetings, workshops, consultations, and visits, especially in regard to cooperation with international and other regional human rights systems. Still, it is difficult to assess the achievements of the Commission because the reports made available so far did not give enough details for any objective assessment. They tend to just enumerate the activities implemented rather than outlining what have been the impacts of the activities; a good example is whether the visibility AICHR has increased or if the AHRD has been implemented and in which way(s). The AICHR as an "overarching" human rights institution in the region has been constrained by a number of factors. The issue of challenges faced by the AICHR will be dealt with after the examination of the ACWC.

The ASEAN Commission on the Promotion and Protection of the Rights of Women and Children (ACWC)

It was mentioned earlier that the Vientiane Action Program of 2004 had specified the setting up of the ASEAN Commission on the Promotion and Protection of the Rights of Women and Children. This was reiterated in the ASEAN Socio-Cultural Community (ASCC) Blueprint adopted in 2009 as part of the Roadmap for the ASEAN Community (2009–2015). "The ASEAN Commission on the Promotion and Protection of the Rights of Women and Children (ACWC) was inaugurated on 7 April 2010 in Ha Noi, Viet Nam, on the occasion of the 16th ASEAN Summit" (ACWC). It has to be noted that the process of drafting the TOR of the ACWC had gone relatively unnoticed as attention was more focused on the AICHR.

Like the AICHR, the ACWC is an intergovernmental and consultative body as clearly stated in Article 4 of the TOR of ACWC. It is interesting to note here that even though the AICHR and the ACWC are given the same status as "intergovernmental" bodies, such a term was not articulated in the name of the ACWC.

The ACWC is composed of 20 representatives, 2 from each AMS. According to the TOR, one is a representative on women's rights and one on children's rights, and both are appointed by the respective government. The representatives serve for a 3-year term but may be consecutively reappointed for another term. Interestingly, the TOR of ACWC was designed in a slightly different way than the TOR of AICHR as it provides for a "staggering system" of its representatives to ensure continuity for the work of the ACWC. Article 6.0 of the TOR of ACWC states that "[e]ach ASEAN Member State shall appoint one of its two representatives to serve an initial term of four and a half years." Another notable difference between the members of the two Commissions is who serves as Chair of the institution. While the Chair of the AICHR rotates in accordance with the Chair of ASEAN, both the Chair and Vice-Chair of the ACWC are elected by the appointed representatives for the first term, but the positions are then rotated consecutively among the AMS in alphabetical order. Under the TOR, the Chair and the Vice-Chair of the ACWC should not be representatives from the same Member State and should not have the same area of competence. They should also follow an opposite cycle. The ACWC reports to the

ASEAN Ministers Meeting on Social Welfare and Development (AMMSWD) with a copy to the ASEAN Committee on Women (ACW) and other relevant ASEAN sectoral bodies (ACWC TOR 2010). It has to be noted that many provisions of the TORs of both the AICHR and the ACWC are more or less identical (such as the provision on principles which appears in Article 3 of the TOR of ACWC and Article 2 of the TOR of the AICHR) and some differ slightly, while some are rather distinctive, as highlighted above.

The composition of the ACWC seems to be more diverse than the one of the AICHR. Although some of the members of the ACWC are retired from or still serving in government agencies, a number of them are from NGOs, charitable organizations, or academia. Some have long years of experience in the field of their respective competence. As may be expected, the gender balance may be a bit problematic as most if not all representatives for women's rights are women. As for representatives for children, the majority are usually also women.

Mandate and Functions of the ACWC

The TOR of ACWC provide for 16 mandate and functions for the Commission to perform. As a specialized body, the mandate covers, in principle, both promotion and protection of the rights of women and children. However, like the AICHR, most of the functions specified in the TOR focus more on the promotional part of the mandate. What is also interesting is that the TOR requires the ACWC in Article 5.6 "[t]o assist, upon request by ASEAN Member States, in preparing for CEDAW and CRC Periodic Reports, the Human Rights Council's Universal Periodic Review (UPR) and reports for other Treaty Bodies, with specific reference to the rights of women and children in ASEAN" and Article 5.7 expects the Commission "[t]o assist, upon request by ASEAN Member States, in implementing the Concluding Observations of CEDAW and CRC and other Treaty Bodies related to the rights of women and children."

This is problematic as the very nature of the human rights bodies around the globe (including specialized regional human rights bodies such as the ACWC) is to "monitor" the fulfillment of state obligations under international human rights instruments, which includes the states' obligations to prepare and submit country reports to treaty bodies and the UPR. The regional human rights bodies are not supposed to implement the recommendations or concluding observations made by the treaty bodies. Their role is basically to ensure proper and effective implementation and fulfillment of state duties and responsibilities as prescribed by the international, regional, and national human rights standards. Another notable point appears in Article 5.16 of the TOR of ACWC which prescribes that the Commission has to "perform any other tasks related to the rights of women and children as may be delegated by the ASEAN Leaders and Foreign Ministers." The fact that the ACWC is directly reporting to the AMMSWD and that the AICHR is under a direct reporting line of the Foreign Ministers, for the ACWC to be delegated or tasked to perform anything even relating to the rights of women and children by the Foreign Affairs is rather unusual especially considering the fact that the AICHR has an "overarching" mandate and functions to protect everybody including women and children.

Like the AICHR, the TOR of ACWC do not provide for any explicit function to receive and investigate complaints or petitions of human rights violations against women and children. As already analyzed in the previous section, some of the functions of the AICHR could be creatively interpreted to perform protection mandates (even if this does not mean directly investigating human rights cases); none of the functions of the ACWC could be easily directed toward the protection mandate. The functions include promoting implementation, developing programs and strategies, promoting public awareness, advocating on behalf of women and children, building capacities, assisting states to prepare reports or implement concluding observations, encouraging states to ratify international human rights treaties, undertaking review of laws and policies, collecting and analyzing disaggregated data, facilitating sharing of experiences and good practices, proposing measures and mechanisms for the prevention of violence against women and children, supporting participation of women and children, and providing advisory services upon request (ACWC TOR 2010). Article 5.9 of the TOR direct the ACWC "to promote studies and research related to the situation and well-being of women and children." However, the language is weaker here than in the similar mandate of the AICHR which asks the Commission to prepare studies. Nevertheless, the ACWC has initiated a few studies such as the baseline study on building the mechanism on implementation and reporting of CRC Concluding Observations in AMS and a baseline study on the right to identity for marginalized children in AMS which was included in the ACWC Work Plan 2016–2020 (ACWC Work Plan 2017). It is interesting to observe that both the AICHR and the ACWC are comfortable with the concept of "baseline" studies.

So far, the ACWC has produced a number of publications which include, among others, the Gender Sensitive Guidelines for Handling Women Victims of Trafficking in Persons and the Good Practices in ASEAN Member States on the Elimination of Violence Against Women and Children. The Commission has prepared a few campaign materials in the form of multimedia on violence against women throughout the life cycle, including a public campaign on anti-violence against women and children. It has adopted the ASEAN Regional Plan of Action on the Elimination of Violence against Women and the ASEAN Regional Plan of Action on the Elimination of Violence against Children (ACWC). The Commission has also, on a regular basis, organized various meetings, workshops, and seminars as well as consultation forums with stakeholders. In fact, activities of both the AICHR and the ACWC seem to be rather similar. The ACWC also adopted, in 2013, the Declaration on the Elimination of Violence against Women and Violence against Children in ASEAN, which is an updated version of the ASEAN Declaration on the Elimination of Violence against Women in the ASEAN Region adopted by ASEAN leaders in 2004.

As mentioned earlier, the establishments of the AICHR and the ACWC by ASEAN have raised high expectations by people in ASEAN, given that the region has traditionally avoided (and continues to avoid) dealing with human rights on the premise that they are considered internal affairs of member states. However, it seems that the two Commissions have failed to meet such expectations because of various conceptual and structural as well as logistical challenges.

The ASEAN Human Rights Commissions and Their Challenges

A human rights advocate from Indonesia wrote in 2014 that:

> since its inception, AICHR has faced major problems regarding capacity, independence, ability to balance its role as a political body and as a human rights commission, ability to engage its stakeholders, work priority-setting and self-perception. It is significant to note that the lack of technical and financial support from ASEAN member- states contributes to the slow progress in the work of AICHR. (Wahyuningrum 2014)

Most if not all challenges identified have been repeated by those who follow the human rights situation in ASEAN and who pushed for effective human rights system in the region. Let us now examine those factors identified in a more systematic way.

The first concern relates to the independence of the two Commissions. There has been no intention of ASEAN leaders to establish any independent human rights bodies in ASEAN. This can be seen in the TOR of both Commissions which provide for the appointment of representatives by the government and the fact that these representatives are required to be accountable to their respective governments. In addition, the TOR of AICHR say very clearly that although the term of services of the representatives is 3 years, "the appointing government may decide, at its discretion, to replace its representative." The TOR of ACWC contains a similar provision which adds that "whenever appropriate the Government shall inform the ACWC of the reason of the replacement." In practice, no government feels obliged to explain why a representative was replaced because it does not feel "appropriate" to do so. Another point is how the members of the two Commissions are referred to. The term "commissioner" has not been used in the TOR and has not been allowed to be used in practice. They are called "representatives" which implies they are expected to represent the government. Although a few representatives, Thailand and Indonesia and now Malaysia in particular, have been acting in their own capacity and are given full freedom to perform (or a high level thereof) by the Thai and Indonesian Ministry of Foreign Affairs, this has not been the case for the majority of representatives. At some point, they were reminded that the AICHR is not an independent body. The term "intergovernmental" was added to the name of the AICHR or included in the TORs to remind the representatives that the mechanism is a government established and they are expected to act on behalf of their respective government.

Second, there is a lack of institutional support of the Commission. None of the two Commissions was equipped with an office or its own secretariat. This matter is still being discussed within the AICHR on regular basis. Representatives are not working full-time. Most of them are not remunerated; they do not have any full-time assistant provided by the respective government or an efficient and dedicated secretariat. This makes it difficult for them to perform adequately. In fact, the Human Rights Division within the ASEAN Political-Security Community Department is only a small unit with a few staff of the Directorate. The officers of the unit are not expected to perform any substantial works except providing logistical and procedural support to the AICHR. Likewise, the ACWC has been supported by the officers of the ASEAN Socio-Cultural Community Department who are serving other bodies as well. A dedicated secretariat and a separate office (as is the case of all other regional human rights bodies) would be needed if the ASEAN human rights bodies are meant to perform properly. Unfortunately, ASEAN does not, again, intend to equip them with institutional support. The two Commissions were designed to be institutionally weak, which prevents them from performing better.

Third, apart from weak institutional design, the two Commissions also lack relevant competence. The TOR of the two Commissions prescribe that in appointing the representatives to the AICHR and the ACWC, the Member States shall give due consideration to competence in the field of human rights in the case of the AICHR and in the field of the rights of women and children for representatives to the ACWC (TOR of AICHR 2009; ACWC TOR 2010). In practice, states exercise their discretion to appoint the person they see fits. This is evident in the countries in which the process of appointment has not been open to the participation of different relevant stakeholders. In some cases, the qualifications of representatives seem less important than the relationships with and the trust of the government. Many governments are not looking for someone who is necessarily committed to the promotion and protection of human rights of the people. Rather they are expected to represent the voice and concerns of their respective government. Already handicapped by the lack of institutional support, representatives without proper qualifications are not able to do much except making sure that they participate in the meetings and other activities they deem sensitive and important to their country.

Fourth, the mandates of the two Commissions are limited. As one commentator noted, "AICHR has been given very weak terms of reference that limit its mandates, authority and powers to promote and protect human rights" (Dursin 2012). This comment was echoed by the former representative of Indonesia to the AICHR, Rafendi Djamin, who said "we [AICHR] are not mandated to deal with individual claims" (Quoted by Dursin 2012). The same critique comes also from human rights organizations. As already analyzed in the earlier section about the mandate and functions of the AICHR and the ACWC, both institutions were not provided with an explicit protection mandate. This is more so in the case of the ACWC, while the AICHR, as already stated, could be progressively interpreting its TOR to perform protection functions.

Fifth is the working principles that ASEAN has been applying in its relations with member states and other partners. Even if the two Commissions were independent and had proper institutional support with the necessary competence, they still could not meet the expectations of the ASEAN people and human rights groups because of the ASEAN principles. Article 2 of the TOR of AICHR and Article 3 of the TOR of ACWC refer to the "respect for principles of ASEAN as embodied in

Article 2 of the ASEAN Charter." The TOR of AICHR elaborates further by stating in particular "d) adherence to the rule of law, good governance, the principles of democracy and constitutional government; e) respect for fundamental freedoms, the promotion and protection of human rights, and the promotion of social justice; f) upholding the Charter of the United Nations and international law, including international humanitarian law, subscribed to by ASEAN Member States (Art. 2 TOR of AICHR)." This obligation is countered by the working principles of ASEAN which include "a) respect for the independence, sovereignty, equality, territorial integrity and national identity of all ASEAN Member States; b) non-interference in the internal affairs of ASEAN Member States; c) respect for the right of every Member State to lead its national existence free from external interference, subversion and coercion; g) respect for different cultures, languages and religions of the peoples of ASEAN, while emphasising their common values in the spirit of unity in diversity" (Art. 2 TORs of AICHR). These latter principles determine the way the two bodies have (not) been dealing with serious human rights abuses so far. The case of almost a million of the Rohingya, an ethno-religious group from Rakhine State in Myanmar who have fled to Bangladesh and a few other countries in ASEAN because of discrimination and violence against them in their country of origin, is rather telling. The exodus of Rohingya has been attracting international attention and is considered a human rights, and humanitarian crisis has never been properly discussed in AICHR. While it is true that a meeting was held in June 2013 under the chairpersonship of Brunei behind closed doors, this meeting concluded that there would be no further discussions, given that the matter was considered an internal affair of Myanmar (as the author of the present chapter learned in conversations with the then Indonesian and Thai representatives to the AICHR in June 2013). In addition, in order for the AICHR or the ACWC to address any issues, they need a consensus which needs to be achieved through a consultative process. A single objection raised openly by a representative is sufficient to stop any action taken by any of the two bodies. Moreover, the AMS adhere to another principle which puts "cooperation" above "confrontation." Any call for actions to address any issues deemed sensitive is perceived as confrontational. As a consequence, all ASEAN bodies refrain from questioning other ASEAN Member States openly. AICHR and ACWC are inhibited by these principles which form part of what is known as the "ASEAN Way." Any real efforts if made by the two Commissions can be easily undermined by these major challenges.

Conclusions: The Future of the ASEAN Human Rights System

Despite challenges faced by the two ASEAN regional human rights bodies, there may be some promising prospects. As stated in the previous section, the Commissions have begun to engage with civil society groups. The fact that some organizations, such as the FORUM-ASIA, a regional human rights group based in Bangkok which were perceived as too critical to AICHR a few years ago, are now registered by the AICHR indicates the level of progress made in engaging with stakeholders. It can be hoped that by engaging with civil society organization more thoroughly, the work of the two Commissions will become more transparent. Moreover, the fact that the two Commissions are now making their annual report available on their respective websites is a good start.

More substantial progress has been made in different areas, notably with the adoption by ASEAN of a number of pertinent declarations such as the ASEAN Human Rights Declaration and other human rights-related documents. They include a legally binding ASEAN Convention Against Trafficking in Persons, Especially Women and Children, which was adopted in November 2015 and entered into force in March 2017 after having received six ratifications. Most recently, the ASEAN Consensus on the Protection and Promotion of the Rights of Migrant Workers was signed by the Heads of States and Governments in November 2017. In fact, there is no lack of ASEAN documents regarding human rights. In addition, the adoption of the document "ASEAN 2025: Forging Ahead Together" brought about some prospects for better promotion and protection of human rights in ASEAN.

The ASEAN Community Vision 2025 emphasizes a rules-based, people-oriented, people-centered ASEAN Community, where "peoples enjoy human rights and fundamental freedoms, higher quality of life and the benefits of community building" (ASEAN Vision 2025). One of the priorities for the ASEAN Community over the next 10 years will be guided by, but not limited to, broad goals that will further consolidate and strengthen the regional grouping. These goals include, among others, "greater emphasis on the peoples of ASEAN and their well-being" and "ensur[ing] fundamental freedoms, human rights and better lives for all ASEAN peoples" (ASEAN Vision 2025). The ASEAN Community Vision 2025 also commits member states to an effort to realizing "an inclusive and responsive community that ensures our peoples enjoy human rights and fundamental freedoms as well as thrive in a just, democratic, harmonious and gender-sensitive environment in accordance with the principles of democracy, good governance and rule of law" (ASEAN Vision 2025). For a region where democracy seems to be deficient in a majority of the Member States and where human rights violations are rampant, the 2025 ASEAN Vision is ambitious. Nevertheless, human rights and fundamental freedoms are themes that are found in all three Community Blueprints, which could be a step toward a more human rights-friendly community, which may then contribute to strengthening the existing ASEAN human rights regime.

Moreover, in 2015, there was also a rather strong political commitment by the ASEAN Foreign Ministers Meeting. For the first time since the establishment of the AICHR in 2009, the AMM Joint Communiqué devoted one separate section of five full paragraphs to the Commission. The Joint Communique "reaffirmed the role of the ASEAN Intergovernmental Commission on Human Rights (AICHR) as the overarching human rights institution in ASEAN for the promotion and protection of human rights and fundamental freedoms of the peoples in the region" (ASEAN Ministerial Meeting 2015). It also "encouraged AICHR to engage more in current human rights challenges in the region" (ASEAN Ministerial Meeting 2015). It immediately referred, though, to the principles enshrined in the ASEAN Charter, the ASEAN Human Rights Declaration (AHRD), as well as the TOR of AICHR, all of them refer to the working principles of ASEAN as already elaborated in earlier section. The most important point was registered in paragraph 22 of the said Joint Communique where it said that "we also encouraged AICHR to acquire a long-term perspective to planning and implementation which will help it realise its human right protection mandate alongside its promotion mandate, as provided for in its TOR" (ASEAN Ministerial Meeting 2015). This suggests that the AMM recognizes the weak implementation of the AICHR's protection mandate and encourages the Commission to balance it.

As already mentioned throughout the chapter, the AICHR and ACWC although inhibited by the weak institutional structure, the ASEAN working principles, and their own TORs, there are some positive move toward becoming a more effective subregional human rights mechanisms. At least, a few countries especially Indonesian as expressed by its Minister of Foreign Affairs, Retno L.P. Marsudi, in 2015 wanted to see the strengthening of its protection mandate. The Indonesian Foreign Minister even went further by emphasizing that the AICHR could within its mandate address human rights issues without waiting for instructions from the AMM, which would raise the Commission's credibility as a human rights institution in the region. She also expressed the hope that recommendations on the review of the TOR of AICHR could be incorporated in the current TOR in order to strengthen its protection mandate. The Minister also suggested strengthening the Human Rights Division in the ASEAN Secretariat and selecting independent representatives through democratic processes and AMS (Dylan 2015). If ASEAN and the AMS are moving toward the direction outlined by the Indonesian Foreign Minister, the ASEAN Human Rights Mechanism will be becoming more relevant in the eyes of ASEAN people. It's really for the ASEAN leaders to decide how to improve the ASEAN human rights bodies's effectiveness in order to enable them to face current challenges.

References

ACWC (2010) Terms of Reference (TOR) of the ASEAN Commission on the Promotion and Protection of the Rights of Women and Children. Available at http://www.asean.org/storage/images/2012/Social_cultural/ACW/TOR-ACWC.pdf. Accessed 28 Feb 2018

AICHR (2009) Terms of Reference (TOR) of the ASEAN Intergovernmental Commission on Human Rights. Available at http://aichr.org/documents. Accessed 26 Feb 2018

AICHR (2010) Five Year Work Plan of the AICHR (2010-2015). Available at http://aichr.org/documents/. Accessed 28 Feb 2018

AICHR (2014) Thematic Study on CSR and Human Rights in ASEAN. Available at http://aichr.org/documents. Accessed 28 Feb 2018

AICHR (2015) Guidelines on the AICHR's Relations with Civil Society Organisations. Available at http://aichr.org/documents. Accessed 28 Feb 2018

AICHR. Consultative Relationship with the AICHR. http://aichr.org/external-relations/consultative-relationship-with-the-aichr. Accessed 26 Feb 2018

ASEAN (1967) Bangkok Declaration. Available at http://asean.org/the-asean-declaration-bangkok-declaration-bangkok-8-august-1967. Accessed 28 Feb 2018

ASEAN (1978) Joint declaration the ASEAN-EC ministerial meeting Brussels, 21 November 1978. Available at http://asean.org/?static_post=external-relations-european-union-asean-eu-ministerial-meetings-joint-declaration-of-the-first-asean-ec-ministerial-meeting-1978. Accessed 28 Feb 2018

ASEAN (1997) ASEAN Vision 2020. Centre for International Law, National University of Singapore. Available at https://cil.nus.edu.sg/wp-content/uploads/formidable/18/1997-ASEAN-Vision-2020-1.pdf. Accessed 28 Feb 2018

ASEAN (2004) Vientiane Action Program VAP. Available at http://www.asean.org/storage/images/archive/VAP-10th%20ASEAN%20Summit.pdf. Accessed 28 Feb 2018

ASEAN (2005) Kuala Lumpur Declaration on the Establishment of the ASEAN Charter Kuala Lumpur. Available at http://asean.org/?static_post=kuala-lumpur-declaration-on-the-establishment-of-the-asean-charter-kuala-lumpur-12-december-2005. Accessed 28 Feb 2018

ASEAN (2006) Report of Eminent Persons Group on the ASEAN Charter. Available at http://www.asean.org/wp-content/uploads/images/archive/19247.pdf. Accessed 28 Feb 2018

ASEAN (2008a) ASEAN Charter. Available at http://asean.org/asean/asean-charter. Accessed 28 Feb 2018

ASEAN (2008b) Terms of Reference for High Level Panel on an ASEAN human rights body. Available at http://www.asean.org/storage/images/archive/HLP-TOR.pdf. Accessed 28 Feb 2018

ASEAN. University network. About ASEAN. Available at http://www.aunsec.org/historyofasean.php. Accessed 28 Feb 2018

ASEAN Ministerial Meeting (1991) Joint communique of the 24th ASEAN ministerial meeting, 20 July 1991. Centre for International Law, National University of Singapore. Available at https://cil.nus.edu.sg/wp-content/uploads/formidable/18/1991-24th-AMMJC.pdf. Accessed 28 Feb 2018

ASEAN Ministerial Meeting (1992) Joint communique of the 25th ASEAN ministerial meeting, 22 July 1992. Centre for International Law, National University of Singapore. Available at https://cil.nus.edu.sg/wp-content/uploads/formidable/18/1992-25th-AMMJC.pdf. Accessed 28 Feb 2018

ASEAN Ministerial Meeting (1993) Joint Communique of the Twenty-Sixth ASEAN Ministerial Meeting Singapore, 23-24 July 1993. Available at http://asean.org/?static_post=joint-communique-of-the-twenty-sixth-asean-ministerial-meeting-singapore-23-24-july-1993. Accessed 26 March 2018

ASEAN Ministerial Meeting (1998) Joint communique of the 31st ASEAN ministerial meeting, 24–25 July 1998. Centre for International Law, National University of Singapore. Available at https://cil.nus.edu.sg/wp-content/uploads/formidable/18/1998-31st-AMMJC.pdf. Accessed 28 Feb 2018

ASEAN Ministerial Meeting (1999) Joint communique of the 32nd ASEAN ministerial meeting, 23–24 July 1999. Available at http://asean.org/?static_post=joint-communique-of-the-32nd-amm-singapore-23-24-july-1999-2. Accessed 28 Feb 2018

ASEAN Ministerial Meeting (2015) Joint Communiqué of the 48th ASEAN Foreign Ministers Meeting. Available at http://www.asean.org/wp-content/uploads/images/2015/August/48th_amm/JOINT%20COMMUNIQUE%20OF%20THE%2048TH%20AMM-FINAL.pdf. Accessed 28 Feb 2018

Asia Pacific Forum of National Human Rights Institutions (2018) Regional Human Rights Mechanisms. Available at https://www.asiapacificforum.net/support/international-regional-advocacy/regional-mechanisms. Accessed 28 Feb 2018

Dursin K (2012) Critics slam ASEAN rights commission. IPS 29 November 2012. Available at http://www.ipsnews.net/2012/11/critics-slam-asean-rights-commission. Accessed 28 Feb 2018

Dylan A (2015) RI'rolesmodel' on human rights in ASEAN, The Jakarta Post, August 7,2015,. Available at http://www.thejakartapost.com/news/2015/08/07/ri-role-model-human-rights-asean.html. Accessed 26 April 2018

Feeney P (2013) The UN world conference on human rights, Vienna, June 1993. Dev Pract 3(3):218–221

Final Declaration of the Regional Meeting for Asia of the World Conference on Human Rights (1993) Available at http://faculty.washington.edu/swhiting/pols469/Bangkok_Declaration.doc. Accessed 28 Feb 2018

Matthew D (2014) An agreement to disagree: the ASEAN human rights declaration and the absence of regional identity in Southeast Asia. J Curr Southeast Asian Aff 33(3):107–129

O'Flaherty M (2013) Vienna declaration and Programme of action +20. Hum Rights Monit Q 1:7–18. Available at https://www.ishr.ch/sites/default/files/article/files/vdpa.pdf. Accessed 28 Feb 2018

Petcharamesree S (2013) The ASEAN human rights architecture: its development and challenges. Equal Rights Rev 11:46–60. Available at http://www.equalrightstrust.org/ertdocumentbank/Sriprapha%20Petcharamesree%20ERR11.pdf. Accessed 28 Feb 2018

Sherlock S (1998) Crisis in Indonesia: economy, society and politics. Parliam Aust, Curr Issues Brief 13:1997–1998. Available at https://www.aph.gov.au/About_Parliament/Parliamentary_Departments/Parliamentary_Library/Publications_Archive/CIB/CIB9798/98cib13. Accessed 28 Feb 2018

tni (2005) EU-ASEAN and the case of Burma – ASEAN-EU meeting postponed over Myanmar issue (Reuters, Singapore, 23 January 1999) 17 November 2005. Available at https://www.tni.org/en/archives/act/2743. Accessed 28 Feb 2018

United Nations (1993) Bangkok NGO declaration on human rights, UN Doc. A/CONF.157/PC/83, 19 April 1993. Available at http://www.internationalhumanrightslexicon.org/hrdoc/docs/bangkokNGO.pdf. Accessed 28 Feb 2018

Vienna Declaration and Plan of Action 1993. Available at http://www.refworld.org/docid/3ae6b39ec.html. Accessed 28 Feb 2018

Wahyuningrum Y (2014) AICHR after five years: progress, challenges and opportunities. Asia-Pacific Human Rights Information Centre FOCUS June 76. Available at https://www.hurights.or.jp/archives/focus/section3/2014/06/aichr-after-five-years-progress-challenges-and-opportunities.html. Accessed 28 Feb 2018

Working Group for an ASEAN Human Rights Mechanism (2000) Draft Agreement for the Establishment of the ASEAN Human Rights Commission. Available at http://www.aseanhrmech.org/downloads/draft-agreement.pdf. Accessed 28 Feb 2018

Working Group for an ASEAN Human Rights Mechanism (2018) About us. Available at http://www.aseanhrmech.org/aboutus.html. Accessed 28 Feb 2018

Agenda for Strengthening Human Rights Institutions

Gerd Oberleitner

Contents

Introduction 552
From Standards to Implementation: Human Rights Institutions Matter 553
Law, Politics, and Coherent Multilateralism 554
The Implementation Crisis: State Sovereignty and the Pitfalls of Bureaucracy 556
Persuasion, Coercion, and the Good Faith of States 558
Designing Human Rights Institutions: Participative Multilevel Human Rights
Governance 560
The Importance of Follow-Up 562
Impact and Success: Measuring Compliance 565
Conclusion 566
References 567

Abstract

This chapter reflects on ways and means to strengthen international human rights institutions, courts, and tribunals in light of current challenges and future opportunities. It argues that despite their shortcomings and even though they represent not the only possible way to realize human right, international human rights institutions, courts, and tribunals still matter as pragmatic, formalized, and legalized channels for human rights politics. They perform a variety of functions within the formalized setting of international organizations which could not be undertaken outside: debate, agenda-setting, creating standards, interpreting norms, monitoring compliance, diffusing, sharing and understanding human rights, and fostering social change. They allow states and other actors to share perceptions of problems, identify goals, devise, and adapt the means for achieving them. In order to be successful, they need to be designed as legitimate

G. Oberleitner (✉)
Faculty of Law, University of Graz, Graz, Austria
e-mail: gerd.oberleitner@uni-graz.at

© Springer Nature Singapore Pte Ltd. 2018
G. Oberleitner (ed.), *International Human Rights Institutions, Tribunals, and Courts*,
International Human Rights, https://doi.org/10.1007/978-981-10-5206-4_21

institutions, embedded in a coherent multilateralism and respond to criticism that their success is limited and they are prone to bureaucratic pitfalls. We must tackle the current implementation crisis and the increasingly hostile attitude of many states towards human rights institutions. Given that international human rights institutions rely on persuasion rather than coercion, their recommendations and judgments need to be followed up more robustly and they must be better linked with civil society and actors on the state level. Measuring their impact remains a challenge. Ultimately, they need to be defended as the best available means to foster incremental progress in human rights.

Keywords
Human rights · United Nations · Human rights bodies · Human rights court · Enforcement · Implementation · Compliance

Introduction

The creation and expansion of the human rights infrastructure since 1945 reflects a general move towards international organizations, which had started already with the League of Nations, and the International Labour Organisation, the two prime institutions created in the interwar period in the first half of the last century. Today, the range and diversity of human rights bodies, courts, and tribunals on the universal and regional level is impressive. Since the establishment of the United Nations (UN) in 1945 and the subsequent emergence of regional organizations, human rights institutions set up within these frameworks embody the hope that appropriate responses to global and regional problems and challenges can be found in such institutions. Just as well, disappointment has been voiced whenever they did not live up to such expectations and when the faith in the power of international norms, organizations, and mechanisms to induce, facilitate, or enforce positive changes was betrayed. Human rights institutions, courts, and tribunals rest on the underlying assumption that they are different from technical or economic international arrangements because they rest on fundamental and universal ideas of upholding or restoring human dignity. Human rights institutions represent the aspiration to transform the idea of human rights into law and law into social change. Where once there was charitable concern for somebody's needs, there is now supposed to be legally binding international document. Where once there was a dream of equality, there is now a mechanism for agreeing on equality's legal form. Ultimately, human rights institutions are not meant to be diffident facilitators of interstate cooperation but autonomous agents of social change and tools to turn rhetoric to action.

These high aspirations may easily remain unfulfilled. Casting the empowering language of human rights in the form international law and framing their transformative potential within commissions and committees may come with substantial costs. When things go wrong, legalizing and institutionalizing human rights leads to the creation of an overburdened and under-performing infrastructure, a bureaucratic straitjacket in which the empowering force of human rights is suffocated by procedural dullness and denigrated by unfulfilled promises. Somewhere in between this hope and despair is the daily reality of human rights institutions, courts, and tribunals. Do these institutions still matter 70 years after the founding of United? And if so, how can their obvious shortcomings be minimized and their hidden strengths be maximized? Which elements of an agenda for strengthening human rights institutions can be discerned?

From Standards to Implementation: Human Rights Institutions Matter

When the Universal Declaration of Human Rights expressed the idea of human rights in 1948 in the language of international law, these newly constituted rights were meant as a common standard of achievement of all peoples and all nations. Human rights bodies or courts were not mentioned in the Declaration. Even so, it was obvious that international institutions had to be the vessels in which human rights needed to be stored. The UN Charter had already envisaged (in its Article 68) a commission on human rights, even though its mandate was left open. After 1948, standard setting became the most pressing task to give meaning and legally binding force to the vague language of the Declaration. However, there was no doubt that securing the implementation of these standards within nation states would be decisive for the long-term success of the human rights project and that some form of guidance for states and supervision of their performance would be necessary. Grand promises on paper alone would not do. Soon, those eagerly advocating meaningful human rights enforcement against oppressive governments and those equally emphatically upholding state sovereignty and nonintervention as key principles of the international legal order were at odds with each other. However, whether they supported or rejected the idea of human rights enforcement, it was obvious to both of them that moving from rhetoric to action was the inevitable next step once the substance of human rights law had been fleshed out. Indeed, while the creation of standards and norms on paper is the prerequisite for their realization, there is ultimately little value in creating abstract rules if governments can ignore and deride them at will and the beneficiaries of such rules can never experience their worth. Realizing standards through legal and institutional means is as important for those for whom the norms were created as it is for the legitimacy of human rights themselves.

Today, we live in the "era of implementation" (Hunt 2017). The law and language of human rights can still be refined, but the main challenge is realizing their potential on the ground. We need to understand how to construct the enabling environment in which human rights can thrive (or at least be kept alive) and consider potential pitfalls within this infrastructure. International human rights institutions and courts now fulfil a range of functions (Oberleitner 2007); they are agora for debates and forum for setting agendas and creating standards, interpreting norms and monitoring compliance, they spell out community norms and lay down their contours, coax, states into making human rights a reality and (occasionally) sanction deviant behavior. They assist governments, adjudicate criminals, provide relief, and try to prevent atrocities. They allow for diffusing, sharing, learning, and understanding human rights globally, and they foster social change. Occasionally, they even substitute domestic processes. Above anything else, they have a supervisory function by which they guide states towards realizing human rights. The various aspects of this function are often brought together under the rubric of monitoring: gathering information through data accumulation, ascertaining of facts, investigating, undertaking comparative analyses, assessing human rights situations, measuring performance, rendering judgments and providing recommendations for change. Monitoring entails processes of consultation, justification, recommendation, and persuasion, whether it is in peer groups (such as in the Universal Periodic Review of the UN Human Rights Council) or by independent bodies (such as Special Rapporteurs of the Human Rights Council). Human rights institutions allow states and other actors to share perceptions of problems, identify goals, and devise and adapt the means for achieving them.

Human rights courts also allow individuals to bring complaints and ask for remedies. The resulting judgments address not only individual grievances but develop the human rights framework further. Strategic human rights litigation before human rights courts by advocacy groups has become an important tool for achieving individual remedies and developing human rights at the same time. The issue of restitution of ancestral land of indigenous communities may serve as one of many examples how different types of impacts can be created through litigation. They comprise material impacts (such as the actual restitution of land), legal and political impacts (such as changes to of specifications of laws or the adoption of national action plans), operational impacts (the setting up of dedicated national institutions, such as investigative commissions), and transformative impacts (when disagreements are being reframed as human rights problems or the cultural regeneration of indigenous communities is placed within a broader human rights discourse) (Open Society Justice Initiative 2016). Even where litigation fails because no immediate remedy is provided by the respondent state, long-term effects can occur; the case law may be of importance elsewhere, new human rights standards may be established, or facts can be ascertained and "truth" established (Leach 2017). And with the fusing of human rights and international criminal law, international criminal tribunals and the International Criminal Court can adopt judgements on a limited range of "human rights crimes" (Schabas 2003, p. 281) such as genocide, war crimes, and crimes against humanity. Despite their limited remit and questionable deterrent force, international criminal courts ensure that impunity for atrocities is not a given anymore.

Law, Politics, and Coherent Multilateralism

The creation, development, and growth of such human rights institutions needs to be understood within David Kennedy's axiom that all ideas need to either materialize or die: what begins as a utopian aspiration for improving the world either wanes or necessarily ends as institutional accomplishment (Kennedy 1987, p. 985). If that is so, we have not much of a choice anyway. Today, we can hardly imagine human rights without the associated institutional framework. Where else would we define problems, fix meanings, and create norms, standards, and principles? It is from the work of the Special Rapporteurs on the right to housing and on the right to health that we have gained a better understanding of the scope, content, and consequences of reframing housing or health issues as human rights concerns. It is from the work of torture prevention bodies that we have reached more clarity on the forms of torture, inhuman, and degrading treatment. Human rights institutions can offer stability, durability, and predictability beyond ever-changing state interests. They are as close as we have yet come in trying to put community interests before national interests.

Even so (and regardless of the design of human rights institutions) power, law, and politics will remain intertwined. Despite all the critique of the "politicization" of human rights institutions and how this endangers their credibility and legitimacy, these institutions are neither a level playing field nor does their subject-matter – human rights – elevate them above politics. Decrying this "politicization" and wishing to drive the political out of their meeting rooms is unrealistic. Human rights are essentially political and so are human rights institutions. Still, they offer space for the kind of formalized political struggle and the exercise of power through legal channels and insist, albeit insufficiently, on law rather than merely imposing ideologies through might. To live up to such a demand, human rights institutions, courts, and tribunals need to imagined (to paraphrase Jan Klabber's more general defense of international organizations) "not as the *deus ex machina* of yesteryear, entering the scene to save the day or save the world, but rather as a type of bounded political community which facilitates discussion and debate; no longer as a regulatory agency par excellence, but simply (and most importantly) as a place where international politics is conducted" (Klabbers 2009, p. 318). Transparent processes, civil society participation, and accountability are necessary to ensure the legitimacy of international human rights without ignoring their political purpose. Important as other forms of global governance outside international organizations may be, the fragility of such network-like governance structures without a legal form do not deliver what international organizations can. We can neither return to mere interstate power configurations as before the rise of global institutions nor can we (yet) put our trust in forms of governance which dispense with formalities altogether. This seems to make international human rights institutions, courts, and tribunals – like other international institutions – not as the ultimately desirable but presently best available format for realizing human rights.

This, however, presupposes a belief that formalized and legalized institutions can effectively respond to human rights violations, which are ultimately results of failures in the political, social, or societal spheres. Consequently, human rights institutions need to be embedded in a "coherent multilateralism" which understands problems of international relations as multidimensional (Leary 2001). Whenever human rights violations are not a one-dimensional occurrence but result from economic inequality, armed conflict, or climate change, then such problems cannot meaningfully be put before a single institution with the corresponding doorplate. Human rights were rightly designated a cross-cutting issue in the 1997 program of reform for the UN. Paul Hunt is right when he argues that what he calls the "mainland" of human rights institutions (the UN Human Rights Council and human rights treaty bodies) cannot alone do justice to the challenge of implementing human rights. The specialized agencies, funds, programs, and other UN bodies that make up the "archipelago" of human rights need to mainstream human rights into policies, programs, projects, plans, and practices, particularly in the field of economic, social, and cultural rights (Hunt 2017). Mainland and archipelago must work in a mutually supportive way, with central human rights institutions providing guidance and specialized agencies focusing on their field of expertise. There is an advantage in further "institutionalizing" human rights and, in doing so, dispersing them in a formalized and coherent way into the management of a range of global concerns (Oberleitner 2008). We find ourselves, however, in difficult times, with many states being increasingly reluctant to accept that human rights are such a cross-cutting issue and seeking to roll back the influence of human rights in international organizations beyond dedicated meeting rooms in the UN.

The Implementation Crisis: State Sovereignty and the Pitfalls of Bureaucracy

There is no shortage of criticism on the performance and lack of impact of human rights institutions, courts, and tribunals. Despite the proliferation of human rights bodies and courts, the overall perception is that they have comparatively limited success to show and that despite all their efforts, gross human rights violations continue to occur, and this is certainly true. While they produce a considerable "output" of reports, conclusions, observations, views, resolutions, decisions, judgments, findings, and recommendations with regard to states' performance and structural and individual human rights problems, we nevertheless find ourselves in an "implementation crisis" (Open Society Justice Initiative 2010, p. 11). Despite lip service which is paid to the importance of human rights and to the significance of making them a reality, states are often unwilling to allow meaningful roles for human rights institutions and their work and are reluctant to follow their guidance. It is estimated that overall only 10–50% of decisions of human rights bodies are effectively implemented (Open Society Justice Initiative 2010, p. 94–5), and that in the Universal Periodic Review, only about half of all recommendations trigger some sort of action, with an even smaller percentage being fully implemented (UPR Info 2014).

Human rights institutions mirror the tension between state sovereignty and community interests. Inadequate as though these institutions may be, we should not forget how radical and politically improbable they seemed when the human rights movement started to form when the UN Charter and the Universal Declaration of Human Rights were adopted. Looking back, it seems rather remarkable how states have allowed cracks to open in the once impenetrable wall of state sovereignty.

Today, simply invoking the Charter's prohibition to intervene in domestic affairs no longer carries sufficient authority so that even states that are hostile towards any form of international scrutiny of their human rights situation usually resort to more sophisticated arguments in defense of their position. This tune has changed, and human rights institutions, courts, and tribunals can take credit for this. They have, in different measure, succeeded to accumulate independence and autonomy, be it by design (such as the independence of judges) or through the persuasiveness of expert knowledge (such as in the case of Special Rapporteurs) or through exercising moral authority and humanitarian leadership. In line with constructivist theories, there is evidence that at least some human rights institutions can assert themselves as autonomous actors operating in accordance with their human rights mandate even against the preferences of states (Alvarez 2006).

They do so in the difficult environment of international law. Many features of international law – the consensually produced treaty arrangements between sovereign nation states, the limited participation of civil society, and the absence of central enforcement authorities – combine to make the international legal order a less than conducive framework for the effective enforcement of human rights; yet it is the only one at our disposal. Most of the time, international human rights institutions say what they have to say in the form of "soft law" – nonbinding resolutions and recommendations and programmatic principles and guidelines – rather than as legally binding "hard law." Security Council resolutions are the exception that proves the rule, as they can be legally binding under Article 25 of the UN Charter. Judgements of human rights courts are also placed within the realm of "hard law," but their legally binding character still means little in the absence of a government's will to abide or the lacking power of state parties to the respective treaty to apply pressure on noncompliant members of the treaty community. This is not necessarily a bleak picture, though. Soft law and soft forms of compliance control are not necessarily worthless but merely different from coercive measures for the way they can induce change (Shelton 2006, p. 319). However, for such processes of justification, rationalization, recommendation, and persuasion to succeed some conditions need to be met, not least that these institutions are perceived as legitimate and operate in a nonselective, consistent, and coherent fashion.

It also needs to be remembered that despite their importance, international human rights institutions remain only subsidiary means for the protection of human rights. The primary responsibility to guarantee human rights remains with states while international institutions provide can more or less robust supportive backup. The rule that local remedies need to be exhausted before cases can be brought to international courts, the required consent of states before the Office of the High Commissioner for Human Rights can enter into a technical cooperation program, or the existence of "opt-in" and "opt-out" clauses in human rights treaty mechanisms are reminders of this subsidiary role of human rights institutions.

Finally, like all bureaucracies, international organizations are prone to developing institutional sclerosis: insulation from reality, self-referential attitudes, alienation of stakeholders, focus on process rather than output, ritualized adoptions of repetitive resolutions, or lack of coordination and coherence, to name just a few. Human rights institutions are not immune to such developments. Where they succumb to them, they turn into empty rituals and are easily perceived as remote, unresponsive, and intransparent, as the embodiment of an elite project devoid of meaning to anyone but a small class of self-absorbed human rights experts. Even where they avoid drifting into this abyss, the intertwined processes of legalization, professionalization, and bureaucratization necessarily shape a discrete understanding of human rights, which may be perceived as remote from the realities on the ground. Human rights litigation, too, is not immune from creating backlashes. Regressive human rights jurisprudence or contradictory judgments may occasionally obscure rather than clarify states' obligations. And the extent to which human rights institutions contribute to the perception that 70 years of international human rights protection have done so preciously little to confront larger and more complex social and economic root causes for inequality and injustice needs to be carefully analyzed. Samuel Moyn has recently highlighted this mismatch between an ever-tighter web of human rights norms and institutions and the accompanying drifting apart of entire segments of societies in an ever more unequal world (Moyn 2018).

Persuasion, Coercion, and the Good Faith of States

Human rights bodies, courts, and tribunals have no means to coerce states to follow their recommendations or judgments: "[p]ersuasion is ultimately the only remedy" (Tomuschat 2014, p. 431). International human rights institutions have to rely on persuasion and appeals to legitimacy or morality, occasionally supported by political and economic incentives or pressure. Again, the Security Council is set apart for the way the UN Charter allows the Council not only to adopt binding resolutions but also to use military force to achieve goals which may occasionally be cloaked in human rights terms. Otherwise, however, human rights institutions rely on persuasion when they seek to compel states to induce change on the domestic level. Even where international courts issue binding judgements, the execution of such judgments is ultimately relegated to the realm of international politics when states need to ensure that their peers comply. It has been suggested that for this reason one might further explore the potential of friendly settlements of human rights cases before courts to see what they can offer to victims of human rights violations (Leach 2017). Such critique on the weakness of human rights institutions' pronouncements is even more obvious for the "views" and "observations" of treaty bodies or the recommendations of Special Rapporteurs. Their output is "soft law." Even so, it can carry authority and its persuasive power should not be dismissed, as long as it is nonselective, produced in a consistent manner, and backed up by some larger form of political organization (Shelton 2006).

Human rights institutions cannot coerce wrongdoers. Instead, they are compliance managers. This, in turn, presupposes the capacity to identify, understand, and counter situations of noncompliance (Brunné 2007, p. 374). Human rights institutions cannot "command and control." They represent a form of international regulation. Their use of legal and moral authority to persuade states to adhere to norms is based on rationalist and constructivist perceptions of international relations (Davies 2010, p. 646). The emphasis must be on understanding how they can best persuade states to implement human rights. For this to happen, one has to take into account the sender as well as the recipient of recommendations or judgements, anticipate the posture a state may take towards them, and align follow-up measures with the nature of recommendations. This requires insights from the scholarship and practice of regulatory mechanisms in international relations to understand (and possibly counter) such postures by states. With this, one may better understand why some states embrace regulatory norms and goals while others disengage or deny the legitimacy of specific regulatory goals even where they accept the rationale of human rights norms in general (Charlesworth and Larking 2015).

The question why states obey international law at all continues to puzzle scholars. It is particularly difficult to answer in the field of human rights, where ideas of reciprocity and theories of rational choice theories are less likely to explain the behavior of states, given that adherence to human rights norms seems to offer them comparatively few incentives (Donoho 2006, p. 12). A realist perspective, which sees norm implementation driven by either the self-interest of states or by external pressure, may often fall short of explaining compliance with human rights norms. Conceptual approaches such as Harold H. Koh's transnational legal process are better suited to explain how the transformation of international norms makes states interact with the international legal system, interpret norms, and internalize them in their legal system, so that attitudes and beliefs change in accordance with international human rights norms and become constitutive behavior (Koh 1999). One may also consider that, in general, states accept international obligations with an intention to comply, and that noncompliance is not always due to the explicit with to break a rule but stems from other reasons such as ambiguous norms, conflicting political priorities, or constraints on the capacity to comply (Chayes and Chayes 1995, p. 1–28). In the absence of dedicated third-party enforcement mechanisms, international human rights bodies and courts need to rely on the cooperation of states. Combining incentives and persuasion may lead to success: "A concept that would visualize human rights exclusively as a burden on the governmental apparatus would be doomed from the very outset" (Tomuschat 2014, p. 432).

When international human rights institutions seek to ensure that human rights are realized within states, they borrow from the three distinct ideas of law enforcement, compliance control, and dispute settlement under international law. It needs to be understood that when an international human rights institution takes up a human rights violation, it engages with this on three levels. It provides redress for the grievances of an individual, it responds to a breach of an interstate promise (usually given in a human rights treaty), and it offers itself as a means of dispute-settlement for states (Paulus 2007, p. 359). Successful human rights implementation needs to play along all three levels. Moreover, while international law positions states as the primary subjects of international law, able to assert their interests at will, the reality is a much more nuanced, with other stakeholders – civil society actors, non-state armed groups or business corporations – playing a potentially powerful role (McCorquodale 2004). Human rights institutions need to accommodate multifaceted processes of acculturation, adaptation, and learning beyond coercive measures to translate international obligations into domestic law and reality. Ultimately, they should be able to make a contribution to creating a domestic human rights culture within societies and communities (Oberleitner 2012).

The effectiveness of human rights institutions presumes, however, a minimum of good faith by governments. Presently, such good faith seems to decline. The past decade has seen a backlash against human rights even from states that so far had supported the idea of human rights and the corresponding international legal and institutional framework. An increasing number of countries have passed laws preventing the financing and functioning of human rights NGOs and have instigated or allowed reprisals against human rights defenders and threats against officials working for human rights institutions. Women's human rights are cut back in many places, genocidal acts against minorities occur unhindered, and in conflict zones not even the barest minimum of humanity can be taken for granted. Human rights are sometimes rejected in their entirety on the grounds of religion or national supremacy, counter-terrorism laws are thriving at the expanse of individual liberty, and new technological developments undermine established views of privacy and date protection. International human rights institutions operate in difficult and hostile times with many states seeking to cut back funding and refusing to accept human rights as a cross-cutting issue in UN special agencies, funds, and programs. If good faith is also expressed through adequately financing human rights institutions, then the continuous underfunding of human rights institutions (which dispose of a fraction of budgets devoted to other fields) is further proof that states are not putting their money where their mouth is. The entire human rights activities of the UN, for example, still receive around 3% of the organization's overall regular budget (OHCHR funding and budget 2018). The struggle over the form and composition of human rights bodies and their procedural rules, their meeting time, location, geographic composition, financing, and about every single staff member employed is always also a political struggle about human rights which reveals state interests, inequality of power, and diverging views of human rights.

Designing Human Rights Institutions: Participative Multilevel Human Rights Governance

Human rights institutions are constructions and consequently their form affects their function and ultimately decides about success or failure. This interplay between form and function matters and adequately designing human rights institutions within an inadequate international legal order is a challenge. Which design elements strengthen and which design elements constrain effectiveness? For one, human rights institutions are largely state-owned and state-driven (as it should be in the international legal order). Yet, while it is the prerogative of states to create norms by which they can ultimately feel bound and ensure representation in their institutions, the importance of civil society participation and the benefits of linking international institutions with domestic constituencies has repeatedly been demonstrated

(Dai 2014). Nongovernmental organizations, National Human Rights Institutions, advocacy groups, national legislators, the legal profession, the media, and other groups need to be connected with international human rights institutions so that they can provide information and have a voice.

There is no uniform attitude towards such participation of actors other than governments. The tripartite composition of the governing bodies of the International Labour Organisation (with their representation of governments and employers' and employees' organizations) and the UN Forum on Indigenous Issues (with half its members coming from indigenous communities) are progressive examples beyond the mere assignation of formal consultative status for NGOs in international organizations (which allows for very limited participation rights). Reaching out to business corporations and non-state armed actors and monitor their human rights performance is another challenge ahead. Such "horizontal" effects of human rights (the violation of human rights but actors other than state agents) attract ever-greater interest and need to be dealt with, whether they are committed by organized entities or private individuals, who commit acts such as domestic violence, trafficking of human beings, sexual abuse, or domestic servitude. When it comes to litigation before human rights courts, it may be equally important to consider the rules of standing and possibly expand the range of actors who can claim "victim status." The European Court of Human Rights has done so in recent cases such as in Câmpeanu v Romania, where it granted victim status to a Romanian NGO which had assisted a young mentally and physically disabled men without any relatives, and allowed the case to be brought forward after the actual had died in a state-run hospital (European Court of Human Rights, Centre for Legal Resources on behalf of Valentin Câmpeanu v Romania 2014).

Ensuring the responsibilities of local and regional authorities in implementing human rights is another challenge ahead for human rights institutions. It is now widely understood that in addition to national governments all levels of governance and, in particular, local and regional authorities have a responsibility for implementing of human rights. Local authorities deliver services in housing, education, health care, water supply, public safety, and other fields are of direct importance for communities and individuals. All these activities raise questions of human rights on a daily basis and in practical manner. With the global rise of urbanization, the role of cities and regions in promoting and guaranteeing human rights becomes ever more important. Documents such as the Agenda 2030 or the New Urban Agenda are aware of this and pursue a human rights approach to local (good) governance. Current economic and societal challenges are primarily felt in cities: managing migration flows, protecting marginalized groups, battling climate change, regulating business corporations, balancing security and liberty in public spaces, or coping with decentralization in times of economic crises and austerity measures. The shift of power and law from the national to the local and regional needs to be accommodated within a state-centered international human rights system which gives as yet little space for local and regional inputs. The increasing engagement of cities and regions in matters of human rights and the perceived "localization" of the international human rights framework leads to questions as to the role and responsibility of local state vis-à-vis the nation state. The consequences of shifting the burden of human rights promotion and protection from the national to the regional and local level will be felt by international human rights institutions, and they will need to find responses.

Finally, the status and power of international institutions needs to be matched by their accountability. Human rights institutions need not only be aware of the pitfalls of bureaucratization and accommodate the political nature of human rights but also have to develop adequate responses to their own potential failures. Unaccountable international human rights institutions, even of only in perception, damage the legitimacy and impair the very idea of human rights and the principles of the rule of law, nondiscrimination, due process, fair trial, and gender equality. The legitimacy of human rights institutions must be grounded in their rules of procedure, in their composition and work ethics, and there must be no gaps in accountability for misconduct. At the same time, one must not fall into the trap set up by those who, under the pretext of "streamlining" and "rationalizing" procedures, seek in effect to curtail the independence and autonomy of human rights bodies by ever-tighter codes of conduct and oversight. Regulating the accountability of human rights institutions is necessary to protect the integrity of the institution and not to open up avenues for excessive governmental control. This is not to say that human rights institutions are not in need of reform. Indeed, some of them, such as the UN human rights treaty bodies, find themselves in a long-running reform process with a view towards ensuring consistency and coherence while preserving their independence and competitive advantages (Keller and Ulfstein 2012; Report of the Secretary General 2016).

The Importance of Follow-Up

Today, the success of the idea of human rights depends largely on the ability of the international human rights system to initiate and foster visible change. When recommendations and judgments of human rights bodies do not lead to noticeable progress, the belief in the system is easily shattered. When human rights institutions do not deliver results, they are little more than self-serving exercises in ritualism which allow states to accept norms in a superficial manner and participate in formal legal procedures in the absence of substantial commitments to human rights. Ensuring that recommendations of human rights bodies are implemented effectively is perhaps the greatest current challenge to the international human rights system (Gaer 2009).

At the same time, such follow-up processes are a surprisingly poorly understood part of international regulatory networks in the field of human rights (Open Society Foundation, Brookings Institution and UPR Watch 2010). When human rights institutions are created, there is usually interest in how they receive and process information and produce recommendations or judgements but there is limited attention to ensuring adequate follow-up once their immediate job is done (Response of Non-Governmental Organizations to the Dublin Statement on the Process of

Strengthening the United Nations Human Rights Treaty Body System 2011, p. 10). Often, there is only a vague expectation or hope that somehow states will do as a monitoring body is telling them, and even where specific regulations on follow-up exist, they are usually vague, as if added as an afterthought to more concrete procedural prescriptions. Following up the implementation of recommendations or judgments creates effectively an additional layer of obligations for human rights bodies which has attracted comparatively little attention (Bernaz 2013, p. 718). Follow-up activities are usually also under-financed in comparison to other activities of human rights institutions (Strengthening the United Nations Human Rights Treaty Body System – Dublin II Meeting: Outcome Document 2011, p. 20).

The output of human rights institutions is not uniform and ranges from sweeping and tentative suggestions to complex recommendations and from suggestions of vague ideals to specific, clear, and implementable prescriptions (United Nations 2016). More often than not, states find themselves confronted with a large number of recommendations by different human rights institutions. This has led to suggestions to ease the burden for the recipient of recommendations, as even states with the intention to adhere to them may find themselves overwhelmed. Adopting joint recommendations, cross-referencing between different recommendations or establishing inter-committee structures to avoid duplication and ensure consistency are possible. There is, however, no blueprint for a "good" recommendation; if it is vague, the state may not understand its intention, but on the other hand, a vague recommendation may make it easier for a state to act on its own impulse rather than reluctantly follow a specific advice. A study on the acceptance of recommendations made in the Universal Periodic Review concluded that it depends on the subject-matter rather than the wording of a recommendation. States which are opposed to discussing sexual orientation before a human rights body will reject even a general mentioning of the topic while they may well be prepared to accept specific and action- recommendations on other issues without hesitation (McMahon 2010). The sender may also matter to the recipient; some states prefer advice from independent sources such as Special Rapporteurs of the Human Rights Council while others would rather accept harsh criticism from their peers than friendly advice from a nongovernmental source (Open Society Foundation 2010, p. 11). The level of compliance also reflects the nature of the remedy; compliance with monetary damages by the European Court of Human Rights is on average high but drops once the Court requests other specific remedies (Open Society Justice Initiative 2010, p. 16).

While judgments of human rights courts and international criminal tribunals can claim legally binding force under international law, the pronouncements of all other institutions are nonbinding recommendations. While this nonbinding nature has its advantages (it allows, for example, to make policy suggestions in a dialogue process without raising expectations of "enforcement"), it remains troublesome. Obviously, such recommendations are not meant to be meaningless but are rather a specific type of obligation. They remain governed by general principles of international law, particularly the principle of bona fide – the duty of states to adhere to international law in good faith. The Committee on Human Rights, for example, considers its views on individual complaints as "exhibit[ing] some important characteristics of a judicial decision" which triggers obligation to respect (Human Rights Committee, General Comment No. 33 2008, para. 11). Even so, more clarity on what is legally expected by states (if anything) would be necessary.

Most human rights institutions are able take steps to ensure follow-up to their decisions. Under Rule 115 of its Rules of Procedure, the African Commission on Human and Peoples' Rights, for example, wants to be kept informed on implementation measures within 6 months of a decision, and then requests further information within 3 months after this report, and sends reminders every 3 months thereafter. Sometimes, human rights bodies entrust rapporteurs with keeping track of follow-up to recommendations, ensuring the flow of information and assessing steps taken by states. Human rights bodies mandated to conduct country visits may resort to the practice of follow-up country visits during which they remind states of their obligations and ask for progress reports. Under Rule 96(2) of its Rules of Procedure, the Inter-American Court of Human Rights can hold compliance hearings with representatives of the state, victims and expert witnesses. The Court also occasionally asks states to identify agents responsible for implementing its decisions on the national level (Open Society Justice Initiative 2010, p. 82–3). Some human rights institutions make cases of noncompliance public. Thematic special procedures of the Human Rights Council can organize events to discuss their reports or hold thematic discussion days, and in doing so reach out to noncomplaint states. The importance of civil society organizations in critically accompanying the implementation process and the follow-up to recommendations is evident. National stakeholders, for example, legislative organs, need to be drawn into this process, for example, by inviting parliamentarians to submit information or ensure their attendance in sessions of the human rights bodies, where relevant (University of Bristol 2011, p. 3).

Human rights institutions usually function in a broader organizational framework so that their respective "parent bodies" can provide additional legitimacy and political weight and can be used in follow-up processes. Information on noncompliance with recommendations is usually found in reports to these bodies. Under Rule 115 of its Rules of Procedure, the African Commission on Human and Peoples' Rights can alert the Sub-Committee of the Permanent Representatives' Committee and the African Union's Executive Council on the implementation of decisions. The European Court of Human Rights turns to the Committee of Ministers of the Council of Europe for the execution of its judgments, which has devised ways to deal with such situations (Gori 2013, p. 908). Under the Committee's Rules of Procedure, states have to abide by a strict reporting timeline on implementation measures and provide the Committee with a plan of action on implementation. The status of implementation can be traced through publicly accessible "status sheets" and cases of noncompliance are put on the Committee's agenda for discussion, with priority given to urgent cases, pilot judgments, or judgments which disclose major structural problems. Cases of noncompliance can then be reverted to the European Court of Human Rights. Similarly, Rule 121(4) of the Rules of Procedure of the African Court on Human and Peoples' Rights allows the African Commission on Human and Peoples' Rights to seize the Court on cases of noncompliance.

Further efforts need to be undertaken to link international human rights institutions with national actors beyond national NGOs and National Human Rights Institutions. This means drawing legislative bodies; administrative units; and the judiciary, local, and regional authorities, trade unions, professional associations, and religious communities into the discussion of human rights matters, based on the decision by international human rights bodies. The national preventative mechanisms under the Optional Protocol to the UN Convention against Torture are a prime example for such an approach, which combines international efforts with domestic institution-building. Web-based "National Implementation Portals" with accessible data, "implementation charts" on the state of implementation of recommendations in the respective national language(s), and compilations of "best practice" examples of how to improve monitoring processes, submit information to human rights bodies, create stakeholder coalitions, and involve epistemic communities and legislators could be envisaged (Strengthening the United Nations Human Rights Treaty Body System – Dublin II Meeting: Outcome Document 2011).

Only very few countries have gone a decisive step further and given legal force to recommendations of human rights bodies. The government of Peru commits itself to implementing nonbinding recommendations as an expression of the principle of good faith in international law and has entrusted a special national institution with directing, monitoring, and coordinating implementation activities, suggesting legal and administrative changes and cooperating with civil society. In Colombia, an interministerial committee decides on the implementation of decisions of international bodies and the payment of damages. Costa Rica has signed an agreement with the Inter-American Court of Human Rights, which gives nonbinding resolutions of the Court the same effect as its legally binding judgments and similar initiatives are under way in Argentina and Brazil (Open Society Justice Initiative 2010, p. 85–8).

Impact and Success: Measuring Compliance

Measuring the impact of human rights institutions is notoriously difficult. Success and failure may depend on the observer's position and expectations. While the human rights activist may decry an inherent structural deficit of a human rights body, states may be satisfied that they have managed to create an institution sufficiently vague to allow broad acceptance and participation. So far, empirical scholarship has produced diverging results on the successes and failures of human rights institutions and on the methodologies to measure them. Positive findings exist which show that human rights institutions contribute to social mobilization for human rights on the national level and strengthen national and transnational activist networks (Simmons 2009). Such results are countered by critics who argue that the existence of a certain level of domestic receptiveness for human rights (in the form of functioning democracies or active civil societies) is a precondition for any success, and that without this precondition, human rights fail where they ought to deliver, namely in autocratic states and against abusive governments (Neumayer 2005; Hafner-Burton and Tsutsui 2007; Hathaway 2002). On the other hand, no certainty exists that human rights do *not* work; scholarship seems to agree that in certain situations and under certain conditions, human rights institutions can produce positive results. The way in which human rights institutions contribute to change is thus "path-dependend and conditional in complex ways" (Dai 2014, p. 572). Most recently, Kathryin Sikkink has defended human rights institutions against the accusation of being mere window-dressing. Especially where states undergo transformations towards greater democracy, the international institutional framework provides measurable support, provided human rights institutions play their role within a mutually influencing matrix of social movements in states, governmental policy, and the domestic judiciary (Sikkink 2017). Within complex social transformation processes, causality is obviously difficult to establish, so that attributing changes directly to the work of human rights institutions is difficult, if not impossible.

In addition, the focus on output may be misplaced, given that the process of scrutinizing states' performance may matter in equal measure (Goodman and Jinks 2004). In human rights monitoring procedures, state representative have to argue their case rather than simply assert a position. The encounters of human rights diplomats can help to shape a distinct epistemic community and participation in such human rights negotiation and monitoring procedures may induce long-term structural changes within a given state and its administration, among legislators and policy-makers. Participation in global institutions and the accompanying processes of socialization and learning can build habits and attitudes, which can be as important as immediate results of human rights monitoring procedures (Goodman and Jinks 2008; Smith 2006, p. 291–4).

Conclusion

Do we have enough human rights institutions, courts, and tribunals? Do we have the right type of institutions? Scholarship has not found indications that the existence of multiple human rights institutions poses a serious danger to the system. The proliferation of human rights institutions since 1945 may pose problems of coherence and consistency, strain resources, and put demands on states but it has not led to a fragmentation that threatens the system as a whole. Normative conflicts are the exception, while reciprocal citations, cross-fertilization and normative "catching-up" towards the highest human rights standard allow human rights institutions in various subregimes of human rights to cooperate and put cumulative pressure on states. The multitude of human rights bodies is thus an asset rather than a problem (Shany 2016). Quite to the contrary, the absence of human rights institutions in the Southeast Asian region, the weak supervisory means in the Arab region, and the discussion on a possible international court of human rights demonstrate that there is room for further development.

Whether we have the right kind of human rights institutions is an altogether different question. There can be no uniform agenda for strengthening human rights institutions, given the diversity of commissions, committees, councils, courts, and tribunals with their distinct mandates. We need to understand the different types of remedies for human rights violations better and analyze their respective impact within a given context, their interactions, and constraints. Human rights institutions may be in constant need of reform but they deserve to be preserved and defended as the best available tools for assisting and supporting human rights and inducing change. The project of making human rights a reality is certainly larger than the narrow focus on committees and commissions, recommendation and judgments seems to suggest, and human rights institutions are not the only answer to the ills of the world (and sometimes not the right answer at all). Still, they are important cornerstones of the growing global human rights edifice. Where change occurs through international human rights institutions, courts, and tribunals, it is usually incremental. Reporting, discussing, justifying, and engaging with recommendations of human rights bodies or judgements of human rights courts in never-ending monitoring cycles may sound tedious (and occasionally is) and the effects are hard to measure. However, while sometimes there may be the need for a revolution, more often change is brought about through the kind of gradual transformation that human rights institutions can facilitate.

References

Alvarez JE (2006) International organizations as law-makers. Oxford University Press, Oxford

Bernaz N (2013) Continuing evolution of the United Nations treaty bodies system. In: Sheeran S, Rodley N (eds) Routledge handbook of international human rights law. Routledge, London/New York

Brunné J (2007) Compliance control. In: Ulfstein G (ed) Making treaties work. Human rights, environmental and arms control. Cambridge University Press, Cambridge, pp 373–390

Charlesworth H, Larking E (2015) Introduction: the regulatory power of the universal periodic review. In: Charlesworth H, Larking E (eds) Human rights and the universal periodic review: rituals and ritualism. Cambridge University Press, Cambridge, pp 1–21

Chayes A, Handler Chayes A (1995) The new sovereignty. Compliance with international regulatory agreements. Harvard University Press, Cambridge MA

Dai X (2014) The conditional effects of international human rights institutions. Hum Rights Q 36(3):569–589

Davies M (2010) Rhetorical inaction? Compliance and the Human Rights Council of the United Nations. Alternatives 35:449–468

Donoho D (2006) Human rights enforcement in the 21st century. Georgia J Int Comp Law 35(1):1–52

European Court of Human Rights (2014) Centre for Legal Resources on behalf of Valentin Câmpeanu v Romania, judgment of 14 July 2014, application no. 47848/08

Gaer F (2009) Sustaining scrutiny: lessons from treaty body follow up procedure. In: Benedek W et al (eds) Global standards – local action. 15 years Vienna world conference on human rights. Intersentia, Vienna, pp 459–564

Goodman R, Jinks D (2004) How to influence states: socialization and international human rights law. Duke Law J 54(3):621–703

Goodman R, Jinks D (2008) Incomplete internationalization and compliance with human rights law. Eur J Int Law 19(4):725–748

Gori G (2013) Compliance. In: Shelton D (ed) The Oxford handbook of international human rights law. Oxford University Press, Oxford

Hafner-Burton E, Tsutsui K (2007) Justice lost! The failure of international human rights law to matter where needed most. J Peace Res 44(4):407–425

Hathaway O (2002) Do human rights treaties make a difference? Yale Law J 111(8):1935–2042

Human Rights Committee, General Comment No. 33 (2008) UN Doc. CCPR/C/GC/33

Hunt P (2017) Configuring the UN human rights system in the "era of implementation": mainland and archipelago. Hum Rights Q 39:489–538

Keller H, Ulfstein G (2012) Conclusions. In: Keller H, Ulfstein G (eds) UN human rights treaty bodies – law and legitimacy. Cambridge University Press, Cambridge, pp 414–425

Kennedy D (1987) The move to institutions. Cardozo Law Rev 8(5):841–988

Klabbers J (2009) An introduction to international institutional law. Cambridge University Press, Cambridge

Koh HH (1999) How is international human rights law enforced? Indiana Law J 74:1397–1417

Leach P (2017) The continuing utility of international human rights mechanisms? Available at https://www.ejiltalk.org/the-continuing-utility-of-international-human-rights-mechanisms. Accessed 28 Mar 2018

Leary VA (2001) International institutions: towards coherent multilateralism. In: Boisson de Chauzournes L, Gowlland-Debbas V (eds) The international legal system in quest of equity and universality: liber amicorum Georges Abi-Saab. Nijhoff, The Hague, pp 823–829

McCorquodale R (2004) An inclusive international legal system. Leiden J Int Law 17(3):477–504

McMahon ER (2010) Herding cats and sheeps: assessing state and regional behaviour in the Universal Periodic Review mechanism of the United Nations Human Rights Council. Available at https://www.upr-info.org/sites/default/files/general-document/pdf/-mcmahon_herding_cats_and_sheeps_july_2010.pdf. Accessed 13 Apr 2018

Moyn S (2018) Not enough. Human rights in an unequal world. Harvard University Press, Cambridge MA

Neumayer E (2005) Do international human rights treaties improve respect for human rights? J Confl Resolut 49(6):925–953

Oberleitner G (2007) Global human rights institutions. Polity, Cambridge

Oberleitner G (2008) A decade of mainstreaming human rights in the UN: achievements, failures, challenges. Netherlands Q Hum Rights 26(3):359–390

Oberleitner G (2012) Does enforcement matter? In: Gearty C, Douzinas C (eds) Cambridge companion to human rights. Cambridge University Press, Cambridge, pp 249–268

OHCHR funding and budget (2018). Available at http://www.ohchr.org/EN/AboutUs/Pages/FundingBudget.aspx. Accessed 13 Apr 2018

Open Society Foundation, Brookings Institution and UPR Watch (2010) Improving implementation and follow-up – treaty bodies, special procedures, Universal Periodic Review. Report of the proceedings (22–23 November 2010). Available at http://www.opensocietyfoundations.org/reports/improving-implementation-and-follow-treaty-bodies-special-procedures-and-universal-periodic. Accessed 13 Apr 2018

Open Society Justice Initiative (2010) From judgement to justice – implementing international and regional human rights decisions. Open Society Foundation, New York

Open Society Justice Initiative (2016) The impacts of strategic litigation on indigenous peoples' land rights. Available at https://www.opensocietyfoundations.org/sites/default/files/slip-landrights-nairobi-20161014.pdf. Accessed 13 Apr 2018

Paulus AL (2007) Dispute resolution. In: Ulfstein G (ed) Making treaties work. Human rights, environment and arms control. Cambridge University Press, Cambridge, pp 251–372

Report of the Secretary-General (2016) Status of the human rights treaty body system. UN Doc. A/71/118 (18 July 2016)

Response of Non-Governmental Organizations to the Dublin Statement on the Process of Strengthening the United Nations Human Rights Treaty Body System (2011) Available at http://www.ohchr.org/EN/HRBodies/HRTD/Pages/Documents.aspx. Accessed 13 Apr 2018

Schabas W (2003) Criminal responsibility for violations of human rights. In: Symonides J (ed) Human rights: protection, monitoring, enforcement. Ashgate, Aldershot, pp 281–302

Shany Y (2016) International human rights bodies and the little-realized threat of fragmentation. Hebrew University of Jerusalem Legal Studies Research Paper Series No. 16-06. Available at https://papers.ssrn.com/sol3/papers.cfm?abstract_id=2722663. Accessed 13 Apr 2018

Shelton D (2006) Normative hierarchy in international law. AJIL 100(2):291–323

Sikkink K (2017) Evidence for hope. Making human rights work in the 21st century. Princeton University Press, Princeton

Simmons BA (2009) Mobilizing for human rights: international law in domestic politics. Cambridge University Press, Cambridge

Smith CB (2006) Politics and process at the United Nations. Lynne Rennier, Boulder

Strengthening the United Nations Human Rights Treaty Body System – Dublin II Meeting: Outcome Document (2011) Available at http://www.ohchr.org/EN/HRBodies/HRTD/Pages/Documents.aspx. Accessed 13 Apr 2018

Tomuschat C (2014) Human rights between idealism and realism, 3rd edn. Oxford University Press, Oxford

United Nations (2016) National mechanisms for reporting and follow-up. A study of state engagement with international human rights mechanisms. United Nations, Geneva

University of Bristol (2011) Implementation of UN treaty body concluding observations: the role of national and regional human rights mechanisms in Europe – summary and recommendations (19–20 September 2011). Available at http://www2.ohchr.org/english/bodies/HRTD/docs/Summary_Proceedings_Bristol_Sept2011_24.10.2011.pdf. Accessed 13 Apr 2018

UPR Info (2014) UPR Info and states discuss follow-up and mid-term reporting (23 September 2014). Available at http://www.upr-info.org/en/news/upr-info-and-states-discuss-follow-and-mid-term-reporting. Accessed 13 Apr 2018

Selected Human Rights Instruments

Selected Legal Texts (Excerpts)

Resolution 60/251 adopted by the United Nations General Assembly on 15 March 2006: Human Rights Council

The General Assembly [. . .]

1. Decides to establish the Human Rights Council, based in Geneva, in replacement of the Commission on Human Rights, as a subsidiary organ of the General Assembly; the Assembly shall review the status of the Council within five years;
2. Decides that the Council shall be responsible for promoting universal respect for the protection of all human rights and fundamental freedoms for all, without distinction of any kind and in a fair and equal manner;
3. Decides also that the Council should address situations of violations of human rights, including gross and systematic violations, and make recommendations thereon. It should also promote the effective coordination and the mainstreaming of human rights within the United Nations system;
4. Decides further that the work of the Council shall be guided by the principles of universality, impartiality, objectivity and non-selectivity, constructive international dialogue and cooperation, with a view to enhancing the promotion and protection of all human rights, civil, political, economic, social and cultural rights, including the right to development;
5. Decides that the Council shall, inter alia:
   (a) Promote human rights education and learning as well as advisory services, technical assistance and capacity-building, to be provided in consultation with and with the consent of Member States concerned;
   (b) Serve as a forum for dialogue on thematic issues on all human rights;
   (c) Make recommendations to the General Assembly for the further development of international law in the field of human rights;
   (d) Promote the full implementation of human rights obligations undertaken by States and follow-up to the goals and commitments related to the promotion and protection of human rights emanating from United Nations conferences and summits;

© Springer Nature Singapore Pte Ltd. 2018
G. Oberleitner (ed.), *International Human Rights Institutions, Tribunals, and Courts*,
International Human Rights, https://doi.org/10.1007/978-981-10-5206-4

    (e) Undertake a universal periodic review, based on objective and reliable information, of the fulfilment by each State of its human rights obligations and commitments in a manner which ensures universality of coverage and equal treatment with respect to all States; the review shall be a cooperative mechanism, based on an interactive dialogue, with the full involvement of the country concerned and with consideration given to its capacity-building needs; such a mechanism shall complement and not duplicate the work of treaty bodies; the Council shall develop the modalities and necessary time allocation for the universal periodic review mechanism within one year after the holding of its first session;

    (f) Contribute, through dialogue and cooperation, towards the prevention of human rights violations and respond promptly to human rights emergencies;

    (g) Assume the role and responsibilities of the Commission on Human Rights relating to the work of the Office of the United Nations High Commissioner for Human Rights, as decided by the General Assembly in its resolution 48/141 of 20 December 1993;

    (h) Work in close cooperation in the field of human rights with Governments, regional organizations, national human rights institutions and civil society;

    (i) Make recommendations with regard to the promotion and protection of human rights;

    (j) Submit an annual report to the General Assembly;

6. Decides also that the Council shall assume, review and, where necessary, improve and rationalize all mandates, mechanisms, functions and responsibilities of the Commission on Human Rights in order to maintain a system of special procedures, expert advice and a complaint procedure; the Council shall complete this review within one year after the holding of its first session;

7. Decides further that the Council shall consist of forty-seven Member States, which shall be elected directly and individually by secret ballot by the majority of the members of the General Assembly; the membership shall be based on equitable geographical distribution, and seats shall be distributed as follows among regional groups: Group of African States, thirteen; Group of Asian States, thirteen; Group of Eastern European States, six; Group of Latin American and Caribbean States, eight; and Group of Western European and other States, seven; the members of the Council shall serve for a period of three years and shall not be eligible for immediate re-election after two consecutive terms;

8. Decides that the membership in the Council shall be open to all States Members of the United Nations; when electing members of the Council, Member States shall take into account the contribution of candidates to the promotion and protection of human rights and their voluntary pledges and commitments made thereto; the General Assembly, by a two-thirds majority of the members present and voting, may suspend the rights of membership in the Council of a member of the Council that commits gross and systematic violations of human rights;

9. Decides also that members elected to the Council shall uphold the highest standards in the promotion and protection of human rights, shall fully cooperate with the Council and be reviewed under the universal periodic review mechanism during their term of membership;

10. Decides further that the Council shall meet regularly throughout the year and schedule no fewer than three sessions per year, including a main session, for a total duration of no less than ten weeks, and shall be able to hold special sessions, when needed, at the request of a member of the Council with the support of one third of the membership of the Council;

11. Decides that the Council shall apply the rules of procedure established for committees of the General Assembly, as applicable, unless subsequently otherwise decided by the Assembly or the Council, and also decides that the participation of and consultation with observers, including States that are not members of the Council, the specialized agencies, other intergovernmental organizations and national human rights in situations, as well as non-governmental organizations, shall be based on arrangements, including Economic and Social Council resolution 1996/31 of 25 July 1996 and practices observed by the Commission on Human Rights, while ensuring the most effective contribution of these entities;

12. Decides also that the methods of work of the Council shall be transparent, fair and impartial and shall enable genuine dialogue, be results-oriented, allow for subsequent follow-up discussions to recommendations and their implementation and also allow for substantive interaction with special procedures and mechanisms;

13. Recommends that the Economic and Social Council request the Commission on Human Rights to conclude its work at its sixty-second session, and that it abolish the Commission on 16 June 2006;

14. Decides to elect the new members of the Council; the terms of membership shall be staggered, and such decision shall be taken for the first election by the drawing of lots, taking into consideration equitable geographical distribution;

15. Decides also that elections of the first members of the Council shall take place on 9 May 2006, and that the first meeting of the Council shall be convened on 19 June 2006;

16. Decides further that the Council shall review its work and functioning five years after its establishment and report to the General Assembly.

Resolution 48/141 Adopted by the United Nations General Assembly on 7 January 1994: High Commissioner for the Promotion and Protection of all Human Rights

The General Assembly [. . .]

1. Decides to create the post of the High Commissioner for Human Rights;

2. Decides that the High Commissioner for Human Rights shall:

   (a) Be a person of high moral standing and personal integrity and shall possess expertise, including in the field of human rights, and the general knowledge and understanding of diverse cultures necessary for impartial, objective, non-selective and effective performance of the duties of the High Commissioner;

   (b) Be appointed by the Secretary-General of the United Nations and approved by the General Assembly, with due regard to geographical rotation, and have a fixed term of four years with a possibility of one renewal for another fixed term of four years;

   (c) Be of the rank of Under-Secretary-General;

3. Decides that the High Commissioner for Human Rights shall:

   (a) Function within the framework of the Charter of the United Nations, the Universal Declaration of Human Rights, other international instruments of human rights and international law, including the obligations, within this framework, to respect the sovereignty, territorial integrity and domestic jurisdiction of States and to promote the universal respect for and observance of all human rights, in the recognition that, in the framework of the purposes and principles of the Charter, the promotion and protection of all human rights is a legitimate concern of the international community;

   (b) Be guided by the recognition that all human rights - civil, cultural, economic, political and social - are universal, indivisible, interdependent and interrelated and that, while the significance of national and regional particularities and various historical, cultural and religious backgrounds must be borne in mind, it is the duty of States, regardless of their political, economic and cultural systems, to promote and protect all human rights and fundamental freedoms;

   (c) Recognize the importance of promoting a balanced and sustainable development for all people and of ensuring realization of the right to development, as established in the Declaration on the Right to Development;

4. Decides that the High Commissioner for Human Rights shall be the United Nations official with principal responsibility for United Nations human rights activities under the direction and authority of the Secretary-General; within the framework of the overall competence, authority and decisions of the General Assembly, the Economic and Social Council and the Commission on Human Rights, the High Commissioner's responsibilities shall be:

   (a) To promote and protect the effective enjoyment by all of all civil, cultural, economic, political and social rights;

   (b) To carry out the tasks assigned to him/her by the competent bodies of the United Nations system in the field of human rights and to make recommendations to them with a view to improving the promotion and protection of all human rights;

   (c) To promote and protect the realization of the right to development and to enhance support from relevant bodies of the United Nations system for this purpose;

(d) To provide, through the Centre for Human Rights of the Secretariat and other appropriate institutions, advisory services and technical and financial assistance, at the request of the State concerned and, where appropriate, the regional human rights organizations, with a view to supporting actions and programmes in the field of human rights;

(e) To coordinate relevant United Nations education and public information programmes in the field of human rights;

(f) To play an active role in removing the current obstacles and in meeting the challenges to the full realization of all human rights and in preventing the continuation of human rights violations throughout the world, as reflected in the Vienna Declaration and Programme of Action;

(g) To engage in a dialogue with all Governments in the implementation of his/her mandate with a view to securing respect for all human rights;

(h) To enhance international cooperation for the promotion and protection of all human rights;

(i) To coordinate the human rights promotion and protection activities throughout the United Nations system;

(j) To rationalize, adapt, strengthen and streamline the United Nations machinery in the field of human rights with a view to improving its efficiency and effectiveness;

(k) To carry out overall supervision of the Centre for Human Rights;

5. Requests the High Commissioner for Human Rights to report annually on his/her activities, in accordance with his/her mandate, to the Commission on Human Rights and, through the Economic and Social Council, to the General Assembly;

6. Decides that the Office of the High Commissioner for Human Rights shall be located at Geneva and shall have a liaison office in New York;

7. Requests the Secretary-General to provide appropriate staff and resources, within the existing and future regular budgets of the United Nations, to enable the High Commissioner to fulfil his/her mandate, without diverting resources from the development programmes and activities of the United Nations;

8. Also requests the Secretary-General to report to the General Assembly at its forty-ninth session on the implementation of the present resolution.

International Covenant on Civil and Political Rights

(adopted on 16 December 1966, entered into force 23 March 1976)

PART IV

Article 28

1. There shall be established a Human Rights Committee (hereafter referred to in the present Covenant as the Committee). It shall consist of eighteen members and shall carry out the functions hereinafter provided.

2. The Committee shall be composed of nationals of the States Parties to the present Covenant who shall be persons of high moral character and recognized competence in the field of human rights, consideration being given to the usefulness of the participation of some persons having legal experience.
3. The members of the Committee shall be elected and shall serve in their personal capacity.

Article 29

1. The members of the Committee shall be elected by secret ballot from a list of persons possessing the qualifications prescribed in article 28 and nominated for the purpose by the States Parties to the present Covenant.
2. Each State Party to the present Covenant may nominate not more than two persons. These persons shall be nationals of the nominating State.
3. A person shall be eligible for renomination.

Article 30

1. The initial election shall be held no later than six months after the date of the entry into force of the present Covenant.
2. At least four months before the date of each election to the Committee, other than an election to fill a vacancy declared in accordance with article 34, the Secretary-General of the United Nations shall address a written invitation to the States Parties to the present Covenant to submit their nominations for membership of the Committee within three months.
3. The Secretary-General of the United Nations shall prepare a list in alphabetical order of all the persons thus nominated, with an indication of the States Parties which have nominated them, and shall submit it to the States Parties to the present Covenant no later than one month before the date of each election.
4. Elections of the members of the Committee shall be held at a meeting of the States Parties to the present Covenant convened by the Secretary General of the United Nations at the Headquarters of the United Nations. At that meeting, for which two thirds of the States Parties to the present Covenant shall constitute a quorum, the persons elected to the Committee shall be those nominees who obtain the largest number of votes and an absolute majority of the votes of the representatives of States Parties present and voting.

Article 31

1. The Committee may not include more than one national of the same State.
2. In the election of the Committee, consideration shall be given to equitable geographical distribution of membership and to the representation of the different forms of civilization and of the principal legal systems.

Article 32

1. The members of the Committee shall be elected for a term of four years. They shall be eligible for re-election if renominated. However, the terms of nine of the members elected at the first election shall expire at the end of two years; immediately after the first election, the names of these nine members shall be chosen by lot by the Chairman of the meeting referred to in article 30, paragraph 4.
2. Elections at the expiry of office shall be held in accordance with the preceding articles of this part of the present Covenant.

Article 33

1. If, in the unanimous opinion of the other members, a member of the Committee has ceased to carry out his functions for any cause other than absence of a temporary character, the Chairman of the Committee shall notify the Secretary-General of the United Nations, who shall then declare the seat of that member to be vacant.
2. In the event of the death or the resignation of a member of the Committee, the Chairman shall immediately notify the Secretary-General of the United Nations, who shall declare the seat vacant from the date of death or the date on which the resignation takes effect.

Article 34

1. When a vacancy is declared in accordance with article 33 and if the term of office of the member to be replaced does not expire within six months of the declaration of the vacancy, the Secretary-General of the United Nations shall notify each of the States Parties to the present Covenant, which may within two months submit nominations in accordance with article 29 for the purpose of filling the vacancy.
2. The Secretary-General of the United Nations shall prepare a list in alphabetical order of the persons thus nominated and shall submit it to the States Parties to the present Covenant. The election to fill the vacancy shall then take place in accordance with the relevant provisions of this part of the present Covenant.
3. A member of the Committee elected to fill a vacancy declared in accordance with article 33 shall hold office for the remainder of the term of the member who vacated the seat on the Committee under the provisions of that article.

Article 35

The members of the Committee shall, with the approval of the General Assembly of the United Nations, receive emoluments from United Nations resources on such terms and conditions as the General Assembly may decide, having regard to the importance of the Committee's responsibilities.

Article 36

The Secretary-General of the United Nations shall provide the necessary staff and facilities for the effective performance of the functions of the Committee under the present Covenant.

Article 37

1. The Secretary-General of the United Nations shall convene the initial meeting of the Committee at the Headquarters of the United Nations.
2. After its initial meeting, the Committee shall meet at such times as shall be provided in its rules of procedure.
3. The Committee shall normally meet at the Headquarters of the United Nations or at the United Nations Office at Geneva.

Article 38

Every member of the Committee shall, before taking up his duties, make a solemn declaration in open committee that he will perform his functions impartially and conscientiously.

Article 39

1. The Committee shall elect its officers for a term of two years. They may be re-elected.
2. The Committee shall establish its own rules of procedure, but these rules shall provide, inter alia, that:
   (a) Twelve members shall constitute a quorum;
   (b) Decisions of the Committee shall be made by a majority vote of the members present.

Article 40

1. The States Parties to the present Covenant undertake to submit reports on the measures they have adopted which give effect to the rights recognized herein and on the progress made in the enjoyment of those rights:
   (a) Within one year of the entry into force of the present Covenant for the States Parties concerned;
   (b) Thereafter whenever the Committee so requests.
2. All reports shall be submitted to the Secretary-General of the United Nations, who shall transmit them to the Committee for consideration. Reports shall indicate the factors and difficulties, if any, affecting the implementation of the present Covenant.
3. The Secretary-General of the United Nations may, after consultation with the Committee, transmit to the specialized agencies concerned copies of such parts of the reports as may fall within their field of competence.
4. The Committee shall study the reports submitted by the States Parties to the present Covenant. It shall transmit its reports, and such general comments as it

may consider appropriate, to the States Parties. The Committee may also transmit to the Economic and Social Council these comments along with the copies of the reports it has received from States Parties to the present Covenant.

5. The States Parties to the present Covenant may submit to the Committee observations on any comments that may be made in accordance with paragraph 4 of this article.

Article 41

1. A State Party to the present Covenant may at any time declare under this article that it recognizes the competence of the Committee to receive and consider communications to the effect that a State Party claims that another State Party is not fulfilling its obligations under the present Covenant. Communications under this article may be received and considered only if submitted by a State Party which has made a declaration recognizing in regard to itself the competence of the Committee. No communication shall be received by the Committee if it concerns a State Party which has not made such a declaration. Communications received under this article shall be dealt with in accordance with the following procedure:
   (a) If a State Party to the present Covenant considers that another State Party is not giving effect to the provisions of the present Covenant, it may, by written communication, bring the matter to the attention of that State Party. Within three months after the receipt of the communication the receiving State shall afford the State which sent the communication an explanation, or any other statement in writing clarifying the matter which should include, to the extent possible and pertinent, reference to domestic procedures and remedies taken, pending, or available in the matter;
   (b) If the matter is not adjusted to the satisfaction of both States Parties concerned within six months after the receipt by the receiving State of the initial communication, either State shall have the right to refer the matter to the Committee, by notice given to the Committee and to the other State;
   (c) The Committee shall deal with a matter referred to it only after it has ascertained that all available domestic remedies have been invoked and exhausted in the matter, in conformity with the generally recognized principles of international law. This shall not be the rule where the application of the remedies is unreasonably prolonged;
   (d) The Committee shall hold closed meetings when examining communications under this article;
   (e) Subject to the provisions of subparagraph (c), the Committee shall make available its good offices to the States Parties concerned with a view to a friendly solution of the matter on the basis of respect for human rights and fundamental freedoms as recognized in the present Covenant;
   (f) In any matter referred to it, the Committee may call upon the States Parties concerned, referred to in subparagraph (b), to supply any relevant information;
   (g) The States Parties concerned, referred to in subparagraph (b), shall have the right to be represented when the matter is being considered in the Committee and to make submissions orally and/or in writing;

  (h) The Committee shall, within twelve months after the date of receipt of notice under subparagraph (b), submit a report:
- (i) If a solution within the terms of subparagraph (e) is reached, the Committee shall confine its report to a brief statement of the facts and of the solution reached;
- (ii) If a solution within the terms of subparagraph (e) is not reached, the Committee shall confine its report to a brief statement of the facts; the written submissions and record of the oral submissions made by the States Parties concerned shall be attached to the report. In every matter, the report shall be communicated to the States Parties concerned.

2. The provisions of this article shall come into force when ten States Parties to the present Covenant have made declarations under paragraph I of this article. Such declarations shall be deposited by the States Parties with the Secretary-General of the United Nations, who shall transmit copies thereof to the other States Parties. A declaration may be withdrawn at any time by notification to the Secretary-General. Such a withdrawal shall not prejudice the consideration of any matter which is the subject of a communication already transmitted under this article; no further communication by any State Party shall be received after the notification of withdrawal of the declaration has been received by the Secretary-General, unless the State Party concerned has made a new declaration.

Article 42

1. (a) If a matter referred to the Committee in accordance with article 41 is not resolved to the satisfaction of the States Parties concerned, the Committee may, with the prior consent of the States Parties concerned, appoint an ad hoc Conciliation Commission (hereinafter referred to as the Commission). The good offices of the Commission shall be made available to the States Parties concerned with a view to an amicable solution of the matter on the basis of respect for the present Covenant; (b) The Commission shall consist of five persons acceptable to the States Parties concerned. If the States Parties concerned fail to reach agreement within three months on all or part of the composition of the Commission, the members of the Commission concerning whom no agreement has been reached shall be elected by secret ballot by a two-thirds majority vote of the Committee from among its members.
2. The members of the Commission shall serve in their personal capacity. They shall not be nationals of the States Parties concerned, or of a State not Party to the present Covenant, or of a State Party which has not made a declaration under article 41.
3. The Commission shall elect its own Chairman and adopt its own rules of procedure.
4. The meetings of the Commission shall normally be held at the Headquarters of the United Nations or at the United Nations Office at Geneva. However, they may be held at such other convenient places as the Commission may determine in consultation with the Secretary-General of the United Nations and the States Parties concerned.

5. The secretariat provided in accordance with article 36 shall also service the commissions appointed under this article.

6. The information received and collated by the Committee shall be made available to the Commission and the Commission may call upon the States Parties concerned to supply any other relevant information.

7. When the Commission has fully considered the matter, but in any event not later than twelve months after having been seized of the matter, it shall submit to the Chairman of the Committee a report for communication to the States Parties concerned:

   (a) If the Commission is unable to complete its consideration of the matter within twelve months, it shall confine its report to a brief statement of the status of its consideration of the matter;

   (b) If an amicable solution to the matter on the basis of respect for human rights as recognized in the present Covenant is reached, the Commission shall confine its report to a brief statement of the facts and of the solution reached;

   (c) If a solution within the terms of subparagraph (b) is not reached, the Commission's report shall embody its findings on all questions of fact relevant to the issues between the States Parties concerned, and its views on the possibilities of an amicable solution of the matter. This report shall also contain the written submissions and a record of the oral submissions made by the States Parties concerned;

   (d) If the Commission's report is submitted under subparagraph (c), the States Parties concerned shall, within three months of the receipt of the report, notify the Chairman of the Committee whether or not they accept the contents of the report of the Commission.

8. The provisions of this article are without prejudice to the responsibilities of the Committee under article 41.

9. The States Parties concerned shall share equally all the expenses of the members of the Commission in accordance with estimates to be provided by the Secretary-General of the United Nations.

10. The Secretary-General of the United Nations shall be empowered to pay the expenses of the members of the Commission, if necessary, before reimbursement by the States Parties concerned, in accordance with paragraph 9 of this article.

Article 43

The members of the Committee, and of the ad hoc conciliation commissions which may be appointed under article 42, shall be entitled to the facilities, privileges and immunities of experts on mission for the United Nations as laid down in the relevant sections of the Convention on the Privileges and Immunities of the United Nations.

Article 44

The provisions for the implementation of the present Covenant shall apply without prejudice to the procedures prescribed in the field of human rights by or under the constituent instruments and the conventions of the United Nations and of the specialized agencies and shall not prevent the States Parties to the present Covenant from having recourse to other procedures for settling a dispute in accordance with general or special international agreements in force between them.

Article 45

The Committee shall submit to the General Assembly of the United Nations, through the Economic and Social Council, an annual report on its activities.

Economic and Social Council resolution 1985/17, Adopted on 28 May 1985: Review of the Composition, Organization and Administrative Arrangements of the Sessional Working Group of Governmental Experts on the Implementation of the International Covenant on Economic, Social, and Cultural Rights

The Economic and Social Council [. . .]
Decides that:

(a) The Working Group established by Economic and Social Council decision 1978/10 and modified by Council decision 1981/158 and resolution 1982/33 shall be renamed "Committee on Economic, Social and Cultural Rights" (hereinafter referred to as "the Committee");

(b) The Committee shall have eighteen members who shall be experts with recognized competence in the field of human rights, serving in their personal capacity, due consideration being given to equitable geographical distribution and to the representation of different forms of social and legal systems; to this end, fifteen seats will be equally distributed among the regional groups, while the additional three seats will be allocated in accordance with the increase in the total number of States parties per regional group;

(c) The members of the Committee shall be elected by the Council by secret ballot from a list of persons nominated by States parties to the International Covenant on Economic, Social and Cultural Rights under the following conditions:

    (i) The members of the Committee shall be elected for a term of four years and shall be eligible for re-election at the end of their term, if renominated;

    (ii) One half of the membership of the Committee shall be renewed every second year, bearing in mind the need to maintain the equitable geographical distribution mentioned in subparagraph (b) above;

    (iii) The first elections shall take place during the first regularsession of 1986 of the Council; immediately after the first elections, the President of the Council shall choose by lot the names of nine members whose term shall expire at the end of two years;

    (iv) The terms of office of members elected to the Committee shall begin on 1 January following their election and expire on 31 December following the election of members that are to succeed them as members of the Committee;

    (v) Subsequent elections shall take place every second year during the first regular session of the Council;

(vi) At least four months before the date of each election to the Committee the Secretary-General shall address a written invitation to the States parties to the Covenant to submit their nominations for membership of the Committee within three months; the Secretary-General shall prepare a list of the persons thus nominated, with an indication of the States parties which have nominated them, and shall submit it to the Council no later than one month before the date of each election;

(d) The Committee shall meet annually for a period of up to three weeks, taking into account the number of reports to be examined by the Committee, with the venue alternating between Geneva and New York;

(e) The members of the Committee shall receive travel and subsistence expenses from United Nations resources;

(f) The Committee shall submit to the Council a report on its activities, including a summary of its consideration of the reports submitted by States parties to the Covenant, and shall make suggestions and recommendations of a general nature on the basis of its consideration of those reports and of the reports submitted by the specialized agencies, in order to assist the Council to fulfil, in particular, its responsibilities under articles 21 and 22 of the Covenant;

(g) The Secretary-General shall provide the Committee with summary records of its proceedings, which shall be made available to the Council at the same time as the report of the Committee; the Secretary-General shall further provide the Committee with the necessary staff and facilities for the effective performance of its functions, bearing in mind the need to give adequate publicity to its work;

(h) The procedures and methods of work established by Council resolution 1979/43 and the other resolutions and decisions referred to in the preamble to the present resolution shall remain in force in so far as they are not superseded or modified by the present resolution;

(i) The Council shall review the composition, organization and administrative arrangements of the Committee at its first regular session of 1990, and subsequently every five years, taking into account the principle of equitable geographical distribution of its membership.

European Convention for the Protection of Human Rights and Fundamental Freedoms

(adopted on 4 November 1950, entered into force 3 September 1953)

Section II
European Court of Human Rights

Article 19
Establishment of the Court
To ensure the observance of the engagements undertaken by the High Contracting Parties in the Convention and the Protocols thereto, there shall be set up a European

Court of Human Rights, hereinafter referred to as "the Court". It shall function on a permanent basis.

Article 20
Number of judges

The Court shall consist of a number of judges equal to that of the High Contracting Parties.

Article 21
Criteria for office

1. The judges shall be of high moral character and must either possess the qualifications required for appointment to high judicial office or be jurisconsults of recognised competence.
2. The judges shall sit on the Court in their individual capacity.
3. During their term of office the judges shall not engage in any activity which is incompatible with their independence, impartiality or with the demands of a full-time office; all questions arising from the application of this paragraph shall be decided by the Court.

Article 22
Election of judges

The judges shall be elected by the Parliamentary Assembly with respect to each High Contracting Party by a majority of votes cast from a list of three candidates nominated by the High Contracting Party.

Article 23
Terms of office and dismissal

1. The judges shall be elected for a period of nine years. They may not be re-elected.
2. The terms of office of judges shall expire when they reach the age of 70.
3. The judges shall hold office until replaced. They shall, however, continue to deal with such cases as they already have under consideration.
4. No judge may be dismissed from office unless the other judges decide by a majority of two-thirds that that judge has ceased to fulfil the required conditions.

Article 24
Registry and rapporteurs

1. The Court shall have a Registry, the functions and organisation of which shall be laid down in the rules of the Court.
2. When sitting in a single-judge formation, the Court shall be assisted by rapporteurs who shall function under the authority of the President of the Court. They shall form part of the Court's Registry.

Article 25
Plenary Court
The plenary Court shall

(a) elect its President and one or two Vice-Presidents for a period of three years; they may be re-elected;
(b) set up Chambers, constituted for a fixed period of time;
(c) elect the Presidents of the Chambers of the Court; they may be re-elected;
(d) adopt the rules of the Court;
(e) elect the Registrar and one or more Deputy Registrars;
(f) make any request under Article 26, paragraph 2.

Article 26
Single-judge formation, Committees, Chambers and Grand Chamber

1. To consider cases brought before it, the Court shall sit in a single-judge formation, in committees of three judges, in Chambers of seven judges and in a Grand Chamber of seventeen judges. The Court's Chambers shall set up committees for a fixed period of time.
2. At the request of the plenary Court, the Committee of Ministers may, by a unanimous decision and for a fixed period, reduce to five the number of judges of the Chambers.
3. When sitting as a single judge, a judge shall not examine any application against the High Contracting Party in respect of which that judge has been elected.
4. There shall sit as an ex officio member of the Chamber and the Grand Chamber the judge elected in respect of the High Contracting Party concerned. If there is none or if that judge is unable to sit, a person chosen by the President of the Court from a list submitted in advance by that Party shall sit in the capacity of judge.
5. The Grand Chamber shall also include the President of the Court, the Vice-Presidents, the Presidents of the Chambers and other judges chosen in accordance with the rules of the Court. When a case is referred to the Grand Chamber under Article 43, no judge from the Chamber which rendered the judgment shall sit in the Grand Chamber, with the exception of the President of the Chamber and the judge who sat in respect of the High Contracting Party concerned.

Article 27
Competence of single judges

1. A single judge may declare inadmissible or strike out of the Court's list of cases an application submitted under Article 34, where such a decision can be taken without further examination.
2. The decision shall be final.
3. If the single judge does not declare an application inadmissible or strike it out, that judge shall forward it to a committee or to a Chamber for further examination.

Article 28

Competence of Committees

1. In respect of an application submitted under Article 34, a committee may, by a unanimous vote,
   (a) declare it inadmissible or strike it out of its list of cases, where such decision can be taken without further examination; or
   (b) declare it admissible and render at the same time a judgment on the merits, if the underlying question in the case, concerning the interpretation or the application of the Convention or the Protocols thereto, is already the subject of well-established case-law of the Court.
2. Decisions and judgments under paragraph 1 shall be final.
3. If the judge elected in respect of the High Contracting Party concerned is not a member of the committee, the committee may at any stage of the proceedings invite that judge to take the place of one of the members of the committee, having regard to all relevant factors, including whether that Party has contested the application of the procedure under paragraph 1(b).

Article 29

Decisions by Chambers on admissibility and merits

1. If no decision is taken under Article 27 or 28, or no judgment rendered under Article 28, a Chamber shall decide on the admissibility and merits of individual applications submitted under Article 34. The decision on admissibility may be taken separately.
2. A Chamber shall decide on the admissibility and merits of inter-State applications submitted under Article 33. The decision on admissibility shall be taken separately unless the Court, in exceptional cases, decides otherwise.

Article 30

Relinquishment of jurisdiction to the Grand Chamber

Where a case pending before a Chamber raises a serious question affecting the interpretation of the Convention or the Protocols thereto, or where the resolution of a question before the Chamber might have a result inconsistent with a judgment previously delivered by the Court, the Chamber may, at any time before it has rendered its judgment, relinquish jurisdiction in favour of the Grand Chamber, unless one of the parties to the case objects.

Article 31

Powers of the Grand Chamber

The Grand Chamber shall

(a) determine applications submitted either under Article 33 or Article 34 when a Chamber has relinquished jurisdiction under Article 30 or when the case has been referred to it under Article 43;

(b) decide on issues referred to the Court by the Committee of Ministers in accordance with Article 46, paragraph 4; and

(c) consider requests for advisory opinions submitted under Article 47.

Article 32
Jurisdiction of the Court

1. The jurisdiction of the Court shall extend to all matters concerning the interpretation and application of the Convention and the Protocols thereto which are referred to it as provided in Articles 33, 34, 46 and 47.
2. In the event of dispute as to whether the Court has jurisdiction, the Court shall decide.

Article 33
Inter-State cases

Any High Contracting Party may refer to the Court any alleged breach of the provisions of the Convention and the Protocols thereto by another High Contracting Party.

Article 34
Individual applications

The Court may receive applications from any person, non-governmental organisation or group of individuals claiming to be the victim of a violation by one of the High Contracting Parties of the rights set forth in the Convention or the Protocols thereto. The High Contracting Parties undertake not to hinder in any way the effective exercise of this right.

Article 35
Admissibility criteria

1. The Court may only deal with the matter after all domestic remedies have been exhausted, according to the generally recognised rules of international law, and within a period of six months from the date on which the final decision was taken.
2. The Court shall not deal with any application submitted under Article 34 that
   (a) is anonymous; or
   (b) is substantially the same as a matter that has already been examined by the Court or has already been submitted to another procedure of international investigation or settlement and contains no relevant new information.
3. The Court shall declare inadmissible any individual application submitted under Article 34 if it considers that:
   (a) the application is incompatible with the provisions of the Convention or the Protocols thereto, manifestly ill-founded, or an abuse of the right of individual application; or
   (b) the applicant has not suffered a significant disadvantage, unless respect for human rights as defined in the Convention and the Protocols thereto requires an examination of the application on the merits and provided that no case may be rejected on this ground which has not been duly considered by a domestic tribunal.

4. The Court shall reject any application which it considers inadmissible under this Article. It may do so at any stage of the proceedings.

Article 36
Third party intervention

1. In all cases before a Chamber or the Grand Chamber, a High Contracting Party one of whose nationals is an applicant shall have the right to submit written comments and to take part in hearings.
2. The President of the Court may, in the interest of the proper administration of justice, invite any High Contracting Party which is not a party to the proceedings or any person concerned who is not the applicant to submit written comments or take part in hearings.
3. In all cases before a Chamber or the Grand Chamber, the Council of Europe Commissioner for Human Rights may submit written comments and take part in hearings.

Article 37
Striking out applications

1. The Court may at any stage of the proceedings decide to strike an application out of its list of cases where the circumstances lead to the conclusion that
   (a) the applicant does not intend to pursue his application; or
   (b) the matter has been resolved; or
   (c) for any other reason established by the Court, it is no longer justified to continue the examination of the application. However, the Court shall continue the examination of the application if respect for human rights as defined in the Convention and the Protocols thereto so requires.
2. The Court may decide to restore an application to its list of cases if it considers that the circumstances justify such a course.

Article 38
Examination of the case
   The Court shall examine the case together with the representatives of the parties and, if need be, undertake an investigation, for the effective conduct of which the High Contracting Parties concerned shall furnish all necessary facilities.

Article 39
Friendly settlements

1. At any stage of the proceedings, the Court may place itself at the disposal of the parties concerned with a view to securing a friendly settlement of the matter on the basis of respect for human rights as defined in the Convention and the Protocols thereto.
2. Proceedings conducted under paragraph 1 shall be confidential.

3. If a friendly settlement is effected, the Court shall strike the case out of its list by means of a decision which shall be confined to a brief statement of the facts and of the solution reached.
4. This decision shall be transmitted to the Committee of Ministers, which shall supervise the execution of the terms of the friendly settlement as set out in the decision.

Article 40
Public hearings and access to documents

1. Hearings shall be in public unless the Court in exceptional circumstances decides otherwise.
2. Documents deposited with the Registrar shall be accessible to the public unless the President of the Court decides otherwise.

Article 41
Just satisfaction
If the Court finds that there has been a violation of the Convention or the Protocols thereto, and if the internal law of the High Contracting Party concerned allows only partial reparation to be made, the Court shall, if necessary, afford just satisfaction to the injured party.

Article 42
Judgments of Chambers
Judgments of Chambers shall become final in accordance with the provisions of Article 44, paragraph 2.

Article 43
Referral to the Grand Chamber

1. Within a period of three months from the date of the judgment of the Chamber, any party to the case may, in exceptional cases, request that the case be referred to the Grand Chamber.
2. A panel of five judges of the Grand Chamber shall accept the request if the case raises a serious question affecting the interpretation or application of the Convention or the Protocols thereto, or a serious issue of general importance.
3. If the panel accepts the request, the Grand Chamber shall decide the case by means of a judgment.

Article 44
Final judgments

1. The judgment of the Grand Chamber shall be final.
2. The judgment of a Chamber shall become final
   (a) when the parties declare that they will not request that the case be referred to the Grand Chamber; or

(b) three months after the date of the judgment, if reference of the case to the Grand Chamber has not been requested; or

(c) when the panel of the Grand Chamber rejects the request to refer under Article 43.

3. The final judgment shall be published.

Article 45
Reasons for judgments and decisions

1. Reasons shall be given for judgments as well as for decisions declaring applications admissible or inadmissible.

2. If a judgment does not represent, in whole or in part, the unanimous opinion of the judges, any judge shall be entitled to deliver a separate opinion.

Article 46
Binding force and execution of judgments

1. The High Contracting Parties undertake to abide by the final judgment of the Court in any case to which they are parties.

2. The final judgment of the Court shall be transmitted to the Committee of Ministers, which shall supervise its execution.

3. If the Committee of Ministers considers that the supervision of the execution of a final judgment is hindered by a problem of interpretation of the judgment, it may refer the matter to the Court for a ruling on the question of interpretation. A referral decision shall require a majority vote of two-thirds of the representatives entitled to sit on the committee.

4. If the Committee of Ministers considers that a High Contracting Party refuses to abide by a final judgment in a case to which it is a party, it may, after serving formal notice on that Party and by decision adopted by a majority vote of two-thirds of the representatives entitled to sit on the committee, refer to the Court the question whether that Party has failed to fulfil its obligation under paragraph 1.

5. If the Court finds a violation of paragraph 1, it shall refer the case to the Committee of Ministers for consideration of the measures to be taken. If the Court finds no violation of paragraph 1, it shall refer the case to the Committee of Ministers, which shall close its examination of the case.

Article 47
Advisory opinions

1. The Court may, at the request of the Committee of Ministers, give advisory opinions on legal questions concerning the interpretation of the Convention and the Protocols thereto.

2. Such opinions shall not deal with any question relating to the content or scope of the rights or freedoms defined in Section I of the Convention and the Protocols

thereto, or with any other question which the Court or the Committee of Ministers might have to consider in consequence of any such proceedings as could be instituted in accordance with the Convention.

3. Decisions of the Committee of Ministers to request an advisory opinion of the Court shall require a majority vote of the representatives entitled to sit on the committee.

Article 48

Advisory jurisdiction of the Court

The Court shall decide whether a request for an advisory opinion submitted by the Committee of Ministers is within its competence as defined in Article 47.

Article 49

Reasons for advisory opinions

1. Reasons shall be given for advisory opinions of the Court.
2. If the advisory opinion does not represent, in whole or in part, the unanimous opinion of the judges, any judge shall be entitled to deliver a separate opinion.
3. Advisory opinions of the Court shall be communicated to the Committee of Ministers.

Article 50

Expenditure on the Court

The expenditure on the Court shall be borne by the Council of Europe.

Article 51

Privileges and immunities of judges

The judges shall be entitled, during the exercise of their functions, to the privileges and immunities provided for in Article 40 of the Statute of the Council of Europe and in the agreements made thereunder.

American Convention on Human Rights

(adopted on 22 November 1969, entered into force 18 July 1978)

Part II – Means of Protection
Chapter VI – Competent Organs

Article 33

The following organs shall have competence with respect to matters relating to the fulfillment of the commitments made by the States Parties to this Convention:

(a) the Inter-American Commission on Human Rights, referred to as "The Commission;" and
(b) the Inter-American Court of Human Rights, referred to as "The Court."

Chapter VII – Inter-American Commission on Human Rights
Section 1. Organization

Article 34

The Inter-American Commission on Human Rights shall be composed of seven members, who shall be persons of high moral character and recognized competence in the field of human rights.

Article 35

The Commission shall represent all the member countries of the Organization of American States.

Article 36

1. The members of the Commission shall be elected in a personal capacity by the General Assembly of the Organization from a list of candidates proposed by the governments of the member states.
2. Each of those governments may propose up to three candidates, who may be nationals of the states proposing them or of any other member state of the Organization of American States. When a slate of three is proposed, at least one of the candidates shall be a national of a state other than the one proposing the slate.

Article 37

1. The members of the Commission shall be elected for a term of four years and may be reelected only once, but the terms of three of the members chosen in the first election shall expire at the end of two years. Immediately following that election the General Assembly shall determine the names of those three members by lot.
2. No two nationals of the same state may be members of the Commission.

Article 38

Vacancies that may occur on the Commission for reasons other than the normal expiration of a term shall be filled by the Permanent Council of the Organization in accordance with the provisions of the Statute of the Commission.

Article 39

The Commission shall prepare its Statute, which it shall submit to the General Assembly for approval. It shall establish its own Regulations.

Article 40

Secretariat services for the Commission shall be furnished by the appropriate specialized unit of the General Secretariat of the Organization. This unit shall be provided with the resources required to accomplish the tasks assigned to it by the Commission.

Section 2. Functions

Article 41

The main function of the Commission shall be to promote respect for and defense of human rights. In the exercise of its mandate, it shall have the following functions and powers:

(a) to develop an awareness of human rights among the peoples of America;
(b) to make recommendations to the governments of the member states, when it considers such action advisable, for the adoption of progressive measures in favor of human rights within the framework of their domestic law and constitutional provisions as well as appropriate measures to further the observance of those rights;
(c) to prepare such studies or reports as it considers advisable in the performance of its duties;
(d) to request the governments of the member states to supply it with information on the measures adopted by them in matters of human rights;
(e) to respond, through the General Secretariat of the Organization of American States, to inquiries made by the member states on matters related to human rights and, within the limits of its possibilities, to provide those states with the advisory services they request;
(f) to take action on petitions and other communications pursuant to its authority under the provisions of Articles 44 through 51 of this Convention; and
(g) to submit an annual report to the General Assembly of the Organization of American States.

Article 42

The States Parties shall transmit to the Commission a copy of each of the reports and studies that they submit annually to the Executive Committees of the Inter-American Economic and Social Council and the Inter-American Council for Education, Science, and Culture, in their respective fields, so that the Commission may watch over the promotion of the rights implicit in the economic, social, educational, scientific, and cultural standards set forth in the Charter of the Organization of American States as amended by the Protocol of Buenos Aires.

Article 43

The States Parties undertake to provide the Commission with such information as it may request of them as to the manner in which their domestic law ensures the effective application of any provisions of this Convention.

Section 3. Competence

Article 44

Any person or group of persons, or any nongovernmental entity legally recognized in one or more member states of the Organization, may lodge petitions with the

Commission containing denunciations or complaints of violation of this Convention by a State Party.

Article 45

1. Any State Party may, when it deposits its instrument of ratification of or adherence to this Convention, or at any later time, declare that it recognizes the competence of the Commission to receive and examine communications in which a State Party alleges that another State Party has committed a violation of a human right set forth in this Convention.
2. Communications presented by virtue of this article may be admitted and examined only if they are presented by a State Party that has made a declaration recognizing the aforementioned competence of the Commission. The Commission shall not admit any communication against a State Party that has not made such a declaration.
3. A declaration concerning recognition of competence may be made to be valid for an indefinite time, for a specified period, or for a specific case.
4. Declarations shall be deposited with the General Secretariat of the Organization of American States, which shall transmit copies thereof to the member states of that Organization.

Article 46

1. Admission by the Commission of a petition or communication lodged in accordance with Articles 44 or 45 shall be subject to the following requirements:
   (a) that the remedies under domestic law have been pursued and exhausted in accordance with generally recognized principles of international law;
   (b) that the petition or communication is lodged within a period of six months from the date on which the party alleging violation of his rights was notified of the final judgment;
   (c) that the subject of the petition or communication is not pending in another international proceeding for settlement; and
   (d) that, in the case of Article 44, the petition contains the name, nationality, profession, domicile, and signature of the person or persons or of the legal representative of the entity lodging the petition.
2. The provisions of paragraphs 1.a and 1.b of this article shall not be applicable when:
   (a) the domestic legislation of the state concerned does not afford due process of law for the protection of the right or rights that have allegedly been violated;
   (b) the party alleging violation of his rights has been denied access to the remedies under domestic law or has been prevented from exhausting them; or
   (c) there has been unwarranted delay in rendering a final judgment under the aforementioned remedies.

Article 47

The Commission shall consider inadmissible any petition or communication submitted under Articles 44 or 45 if:

(a) any of the requirements indicated in Article 46 has not been met;

(b) the petition or communication does not state facts that tend to establish a violation of the rights guaranteed by this Convention;

(c) the statements of the petitioner or of the state indicate that the petition or communication is manifestly groundless or obviously out of order; or

(d) the petition or communication is substantially the same as one previously studied by the Commission or by another international organization.

Section 4. Procedure

Article 48

1. When the Commission receives a petition or communication alleging violation of any of the rights protected by this Convention, it shall proceed as follows:

   (a) If it considers the petition or communication admissible, it shall request information from the government of the state indicated as being responsible for the alleged violations and shall furnish that government a transcript of the pertinent portions of the petition or communication. This information shall be submitted within a reasonable period to be determined by the Commission in accordance with the circumstances of each case.

   (b) After the information has been received, or after the period established has elapsed and the information has not been received, the Commission shall ascertain whether the grounds for the petition or communication still exist. If they do not, the Commission shall order the record to be closed.

   (c) The Commission may also declare the petition or communication inadmissible or out of order on the basis of information or evidence subsequently received.

   (d) If the record has not been closed, the Commission shall, with the knowledge of the parties, examine the matter set forth in the petition or communication in order to verify the facts. If necessary and advisable, the Commission shall carry out an investigation, for the effective conduct of which it shall request, and the states concerned shall furnish to it, all necessary facilities.

   (e) The Commission may request the states concerned to furnish any pertinent information and, if so requested, shall hear oral statements or receive written statements from the parties concerned.

   (f) The Commission shall place itself at the disposal of the parties concerned with a view to reaching a friendly settlement of the matter on the basis of respect for the human rights recognized in this Convention.

2. However, in serious and urgent cases, only the presentation of a petition or communication that fulfills all the formal requirements of admissibility shall be necessary in order for the Commission to conduct an investigation with the prior consent of the state in whose territory a violation has allegedly been committed.

Article 49

If a friendly settlement has been reached in accordance with paragraph 1.f of Article 48, the Commission shall draw up a report, which shall be transmitted to the petitioner and to the States Parties to this Convention, and shall then be communicated to the Secretary General of the Organization of American States for publication. This report shall contain a brief statement of the facts and of the solution reached. If any party in the case so requests, the fullest possible information shall be provided to it.

Article 50

1. If a settlement is not reached, the Commission shall, within the time limit established by its Statute, draw up a report setting forth the facts and stating its conclusions. If the report, in whole or in part, does not represent the unanimous agreement of the members of the Commission, any member may attach to it a separate opinion. The written and oral statements made by the parties in accordance with paragraph 1.e of Article 48 shall also be attached to the report.
2. The report shall be transmitted to the states concerned, which shall not be at liberty to publish it.
3. In transmitting the report, the Commission may make such proposals and recommendations as it sees fit.

Article 51

1. If, within a period of three months from the date of the transmittal of the report of the Commission to the states concerned, the matter has not either been settled or submitted by the Commission or by the state concerned to the Court and its jurisdiction accepted, the Commission may, by the vote of an absolute majority of its members, set forth its opinion and conclusions concerning the question submitted for its consideration.
2. Where appropriate, the Commission shall make pertinent recommendations and shall prescribe a period within which the state is to take the measures that are incumbent upon it to remedy the situation examined.
3. When the prescribed period has expired, the Commission shall decide by the vote of an absolute majority of its members whether the state has taken adequate measures and whether to publish its report.

Chapter VIII – Inter-American Court of Human Rights
Section 1. Organization

Article 52

1. The Court shall consist of seven judges, nationals of the member states of the Organization, elected in an individual capacity from among jurists of the highest moral authority and of recognized competence in the field of human rights, who

possess the qualifications required for the exercise of the highest judicial functions in conformity with the law of the state of which they are nationals or of the state that proposes them as candidates.

2. No two judges may be nationals of the same state.

Article 53

1. The judges of the Court shall be elected by secret ballot by an absolute majority vote of the States Parties to the Convention, in the General Assembly of the Organization, from a panel of candidates proposed by those states.

2. Each of the States Parties may propose up to three candidates, nationals of the state that proposes them or of any other member state of the Organization of American States. When a slate of three is proposed, at least one of the candidates shall be a national of a state other than the one proposing the slate.

Article 54

1. The judges of the Court shall be elected for a term of six years and may be reelected only once. The term of three of the judges chosen in the first election shall expire at the end of three years. Immediately after the election, the names of the three judges shall be determined by lot in the General Assembly.

2. A judge elected to replace a judge whose term has not expired shall complete the term of the latter.

3. The judges shall continue in office until the expiration of their term. However, they shall continue to serve with regard to cases that they have begun to hear and that are still pending, for which purposes they shall not be replaced by the newly elected judges.

Article 55

1. If a judge is a national of any of the States Parties to a case submitted to the Court, he shall retain his right to hear that case.

2. If one of the judges called upon to hear a case should be a national of one of the States Parties to the case, any other State Party in the case may appoint a person of its choice to serve on the Court as an ad hoc judge.

3. If among the judges called upon to hear a case none is a national of any of the States Parties to the case, each of the latter may appoint an ad hoc judge.

4. An ad hoc judge shall possess the qualifications indicated in Article 52.

5. If several States Parties to the Convention should have the same interest in a case, they shall be considered as a single party for purposes of the above provisions. In case of doubt, the Court shall decide.

Article 56
Five judges shall constitute a quorum for the transaction of business by the Court.

Article 57

The Commission shall appear in all cases before the Court.

Article 58

1. The Court shall have its seat at the place determined by the States Parties to the Convention in the General Assembly of the Organization; however, it may convene in the territory of any member state of the Organization of American States when a majority of the Court considers it desirable, and with the prior consent of the state concerned. The seat of the Court may be changed by the States Parties to the Convention in the General Assembly by a two-thirds vote.
2. The Court shall appoint its own Secretary.
3. The Secretary shall have his office at the place where the Court has its seat and shall attend the meetings that the Court may hold away from its seat.

Article 59

The Court shall establish its Secretariat, which shall function under the direction of the Secretary of the Court, in accordance with the administrative standards of the General Secretariat of the Organization in all respects not incompatible with the independence of the Court. The staff of the Court's Secretariat shall be appointed by the Secretary General of the Organization, in consultation with the Secretary of the Court.

Article 60

The Court shall draw up its Statute which it shall submit to the General Assembly for approval. It shall adopt its own Rules of Procedure.

Section 2. Jurisdiction and Functions

Article 61

1. Only the States Parties and the Commission shall have the right to submit a case to the Court.
2. In order for the Court to hear a case, it is necessary that the procedures set forth in Articles 48 and 50 shall have been completed.

Article 62

1. A State Party may, upon depositing its instrument of ratification or adherence to this Convention, or at any subsequent time, declare that it recognizes as binding, ipso facto, and not requiring special agreement, the jurisdiction of the Court on all matters relating to the interpretation or application of this Convention.

2. Such declaration may be made unconditionally, on the condition of reciprocity, for a specified period, or for specific cases. It shall be presented to the Secretary General of the Organization, who shall transmit copies thereof to the other member states of the Organization and to the Secretary of the Court.

3. The jurisdiction of the Court shall comprise all cases concerning the interpretation and application of the provisions of this Convention that are submitted to it, provided that the States Parties to the case recognize or have recognized such jurisdiction, whether by special declaration pursuant to the preceding paragraphs, or by a special agreement.

Article 63

1. If the Court finds that there has been a violation of a right or freedom protected by this Convention, the Court shall rule that the injured party be ensured the enjoyment of his right or freedom that was violated. It shall also rule, if appropriate, that the consequences of the measure or situation that constituted the breach of such right or freedom be remedied and that fair compensation be paid to the injured party.

2. In cases of extreme gravity and urgency, and when necessary to avoid irreparable damage to persons, the Court shall adopt such provisional measures as it deems pertinent in matters it has under consideration. With respect to a case not yet submitted to the Court, it may act at the request of the Commission.

Article 64

1. The member states of the Organization may consult the Court regarding the interpretation of this Convention or of other treaties concerning the protection of human rights in the American states. Within their spheres of competence, the organs listed in Chapter X of the Charter of the Organization of American States, as amended by the Protocol of Buenos Aires, may in like manner consult the Court.

2. The Court, at the request of a member state of the Organization, may provide that state with opinions regarding the compatibility of any of its domestic laws with the aforesaid international instruments.

Article 65

To each regular session of the General Assembly of the Organization of American States the Court shall submit, for the Assembly's consideration, a report on its work during the previous year. It shall specify, in particular, the cases in which a state has not complied with its judgments, making any pertinent recommendations.

Section 3. Procedure

Article 66

1. Reasons shall be given for the judgment of the Court.

2. If the judgment does not represent in whole or in part the unanimous opinion of the judges, any judge shall be entitled to have his dissenting or separate opinion attached to the judgment.

Article 67

The judgment of the Court shall be final and not subject to appeal. In case of disagreement as to the meaning or scope of the judgment, the Court shall interpret it at the request of any of the parties, provided the request is made within ninety days from the date of notification of the judgment.

Article 68

1. The States Parties to the Convention undertake to comply with the judgment of the Court in any case to which they are parties.
2. That part of a judgment that stipulates compensatory damages may be executed in the country concerned in accordance with domestic procedure governing the execution of judgments against the state.

Article 69

The parties to the case shall be notified of the judgment of the Court and it shall be transmitted to the States Parties to the Convention.

Chapter IX – Common Provisions

Article 70

1. The judges of the Court and the members of the Commission shall enjoy, from the moment of their election and throughout their term of office, the immunities extended to diplomatic agents in accordance with international law. During the exercise of their official function they shall, in addition, enjoy the diplomatic privileges necessary for the performance of their duties.
2. At no time shall the judges of the Court or the members of the Commission be held liable for any decisions or opinions issued in the exercise of their functions.

Article 71

The position of judge of the Court or member of the Commission is incompatible with any other activity that might affect the independence or impartiality of such judge or member, as determined in the respective statutes.

Article 72

The judges of the Court and the members of the Commission shall receive emoluments and travel allowances in the form and under the conditions set forth in their statutes, with due regard for the importance and independence of their office. Such emoluments and travel allowances shall be determined in the budget of the

Organization of American States, which shall also include the expenses of the Court and its Secretariat. To this end, the Court shall draw up its own budget and submit it for approval to the General Assembly through the General Secretariat. The latter may not introduce any changes in it.

Article 73

The General Assembly may, only at the request of the Commission or the Court, as the case may be, determine sanctions to be applied against members of the Commission or judges of the Court when there are justifiable grounds for such action as set forth in the respective statutes. A vote of a two-thirds majority of the member states of the Organization shall be required for a decision in the case of members of the Commission and, in the case of judges of the Court, a two-thirds majority vote of the States Parties to the Convention shall also be required.

Part III – General and Transitory Provisions
Chapter XI – Transitory Provisions
Section 1. Inter-American Commission on Human Rights

Article 79

Upon the entry into force of this Convention, the Secretary General shall, in writing, request each member state of the Organization to present, within ninety days, its candidates for membership on the Inter-American Commission on Human Rights. The Secretary General shall prepare a list in alphabetical order of the candidates presented, and transmit it to the member states of the Organization at least thirty days prior to the next session of the General Assembly.

Article 80

The members of the Commission shall be elected by secret ballot of the General Assembly from the list of candidates referred to in Article 79. The candidates who obtain the largest number of votes and an absolute majority of the votes of the representatives of the member states shall be declared elected. Should it become necessary to have several ballots in order to elect all the members of the Commission, the candidates who receive the smallest number of votes shall be eliminated successively, in the manner determined by the General Assembly.

Section 2. Inter-American Court of Human Rights

Article 81

Upon the entry into force of this Convention, the Secretary General shall, in writing, request each State Party to present, within ninety days, its candidates for membership on the Inter-American Court of Human Rights. The Secretary General shall prepare a list in alphabetical order of the candidates presented and transmit it to the States Parties at least thirty days prior to the next session of the General Assembly.

Article 82

The judges of the Court shall be elected from the list of candidates referred to in Article 81, by secret ballot of the States Parties to the Convention in the General Assembly. The candidates who obtain the largest number of votes and an absolute majority of the votes of the representatives of the States Parties shall be declared elected. Should it become necessary to have several ballots in order to elect all the judges of the Court, the candidates who receive the smallest number of votes shall be eliminated successively, in the manner determined by the States Parties.

African Charter on Human and Peoples' Rights

(adopted 28 June 1081, entered into force 21 October 1986)

Part II: Measures of Safeguard
Chapter I: Establishment and organisation of the African Commission on Human and Peoples Right'

Article 30

An African Commission on Human and Peoples' Rights, hereinafter called "the Commission", shall be established within the Organisation of African Unity to promote human and peoples' rights and ensure their protection in Africa.

Article 31

(1) The Commission shall consist of eleven members chosen from amongst African personalities of the highest reputation, known for their high morality, integrity, impartiality and competence in matters of human and peoples' rights; (2) particular consideration being given to persons having legal experience. The members of the Commission shall serve in their personal capacity.

Article 32

The Commission shall not include more than one national of the same State.

Article 33

The members of the Commission shall be elected by secret ballot by the Assembly of Heads of State and Government, from a list of persons nominated by the State Parties to the present Charter.

Article 34

Each State Party to the present Charter may not nominate more than two candidates. The candidates must have the nationality of one of the State Parties to the present Charter. When two candidates are nominated by a State, one of them may not be a national of that State.

Article 35

1. The Secretary General of the Organisation of African Unity shall invite State Parties to the present Charter at least four months before the elections to nominate candidates.
2. The Secretary General of the Organisation of African Unity shall make an alphabetical list of the persons thus nominated and communicate it to the Heads of State and Government at least one month before the elections.

Article 36

The members of the Commission shall be elected for a six year period and shall be eligible for re-election. However, the term of office of four of the members elected at the first election shall terminate after two years and the term of office of three others, at the end of four years.

Article 37

Immediately after the first election, the Chairman of the Assembly of Heads of State and Government of the Organisation of African Unity shall draw lots to decide the names of those members referred to in Article 36.

Article 38

After their election, the members of the Commission shall make a solemn declaration to discharge their duties impartially and faithfully.

Article 39

1. In case of death or resignation of a member of the Commission, the Chairman of the Commission shall immediately inform the Secretary General of the Organisation of African Unity, who shall declare the seat vacant from the date of death or from the date on which the resignation takes effect.
2. If, in the unanimous opinion of other members of the Commission, a member has stopped discharging his duties for any reason other than a temporary absence, the Chairman of the Commission shall inform the Secretary General of the Organisation of African Unity, who shall then declare the seat vacant.
3. In each of the cases anticipated above, the Assembly of Heads of State and Government shall replace the member whose seat became vacant for the remaining period of his term, unless the period is less than six months.

Article 40

Every member of the Commission shall be in office until the date his successor assumes office.

Article 41

The Secretary General of the Organisation of African Unity shall appoint the Secretary of the Commission. He shall provide the staff and services necessary for the effective discharge of the duties of the Commission. The Organisation of African Unity shall bear cost of the staff and services.

Article 42

1. The Commission shall elect its Chairman and Vice Chairman for a two-year period. They shall be eligible for re-election.
2. The Commission shall lay down its rules of procedure.
3. Seven members shall form the quorum.
4. In case of an equality of votes, the Chairman shall have a casting vote.
5. The Secretary General may attend the meetings of the Commission. He shall neither participate in deliberations nor shall he be entitled to vote. The Chairman of the Commission may, however, invite him to speak.

Article 43

In discharging their duties, members of the Commission shall enjoy diplomatic privileges and immunities provided for in the General Convention on the Privileges and Immunities of the Organisation of African Unity.

Article 44

Provision shall be made for the emoluments and allowances of the members of the Commission in the Regular Budget of the Organisation of African Unity.

Chapter II: Mandate of the Commission

Article 45

The functions of the Commission shall be:

1. To promote human and peoples' rights and in particular: (a) to collect documents, undertake studies and researches on African problems in the field of human and peoples' rights, organise seminars, symposia and conferences, disseminate information, encourage national and local institutions concerned with human and peoples' rights and, should the case arise, give its views or make recommendations to Governments; (b) to formulate and lay down, principles and rules aimed at solving legal problems relating to human and peoples' rights and fundamental freedoms upon which African Governments may base their legislation; (c) cooperate with other African and international institutions concerned with the promotion and protection of human and peoples' rights.
2. Ensure the protection of human and peoples' rights under conditions laid down by the present Charter.
3. Interpret all the provisions of the present Charter at the request of a State Party, an institution of the OAU or an African Organisation recognised by the OAU.
4. Perform any other tasks which may be entrusted to it by the Assembly of Heads of State and Government.

Chapter III: Procedure of the Commission

Article 46

The Commission may resort to any appropriate method of investigation; it may hear from the Secretary General of the Organisation of African Unity or any other person capable of enlightening it.

Communication from States

Article 47

If a State Party to the present Charter has good reasons to believe that another State Party to this Charter has violated the provisions of the Charter, it may draw, by written communication, the attention of that State to the matter. This Communication shall also be addressed to the Secretary General of the OAU and to the Chairman of the Commission. Within three months of the receipt of the Communication, the State to which the Communication is addressed shall give the enquiring State, written explanation or statement elucidating the matter. This should include as much as possible, relevant information relating to the laws and rules of procedure applied and applicable and the redress already given or course of action available.

Article 48

If within three months from the date on which the original communication is received by the State to which it is addressed, the issue is not settled to the satisfaction of the two States involved through bilateral negotiation or by any other peaceful procedure, either State shall have the right to submit the matter to the Commission through the Chairman and shall notify the other States involved.

Article 49

Notwithstanding the provisions of Article 47, if a State Party to the present Charter considers that another State Party has violated the provisions of the Charter, it may refer the matter directly to the Commission by addressing a communication to the Chairman, to the Secretary General of the Organisation of African unity and the State concerned.

Article 50

The Commission can only deal with a matter submitted to it after making sure that all local remedies, if they exist, have been exhausted, unless it is obvious to the Commission that the procedure of achieving these remedies would be unduly prolonged.

Article 51

1. The Commission may ask the State concerned to provide it with all relevant information.
2. When the Commission is considering the matter, States concerned may be represented before it and submit written or oral representation.

Article 52

After having obtained from the States concerned and from other sources all the information it deems necessary and after having tried all appropriate means to reach an amicable solution based on the respect of human and peoples' rights, the Commission shall prepare, within a reasonable period of time from the notification referred to in Article 48, a report to the States concerned and communicated to the Assembly of Heads of State and Government.

Article 53

While transmitting its report, the Commission may make to the Assembly of Heads of State and Government such recommendations as it deems useful.

Article 54

The Commission shall submit to each Ordinary Session of the Assembly of Heads of State and Government a report on its activities.

Article 55

1. Before each Session, the Secretary of the Commission shall make a list of the Communications other than those of State Parties to the present Charter and transmit them to Members of the Commission, who shall indicate which Communications should be considered by the Commission.
2. A Communication shall be considered by the Commission if a simple majority of its members so decide.

Article 56

Communications relating to Human and Peoples' rights referred to in Article 55 received by the Commission, shall be considered if they:

1. Indicate their authors even if the latter requests anonymity,
2. Are compatible with the Charter of the Organisation of African Unity or with the present Charter,
3. Are not written in disparaging or insulting language directed against the State concerned and its institutions or to the Organisation of African Unity,
4. Are not based exclusively on news disseminated through the mass media,
5. Are sent after exhausting local remedies, if any, unless it is obvious that this procedure is unduly prolonged,
6. Are submitted within a reasonable period from the time local remedies are exhausted or from the date the Commission is seized with the matter, and
7. Do not deal with cases which have been settled by those States involved in accordance with the principles of the Charter of the United Nations, or the Charter of the Organisation of African Unity or the provisions of the present Charter.

Article 57

Prior to any substantive consideration, all communications shall be brought to the knowledge of the State concerned by the Chairman of the Commission.

Article 58

1. When it appears after deliberations of the Commission that one or more Communications apparently relate to special cases which reveal the existence of a series of serious or massive violations of human and peoples' rights, the Commission shall draw the attention of the Assembly of Heads of State and Government to these special cases.
2. The Assembly of Heads of State and Government may then request the Commission to undertake an in-depth study of these cases and make a factual report, accompanied by its finding and recommendations.
3. A case of emergency duly noticed by the Commission shall be submitted by the latter to the Chairman of the Assembly of Heads of State and Government who may request an in-depth study.

Article 59

1. All measures taken within the provisions of the present Chapter shall remain confidential until the Assembly of Heads of State and Government shall otherwise decide.
2. However the report shall be published by the Chairman of the Commission upon the decision of the Assembly of Heads of State and Government.
3. The report on the activities of the Commission shall be published by its Chairman after it has been considered by the Assembly of Heads of State and Government.

Chapter IV: Applicable Principles

Article 60

The Commission shall draw inspiration from international law on human and peoples' rights, particularly from the provisions of various African instruments on Human and Peoples' Rights, the Charter of the United Nations, the Charter of the Organisation of African Unity, the Universal Declaration of Human Rights, other instruments adopted by the United Nations and by African countries in the field of Human and Peoples' Rights, as well as from the provisions of various instruments adopted within the Specialised Agencies of the United Nations of which the Parties to the present Charter are members.

Article 61

The Commission shall also take into consideration, as subsidiary measures to determine the principles of law, other general or special international conventions, laying down rules expressly recognised by Member States of the Organisation of African Unity, African practices consistent with international norms on Human and Peoples' Rights, customs generally accepted as law, general principles of law recognised by African States as well as legal precedents and doctrine.

Article 62

Each State Party shall undertake to submit every two years, from the date the present Charter comes into force, a report on the legislative or other measures taken, with a view to giving effect to the rights and freedoms recognised and guaranteed by the present Charter.

Protocol to the African Charter on Human and Peoples' Rights on the Establishment of an African Court of Human and Peoples' Rights

(adopted 10 June 1989, entered into force 25 January 2004)

Article 1 Establishment of the Court

There shall be established within the Organization of African Unity an African Court on Human and Peoples' Rights (hereinafter referred to as "the Court"), the organization, jurisdiction and functioning of which shall be governed by the present Protocol.

Article 2 Relationship between the Court and the Commission

The Court shall, bearing in mind the provisions of this Protocol, complement the protective mandate of the African Commission on Human and Peoples' Rights (hereinafter referred to as "the Commission") conferred upon it by the African Charter on Human and Peoples' Rights (hereinafter referred to as "the Charter").

Article 3 Jurisdiction

1. The jurisdiction of the Court shall extend to all cases and disputes submitted to it concerning the interpretation and application of the Charter, this Protocol and any other relevant Human Rights instrument ratified by the States concerned.
2. In the event of a dispute as to whether the Court has jurisdiction, the Court shall decide.

Article 4 Advisory Opinions

1. At the request of a Member State of the OAU, the OAU, any of its organs, or any African organization recognized by the OAU, the Court may provide an opinion on any legal matter relating to the Charter or any other relevant human rights instruments, provided that the subject matter of the opinion is not related to a matter being examined by the Commission.

2. The Court shall give reasons for its advisory opinions provided that every judge shall be entitled to deliver a separate or dissenting decision.

Article 5 Access to the Court

1. The following are entitled to submit cases to the Court
   (a) The Commission;
   (b) The State Party which has lodged a complaint to the Commission;
   (c) The State Party against which the complaint has been lodged at the Commission;
   (d) The State Party whose citizen is a victim of human rights violation;
   (e) African Intergovernmental Organizations.
2. When a State Party has an interest in a case, it may submit a request to the Court to be permitted to join.
3. The Court may entitle relevant Non-Governmental Organizations (NGOs) with observer status before the Commission, and individuals to institute cases directly before it, in accordance with article 34 (6) of this Protocol.

Article 6 Admissibility of cases

1. The Court, when deciding on the admissibility of a case instituted under article 5 (3) of this Protocol, may request the opinion of the Commission which shall give it as soon as possible.
2. The Court shall rule on the admissibility of cases taking into account the provisions of Article 56 of the Charter.
3. The Court may consider cases or transfer them to the Commission.

Article 7 Sources of law
The Court shall apply the provisions of the Charter and any other relevant human rights instruments ratified by the States concerned.

Article 8 Consideration of cases
The Rules of Procedure of the Court shall lay down the detailed conditions under which the Court shall consider cases brought before it, bearing in mind the complementarity between the Commission and the Court.

Article 9 Amicable settlement
The Court may try to reach an amicable settlement in a case pending before it in accordance with the provisions of the Charter.

Article 10 Hearings and representation

1. The Court shall conduct its proceedings in public. The Court may, however, conduct proceedings in camera as may be provided for in the Rules of Procedure.

2. Any party to a case shall be entitled to be represented by a legal representative of the party's choice. Free legal representation may be provided where the interests of justice so require.

3. Any person, witness or representative of the parties, who appears before the Court, shall enjoy protection and all facilities, in accordance with international law, necessary for the discharging of their functions, tasks and duties in relation to the Court.

Article 11 Composition

1. The Court shall consist of eleven judges, nationals of Member States of the OAU, elected in an individual capacity from among jurists of high moral character and of recognized practical, judicial or academic competence and experience in the field of human and peoples' rights.

2. No two judges shall be nationals of the same State.

Article 12 Nominations

1. States Parties to the Protocol may each propose up to three candidates, at least two of whom shall be nationals of that State.

2. Due consideration shall be given to adequate gender representation in the nomination process.

Article 13 List of candidates

1. Upon entry into force of this Protocol, the Secretary-General of the OAU shall request each State Party to the Protocol to present, within ninety (90) days of such a request, its nominees for the office of judge of the Court.

2. The Secretary-General of the OAU shall prepare a list in alphabetical order of the candidates nominated and transmit it to the Member States of the OAU at least thirty days prior to the next session of the Assembly of Heads of State and Government of the OAU hereinafter referred to as "the Assembly".

Article 14 Elections

1. The judges of the Court shall be elected by secret ballot by the Assembly from the list referred to in Article 13 (2) of the present Protocol.

2. The Assembly shall ensure that in the Court as a whole there is representation of the main regions of Africa and of their principal legal traditions.

3. In the election of the judges, the Assembly shall ensure that there is adequate gender representation.

Article 15 Term of office

1. The judges of the Court shall be elected for a period of six years and may be re-elected only once. The terms of four judges elected at the first election shall

expire at the end of two years, and the terms of four more judges shall expire at the end of four years.

2. The judges whose terms are to expire at the end of the initial periods of two and four years shall be chosen by lot to be drawn by the Secretary-General of the OAU immediately after the first election has been completed.

3. A judge elected to replace a judge whose term of office has not expired shall hold office for the remainder of the predecessor's term.

4. All judges except the President shall perform their functions on a part-time basis. However, the Assembly may change this arrangement as it deems appropriate.

Article 16 Oath of office

After their election, the judges of the Court shall make a solemn declaration to discharge their duties impartially and faithfully.

Article 17 Independence

1. The independence of the judges shall be fully ensured in accordance with international law.

2. No judge may hear any case in which the same judge has previously taken part as agent, counsel or advocate for one of the parties or as a member of a national or international court or a commission of enquiry or in any other capacity. Any doubt on this point shall be settled by decision of the Court.

3. The judges of the Court shall enjoy, from the moment of their election and throughout their term of office, the immunities extended to diplomatic agents in accordance with international law.

4. At no time shall the judges of the Court be held liable for any decision or opinion issued in the exercise of their functions.

Article 18 Incompatibility

The position of judge of the Court is incompatible with any activity that might interfere with the independence or impartiality of such a judge or the demands of the office, as determined in the Rules of Procedure of the Court.

Article 19 Cessation of office

1. A judge shall not be suspended or removed from office unless, by the unanimous decision of the other judges of the Court, the judge concerned has been found to be no longer fulfilling the required conditions to be a judge of the Court.

2. Such a decision of the Court shall become final unless it is set aside by the Assembly at its next session.

Article 20 Vacancies

1. In case of death or resignation of a judge of the Court, the President of the Court shall immediately inform the Secretary General of the Organization of African

Unity, who shall declare the seat vacant from the date of death or from the date on which the resignation takes effect.

2. The Assembly shall replace the judge whose office became vacant unless the remaining period of the term is less than one hundred and eighty (180) days.

3. The same procedure and considerations as set out in Articles 12, 13 and 14 shall be followed for the filling of vacancies.

Article 21 Presidency of the Court

1. The Court shall elect its President and one Vice-President for a period of two years. They may be re-elected only once.

2. The President shall perform judicial functions on a full-time basis and shall reside at the seat of the Court.

3. The functions of the President and the Vice-President shall be set out in the Rules of Procedure of the Court.

Article 22 Exclusion

If a judge is a national of any State which is a party to a case submitted to the Court, that judge shall not hear the case.

Article 23 Quorum

The Court shall examine cases brought before it, if it has a quorum of at least seven judges.

Article 24 Registry of the Court

1. The Court shall appoint its own Registrar and other staff of the registry from among nationals of Member States of the OAU according to the Rules of Procedure.

2. The office and residence of the Registrar shall be at the place where the Court has its seat.

Article 25 Seat of the Court

1. The Court shall have its seat at the place determined by the Assembly from among States parties to this Protocol. However, it may convene in the territory of any Member State of the OAU when the majority of the Court considers it desirable, and with the prior consent of the State concerned.

2. The seat of the Court may be changed by the Assembly after due consultation with the Court.

Article 26 Evidence

1. The Court shall hear submissions by all parties and if deemed necessary, hold an enquiry. The States concerned shall assist by providing relevant facilities for the efficient handling of the case.

2. The Court may receive written and oral evidence including expert testimony and shall make its decision on the basis of such evidence.

Article 27 Findings

1. If the Court finds that there has been violation of a human or peoples' right, it shall make appropriate orders to remedy the violation, including the payment of fair compensation or reparation.
2. In cases of extreme gravity and urgency, and when necessary to avoid irreparable harm to persons, the Court shall adopt such provisional measures as it deems necessary.

Article 28 Judgment

1. The Court shall render its judgment within ninety (90) days of having completed its deliberations.
2. The judgment of the Court decided by majority shall be final and not subject to appeal.
3. Without prejudice to sub-article 2 above, the Court may review its decision in the light of new evidence under conditions to be set out in the Rules of Procedure.
4. The Court may interpret its own decision.
5. The judgment of the Court shall be read in open court, due notice having been given to the parties.
6. Reasons shall be given for the judgment of the Court.
7. If the judgment of the Court does not represent, in whole or in part, the unanimous decision of the judges, any judge shall be entitled to deliver a separate or dissenting opinion.

Article 29 Notification of judgment

1. The parties to the case shall be notified of the judgment of the Court and it shall be transmitted to the Member States of the OAU and the Commission.
2. The Council of Ministers shall also be notified of the judgment and shall monitor its execution on behalf of the Assembly.

Article 30 Execution of judgement

The States parties to the present Protocol undertake to comply with the judgment in any case to which they are parties within the time stipulated by the Court and to guarantee its execution.

Article 31 Report

The Court shall submit to each regular session of the Assembly, a report on its work during the previous year. The report shall specify, in particular, the cases in which a State has not complied with the Court's judgment.

Article 32 Budget

Expenses of the Court, emoluments and allowances for judges and the budget of its registry, shall be determined and borne by the OAU, in accordance with criteria laid down by the OAU in consultation with the Court.

Article 33 Rules of Procedure

The Court shall draw up its Rules and determine its own procedures. The Court shall consult the Commission as appropriate.

Index

A

Abkhazia, 79, 84, 90
Access to justice, 433
Accountability, 320, 321, 327
Addis Ababa Guidelines, 122
  on independence and impartiality of
    members of human rights treaty
    bodies, 183
Advisory Committee, 62
Advisory Group of Experts, 73
Advisory opinions, 284, 496, 499
Afghanistan, 79, 310
African Charter on Human and Peoples Rights,
  305, 386, 480, 494, 498, 499, 514
African Charter on the Rights of Women in
  Africa, 387
African Commission on Human and Peoples'
  Rights, 480, 481, 484–486, 489,
  493–495, 498, 500, 564
  background and context, 508
African Committee of Experts on the Rights
  and Welfare of the Child, 482
African Court on Human and Peoples' Rights,
  480, 481, 498, 506, 519, 564
African Union (AU), 481
  exhaustion of domestic remedies, 483, 500
Agenda 2030, 561
Agenda for Sustainable Development, 175
Akayesu, 337
Al Bashir, 362
Alston, Philip, 273, 276–278, 279, 281–284,
  286–288
American Anthropological Association
  (AAA), 36
American Convention on Human Rights,
  465, 514
American Declaration of the Rights and Duties
  of Man, 31, 464

American Law Institute (ALI), 37
Amnesty International, 41
Annan, Kofi, 207
Apartheid, 480
Arab Charter on Human Rights, 514–516,
  518
Arab Court of Human Rights, 516–518
Arab Human Rights Committee, 514–516
Arab Plan for Enhancing the Culture of Human
  Rights, 513
Arab Plan of Action for Human Rights
  Education, 513
Arab Spring, 512, 519
Arbour, L., 72
Armed conflict, 432
Arms Trade Treaty, 382
Arria-formula, 204, 206, 207, 211
ASEAN Commission on the Promotion and
  Protection of the Rights of Women and
  Children (ACWC), 541–542
  mandate and functions of, 542–544
ASEAN Inter-Governmental Commission on
  Human Rights (AICHR), 537–538
Assembly of States Parties, 524
Association of Southeast Asian Nations
  (ASEAN)
  Bangkok Declaration, 529
  and human rights, 529–530, 533, 534
  turning point in, 530–533
  Vision 2020, 534
Asylum, 429
AU Convention for the Protection and
  Assistance of Internally Displaced
  Persons in Africa, 387
Austerity measures, 164
Aut dedere aut judicare, 383
Authority, 3–5
Azerbaijan, 307

B

Bangkok NGO Declaration on Human
    Rights, 532
Barayagwiza, Jean-Bosco, 342
Beijing+5, 180
Beijing Declaration and Platform for
    Action, 172
Beijing Platform for Action, 180
Bizimana, Augustin, 341
Bosnia and Herzegovina, 300, 340
Burgh House Principles, 524
Burundi, 82, 85, 88, 90, 206, 207, 212, 215,
    308–311
Bush, George H. W., 201

C

Cairo Declaration on Human Rights in
    Islam, 514
Canada, 107, 192
Capacity building, 75–76
Cassin, René, 27
Central African Republic (CAR), 84,
    213, 218
Centre for Civil and Political Rights, 121
Chang, Peng Chun, 27
Charter of the International Military
    Tribunal, 326
Charter of the United Nations, 5
Chivalry, 380
Civil society, 179
Clawback clauses, 486
Climate change, 163
Coercion, 558
Cold War, 34, 40, 43, 70, 120, 135, 201, 202,
    214, 272, 273
Collective bargaining, 236, 239
Colonialism, 26, 29, 35, 480
    European, 36
Commission of Fifteen, 323
Commission on Human Rights (CHR), 27, 51,
    202, 205, 210, 214
Commission on the Disappearance of Persons,
    402, 418
Committee Against Torture, 307
Committee of Experts on Indigenous
    Labour, 243
Committee of Experts on the Application of
    Conventions and Recommendations,
    232
Committee of Ministers, 424, 438
Committee on Conventions and
    Recommendations, 258

Committee on Economic, Social and Cultural
    Rights, 241
Committee on Freedom of Association,
    235, 236
Committee on the Application of Standards,
    230
Committee on the Elimination of all Forms of
    Discrimination against Women, 2
Committee on the Elimination of
    Discrimination against Women
    (CEDAW), 182, 304
Committee on the Rights of the Child, 304
Communications, 481, 483, 485, 486–491,
    497, 506
    to African Court, 504
Compensation, 490
Complementarity, 369
Compliance, 559, 564–566
Concluding Observations, 11, 101, 126, 147
Congo, 201, 211, 220
Constitutional Court of South Africa, 154
Consultative status, 179
Convention against Discrimination in
    Education, 255
Conventionality control, 472, 473
Convention concerning the Protection of the
    World Cultural and Natural
    Heritage, 256
Convention on the Elimination of All Forms of
    Discrimination against Women
    (CEDAW), 83, 180, 521
Convention on the Prevention or Punishment of
    the Crime of Genocide, 327
Convention on the Protection and Promotion of
    the Diversity of Cultural Expressions, 256
Convention on the Protection of the Underwater
    Cultural Heritage, 256
Convention on the Rights of Persons with
    Disabilities, 273, 276
Convention on the Rights of the Child, 90
Convention on the Safeguarding of the
    Intangible Cultural Heritage, 256
Core labour standards, 232
Core obligations, 159
Costa Rica, 301
Côte d'Ivoire, 207, 212
Council of Europe, 304, 428, 429
Council of the League of Arab States, 516
Court of Justice of the European Union, 440
Crime of aggression, 367
Crimes against humanity, 362
Cultural heritage, 256
Culture, 252

D

Darfur, 212, 217
Days of General Discussion, 148
Death penalty, 53, 494
Death sentence, 521
Declaration of the Regional Meeting for Asia of the World Conference on Human Rights, 532
Declaration on Bioethics and Human Rights, 256
Declaration on the Rights of Indigenous Peoples, 53
Declaration on the Right to Development, 158
Declaration on Violence against Women, 176
Democracy, 240–241, 403, 408–410, 414, 418
Democratic People's Republic of Korea (DPRK), 204, 206, 209
Democratic Republic of the Congo (DRC), 86
Denial of justice, 429
Department for International Development, 87
Department of Political Affairs (DPA), 219
Derogation, 385
Development cooperation, 158
Dignity, 406, 407, 415
Director General, 253, 257, 259, 261–263
Domestic implementation of international human rights standards, 305
Dublin Regulation, 429
Due diligence approach, 161
Due process, 341, 345

E

East African Court of Justice, 482
East Timor, 207, 214–216
Economic and Social Council (ECOSOC), 145, 202, 295
Economic Community of West African States (ECOWAS), 482
Economic, social and cultural rights, 145–146
ECOSOC Resolution 1235, 8
ECOSOC Resolution 1503, 8
Ecuador, 238
Education, 252
El Salvador, 70, 209, 211
Enforced disappearances, 432
Enforcement, IHL, 378
  domestic mechanisms, 381–383
  General Assembly, 391
  International Court of Justice, 393
  international criminal law mechanisms, 393
  international level, 388
  mechanisms, 388–389

non-State actors, 394
regional organizations, 384
Security Council, 390–391
UN system, 389–390
Eritrea, 81, 218
Ethiopia, 81
Ethnic cleansing, 212, 213
European Convention on Human Rights, 11, 346, 384, 424, 514
European Court of Human Rights, 11, 130, 188, 241, 275, 278–280, 282, 285, 305, 424, 564
European Union (EU), 444, 446, 451
  agency for Fundamental Rights (FRA), 445
  Charter of Fundamental Rights, 445–447, 449, 450, 452–454
  Council of, 451
  law, 449, 450
  and treaty of Lisbon, 450
Evidence-based advise, 449, 452, 453
Executive Board, 252–253, 257–265
Exhaustion of domestic remedies, 280, 483–485
Exhaustion of local remedies, 263
Extraordinary rendition, 429
  program, 383
Extraterritorial application of Covenant, 157–159
Extraterritorial human rights obligations, 159–161
Extra-territorial jurisdiction, 431

F

Field operations, 72, 78
First World War, 323
Forced Labour Convention, 242
FRA, see Fundamental Rights Agency (FRA)
Freedom of association
  procedures concerining, 235–237
  and trade union rights, 237–239
Freedom of expression, 255, 261
Freedom of speech, 430
French Declaration of the Rights of Man and Citizen, 31
Friendly settlements of human rights, 558
Friendship, 407
Fundamental Rights Agency (FRA), 305
  contributions show, 458
  data and analysis, 454
  EU, 444–446
  legal expertise, 455
  practical guidance, 458

G

Gender-based violence, 339
General Assembly, 391–392
General Comments, 12, 103, 127–130, 148
General Conference, 252–253, 256–259, 261, 264
General recommendations, 103
Geneva Conventions, 380
Genocide, 327, 337, 357, 361–362
Globalisation, 156
Grand Chamber, 425
Grave breaches of the Geneva Conventions,
      365, 382
Guiding Principles for Human Rights Field
      Officers Working in Conflict and
      Post-Conflict Environments, 91
Guiding Principles on Business and Human
      Rights, 56

H

Haiti, 71, 87, 211, 217
Helsinki Final Act, 40
High Commissioner for Human Rights, 201,
      203, 206, 210, 213, 215, 217, 219–221
Holocaust, 5, 35
Human rights, 50, 200, 209–210, 252, 254, 417
   in DPRK, 204
   impact on, 201
   protection of, 201
   standard-setting and monitoring, 257–258
   truth commissions (*see* Truth commissions;
      UN Security Council and Human Rights)
   within UNESCO's competence, 254
   violations, 200, 202, 403, 407, 408,
      411, 413
Human Rights Commission, 259
Human Rights Committee, 12, 145, 304
Human Rights Council (HRC), 8, 201–205,
      265, 266, 297, 302, 303, 392
   achievements of, 52
   Advisory Committee to, 62–63
   challenges, 59
   election, 64–65
Human rights courts, 554, 563
Humphrey, John P., 27, 174

I

IACHR, *see* Inter-American Commission on
      Human Rights (IACHR)
ICESCR, *see* International Covenant on
      Economic, Social and Cultural Rights
      (ICESCR)

ICRC, 380, 389
ICTR, 381, 394
ICTY, 381
Immigration, 489
Immunity, 383
Impact of truth commissions, *see* Truth
      commissions
Implementation, 437–438, 553–554
Independence of the court and judges, 523–524
Independent Expert on Sexual Orientation and
      Gender Identity, 61
Indigenous and Tribal Populations Convention,
      243, 244
Indigenous communities, 554
Indigenous peoples' rights, 242, 496
Individual application, 12
Individual communications, 130–135
Individual complaints, 104, 145, 152, 273, 274,
      275, 278, 280, 285, 288
Infringement proceedings, 438
Inquiry procedure, 106
Inter-American Commission on Human Rights
      (IACHR), 464, 469, 471, 472
   precautionary measures, 471
Inter-American Commission on Women, 173
Inter-American Convention on Human
      Rights, 385
Inter-American Court of Human Rights
      (IACourtHR), 241, 244, 465, 469, 564
   provisional measures, 471
Inter-American Democratic Charter, 468
Inter-American human rights instruments, 473
Interim measures, 281
International Agreement for the Suppression of
      the 'White Slave Trade, 170
International Center for Transitional Justice
      (ICTJ), 405
International Conference on the Repression of
      Terrorism, 357
International Convention for the Protection of
      all Persons from Enforced
      Disappearance, 53
International Convention for the Suppression of
      Traffic in Women and Children, 170
International Convention for the Suppression of
      Traffic in Women of Full Age, 170
International Convention on Civil and Political
      Rights (ICCPR), 521
International Convention on the Elimination of
      All Forms of Racial Discrimination, 10
International Convention on the Rights of
      Persons with Disabilities, 53
International Court of Human Rights, 272

International Court of Justice (ICJ), 118, 122, 234, 381, 393
International Covenant on Civil and Political Rights (ICCPR), 118, 119, 135, 259, 346
International Covenant on Economic, Social and Cultural Rights (ICESCR), 144, 150, 259
International crimes, 320, 321
International Criminal Court (ICC), 356–358, 381, 391, 554
  admissibility issues, 369–371
  crime of aggression, 367
  crimes against humanity, 362–364
  genocide, 361–362
  structure of, 358–360
  trigger mechanisms and jurisdiction, 367–369
  war crimes, 364–367
International criminal law, 336, 338, 348, 364–366
International Criminal Tribunal for Rwanda, 335, 358
International Criminal Tribunal for the former Yugoslavia, 279, 335, 358
International Declaration on Human Genetic Data, 256
International Fact-Finding Commission, 389
International humanitarian law (IHL)
  African Charter on Human and Peoples Rights, 386–387
  considerations and factors, compliance with, 380
  enforcement (see Enforcement, IHL)
  European Convention on Human Rights, 384
  Inter-American Convention on Human Rights, 385–386
International Labour Conference, 230
International Labour Office, 231
International Labour Organization (ILO), 33, 170, 228
  indigenous peoples' rights, 242
  mandate and institutional framework, 229
  regular supervisory systems, 233–234
  right to collective bargaining, 239–240
  standard review mechanism, 246
  trade union rights, 240–241
  tripartism, 230
International labour standards, 231
International Law Commission, 16, 382, 392
International Military Tribunal of Nuremberg, 357
International Military Tribunal of Tokyo (IMT), 321, 322, 357

International Monetary Fund, 158
International Women's Year, 180
Interpretive authority, 2, 11, 16, 17
Inter-state application, 427
Inter-state complaints, 12, 104
Iran, 174
Islamic Shari'a, 520

J
Jose Ayala Lasso, 70
Judicial misconduct, 524
Jurisprudence, 428–432
Jus cogens, 394
Jus in bello, 378
Justice, 407
Justiciability, 153, 161, 165

K
Kabuga, Félicien, 341
Kambanda, 337
Kellog-Briand Pact, 322
Kenya, 310
Kosovo law, 346
Kosovo Specialist Chambers (KSC), 346–348
Krstić, Radislav, 337
Kuala Lumpur Declaration on the Establishment of the ASEAN Charter, 535

L
Lasso, José Ayala, 206
Lauterpacht, Hersch, 43
Law Association for Asia and the Pacific (LAWASIA), 534
Law of armed conflict, 378
  See also International humanitarian law (IHL)
League of Arab States, 513–514, 519
League of Nations, 170, 356
Lebanon, 343
Legislative authority, 2
Legitimacy, 2, 4
Leipzig Trials, 324
Leipzig war crime tribunal, 356
Lemkin, Raphael, 34, 327, 361
Lex specialis, 386
Liberia, 90
Libya, 218, 220, 221

Limburg Principles on the Implementation of the
International Covenant on Economic,
Social and Cultural Rights, 149
London Charter, 321

M

Maastricht Guidelines on Violations of
Economic, Social and Cultural
Rights, 152
Maastricht Principles on the Extraterritorial
Obligations of States, 160, 165
Malik, Charles, 27
Margin of appreciation, 427
Mechanism for International Criminal
Tribunals, 335
Mexico, 192
Middle East and North Africa (MENA)
region, 513
Minimum core obligations, 150
Mladic case, 335
Monetary damages, 490
Monitoring, 76, 79
Mpiranya, Protais, 341
Multilateralism, 555
Myanmar, 235

N

National Commissions for UNESCO, 253
National Human Rights Institutions (NHRIs),
125, 126, 129, 561
achievements and challenges, 306
origins, mandate and functions, 295
Paris Principles and Sub-Committee on
accreditation, 296
terminology and typology, 293–295
National Preventive Mechanisms, 108
Nepal, 78
New Urban Agenda, 561
Non Aligned Movement (NAM), 209
Non-discrimination, 238
Non-governmental organizations (NGOs), 147,
519, 561
Non-State actors, 274, 276, 286, 288, 394, 487
Nuremberg trials, 320, 321
international crimes and, 321
Nyerere, Julius, 41

O

Office of the High Commissioner for Human
Rights (OHCHR), 99, 203, 297
Office of the Prosecutor, 360

Optional Protocol, 152, 153
to the Convention Against Torture, 307
and the work of the Committee, 188
Organisation for Security and Cooperation in
Europe, 87
Organisation of African Unity (OAU), 42, 480
Organization for Security and Cooperation in
Europe, 305
Organization of American States (OAS), 305,
464, 465, 467, 468, 470, 472, 475

P

Palestine, 252
Paris Peace Conference, 356
Paris Principles, 186, 292, 294–300, 308
Parliamentary Assembly of the Council of
Europe, 305, 436–437
Peace, 403, 406, 408–411, 416, 418
Peacekeeping, 72, 75, 80, 390
Peace missions, 76
Peace of Westphalia, 322
Permanent Court of International Justice, 230
Persuasion, 558
Persuasive authority, 17
Peru, 411, 413
Philadelphia declaration, 229
Philippines, 107, 131, 192, 310
Pilot judgment procedure, 436
Politicization, 555
Potsdam Agreement, 321
Poverty, 480
Precautionary measures, 467, 471, 472
Pre-Trial Chambers, 358
Principle of autonomy, 239
Proclamation of Tehran, 7
Pro homine approach, 16
Proprio motu investigation, 368
Protecting Powers, 380, 388
Protocol to the African Charter on Human and
Peoples' Rights on the Establishment of
the African Court on Human and
Peoples' Rights, 519
Protocol to the African Charter on Human and
Peoples' Rights on the Rights of Women
in Africa, 483
Provisional measures, 492, 502
Public emergency, 425

R

Reconciliation, 403, 406, 409, 411–413, 418
Redress, 435–436

Remedies, 273, 275, 276, 279, 280, 286, 288
Reparations, 468, 470, 487
Reporting procedure, 100
Responsibility to protect doctrine, 391
Rettig Commission, 402
Rights for the defendant, 342
Right to adequate housing, 486
Right to counsel, 342
Right to health, 159
Right to life, 431, 495
Right to strike, 239
Right to water, 150
Robinson, Mary, 206
Rome Statute, 360
Roosevelt, Eleanor, 27, 173
Ruggie Principles, 160
Rule of law, 74, 86
Rwanda, 72, 203, 210, 212, 213, 215, 219, 339

S
Sanctions, 216
San Francisco Conference, 170
San José Guidelines, 123, 189
Saudi Arabia, 28, 174
Science, 252
Secondary agents of justice, 6–7
Second World War, 321, 323, 329, 330
Secretary General of the League of Arab
     States, 517
Security Council, 390, 557
     See also UN Security Council and
         Human Rights
Self-referrals, 368
Self-representation, 342
Sexual minorities, 491
Sexual violence, 338
Sharpeville Massacre, 6
Sierra Leone, 85, 90, 207, 214, 215
Slavery, 242
Somalia, 211, 218
South Africa, 29, 201, 202, 217, 220
South African Truth and Reconciliation
     Commission, 402, 415, 418
South Asian Association for Regional
     Cooperation, 528
South Sudan, 207, 216, 218
Soviet Union, 119, 273
Special Adviser on the Prevention of
     Genocide, 219
Special Procedures, 8, 54, 60–62
Special Rapporteur(s), 82, 483, 496, 497, 507
     on extreme poverty and human rights, 55
     on the right to food, 55

Special Tribunal for Lebanon (STL),
     343–345
Sri Lanka, 107
Standard review mechanism, 246
Standing Committee on Human Rights, 513
Statement on Public Debt, Austerity
     Measures, 150
State of emergency, 385
State reports, 145, 146, 498
State sovereignty, 556
Statute of the Arab Court of Human Rights,
     516, 525
Sub-commission on the Status of Women, 173
Sub-Committee on Accreditation, 296
Subcommittee on Prevention of Torture and
     Other Cruel, Inhuman or Degrading
     Treatment or Punishment (SPT), 97
Subject matter jurisdiction, 520–521
Sudan, 82
Superior responsibility, 339
Supreme Court of India, 188
Sustainable Development Goals, 74, 163,
     175, 184
Syria mechanism, 348–350

T
Terrorism, 344, 429
Timor Leste, 83, 85, 90, 212
Tokyo trials, 320
     international crimes and, 321–325
Torture, 429, 521
Trade union rights, 240
     and democracy, 241
Transitional justice (TJ), 402, 403, 408
     conceptualization of, 405
     truth commissions in (see Truth
         commissions)
Transitional Justice Database (TJDB), 404
Treaty bodies, 262, 264, 266
Treaty body reform, 96
Treaty of Lausanne, 325
Treaty of Lisbon, 450
Treaty of Sèvres, 325
Treaty of Versailles, 229, 237, 242, 323
Trial Chamber, 359
Trials in absentia, 345
Tripartism, 230
Truth commissions, 417–418
     claims and evidence, 409–410
     definitions of, 403–405
     on democracy, 410–411
     function of, 402, 407–408

Truth commissions (*cont.*)
mandates of, 407–408
multiple objectives of, 406–407
on peace, 411–413
on reconciliation, 413–416
reports and recommendations, 417
in transitional justice, 408–409

U
Ukraine, 310
UN Assistance Mission for Rwanda
(UNAMIR), 203, 211
UN Basic Principles and Guidelines on the
Right to a Remedy and Reparation for
Victims of Gross Violations of
International Human Rights Law and
Serious Violations of International
Humanitarian Law, 275
UN Committee on Economic, Social and
Cultural Rights, 278
UN Decade for Human Rights Education, 255
UN Declaration on the Rights of Indigenous
Peoples, 244
UN Department of Political Affairs, 70
UNESCO
Associated Schools, 254
Chairs, 254
competence, human rights within, 254–256
Constitution, 252
procedure on human rights violations,
258–264
structure and functions of, 252–254
UN Guiding Principles on Business and Human
Rights, 160
UN High Commissioner for Human Rights, 13,
70, 72
UN Human Rights Field Officers, 75
United Kingdom, 107
United Nations, 3, 7, 10, 75, 200, 204, 552
See also UN Security Council and Human
Rights
United Nations Charter, 5, 50, 252, 553
United Nations (UN), human rights treaty
bodies, 96
achievements, 108–110
challenges, 110–112
complaints procedure, 104–106
development and mandate, 98–100
general comments, 103–104
inquiry procedure, 106–107
OPCAT model, 108
reporting procedure, 100–103

United Nations Independent Investigation on
Burundi, 308
United Nations Security Council, 343
United States Agency for International
Development, 87
Universal Declaration of Human Rights
(UDHR), 5, 26–28, 30, 31, 33–35,
254, 553
debates, 37
Universal Declaration on Cultural Diversity, 256
Universal Declaration on the Human Genome
and Human Rights, 256
Universal jurisdiction, 383
Universal Periodic Review (UPR), 8, 56–59,
125, 126, 134, 274, 287, 303, 392, 554
UN Mission in Haiti (UNMIH), 211
UN Observer Mission in El Salvador, 71
UN Protection Force, 209
UN Security Council and Human Rights, 209
CHR, 202
Cold War period, 201
commissions of inquiry, 212–213
conflict prevention action, 219–220
Council dynamics, 220–221
discussions of human rights, 208–209
DPRK, 204
ECOSOC, 202
judicial mechanisms, 213–214
OHCHR, 203
peace operations, components in, 210–211
sanctions, 216–219
summit-level meeting, 201
UNAMIR, 203
UN High Commissioner for Human Rights,
interaction with, 206–207
UN human rights investigators, interaction
with, 205–206
visiting missions, 214–216
UN specialized agencies, 162
UN Stabilization Mission in Haiti, 83
UN Transitional Administration in East Timor
(UNTAET), 214
UN Transitional Authority in Cambodia, 211
UN Trusteeship Council, 41
UN Women, 173
Uruguay, 132, 411, 413
US Bill of Rights, 31
Uwinkindi, 339

V
Venezuela, 241, 307
Victim reparation, 328

Victim status, 561
Vienna Convention on the Law of Treaties, 13, 18
Vienna declaration, 153
Vienna Declaration and Programme of Action, 172
Vientiane Action Program (VAP), 535

W
War crimes, 364, 381
Western European and Others Group (WEOG), 130
Western Sahara, 211
Working Group for an ASEAN Human Rights Mechanism, 534
Working Group of Governmental Experts, 145
Working Group on Communications on the Status of Women, 177
Working Group on Enforced or Involuntary Disappearances, 54
World Bank, 158, 163
World Conference on Human Rights, 530

World Court of Human Rights (WCHR), 284, 287
advisory opinions, 283–284
Alston's fundamental critique, 276
arguments for, 273
bindingness, 282–283
budget, 279
creation of, 274
draft Statute of, 275–276
Entities, 286
exhaustion of domestic remedies, 280–281
fact-finding powers, 279–280
hierarchy, 285–286
interim measures, 281–282
justiciability of human rights, 277–278
legalism, 284–285
ratification process of, 274
universality, 278–279, 286–287
World Press Freedom Day, 256
World Press Freedom Prize, 256
World Programme on Human Rights Education, 255

Y
Yemen, 218

Printed by Printforce, the Netherlands